John Dickson CARR

The Man Who Explained MIRACLES

Douglas G. Greene

OTTO PENZLER
NEW YORK

**OTTO
PENZLER
BOOKS**

OTTO PENZLER BOOKS
129 West 56th Street
New York, NY 10019
(Editorial Offices only)

Simon & Schuster Inc.
Rockefeller Center
1230 Avenue of the Americas
New York, NY 10020

Designed by Songhee Kim

Manufactured in the United States of America

1   3   5   7   9   10   8   6   4   2

Library of Congress Cataloging-in-Publication Data
Greene, Douglas G.
John Dickson Carr: the man who explained miracles/Douglas G. Greene.
p.   cm.
Includes bibliographical references.
1. Carr, John Dickson, 1906–1977—Biography.   2. Authors,
American—20th century—Biography.   3. Detective and mystery
stories—Authorship.   I. Title.
PS3505.A763Z67   1995   94-23283   CIP
8139.52—dc20
[B]
ISBN: 1-883402-47-6

Contents

Preface

For more than forty years, John Dickson Carr created and explained miracles in novels, short stories, and scripts. His detective stories have a special flavor that is found nowhere else in mystery fiction, or indeed in fiction generally. What can be called the "Carrian synthesis" is made up of supernatural atmosphere, fair-play detection, complex but lively narratives, uproarious comedy, and a romantic interest in the past and in Adventure in the Grand Manner. Carr was the unchallenged master of ingenuity of method, especially in the "locked-room murder." His stories normally ask not only "Whodunit?" but also "How could it have been done?" Carr's crimes seem to have been committed without human agents. Murders take place in rooms all of whose entrances are locked and sealed; bodies are found alone in buildings surrounded by unmarked snow or sand; people enter a house or dive into a swimming pool and utterly disappear. And for fully three-quarters of the story, Carr suggests that only a vampire, a witch, or a ghost could have committed the crimes. "Let there be a spice of terror," Carr wrote, "of dark skies and evil things."[1] Striding through these adventures, bringing order and reason to what seems a world dominated by the dark powers, are four towering figures of detective fiction—Henry Bencolin of the Sûreté, Dr. Gideon Fell, Sir Henry Merrivale, and Colonel March of Scotland Yard's Department of Queer

Complaints. This relationship between chaos and order, the supernatural and the material, the irrational and human reason is fundamental to Carr's writings.

In his novels, short stories, and radio plays, John Dickson Carr created worlds that never actually existed but that were immensely attractive to Carr, and as the continuing sales of his books indicate, to generation after generation of readers. His early books featuring the French detective Bencolin describe an eerie, Poe-esque Old World, which despite specific references that set the stories in Paris, in London, and on the Rhine, existed only in Carr's imagination. His first Dr. Gideon Fell novels, *Hag's Nook* and *The Mad Hatter Mystery*, published in 1933, are filled with anglophilic warmth—connected with his love of the tales of G. K. Chesterton—but they don't tell the full story of an England at a time when, after all, the Depression was at its height. For many Americans, however, they show England as it *should* be, as a place where, Carr wrote, "The earth is old and enchanted."[2] Soon, especially in the early Sir Henry Merrivale novels such as *The Red Widow Murders*, he showed London as "Baghdad-on-the-Thames," a *New Arabian Nights* world with adventure behind every doorway. Even after he became acclimated to Britain, and his books more accurately describe the background (in, for example, the wartime novels, *She Died a Lady* and *He Wouldn't Kill Patience*), the stories still reflect a world that he could escape to, a place of order and values. After World War II, when shortages and his hatred of socialism drove him back to the United States, and indeed through the rest of his life, Carr expressed himself mainly in re-creations of the past—meticulous accounts of the sights and sounds and smells of earlier centuries, but nonetheless seen with a golden glow of romance.

When they first met on shipboard in 1930, John Dickson Carr told his future wife, Clarice Cleaves, that he had been born in Paris when his father was there on a diplomatic mission. Visiting John's parents in Uniontown, Pennsylvania, six years after their marriage, she discovered that this story was not true.[3] Carr loved to color his accounts of events, to make them more dramatic than they had in fact been. Life never quite measured up to the adventure that he knew should be there. He was like the character in one of his early books, *The Bowstring Murders*, who dreams of having "adventures . . . in the grand manner [and meeting] a slant-eyed adventuress, sables and all, who suddenly slips into this [railway] compartment, whispers 'six of diamonds—north tower at midnight—beware of Orloff.'"[4] In publicity material he prepared for his publisher around 1935, Carr complained that in roaming through Cairo, Paris, and the Limehouse section of London he had never met "a mysterious master mind or a really good looking adventuress with slant eyes. This," he concluded, "is discouraging."[5] Carr was a storyteller, not only in his books but in his everyday life, and he seldom admitted that some of his tales were fantasies until his wife challenged him. "Oh, come on," she would say, and he would grin happily and answer, "Well, it's a good story; I might use it in a book."[6]

This trait, which is entertaining in the man, can bedevil his biographer. Carr knew the value of retaining papers; he was delighted that the Doyle family had done so, thereby making research for his *Life of Sir Arthur Conan Doyle* relatively straightforward. But he never believed that his own papers would become important, even though his agents told him that libraries might be interested. Each time the Carrs moved—and during one decade they pulled up stakes about every other year—they discarded letters and documents. Not a single typescript is known to survive of a John Dickson Carr novel, and his immediate family has only a handful of his letters. Fortunately, the factual basis of many of Carr's stories can be judged from other sources. He had a vivid personality. His friends and acquaintances remember him distinctly and almost always with great fondness, not only for his detective novels but also for his generosity and courtesies. It is difficult to find instances where he consciously hurt anyone, even on those occasions when, by strict standards (and using a prim and proper Victorian word), his life was irregular. In interviewing Carr's childhood friends as well as his preparatory school and college classmates, I found that even after sixty or more years almost everyone recalled some colorful anecdote about him. In many instances, several different accounts of the same event survive, and Carr's version can be balanced against the memory of his friends.

Fortunately, the survival of other material makes up, in large measure, for the lack of family papers. From an early age, John Carr loved to write, and beginning when he was fifteen years old, his essays on various topics were published in his hometown newspaper. By 1935 various correspondents had begun to preserve his letters. Fellow detective-story writers Dorothy L. Sayers, Anthony Boucher, Clayton Rawson, and Frederic Dannay (who was half of Ellery Queen) kept correspondence, and less consistently so did Carr's publishers and agents. By the 1960s, when Carr was recognized as one of the greatest of grand masters of detective fiction, fans (including me) were showering him with letters, and these fans have courteously made Carr's answers available. I have located some 350 letters from John Dickson Carr, but these letters leave gaps in subject matter that will necessarily be reflected in this biography. Almost all of Carr's correspondence with Hamish Hamilton, who published Carr's books under his own name, are still in the possession of that company, and his American publishers, Harper & Brothers, have a scattering of Carr's letters. But the publishers of his books under the Carter Dickson pseudonym, William Morrow of New York and William Heinemann of London, told me that their correspondence with John Dickson Carr was destroyed. Some of the gaps in publishers' files can be filled with material preserved by his British agents, Pearn, Pollinger and Higham, beginning in 1950, and by his United States agents, Rene de Chochor and James Oliver Brown, beginning in 1952, but we still know more about the writing of the books published under Carr's own name than about those published as by Carter Dickson.

Still, despite all the documentary evidence, some of the stories that Carr told cannot be verified. Did he as a lad change the organ pipes around at a church or chapel? (Answer: probably.) Did he plan to attend the Sorbonne in Paris during 1927 and 1928? (Perhaps.) Did he attend Harvard University? (Probably not.) Did he and a friend create an upside-down room? (Almost certainly not.) Did he have an emergency appendectomy at college performed by an untrained classmate? (Definitely not.) Some of these tales and others in a similar category will be discussed later, but in all cases a clear warning will be added when the source is only John Dickson Carr.

S. T. Joshi has recently written a book about Carr's works, entitled simply *John Dickson Carr, a Critical Study* (Bowling Green State University Popular Press, 1990). Joshi's book is filled with insights about Carr's writings and attitudes. I have learned much from it, but the reader of this biography will soon discover that I disagree with some of its judgments. Besides Joshi's book, readers should consult an important chapter devoted to John Dickson Carr in LeRoy Lad Panek's *Watteau's Shepherds, The Detective Novel in Britain, 1914–1940* (Bowling Green University Popular Press, 1979), which contains the best analysis of how Carr's books work as detective fiction.

John Dickson Carr was a complex man, who impressed different people in different ways. His widow says that "I do not think anyone saw the same person in him."[7] There is an irony in writing a biography of John

Dickson Carr that tries to make a contribution to understanding the forces that made him, for Carr himself did not think that psychological analysis is the proper role of either fiction or biography. His dislike of realistic novels that analyze character was almost as great as his hatred of mathematics. Detective stories, he said, should tell *"who* or *how* rather than the not-very-appealing *why*."[8] In writing about Doyle's Professor Challenger, Carr complained, "Novelists, nowadays, are sometimes praised for the art with which they 'put a character under the microscope and dissect him.' Conan Doyle never did this. He never needed to do it. To be dissected, a character must be dead. And there is nothing dead about George Edward Challenger. Subjected to the process of dissection, it is to be feared, he would arise bodily from the page and retaliate with a punch in the nose."[9] This argument will not impress a logician, but there is no denying that Carr felt strongly that clinical or formal psychology has no legitimate place in literature, even in nonfiction. When he wrote his biography of Sir Arthur Conan Doyle as "a story of adventure,"[10] he quite consciously decided that it was enough to describe what Doyle did and what he said, not what created the personality that did and said such things.

Carr would be pleased to know that not enough material survives about his formative years to place him metaphorically upon a couch and ask, in the words of Dr. Fell (disguised as a Viennese psychologist, Sigismund von Hornswoggle), "Vot you dream?"[11] On the other hand, Carr did think that at an early age—he suggested the age of seven—"our essential tastes begin to be stamped on us by outside impressions. They are never eradicated, even when we think we have forgotten them."[12] But although he might forgive me for trying to locate his essential tastes during his childhood, he would be less pleased by my suggestion that his early relations with his mother were important. That idea, though I don't draw any Oedipal conclusions from it, might seem too close to the theories of Sigmund Freud, whose work he especially despised. The reader, however, will be able to judge the persuasiveness of this and other suggestions.

In writing this book, I have incurred many debts. I believe that I have recorded the names of all those whom my allies in research have interviewed, but if I have missed anyone on the following pages, please accept my apologies.

First I must express my deep gratitude to Old Dominion University and especially Dr. Charles O. Burgess, dean of the College of Arts and Letters, for granting me a leave of absence in order to write this book.

For locating letters and other papers, I am grateful to the following, several of whom supplied copies of their own correspondence with John Dickson Carr: Donna Slawsky of Harper & Row, Publishers (now Harper-Collins); Roger Smith of William Heinemann, Publishers; James Woodall of Hamish Hamilton, Ltd.; the late John G. Murray of John Murray, Publishers; Bruce Hunter of David Higham Associates; Austin J. McLean, Special Collections, University of Minnesota Library; Cynthia Farar, Harry Ransom Humanities Research Center, University of Texas at Austin; Loretta A. Alfaro, Research and Liaison, Passport Office, Department of State; Bernard Crystal, Columbia University Library; Virginia Kolb, Wheaton College Library; Margaret Goostray, Mugar Memorial Library, Boston University; Lilly Library, Indiana University; Rhoda Cousins and John Jordan, Written Archive Center, British Broadcasting Corporation; BBC Radio Drama Library; British National Sound Archive; Samuel Brylawski, Library of Congress; Edda Tasiemska, the Hans Tasiemska Archives; British Library (Newspaper Division) at Colindale; Leslie Baldwin, City University Library, London; Rosalie Abrahams; Jan Broberg; Richard Clark; Benjamin F. Fisher IV; Allen J. Hubin; Otto Penzler; Norma Schier; the late Eleanor Sullivan, editor of *Ellery Queen's Mystery Magazine*; Nick Utechin; and Francis Wilford-Smith.

For material relating to John Carr's childhood in Uniontown, Pennsylvania, I am especially grateful to the Honorable Edward Dumbauld, senior district judge, Western District of Pennsylvania. Judge Dumbauld, who was probably John's closest boyhood friend, not only recorded his memories for this book, but also put me in contact with others who remember John as a boy: Mary Rosboro Carroll, Louise Shelby Connor, Mrs. Stuart Forstall, Hannah Messmore Henderson, Mary White Hubbard, Anna Jones, John Messmore, Sr., Winifred Woodfill. When I visited Uniontown, I met David J. Beeson and he recorded some memories of John. Among others in Uniontown, I am also grateful to Helen Snaith, librarian, Uniontown High School, for locating Carr's earliest published works; Delores Rhodes of Uniontown Public Library for access to copies of the *Uniontown Daily News Standard;* and Walter J. (Buzz) Storey for recollections of William O'Neil Kennedy and for a photocopy of Kennedy's pamphlet, *Bachelor Abroad.*

For memories of The Hill School, I am in debt to Carr's classmates, the Honorable Herbert S. MacDonald and Dr. William B. Willcox. I am also grateful to James A. Gundy III, director of development, The Hill School;

William F. Hallstead III; and Shannon Hunt Wilson and Dr. Barbara Koelle, who located Carr's preparatory-school writings.

For material on Haverford College, I am grateful to Carr's coworkers on *The Haverfordian*, John Rodell, Samuel Cook, and the late Frederic Prokosch, as well as Diana Alten, Haverford College Library, who arranged to lend me copies of the Carr-edited issues of *The Haverfordian*. Through the kindness of John Loughname and Timothy Wilson, of Haverford's alumni association, a request for information appeared in the alumni magazine, with the result that I obtained the valuable assistance of John's classmates: Dr. Herbert Ensworth, the late Francis C. Jameson, the Reverend Joe McNamee, James Partington, Jr., and Walter Sondheim, Jr. Donald Rumbelow put me in contact with Mrs. Beatrice Clifford McDade, whom John Carr dated at Haverford and who has kindly supplied information. Professor Robert Greenfield, who is writing a critical study of the works of Frederic Prokosch, has helped to identify the authorship of some *Haverfordian* material. Rebecca J. Bates, curatorial assistant, Harvard University Archives, examined Harvard records.

For material on John Dickson Carr's years at Columbia Heights, I thank Edward Coleman Delafield, Jr., and John Murray Reynolds. Ray Stanich has checked on locations in the area. Roland Lacourbe, the French expert on John Dickson Carr (and on the cinema), has provided material on Carr's visits to Paris.

For information on the world of the pulp magazines in the middle 1930s, I am grateful to the late Henry Steeger, founder of Popular Publications; pulp writers Ryerson Johnson, Hugh B. Cave, and the late Theodore Roscoe; and pulp experts Robert Weinberg, Ron Goulart, Stephen Miller, and Jack Deveny.

For material on John and Clarice Carr's years in England, I am deeply obligated to Tony Medawar, whose indefatigable research unearthed lost or little-known writings of John Dickson Carr and who interviewed many people in London and elsewhere. Robert C. S. Adey, Ken Cowley, John Curran, John Jeffries, Nick Kimber, B. A. Pike, Derek Smith, Collin Southern, Geoffrey H. Webster, and Dr. James E. Keirans gathered information that for geographical or temporal reasons I could not obtain myself. I should add too that Jim Keirans has photographed Carr residences in America and Britain, and his sharing the photographs with me has allowed me to describe those buildings with some precision. Others in England who supplied important material or memories include Alan Wykes;

D. G. White; Barry Mann, hon. archivist, Savage Club; Kay Hutchings, librarian, Garrick Club; Philippa Boland, Writers' Summer School; Geoffrey Bush of the Carr Society; Edwin A. Dawes and John Wade of the Magic Circle; Jill Elly Riley, the Museum of Broadcasting; Richard Mangan, the Raymond Mander and Joe Mitchener Theatrical Archive; June Whitfield (who acted in the play *She Slept Lightly*); Ernest Dudley; Toni Naldrett; Leonard Huckman; Richard Usborne; Max Martyn; and Rupert Allason (Nigel West).

For information on The Detection Club and associated material on British writers, I am indebted to the honorary president of The Detection Club, H. R. F. Keating, the late Christianna Brand and her husband, Roland Lewis, Elizabeth Ferrars, Michael Gilbert, Michael Innes, Anthony Lejeune, the late Gladys Mitchell, Julian Symons, Sir Kingsley Amis, Lady Wykeham (daughter of J. B. Priestley), Nicky Stoddard (of J. B. Priestley's agents, Peters, Fraser, & Dunlop), Janet Morgan (biographer of Agatha Christie), Rosalind Hicks (daughter of Agatha Christie), Betty D. Vernon (biographer of Margaret Cole), and David Whittle (who is writing a biography of Edmund Crispin).

For details on Carr's association with Adrian Conan Doyle, I am especially grateful to Richard Lancelyn Green, whose transcriptions of the correspondence between Adrian and his brother Denis Conan Doyle were invaluable. I am also grateful to Peter E. Blau, Dame Jean Conan Doyle, the late Michael Harrison, Jon Lellenberg, and Howard Lachtman.

For information on the Mystery Writers of America and associated material on United States writers and editors, as well as material on the Mamaroneck years, I thank Michael Avallone, Elaine Budd, Mary Cantwell, Dorothy Salisbury Davis, Lillian de la Torre, Edward D. Hoch, Joan Kahn, Harold Q. Masur, Francis M. Nevins, Jr., Bill Pronzini, Katherine Rawson, Hugh Rawson, Clayton Rawson, Jr., Phyllis P. White, and Barry Zeman. For material about the Carrs' holiday in Sweden, I thank Johan Wopenka and Ake Runnquist.

For material on the years at Greenville, South Carolina, I thank Norvin Duncan, Sally Edwards, Carol McCarthy, Mr. and Mrs. Arthur Magill, Edna Seamans, and Penny Forrester of Greenville County Library. Paul E. Greene supplied information on Social Security and tax matters. Dr. Susan Mandell helped me to understand medical matters related to Carr's last years.

Others whose assistance has been invaluable include Ramon Nadal Albiol, Hugh Abramson of International Polygonics, Ltd., William S. Armstrong IV, Victor Berch, Matthew Berger, Mauro Boncompagni, Gary G. Brockman, John W. Campanella, Gilbert J. Chin, William Dunn, the late Larry L. French, David L. Godwin, Paul Halter, Paul M. James, Jerry Kaiz, the late Roger Kuehl, Stephen Leadbetter, Charles MacDonald, Daniel P. Mannix, Christine May, Christopher Lee Phillips, L. Sayer, Jim Schoenberger, Anthony Shaffer, David S. Siegel, Steven Steinbock, and Douglas Waugh. Ruth Bradberry and David L. Greene, along with the ever generous and energetic Jim Keirans and Tony Medawar, read the typescript of this book and caught errors and suggested improvements. I am also grateful to the people at Otto Penzler Books—Otto Penzler, Kate Stine, Teresa Huddleston, and my editor, Michele Slung—for their many contributions to the final version of this book.

John Young has been a constant source of enthusiasm, encouragement, and support. I owe much to him.

I doubt that any biographer has received more friendly assistance from the subject's family. John Dickson Carr's cousin Wooda (Nick) Carr first suggested that I write this book, and he supplied photographs, letters, and other family material. Two other cousins, Phillip Carr and William Kisinger, courteously answered my questions. I am grateful also to John's brother-in-law, Roy Cleaves, for recording his memories about the Carrs' Kingswood days. John's widow, Clarice Cleaves Carr, authorized this biography, and she and her daughters, Julia McNiven, Bonita Cron, and Mary Howes, have been unfailingly helpful. After more than fifteen telephone interviews with Clarice and fewer but lengthy interviews with Julia and Mary, I am sure that they began to feel squeezed dry of information; Bonnie has avoided my onslaught, at least partly, only because she lives in New Zealand, but she has kindly answered my questions by letter, and by telephone on those occasions when I caught her while she was visiting the United States. Julia's husband, Richard McNiven, has also patiently answered my questions. The Carrs tried to ensure that I have accurately recorded facts, but they exercised no control over my interpretations or on the emphasis of the presentation. My inability to get something right or to understand something fully must be laid entirely on my shoulders. If this book deserves any praise, it should go to those who so willingly and generously gave their time and information to the project.

Douglas G. Greene
Norfolk, Virginia
May 1994

A Note on Solutions

John Dickson Carr remarked that the one thing a critic must not do is reveal the solution to a detective novel, and most mystery fans rightly agree. Nonetheless, how Carr resolved the puzzle is often significant in understanding his life and works. When I find it necessary to give away the ending of a story, I have placed four asterisks (****) immediately before the offending passage, and have placed the passage's opening sentence within brackets and in boldface type. Some readers may wish to skip to the succeeding paragraph.

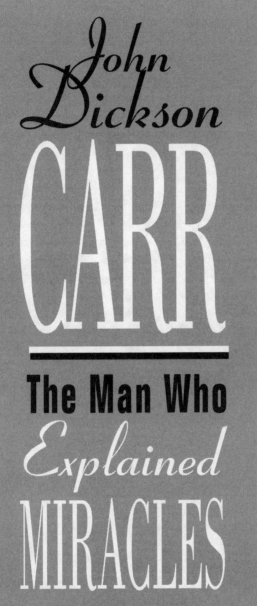

John Dickson

CARR

The Man Who

Explained

MIRACLES

Chapter 1

UNIONTOWN

Looking back at Uniontown, Pennsylvania, where he had been born and spent his childhood, John Dickson Carr invested the community with romance:

> The lamps of the old town were brightening in winter dusk. The seven-thirty train whistled, far away, and you could see the yellow face of the court-house clock. A few snowflakes drifted as shadows across bright and clean-swept streets. They had laid out these streets in the year Washington took command of the continental army. Through them would always blow the wind of stage-coaches, and the note of the key-bugle from the great days of the National Highway; the town below the blue mountains would keep its rattling hum, its muddy yellow creek, and its ghosts.[1]

What others less poetically inclined would have seen was a bustling commercial community, wealthy from the profits of the coal mining and the coke furnaces (or "beehive ovens") that glowed in the hills surrounding the town. The mines were worked by immigrant laborers, primarily from central Europe, who lived in what were called "patches" outside town, while the owners had homes in Uniontown itself. Current inhabitants look back on that period almost as a golden age. There were about a dozen men considered millionaires in the community; the leaders of society gathered around the Episcopal and Presbyterian churches; and as Uniontown was the county seat of Fayette County, there was a lively interest in legal and political affairs. A point of pride for Uniontown and the surrounding valley was the mansion on the Barnes estate in the small community of Hopwood, just off one of the main roads leading from Uniontown to West Virginia. Uniontown was also proud of its past. In the narrow yard outside the courthouse was a gilt-covered statue of the Marquis de Lafayette, erected to honor that statesman's visit to Uniontown in 1825.[2] As a boy, John Carr looked at the statue and thought of romance—of swordsmen, and honor, and dedication to a cause.

Uniontown lies about fifty miles south of Pittsburgh, and despite the fact that the trip through the mountains might take three and a half or four hours by automobile, many touring companies used to come by way of Pittsburgh to put on shows at one of Uniontown's several theaters. Uniontown had, and still retains, the atmosphere of a small town, enclosed metaphorically as well as physically by its coal-producing mountains. But it kept windows to the outer world through Pittsburgh, through the theatrical companies, and through politics. And one of its leading politicians was John Dickson Carr's father, Wooda Nicholas Carr.

As genealogists might put it, the immigrant of this branch of the Carr family was Nicholas Carr, who was born in Ireland in 1819 of Scots-Irish stock. He settled in Allegheny County, Pennsylvania, where in the words of a book of local puffery "he became identified with the livestock business. . . . His business was very extensive among the butchers."[3] His son, John Dickson Carr I, born in 1849, was a contractor who dealt in marble cabinets and other interior furnishings, as well as more prosaic items, including concrete paving. Sidewalks can still be found in Uniontown with the imprint "Jno. D. Carr." He married Amanda M. Cook, who according to family tradition was a descendant of Colonel Edward Cook, a Revolutionary War hero and founder of Cookstown on the Monongahela.[4] She would become a doting grandmother to young John Carr, encouraging the boy's interest in reading. When John became an author himself, he presented her with a copy of his second book, with the note that it was "in memory of the days when he read her better stories than this."[5]

John D. and Amanda Carr had seven children, the first of whom was Wooda Nicholas Carr, born February 6, 1871, in Allegheny City (now part of Pittsburgh), Pennsylvania. The family moved to Uniontown in 1885. Six years later, Wooda graduated from Monongahela College with plans to become a journalist. His father had a financial interest in a local newspaper, and in 1891 "Wood" or "Woody" (as his friends generally called him) became editor of the *Uniontown Standard* and in 1893 of another local paper, the *Democrat*. Soon, however, he withdrew from the newspaper business in order to study law. At that time, it was more common for a prospective lawyer to work with an older member of the bar than to attend law school. In *Poison in Jest*, John's early novel set outside Uniontown, he remembered "the hard-drinking, hard-thinking, whisky-and-spittoon lawyers who did not study laws, but made them," and he contrasted them with the newer generation, who bragged about attending law school: "Under the shadow of the great lawyers whose voices boom from the old days, you will grub forever among deeds and minor litigations and catch-penny knavery, and on your grave shall be written: 'He went to law school.'"[6]

Wooda Carr was admitted to the bar in 1895, and soon became one of Fayette County's most prominent lawyers. He practiced before the supreme courts of Pennsylvania and the United States, and in 1908 he formed a partnership with his younger brother, W. Russell Carr, who had studied under his guidance for two years. Contemporaries recall that the personalities of the brothers complemented each other: Russell was the studious member of the firm and he handled its business side; Wooda, although also interested in scholarship, enjoyed more the give and take of the courtroom. W. Russell Carr later became president judge of the Court of Common Pleas of Fayette County. Another of Wooda's brothers was, like his father, named John D. Carr—in this case, however, the middle name was Dennis. He was a physician who eventually moved to North Dakota, where he became head of a psychiatric hospital.

Wooda N. Carr was married on October 21, 1903, to the twenty-five-year-old Julia May Lenox Kisinger of the nearby town of Brownsville. In the early years of their marriage, they lived in an apartment in the eleven-story, yellow brick National Bank Building (now Fayette Bank) at the corner of Main and Morgantown streets, and it was there that their son John Dickson Carr was born on November 30, 1906. Although some sources have suggested that John had siblings, he was—except for an earlier child who died in infancy—an only child. He was named after his grandfather, and because of the two John D. Carrs in previous generations, he was generally referred to as John III.

Beginning with the Bryan–McKinley campaign of 1896, Wooda Carr had been active in Democratic party politics as an old-fashioned stump

orator. His general appearance—short, bald, and tending toward plump-
ness—reminded his listeners of William Jennings Bryan. Bryan, in fact,
was an occasional visitor at Wooda Carr's home. (Julia Carr said that of all
her husband's political associates, Bryan was the greatest trencherman:
"He ate everything you put in front of him!")[7] Like Bryan, Wooda loved
the power and rhythm of language. Edward Dumbauld, one of young
John's closest friends, recalls Wooda Carr proclaiming that:

> I have looked upon this Republican Party in its concavity and in its
> convexity, in its magnitude and in its pulchritude, in its obliquity and
> in its iniquity; and I am moved to exclaim with King Lear of old,
> "Give me an ounce of civet, good apothecary, to sweeten my imagi-
> nation."[8]

Fayette County usually voted Republican during this period, but in 1900
Wooda at the age of twenty-nine bravely ran for Congress. He was defeated, and so was his father when the older man was a candidate eight
years later.

A political opportunity for the Fayette County Democrats and for
Wooda Carr came in 1912. The Republicans had been split by Theodore
Roosevelt's Progressive party or "Bull Moose" bid for the presidency.
Wooda received the unanimous Democratic nomination to run against
the sitting Republican member of Congress, Thomas S. Crago, whose
party had been weakened by the decision of the Bull Moose party to run a
candidate. A story that is still current in Uniontown has young John being
enlisted in his father's cause. The boy had always been, in a sense, on dis-
play. At the age of three, he had been taught to recite the names of the
presidents of the United States, and in 1912, almost six years old and
dressed in his best sailor suit and boater hat, he would stand on a table at
political rallies and recite poems.[9] Whatever the effect of young John's appearances, the vote on November 6 came as a surprise: Wooda Carr received an absolute majority, 7,040 of a total vote of 13,518. Pennsylvania
was one of the states won by Theodore Roosevelt, but Woodrow Wilson
took the presidency and the Democrats dominated the House of Representatives by the greatest margin of the past twenty years.[10]

Wooda Nicholas Carr, member of Congress from the Twenty-third District of Pennsylvania, arrived with his family in Washington, D.C., at the
end of 1912 or early in 1913, where, to quote a rather strange Uniontown
comment, he became "one of the honest and sincere young men who
could always be counted upon to uphold the hands of the Wilson admin-

istration."[11] Although John always said that he had "very vivid childhood memories" of Washington, he recorded only a few anecdotes:

> While my father thundered in Congress, I stood on a table in the members' anteroom, pinwheeled by a God-awful collar, and recited Hamlet's Soliloquy to certain gentlemen named Thomas Heflin and Pat Harrison and Claude Kitchin and others whom I have apparently since inspired along that line.

He crawled onto the lap of the former speaker of the House, "Uncle" Joseph Cannon to hear ghost stories; he asked President Wilson what his name was; and he learned how to shoot craps from congressional page boys.[12]

The Carrs lived in the Congressional Apartments, at the corner of East Capitol Street across from the Library of Congress. The apartments are the setting for an early scene in one of John's last novels, *The Ghosts' High Noon*. Unfortunately, he recorded little more than that the building was small and built of red brick, and that the basement had a "cramped and raftered" bar and grill. Much to his mother's displeasure, John often sneaked out of the apartment to sell newspapers on the street with a paperboy, who was black.[13] There were very few black people in Uniontown, and John grew up with almost no racist preconceptions. Unlike the works of many other popular authors of the era, John Dickson Carr's novels and short stories would rarely reflect fears and stereotypes about blacks. In the immediate context, however, the connection with newspapers is more indicative of what would come. Probably because of his grandfather's and father's earlier association with the Uniontown papers, anything to do with journalism had a tremendous attraction for John. Along with his two years in the nation's capital, newspapers showed him that there was a large world beyond southwestern Pennsylvania.

But the Washington period was only a brief interlude for Wooda and Julia Carr and their son. In the election of November 3, 1914, the Democrats took a beating. Their 185-seat majority in the House of Representatives was reduced to only nineteen, and they lost six of their twelve seats in Pennsylvania. Congressman Wooda N. Carr was defeated by almost three thousand votes as Fayette County reverted to its traditional Republicanism.[14] Around 1910, the Carrs had moved to a large turreted Victorian house at 25 Ben Lomond Street. Five or six years later, they moved to 52 South Mount Vernon Avenue—another rambling house, with carved marble chimneypieces and a staircase in the central hallway. Here they remained until John went off to preparatory school in 1922. The Carrs' next house, at 60 Ben Lomond Street, was slightly smaller, but it was still a spacious dwelling because it had to house Wooda's impressive library.

In 1912 it was said of Wooda Carr that "his recreation is taken with his books, he having probably the best selected if not the largest private library in the state."[15] The walls of his houses on Mount Vernon Avenue and Ben Lomond Street were lined with leather-bound sets of the great authors—Charles Dickens, Mark Twain, William Shakespeare, William Makepeace Thackeray, and above all O. Henry, probably his favorite writer. Wooda's library had many volumes of poetry from which he liked to quote in his political speeches. John later remembered that his father had "a strong taste for sensationalism," and that he owned numerous accounts of criminal trials in addition to novels of adventure, mystery, and espionage. He also had books of American history, including a multivolume account of the Civil War illustrated with Mathew Brady photographs. Wooda Carr could often be found sitting with a book in front of him, and he was always willing to lend volumes even to neighborhood children. Children adored him because he made time to listen to them, to treat their ideas with polite respect, and to tell them stories.[16]

Perhaps more than anything else Wooda Carr was a storyteller. Sometimes he used a Pennsylvania Dutch accent to tell amusing anecdotes, but more often—gesturing with his cigar and speaking in a sonorous voice—he talked about great events. Life to him was a thunderous drama; everything that happened was writ large, like the clash of debate and personality in the courtroom. As his son listened avidly, Wooda told tales of the criminal cases that he was involved in. In his later letters John often told anecdotes inspired by his "father, an old warhorse of many criminal trials."[17]

To Wooda N. Carr history was not about the slow growth of social and economic patterns but about events and personalities and clashing ideals. From Wooda's viewpoint, history confirmed his fervent patriotism: The story of the American Revolution proved the benefits of American democracy. He impressed on his son that the family had come from Ireland, not England, and that the British had oppressed both the Irish and the American colonists. In contrast to his later stance, John in his youth was an anglophobe, hating what he called "Jawn Bull" for his oppression of Ireland. When, for example, the English proposed an agreement with Ireland in 1922, the fifteen-year-old John D. Carr III thundered, "Ireland needs an-

other champion as fearless as St. Patrick to tell J. Bull where to head in
when he springs another trick 'compromise.'"[18]

As a boy, John echoed his father's opinions. When Rudyard Kipling in
1922 was quoted as criticizing the United States' participation in the
World War, John wrote:

> It is not what we did in the world war that hurts Kipling so much as
> what we did in that little scrap in 1776. . . . He speaks for that poison
> in the English system, the royalist element, whose numbers are hap-
> pily diminishing. The English throne is none too secure and there are
> evidences that George V may be the last of his tribe.[19]

The early influence of his father's views may explain the odd quality in
some of John's historical novels, a quality that can only be called "aristocratic egalitarianism."

John Dickson Carr eventually gave up his dislike of England, and
shortly before his father died, John found the temerity to question the
depth of his father's oft-expressed opinions of British/American relations.
In *The Cavalier's Cup*, a book that he wrote during July and August 1952,
John based one of the characters at least partly on Wooda. Congressman
William T. Harvey of the "23 1/2 congressional district of Pennsylvania . . .
just outside Pittsburgh," is described as the son of "old John D." In fairness, however, it must be pointed out that as colorful as Wooda N. Carr
undoubtedly was, he certainly did not engage in all the highjinks attributed to Congressman Harvey, including chasing (and catching) a female
member of Parliament clad only in her underwear. However, when Sir
Henry Merrivale points out that "Harvey" is an English name, the congressman's enraged answer may have been taken from John's childhood:
"It's despicable Republican propaganda. My forebears were all Scottish
and Irish, every single one of them. There's not a drop of English blood in
my veins! Not one drop!"[20]

Julia Kisinger Carr was so different from her husband that neighbors
often wondered how the two came to marry. While Wooda was mild, and
his speech rolled out sonorously, Julia was emotional, temperamental, exuberant, and frequently sarcastic. She had a sharp tongue, and she liked
to tease the menfolk around her in the hope of getting a rise out of them;
then when everyone else had become furious, she would laugh uproariously. She had absolutely no interest in books, and would berate her husband—with no effect at all—in an attempt to drag his attention away

from his reading. She was heard to say, "If I ever marry again, I'm going to marry a man who can't read." The difference between husband and wife extended even to the church they attended. Julia was an Episcopalian, and Wooda a Presbyterian; young John generally went with his father to the First Presbyterian Church.

The neighborhood children tended to goggle at Julia's hennaed hair, which was always an unlikely black-red combination. Her three sisters, who lived a staid antebellum life in Brownsville, saw her as a "New Woman," an independent soul at a time that female independence seemed radical. Others, however, found her a limited woman who could not understand her intellectual husband and her imaginative son. Mrs. Anna Carroll Jones, whose brother Jim was a childhood friend of John's, has perhaps the most balanced view: "A sort of harried general, she had the daily task of prodding her detached and procrastinating troops into action." Her husband and her son could retreat so thoroughly into their own worlds that managing the family must have been a constant challenge. Neighbors still recall her calling in strong voice "Wood" or "John" when she wanted something, and not always getting a response.[21]

For many years, Wooda was a heavy drinker. Later in life, he would have to be hospitalized for alcoholism before finally giving up the bottle.[22] However, around 1916 he was offered the chance to indulge away from his wife's scrutiny. Parents on Ben Lomond Street and nearby decided that it would do their sons good to spend two weeks camping in the mountains. Except for a lifelong love of baseball, Wooda Carr was not athletic, but he was the only father to volunteer to be the leader of "Camp Ben Lomond," and he managed to take along a private supply of refreshment. Long after, some of the boys still remembered the strange effects his thirst quenching had on baseball games he umpired at Camp Ben Lomond. The camp did not become an annual affair.

In spite of their differences, however, Wooda and Julia Carr seemed always to enjoy each other's company. As they grew older, whenever Wooda was in the sitting room in his favorite chair with a book, Julia would be in the same room listening to the radio. They often spent their evenings sitting together on the front porch. Toward the end of his life, when Wooda was quite ill, his wife devotedly and uncomplainingly acted as his nurse.[23]

However one tries to understand Julia Kisinger Carr, there is no doubt that she and her son never got along. Some people who knew both say that he loathed her. To take one example of how she could anger him, he was known as Johnny as a child, but when he grew older he hated the name, and indeed denied that he ever had a nickname. When he was an adult, his mother could drive him out of a room by addressing him as Johnny, and sometimes did so. Probably the most fundamental part of their relationship was that she did not understand a boy who often lived in his own world and who, like his father, found the drama of history and of books more compelling than life in small-town America. Ironies, even contradictions, abound in this situation. Julia could certainly be an iconoclast, yet her iconoclasm was limited by her strong sense of the fitness of things. She wanted John to behave like a perfect child, while John himself admired the heroes of romance who did not have to be concerned about what the world thought. John himself also tended to iconoclasm, opposing fashionable ideas, but—again ironically—he too thought that correct behavior was important.

No biographer should try to make all of this consistent, because neither Julia Kisinger Carr nor John Dickson Carr was ever able to resolve the contradictions. But Julia's caustic remarks when John was less than a complete gentleman made things worse, and he responded by retreating to an attic room to read or to write: For the rest of his life, he preferred to have his study in an attic. Punishments didn't help either; threats with a hairbrush had no effect, nor did the extraordinary solution promoted by Julia's sisters of wrapping the boy's forehead with wet towels to drive the strange ideas out of his brain. The ideas never left John, nor did his dislike of his mother. Even during his final months confined to a nursing home—when his mother had been dead for ten years—he still talked about her with dislike.[24] It seems safe to assume that every time a strong-minded or man-dominating woman appears as a character in one of his books, she is based at least in part on Julia Kisinger Carr.

Although John had bouts with the usual childhood diseases—whooping cough when he was seven years old, chicken pox when he was eight, and measles when he was fourteen—he was on the whole an active child.[25] He enjoyed sports, but, because he was smaller than most boys his age, he was unable to participate in many of them. Size, however, did not keep him from baseball. In the summers his father took him on day trips to Pittsburgh to see the Pirates play. John could become almost lyrical when, as a teenager, he wrote about the game:

> To see a slugger meet the ball with the sharp, clean crack of the bat that is the harbinger of a long, powerful drive; to see the gray pellet

speeding far above the heads of the infield, and then to see a fielder
leap high and pluck it from the air in a spectacular catch that robs the
batter of a possible home run—that, we think, provides the greatest
satisfaction.[26]

John played baseball with the other boys in the neighborhood, usually as
catcher or second baseman. In later years, he recalled an automatic pitching machine in Uniontown, frequented by young ballplayers, and he described it in one of his novels:

> At the far end, in what appeared to be a padded rear wall, they could
> see a dark aperture like an open doorway. In the middle of the aper-
> ture loomed some box-like metal contrivance which grotesquely sug-
> gested an altar. . . . A shiny white baseball appeared up over the back
> of the altar, where metal glinted faintly. After seeming to hang there
> for an instant, it flew towards the plate.[27]

Baseball would often play a part in John's novels, from Dr. Gideon Fell's
attempts to construe baseball slang into Latin, to Sir Henry Merrivale's
blasting one out of the park, to (in some of the final stories) grown men attempting to settle competition over women by playing ball. A Carr expert,
Dr. James E. Keirans, has taken an inventory of the characters in Carr's
books and found that he mentioned at least seven real-life players, from
Christy Mathewson to Roger Maris. According to young John Carr's application for admission to preparatory school, he was also interested in
horseback riding and swimming.

Although John was not naturally mechanically inclined, he was fascinated by gadgets of all sorts (including pitching machines), and these too
would leave marks in his stories. For example, as a boy he was intrigued
by the relatively new phenomenon of radio—even to the point of learning how to wire a set. In 1922, he called radio "the greatest invention of
the age. . . . It will not die." He believed that Marconi was one of the six
greatest men of history—the others being Aristotle, Caesar, Roger Bacon,
Francis Bacon, and Abraham Lincoln.[28] When he was about sixteen years
old, a neighbor, John Messmore, taught him how to drive, in a Dodge
owned by Wooda Carr. John did learn, but not easily, and he nicknamed
the automobile "True Love" because its course did not run smoothly.[29] As
an adult, he much preferred having others drive.

Among John's lifelong enthusiasms were the theater and the movies.
He escorted neighboring girls to see touring theatrical productions that

played in Uniontown. The town also had four or five movie theaters, and John preferred stories that featured swashbuckling heroes like Douglas Fairbanks, Sr., swinging from one balcony to another.[30] One of his favorites was the 1917 silent film *A Tale of Two Cities*. Sound wasn't necessary for an enthusiastic audience:

> They can see [Carton's] lips move (John said) in the speech whose closing words are known in every civilized country on the face of the earth. They can see the jeering crowd surging like an angry sea about the base of the guillotine. Then, through the mist, they can see the heavy knife flash downward.

Other pictures that he praised included such stirring epics as *Les Miserables* and *The Last of the Mohicans*. He also liked westerns, though he complained about the tendency of some audience members of such fare to read the title frames out loud. A quarter-century later, he also remembered movies about scientific detective Craig Kennedy, whose "early film serials . . . held us petrified."[31]

As a fifteen-year-old, he felt so strongly about the movies that he objected when, in response to the Fatty Arbuckle scandal and the William Desmond Taylor murder, the suggestion was bruited that the film industry appoint some kind of dictator to clean things up. In words that were something less than a ringing endorsement, John wrote that "the movies are not as a rule depraved. . . . They condemn the movies on the strength of two or three paltry crimes!" More positively, he praised the films for teaching morality when they showed villains getting their comeuppance, and for presenting classic literature in a way that was easy to understand. Rather than trying to censure films, John proposed that moralists should make certain that all schools have movie projectors for classroom use.[32]

Perhaps showing films in the classroom would have made John Carr a more attentive high school student. His classmates, amused by the "III" after his name, nicknamed him "John D. Three Eyes." He was looked upon as bright but not always involved in the classes, and somewhat offbeat. Wearing his hair a bit longer than the other boys (for reasons no one seems to have recorded), John would often arrive for classes "laughing and talking," recalls one of his schoolmates, Winifred Woodfill, "and usually a little late." His favorite classes were the literature classes taught by Reardon S. Cotton, who encouraged John to become a writer and who also took an interest in his pupils outside school. For example, Cotton taught John, Edward Dumbauld, and others the rudiments of chess.[33]

Probably influenced by his father's interest in politics, John enjoyed his civics class, too. Winifred Woodfill remembers that when the teacher, Mr. Mosier, assigned students to draw a plan for a model town, all of them except John came in with amateurish papers. John, however, had produced an elaborately detailed map of a town that he had named Brysonville after the principal. The streets and squares were named for John's teachers—Mr. Mosier had Mosier Boulevard, the Latin teacher, Miss Clutter, was remembered in Clutter Street, and so on.[34] On the other hand, John was not particularly interested in his science classes, and he positively hated mathematics. He had no aptitude for the subject and no interest in struggling through it, and when John was bored by something he could not imagine why it might appeal to others. For example, after what must have been a frustrating day in a mathematics class, John was walking home with Edward Dumbauld. "I unctuously spoke the word 'algebra,'" Dumbauld reports, "whereupon John turned and struck me in the chest, breaking the glasses in my pocket."[35] He called mathematics "the last refuge of the halfwit," and peppered his books with unkind comments on the subject. More than forty years later, he still recalled his frustrations in trying to solve algebraic problems. One of his characters remarks:

> To me mathematics means the activities of those mischievous lunatics, A, B, and C. In my time they were always starting two trains at high speed from distant points to see where the trains would collide somewhere between. . . . And when the silly dopes weren't wrecking trains or computing the ages of their children without seeming to know how old the brats were, two of 'em had a passion for pumping water out of a tank while the third mug pumped water into it.[36]

John certainly meant these lines as a comic rather than a persuasive critique of mathematics, but they do indicate that, when it came to algebra, John could hold a grudge.

As a teenager, John Carr was fascinated by newspaper work—what he called in a youthful poem "the smoky dens of press."[37] He spent summers and after-school hours hanging about the *Uniontown Daily News Standard*'s offices. He later was to recognize that he had been something of a pest and that "experienced old newshawks rightly cursed obedient servant to blister."[38] A few legends about his early newspaper work, sometimes promulgated by John himself and recorded as fact in several references, should be dispelled here. For one thing, despite John's own claims, his grandfather did not own the *Daily News Standard* at the time that the boy worked for it. For another, he never ran a boxing column called "Ignatz the Oracle"; there was no such column, but pithy statements about sports in general were contributed by various staff members, and these were signed by "Ignatz." Some must have been written by John, but they cannot be singled out. Certainly, the statement that has appeared in print several times that John began writing for the newspaper at the age of eleven is not true. There is, however, no reason to doubt his own statement that, starting at the age of fourteen, he began covering murder trials and sporting events. Unfortunately, because the paper rarely included bylines, John's earliest articles cannot be identified.[39]

John's closest friend on the newspaper was William O'Neil Kennedy, who was then about forty-five years old. Although he died almost fifty years ago, O'Neil Kennedy is still remembered vividly in Uniontown. Tall, immaculately dressed, with waxed, spiked mustaches, Kennedy impressed the town with his culture and sophistication. He had traveled widely in America and Europe, and, a lifelong bachelor, he was charming and attractive to women. As a writer and editor, he was a stickler for exact grammar and precise word usage. When John Carr began writing for the *Daily News Standard*, John O'Donnell was the editor, and Kennedy handled the sports pages. John's attitude toward Kennedy had an element of hero worship; indeed, in many ways, he wanted to *be* O'Neil Kennedy. For one thing, the newspaperman was about six feet two inches in height, some six or seven inches taller than John, who was always very slight in build. He had experienced the wider world that John dreamed about. Like most fifteen-year-old males, John was most impressed by the success with women that Kennedy was reputed to have.

John's unsigned articles must have been good enough to persuade O'Donnell to let the boy have his own bylined columns. He wrote a handful of articles called "High School News," but these are almost entirely lists of what his classmates were doing. Much more significant was "As We See It," a general column in which the young John D. Carr III expressed his opinion on any subject that interested him. The column began as a daily feature, but toward the end of its run appeared much less frequently. All in all some sixty columns appeared between February 22 and September 16, 1922.

Some of John's teenage writings tell us more about his admiration for his father than about his own opinions. For example, nine of his "As We See It" columns criticize Warren G. Harding and other Republicans and discuss specific political issues. One of John's strangest contributions is his defense of family friend William Jennings Bryan's attack on the Darwinian theory of evolution, an article that shows that John had never read Darwin: "According to Darwin," he wrote, "man descended from a monkey. . . . The Bible says that God created man in his own image. Now if Darwin be right, then the Deity we know is a monkey and Christianity a mockery." It is only fair to add that John did not hold this opinion in later life; in addition the article praised Bryan "because he was fearless enough to advocate prohibition," and it may not have reflected his views even in 1922.[40]

It is easy to criticize the naive remarks of someone not yet sixteen years old—so easy that I hope readers will forgive me for doing so. For instance, John's articles defending Christianity cannot be called persuasive: his argument that the defeat of Napoleon at Waterloo and the failure of the Puritans to control England prove the existence of God would not impress a theologian—or, I suspect, one of the older newspapermen.[41] John's dislike of Puritanism reappears in several "As We See It" columns condemning "leather-lunged balloon-winded glooms who call themselves reformers"[42]—a group that included the family hero, William Jennings Bryan. Never mind; columnists are not always consistent.

What is most impressive is how many of the columns are better written and express views that are more mature than might be expected of someone John's age. The articles show an early interest in spiritualism, but not from the view of its possible legitimacy; he was more interested in what tricks might have fooled its advocates. In 1922, Sir Arthur Conan Doyle was touring the United States lecturing on the subject. Doyle had long been interested in spiritualism, but he became certain of its reality when, using his wife as a medium, he contacted, he believed, the spirit of his son, killed during the First World War. In commenting on Doyle's lecture tour, John raised several points that would reappear in his later writings. For one thing, according to John D. Carr III, Doyle's claims did not make artistic sense: "We do not believe that those who have passed into a transcendent world can be recalled to bang tambourines or maltreat furniture." And again: "If the inhabitants of that land can span the shadowy abyss, then it is silly to imagine that they would waste time tipping tables and writing on slates for the benefit of the medium's exchequer." John suggested that mediums use tricks to fool those who are in a receptive frame of mind because of the recent loss of a loved one.[43]

John's youthful literary opinions can be discerned by combining references to books and writers in "As We See It" with remarks that he made later in life. It comes as no surprise that the sort of books that the young John Dickson Carr most enjoyed were those that appealed to the imagination, not the type that explored everyday life. In 1935, he wrote that his earliest heroes had been "Sherlock Holmes, D'Artagnan, Admiral Dewey, and The Wizard of Oz."[44] Putting aside the single nonliterary reference (and after all, Dewey was the hero to many boys born shortly after the turn of the century), it's obvious that his boyhood reading, like his later writing, combined fantasy, historical romance, and detection.

Reading L. Frank Baum's Oz books helped develop John's imagination, and indeed the imaginations of other future mystery writers of Carr's generation, including Frederic Dannay (half of the writing duo using the pseudonym Ellery Queen) and Anthony Boucher. The thirteen Oz books, beginning with *The Wonderful Wizard of Oz* in 1900, are the most important and influential children's books written by an American. It may have been their very Americanness that brought them into Wooda Carr's house, but their appeal to John was probably different. Baum's biographer, Russell P. MacFall, points out that Oz was for children what Anthony Hope's Ruritania and George Barr McCutcheon's Graustark were for adults—an escape to a fanciful kingdom that was a testing ground for British or American virtues. Baum himself was fond of mystery stories, and at least three of the Oz books come very near to being genuine detective novels—*Ozma of Oz*, *The Lost Princess of Oz*, and *Glinda of Oz*. John must have been intrigued by Baum's claim that many seemingly magical effects are gimmicks, the production of humbug wizards. He certainly never forgot the Oz books. When he moved to England in the early 1930s, he was astonished that no one there seemed to have heard of Baum's creation, but he told his daughter Julia tales about the Deadly Desert that surrounds Oz, took his family to see the MGM movie *The Wizard of Oz*, starring Judy Garland, in London in 1940, and when he returned to America during World War II, he gave Julia many of the Oz books.[45] Unfortunately, John recorded little about other children's books, though the frequent mentions of *Alice in Wonderland* in his first novel, *It Walks By Night*, published in 1930, suggest that Lewis Carroll's classic was on his childhood shelves. While Baum and Oz were friends to John, however, Carroll and *Alice* were symbols of incongruity, even of the bizarre: "I could fancy this horrible robot walking the halls," says one of Carr's characters, "with a copy of *Alice in Wonderland* under its arm."[46]

John Carr was not fond of the boys' series books—the *Tom Swift* and *Boy Scouts Adventures* volumes that dominated the Uniontown Public Library shelves.[47] He much preferred adult versions of swashbuckling. Anna Carroll Jones recalls that his favorite books as a teenager "were stories of high adventure and derring-do, with *The Three Musketeers* a great favorite." Other favorites included almost the entire works of Robert Louis Stevenson and Charles Dickens. Of adventure novels popular during the 1920s, he liked some of Zane Grey's western stories, but thought that his characters were forgettable. He also admired the now-forgotten A. S. M. Hutchinson ("in the front rank of modern authors"), James Oliver Curwood ("always engrossing"), and Floyd Dell ("a very clever author"). One of the era's more shocking bestsellers, E. M. Hull's *The Sheik*, he found interesting but "not the great book it is made out to be."[48]

That his third fictional hero was Sherlock Holmes leads us to discuss the influence of various mystery and detective-story writers on the young John Dickson Carr. He later said that his reading of mystery stories began "as a boy in my early teens . . . about 1919," and that he was encouraged by his father's own love of sensational literature.[49] From John's later comments, a list of the detective writers whom he read around this time can be compiled: G. K. Chesterton, Arthur Conan Doyle, Jacques Futrelle, Anna Katharine Green, Thomas W. and Mary E. Hanshew, Gaston Leroux, Isabel Ostrander, Melville Davisson Post, Arthur B. Reeve, and Carolyn Wells. We can also add espionage and thriller writers whom the young Carr also enjoyed: John Buchan, E. Phillips Oppenheim, Sax Rohmer, and Valentine Williams. More than half a century later, he remarked that many of these writers "had no great merit . . . but they impressed a callow youth who had already chosen his profession."[50]

Beginning with the writers of thrillers, let's sort out some of these influences. Touches drawn from Buchan, Oppenheim, and other espionage writers appear in Carr's tales written as a teenager, and references in his mature writings to "adventures in the grand manner" with "slant-eyed adventuresses" were drawn from novels of international intrigue. When he was fifteen years old, John commented that "high among the mystery yarn-spinners is Sax Rohmer, whose stories for sheer gripping action and uncanny happenings are surpassed nowhere."[51] On the other hand, in his first book, published in 1930, he made fun of Rohmer's use of venomous creatures in his tales about Fu-Manchu, the Devil Doctor:

> And then there's the equally poisonous pretzel adder from the Swiss Congo. It is so called because it curls up like a pretzel and is a convenient salty yellow color; it can be sent to your victim in a box of harm-

less pretzels. Sax Rohmer says there is only one way to detect the presence of this viper. You should always drink beer with your pretzels, for at the sight of beer this adder emits a faint but audible smacking of the lips.[52]

Some of the detective-story writers whom John read as a boy left little trace on his later writings. Although he liked Isabel Ostrander's novels about detective Timothy McCarty (and shortly before he died he attempted to complete a collection of her work), it is difficult to find an indication that Ostrander had any effect on his own fiction. He once said that Ostrander as well as Anna Katharine Green and Carolyn Wells had become "lost ladies now well lost."[53] Arthur B. Reeve, creator of Craig Kennedy, scientific detective, is almost forgotten today, but about 1920 he was the most popular of all American mystery writers. Carr's early stories were influenced by Reeve's tale called "The Silent Bullet," which introduced the Maxim Silencer to fiction. The silenced gun became the teenaged Carr's favorite plot gimmick.

In 1968, Carr wrote that Arthur Conan Doyle and G. K. Chesterton "together with Melville Davisson Post, a touch from Jacques Futrelle, or even a whisper from the Hanshews—not forgetting Gaston Leroux's *The Mystery of the Yellow Room*—really influenced your obedient servant. All of them loved an impossible situation, and gave me the push in that direction."[54] What connects these writers is their love not only of tricks, seeming impossibilities, and murders in locked rooms, but (except in some of Post's stories) of the sensational in general. Carr was less interested in the comedy of manners, which was to dominate the British school of detective fiction, especially a few years later with Dorothy L. Sayers and Agatha Christie. John did read one of the early country house novels, A. A. Milne's *The Red House Mystery*, on its publication in 1922, but he didn't like it very much because it wasn't as thrilling as the tales of Fu-Manchu.[55] As a teenager he preferred authors who liked to dispatch victims with poisons unknown to science, administered by strange foreigners who were members of secret societies or newly arrived from the Andaman Islands.

Of the authors whom John especially admired, Post is best remembered for his well-crafted stories of Uncle Abner, the antebellum Virginian who solved one classic locked-room case, "The Doomdorf Mystery," which Carr believed one of the four finest detective short stories ever written. Another of John's favorite writers was Jacques Futrelle, a journalist who, before his death in the *Titanic* disaster, wrote two volumes of short stories about Professor S. F. X. Van Dusen, the "Thinking Machine." The style was flat, but Futrelle's ingenuity still makes his stories memorable. For example, the Thinking Machine explained how someone can be gassed in a locked bedroom, how a murder can be seen in a crystal ball, and how an automobile can vanish from a road almost under the eyes of witnesses. In his most famous case, "The Problem of Cell 13," the Thinking Machine himself escaped from a locked jail cell. Also influential on the young Carr was *The Mystery of the Yellow Room* by Gaston Leroux. In 1935, Carr had Dr. Fell describe the story as "the best detective novel ever written."[56] It has seldom been surpassed in puzzling readers about a murderous attack in which the victim is alone in a locked room, but Carr may have been equally impressed by the structure of the book, in which Leroux challenges the reader time after time to unravel the mystery.

Thomas W. and Mary E. Hanshew are almost unknown today because, as Carr admitted, their tales were told "in prose of a hilarious nature." The adventures of their sleuth, Hamilton Cleek (who is also the true prince of the Balkan kingdom of Maurevania), are marvelous exercises in the improbable, but—leaving aside Sherlock Holmes and Father Brown—if I had to pick a detective who had the greatest effect on John's imagination it would be Cleek, the Man of the Forty Faces. Like Carr's Dr. Gideon Fell and Sir Henry Merrivale, Cleek is an amateur called in by Scotland Yard to assist in only the strangest cases, and Cleek's solutions are almost as strange. It's only Hamilton Cleek who can discover that the jewels that vanished in a seemingly impossible manner were secreted in the pouch of a kangaroo. No one but Cleek understands that poison was brought into the locked room on the wings of a moth. Cleek alone knows how someone can turn a somersault and disappear in midair. While realizing that no one could call the Hanshews great writers, John always had a sentimental fondness for their works. Much later, he wrote to Frederic Dannay:

> If you told me a new Cleek story had been discovered, I would rather read that story than any discovery except a new story about Father Brown. . . . Almost every Cleek story contains a new—and usually spectacular or apparently supernatural—method of committing murder. Men walk into rooms and vanish, or die without discernible cause. The nine-fingered skeleton, the empty hypodermic, the monster footprint: such conceptions have real imagination. The Hanshews used ideas. They spun plots.[57]

In addition to the Hanshews, the main influences on John Dickson Carr as a detective-story writer came from Sir Arthur Conan Doyle and G. K. Chesterton. The great detective with his eccentricities, the cryptic remark, the clue that seems to point in one direction but actually means something else—all of this came from Doyle. John was so impressed by Holmes's methods that, in "As We See It," he argued that "in the case of a robbery or murder Sherlock Holmes' inductive reasoning . . . would run to cover the criminal while Scotland Yard floundered about in a sea of suspects and conjecture."[58] Carr's books contain many references to Doyle, some of which are so much a part of the texture of Carr's world that they need no glossing. When Sir Henry Merrivale is nicknamed "Mycroft" in *The Plague Court Murders,* the reference is immediately obvious. When a police surgeon is named Dr. Watson in *The Mad Hatter Mystery,* we don't require an explanation of his Holmesian references: "People hiss at me round corners. They ask me for needles and fourwheelers and Shag Tobacco, and have I my revolver handy? Every fool of a plainclothes constable waits patiently for my report so he can say, 'Elementary my dear. . . .'"[59]

When he was fourteen years old, John discovered the writings of Gilbert Keith Chesterton. The first Chesterton book he read was not a Father Brown story, but that extraordinary phantasmagoria of mystery and fantasy, *The Man Who Was Thursday.* It was, however, Father Brown who captured his imagination. "Though my youth was much influenced by Conan Doyle and Sherlock Holmes," he wrote to a young fan in 1967, "a still greater influence came from Chesterton's short detective stories about Father Brown." The next year, he told a college audience:

> My extravagant admiration for Chesterton . . . has never died to this day. . . . Chesterton is great in the little priest Father Brown, the brilliance of his plots, the superb writing which carries the reader along both by curiosity of the problem and by the strength of the situation and the characters he presents.

Carr often called Chesterton "my literary idol."[60] I could continue at some length about John's literary debt to Chesterton, and in fact I did so in a detailed article I wrote a few years ago.[61] I can summarize the article by saying that John was influenced by more than Chesterton's mastery of the locked room and other so-called miracle crimes. Chesterton's interest in the incongruous, in paradoxes, in the pattern of the crime rather than in physical clues, in setting out the case so that the reader thinks that one course of events has occurred when in fact an entirely different series of happenings has taken place—all these became integral parts of Carr's own fiction.

While discussing John's teenage reading of mystery writers, I should mention his father's favorite writer, O. Henry, who although he did not write genuine detective stories contributed to John's later style by emphasizing the surprise ending. In 1969, Carr wrote that O. Henry had had a "fairly strong influence" on him.[62] As a boy, he had echoed his father's sentiments in saying with notable hyperbole that O. Henry "shaped with his master hand the destiny of American literature." After praising O. Henry for his characters and for avoiding "tedious moralizing" and "stilted phrases," the youthful John D. Carr III pointed out what really characterized O. Henry's tales: "And then, sudden and dazzling, there occurred that unexpected twist that gave the reader a real thrill."[63]

Detective stories, John had already decided by the age of fifteen, should play fair with the reader, presenting all the available evidence. But the clues need not be physical; the master of the craft will put "here and there a casual remark that, unknown to the reader, is the keynote to the plot." He criticized Mary Roberts Rinehart for not making the murderer a main character: She simply did not have the ability, he complained, to keep the murderer in the reader's attention, and therefore her denouement falls flat. "Though she falls down woefully as a writer of detective fiction," John admitted, "she is an especial favorite with the flapper, who eagerly devours her stories and shouts loudly for more."[64]

But while the structure of John Carr's early writing was taken primarily from the Hanshews and Chesterton, with a dash of O. Henry, Futrelle, Post, and Leroux, the atmosphere was pure Edgar Allan Poe. John loved ghost stories by various writers, including Rudyard Kipling, F. Marion Crawford, and Washington Irving—although he disliked Irving's tendency to be whimsical: "If you must write terror stories," John wrote in 1922, "disgorge your ghastly faces and bloodstains on the floor, but discard your humor." He was, however, unrestrained in his enthusiasm about Poe. John said that his stories have "a terrible power." It's worth quoting John's youthful comments on his favorite stories and poems to show how his own style was affected by Poe's haunted imaginings:

> Poe wrote of ravens perching on pallid busts in "purple-curtained" rooms at midnight, when the embers died on the hearth and black memories of a departed brooded in man's mind—surely an exquisite

setting, had he chosen to make of "The Raven" a ghost story instead
of the most musical poem in the English language. He wrote of men
doomed to death by great mental torture in the dungeons of the Inquisition; of yawning pits sheltering horrors unnamable; of sweeping pendulums whose undersides were razor-like knives swinging
ever closer above the breast of the prisoner. He told of strange houses
wherein dwelt stranger inmates; women, imprisoned alive in the
tomb, breaking out while a storm roared about the towers of the grim
house. He dealt with a terrible pestilence whose "avatar and seal"
was blood—"the redness and horror of blood"; and of the Red Death
coming like a thief in the night to strike down the revellers at a
masked ball. These are all horror stories supreme carrying an atmosphere and an uncanny fascination that is their own.[65]

These passages contain some of John's best writing as a teenager—purple
prose perhaps, but powerful.

By this point, it should be obvious that the young John Dickson Carr
preferred a very specific sort of fiction, and disliked—indeed, abhorred—
another specific type. Without getting into an elaborate debate about literary definitions of "realism" and "naturalism," we should note that John
objected to novels that claim to depict life as it is. His opinions on this
matter are so important for the direction his own writings were to take
that I have included in Appendix 1 a complete essay from his newspaper
column comparing realism with detective fiction. His two *bêtes noires* were
Sinclair Lewis and F. Scott Fitzgerald. *Main Street* he called "insufferable"
because Lewis "mistakes vulgarity for realism." The characters in the novels of both authors "are frightful parodies of real men and women, whose
every action is unnatural. . . . These authors try to be terrible in their 'revelation of human character'; and they so impress the gullible that they are
regarded as great writers."[66]

Whenever Carr wrote about authors who emphasized character over
plot, he tended to proclaim rather than prove his judgments, but he was
making an important point that tends to be overlooked in literary criticism. Textbooks and college courses on British and American literature
generally follow a progression that sees the Dickensian novel leading to
the domestic novel to the realistic to the naturalistic, and so on. That of
course did happen, but it's not the entire story nor, to Carr, the main one.
The emphasis on plot and narrative that was so much a part of Dickens,
Wilkie Collins, and their contemporaries was picked up in late Victorian

and Edwardian times by novelists who are often nowadays considered genre writers, outside the mainstream. These authors include Stevenson and H. Rider Haggard in the adventure story and the imperialist romance, Bram Stoker and Montague Rhodes James in the supernatural story, H. G. Wells in the scientific romance, and A. Conan Doyle and G. K. Chesterton in the detective story.

Carr saw detective fiction in the 1920s as continuing the Victorian mainstream, and he objected to realism, which, he thought, was taking fiction in the wrong—in fact, in almost a nonliterary—direction. Carr's view was of course a narrow one, especially in his extreme comments of later years in which he lumped together some of the greatest writers—Dostoyevski, Tolstoy, Proust, Joyce—as "sacred cows . . . with reputations overblown out of all proportion to their merits."[67] In its more general sense—that the plot is necessary for fiction—Carr's attitude is defensible. But he expressed it with such vehemence that we are left with the impression that it was more than simply a literary argument, that it was something fundamental to him. For him, literature was fantasy and adventure and mystery, Oz and D'Artagnan and a puzzle that can be solved; it was a means to escape his mother's sarcasm and to find a larger world than his small hometown. In short, for John Dickson Carr, writing that emphasizes what he called in his college days "the realistic thump of a janitor's mop"[68] misses the point of what a good narrative is all about.

John D. Carr III's first attempt at writing fiction apparently does not survive. At about the age of ten, he and Edward Dumbauld wrote, edited, and copied out by hand on white tablet paper a newspaper that they called *The Speed*. It chronicled family and neighborhood doings, and any extra space that remained on the bottom of the page John filled with a serialized story.[69] His earliest known appearance in print, a short story called "The Ruby of Rameses" (in the Thanksgiving 1921 issue of the Uniontown High School magazine, *The Maroon and White*), contains many elements that would reappear in his mature works. In atmosphere, it is an attempt to imitate Poe's eeriness: The story begins, "The mysterious voice of the night wind wailed its melancholy dirge through the dark sombre aisles of the woodland." (John must have recently read Poe's "Ulalume.") In plot, it is an odd combination of pseudo-Egyptian occultism and rational detection, and it makes even less sense than the Hanshews' Cleek stories. The narrator, Radbourne, arrives at the grim pile of Pollard Hall to see his old Oxford classmate, Brandon Pollard. (John must also recently have read Poe's "The Fall of the House of Usher.") There he meets a scarecrowlike attendant named Alloway and a witchlike woman servant named Marie. After going up interminable staircases, he enters the room where Pollard, sadly changed, waits for him. Pollard's face—like the faces of many later Carr characters—is "a grotesque mask; withered, yellow, furrow-fretted, his shrunken flesh reminded me of fine parchment drawn skin-tight over the features of a Laocoon."

Pollard tells his tale. Pharaoh Rameses I possessed a jewel, the Fire Ruby of Rameses, which was buried with him. Thousands of years later, a religious fanatic named Ahrida started a new religion, which worshiped Rameses and had its temple in the Pharaoh's pyramid. Plummeting to the mundane, the young author says that "despite the radical unsoundness of his ideas," Ahrida's religion caught on. Five years ago, a band of archaeologists found the Fire Ruby, and took it to England, where Pollard gained possession of it. Pollard has been fleeing Ahrida ever since that time, and "the black dread that shrivelled my very soul" had resulted in his physical changes. After showing Radbourne the ruby, he then asks to be alone. As Radbourne closes the door behind him, Pollard bolts himself into the room.

On the way downstairs, Radbourne hears a pistol shot—which John describes as a "short, staccato bark"—and, following Alloway, he dashes back up the stairs. Alloway breaks down the door, and the two find the body of Brandon Pollard. As the first description of a locked room in Carrian fiction, the following passage is worth quoting:

> Our subsequent search of the great, bare apartment had yielded us but one discovery—the paradoxical fact that the room's lone window had likewise been locked—on the inside. Both the servant and I would be prepared to swear that no one had passed us on the staircase. . . . There was, moreover, absolutely no secret means of ingress or egress,* as an exhaustive search of the walls, the floor, and even the ceiling had convinced me. How, then, had the assassin been able to enter and leave a locked room?

Back in the hall, Radbourne comes upon a mysterious, beautiful woman: "There was about her a vague, exotic perfume, hauntingly reminiscent of the bazaars and shops of Cairo." She hurls the Fire Ruby at Radbourne's feet, and when he tries to follow her, she fires a revolver (this time with a

*This may be the last time that anyone "ingressed" or "egressed" in one of John Dickson Carr's stories.

"venemous crack") in his direction. She runs into a room and bolts the door. Radbourne bursts in, but the exotic woman has disappeared.

The scene turns to a coroner's court, and to John Dickson Carr's first detective, the blind Frenchman, Lieutenant Rene Lamar, who says that it is "a very pretty little problem, monsieur, but not in the least a difficult one." The shot that Alloway and Radbourne had heard was a fake—how faked and by whom is not explained—and when Alloway burst into the room, Pollard was still alive. (Don't ask why he didn't move when Alloway and Radbourne arrived.) At any rate, Alloway killed him by firing a silenced gun, unnoticed by Radbourne, who was just behind him. (John apparently believed that guns with silencers make no sound at all and are so small that no one can see them being fired.) Fortunately for Alloway, as he burst through the door, Pollard conveniently said nothing and did not move, and Radbourne did not notice that he was still alive. The Ruby of Rameses was stolen independently by the mysterious woman, whose real name is Jeanne Darin and who with "a mask of painted wax" was masquerading as the old servant Marie. And if that's not enough, it turns out that the ruby was a fake. Pollard had a disease called "Insanitas Diaboli" and the entire tale of Rameses and the vengeful Egyptians was a self-delusion. When Jeanne discovered that the ruby was mere paste, she threw it at Radbourne, and "instead of entering the apartment itself, she went into a secret passage opening into the corridor side by side with the door." The roller-coaster of a story ends as Alloway swallows poison with "his thin lips contriving to articulate."

As Dr. Fell might have said, *Wow*. In later years, John shunned such primitive devices as the secret passage, and eventually he would learn how a silencer works. More significantly, the story has the first mention of masks, an image that John would use over and over. He seems to have seen the world as full of people hiding their true feelings with public masks. Influences in this story include Sax Rohmer, whose *Tales of Sacred Egypt* had been published in New York two years earlier. The idea of a blind detective may have been taken from Ernest Bramah's Max Carrados or, more likely, from Clinton Stagge's Thornley Colton, who had enjoyed a brief vogue in America between 1915 and 1920. The personality of Rene Lamar and the trial scene may have come from Gaston Leroux's *The Mystery of the Yellow Room*. John probably based his locked room on the Hanshews' Hamilton Cleek stories. Stolen Oriental jewels were stock in trade for the Man of Forty Faces.

John's next story, "The House of Terror," published in *The Maroon and*

White, Midwinter, 1922, is also overwritten, full of such lines as "evil, ma-lignant eyes they were, glowing like red-hot coals, and seeming to Melford to sear his very flesh." Like "The Ruby of Rameses," the tale be-gins at a desolate house: "Above him loomed Heatherby House—gaunt, grim, and forbidding." (At this stage in his writing—and in fact in many of his apprentice stories—John thought that all that was necessary to create a mood of terror was an adjective, or several, but such words as "gaunt," "grim," and "forbidding" are too vague to add up to much.) Melford shows up at Heatherby House, having been summoned there by his late grandfather's solicitor, Basil Spencerton. As he arrives, he sees a Thing (capitalized throughout the story), which is "devoid . . . of all semblance of human shape." Then Melford hears a pistol shot, this time "a spiteful crack," and a bullet tears through his hat brim. This is followed by a "hideous, choking cry," and Melton discovers the body of Basil Spencer-ton, stabbed with a dagger whose handle is in the form of a serpent twist-ing about a tree. He is clutching a crumpled envelope in his hand, and a broken cuff link is beside his body. The cuff link belongs to Sir Eric Hirth, who threatened the previous day to kill Spencerton. Hirth himself stum-bles out of the house, crying about "those eyes," then collapses in a faint.

The crumpled envelope contains a letter from Melford's grandfather: "I am neither a nervous nor an imaginative man, and I never believed in ghosts—until I saw that THING. But it hates me in death as Philip Dar-worth hated me in life."* He goes on to say that Darworth had stolen some jewels and prepared to leave England, but that he had planned to kill Melford's grandfather first. Darworth, however, was killed first, but Melford's grandfather continued to see the eyes of the dead man burning into him. After reading this letter, Melford decides to return the jewels to their rightful owner, but runs into "the Thing" again. "Its body, though blurred and indistinct in contour, shone with an infernal light of its own." An intruder then knocks Melford unconscious. When he wakes, he finds Constable Brant and the coroner, Dr. Ennisthory, hovering over him.

It turns out that the ghost was a fake, played by an American who has been hired by the murderer to scare first Melford's grandfather then other people away while he searched for the jewels. The indistinct outline and

*This is a paraphrase of the opening lines of one of Carr's favorite ghost stories, F. Marion Crawford's "The Screaming Skull": "I have often heard it scream. No, I am not nervous or imaginative; and never believed in ghosts, unless that thing is one. But it hates me as it hated Luke Pratt, and it screams at me."

infernal light and strange eyes are never explained. In the final line of the story, the pseudoghost identifies Constable Brant as the murderer.

"The House of Terror" was John's attempt to write a horror story, and his first effort at providing material explanations (unconvincing and incomplete as they are) for apparently supernatural events. Otherwise, it should be noted that the influence of the Hanshews—with the jewels, the strange dagger, and the sprinkling of clues about the body—is again paramount.

In its maturity as well as its subject matter, John's third short story, "The Will-o'-the-Wisp," published in the Easter, 1922, *Maroon and White*, belongs in a different world. It is a swashbuckling tale of swordplay and highwaymen, and like several of Carr's novels written thirty years later, it is based on time travel. At one o'clock in the morning, the unnamed narrator is musing about Uniontown's statue of Lafayette, which he can barely see by the mist-blurred street lights. Suddenly, the mist increases and he finds that he has returned to the Uniontown of 1825 in the body of one Rupert Brixley. At a party for Lafayette, he meets a beautiful woman named Marcia, who it turns out had thrown Brixley over for Juan Alvez. She is a femme fatale, the type who enjoys teasing men and who would show up under different names in many of Carr's books. Her beryl eyes, John says,

> added an almost sinister aspect to her Lorelei-like face. I put her
> down at once as a girl dangerous to the nth degree. She was the sort
> of beauty who is not content with being merely coquettish, but must
> stir up trouble among her suitors, ostensibly to test their love for her,
> but really in a spirit of malicious delight at being quarrelled over.

Alvez thinks that Lafayette is competing for Marcia's attention. Alvez announces, "I'll wait until after the ball. Just now, however, I'm going to get drunk."

Meanwhile, the crowd is obsessed with the recent activities of a mysterious masked highwayman known as the Will-o'-the-Wisp: "Why, sir, the audacious fellow does things Turpin would never dream of attempting." Lafayette says that in France such a criminal would not stay free long. Then the highwayman himself turns up, challenging Lafayette to a duel. Lafayette disarms him and is about to make the final swordthrust when Alvez aims a pistol at the marquis. Brixley leaps forward, deflects the gun, which "vomited forth its winged messenger of death" and struck down the Will-o'-the-Wisp. The mask is pulled off the dying highwayman to reveal the face of . . . Marcia. Suddenly, the mist returns, and the narrator hears a coal truck lumbering through the street beneath his window.

"The Will-o'-the-Wisp" has a surprise ending but no mystery or detection (or Hanshews). The purple prose of the two earlier stories is a bit less evident, and John clearly put more of himself into the story. When the narrator realizes that he has gone back a century, "The wine of the only adventure I had ever experienced in the course of my drab, prosaic life mounted swiftly to my brain; I felt gay, confident, reckless." A few months later, in one of his final columns for the *Daily News Standard*, John mused about what he would do if he had five million dollars:

> We thought of trips to Europe; of solitary rambles along the gaunt, crumbling ruins of ancient Rome; the cool, airy emptiness of a languorous Egyptian night; of glassy moonlit waters beneath the Southern Cross; of all the thousand scenes that bring with them the faint, musty breath of the past; suggestions of forgotten splendor and dynasties that are dust.[70]

Chapter 2

THE HILL
AND HAVERFORD

In August 1922, Wooda and Julia Carr decided to send their son to The Hill School, a preparatory school in Pottstown, Pennsylvania. The Hill was known for preparing young men for the College Board Examinations and having them accepted by the finest Ivy League colleges. John's parents hoped that his years at The Hill would lead to John's admission to Harvard and then to training in his father's profession as a lawyer. The superintendent of the Uniontown School District certified that John was "a first class student, industrious, studious, brilliant, dependable and exemplary in habits and character." This statement ignored John's hatred of mathematics and all its works, but the superintendent assured The Hill that "you will find him a gentleman in training, disposition and character." John was admitted, and headed off to preparatory school for the opening of classes on September 19; he was not yet sixteen years old.[1]

Carr recalled in one of his early novels what it was like to be going off to Hill School: "We were in the first triumphant flush of being allowed to drive automobiles; when a room which was to be our own, at a preparatory school, made us feel that we were already men of the world."[2] He later said that the change from Uniontown to The Hill School was not always easy, but that he was glad to be away from his mother.[3] He was one of about 430 students to be taught by around fifty faculty members. His classmates called him "Johnny." An aerial photograph of The Hill School, taken in 1921, shows a spacious campus with large academic buildings and dormitories and an impressive chapel surrounding a central mall. Nearby was the Dell, a quiet area of woods and lake, with the school's theater. The Hill was organized according to "forms" rather than "classes," with the sixth form being the highest.[4] John entered the fourth form, but his application admitted that he could not succeed on that level in algebra or in French.

During John's first year at The Hill (1922–23), he was in second-form algebra and third-form French. He did well in them: With 65 being passing, he actually averaged a grade of 82 in algebra. His parents must have been astonished: He never admitted in later years that he had once done so well in a mathematics course, and in fact he would never do so well again. His French grade was 71, with English and Latin in the low 80s. During his second year at The Hill, however, he barely passed French and algebra, and during the third year all of his grades were in the 60s and 70s. Three decades later, he recalled that his academic career had been "absolutely undistinguished except for beating everybody else at my kind of writing, English literature, or Latin."[5] He was correct about the lack of distinction—and his memories notwithstanding, during his final year that lack of distinction extended even to English and Latin. He may have identified the problem when he wrote in an editorial in The Hill Record, "How could we presume to tell others how hard to study when we didn't know ourselves."[6]

As John's grades declined, his extracurricular activities increased. After writing about duels in two of his Uniontown High School stories—and loving swashbuckling in general—he was delighted to join fellow student William B. Willcox (later professor of history at Yale) and others in hiring a White Russian émigré to instruct them in fencing during after-class hours. Willcox remembers that his friend was small and pale-featured (and his pictures at this period do show John to be unprepossessing), but fencing allowed him to be at an equal level with the others. The fencing master taught the boys various tricks that were irrelevant to American fencing, but John would remember them years afterward and describe them in his historical novels. Among these tricks was maneuvering your opponent so that the sun was in his eyes. John was so taken with becoming directly involved with swordplay that he and Willcox went fencing by moonlight. But one day their Russian failed to show up for the lessons; they never did discover what happened to him.[7]

John loved to tell one particular story about The Hill School. Macon

Fry, a friend from Uniontown, visited one weekend, and the two of them decided to shift around some of the organ pipes in the chapel—something that would not have been difficult, as the pipes simply sat in their positions. On Sunday morning, the organist was astonished when he began to play the hymns and the wrong notes came from the instrument, but he gamely continued. The mischief of the shifted organ pipes is one of those stories that cannot be independently confirmed, but the Carr family remains convinced that it did happen.[8] It was the sort of prank that might have been committed by his detective Sir Henry Merrivale and, in fact, in *Seeing Is Believing* (1941), Carr actually did attribute it to H.M. in his youth.

Although John never attached a year to another story he often told about himself, this is probably the best place to mention the episode of the upside-down room. According to Carr, he and Macon Fry built a room in which the chandelier was attached to the middle of the floor and projected upward. The boys bolted some furniture onto the carpeted ceiling. They then entertained some guests at a drinking bout, and as each guest collapsed with too much whiskey, the two jokers would drag him into the inverted room. When the victim woke, he invariably would frantically grab the chandelier to prevent himself from falling to what was actually the ceiling. When John told this tale, he had some trouble persuading his audience that he and his boyhood friend had the expertise (or indeed the room) to work the trick, and when pressed he admitted that he had read about it "in an old joke-book I vaguely remember picking up in my boyhood."[9] The joke-book may have, in turn, obtained the idea from a genuine upside-down room that had been part of the attractions of the St. Louis Exposition in 1904. John's interest may also have been piqued by the fact that L. Frank Baum had described such a room in *The Lost Princess of Oz* (minus, of course, the drunken revelers). Whatever the case, he was so intrigued by the idea that he mentioned as one of Dr. Fell's unrecorded cases "the still more curious problem of the inverted room at Waterfall Manor."[10]

Some activities outside the classroom were mandatory for all Hill students, including debate and other forms of public speaking, in which "Johnny" Carr excelled. He was a member of a debating group called Q.E.D. II during his three years at The Hill, winning the Colgate Cup twice for debate. On April 18, 1925, as the representative of Q.E.D. II, John won the Stronge Trophy in extemporaneous speaking. His subject was "The Flag." The text of the speech doesn't survive, but undoubtedly it reflected some of the political orations of his father.[11]

John's main activities involved writing. In 1924, he described himself as "a lazy devil ... except when it comes to hammering a typewriter and other things that never do us any good."[12] Some of his work done at The Hill has been lost. It would be valuable, for instance, to know more about his first attempt to write a play, but all that is recorded of *Arms and the God*, which he wrote with another student, Sheldon Dick, is that it was performed at the Dell Theater. Just as unfortunately, we don't have copies of all of John's earliest comic publications. Both William Willcox and another boy from Uniontown, Herbert MacDonald, remember him as the class punster. Professor Willcox wrote to me that he could recall only one of Johnny's effusions—and wished that he couldn't. In an essay done for class assignment about the predawn hours in a city when workers going to an early shift pass by late revelers weaving their way home, Carr wrote, "The hardy sons of toil passed by the tardy sons of boil."[13]

John's more serious writings were published in the monthly literary magazine, *The Hill Record*, and in the 1927 volume *A Book of Hill School Verse*. It's an impressive body of work for a teenager: two detective stories, a mystery story that comes near detection, a serialized adventure novelette, a boxing tale, a contemporary comedy of swordplay, two drinking tales, a historical romance, two ghost stories, three essays, and eight poems. John wrote some of this material for the English Club, organized by former headmaster Alfred G. Rolfe and made up primarily of sixth-form students as well as a few faculty members. One of the great honors at The Hill was to be elected a member of the club, and John was one of the few chosen in his fifth form.[14] At many of the meetings, the students read their own works, primarily poems.

In subject matter most of John's poems are praises of heroes and lost causes, often stirring but occasionally leaning toward bombast. In rhyme and meter, they show considerable influence from Rudyard Kipling with a bit from Robert Browning. They usually have internal rhymes and strongly accented rhythm. Typical is the opening of Johnny Carr's "Hunting Song":

> To saddle, to saddle, to spur and away,
>   In the gray of the glancing dawn,
> When the hounds are out with a treble shout
> And the whip and spur of the merry rout
>   To the vales and the dales have gone!

John won prizes at The Hill for his poetry, including the headmaster's prize in 1924, but on the whole, he did not have a strong poetic sense; he liked the sound of words but was less interested in depth of feeling. Most of his poems were written to arouse fervor, rather than to examine meaning or emotions. But within those limitations, some of his youthful verses are still effective. As part of one of his short stories, he included the following lines, which are more closely related to Swinburne than to Kipling:

> *If this could be!*
> *From out the sea to raise the crystal spires*
> *Of cities dimly known to me*
> *Where move the shapes of fantasy*
> *And bards of dreams in fancy free awake their sleeping lyres.*

John's earlier interest in fantasy had shown a strong Poe-esque influence toward the weird and terrible, but in his poems written at The Hill School, he combined the weird with a more lyrical sense taken from Swinburne. Despite an occasional lapse in rhythm, probably his best poem is "Helmsmen of Atlantis," combining his interest in lost causes, in stirring visions, and in romance. He was then eighteen years old. Two stanzas follow:

> *In dim and dark Atlantis,*
> *Where now the white shark gleams,*
> *A marble monster comes to life*
> *Within a world of dreams;*
> *In brooding old Atlantis*
> *The ghosts of temples rise,*
> *And tipped with blood, the shattered sun*
> *Along its roof-top dies.*
> . . . .
> *(A watch on deck in the dying night,*
> *A figure black on the moon,*
> *And a voice that sings of distant things*
> *In an old, forgotten tune.)*

Several of John's poems praised Ireland, connecting her with songs, tragedy, dreams, and the perfidy of the English. His most interesting, and least typical, poetic subject was "Election Night," which has a drive and fervor that, unlike his other poems, was based on direct observation. Not all the rhythms and images work, but a few lines are worth quoting for their capturing of Uniontown elections:

> *Blear-eyed men in shirt sleeves toiling at the dim-lit poll,*
> *Grimy miners raising now the mighty voice of coal;*
> *Silent clans in offices stare down upon the street,*
> *Throb of pounding foreheads and the stamp of restless feet.*

John Carr's stories and essays published in *The Hill Record* (of which he was managing editor) were still immature, especially in their adolescent daydreaming, but they have more control and a greater focus than his detective/horror stories written at Uniontown High School; even "The Will-o'-the-Wisp" is not as good as his finest tales at The Hill School. His first story for *The Hill Record*, "The Marked Bullet," published in the March and April 1923 issues, is difficult to evaluate, for the magazine printed some pages of John's typescript in the wrong order and apparently omitted some sections. "The Marked Bullet" begins, like two of his earlier tales, at an eerie English mansion, and the first two paragraphs are filled with such words as "grotesque," "ghostly," "writhe," "deadness," "silent spectre," and "dingy." Nevertheless, the story is not horror but straight detection, the murder being solved by a Constable Marden. The body is found in a locked room: Its doors and windows are bolted, and there is no secret entrance. One character explains: "Walls and floor and ceiling are all intact. Not even a crack. Fireplace bricked up. The room might have been made of concrete, to all practical purposes." The solution is exactly the same as in "The Ruby of Rameses," and is based on the same utter impossibility: The first man into the room killed his victim with a silenced gun that no one heard or saw. Yet, though a florid style dominates the tale, John occasionally includes some sharply delineated descriptions—for example: "His neat mustache drooped a little; his colorless hair was scraggly without oil; and his hasty toilet made him look lopsided."

John's second detective story for *The Hill Record*, "Ashes of Clues" (October 1923), is much better, though it too suffers from excessively atmospheric language. Once again, John inflicted on the reader such words as "gaunt," "creakings," and "withered." The structure of the story, however, is sophisticated. The first part describes how a man named Saunders murders an unidentified enemy in the dressing room of a theater. Saunders, who resembles his victim, then takes the murdered man's place. In the second part, we follow Detective Sergeant Mattison's investigation of the crime. The main mysteries in the story, consequently, are which character

Saunders is now playing and what mistake he has made that will reveal his guilt. The influence behind this tale is probably R. Austin Freeman's classic volume of "inverted" detective stories, *The Singing Bone,* which was published in book form in the United States in 1923. Like Freeman, Carr had the reader follow the commission of the crime, but with its double mystery Carr's story is actually more daring than anything Freeman attempted. It is also less smoothly told, however, and it is solved by evidence not given to the reader.

"E'en Though It Be a Cross" (April 1924) contains a bit of detection, but it is of more interest for the sentiments its author expressed. Or attempted to express. Filled with some extremely tortured metaphors, it tells the tale of Lane Hardmann, a musician with "a gaunt face almost like a death mask," who prays to God that his wounded father will survive. When the father dies, Hardmann expresses all sorts of antireligious sentiments. Hardmann investigates and finds that his friend Travers shot his father with what seems by this time the inevitable silenced revolver. With eyes "that now reflected fires more baleful than those that ever lit up Gehenna's sulphurous valleys," he threatens to kill Travers but is himself killed. Dying, he sees an undefined "vision." The story needed to be much more sharply written for the reader to work out what John was trying to say about religion.*

John's most ambitious story while at The Hill was "The Blindfold Quest," a novelette of almost ten thousand words, which was published in three parts between November 1923 and January 1924. Influenced by *The Prisoner of Zenda* and *Graustark*—both of which are mentioned in the story—"The Blindfold Quest" recounts the adventures of three American boys who become involved in the politics of the Balkan kingdom of Brokovia. Except for a clumsy use of slang, it is a clearly written story, full of exciting incidents and unexpected twists. Though the plot is not straightforward, the writing is; for once, the young John Carr didn't feel that he had to overuse grim adjectives. The story begins with the three lads traveling by train to Bordeaux and dreaming of being "heroes in a story." The French police burst into their compartment and arrest Frederick Brotheurs, a jewel thief.

When by mistake the *gendarmes* also try to arrest one of our heroes, the

---

*Whatever the point John was trying to make in this story, the tone is quite different from his defense of religion in his newspaper column. From this point on, John Dickson Carr was sturdily agnostic on questions of religion.

three boys escape from the train and steal Brotheurs's car. Brotheurs has inconveniently left his latest haul—the crown jewels of Brokovia—in the car, and even more inconveniently, in the backseat is the body of King Gustave, who was shortly to marry the princess of the neighboring country of Barnehasset. The boys dash to Brokovia in the car, pursued by the French police. "Somehow," one of them announces, "I sort of like this thing, dangerous or not." They are saved from arrest by the female lead, Lady Katherine Ness, and they discover that, despite the fact that the groom is dead, the wedding is still scheduled. In *Zenda* fashion, King Gustave has been replaced by a lookalike, played by the now freed jewel thief. When this fact is revealed, Barnehasset declares war. One of the boys and a French ace take a plane to Barnehasset, where they witness a swordfight between the old king and an unidentified spy. In a manner too complicated to relate, the revelation of the identity of the spy ends the war. This brief summary doesn't do justice to this lighthearted tale, which is entertaining throughout.

John's ghost stories for *The Hill Record* are generally overwritten and a bit obscure. "The Riddle of the Laughing Lord" (February 1924) is heavy-handed, but it offers glimpses of ideas and images that Carr would later use more effectively. By now, we expect many of John's tales to start in a mysterious house, and this one is no exception. Greytowers, the home of Morgan Grimm, "resembled a watchful old beast, the ivy patching its stolid face like scars." Like later Carr characters, Grimm collects artifacts of murder, the most important being a statue called the Laughing Lord, showing a handsome young Austrian nobleman who "had the gift of laughter; they could hear him laughing in the halls of his castle at night when he was using the strangling-cord or the dagger or the poison cup on one of his nearest and dearest." The atmosphere of brooding terror and madness is, unfortunately, damaged by the assertion that the Laughing Lord will retain its horrid laugh until, like a ghostly Boy Scout, "some good deed liberates his soul." Grimm invites his enemy, Blade, whom he fears is in love with his "full-lipped, dark-eyed" wife, to view the statue. When Grimm tries to poison Blade, however, the lights go out, and Grimm himself is found strangled. A serene expression is now on the face of the Laughing Lord.

"Candlelight: A Ghost Story of Christmas," is a much lighter (and less successful) story. In his youthful works John had difficulty in matching mood with plot, and he fills the tale with inappropriately eerie language. The story goes like this: Three men always meet before Christmas, including Holmes Danforth, who "at nineteen had been expelled from college for drunkenness." Two of the men announce that they are in love with the same woman, Jane Wainwright. Charles Dickens is the most important influence on "Candlelight," as ghosts of a past Christmas show up to explain the competition for the woman's hand. But when we return to the present, we find that it is the third man who is engaged to marry Jane.

In several of John's stories written at The Hill, drinking is presented as something men do at important moments. He clearly saw it as a sign of being an adult, perhaps of being like his father. He wrote two stories for *The Hill Record* whose subject is drinking, the first of which, "The Kindling Spark" (June 1923), is a well-written but rather silly bit of adolescent daydreaming. Jimmy O'Brien is a bookish newspaperman of Irish lineage. He believes that war is useless, and therefore when the United States decides to enter World War I, he reacts by getting drunk. He then sees Peggy Lynn, whom he has hankered after from a distance; she is with a man named Cormack. Jimmy fights Cormack, beats him, then offers to take on the kaiser singlehandedly. Like the true woman she is, Peggy falls in love with Jimmy.

Written two years later, just before John left The Hill School, "The Gordon Djinn" is another story filled with touches that would become typical of his writing. And in this case, tone and plot do come together; both the story and the language used to tell it are very funny. "The Gordon Djinn" is narrated by Ken Blake, a newspaperman and detective-story writer. He begins the story:

> Virginia was going to marry a spiritualist, and that was why I got
> drunk. People have a great many excuses for getting drunk; they do
> it both to accentuate joy and drown sorrow—to celebrate the Fourth
> of July to glorify independence, and again on the birthday of the
> eighteenth amendment to bewail servitude.

The spiritualist, Floyd Bannerman, is "an apostle of immorality who was never immoral, and . . . a poet who had got so far into the future that nobody knew where he was. To him life was a puzzle, and whenever the pieces made some design he jumbled them up again." Bannerman speaks paradoxes: "Life is simply a noisy little alarm-clock ticking in eternity. Nothing is really important except what is unimportant." "Nothing is bound to happen except what is impossible." "In God we rust." And, a sentiment that John agreed with: "Mathematics is the refuge of the half-witted curious." When Bannerman comes up with one of his paradoxes,

Ken Blake says simply, "Some day you're going to turn one of those verbal somersaults and meet yourself coming the other way. I hope both of your-selves break your necks." As he leaves Bannerman's apartment rather than fight to win Virginia, she shouts at him in despair, "Damn you." Ken then returns to the rooms he shares with Holmes Lamoreux, who has "a long, lean diabolical face," and who comforts Ken with the sentiment that "the female of the species is more dead wood than the male."

After an evening spent drinking gin, Lamoreux shows Ken a lamp that he claims once belonged to Aladdin. Ken rubs it, and a djinn appears (hence the punning title). The djinn speaks in languorous words—"I come from the land where the drowsy sea woos white blossoms, and the cypress trees are black as sorrowing ghosts, and the great golden moon lures the tides from a silver sky"—but Ken keeps interrupting him. He has the djinn take him to Virginia's home, where he sees her mother—"a Mat-terhorn in white lace, looking down stonily over the icy slopes of herself." Ken tells her that "you are entitled to this pursuit of sappiness if you like," but that he is a better spiritualist than Bannerman. He then has the djinn perform all sorts of tricks—trombones drop from the ceiling, three mice march across the table with flag, drum, and fife, books "emit tiny armies of words," and a cuckoo comes out of a clock to complain "what the hell do you want."

Ken wakes up the next day still hugging the lamp and with a monu-mental hangover. Virginia rings on the phone. It turns out that someone sent Bannerman a case of gin last night, he got drunk, thought he was Aladdin, and insulted Virginia's mother. The wedding is off, and Virginia and Ken are free to marry. The praise of drinking, the wild humor, the male-female tension, the desire of a woman for men to compete for her, and much else in "The Gordon Djinn" would reappear time and time again in John's later writing.

John was clearly trying different types of themes for his short tales. "The God of the Gloves" (January 22, 1925) was his only attempt to write a sports story. It's quite well done, with good descriptions of a boxing match. Dinny McFarlane is typical of John's early heroes—bookish and Irish—and newspaper scenes fill much of the background. Before the story opens, Dinny's father was almost killed in the ring by a sadistic fighter. The son now decides to become a professional boxer to gain revenge on his father's opponent, and of course, to do this in front of his fiancée. He has no chance of defeating an experienced boxer, and a newspaperman says viciously, "Don't they ever think of fair play? Don't they ever think of giving anyone a chance?" The fight is fixed; the champ has a hypodermic in his glove. But he mistakenly jabs himself with it, and Dinny wins.

Two other stories written at The Hill are also worth examining. "The Harp of Tairlaine" (April 1925) is John's first straightforward historical romance, and in a different way from "The Gordon Djinn" it too is filled with his favorite themes—in this case, romance, royalism, and lost causes. John had moved away from his father's fervid Americanism and in "The Harp of Tairlaine" finds monarchy an ideal worth dying for, at least when it's opposed by Cromwell's Puritans. "The Harp of Tairlaine" takes place in 1649 in England, and at the beginning we find Michael Tairlaine, an Irish bard, sitting in a tavern in "a quiet, inoffensive way." Clearly John, who had already written poems of Ireland, was thinking of himself. Sir Gareth Ardell looks on him as weak: "The poet's sword-arm ever winces." Tairlaine agrees to help free the imprisoned King Charles I: "The Puritan must fall, for he has forgotten how to laugh." Sir Gareth, however, really plans to trick Tairlaine into rescuing his sweetheart, Lady Joan. Sir Gareth, like the braggart he is, proves weak, but Tairlaine saves Lady Joan. The poet, however, is wounded and collapses believing that he has rescued the king. Tairlaine lies dying in the street with "the smiles of a great ideal realized, of a king escaping in safe hands." His shattered harp is at his side; he touches some strings; then the story ends "The Harp of Tairlaine was still." Although, as with John's detective and ghost tales, "The Harp of Tairlaine" overuses atmosphere, it is a most impressive story expressing those emotions that sometimes only the young are able to summon up for an ideal and for what John called "the blood-red of romance."

"The Cloak of D'Artagnan" (June 1924) is yet another piece of wish-fulfillment on John's part. Terence O'Riordan—Irish, of course—thinks of himself as a Cavalier: "He loved stories of swashbucklers with courtly manners and ready swords, who fought duels by moonlight." He is in love with Milly Langworth, who is "very practical and up-to-date" but with an "innate spirit of romance." To impress her, Terence plans a masked ball at which he will appear as D'Artagnan. He hires a man named Dodd to appear as "the masked mystery," who will pretend to steal his mother's diamonds. Terence will arrive at the nick of time, stage a swordfight, and recover the diamonds. Dodd, however, is not playing a part; he is a genuine jewel thief after the diamonds. When Terence shows up, Dodd hides the diamonds in the visor of a suit of armor. As luck would have it, the armor happens to have an occupant, and Terence realizes that Dodd has been playing a double game. They end up in a rip-roaring wrestling and boxing match up and down the staircases, before Terence knocks Dodd out. Milly breathes, "Wonderful," and Terence's father says that he's not wearing the Cloak of D'Artagnan: "'Tis the cloak of Dempsey."

In looking at his *Hill Record* stories as a whole, it is surprising that John Dickson Carr's least effective stories are the types that he excelled in writing as an adult—detective and supernatural stories. In none of these was he able successfully to combine plot structure and atmosphere. But even the best of his efforts written at The Hill—"The Blindfold Quest," "The Gordon Djinn," "The Harp of Tairlaine," and "The Cloak of D'Artagnan"—are still apprentice work. Yet because some of his descriptive passages are so good, some of his story ideas so compelling, some of his characterizations so sharp, it is easy to overlook the fact that John was between fifteen and eighteen years old when he wrote these stories. It is also easy to fall into the trap of expecting too much maturity in them and to feel let down when we find that his attitudes were still those of a teenager. He was, nevertheless, a very talented teenager.

As an adult, John said that "I mention the Hill School with pride because it was the only institution of learning from which I wasn't fired."[15] This statement is a bit misleading; he wasn't "fired" from The Hill, but he did not successfully complete its program. Even though he gave the commencement speech in June 1925, he never received his diploma because he failed his final course in mathematics. He was given the opportunity to retake the examination before October 1, 1925, but either he refused to take the exam or he failed it again, for The Hill's records indicate that he did not graduate.[16]

In later years, John Dickson Carr told his wife and children, and recorded in some autobiographical notes, that he had briefly attended Harvard University after leaving The Hill School, but the authorities discovered that he lacked the required mathematics course and threw him out. There was certainly some truth to this story. His parents had planned to send him to Harvard. The university, however, has no record of his admission. In September 1925, Wooda Carr explained simply that

> we have concluded to send John to Haverford College instead of Harvard, believing that he would do better work at the former institution. Moreover, we feel that John needs the personal attention that he would get at Haverford, which is entirely lacking at Harvard.[17]

Haverford College, on the Philadelphia Main Line south of Bryn Mawr, was the type of institution that would supply individual attention. A

Quaker school with the reputation of training proper young gentlemen, it offered an outstanding education, along with a warm humanism exemplified by its classics professor Rufus M. Jones. One of John's classmates remembered that Haverford enjoyed a pastoral setting: "A park led through a thicket of willows and dogwood and opened into an immensity of smooth sloping lawn. Two swans floated idly on a round reedy pond and a big granite spire rose from the crest of the hill."[18]

John Dickson Carr was known as "Jack" at Haverford, the nickname bestowed to avoid confusing him with his freshman roommate, John Lineaweaver. Carr and Lineaweaver soon became associated with the literary group at Haverford, then dominated by Frederic Prokosch, who would become an important novelist and poet, but at the time was working on his master's degree. The roommates' attitudes and tastes in literature differed greatly. Lineaweaver admired the avant-garde writers, especially Proust and Joyce and Gertrude Stein, and his greatest delight was to read the literarily progressive magazine *The Dial.* Prokosch, who was Lineaweaver's closest friend at Haverford, recalled that Lineaweaver "lived in a constant anguish of insomnia and hemorrhoids but his dedication to the works of Gertrude Stein was heroic." Any kind of devotion to Stein, especially a heroic one, was unlikely to appeal to John Dickson Carr. He himself was firmly in the neoromantic school, and classmates recall that Carr and Lineaweaver would continue a running argument late into the night, their room filled with cigarette smoke and literary passion.

In a series of letters written shortly before his death, Prokosch recorded in vivid language his memories of John Dickson Carr:

> He was a grayish, rather imploring-looking boy, with dark rings around his eyes, an air of dejection but also a sense of humor and gaiety and mischief. I rather liked him, though he wasn't quite my cup of tea. . . . [He was] a small, sickly boy who smoked incessantly, who wrote all night long, romantically and insatiably, and who would suddenly walk into my room and declaim, from memory, poems by Noyes, Housman, Chesterton. . . . His physical smallness no doubt stimulated his bravado and "swordplay," but of course those athletic postures were ingrained in his character. Our friend John Lineaweaver used to jeer most cruelly at all this nonsense, but there was something disarming and vulnerable about Carr.[19]

In his memoirs, *Voices,* Prokosch called Carr "eccentric," and this was true in more than his literary interests. Unlike most students, who dressed informally for class, Carr always wore a suit coat and sometimes a topcoat, and he was one of the few students who often wore a vest. As he had done back in Uniontown High School, he tended to wear his hair long—"he always just let it dangle," one fellow student remembers. Samuel Cook, who ran the student bookstore, recalls that both Carr and Prokosch were soft-spoken and had to be approached before they would talk with others. Through the bookstore's windows, Cook watched Carr go back and forth between classes, almost always alone. Carr built up what was for that time a large debt at the bookstore—some twenty-five dollars—and when Cook refused to let him have anything more on account unless he paid the bill, Carr simply said (rather abruptly but, Cook remembers, not insolently), "Send it to my father." Wooda Carr paid immediately. From this story, one might conclude that "Jack" Carr felt he was better than others at Haverford, but other evidence points in a different direction. He seems to have been more lonely than a loner, someone who adopted affectations, whether of appearance or attitude, as a defense against the opinions of his classmates. He wanted to be different from the general run of college students, and he succeeded. As one acquaintance from the time put it, "He worked very hard at being out of step."[20]

As Prokosch recalled, Carr had taken to smoking cigarettes. Friends don't remember that he smoked in earlier years, but beginning at Haverford, he was a chain smoker. He often carried a pipe as well, but that was to create an image: He seldom lit it.[21]

During his sophomore year, Carr became acquainted with the freshmen who moved into Merion Annex, where he had his room. He did not fall in with the Haverford tradition of looking down on, and even harassing, the "Rhinies," as freshmen were called. When James Partington, Jr., entered Haverford in autumn 1926, he was assigned a room near Carr's in Merion Annex. He quickly found that "Jack" was the only sophomore "who did not behave like the rest of his classmates." Rhinies were required to put on a show for the rest of the college, and Partington went to Carr for help, since he was known to be a writer and "no matter how late at night I hit the books I could still hear the pounding of the typewriter in Jack's room." Carr wrote and even choreographed a ten- or fifteen-minute playlet that parodied the popular operetta *The Student Prince*. Entitled *The Stewed Prince of Haverburg,* it was filled with topical reference to Haverford events and professors, including Lunt (history) and Post (Greek). Partington and others belted out the following verse:

I'm a rollicking lord from Haverburg
  And a helluva Stewed Prince.
I've learned the means of eating the beans
  With never a single wince.
I've taken the most from Lunt and Post
  And never pulled a quince.
I'm a rollicking lord from Haverburg
  And a helluva Stewed Prince.

The show was a great success, and the 1926–27 Rhinies had a relatively easy time of it from upperclassmen.

Carr had a mischievous sense of humor. At about ten o'clock one night in April 1927, Partington heard a commotion in Carr's room and something that sounded like a shot. He rushed there and found the room almost totally dark, with the only lamp turned toward the wall. In the shadows was a tuxedo-clad figure, a hat covering its face, and a red stain on the left side of its white dress shirt. Partington didn't realize it was a dummy until Carr removed the hat. The two of them then invited some of the residents of another floor to see the effect. Someone called the college police to the scene of the crime. "After Jack with his usual facility explained the prank," Partington wrote, "the policemen started to leave with big smiles on their faces." They were followed by another student, stammering, "You're not going to leave that body there."[22]

Partington and his roommate, George Rogers, took Jack Carr to nondenominational meetings at an Episcopal church in nearby Ardmore. The church invited college students and young people to meet on weekend evenings as a way of getting them together under supervision. These gatherings were not overtly religious, but the minister was there, and that made the arrangement acceptable to parents. At one of the meetings, Carr met a high school student named Beatrice Clifford (now Beatrice McDade), and they began dating. She believes that they were drawn together because their friends considered both of them misfits. Neither was athletic, and both had literary interests. The relationship can hardly be considered passionate. The most they did was hold hands and occasionally play "sardines" at the home of Janet Hayes, who was George Rogers's girlfriend. Sardines was an innocent sort of game in which one person hid in the dark, and whoever found him or her had to try to squeeze into the same place, and eventually a whole crowd was crammed together with a good amount of grabbing and tickling. This impressed Carr enough that in his novel *The Eight of Swords,* he referred to "that noble pastime called sardines." Bea and Jack were seldom alone together. Their only real dates were to attend cricket matches. Haverford was the only American college to have a cricket team, and it played local amateur cricket clubs. Jack had wanted to play on the team, but as he said later, "I was a little runty." While Bea's friends went to football games, she and Jack would attend cricket and drink interminable cups of tea while the match proceeded, or (more commonly with cricket) didn't proceed.[23]

Bea McDade remembers Carr as covering his fundamental shyness by playing a role: He tried by dress and attitude to look like a writer. He walked about slowly as though, in professorial fashion, he were musing about some intellectual problem. Whenever he praised writers, he would choose an esoteric figure. For example, he spoke highly of the poetry of Christopher Smart and Charles Pierre Baudelaire, and he would quote the least popular of Shakespeare's sonnets. He also liked the lyrical tales of Donn Byrne, whose romanticized view of Ireland and the Irish appealed to someone like Carr, who still affected anglophobia. Another of Carr's favorite writers at this time was James Branch Cabell, author of the once-scandalous book *Jurgen.* A writer of fantasies set in the imaginary medieval kingdom of Poictesme, Cabell was the sort of author whose work appealed to a young man whose hero had once been the Wizard of Oz.

Bea Clifford and Jack Carr found in each other an audience. Bea would read her poetry to him, and he would read his short stories. The crowd made up of Bea Clifford, Janet Hayes, and others formed a sort of salon, and Carr would read with much expression, and occasionally act out, the story that he was currently writing for *The Haverfordian.*

Some of Carr's stories for *The Haverfordian* were of such quality that, unlike his writings at The Hill, we no longer have to look upon them merely as an apprenticeship. The atmosphere in most of his college tales is too synthetic to place them at the highest level of his productions. Nonetheless they remain impressive accomplishments—so impressive, in fact, that after his death, six of his college stories were published in posthumous collections by commercial publishers, and two have been reprinted in anthologies. S. T. Joshi, in the only lengthy critical study of Carr's works, states that in his detective stories for *The Haverfordian,* "Carr already reveals a surety of touch, a vividness of prose style, and deftness in plot-weaving that would be hallmarks of his entire career."[24]

Carr's first three stories for *The Haverfordian* are historical romances, though the earliest, "'As Drink the Dead . . . ,'" moves from present to past with great facility. All three are based on the classic motif of *la belle dame sans merci*. Each features a woman who has, as one story puts it, "the fiery, swirling beauty of Castille, the passion of the Moor, the cruelty of the Inquisition." According to Jack Carr, a woman is "all ice and fire." When a man asks a woman whether she wants something, she responds, "Why, yes, there is something I would have; is it not natural? For what purpose do we women exist, if not for wanting something? You die, finally, because you cannot give us our last wish." In the story from which this quotation is taken, what she, like Salome, wants is the head of her enemy.[25] Whatever such comments may reveal about the author's psychological condition, it is obvious that he was inexperienced where the opposite sex was concerned: Attracted to women, he also feared them. Female characters never become real in these early stories; good or bad or both, they remain dim figures of romance.

"'As Drink the Dead . . .'" was published in the March 1926 issue of *The Haverfordian*, illustrated with a woodcut by Frederic Prokosch. It was collected posthumously in book form in *The Door to Doom and Other Detections*. The story begins in contemporary Italy, as a German author named Von Arnheim asks an Italian count to show him the famed della Trebbia cup. Within the modern tale is a story of Renaissance Italy, written by Von Arnheim, about Lucrezia Borgia and the deaths of her father and brother. When Von Arnheim calls the cup "The Devil's Grail," the Count shouts "Blasphemy." "Well, blasphemy, if you like," Von Arnheim replies, "but a picturesque touch." The legend behind this cup was that it would spare the innocent, but the guilty who drank from it would die of poison. Garcini della Trebbia gave the Borgia pope Alexander VI and his son Cesare Borgia the cup. They died, but he then drank from it and was unharmed.

The story that Von Arnheim tells offers clues to the solution of this seeming miracle, but he explains to the count that he must see the cup to confirm it. The count insists that Garcini della Trebbia's preservation was the will of God. The key statement is Von Arnheim's response, "The will of God if you wish it." The count insists on drinking from the cup to test God's will. As the count raises the cup, Von Arnheim sits at a table writing the conclusion to his story—that della Trebbia had by trickery killed the pope and his son because he thought it was Lucrezia Borgia's wish. The count gradually drops limply on the table, but only when Von Arnheim has finished writing does he call for help. The explanation of the miracle problem is far better than the solutions in Carr's earlier locked-room stories, but he tossed in an unexplained and unnecessary supernatural touch—a servant thinks he sees the count's body in bed before he drinks from the Devil's Grail—but the tale as a whole is beautifully written, with such lines as: "Strange dragons of boats swam the canals, which by night were a far shimmer of torches on water."

In the April 1926 *Haverfordian*, Carr was listed as one of four associate editors working with the editor, Robert Barry. For this issue, he contributed a less satisfactory historical romance, "The Red Heels," about drinking and swordplay and a woman's treachery in the Paris of the Reign of Terror. It's a confusing tale, with Napoleon popping in and out of it, and various people being in love with a cruel woman. (One of them even chooses to die with her at the conclusion.) The reader (or at least, *this* reader) is left feeling that it was a stupid rather than a noble decision.

The theme of magnificent but futile gestures is much more successfully handled in Carr's May 1926 contribution, "The Dim Queen," collected in another posthumous volume, *Fell and Foul Play*. Retif, a soldier of Napoleon who "lost a fortune at the gaming-table and won the cross of honor at Austerlitz," travels to Seville. There he meets a poverty-stricken Spanish swordsman who insists on selling his cloak so that they may have a bottle of wine. They talk of a woman who, though young, "is old, old as the Alhambra, old as the art of poison." She is also a matador who enjoys "the thrust of the blade that blocks the great bulls and crushes them to their knees in blood." She challenges Retif, who, unknown to her, is one of Europe's greatest swordsmen, but he refuses to defend himself. She responds by "the foulest stroke known to fencers" and blinds him. Nevertheless, he still will not reveal his identity, and the story ends as he travels north—now accompanied by a good woman—to join Napoleon at Waterloo. For all its adolescence, "The Dim Queen" is a powerful tale whose theme meant a great deal to John: "It shall be of romance; are you not pleased to call her your dim queen? Yes, as romance always drowns reality?"

John Dickson Carr became editor of *The Haverfordian* for the June 1926 issue. Students were surprised that Carr, then only a freshman, was selected for such a position. Samuel Cook, who was advertising manager for the magazine, remembers a rumor that Frederic Prokosch was instrumental in the choice. Prokosch, who had received his master's degree the previous month, was, as he described himself, "a kind of adviser in the English Department." Sadly, I had not asked Prokosch about this matter before he died, and it is now unlikely that we will ever know the extent of his involvement.

During Carr's editorship of *The Haverfordian*, 1926–27, it is not always obvious which poems and stories were written by which member of the staff. Professor Edward Snyder of the English Department said that, using various pen names, young Carr on at least one occasion wrote an entire issue himself.[26] Sixty years later, Prokosch recalled that they had invented "prankish pseudonyms." "There was," he said, "certainly a great deal of playfulness in the atmosphere and an intermingling of pseudonyms. . . . I suppose the staff did sit around and assign names to each other."[27] (The word "staff," incidentally, is an overstatement. During the school year of 1926–27, Carr and Prokosch did all the editorial work, joined in spring 1927 by John Rodell, who would succeed Carr as editor later that year.)

Carr and Prokosch published some material under their own names, some anonymously, and some pseudonymously. Their first pseudonym was "Eric Hirth," the name of a character in Carr's first story published at Uniontown High School. They also used the pen names "C. G. Baker" and "Caliban." Both names appeared several times during Carr's tenure at *The Haverfordian* and continued to be used after Carr left the college. Other pseudonyms, such as "Richard Westcott," appeared only once. In addition, Carr and Prokosch often attributed their poems to people identified only by initials: "M.R.P.," "E.S.D.," and so on. The greatest bibliographical headache is that they sometimes wrote stories or verse under each other's names or signed the names of their classmates to various pieces. This sounds like the plots of Carr's later novels, and in fact Prokosch claimed that "Carr was the instigator of all this nonsense, and the rest of us merely consenting co-conspirators."[28]

Fortunately, even after sixty years a great deal of this confusion can be straightened out, though some questions do remain. A poem, "Hunting Song," attributed to "M.R.P.," is a reprint of a verse that Carr wrote at The Hill and that was published in *A Book of Hill School Verse*. He reused one of his Hill stories, "The God of the Gloves," in *The Haverfordian* under the name of his friend George P. Rogers. "Song of the Sword," a poem published under Frederic Prokosch's name, was (Prokosch told me in a letter) actually written by Jack Carr. It has many of Jack's early themes, including swordplay and references to D'Artagnan, and, as the following excerpt shows, it is full of color:

> *Wine a-crawling ruddy*
> *Gauzy ruffles bloody,*
> *Wrists that flash and twinkle in the gloom—*

Falling drops a-spatter,
Drive and dart and clatter,
Red tears on the wigged white face of doom.

"The Haunting of Tarnboys," an interesting tale with its medieval super-naturalism, was supposedly written by Francis C. Jameson, a classmate at Haverford, but in a recent letter Jameson confirmed what the stylistic points indicate—it was written by John Dickson Carr.[29] "That Ye Be Not Judged," a story of Cavaliers and Puritans shortly before the English Civil War, has the name of Ira B. Rutherford attached to it. Rutherford is no longer alive, but his classmates do not remember him as a writer; again, subject matter and stylistic considerations indicate that Carr was the actual author.

The authorship of some *Haverfordian* stories and poems during Carr's editorship, however, will never be entirely resolved, especially in cases in which Carr, Prokosch, and Rodell used the same pseudonym. I have discussed some of these pieces with Rodell, and with his help have been able to decide on some probable attributions. Only one contribution by "Eric Hirth," a poem called "Song of the Toy Shops," was probably written by Carr. Other poems under that name were by Rodell and Prokosch—one in fact was reprinted in a book a short while later under Prokosch's name. The authorship of a short prose work, "Après Midi" by "Hirth," is a mystery. It was not written by Rodell, and its precious, almost brittle language is not typical of either Carr or Prokosch, but perhaps the two of them wrote it together. "Caliban" contributed only two pieces during Carr's editorship. The first, a ghost story called "The Devil-Gun," is full of Carr's stylistic and plot tricks. The second, a verse called "Navalis," was written by Rodell. The situation is similar with "C. G. Baker." His first contribution, "Pygmalion," can be attributed, with slight hesitation, to Carr. Baker's second, "Casanova's Lament," was by Rodell.

The most intriguing problem is "The Cross and the Crown," a story by W. A. Reitzel. It is a clumsy effort, especially in its use of English dialects, but it is filled with Carrian echoes, including its Chestertonian title, its emphasis on drinking, and the presence of such lines as: "In the *Black Bull* at Clannerton, far south, a thin little man with a grizzle of beard under his chin, who sat at the back of the room, rose and bowed and drank." The tale is also strongly anticlerical, like many of Carr's writings of this period. But Reitzel was Carr's English professor, and though Jack could attribute his works to classmates, I doubt that he would have dared sign his professor's name to one of his own stories, or even to revise Reitzel's work. For lack of a better solution, I hazard a guess that Reitzel and Carr collaborated on the story. Whatever the case about "The Cross and the Crown," Rodell in 1929 wrote a good summary of Carr's and his successive editorships: "Both were intimate friends and sponsors of the work of such well-known men as Eric Hirth and C. G. Baker . . . and Caliban without whose friendship they would, indeed, have been frequently obliged to write entire issues unaided and alone."[30]

Carr received Haverford College's Hibberd Garrett prize in poetry, and the college's student yearbook, *The Record*, stated that Jack Carr "had poetry reprinted in selections of the best college literary work of the country."[31] These reprints have not been located, but Carr's poetry published in *The Haverfordian* shows little development from his Hill School days—and, in fact, even some later poems (such as "Kentish Sir Byng" in the 1953 novel *The Cavalier's Cup*) have the same emphasis on strong (even bouncy) rhythm, internal rhymes, and lofty subjects. But a few of his verses, though without depth of feeling, can still be stirring—for example, "Song of the Jolly Roger" by "E.S.D.":

> The wind is in the halyards and the death's-head sings before,
> (But the dead men swing in a grisly ring and dance on the
> ⠀⠀⠀ocean's floor!)
> . . . .
> Now a cup, a cup to the life (fill up!)
> ⠀⠀Drink deep to your lover's vow;
> ⠀⠀Drink to the lass, and drink to the glass,
> ⠀⠀⠀And—drink to the hangman now!

More interesting is the anonymous "Song of the Legionary," which in a letter to me John Rodell attributed to Carr. It shows a lyrical sense taken from Swinburne and A. E. Housman:

> Shall I see you in the brown leaves
> ⠀⠀And will you think of me?
> Shall I see you in the twilight
> ⠀⠀By an old and tangled tree?
> You smiled, and all so duskily;
> ⠀⠀Your touch brushed lightly by,
> As linnets brush the white rose-bloom
> ⠀⠀And, pierced with singing, die.

In the Haverford students' yearbook, Rodell wrote that he and Carr "developed equal facility and felicity in supplying their magazines with specimens of any given literary genre that happened to be needed at the time." The works signed by Carr and those that can be attributed to him confirm the truth of Rodell's statement. It would be repetitious to go over in detail all of Carr's prose work during his editorship of *The Haverfordian*, but a few of his historical romances and supernatural tales should be mentioned before we examine his detective stories. "The Blue Garden" (November 1926) is again about the Borgias and women who bait and betray men, and we need not linger over it. More important is "The Devil-Gun" (December 1926), published under the pseudonym "Caliban." It is one of the few pure horror stories that John Dickson Carr ever wrote, and an amazingly mature one. The influence here may be the famous pulp magazine *Weird Tales*, which Carr mentioned in another story written at Haverford.[32] Carr describes Russia, where the story takes place, as a bleak, windswept country inhabited by empty people:

> Anstruther has often told me that the people he saw there were not human at all. In those days before the war they were brutes who seemed all the more horrible because they had the forms of men, with their square faces and wooly caps. They would stand motionless to stare at you in the snow—the snow which is not calm and holy, as of Christmas eve, but dreary and streaked on the black hills.

Years earlier, Sir Lionel Barnstow had left England "talking hell-fire and throwing duel challenges to everyone" and disappeared into Africa. Rumors spread of what he had been doing, but now he has emerged in southern Russia, near the Black Sea. In response to a plea from Sir Lionel, his nephew Noel Barnstow and Noel's friend Anstruther go to Russia and arrive at the mysterious mansion that, under various names, had already played such a role in the young Carr's imagination. They find Sir Lionel collapsing from terror. He speaks in a sad facsimile of the manner of a gracious country gentleman, and introduces them to his new wife, Corinne, whom he had met tending bar in Capetown: "Her scanty, straw-colored hair had been piled high, stuck with a red plume; she wore a flowered gown of a decade past, which swept out into a train and almost tripped her." In a magnificent gesture of the type that Jack Carr admired, Noel kisses his new stepmother.

Sir Lionel asks what is the most horrible thing they can imagine. Anstruther replies "fire," but Sir Lionel says that there is something worse: "You never saw this thing when it was dead." In Africa, the natives had cornered him but he escaped when he shot their witch doctor in the face with his elephant gun, the "devil gun." This now faceless thing has come back to terrify Sir Lionel: "Can't imagine a thing worse'n fire, eh? Well, I saw this thing the other night. I came in my room, and lit the lamp, and there it was sittin' in my chair lookin' at me." Noel and Anstruther go to their room, and they hear something climbing toward them along the outside wall of the house. Carr builds up the tension expertly as "the thing" comes closer and climbs through the window. Despite his fear of fire, Anstruther grabs a red-hot poker to threaten it, but the thing jumps at them. Lady Corinne shows up at the door with the devil gun and shoots it. As she kneels before the shapeless object, she begins to scream, "Lionel! . . . Lionel! . . . [I] didn't mean to shoot you."

Carr's detective tales at The Hill School had been the least accomplished of all his juvenile works, but, although the solutions often strain credulity, the early cases of Henri Bencolin, prefect of police of Paris, would be worthy of many writers past the journeyman stage and aspiring to become masters. This development came about because Carr had outgrown the Hanshew period of his interest in impossible crimes and had absorbed the methods of G. K. Chesterton. He read *The Incredulity of Father Brown* at the same time that he decided to create his detective stories for *The Haverfordian*, and in a review of Chesterton's book in the November 1926 issue of the college magazine, Jack did not restrain his enthusiasm:

> Here we have G. K. taking rabbits out of clerical hats in his most mystifying manner. These are the best detective stories of the year, and not even Conan Doyle has ever come within a pistol-shot or a knife-throw of them. We have haunted castles, winged daggers, vanishing men—and over it all the genial, lovable priest who plays detective.

That's what Carr wanted to create in his own stories—mysterious happenings that seem to be supernatural, mystification that lasts until the detective reveals all. And, like Father Brown, Henri Bencolin understands the crime by re-creating it in the mind.

Carr clearly makes this point about the creative (or re-creative) imagination in one of the Bencolin stories published in *The Haverfordian*—adding his usual strictures on mathematics:

> A chess game can be a terrible and enthralling thing, when you play it backwards and blindfolded. Your adversary starts out with his king in check, and tries to move his pieces back to where they were at first;

that's why you can't apply rules or mathematical laws to crime. The
great chess player is the one who can visualize the board as it will be
after his move. The great detective is the one who can visualize the
board as it *has been* when he finds the pieces jumbled. He must have
the imagination to see the opportunities that the criminal saw, and
act as the criminal would act. It's a great, ugly, terrific play of opposite imaginations. Nobody is more apt than a detective to say a lot of
windy, fancy things about reasoning, and deduction, and logic. He
too frequently says "reason" when he means "imagination." I object
to having a cheap, strait-laced pedantry like reason confused with a
far greater thing.[33]

Carr's attitude goes back to Poe. In "The Purloined Letter," Dupin says "as
poet *and* mathematician, he would reason well; as mere mathematician,
he could not have reasoned at all," and he argues that problems can be resolved through "an identification of the reasoner's intellect with that of
his opponent." This idea of the re-creative imagination is also Chestertonian, and it was to dominate Carr's detective fiction, and perhaps also
Carr's attitude toward all creation.

In short, whether Bencolin talks about imagination, or Dr. Fell about
"woolgathering," or Sir Henry Merrivale about "sittin' and thinkin'," all of
Carr's detectives use Father Brown's method of discerning the pattern
that the events form. Unlike the fictional sleuths of many other authors,
they do not make elaborate inferences from, say, a matchstick or a cuff
link left at the scene of the crime.

Why Carr decided to create a French detective is not known. Perhaps
he was thinking back to Poe's C. Auguste Dupin or Leroux's Joseph
Rouletabille; perhaps he was influenced by Chesterton's brief use of a
French detective named Aristide Valentin in the first Father Brown stories;
perhaps the cause was simpler: Carr knew people who had just returned
from Paris and could supply him with some of the color. While John was
in Uniontown during the summer of 1926, O'Neil Kennedy was in France,
and when John went back to Haverford in the autumn, Frederic Prokosch
was full of stories of his summer spent in Paris with Carr's roommate,
John Lineaweaver. John Carr typically invested their stories of France
with a neoromantic melancholy: "Like all good Frenchmen, Bencolin
loved his Paris. He loved the pink-and-white flowered trees, the hurdy-
gurdies, the gaiety that is almost sadness."[34]

Although Chesterton's invention of a French detective may have influenced Carr, Bencolin himself seems to have no real similarities to Valentin. Chesterton described Valentin as having "plodding logic," while according to Carr, Bencolin was sometimes believed to have "far too much imagination." The real influence, at least on the physical description of Bencolin, was O'Neil Kennedy. Admittedly, in the early stories the resemblance is not obvious. In "The Fourth Suspect" (*The Haverfordian*, January 1927), we learn that Bencolin is short and stooped, has a black beard, and wears his top hat at a rakish angle. Already, however, he has Kennedy's "unnecessary theatricality." By the fourth Bencolin short story, "The Murder in Number Four" (June 1928), the resemblance between Bencolin and Jack's friend and mentor has become clear, as the detective's close-parted, glossy hair is emphasized, along with his curling mustache. In the Bencolin books, especially *The Corpse in the Waxworks*, the detective's sartorial sense receives great attention. In short, when Jack Carr decided to create a person of sophistication and elegance with a sense for the dramatic, he automatically thought of O'Neil Kennedy.

For *The Haverfordian*, Carr wrote four detective short stories and a novella featuring Bencolin, and he used Bencolin as a character in the framing story for a group of tales that he called "The New Canterbury Tales." In all of these appearances, Bencolin investigates seemingly impossible crimes or ghostly events. The tone is set in the first story, "The Shadow of the Goat," published in the November and December 1926 issues. It begins in a room at Whitehall where Bencolin has been visiting his friend, Sir John Landervorne, described as "possibly the only man who could have given orders to Scotland Yard." They are discussing the extraordinary events surrounding the disappearance of Cyril Merton, a bearded student of demonology. Words like "sorcery," "ghostly," "witchcraft," and "phantom" fill the first two pages, and throughout the story Carr creates a mood of the supernatural.

Landervorne tells Bencolin about Merton's disappearance. In a Norman castle, Cyril Merton had announced to Sir John, Julian Arbor, and Billy Garrick that he could vanish from a locked and guarded room. He then proceeded to do so, even though witnesses had the room under constant observation. A short while later, a corpse was found in another eerie house, alone in a locked room. To make matters even more inexplicable, Merton seemed to appear and then again to disappear almost before the eyes of onlookers.

At this point, the story stops, and readers were challenged to present a solution, the winner to receive a check for twenty-five dollars. Carr's solution would be given in the next issue. According to a later interview, John didn't have the money but he felt secure in the belief that no one could work out the solution. This was probably the case with most readers of *The Haverfordian*. The story was published anonymously, and Samuel Cook recalls that students who came into the bookstore speculated not only about the solution to Merton's disappearance but also about the authorship of the story. The anonymity, however, must not have been much of a cloak, for immediately after writing each section Jack Carr read the story to Bea Clifford and other friends and challenged them to work out the solution. They didn't, but much to his chagrin a freshman named Edward Taulane showed up about an hour after the issue was published, presented the correct solution, and demanded his prize. John had to beg his father to come through with the money.

[****Those who have not read "The Shadow of the Goat" should skip this paragraph.] Merton disappeared by shaving off his beard in the room, then disguising himself as one of the other characters; the impersonation was not noticed because the room was lit only by candles. No matter how one slices it, this solution is difficult to believe, especially since Merton played the other part for about three hours, but it indicates how strongly Carr believed that masks (in this instance, Merton's beard) could hide a person. The solutions to the other impossibilities in "The Shadow of the Goat" are almost as weak; one involves someone having a duplicate key. Even so, the story is well told, and its twist ending, in which another character, who had seemed to be the hero, had intervened to murder Merton, is excellent. Bencolin comments:

> You do not find it pleasant, or even clever. It upsets our beautiful notion of a story; not only have we shattered our hero, but there is not enough of the theatrical in him to follow a story formula and kill himself. Truth is infinitely more childish than the stories about it.

Carr's second Bencolin story, also published anonymously, was "The Fourth Suspect" (January 1927). It too is atmospheric: Trees are described as "eerie and ghostly," and a person pacing up and down is a "spectral figure." In "The Fourth Suspect," Carr introduced two of the most interesting characters in his early work. M. le Comte de Villon, Bencolin's superior, has a huge, bald head and pendulous lips. He is a descendant of the alcoholic fifteenth-century poet François Villon, who seems to have been one of young Carr's favorite personages, though his remark that the poet "had grinned over Paris like a gargoyle" doesn't seem quite apt. This idea of romantic drunkenness also appears with the second character introduced in the story, the one-armed Irishman Patrick O'Riordan, an agent for the French secret service during the First World War. Among his exploits: He had drunkenly crossed German lines on nerve alone, and in Constantinople had ridden with a German general in his automobile.

"The Fourth Suspect" is Carr's first attempt to write a story with an espionage background. A spy named La Garde carries a paper with the name of his contact in the French government. He has apparently seduced O'Riordan's wife, the gypsy singer Mme. St. Marie. In a fury O'Riordan calls Villon to wait with him for her return from a masked ball hosted by La Garde. Finally, able to wait no longer, they go to La Garde's house. They hear a pistol shot as they approach. O'Riordan breaks down the locked door, and they find La Garde's body, dressed in an eighteenth-century costume of velvet and satin. He is wearing a mask, and in the center of his forehead is a bullet hole looking like another eyehole in the mask. The murderer has disappeared.

[****I suspect that most readers have already worked out the explanation of the locked-room problem.] As in Carr's earlier stories, "The Ruby of Rameses" and "The Marked Bullet," the solution is based on a misunderstanding of the Maxim Silencer: Carr believed that a gun fitted with a silencer could fire a bullet with no sound at all. In "The Fourth Suspect," a gunshot is fired by another character as Villon and O'Riordan approach the room, but La Garde is still alive as O'Riordan bursts in. Unbelievably, La Garde says not a word as O'Riordan enters, and the Irishman shoots him with the silenced gun. Villon, though an experienced police officer, does not notice a thing.

More interesting in this story is the subplot—the mystery of where La Garde hid the important paper and what Bencolin will do with the information. It turns out that the paper reveals that O'Riordan's wife, Mme. St. Marie, is the agent of a foreign power. She is eager to turn her husband, O'Riordan, over to the authorities for La Garde's murder. Like later Carr detectives, Bencolin is less interested in the law than in protecting his friend, and he tells St. Marie that revealing O'Riordan's guilt will make it necessary to tell the full story, including her own treason: "Take part of your information or all of mine—but, in the name of God, let there be an equal falsehood or an equal truth." Bencolin has discovered La Garde's paper in a clever hiding place, just as obvious in its way as that in Poe's "Purloined Letter," which is mentioned in the story. Bencolin then, in another theatrical gesture, tricks Villon into destroying it unread. Neither O'Riordan nor Mme. St. Marie are arrested for their crimes.

Bencolin's next appearance was his most unusual. The March 1927 *Haverfordian* was the traditional "chapbook" issue of the magazine in which all the stories were to be published anonymously. Unfounded rumors, probably started by Carr to increase sales, spread that the chapbook was to be suppressed. Carr named this issue "The New Canterbury Tales," and it contained eight stories, which he called "legends," and a framing tale. Prokosch and Carr wrote the entire issue, but included the initials of six additional authors at the beginning. Two of these authors, however, have the initials of our pseudonymous friends "Eric Hirth" and "C. G. Baker"; two others have the initials of Francis Jameson and George P. Rogers, who did not write for the magazine but on whom Carr foisted his own stories. The remaining two sets of initials ("W.S." and "J.B.") are more mysterious; they are not of contributors to *The Haverfordian*, though "W.S." may be an oblique reference to Caliban through William Shakespeare. Shortly before his death, I sent Prokosch a copy of "The New Canterbury Tales." He replied that he had forgotten all about it, "but I detect Carr's fine Italian hand (for most of it) and my own too (in parts, & to my embarrassment)."[35] An examination of the stories by several experts in Carr's works has resulted in a consensus: The framing story and five of the "legends" are by Carr; two of the stories are by Prokosch; the eighth is more difficult, and it may be a collaboration.[36] The tales, only five to six pages long, are quite compressed, some of them sketches for ideas that would have been better if developed at greater length, but they cover many of Carr's youthful interests—mystery, detection, the supernatural, and historical romance with plenty of swashbuckling.

The framing story takes place "in an ancient, rook-haunted, decaying manor house on the Wessex downs." Henri Bencolin, Sir John Landervorne, Patrick O'Riordan, Ludwig von Arnheim (from "'And Drink the Dead . . .'"), and Stoneman Wood (an American newspaperman) are guests of an Englishman named Dunstan. The men discuss their love of old-fashioned stories, with ghosts and voluptuous ladies, and they agree that each will tell a tale. Wood is fascinated by a legend he has heard about the manor house—the ghost of a monk appears at a window that has a verse scratched in the pane. The first story is consequently "The Legend of the Black Monk," told by the host, Dunstan, and obviously written by John Dickson Carr. It is a medieval romance about a lecherous monk who attacks a beautiful woman and whose ghost still appears. The second story, also by Carr, is called "The Legend of the Softest Lips." It is, says O'Riordan, who tells the tale, a true account of his adventures as a spy for the French government in Turkey. Esmet Pasha asks him to obtain a box from a European woman imprisoned in a harem. The box contains papers that will secure her release. O'Riordan does so in a series of romantic escapades, but finds that the woman is not a prisoner but a hired servant and that the box contains jewels, which she and Esmet Pasha were stealing. Carr liked this tale, and twelve years later he used the same plot in another story, "Harem-Scarem."

The next story, Sir John Landervorne's "The Legend of the Gay Diana," set in Regency England, is another Carrian historical romance with a touch of mystery. It features Lady Diana of Falcondene Court, who is the archetypal man-devouring woman who appears in many early Carr romances. She wants to control men, even to the extent of driving them to violence for her, and she is not interested in protecting her reputation: "Do you expect me to blush every time when they mention a man?—or thrill and be meanly lascivious with myself behind doors, and shut my eyes in wonder and tap a parasol?" Von Arnheim's story comes next. "The Legend of the Neckband of the Carnellians" is a historical tale, but it has none of Carr's stylistic quirks. The language is suggestive of Andrew Lang's translation of *Aucassin and Nicolette*. Probably this legend was written by Prokosch, who was at that time steeped in medievalism.

At this point in the framing story of "The New Canterbury Tales," two stranded travelers, Mr. and Mrs. Mortimer Grimmel, join the five storytellers. Mrs. Grimmel agrees to tell a story, but first Stoneman Wood recounts "The Legend of the Cane in the Dark." The story's central situation must have intrigued Carr, for he later reused the plot three times—in two short stories and a radio script. On the way home to Pittsburgh from Canada, where he had been on a hunting trip, Wood reads a newspaper account of his own death. Hurrying to his house, he is followed by a huge figure wearing a black coat and tapping a cane. At home, he sees his own corpse laid out for a funeral. It turns out that his cousin Stephen, wanting to inherit his money, tried to have him killed in Canada. Stephen then obtained the body of a man who resembled Wood but who had died a natural death. The cane-tapping figure may have been the ghost of Wood's uncle intervening to protect him. This story is followed by "The Legend of the Hand of Ippolita," which was almost certainly written by Prokosch. The final tale, "The Legend of La Bella Duquesa," told by Mrs. Grimmel, has a plot that is probably by Carr—the killing of a boy by an older woman who is his lover—but the writing, with a sort of brittle sophistication, may be Prokosch's.

"The New Canterbury Tales" then returns to the framing story. Carr produced an unexpected conclusion by showing that two of the tales were connected with each other. Bencolin explains that O'Riordan's experience, which he had recounted in "The Legend of the Softest Lips," was true, and that the two main characters were, in fact, Mr. and Mrs. Grimmel. Mrs. Grimmel had been the woman with the "softest lips," and Mr. Grimmel had played the role of Esmet Pasha. Moreover, Mrs. Grimmel's story, "The Legend of La Bella Duquesa," was about herself; she was the woman who had killed her young lover. Years earlier, Bencolin had investigated the murder but had not been able to prove her guilt. Then, in what would soon typify Carr's stories, Bencolin provides a material explanation for the ghost of the black monk that had resulted in the first tale.

"The New Canterbury Tales" ends with "L'Envoi," which defends romance against realism:

> The things which lie closest to the heart are fancies. . . . You in your dreams will unhorse the stoutest opponent, so that you will be the man you might have been had you dared take the open road and the bright eyes of danger. If we lived always in reality, we should all be poor things indeed. Truth? Is there anything more true than what one in his inmost self desires? . . . Realists are the people who look in a mirror and get disgusted. They are the ones who explode all your fine ideas. They would pull down Kenilworth Castle and substitute an efficient gas-station. . . . If, however, we forward romantic propaganda, that is entirely within our realm. If we assume that there is a higher thing in fiction than the realistic thump of the janitor's mop, at least we do little harm. The most dangerous trap about writing is that an author finds it so easy to be scowlingly cynical on paper that he whirls round his Byronic tie and takes a leer at romance.

Bencolin appeared in *The Haverfordian* again two months later in "The Ends of Justice" (May 1927). Carr's early solutions to the problem of murder in a locked room stretched credulity to the breaking point, and "The Ends of Justice" proves no exception. Here, Roger Darworth, a spiritualist, is visited by his cousin Tom Fellowes. Witnesses then hear Darworth screaming. Breaking into the room, they find him handcuffed to his chair, stabbed in the heart. No one is there, and there is fresh, unmarked snow outside the window. Though it is never shown how Fellowes could have left the room, he has been convicted of murder, and will soon be hanged.

[****Once again, I shall give the solution, so readers who find this approach unfair should skip this paragraph.] Bencolin, in England visiting Landervorne and an Anglican bishop named Wolfe, discovers that Darworth in fact committed suicide; even after he stabbed himself in the heart, he managed to put his hands in the cuffs. I don't know whether this would have been physically possible, but it was certainly foolish of Darworth to depend on being able to do anything after he put a knife in his heart.

The real interest in the story is the female lead, who for a refreshing change is not one of the destructive, remote women who had appeared in our young romantic's earlier stories. Cynthia Melford is described by Bishop Wolfe as "an utterly frivolous chit, one of the type called 'saucy' . . . with bobbed hair and what is known as 'make up'"—in short, the type of modern woman who reappears in many of Carr's novels of the 1930s. Also of interest is the portrayal of Bishop Wolfe, a churchman turned detective who had found the evidence to convict Fellowes. Carr had expressed an increasing anticlericalism in his stories, but seldom as bitterly or, one must admit, heavy-handedly as he does with Wolfe. The bishop is a cold, colorless, emotionless caricature, who mouths pious platitudes. Bencolin says that even Pilate was more merciful than the bishop, and the story concludes with the bishop praying for Fellowes's soul. Bencolin responds, "Oh, Bishop, when will you learn? When will you learn?" This tale has been described as "an amazing production for a twenty-year-old,"[37] and in plotting and atmosphere, I agree, it is. But its attitude toward the clergy is a typical youthful piece if iconoclasm. Carr would do better, however, with another sleuthing churchman in a novel called *The Eight of Swords*, in which the odd image of a man of the cloth investigating crime is a source of amusement, not bitterness. In neither "The Ends of Justice" nor *The Eight of Swords*, incidentally, did Carr have Father Brown in mind, for Chesterton's creation is never a conscious criminologist in the sense that Carr's detecting bishops are.

Carr concluded "The Ends of Justice" with the remark that "this is the last of the Bencolin stories." Jack had planned to return to Haverford for his junior year, and he and John Rodell, the next editor of *The Haverfordian*, were going to room together. But Carr's grades, except in his English courses, were disastrous. His classmates recall that he stayed up all night writing; he showed up in class with bloodshot eyes, but not from studying. *The Haverfordian*'s advertising manager, Samuel Cook, says, "I don't believe he ever studied one hour for any class." Another classmate, Walter Sondheim, Jr., recalls the same thing: "He was more interested in writing, I think, than studying."[38] Not even in William Altick Reitzel's English composition class was Carr willing to put in much effort. His classmate, Herbert Ensworth, remembers:

> Because my name starts with "E" and his with "C," we were assigned to the same section in freshman composition. We had to write a short essay every week, then we'd read them to the small number around in the class. I had worked on my composition. He'd get at his about an hour before the class or something like that, and dash it off. I'd read mine. It would be fair. Then he'd read his and it was great.[39]

Carr's mathematics grades at Haverford were especially bad. "From day one," according to fellow student Joe MacNamee, "he let the algebra professor know that he did not want to take the subject. Mr. Carr was a writer and hated the course." His total grade in algebra was 2 points out of a possible 100. In his sophomore year, he took economics with almost the same abysmal result—a grade of 16; Dr. Fell expressed Carr's opinion when he talked about "algebra, economics, and other dismal things."[40]

Jack ended his sophomore year with a combined grade of 52.6. For promotion to the junior class, he needed an average of 65.0. Haverford College, however, was willing to let him return if he could pass the entrance examination for plane geometry. James Partington, Jr., Jack Carr's friend from Merion Annex, recalls that almost for the first time he studied for a mathematics test: "He had memorized the textbook so well that he could tell you the page number of any theorem but he could not solve original problems." Haverford's records show that Carr scored 35 on the plane geometry examination, an astonishing grade for Carr but not even close to passing. A story recalled by two of his fellow students is that the college did not want to throw him out because of his ability as a writer, so the administration offered him a deal: "If you will take what we consider the hardest course in college and pass it, we'll forgive you the math." They assigned him Greek, but Carr refused to take it, and he left Haverford.[41]

Preparing to return to Uniontown, John Dickson Carr wrote what he thought would be his final story for *The Haverfordian*. "The Deficiency Expert," published in the May 1927 issue, is humorous, but it also has a strong undercurrent of bitterness. It is about Rinkey Donovan, who has been asked to withdraw from college for a series of pranks, which the dean claims "persistently overturned everything that is noble and good in the college." One of the pranks was publishing a series of lies in the college newspaper, though Rinkey asserts that "it wasn't lies; it was art." The dean tells Rinkey's father that the boy has a brilliant mind, but that it would be better if he does not return to school. Rinkey's father resembles Wooda N. Carr, "stout and bald-headed and genial. . . . He was proud of Rinkey, and at the Elks' Club [in which Wooda was also active] he was in the habit of referring to 'these damn tame little rabbits who haven't a thing in 'em.'" But he fears that Rinkey's leaving college "will just about kill your mother."

Rinkey wants to become a newspaperman, and his father (who owns the *Humberville Bulletin*) makes him temporary editor. Humberville is a thinly disguised Uniontown, even to Lafayette's visit there a century earlier, and the *Bulletin* is the *News Standard*. The city editor is named "O'Neil, an Irishman who looked like a German and who stuttered." (O'Neil Kennedy had a stammer.) Rinkey decides that, like his college paper, the *Bulletin* will be filled with lies. One of the purposes is to elect his father's candidate, Billy Mugson, to Congress. Mugson has characteristics that Carr would later give to Dr. Gideon Fell and to Sir Henry Merrivale. He sits with his feet on a table and is described as "expansive, red-faced, and white-whiskered, rather like Santa Claus. He was genial and blundering as a threshing machine." Mugson says, "Now I wouldn't buy anybody's vote; you know that. I got ideals, same as anybody else—sure I have! But if we get cars we can line the wenches up at the polls."

Much of "The Deficiency Expert" is taken up with the strange news items that the *Bulletin* prints about Mugson's opponent, Jeffrey Davis. It states that Davis advocates the method of Dr. Sigismund von Stubbenheim of Gottingen for removing alcohol from liquor and feeding the result to infants: "BETTER BEER FOR BIGGER BABIES," says the *Bulletin's* headline. The newspaper also reports that "Mr. Davis, in scientific language, coldly earnest, set forth his plans for a league called 'The Daughters of Chastity,' which should pledge itself to preserve strict continence between husband and wife except for a definite purpose." There is, however, only one meeting of the league; it is stormed by indignant husbands. But Rinkey becomes more and more disillusioned as he finds that Mugson does not deserve victory. Eventually, when Mugson wins the election, Rinkey collapses crying. "He went stupidly down the stairs, wondering whether he was going back to college, wondering whether he was going to be an incurable romanticist all his days."

Chapter 3

PARIS, BROOKLYN HEIGHTS— AND THE SATANIC BENCOLIN

On June 27, 1927, John Dickson Carr applied for a passport so that he could travel abroad, with O'Neil Kennedy signing an affidavit swearing to his citizenship, having "known the applicant personally for 15 years." The application says that John, twenty years old, was five feet, six inches in height, with brown hair and gray eyes. Unlike most passport photographs, John's shows him at his best. The unprepossessing boy had matured into a good-looking young man, with large, almost dreamy eyes and the hint of a smile. At this point, though, a Carr biographer is almost at a loss. It sounds too blunt simply to say that on August 20, 1927, John Dickson Carr embarked from New York City on the ship *Lapland*, remaining in Europe, primarily Paris, for the next five months—but we don't know much more for sure. Five years earlier he had recorded his dreams of traveling to Europe to see "all the thousand scenes that bring with them the faint, musty breath of the past." Why John wanted to travel is clear; why Wooda and Julia Carr permitted him to go (and paid all his expenses) is less so. Carr later told an interviewer, "My father's idea was that I should also go into the legal profession, but he indulged me. I was supported by him. I went off to Paris." Elsewhere, he wrote that he "began to wander about Europe at early age, on pension from father."[1] On his passport application, he stated that he planned to go to France to "study," but he didn't define his plans any more exactly. Later family legend says that John was supposed to attend the University of Paris (the Sorbonne). A local article published on his return says only that the purpose was to perfect his French. At least, the trip was successful on that level, for he did indeed become proficient in the language.

On the way to the ship, John stayed overnight with his Haverford friend James Partington, Jr., and his family in New Jersey. He traveled on the *Lapland* to England; from there he flew across the Channel to France. He told Partington that he had met an attractive Frenchwoman on the plane. When they reached Paris, they went out together and ended up in the same hotel room for the night, with predictable results.[2] Nowadays, when the "first time" is considered of extreme importance, we might wish to know whether the story was true or whether John was engaging in a bit of braggadocio, but as with most other events on this trip, we simply can't be sure of the facts.

John toured Europe before finding an apartment in Paris. He spent time in England, Germany, and Italy. Unfortunately, all that we know about Carr's visit to England in 1927 is a remark in a letter to a fan forty years later. "It's also good that you share my weakness for Englishwomen. This began when I met the original of Dorothy Starberth [of the novel *Hag's Nook*] in London in 1927."[3] October found him in Amsterdam. It was from there that he sent Partington a photograph of himself standing in front of a Fokker single-engine airplane. He cut a natty figure with his fedora, gloves, and cane. On the back of the photograph he wrote:

> A careful attention to detail in this camera-study will repay the effort. It was caught by Mlle. Lucienne Baugouin, about whom M. Carr swears to write a book (privately published). At the left of the plane will be seen M. Eric Hirth superintending the loading of M. Carr's baggage.... To the right are two unidentified ladies, presumed by the Scotland Yard operative hiding in the cockpit to be Mlle. Yvonne Bagatelle and Fraulein Ethel Palozi. Assisting Mlle. Baugouin in taking the picture of this distinguished criminal were M. Henri Bencolin and Sir John Landervorne, who have him under observation, as much as anybody could.—Clipping from "Scotland Yard Bulletin."[4]

At this point in his life, Carr affected the cynical attitude that the various places he had visited had not measured up to his expectations. A few months later, he told a reporter for the *Uniontown Daily News Standard,* "The garbage in the canals of Venice, the peacefulness of Heidelberg, and the tendency of London not to produce any honest-to-God mysteries has ruined everything that has been written about them. . . . But he finds that adventure is not dead."[5]

After these sadly unrecorded adventures, he went to Paris, ostensibly to study—"this being," he said, "probably the only thing in Paris I did not do."[6] He had decided that he was going to make his living as a writer, and at the least he would pick up the atmosphere for more stories about Bencolin. One legend of doubtful authenticity is that during the Paris months Carr wrote a detective novel every two weeks, but, finding them unsatisfactory, made a ritual of piling them up in a fireplace and burning them.[7] Whatever one makes of that tale, it is certainly true that he began and then destroyed a historical romance. It was set in the seventeenth-century England of the Cavaliers and the Puritans, and he described it as having "lots of gadzookses and swordplay," but, or so he told Professor Edward Snyder back at Haverford, he abandoned it because he found he could not treat the Puritans fairly.[8]

The months that Carr spent in France greatly influenced his writing. After the vagueness of the neoromantic, melancholy descriptions of Paris in his college stories, Carr's accounts of Paris came alive with a sensitivity to sights and sounds and moods. In a 1929 novella called "Grand Guignol," he wrote:

> Paris was preening its finery that day: the gigolos were all a-cackle on the Champs Elysees, there was a warm winelike air made luminous around the green of the Tuileries, whose aisles were in bloom with the early-spring crop of artists painting the vista toward the Arc de Triomphe. It was all high lights and water color, with the gray face of the Madeleine peering down her street at the obelisk from the Nile.[9]

In his first novel, *It Walks By Night*, published two years after his return to America, Carr described a morning such as he must have experienced in the City of Light:

> I woke in the warmth of clear blue sunlight, one of those mornings that flood you with a swashbuckling joyousness. . . . The high windows were all swimming in a dazzle of sun, and up in their corners lay a trace of white clouds, like angels' washing hung out on a line over the grey roofs of Paris. The trees had crept into green overnight; they filled the whole apartment with a slow rustling; they caught and sifted the light.[10]

Carr avoided the American writers' colony on Paris's Left Bank; it was made up of expatriates who followed Gertrude Stein and other authors whose works he despised. It may be accounted unlikely that, as one legend has it, he used to drop by the Left Bank once a week and harangue the artists and writers: "Give it up, fellows. Come on across the river and get a decent room. Buy a new suit. Trim your beards. Why don't you stop talking about Art and get some work done." But it is certainly true that he never felt that poverty was beneficial for a writer. "I've always been strictly a Right Bank man," he said about those days. "I liked to dress well, live comfortably, and eat in good restaurants." Lucky enough to have his father paying for his trip—probably in the belief that he was taking classes somewhere—John was able to afford a comfortable suite on the rue des Eaux.[11]

He began his return trip to the United States on January 21, 1928, sailing on the *Empress of Scotland*. Delayed by gales, the return passage took eleven days. His journey made him a celebrity in Uniontown. The *News Standard* headlined an article "John Carr Returns from Paris Study," and the young man addressed various groups about his experiences. At a meeting of the Kiwanis Club, for example, he "dwelt eloquently and intelligently on our international relationships from political, commercial, and social standpoints." He said that travel itself has an educational value, which may have been his way of explaining to his parents that, though he neglected to take any courses in Paris, he became better educated anyway.[12]

After his return home, Carr discovered that *The Haverfordian* had just published a short story in its January 1928 issue called "The Dark Banner," signed by John Dickson Carr. John Rodell remembers that he and Frederic Prokosch had "a formidably impish attitude" toward Carr's belief that he was already prepared to be a professional writer. Looking back on the episode, Rodell now realizes that Carr was right, but at the time Rodell and Prokosch decided to pull his leg by writing a historical romance with all of his atmospheric language, his emphasis on swords, on drinking, on magnificent gestures, and on a hopeless love for an unfeeling woman. In a marvelous imitation of Carr's youthful style, "The Dark Banner" begins: "In those young years in Heidelberg, when faces were scarred and the sword blade was justice, he had drunk and fought and loved with the best." And it ends: "'Is it not enough that we have loved?' 'It is enough.' And struggling to his feet, he waved a dark banner high, high above his head, challenging death as it came." But their friend Jack did not find the story amusing, and according to Rodell, he threatened to sue. A couple of issues later, Rodell published an "Apologia Errataque" in which by implication he and Prokosch pointed out that Carr had done similar things by attributing his stories to classmates.[13]

In spite of Prokosch's close association with Carr during an important time of his life, Carr never mentioned Prokosch in his correspondence or in conversations with his family. Prokosch never read any of Carr's novels, and as far as his family knows, Carr never read anything by Prokosch. It should be pointed out that even at Haverford their styles were completely different. Carr was mainly interested in plot and mood; Prokosch saw fiction as recounting a symbolic quest. In 1935, Prokosch's *The Asiatics*, an extraordinary picaresque novel, was a popular and critical success. Thomas Mann called it "among the most brilliant and audacious achievements of the younger literary generation." Prokosch followed with more novels and volumes of lyric poetry, which were praised by W. H. Auden and which influenced Dylan Thomas.

Prokosch's novels have been described as "determinedly unrealistic fiction,"[14] a phrase that certainly applies to Carr's work as well, and it is curious that, despite their many differences in approach, parallels can be found in their work. Both Carr and Prokosch were interested in fantasy and were influenced by childhood reading of fairy tales. Both men looked to the past for their literary inspiration—Carr to the Victorian novelists, Prokosch to the picaresque tale-tellers. And both were less interested in character or in analysis of the contemporary world than in creating a distant time or place or mood. It's interesting, too, that Carr and Prokosch eventually left America, finding for very different reasons their muse in Europe. Frederic Prokosch died in France in 1989.

Carr retained some contact with John Rodell, calling him on one occasion an "old friend" and noting his success as a dramatist.[15] Rodell won the National Theatre Conference Award for *Jeff Comes Home*, and he also worked in Hollywood as a screenwriter. Much-married, he published *How to Avoid Alimony: A Survival Kit for Men* in 1971.

On John's return from Paris, Wooda Carr agreed to give his son a year to prove that he could make a living as a writer. John did some work for the *Uniontown News Standard*, and O'Neil Kennedy encouraged the young man to write a novel. The first fruit of this period, however, is a short story published not in a paying periodical but in the June 1928 number of *The Haverfordian*. "The Murder in Number Four" is the finest of Carr's early short stories. It opens "During the night run between Dieppe and Paris, on a haunted train called The Blue Arrow, there was murder done," and the rest of the tale continues this mood. Sir John Landervorne is in Paris with Bencolin and Villon when the case of the murder on the Blue Train reaches them. A man has been found strangled in his locked compartment. Except for the locked door, the only entrance to the compartment is a window, opened a mere five or six inches at the bottom. The passengers, including a jeweler named Septimus Depping, report seeing a ghost with a beard and a chopped-off nose. The victim is wearing false whiskers, and as in Carr's later *Arabian Nights Murder,* Carr emphasizes the grotesque:

> It was as though the imagination of all three, focused on a weird train and a strangler's hands, brought a little of the blue mystery of it into that room. A sense of remoteness added to their feeling of nearness to a dead man in a false beard—which somehow made it all the more horrible.

Another character is a militant feminist named Brunhilde Mertz, author of *Woman, the Dominant Sex* and *What Europe Owes to Uncle Sam.* As S. T. Joshi points out, the portrait of Mertz is crude and malicious.[16] Carr never appreciated women with the strength to play a male role. In an earlier story, "The Dim Queen," which has as a main character a female bullfighter, such a woman is seen as destructive; in "The Murder in Number Four," the image is presented comically, and the modern feminist is made equivalent to the Boorish American. Brunhilde Mertz says to Villon:

> Now, none of your parleyvooing on me, sir; you speak English. Everybody ought to speak English over here; the idea of this foolish talk, widdgy-widdgy, and waving your hands, like a lot of crazy people! It isn't natural, *I* say!

Whether the reader enjoys "The Murder in Number Four" depends partly on what he or she thinks of the depiction of Brunhilde Mertz, but as a combination of puzzle, atmosphere, and ingenuity, it is a superb performance. For the first time we cannot fault Carr's solution of the impossible crime; it is simple and convincing, but carefully masked by devious misdirection, and the identity of the murderer is a complete surprise. Carr uses the scheme devised by Chesterton in the Father Brown case "The Invisible Man," of hiding the murderer by making him too much a part of the background to be suspected.

The publication of "The Murder in Number Four" in *The Haverfordian* did not indicate to Wooda and Julia Carr that John was about to make a living as a writer. In June 1929, Wooda asked his nephew, John Carr Duff, principal of the Benjamin Franklin Junior High School in Uniontown, to find out what could be salvaged from the wreckage of John D. Carr III's academic career. Wooda still hoped that his son could receive a college degree and go into the law. Duff wrote to The Hill School, and the result was disappointing: Hill School credit could not be used for College Board examination credit.[17] With his father and cousin making plans for him to pick up his formal education again the coming autumn, John realized that he had to show that his hopes of becoming a writer were practical, or resign himself to preparing for a career in law. He decided to begin work in earnest on a novel featuring Henri Bencolin. Stories are still current in Uniontown that Carr wrote the book that would become *It Walks By Night* in the offices of the *Daily News Standard.* That legend seems to have arisen from John's close association with O'Neil Kennedy, with whom he discussed Bencolin's newest case. Other stories originated with Carr himself. He told some people that he wrote the story not in Uniontown but in Paris, and it is not unlikely that he had devised most of the plot while abroad. On another occasion, he said that he wrote the book at the home of his aunts in nearby Brownsville, but the only record about writing *It Walks By Night* that he ever put on paper is the simple comment, "The first book was written at my parents' home and at my uncle's [W. Russell Carr]."[18]

The first version of the story was a twenty-five-thousand-word novella called "Grand Guignol," with a wonderful subtitle: "Mystery in Ten Parts, Performance Under the Direction of M. Henri Bencolin, Prefect of Police of Paris." The Grand Guignol was the great theater of horrors in the Montmartre section of Paris, where all sorts of exaggerated effects were used to make the audience believe that it really saw decapitations, burnings alive, tortures by acid, and other sadistic pleasantries. Carr had gone to the Grand Guignol in 1927 or 1928, and he presented his story as a performance in which Bencolin opens the curtains to reveal various horrors. The first chapter is called "The Overture: Danse Macabre," the second, "Red Footlights," and so on. He sent the story to *The Haverfordian,* probably as a way of testing its reception. The first part made up the entire "chapbook" issue of March 1929, with a cover showing a robed skeleton opening the curtains. The second appeared the next month, with a frontispiece depicting Bencolin as suavely Mephistophelian.

During the spring and summer of 1929, Carr enlarged his story to about seventy thousand words, and armed with a letter of introduction from O'Neil Kennedy to Henry Tomlinson, Jr., who was a salesman and manuscript-reader for Harper & Brothers, he brought the typescript to New York City. Despite the fact that the novel then had the uninspired title *With Blood Defiled,* Tomlinson read the tale and enthusiastically asked a friend of his, Edward Coleman Delafield, Jr., to read it as well. Delafield, who like Tomlinson doubled as salesman and manuscript reader, was equally enthusiastic about the book. The two of them took *With Blood Defiled* to T. B. Wells, chairman of Harper & Brothers and editor of *Harper's Magazine,* and bet him a dinner that he couldn't guess the murderer.[19] Wells lost, and on August 14, 1929, John Dickson Carr signed a contract with Harpers' president, Eugene F. Saxton, to publish *With Blood Defiled* with an advance of three hundred dollars and an option on Carr's next two novels.[20] Fortunately, the title was soon changed to *It Walks By Night.*

The book was published simultaneously in the United States and Britain—in the latter by Harpers' London branch—on February 5, 1930. The dust jacket showed a gruesomely clawed red hand. Clearly aiming more for the *Weird Tales* than the Sherlock Holmes audience, Harpers took out an advertisement in *The New York Times Book Review,* describing the book as "a weird, satanic, terrifying mystery." It was packaged as one of Harpers' "Sealed Mysteries," with a thin paper seal around the final third of the book. If the reader returned the book with the seal unbroken and the conclusion therefore unread, he or she would receive a refund.*

John dedicated *It Walks By Night* to his parents. He presented one of the copies he received on publication day to the man who had the most influence in encouraging him to be a writer: "For O'Neil Kennedy—to whom Bencolin is no stranger—the first copy of the first edition."[21] Another he sent to the great bookman Christopher Morley, a Haverford graduate whom Carr had met the previous fall: "You expressed a wish to the author," John wrote, "to read this young man's first effusion; and then, after all, even a bad detective story is better than no detective story whatever."[22]

In changing "Grand Guignol" to *It Walks By Night,* Carr retained the overall plot and the main characters, but he fleshed them out, added more descriptions of setting, and used dialogue more effectively. He also added some characters. For example, Dr. Grafenstein, who was killed before "Grand Guignol" began, is very much alive in *It Walks By Night,* probably

---

*Few copies survive with the seal unbroken, though I've seen one in which the purchaser cleverly unglued the seal so that he or she would not have to tear it in order to finish the story.

so that Carr could be sarcastic about modern psychology, which he seems
to have associated with the realistic novels that he despised. Carr believed
that psychologists make the horrifying and the mad commonplace by
talking of psychoses rather than of evil. Dr. Grafenstein is "rather pitiable,
this spectacle of an intelligent man, a dogged and earnest and plodding
man, seeing things undreamed of in his psychology."[23] The other main
character added to *It Walks By Night* is Sharon Grey, who becomes the narrator's love interest. He meets her in a scene most males have fantasized:
She is naked, "a breathless mystery of flesh and shadows against the pil-
lows in the faint light."[24]

In enlarging his story, Carr omitted Villon and promoted Bencolin from
prefect to *juge d'instruction* in his place, though on one occasion Carr forgot the change and called Bencolin the prefect. More important is the development of Bencolin's character. He had begun in the short stories as a
kindly sort; he was becoming almost soulless in "Grand Guignol," and in
It Walks By Night he is satanic. His face is a "devilish and inhuman mask"
with "thin, cruel lines" and "a thin Borgian smile."[25] He moves people
about like chessmen, using them, torturing them. The main plot change
between the two versions of the story is that the earlier ends in a scene
that we would now call "hokey": The suspects are manacled and forced to
see a reenactment of the crime on film, complete with dramatic organ
music. Experience has taught Bencolin, as he explains in "Grand Guignol," that the guilty person will always attempt to escape from the mana-
cles. And sure enough, that's what happens. In *It Walks By Night*,
however, Bencolin merely recounts the solution, and the murderer conveniently confesses.

As Harpers emphasized in its advertisements, *It Walks By Night* is more
of a "weird, satanic" book than the type of detective novel familiar to most
readers. Carr had taken the sense of paradox and seeming impossibility of
Chesterton, combined it with the terrifying atmosphere of Poe, and produced a puzzle story without much direct detection. Bencolin is, of
course, a law officer, and here more than in later cases he does talk about
the use of physical evidence, but the book isn't about any of that. This
Bencolin, like the Bencolin of Carr's college stories, uses imagination, not
fingerprints and ballistics, to unravel the case, and he explains that "I have
never been baffled, and I have never been more than twenty-four hours
in understanding the entire truth of any case on which I have been engaged."[26] He understands the truth of the case; he never really investigates it. The plot is based on misdirection. As one character says:

> The art of the murderer . . . is the same as the art of the magician. And
> the art of the magician does not lie in any such nonsense as "the
> hand is quicker than the eye," but consists simply in directing your
> attention to the wrong place. He will cause you to be watching one
> hand, while with the other hand, unseen though in full view he pro-
> duces his effect.[27]

It Walks By Night is told like a horror story. The mood is almost claustrophobic, with madness at the heart of the events, and the book is filled
with tight, tense, loaded language, grotesque scenes, incongruous images,
and references to Poe and to Baudelaire's *Flowers of Evil*. One of the chapters is entitled "We Talked of Poe," and a main plot element is taken from
"The Black Cat" and "The Cask of Amontillado"—"the most artistic scene
in all literature," says one character. The book begins with references to
"night-monsters . . . with blood-bedabbled claws"; werewolves are mentioned; and it is implied that the murderer can turn himself into a creature
that enters locked rooms at will. None of the characters have any human
warmth. Sharon Grey is at best ambiguous; Bencolin toys with people;
most of the others are vengeful or mad.

It is fair to say that the book is overwritten, in that unnecessary adjectives to heighten the mood are used throughout, and the characters seldom act in ordinary human ways. Carr knew this, and in an important
passage in the book admits it. Commenting on a play written by one of
the characters, the narrator says:

> I do not know whether it was a good play; calmly considered, no
> doubt, the thing was clap-trap in the extreme. The characters spoke
> in a dialogue like nothing in heaven or earth, but behind it was an
> imperially purple imagination . . . and a kind of grotesque smiling
> detachment, like a gargoyle on a tower.[28]

Carr had no interest in writing realistically. If his characters do not speak
the way real Frenchmen do, what does that matter? *It Walks By Night* is a
puzzle story in the form of a Poe-esque fantasy, set in a Poe-esque France,
colored by an imperially purple imagination.

The construction of *It Walks By Night* is brilliant, with suspense carefully
maintained, and red herrings everywhere, and many clues to the solution.
The art of the magician is obvious throughout. We don't investigate the
crime; we are fooled by it. Our attention is directed toward the supernatural, toward the innocent characters, toward everyone and everything except the true solution until Carr, and Bencolin, are ready to reveal it.

The story begins on April 27, 1927. The narrator, Jeff Marle, obviously represents Carr himself. He is an American of Irish descent whose sojourn in Paris is paid for by his father. He is, like Carr, a fencer. Bencolin, who has promised Marle's father to look after him, invites him to a party for the Duc de Saligny and his bride, Louise. Among the guests is Eduard Vautrelle, described in a Chestertonian phrase as having "the material of a general, an artist, a side-show barker."[29] Everyone fears that Louise de Saligny's first husband, Laurent, a homicidal madman who delights in blood, will carry out his threat to murder the Duc de Saligny. Laurent escaped from an asylum, had his face changed by a plastic surgeon, then killed the surgeon. Bencolin describes how the murder of the surgeon was discovered in a horrifying passage that is typical of the book: "For a man of imagination, what a Grand Guignol picture! . . . They found Rothswold's head looking out from one of his own jars of alcohol on a shelf, but there was no trace of the body."[30]

At the wedding party, the Duc de Saligny is seen entering a room. Though the room is under observation at all times and no one else is present, he is decapitated there by a single sword cut. Bencolin finds the head with the breeze blowing through the hair. Later, another corpse is discovered, hidden in a wall, "Cask of Amontillado" fashion, and the whole world appears insane. Already, however, Bencolin has made a comment that is central to the effect of Carr's novels, one that helps explain why he introduces seeming impossibilities, why he suggests irrationality and the supernatural, only to restore order: "There must be sanity to the play somewhere; if there is no meaning in any of these incidents, there is no meaning in all the world."[31]

[****Warning: Here I shall discuss the solution, because it reveals some important points about Carr's writing.] The entire case depends on a confusion between victim and murderer that is, if anything, more impossible than the murder itself. The victim in the guarded room is not Saligny but Laurent. Laurent in fact had earlier killed Saligny, then taken his place. He is then himself murdered at the party by Vautrelle in cooperation with Mme. de Saligny, who has belatedly discovered the change in identities. That an engaged woman would not have soon recognized that her fiancé was no longer the same man, but her first husband—with nose altered and hair dyed, but no other features changed—is ridiculous. Carr could have handled the problem by limiting the contacts between the engaged couple, perhaps even making it an arranged marriage. That he does not do so confirms that he was confident of the effect of "masks" of any sort. A person can hide his real identity by externals, either in appearance or in actions. And Carr is so persuasive about this in *It Walks By Night* that most readers do not realize that they are in fact suspending a huge amount of disbelief.

It Walks By Night is also significant for the biographer investigating John Dickson Carr's interests at this pivotal point in his life. In addition to Baudelaire and Poe, whose works strongly influence the plot and events of *It Walks By Night*, Carr mentions other writers whose influence on him we have already seen—Gaston Leroux, Algernon Charles Swinburne, and François Villon. Nor does it surprise us that he also refers to the French romantic poets Alphonse de Lamartine and Paul Verlaine, and to the English poet Dante Gabriel Rossetti. It was probably the brooding sensuality of these writers that appealed to Carr. The book also contains a reference to William Jennings Bryan's dispute with Darwinism, but no longer does Carr attempt to defend God from science. Perhaps most interesting is a passage mentioning great real-life murderers who produced "the artistry of crimes." In later life, he was fascinated by crime both for itself and as a way of turning it into detective-story plots. As a teenager, he had been interested in the William Desmond Taylor case, and his friend Edward Delafield recalls that about the time of *It Walks By Night* Carr read widely about famous crimes.[32] Among the cases he mentions in his novel are the crimes committed by John Thurtell and Joseph Hunt, Dr. Crippen and Dr. Cream, Henri Landru, George Smith, Jean-Baptiste Troppmann, and "demure Constance Kent." He includes in this list even Spring-Heeled Jack, the fictional criminal who supposedly bounded about England at the time of the Bow Street Runners, and who became the hero of countless penny-dreadfuls.[33]

It Walks By Night sold very well, going through at least seven printings in the United States within two months of publication date. The critics were generally kind, though occasionally bemused. The London *Spectator* was not sure whether Carr's occasionally overwrought style was meant to be taken seriously: "The story may be read either as itself or a burlesque of itself. In both it is above average." *The New York Times* was more straightforward: "The story is beautifully told and offers one surprise after another before it reaches its dramatic denouement." The most negative comments came from the novelist Arnold Bennett. In a lengthy review in the London *Evening Standard*, he announced that he wouldn't have started the book if it hadn't come with the "Sealed Mystery" gimmick— which at least shows that the publisher knew what he was doing but which indicates that Bennett did not approach the story in the best frame of mind. He criticized Carr's style ("full of primeval cliches"), his characters ("the French characters never show a sign of French mentality"), his dialogue ("no human being ever did or could talk as this criminal talks"), and his plot ("a bog and a morass between the full statement of the enigma and the solution"). To put it mildly, Bennett did not like the story, but he judged it not as a fantasy but as an approximation to reality, on which grounds the book fails totally. The reviewer for the *Saturday Review of Literature* saw most clearly what the author was trying to do: "Mr. Carr's story is wildly improbable, but it moves easily within the field of its own assumptions and holds the nerves, if not the commonsense, of the reader pliant to its mood and happenings."[34]

When *It Walks By Night* was published, Carr had moved to Brooklyn Heights. During the autumn of 1929, Carr and Edward Delafield decided to rent together an apartment at 74 Columbia Heights for seventy-five dollars a month. It had three rooms—bedroom, living room, kitchen—on the third floor, with an octagonal front facing New York Harbor. The building no longer exists—that block and the adjoining one were torn down many years ago to make an entrance for a roadway—but the neighborhood still has much of the quiet, middle-class atmosphere of the early 1930s.[35] Henry (Tommy) Tomlinson sometimes shared the apartment with them. The son of the British writer H. M. Tomlinson, he supplied some of the colorful anecdotes about the Carr-Delafield household that were published twenty years later in Robert Lewis Taylor's *New Yorker* article, entitled "Two Authors in an Attic," about John Dickson Carr. Others who formed part of the group of friends were Bob Humphrey, a friend of Delafield's from college, and John Murray (Jack) Reynolds, who met Carr and Delafield at a party given by Harpers to celebrate the release of Carr's second novel, *The Lost Gallows*. Reynolds, who was called the "Gaffer" by the crowd because he was four or five years older than the others, worked for the Munson Steamship Company, of which his father was corporate secretary. He supplemented his income by writing teenage novels and pulp stories, including a few years later the first adventure of "Ki-Gor of the Jungle," one of the most popular of pulp heroes.

Carr later claimed that he read "comparatively few" pulp magazines; in the mid-1970s he explained to his cousin Nick Carr that "the pulps I did see, mostly alleged detective, made me simmer with impatience because no editor told his authors they must play fair with the clues."[36] This was undoubtedly true about many of the detective pulps in which the hard-boiled private-eye style was developing, but his friends from the 1930s recall that he often read other sorts of pulp magazines, especially adventure and horror. Jack Reynolds tried to persuade him to try his hand at a pulp novelette. Reynolds was being paid about five hundred dollars for a fifteen-thousand-word novelette, and that was two hundred dollars more than Carr received as the advance on *It Walks By Night*. The two men even discussed collaborating on a story but never got around to doing so. Reynolds introduced his younger friend to some of his editors, and Carr seriously considered submitting a story. He told Ed Delafield, however, that he wanted to save his plots for novels.[37] Nonetheless, this pulp connection would have results a few years later.

The Brooklyn Heights days, when this group of young men was helling about New York in the final, wild times of Prohibition and when the future possibilities seemed limitless, produced more anecdotes than any other period of Carr's life. Reynolds recalls the period vividly, and Delafield and Tomlinson told various tales to Robert Lewis Taylor, who included them in his *New Yorker* article about Carr. One must, however, be cautious in accepting Taylor's stories at face value. He wrote of the Brooklyn Heights period in tones of broad farce, an attitude that offended Carr. Carr also objected to the substance of the article, denying the reality of most of the events that Taylor related. "Every inaccuracy," he complained, "is meant to make the victim look ridiculous or picture him as the ill-mannered lunatic of all time. . . . Those goings-on in Brooklyn are mythical."[38] Fortunately, in recent correspondence and interviews, Reynolds and Delafield have had the opportunity to compare their memories against Taylor's account and Carr's denials, so we can be fairly certain what actually happened.

Some of the stories included in Taylor's article were false, or at least garbled. One famous anecdote has been repeated by other writers—that every time Carr received a royalty check, he would:

> board ship out of New York Harbor, and ride back and forth to Europe, or to the African Gold Coast, or to Madagascar, until he was financially exhausted. Then his roommates would receive a cablegram, from some remote port, saying, "MUST HAVE TWO HUNDRED AND FIFTY DOLLARS IMMEDIATELY."[39]

Although an incident similar to this happened once, the portrait of John taking off to various corners of the world is wrong. He did on occasion return to Uniontown for visits—often without informing Delafield in advance—and he took two overseas trips. In the spring and summer of 1930, he traveled to Europe, and in May 1931 he went to Cuba. I shall talk about the European trip later, as it was important for several different reasons— including the fact that he ran out of money, thus giving rise to the cable-gram legend. The Cuban trip was arranged by Jack Reynolds, who had him sent as what Carr called "a supercargo" on one of the Munson steamships. Carr described it as a "prank," for which he had to surrender his passport in exchange for a seaman's ticket.[40]

Many of the anecdotes about these years refer to Carr's writing meth-ods and where he found his ideas. Delafield confirms a story published in Taylor's article that Carr would sometimes get them in the shower; he would dash out, and in a phrase (and situation) reminiscent of Archi-medes, shout, "I've got it." Carr might read the crime news in the paper, notice a routine suicide, and then, says Delafield, "he would begin to twist it and turn it around, and before long it would emerge as a full-fledged book plot." Tomlinson told Taylor that on one occasion he asked Carr if he had any trouble devising plots. "I've had exactly one hundred and twenty complete plots outlined, for emergencies," Carr answered, "since I was eleven years old."[41]

Carr's work habits at this time of his life were peculiar. Before putting anything on paper, he worked out all the details of the novel in his head. As one friend put it, he had "a remarkable brain." He could remember in detail what he had read or seen, and he could recall every element of a novel he was mentally constructing without having to make notes or an outline. Once he started to write, he found it difficult to leave the type-writer. When he was working on his second book, he sometimes re-mained at the typewriter for thirty-six hours straight, without sleep or food. The details of plot, character, and setting so dominated him that he had difficulty sleeping, but after finally exhausting himself, he would take a short nap, and then start again. He would, says Reynolds, "sequester himself and come up for air when he had to. A few occasions, I was around when he came up for air, and we would talk briefly; 'I'm having trouble with this, but I'll get it straightened out' and so on." In this man-ner, Carr could finish a book in about three weeks.[42]

He would then take the typescript to Harper's, get an advance against royalties, and proceed on a rip-roaring program of relaxation. Carr and Delafield sometimes went to speakeasies, but more often they had parties at their apartment. At some of these, the group played the game of Mur-der, in which victim and detective were chosen by drawing cards, the lights turned off, and the mock murder committed. The player designated as the detective attempted to identify the culprit through cross-examination. Carr mentioned the game several times in his novels, and it plays important roles in the plots of *The Peacock Feather Murders* (1937) and *The Sleeping Sphinx* (1947). Carr enjoyed the game so much, and suggested playing it so often, that many of his friends thought that he had invented it.[43] Before Carr played Murder, however, the game had already become popular, and in 1929 it had been used as the background of a mystery novel, Frances Noyes Hart's *Hide in the Dark*.

One of Robert Lewis Taylor's anecdotes that has been confirmed by Delafield recounts a trick that Carr played on his guests at a Columbia Heights party. Before the party began, he went down to the empty apartment beneath the one rented by Delafield and Carr and ran a wire from a microphone to the radio in their living room upstairs. During the party, he sneaked downstairs and broke into broadcasts with his own news items. He began by speaking in broken English, identifying himself as Mussolini and cursing the United States and its ambassador. Then he set off a cap pistol and screamed, "Oh, my God, the ambassador's been shot." Every half hour or so, he added further details over the radio, finally reaching a climax with the announcement that a fleet of Italian airplanes had set out for America to bomb New York City. One of the guests at the party, a young woman, suddenly stood up and ran out of the house to warn her mother. Finally, John came upstairs and admitted the joke.[44]

John's primary method for unwinding after putting a book together was alcohol. He did not drink while engaged in the actual writing, but once he had completed the typescript he would often get drunk on the bathtub gin that he, Delafield, and Reynolds produced. They often purchased a gallon of grain alcohol and diluted it by half with water. In their early days of producing their own liquor, they carefully flavored the alcohol with oil of juniper, or orange, but later they simply mixed it with whatever was at hand. If they put nothing more than water in it, they called it gin; if they added cocoa for coloring, it was whiskey; sugar made it rum, and so on.[45]

The subject of alcohol is an important key to understanding John Dickson Carr's life. Because of hints by John's mother, his wife, Clarice, believes that he may have started drinking at the age of fourteen. Julia Carr's hints, however, may have referred to something as minor as a single episode of John's breaking into his father's liquor cabinet. But he certainly was not drinking regularly at that age; no friends from Uniontown, from The Hill School, or from Haverford College recall that he drank at all, and in fact at Quaker Haverford, he would have had almost no opportunity. Carr's regular drinking started in Brooklyn Heights. His motivation, at least in part, was to create an image. At that time, the literary world and the movies idolized figures who partied and drank. It was part of the business of being a writer and of being freed from traditional restraints. Only dreadful people, called teetotalers and bluenoses, could object. For Carr, however, it was more than this. His father drank heavily, and John had inherited this tendency to be what is now called "an addictive personality." The son saw drinking as part of being like his father. It was, he indicated over and over again in his juvenile stories, the thing that men do simply because they are men, and when this belief is combined with a predisposition for addiction, it's not surprising that Carr eventually was to become dependent on alcohol.

A biographer cannot in honesty present this dependency as something Carr fought all his life, for the truth is that until his final years he did not wish to fight it. It was part of being John Dickson Carr, and he had no desire to change. During the early 1930s, he could control his need for alcohol. He did not drink all the time, but only when he was winding down from the intensity of writing a book. When he drank, however, it was heavily. Jack Reynolds remembers that the parties at the Columbia Heights apartment were noisy, especially as the evening wore on and the gin continued to flow, but neither Carr nor any of the crowd became quarrelsome or offensive.[46] Carr, however, sometimes passed out at the parties, and Delafield and Reynolds, who participated in this alcoholic world, were amused rather than worried. Learning on one occasion that he disliked sand, they ended a party by taking the sleeping Carr and leaving him on a beach. He showed up at the apartment the next day without commenting on the outing. Sometimes Carr would borrow Delafield's car, park it somewhere, and wander home without it. This happened so often that the police came to expect Delafield to ask them for help in locating the automobile. When he had been drinking, Carr's fundamental suspicion of authority would assert itself. Robert Lewis Taylor wrote the following, based on information from (and recently confirmed by) Edward Delafield:

He would pick out a cop and follow him around on the beat, carrying on an impertinent monologue that fell just short of being actionable. Sometimes, he'd ask the officer to help him across the street, or salute him pompously when they passed each other. Then he'd search lawns with a magnifying glass, looking for clues, and take notes in a little black book. The police in the area knew him and treated him with heavy patience. "Why don't you go on home, Mr. Carr?" they'd say. "Write some more mysteries. Show us how a real detective works."[47]

In April 1930, Carr took money earned from *It Walks By Night* to make a return trip to England and the Continent. Suffering from a hangover, he arrived in London and called on Hamish (Jamie) Hamilton, representing the British branch of Harper & Brothers, who would be his friend and publisher for more than forty years.[48] As he had the last time, however, Carr spent most of his time abroad in Paris, staying this time at the Hôtel la Bourdannais, near the Champs de Mars and the Eiffel Tower. The room cost around forty francs, and three meals a day added only sixty-five francs to his expenses. With the franc worth about four cents, room and board amounted to a bit more than four dollars a day. Nonetheless, in May, Carr ran into a financial emergency and sent Delafield a cablegram begging him to get three hundred dollars as an advance from Harpers. The publisher sent the money, but in his acknowledgment, Carr never told Harpers exactly why he had needed it: "Considering that this letter may go into the archives* or be read by a female secretary or something, I can't tell you just now what the jam was. But it threatened to have hair-raising complications." Carr indicated that a woman was involved: The troubles, he said, came from "Aphrodite."[49]

The money arrived just in time, for Carr had made arrangements to host his old friend O'Neil Kennedy in Paris. Kennedy arrived toward the end of the first week in June and planned to write a series of articles on his overseas experiences for the *News Standard*. These articles were also collected into a small book, *Bachelor Abroad*, and published by the newspaper in December 1930. The book begins with a near-dedication to John Dickson Carr: "Were [the articles] more pretentious, and more worthy, I should with keenest pleasure dedicate them to my good friend John Dickson Carr, my companion in the rambles herein noted, with whom the trip was one long delight." Although *Bachelor Abroad* is made up primarily of descriptions of tourist sites and activities, it has enough personal comments to make it an important source for Carr's life at this time. Kennedy

---

*It did.

docked at La Havre and took a train for the Gare St. Lazare, where he searched for his host:

> Before I reach the exit into the gare promenade, my roving eye is at-
> tracted (dazzled, rather) by the sight of a French dude. A young man
> garbed in double-breasted plaid of grey and black, a green beret on
> his head, boutonniere in button-hole, and twirling a malacca cane
> with all the insouciance of the Boulevardier, is striding toward me,
> smile a foot wide on his face. I rub my eyes—bless my soul if it isn't
> my boy friend, John Dickson Carr![50]

Kennedy attributed to Carr's Parisian finery their receiving effusive service at restaurants and their often being eyed by young women.[51] Throughout the book, Kennedy mentioned women, both *filles de joie* and more respectable ladies, who looked appraisingly at him and Carr, but he mentioned nothing as disruptive (or expensive) as the earlier difficulty for which John had needed the emergency money.

With John handling the French conversations, the two men visited Paris's nightspots, where jazz was everywhere. They attended the Moulin Rouge and the Folies Bergère (with, Kennedy noted appreciatively, its "daring tableaux"); they went to a performance of the famous theater of horrors, the Grand Guignol; and they heard a chanteuse sing "St. Lazare" at the Lapin Agile in Montmartre. At the conclusion, John explained to Kennedy that St. Lazare was the prison for prostitutes, and that the song is the lament of a prostitute who has lost her lover. The two men also went slumming in the Parisian underworld then existing between the rue de Rivoli and the boulevard de la Chapelle, near the Gare de Lyon. There Carr and Kennedy saw the *apaches* and the "decadents of the bourgeoisie."[52] In common with other tourists, Carr and Kennedy also went to Notre Dame, Versailles, Fontainebleu, and the Louvre. Near the Eiffel Tower, they had a picture taken with their heads looking through holes in a painted scene. The photograph showed them climbing the outside of the tower.

Around June 21, they set off for a two-week tour of Brussels and the Rhineland. After obtaining accommodations at the Hotel Cosmopolite in Brussels, they went to the site of the Battle of Waterloo, but what was most memorable was an elaborate meal they had at a Brussels restaurant called Chapon Fin. Described in Kennedy's book in loving detail—crawfish soup, grilled Dijon sole, chicken in casserole, peche Marie Jose, and for the wine, Château Yquem (1919)—it does seem to have been a notable occasion, and all for fifteen dollars. Memorable for a different reason was their experience at Mainz. They were at the Hotel Germania, with a room overlooking the Rhine, when the last of the Allied occupation troops pulled out. Neither Carr nor Kennedy knew more than a few words of German, but at eleven o'clock that night they went out to a café to order two Pilsner beers. They found themselves in the center of a near riot between German nationalists and an old man who wanted a separate Rhineland state under the protection of France. Fearing that if they spoke English or French the mob would turn on them as representatives of the victorious Allies, they raised their huge glasses of beer in front of their faces and tried to be inconspicuous. At last, they slipped out, but found themselves lost in Mainz before they finally located their hotel.[53]

On July 4, 1930, the two men were in Heidelberg at the Hotel Schloss. The hotel flew the American flag in honor of its guests, and for a reason that Kennedy does not make entirely clear, that sight encouraged him and Carr to return to Paris. They spent two more weeks there, before Kennedy decided to spend the final eight days of his journey in London. John planned to return to the United States at about the same time but on a different ship, and they agreed to meet in New York City.[54]

This June and July spent with O'Neil Kennedy had almost immediate results in John Dickson Carr's writing, especially in providing the settings for two of his Bencolin books. The most detailed and emotive section of *Bachelor Abroad* is the description of the trip that the two men took down the Rhine. Starting at Cologne, where they stayed at the Hotel Hansa, they traveled by steamer to Coblenz and Mainz. Kennedy refers to many of the sights Carr would describe in the second chapter of *Castle Skull*, which was published the next year—the Bridge of Boats, the passengers' singing "Die Lorelei" as the steamboat passed the Lorelei rocks, and the vista of castle after castle. Kennedy's description also makes it likely that Castle Skull itself was based on the twin castles called "The Hostle Brothers." Readers of the book will recall that one of the characters, Brian Gallivan, is the author of a book entitled *Legends of the Rhine* that Jeff Marle purchases at the Mainz railway station. Though Kennedy does not state that either he or Carr bought anything at the Mainz station, it seems obvious that one of them did obtain a copy of Wilhelm Ruland's *Legends of the Rhine*, the most popular book for Rhine steamer travelers; it contains all the legends mentioned in both *Bachelor Abroad* and *Castle Skull*.[55]

In Paris, Carr took his friend to the Musée Grévin, a waxworks on the boulevard Montmartre. Carr renamed it the Musée Augustin, and made it the setting for the murder in *The Corpse in the Waxworks*, published early in 1932. Kennedy records that the Musée Grévin had some modern exhibits, but the main interest was the dramatic scenes in the gallery of horrors— the Christian martyrs in the Roman arena and the catacombs, the assassination of Marat, and the death of Napoleon as a drowsing manservant sits nearby. Carr described these exhibits in almost the same language in Chapter 2 of the *The Corpse in the Waxworks*, and he remarked that the gallery was filled with

> groups of figures in scenes, each in its compartment, each a masterpiece of devilish artistry. . . . I felt it contrary to nature that they did *not* move. They were more ghastly, these shadowy people, than though they had stepped forth in their coloured coats to speak.

Kennedy said the same thing less poetically: "It is bloody, gruesome, terrible—and gripping."[56]

In later life, Carr always preferred to travel first class, but after his financial embarrassment two months earlier, he prudently booked passage back to New York on the Red Star Line ship *Pennland*, one of the less expensive liners. For a one-way fare of about $125, the traveler could expect a ten-day voyage across the Atlantic, as compared with less than seven days on one of the great floating palaces such as the *Mauretania* and the *Leviathan*. The *Pennland* and a few other older ships had low fares because they were considered outmoded, but their accommodations, called by some travelers "solidly tourist third," were perfectly comfortable and the cabins were better than those on ships with "regular tourist third" or, worst of all, the class called "steerage."[57] About the fourth week on July 1930, the *Pennland* began its voyage in Southampton, England, picking up Carr and other passengers late the same night in France.

Two days after the voyage began, John chanced upon a twenty-one-year-old Englishwoman from Kingswood, near Bristol. Clarice Cleaves, making her first trip outside England, went to the women's salon to have her hair bobbed, so that she would be fashionably coiffed when she arrived in New York. Unfortunately, the salon had been booked up, so she bravely decided to go to the men's barbershop. Only one customer was waiting there, reading a book, and when she explained to the barber that she needed to have her hair cut short, the young man gallantly rose and said that she could go before him. He introduced himself as John Carr, and her immediate impression was that he had beautiful, large, dark-gray eyes. That evening, after dinner, John went to her table and requested a dance. He asked her whether she liked detective stories. She had read only a couple of books by Edgar Wallace, the most prolific thriller writer of the time, and she had found them "pretty poor stuff." When she answered honestly that she was not much of a detective-story enthusiast, he said that he had one he wanted her to try. He went off to his cabin, and a few minutes later returned and presented her with a copy of *It Walks By Night*. She already liked John so well that she couldn't refuse the book. She read it on the trip, and as she said much later, "I did think it was for his age extremely well-written and reasonably well-plotted, and so of course I praised it." (When Carr got back to Brooklyn Heights, he told Delafield and Reynolds a slightly different story. He said that he had met a most pleasant girl on shipboard, and that she had volunteered the comment that "my favorite detective story I've read lately is *It Walks By Night*." Clarice's response to learning recently what John had told his friends was, "Well, that's what he *would* say.")[58]

Clarice Cleaves was an extremely pretty young woman, with blond hair, eyes of an unusual navy blue, and what one friend describes as "a kitten face and a typically English complexion of roses-and-milk." She was slim and petite, only about five feet, two inches tall, which, as Jack Reynolds thought when he first met her, was "a suitable size for John."[59] Above all, Clarice Cleaves was charming in 1930, and she still is charming more than sixty years later. I doubt that she has ever realized that she has an ability almost to enchant people with an unusual combination of strength and gentleness. This fact came out over and over as I interviewed people who had known John and Clarice. As soon as they met, John and Clarice got along wonderfully, spending much of their time on shipboard together. In many of John's books, the hero falls in love at first sight. This may seem to be a survival of John's unrealistic romanticism, but in fact it happened to him on board the *Pennland* in July 1930.

Clarice was the daughter of James Henry (usually called "Harry") Cleaves, a mining engineer from Somersetshire who had spent much time in South Africa advising on gold mining. Her mother was Mary Bright Cleaves, from Gloucestershire, just outside Bristol. Clarice was heading for America as something of a birthday present. Her sister had had an elaborate twenty-first birthday celebration two years earlier, but Clarice begged her parents that, rather than being spent for a party, her birthday money be used to send her to the United States. Two of her school friends had moved to Scarsdale, New York, and Clarice dickered with her father and mother to let her visit them there. An agreement was reached: She could make the trip with a friend of the family, Mrs. Hicks, who often sailed from England to America, but if she stayed in the United States, she would have to support herself. Her mother said, "I keep you in your own country, but I will not finance you in somebody else's."[60]

Mrs. Hicks was worried when John and Clarice spent so much time together; she told her charge that "Carr" was an Irish name, and (she thought) who knows but he might be a Catholic. She need not have been concerned on that score, at least: John's background was Presbyterian, his beliefs agnostic, and his early anglophobia had almost disappeared. Probably the last gasp was making Jeff Marle, the narrator of the Bencolin novels, an American of Irish descent. Mrs. Hicks was relieved that the shipboard association seemed to have ended when the *Pennland* docked. John went off to Uniontown to visit his father, who was ill, and Clarice moved in with her friends in Scarsdale. Luckily, since it was the height of the Depression, she found a job doing clerical work at a store called Scarsdale Supply. After Wooda Carr's health improved, John returned to the apartment on Columbia Heights around Christmas, and he phoned Clarice to ask whether he might come out to Scarsdale to reminisce about the voyage. She invited him to come over. They began seeing each other almost every weekend, and she was a frequent guest at the Columbia Heights parties. Incidentally, while at Uniontown, John Dickson Carr had grown a mustache of the narrow, pencil-thin type favored by movie heroes of the day.[61]

Meanwhile, he had continued to write. In France, he'd started work on a book called *Miss Death*. The title hints that the novel was to be another version of his "woman the destroyer" theme, but we know little about the story. Nine years later, he wrote to his friend, the mystery writer Clayton Rawson, "I can still remember my own second book with a shiver. Writing it was the most difficult job I ever had. I twice tore up twenty or thirty thousand words." By May 1930, Carr had sent Delafield the entire typescript of *Miss Death* except for the conclusion, but Harpers must have rejected the book. *Miss Death* may have been the unpublished novel mentioned in a letter of 1935. It was set, he said, in America, and it "was so bad that it couldn't be published."[62]

When John returned to the United States from Paris, Ed Delafield talked to him about his financial habits. Whenever Carr received a check from his publishers, he cashed it and spent lavishly until the money was gone. Delafield discussed the situation with Carr and with Eugene Saxton of Harper & Brothers, and asked that the twice-yearly royalty schedule, standard with most publishers, be changed for Carr. The result was that Carr promised to write two books a year for Harpers and the publisher agreed to a regular payment of one hundred dollars a month against royalties.[63] This arrangement, however, could still lead to problems, because Carr continued to cash checks immediately, and he liked to carry around a roll of bills. Jack Reynolds recalls:

> John and I had been to some party somewhere over in Manhattan, and came back to Columbia Heights late by taxi. It was John's turn to pay. The meter read about $3.75. John, in a burst of tipsy generosity, gave the taxi driver a five-dollar bill and said, "Keep the change." However, on counting his money in the morning, it developed that the bill he had given the taxi driver had been for fifty dollars, and not for five.[64]

Carr's haphazard attitude toward money lasted all his life. It was not so much that he thought that money should be spent rather than hoarded—though he did believe that. It was more that money was never high on his list of priorities. He had little interest in business matters, and even if he had, he had no business sense to manage those interests. In later years, when Carr received royalty checks, he would often fold them, put them in a drawer or in his trousers pockets, and then forget about them. Periodically, his wife and daughters would go through his trousers and locate the checks.[65]

The new financial arrangement with Harpers resulted in a regular spring and fall publication schedule of John Dickson Carr books: *The Lost Gallows* appeared on March 4, 1931; *Castle Skull*, which was dedicated to Edward Delafield and O'Neil Kennedy, was published on October 1, 1931; *The Corpse in the Waxworks* on March 23, 1932; and *Poison in Jest* on September 28, 1932. Hamish Hamilton, who had managed the London branch of Harper & Brothers, formed his own publishing company, which still often issued Harpers books in Britain. He refused, however, to publish *Castle Skull*, which was to remain unpublished in England for more than forty years.

Since it does not feature Bencolin, it is better to delay discussing *Poison in Jest*, but the four Bencolin novels can be treated together. All of them show the strong influence of Poe, and a bit from H. P. Lovecraft and other *Weird Tales* writers. "The Masque of the Red Death" is quoted at the beginning of *The Corpse in the Waxworks* and Poe's ghost seems to be present at every scene. The Bencolin books do accurately describe real places—Paris in *It Walks By Night* and *The Corpse in the Waxworks*, London in *The Lost*

Gallows, the Rhineland in *Castle Skull*—but they have a brooding, macabre feeling to them that place them within the tradition of the horror story. Detective stories of horror or horror stories of detection—whatever we call the Bencolin novels, Carr combined genres in a way that not even Poe had done before him, and that few authors would do after him. Closest would be Hake Talbot with *The Hangman's Handyman* (1942) and *Rim of the Pit* (1944), two books directly influenced by Carr. It is little wonder that such experts on the horror story as S. T. Joshi (who has written widely on H. P. Lovecraft) rate the Bencolin books so highly. I do too, but I think that occasionally the atmosphere becomes so thick that the reader wants some relief. Especially in *Castle Skull*, everything seems a bit synthetic.

The Bencolin stories have a sense of unreality, of morbid fantasy that removes them from the real world; for the most part they exist and are acceptable, as a reviewer of *It Walks By Night* had noted, "within the field of [their] own assumption." Carr creates this world by making everyday things extraordinary. In *The Lost Gallows*, he says that "common things are made alluring by being blurred,"[66] and what struck the young Carr as alluring was often also terrifying. In each of the Bencolin novels, he takes an ordinary setting and exaggerates it. Schloss Schadel, the titular setting of *Castle Skull*, is one of many structures that dot the banks of the Rhine, but Carr doesn't describe it like that:

> In the centre of the walls, built so that the middle of the battlements constituted the teeth of the death's head, reared the vast skull of the stone. The light was too dim to make out details, but I saw the eyes. I saw the two towers on either side, horribly like ears; I saw the whole thin, rain-blacked monstrous pile move slowly above our heads.[67]

The Brimstone Club in *The Lost Gallows* is an extreme version of an English gentleman's club. Members are not passed on by committee, they simply pay outrageous dues, and therefore the club attracts "the wealthy and drifting scum of the world." The Brimstone Club is "curious" and "disreputable" and full of "luridness"; it is "a place more evil and morbid than any hauntings from the past"; it has a "restless doom." In short, "The atmosphere of melancholy and doom . . . seeps into every room. One is hushed by the massive dreariness of its luxury, its sombre lamps, its thick, muffled carpets, its hint of suicide."[68] In *The Corpse in the Waxworks*, the Musée Augustin is described in fantastic language: "I do not know whether you can appreciate what I mean," says Monsieur Augustin himself:

The purpose, the illusion, the spirit of a waxworks. It is an atmosphere of death. It is soundless and motionless. It is walled off by stone grottoes, like a dream, from the light of day; its noises are echoes, and it is filled with a dull green illumination as though it were in the depths under the sea. Do you see? All things are turned dead, in attitudes of horror, of sublimity. . . . This silence, this motionless host in the twilight, is my world. I think it is like death, exactly, because death may consist of people frozen for ever in the positions they had when they died.[69]

Carr also uses minor physical details to contribute to this atmosphere. A staircase, for example, is not merely wide; it is "the sort of staircase which seems exactly suited for bringing coffins down." Even piano playing is atmospheric: "He played Chopin with a kind of exquisite madness, and the throbbing sorrow of the damned."[70]

In this sort of world, the most extraordinary events can seem natural. I have already described the imposture and the seemingly impossible murder in *It Walks By Night*, both of which would seem ridiculous in the consciously realistic world of Dashiell Hammett or Ernest Hemingway. In Carr's next book, *The Lost Gallows*, a car careers down the street driven by a dead man, and another man is captured by an enemy and hanged from a lost gallows in a lost room on a lost street.* This image of a London street—Ruination Street—that has simply disappeared, and yet somehow can be seen in the fog, is one of the most haunting that Carr ever created. A criminal using the traditional name for a hangman, "Jack Ketch," seems able to enter locked rooms at will to leave messages and objects. The image of puppets and the Punch and Judy show is often used in *The Lost Gallows*; the characters seem to Jeff Marle to be merely dolls, and "little blind gods had them and were disposing them mirthfully."[71] In *Castle Skull* the mood is perfectly set by the opening line: "D'Aunay talked of murder, castles, and magic." The story is about the seemingly impossible disappearance many years earlier of a magician named Maleger from a railway carriage. Bencolin competes with the inspector of police in Berlin, Baron Sigmund von Arnheim—whose name but nothing else is taken from Carr's *Haverfordian* stories—in solving that crime and a new murder:

---

*Carr may have gotten the idea of a lost room from M. R. James's story "Number 13" and of a lost street from H. P. Lovecraft's "The Music of Erich Zann" (*Weird Tales*, 1925), but otherwise those two stories are entirely different from *The Lost Gallows*.

The flaming body of Maleger's heir, the actor Myron Allison, is seen on the battlements of another castle. *The Corpse in the Waxworks* has no impossible crime, but it is probably the most tightly plotted of the Bencolin books. The crime and the setting are perfectly integrated, the plotting convoluted, the puzzle element beautifully handled, and the final solution surprising. The recurring image in *The Lost Gallows* is puppets; in *The Corpse in the Waxworks* it is masks. Following the quotation from Poe at the opening of the book, a second quotation is given, this one from George Slocombe: "Beneath the black mask, and below the broad concealing hat, still shine the bright eyes of danger." A body is found in the arms of a wax satyr, and next door to the Musée Augustin is the Club of the Silver Key, where bored aristocrats in masks gather for assignations.

The people who inhabit this extraordinary world of Carr's imagination are as exaggerated and grotesque as the plots and the settings. Carr often describes the characters as "goblins" or "gnomes," and physical descriptions dwell on the grotesque:

> His red-rimmed eyes had an uncanny habit of seeming to grow round and then shrink, as with the beat of a pulse. His straggly mustache and fan of white whiskers were much too large for the bony face; his cheek bones were shiny, but his bald head looked as though it had been covered with dust. Two tufts of white hair stuck up behind the ears.

The Brimstone Club and the houses in Bencolin's cases are decaying, and so are the people who live in them. Colonel Martel in *The Corpse in the Waxworks* is the last in a line of aristocrats, and he dwells in the past consumed by the desire to preserve family honor. He spends all his time playing dominoes with his deaf wife.

Madness born of inbreeding or introspection or desire for vengeance dominates many of the characters in the Bencolin novels. The clearest example is probably Etienne Galant in *The Corpse in the Waxworks*, who is tall, vigorously handsome, with hypnotic yellow-gray eyes—but with a red nose so badly smashed that it was "like the proboscis of an animal." "He smiled at us; the smile lit up his face affably, and the nose made it hideous." Galant is based in part on Sherlock Holmes's nemesis, Professor Moriarty, but rather than a mathematician he is a former professor of English literature—and a current blackmailer:

> A man of extreme brilliance, who has read books until his brain bursts with the weight of them; he is brooding, introspective, vicious

of temper; he begins to look out upon what he considers a crooked world, wherein all moral values are hypocrisies. . . . [He blackmails] to feed this colossal hate of his—which is merely the hate of a misplaced idealist. . . . I do not think it was the money especially. He drew fantastic sums from these people, but what he liked was to rip open reputations, smash idols.[72]

Bencolin himself seems part of this madness. He is perhaps at his most extreme in *The Lost Gallows*, in which he manipulates people and finds the human race dull. He cannot sleep without drugs. *The Lost Gallows* is structured around a wager between Bencolin and Sir John Landervorne, who previously had appeared in Carr's *Haverfordian* stories. Sir John says that Bencolin uses intuition too often, but an English detective must have "practice, patience, and perseverance." Bencolin responds that those are "the qualities most highly developed in a trainer of a flea-circus."[73] After a body is discovered, Bencolin wagers a dinner that he can name the murderer within forty-eight hours.

[****Here I must reveal the ending of the story to show how Carr has presented Bencolin's character.] Bencolin proves that Sir John Landervorne himself is the murderer. Charges that this solution is "underhanded," incidentally, are not relevant:[74] The story is entirely fair to the reader, and clues are sprinkled throughout the book pointing to Sir John's guilt. Having a policeman commit the crime is not new: Carr may have been influenced by Israel Zangwill's *The Big Bow Mystery*, Gaston Leroux's *The Mystery of the Yellow Room*, and G. K. Chesterton's "The Secret Garden." In a way, *The Lost Gallows* twists the famous solution to Agatha Christie's *The Murder of Roger Ackroyd*—which has also suffered under the charge of being unfair. (In one scene, Bencolin, "unutterably bored" by the case, turns for intellectual challenge to a detective novel, which Carr attributes to one "J. J. Ackroyd.") But what is most striking is the heartlessness with which Bencolin unmasks his old friend: "The Frenchman was cool and impersonal; he regarded Sir John as he might have looked at some curious insect." Bencolin bows to Sir John, and Jeff Marle says that he has no idea what is going on behind Bencolin's mask; he sees only "the edge of a cruel politeness and an eyebrow lifted mockingly. I felt he was with difficulty restraining a smile."[75] Bencolin then goads another character, who was guilty in a different way, into taking a literal false step and hanging himself. The book ends: "Bencolin was humming a little tune and smiling." It is a powerful conclusion, and one that fits this inhuman, mad world Carr has created.

Even in *The Lost Gallows*, when Bencolin is at his most Mephistophelian, there are signs that Carr found his detective too unrelievedly sadistic and tried to right the balance. For instance, Bencolin announces that he likes "to see young people have a good time," and somewhat later he seems even to have a human emotion toward his adversary: "I am playing with lives, God help me!"[76] This slightly more human detective is the one we see in *Castle Skull*. In that book, Bencolin even arranges for the murderer to go free. LeRoy Lad Panek, a scholar of detective fiction, suggests that Carr was becoming dissatisfied with Bencolin, preferring characters who retain a boyishness, even a rowdiness. In *Castle Skull*, Panek points out, Carr tried to put a bit of this childlikeness into Bencolin when the detective sings "Mademoiselles from Armentières," and when he recalls riding down New York's Fifth Avenue in a steam calliope.[77] All of this, however, simply doesn't fit the personality that Carr has developed for Bencolin.

The most interesting version of Bencolin is in *The Corpse in the Waxworks*, that book of masks and wax figures. At the opening, Bencolin himself is shown wearing a type of mask: He alters his dress according to whether he is about to arrest a criminal. "When he walks in evening clothes, with the familiar cloak, top-hat, and silver-headed stick, when his smile is a trifle more suave and there is a very slight bulge under his left arm—messieurs that means trouble." Near the end of the book, however, the detective admits that he makes errors—something out of character for the Bencolin of the previous novels. He even has a moment of self-revelation that tells us why he sometimes seems cruel:

I continued to chuckle, like a broken street-organ, and I turned the crank, like a blind man, and I threw my tiny little dissonances against the passion and pity and heart-break that jostled me in the street. — Pass me that brandy like a good fellow, and let me talk foolishness for a minute! I get little enough chance to do it. Yes. So I laughed, because I feared people, feared their opinion or scorn. . . . So because they might take me for less than I was, I tried to be more than I am; like many others. Only my brain was strong, and damn me! I forced myself to become more than I am. There walked Henri Bencolin— feared respected, admired (oh, yes!)—and behind him now begins to appear a brittle ghost, wondering about it. . . . To examine one's own

mind and heart, and explore them fully, is a poisoned doc–
trine. . . . Introspection is the origin of fear, and fear builds these walls
of hate or mirth, and makes me dreaded; and I am paid back, many
times over, by dreading myself.[78]

Bencolin sees behind the mask he has created, and is afraid. His comments help us to understand why Carr's writing is almost never intro-
spective and why he so disliked books that are. Without our masks, we
are naked and unprotected, and we fear what we may find.

Carr understood the weakness of the Bencolin novels. Three years after
the publication of *The Corpse in the Waxworks*, he said, "I used to believe
that all the readers would find my stuff as dull as ditchwater unless I
whooped up the grotesqueness everywhere, and turned all my characters
into jumping-jacks."[79] But this is the strength of these early books as well;
they may not be realistic, but they are colorful, picturesque, terrifying,
and compelling.

Carr probably began his fifth novel, *Poison in Jest*, as a way of bringing
his detective to America. It has all the characteristics of the Bencolin novels—heavy atmosphere, grotesque images, a doom-laden family touched
with madness, and narration by Jeff Marle. But although he is mentioned
in passing, Bencolin himself does not appear. As in the earlier novels, the
description of physical setting is accurate, yet the places exist in a world
that is closer to horrific fantasy than reality. Edgar Allan Poe's spirit, which
had already traveled with John Dickson Carr to France, England, and
Germany, now joined him just outside Uniontown, Pennsylvania, where
Poison in Jest takes place. Uniontown itself is not mentioned by name in
the book, but Fayette County is, and Judge Quayle's estate, where most of
the events occur, is based on the old Barnes estate that still exists in Hopwood next door to Uniontown. Oddly, though, Carr brings little of the
familiar setting to life. The only references that seem directly drawn
from John's experiences—the romantic description of Uniontown and the
memories of setting off to preparatory school—have already been quoted.
For the rest, most of the story could have taken place anywhere. The Vienna scenes, which begin and end the book, are unexpectedly more vivid
than the ones in Pennsylvania.

The plot of *Poison in Jest* also has weaknesses. It is filled with false starts.
For example, several characters see a disembodied hand from a statue
of Caligula, which supposedly creeps along on its own motive power.
(This idea was based on an episode from John's childhood, in which his

mother dashed down the stairs of their Mount Vernon Avenue house and knocked over a classical statue and broke off its arm.)[80] But, after the opening pages, Carr forgets about the crawling hand until he reintroduces it perfunctorily at the very end. Perhaps that is just as well, for it turns out to have almost nothing to do with the plot. Another false start is Judge Quayle himself, who at first seems to be based on Carr's father. John uses the judge as a vehicle to praise old-time lawyers like Wooda Carr, yet it develops that Quayle is a drug addict who is at best an object of pity rather than admiration.

Carr did not think highly of *Poison in Jest*; three years later, he remarked that it was "my most outstanding and sodden flop."[81] He was overstating the matter, for there are good things about *Poison in Jest*. The mystery— the attempted murder of Judge Quayle and the deaths of his daughter and son-in-law—is excellent, and the clues to the final solution are well done. The best part of the book is the character of Carr's new detective, Patrick Rossiter, who seems to have been invented as a complete break from the saturnine Bencolin. We first see him wearing a "disreputable hat," and lighting a homemade cigarette, which flares like a torch. He believes himself to be a great actor, a great musician, and a great detective. His sleuthing is scatterbrained: "His brain did wander in that dizzy fashion, in God knows what fanciful labyrinth."[82] Things that are clear to him are often completely confusing to others:

> Man, man, [he says] don't you see the importance of drawing a picture? Don't you see the momentous and appalling issues which hang on your drawing a picture? Don't you perceive the profound psychological bearing it will have on the solution of this case when you draw a picture?[83]

Above all, Rossiter is like a grownup child who has not lost the wonder of seeing the world as a place of adventure. Carr tells us that he "can't stay away from childish things" and indicates that the clear-sightedness of a child lets Rossiter see matters the way they really are. When, at the end of the story, Rossiter tells Marle, "I'm not such a fool really," the reader agrees: Childishness is not the same as foolishness.[84]

In the evolution of Carr's work, *Poison in Jest* is an important novel: For the first time, Carr made his detective into an exorcist. Having an eerie atmosphere and seemingly impossible crimes build together to the point that the only possible explanation must be supernatural—that would become the structure of many of Carr's books. At the conclusion, the detective would reveal that all had been created by humans for human motives, and a rational universe would be restored. In the Bencolin novels, however, it was difficult to have a detective cast out devils when the detective himself resembled Satan. There is a tension in the Bencolin cases that may reflect an ambivalence in the author's own attitude: At times, Bencolin argues for an ultimately ordered universe; at other times he seems to say that all creation is mad. Insanity plays a part in *Poison in Jest*, but Patrick Rossiter is neither mad nor satanic, and it makes sense when he says, "I'm a wizard, really. I'm an exorcist. Watch me cast out a devil: I just dropped him on the floor. And he looks a bit comical, doesn't he?"[85] Many of Rossiter's characteristics—his bumbling, his wool-gathering, his warm humanity, his cryptic remarks, his ability to cast out devils—would shortly appear in Dr. Gideon Fell, the Carr sleuth who was to solve almost all of his cases in Great Britain.

At this point it should be noted that there was a simple reason why Carr would soon create an English detective: His relationship with Clarice Cleaves confirmed his already emerging anglophilia. During 1931 and the first half of 1932, John and Clarice continued to date, and on June 3, 1932 (without telling John's parents), they were married. Jack Reynolds, the only member of the Brooklyn Heights crowd with any church associations, found a Presbyterian minister in Brooklyn. The group decorated the minister's library with the American flag and the British Union Jack, and Reynolds gave the bride away. There was no money for a honeymoon, so John and Clarice moved immediately into a furnished apartment at 78 Park Avenue in New York City, at a rent of ten dollars a week.[86]

From *Hag's Nook*, written that autumn, we get a picture of John's attitude:

> He thought of himself sitting in a class last year and thinking that if
> he flunked economics (which, like all intelligent people, he detested),
> it would be the end of the world. Possessing a wife, he would become
> suddenly a citizen, with a telephone number and a cocktail shaker
> and everything; and his mother would have hysterics.[87]

John's failure to inform his family in advance about the wedding exacerbated the tension that already existed with his mother. He asked O'Neil Kennedy to be an emissary and break the news to Julia Carr. According to a story still told in Uniontown, which John himself repeated to Clarice, his mother figuratively threw Kennedy out of the house, and told him that if John tried to come home, she would order him to leave as well. John did then telephone home, and his father said that if John was happy, he certainly was also; Julia, however, refused even to talk to her son. She told her sisters that she did not ever want to meet the woman she called "that English adventuress." John did not see his parents for another seven years, and even when the differences were smoothed over, his mother remained bitter about the circumstances of the marriage and never really accepted Clarice.[88]

Many of the heroines in John's books from this period—for example, Patricia Standish in *The Eight of Swords*—are based on Clarice Carr. But unlike some of his fictional women, Clarice was made of stern stuff, and when it became necessary to open or close a home or run the finances or rescue John from what she called a "toot," she was a person of strength. John, though he may never have realized it, needed a strong wife. Although he was not always a faithful husband, everyone who was associated with the family knew that John deeply loved his wife.

In the autumn of 1932, Clarice found that she was pregnant; this came as a surprise to John, because for some reason he had been convinced that he was destined to be childless.[89] The pregnancy meant that some decisions would have to be made. Harry and Mary Cleaves were asking when they would meet their new son-in-law. The Brooklyn Heights crowd, though remaining friendly with one another, was breaking up as a group. Jack Reynolds, in the middle of a divorce, was going his own way, and Ed Delafield had gotten married and moved to an apartment in Greenwich Village. Clarice recalls that there was little to keep them in America: "We hadn't a house of our own and furniture and cars and all those things; we had zilch."

Clarice brought up the idea to John of going to England, explaining that it would be cheaper to live on the other side of the Atlantic, since Great Britain was going off the gold standard and the rate of exchange was favorable for someone with American dollars. Their plan was to leave New York in January 1933 and stay in England for about six months to see how things worked out. But to do that, they needed additional funds. John was receiving his monthly payment of one hundred dollars from Harpers, and during the autumn of 1932 he was working on a book he had already contracted with them, to be called *Hag's Nook*. But that was not enough. To pay for a child and a trip to England, he had to increase his output.

At white-hot speed, Carr wrote a novel entitled *The Bowstring Murders*, but Harpers told him that they could publish only two of his books a year.

Although they probably could not have stopped him from publishing elsewhere as long as he fulfilled his contract with them, Harpers explained that he would be in a sense competing with himself if he used his own name with a different publisher. Harpers had no objection, however, if another publisher issued *The Bowstring Murders* under a pen name. Carr's first thought was apparently to invert the given names of his father and attribute the book to one "Nicholas Wood," but he decided to submit the book under the pseudonym "Christopher Street," taken from Ed and Babs Delafield's Greenwich Village address. Delafield suggested that his friend take the typescript to Frances Phillips of the William Morrow Company. Carr did so, and asked her to check with Harpers about his writings. He made the mistake, however, of saying that he needed the money quickly because he was about to become a father. The result was a contract that was overwhelmingly favorable to the publisher. Carr gave up all rights, receiving what he called a "substantial advance," but he would collect no royalties. He would be paid nothing more even if there were a British edition, and the publisher had all other rights—translations, films, and so on. At least he had the money to go to England.[90]

Reynolds arranged passage for the Carrs on a Munson cargo ship called the *Capulin*. It had only three passenger cabins, but it was a comfortable ship, and John and Clarice sailed from New York on January 30. Seas were heavy, but John loved the trip and he tried to learn as much as he could about the vessel for possible future use in a novel. On one occasion, Clarice left their cabin to find John: He had climbed to the crow's nest and was waving cheerfully to her. They arrived at the Thames dock on Valentine's Day, 1933.[91] Except for a brief period during the war, John and Clarice were to make their home in England for the next sixteen years.

Chapter 4

INTERLUDE— JOHN DICKSON CARR AND DETECTIVE FICTION

When Inspector Hadley objected to Dr. Fell's announcement in *The Three Coffins* that he planned to lecture on locked rooms, Fell responded forthrightly, "All those opposing can skip this chapter." I make the same invitation. If you are interested only in the life of John Dickson Carr, proceed to the next chapter. If, on the other hand, you are interested in having me lecture on the detective story and Carr's place within it, read on.

Let's start by asking what we mean when we use the phrase "detective fiction." We first should look at (and rudely dismiss) a term that has bedeviled anyone who wants to talk about the subject with any precision. The term, "crime fiction," which has recently gained currency, is so broad that it is almost useless. Any term that can embrace such diverse works and authors as *Gilgamesh*, Juvenal, Chaucer, Shakespeare, Cervantes, Fielding, Dickens, Dostoyevski, and P. G. Wodehouse is, to put it mildly, imprecise. Detective fiction certainly uses crime as a subject, but so do many other types of literature, and indeed stories about crime are as old as storytelling itself, as anyone who has read the biblical account of Cain and Abel can attest. The situation has become worse with a few writers claiming that somehow the detective story has led to the crime novel. That, of course, is chronological nonsense, for novels about crime were written long before the first stories about detection, and more seriously, such a claim implies (and sometimes states directly) that crime stories are more sophisticated than detective stories. The truth is that some are and some are not. The point, however, is that in talking about detective fiction, we are not talking about something that is more or less sophisticated than crime novels, but something that is more specific.[1]

Detective stories have features in common, though the weight that each receives can vary. One element is the story's attitude toward crime. For centuries, the hero in popular fiction was often the lawbreaker rather than the one who enforced authority. Many of the episodes in Apuleius' *The Golden Ass* (second century C.E.) are about crimes and criminals. The late medieval and Renaissance tales by Chaucer, Boccaccio, and Rabelais commonly have rogues and robbers (and worse) as protagonists. So do the picaresque works of the sixteenth through eighteenth centuries, whose theme is often the rogue's cleverness; they are, in effect, nose-thumbing novels. The seventeenth- and eighteenth-century gallows speeches printed in pamphlet form and collected as *The Newgate Calendar,* though including moralistic injunctions, in fact glorify highwaymen, cutpurses, and other malefactors. In short, from Robin Hood to Claude Duval and Dick Turpin, the image of the romantic criminal was a common motif in popular fiction.

Several developments during the early part of the nineteenth century, however, shifted this emphasis. For one thing, industrialists, merchants, shopkeepers, and the wealthier working classes (the so-called aristocracy of labor) were rising to positions of economic significance, and as property owners they did not see much to praise in roguery. Robbing from the rich and giving to the poor was not all that attractive to the new middle class. Moreover, literacy had increased to the extent that now the middle classes could read the works that appealed to their interests. And what they often chose to read were accounts of murder. The Victorian age was fascinated with murderers and their victims. Murder was the ultimate challenge to the comfortable assumptions of the Victorians, yet as long as it happened in someone else's family and as long as the criminal was tried and executed (or at least imprisoned), reading about it ultimately confirmed that the social order was secure. The new daily and weekly papers found that headlining the latest sensational crime was a sure way to increase circulation. According to Richard D. Altick, the eminent historian of Victorian murders:

In current murder they found a ready channel both for the release of such rudimentary passion as horror, morbid sympathy, and vicarious aggression and for the sheer occupation of minds otherwise rendered blank or dull by the absence of anything more pleasing or intellectually more elevated.[2]

Well, maybe for some people, but others who read voraciously about murder, including de Quincey, Dickens, and Trollope, did not have minds that had been rendered dull.

The second element of detective fiction is directly connected with the first: Detectives, not criminals, became heroes. The old and often corrupt city watch and Bow Street Runners were being replaced by professional police forces—most important was Scotland Yard in 1829—and policemen became heroes of popular literature. Dickens often showed the police in a positive light, most strikingly with Inspector Bucket in *Bleak House* (1853), and from the 1850s through the end of the century, many books appeared that purported to be genuine diaries of police officers. They had titles like *Recollections of a Detective Police-Officer, Autobiography of an English Detective, The Detective's Note-Book, Clues: Or Leaves from a Chief Constable's Note-Book,* and *The Experiences of a Lady Detective.* These books were usually thinly veiled fictions, but their success shows that law-enforcement officers were perceived favorably.

The third ingredient of detective fiction is the emphasis on mystery. Structuring a story around something unknown, something to be discovered or elucidated is an ancient technique, but having mystery as the major plot element is a characteristic of the gothic novel, beginning with Horace Walpole's *The Castle of Otranto* (1765) and Ann Radcliffe's *The Mysteries of Udolpho* (1794). These books were followed by a flood of volumes: *The Carthusian Friar, or the Mysteries of Montanville, Who's the Murderer? Or the Mysteries of the Forest, The Abbot of Montserrat, or the Pool of Blood,* and many others. By the 1830s, gothic novelettes were appearing in cheap editions called shilling shockers, and a decade or two later, they influenced the even lower priced penny dreadfuls, with titles like *The Mysteries of the Court of London.* All of these books emphasize supernatural occurrences— disembodied hands, ancestors stepping out of their portraits, and so on. The gothic stories that have supernatural resolutions are the ancestors of ghost and horror stories, but many of the gothics (especially those by Ann Radcliffe and William Child Green) conclude with all the mysteries explained rationally. These novels influenced the early detective story, especially through Edgar Allan Poe, who was fundamentally a writer of gothic horror.

For various reasons related to developments of his time—he had read, for example, the memoirs of Vidocq, the founder of the Sûreté—and even more to his own interest in theories about genius, Edgar Allan Poe wrote "The Murders in the Rue Morgue" (1841) and other tales that made him the father of detective fiction. Because other writers did not share his preoccupations, however, his stories had little immediate influence. Instead, the gothic novel had to pass through the sensation novel of the 1860s and the 1870s before detective fiction clearly emerged. Mary Elizabeth Braddon, Mrs. Henry Wood, Wilkie Collins, and others wrote stories structured around secrets—secrets the characters hide from one another, and secrets that the author hides from the reader. This was the age of the fictionalized police reminiscence, so it was natural that the sensation novels often had police detectives arrive to elucidate some of the secrets, and sometimes this resulted in novels that had all the elements of modern detective stories, most notably Mary Elizabeth Braddon's *The Trail of the Serpent* (1861), Charles Felix's *The Notting Hill Mystery* (1865), and Wilkie Collins's *The Moonstone* (1868). It seems unlikely that these authors thought they were doing anything unusual in bringing detection into their novels; it was simply one of many methods they employed in handling the secrets on which their stories were based.

The fourth part of the development of detective fiction can be handled fairly briefly, for it is implied in the gothic stories that have material explanations for their mysteries. In earlier ages, whenever crime was deemed bad—and that was hardly a universal attitude—it was because it upset the natural social or political order (as in *Hamlet* and *Macbeth*) or, which was much the same thing, it sinned against God. A book called *God's Revenge against the Execrable Crime of Murther* went through edition after edition in the seventeenth century. It was made up of stories of murder that in later times would have been investigated by detectives and tried in the courts, but the theme of the book was that God will punish murderers. A major development of the eighteenth century was not only changes in economic and social conditions, but (connected with these) the assumption of the Enlightenment that humans can find answers through reason. Voltaire's *Zadig* (1749) has a famous scene in which Zadig makes deductions from physical evidence much as Sherlock Holmes would do more than a century later. The opening paragraphs of Poe's "The Murders in the Rue Morgue" reflect an enlightened belief in reason, and in spite of fascination with the irrational associated with romanticism, the nineteenth century continued this belief in the power of the human mind, especially with an increasing emphasis on empiricism. The Victorians valued progress, and they expected humans to come up with solutions without waiting for God to intervene. This assumption permeates detective fiction.

To summarize to this point: Detective fiction is based on a mysterious crime, and this crime must be solved because (it is assumed) law and order are in themselves valuable; the detective who investigates the mystery can be official or amateur, but in either case represents the positive values in society; and through human reason rather than divine intervention he or she solves the mystery.

Although these characteristics came together in exceptional instances in Poe's stories and in the sensation novels, the genre really emerged with the stories of the Frenchman Emile Gaboriau and of the American Anna Katharine Green. Gaboriau's novels about Monsieur Lecoq were translated into English and published in America primarily in the 1870s and in Britain in the 1880s. They were immensely popular in both countries; in Britain they were described on the front covers as "Gaboriau's Sensational Novels," and they show the connection between the sensation novels and detective fiction. Gaboriau's books, though clumsy in structure and declamatory in dialogue, have many clever sections. Lecoq investigates clues, makes cryptic remarks, and fingers the criminal. Anna Katharine Green's books, beginning with *The Leavenworth Case* (1878), are much better structured than Gaboriau's, though she too tended to write in melodramatic dialogue. Both Gaboriau and Green concentrated on the mystery and the detection; they did not include those elements for other purposes, as was the case with Wilkie Collins and M. E. Braddon.

By the time that Arthur Conan Doyle introduced Sherlock Holmes in *A Study in Scarlet* (1887), there was a growing market for detective novels. Fergus Hume's *The Mystery of a Hansom Cab*, published a year earlier, was a runaway bestseller, and other authors, now unfairly forgotten, such as B. L. Farjeon and Thomas W. Speight, wrote accomplished detective novels. In fact, the new form had been so clearly defined that writers produced parodies of detective stories—Mark Twain's "The Stolen White Elephant" (1882), "W. Humer Ferguson's" *The Mystery of a Wheelbarrow* (1888), Robert Louis Stevenson's *The Wrong Box* (1889), and Robert Barr's *From Whose Bourne* (1893). Doyle's contribution was not to send the detective story in a new direction, but to sharpen what was already implicit in it. Above all, he placed the emphasis on the Great Detective, who with all his eccentricities would become the focus of the story. Doyle, moreover, was a superb writer. He did not lead the detective story away from the sensationalism that had characterized it; there is plenty of sensationalism in Holmes's cases. But he wrote so well, his descriptions are so precise, his characters so well drawn, that much of the crudity of earlier writers was avoided.

Doyle's main success came not with the early Holmes books, *A Study in Scarlet* and *The Sign of Four*, but with the series of short stories in *The Strand Magazine*, starting with "A Scandal in Bohemia" in July 1891. The popularity of this series meant that most important detective fiction by various authors between 1890 and about 1910 or a bit later was done in the short-story form. A change, however, began to occur shortly before World War I. Starting with R. Austin Freeman's *The Red Thumb Mark* (1907) and, more important, *The Eye of Osiris* (1911), novels of seventy-five thousand to ninety thousand words became the most common length for a detective story. Obviously novels had to be more elaborate in plot than short stories, and some authors added subplots, including international intrigue and love affairs, which were not always germane to the mystery and its solution. In addition, the mystery became more complicated, sometimes by having several different matters that had to be resolved—for example, not only who committed the murder but how it was done—and sometimes by having multiple solutions. The device of having a false solution to be followed by the true (or sometimes by a second false solution before the truth was finally revealed) did not begin in E. C. Bentley's *Trent's Last Case* (1913), but it was that book that made the device popular among the writers of the so-called Golden Age (about 1920 to 1940). It reached its apex with the seven solutions in Anthony Berkeley's *The Poisoned Chocolates Case* (1929).

The pattern that I have laid out in the growth of detective fiction seems straightforward, but like most apparently straightforward things it is too simple. In fact, at around the turn of the century there were many stories featuring detectives that do not fit into this scheme at all. Detectives were popular heroes in fiction, even in stories that have little mystery. In the American dime novels detectives were often protagonists, but they do little detecting. Nick Carter, Old King Brady, Old Sleuth, and (in Britain) Sexton Blake follow people about and wear numerous disguises, but they do not do much thinking, and there is rarely a puzzle to dominate the plot. Digging into turn-of-the-century novels by Fred M. White, Gerald Biss, William LeQueux, and many others finds plenty of characters who call themselves detectives and who may be policemen or work for a "private enquiry" office, but they are usually adventure heroes, often engaged in stopping a plot against the crown—in one instance, an attempt to reverse the results of the fifteenth-century Wars of the Roses and restore the House of York to the British throne. Sax Rohmer's hero, Nayland Smith, the nemesis of Fu Manchu ("The Yellow Peril Incarnate"), is a detective, but he is more closely akin to an adventure hero like H. Rider Haggard's Allan Quartermain than he is to an investigator like Sherlock Holmes. Many of the protagonists in Edgar Wallace's novels are detectives, and occasionally some of them (especially J. G. Reeder) do some actual detecting, but for the most part they are thriller heroes, involved with gangs and super-criminals and exotic adventuresses, and they bound from one adventure to another without much time for thought.

In the early 1930s, John Dickson Carr, in company with other writers, drew a line between thrillers and detective stories:

> Broadly speaking [he wrote] a thriller may be defined as a story in which the detective-problem is not of paramount importance because the detective never sits still long enough to think about it. If you see him sitting quietly in an armchair, it is because someone has just knocked him over the head with a life-preserver; he will awake presently.[3]

But around 1920, when as a teenager John D. Carr III began to write, distinctions were not all that clear. Nayland Smith and Nick Carter were detectives, just as Sherlock Holmes and Father Brown were detectives. Indeed, there were fictional detectives of every variety—police detectives, scientific detectives, "rule-of-thumb" detectives, mystic detectives, thriller detectives, journalist detectives, blind detectives, armchair detectives, lawyer detectives, clergyman detectives, gypsy detectives, jeweler detectives, railroad detectives: The list can be extended almost indefinitely. Some of them were logical thinkers, others were intuitive, and others continued the action-packed thriller tradition. Some detectives had odd combinations of traits from odd combinations of sources. M. P. Shiel's Prince Zaleski, for instance, is perhaps the most eccentric of all detectives—a reclusive drug addict who combines Sherlock Holmes with Nietzsche's *Ubermensch*. Occasionally, as in Richard Marsh's *The Beetle,* the detective investigates genuine supernatural occurrences. Thomas W. Hanshew, creator of Hamilton Cleek, the Man of the Forty Faces, whose influence permeates Carr's first adolescent stories, had been a dime novelist, but he was clearly influenced by the Great Detective tradition—and by just about anything else that would sell.

G. K. Chesterton was probably the first to state the principles of "fair play," that is, that every clue to the solution must be given to the reader at the same time that the detective finds it. For Chesterton as for Carr, the distinguishing element of detective fiction is not investigation of a crime, but mystery and its solution based on clues given to the reader. As early as 1906, Chesterton wrote, "The detective or mystery story need not, of course, be primarily concerned with detectives. . . . The real distinguishing feature is that the reader should be confronted with a number of mysterious facts of which the explanation is reserved till the end." In his Father Brown stories, Chesterton himself adhered to the fair-play rule. So did other writers whose first works were published shortly before World War I, especially R. Austin Freeman in his Dr. Thorndyke stories, the Baroness Orczy in the three volumes about the Old Man in the Corner, Jacques Futrelle in the cases of the Thinking Machine, and Carolyn Wells in her Fleming Stone novels. Moreover, giving all the clues to the reader would become the most firmly held literary principle of John Dickson Carr and of the Golden Age writers in general.

During the Golden Age of the 1920s and the 1930s, the puzzle element of the detective story reigned supreme. The decade following World War I was the great period of games and puzzles, perhaps because they indicated, in spite of all evidence to the contrary, that things could still be solved. The crossword puzzle was invented in the 1920s; board games, especially Monopoly, were popular; people played Mah-Jongg, canasta, contract bridge, and (in Brooklyn Heights and elsewhere) the Murder game. Detective-story authors saw their books as contests in which the goal was to fool their readers, and any trick was legitimate as long as all the clues were honorably displayed. The trickiest practitioner of the genre was Agatha Christie who, starting in 1920 with *The Mysterious Affair at Styles*, developed a gimmick that came to characterize her works: The murderer almost always turns out to be the least-likely suspect. In a Christie, one should be suspicious of everyone—the detective in charge of the case, the little old lady crippled for twenty years, the suspect whom the sleuth is trying to exonerate, even the narrator. The reviewers of the day more commonly praised books for their plots and how fair they were to the reader than for their development of character or setting.

Detective novels from the Golden Age were filled with inventive ways of presenting the clues—sketch maps of the murder site, lists of items found on the corpse, charts, timetables, transcriptions of interviews, and so on. Some authors—most important Ellery Queen, but also including Rupert Penny and Hugh Austin—stopped the action about three-quarters of the way through the story with a note labeled "Challenge to the Reader" informing him or her that all the clues sufficient to solve the crime had now been given. Another writer, Q. Patrick, included in one of his books a tipped-in piece of paper stating that there is an important clue on that page. Clifford Knight had a sealed "Clue Index" at the end of his early books.

In some cases, the puzzle ceased to have any connection to literature at all. Lassiter Wren and Randle McKay produced three *Baffle Books* (1928–30), which had very short mysteries with solutions given at the end. These were used at parties, and points were awarded to the player who solved the most puzzles. A short while later came Austin Ripley's *Minute Mysteries* (1932) and J. C. Cannell's *100 Mysteries for Arm-Chair Detectives* (1932) with even shorter stories whose solutions hinge on tiny details. The final extreme, the Gothic Folly of the challenge-to-the-reader development, was the *Crimefiles* of the late 1930s, designed by J. G. Links and written (if that is the word) by Dennis Wheatley and others. Instead of having any narration, the *Crimefiles* were bound-together collections of clues—police reports, letters, telegrams, photographs, newspaper pages, fingerprints. Physical items were included in glassine envelopes—burned matches, stamps, torn-up photographs, railway tickets, even face powder from the victim. Many of the mysteries in the *Baffle Books* and the *Crimefiles* are still fun to work out, and similar game books are occasionally still produced, but they cannot be considered detective stories. For most authors the challenge was how to maintain the puzzle element while telling an interesting story, with believable characters in realistically described settings.

Many of the writers of the Golden Age believed that detective fiction had reached maturity. No longer did crude sensationalism dominate the form; the emphasis was now on the intellectual challenge implicit in the fair-play principle. Some authors, including S. S. Van Dine and Ronald Knox, produced rules to make certain that mere thrillers could not be accepted into the canon. Knox, who was a Catholic priest as well as an important mystery writer, called his list (like Moses') a Decalogue and included such rules as: "The criminal must be someone mentioned in the early part of the story"; "All supernatural or preternatural agencies are ruled out as a matter of course"; "Not more than one secret room or passage is allowable"; "No hitherto undiscovered poisons may be used"; and of course, "The detective must not light on any clues which are not instantly produced for the inspection of the reader."[4] In words similar to ones that Carr would later use, S. S. Van Dine, author of the popular Philo Vance mysteries, summarized detective fiction of the Golden Age: "The detective story is a kind of intellectual game. It is more—it is a sporting event. And the author must play fair with the reader. . . . He must outwit the reader, and hold the reader's interest, through sheer ingenuity."[5] This emphasis on fair play in the clueing dominated The Detection Club, founded in London in 1930 by Anthony Berkeley, which was made up of almost all of the major writers of the Golden Age.[6]

As with Doyle and his followers, the focus of Golden Age authors was usually on the detective. It is true that some of them created relatively colorless sleuths; it is hard to remember anything about the personalities of John Rhode's Dr. Priestley, Freeman Wills Crofts's Inspector French, and G. D. H. and M. Coles's Superintendent Wilson. For the most part, however, the tradition of the Great Detective with all his eccentricities continued, though he or she had become more human and even occasionally fallible. H. C. Bailey's chubby Reggie Fortune moaned and groaned throughout his cases like, Carr said, "an animated cream-puff."[7] In his early cases, Dorothy L. Sayers's Lord Peter Wimsey was an aristocrat who collected incunabula and spoke in an affected drawl. Christie's Hercule Poirot was a tiny Belgian with an egg-shaped head, who was vain about his mustaches and spoke about his "little gray cells." A fictional detective was still expected to be larger than life, to make cryptic remarks, to have esoteric knowledge, and to be an amateur. Superintendent So and So, Inspector This and That continued to solve fictional cases, but they paled before the successes of the amateurs. Carr summarized the appeal of the amateur:

> To begin with, we object to the professional merely because he is a professional. This may seem to be carrying the Anglo-Saxon love of amateurism too far: but the reasons, if irrational, are sincere. Nothing galls our romantic minds more than the statement, "It's all in a day's work." A fine corpse, strangled with a green cord and having its mouth stuffed full of gold coins, is not in our day's work. A knifed baronet, with nine suspects skulking in one long procession round

the drawing-room windows, is not in our day's work. And if you protest that it is seldom in anybody's day's work, including that of the police, you only stress the reason why we do not like any such admirable carryings-on measured by any rule of thumb—or thumb-print.[8]

Fortunately, if implausibly, the police were always ready to welcome the counsel of these amateur sleuths. Wimsey assisted Inspector Parker, Poirot helped Inspector Japp, Anthony Berkeley's Chief Inspector Moresby was amazingly patient with self-styled detective Roger Sheringham. This pattern can be traced all the way back to our friends the Hanshews, in whose books Superintendent Maverick Narkom is touchingly depending on the brilliance of Hamilton Cleek. Perhaps the apotheosis of this development is in the clever, though turgidly written, stories by Max Afford, whose amateur detective is the roommate of a Scotland Yard chief inspector.

John Dickson Carr's principles about the craft and structure of detective fiction remained much the same throughout his writing career. Besides his novels and short stories themselves, the major sources for a discussion of his ideas about the genre are Basil Hogarth's *Writing Thrillers for Profit* (1936), which contains extensive excerpts from letters from Carr and other Golden Age writers; Carr's lengthy essay on detective fiction entitled "The Grandest Game in the World," written in 1946 but not published until 1963, and then only in truncated form (the complete essay was first printed in the revised edition of *The Door to Doom* in 1991); Carr's panel discussions and speeches at the Mystery Writers of America meetings during the late 1940s and the early 1950s; and many remarks in his review column in *Ellery Queen's Mystery Magazine* from 1969 to 1976.

The most fundamental point, repeated over and over in all of these sources, is that John Dickson Carr was a vehement exponent of the fair-play tradition. In Chestertonian fashion, his definition of detective fiction did not emphasize investigation but rather the contest:

> The detective story is a conflict between criminal and detective, in which the criminal, by means of some ingenious device—alibi, novel murder method, or what you like—remains unconvicted or even unsuspected until the detective reveals his identity by means of evidence which has also been conveyed to the reader. . . . The detective novel at its best will contain three qualities seldom found in the thriller. It will contain the quality of fairplay in presenting the clues. It

will contain the quality of sound plot construction. And it will contain the quality of ingenuity.

Carr began his essay, "The Grandest Game in the World," with a quotation from the oath taken by new members of The Detection Club requiring fair play in the revealing of clues, "and this rule," Carr says, is "the *sine qua non* of the profession." He argues that the best sort of clueing should not be based on a single clue, or on one inconsistency, but on "a ladder of clues, a pattern of evidence, joined together with such cunning that even the experienced reader may be deceived: until, in the blaze of the surprise ending, he suddenly sees the whole design."[9] In the complete version of "The Grandest Game in the World," Carr analyzes the techniques used by various mystery writers to provide clues yet fool the reader. Sometimes, it must be admitted, Carr engages in special pleading, as when he tries to show that Doyle's Sherlock Holmes stories accepted the fair-play rule long before it was invented, but his analysis of the novels of such Golden Age authors as Berkeley, Christie, Queen, Sayers, and Van Dine is brilliant.

Carr enjoyed speaking about the art of misdirection. "Once the evidence is presented," he said, "there are very few things which are not permissible." Mystery writer Harold Q. Masur recalls that at a luncheon meeting, probably around 1949 or 1950, Carr advised him, "Tell every lie as though it were the truth, and every truth as though it were a lie."[10] Carr described this technique in more detail at a craft meeting of the New York chapter of the Mystery Writers of America during the late 1940s. Carr shared a panel with Hugh Pentecost and Ellery Queen (both Frederic Dannay and Manfred Lee) on the topic "Writing the Mystery Story." According to the report of the session recorded by another writer, Dorothy Gardiner, Carr said:

> Write a lie as though it were true, and the reader, intent on his own detecting, will swallow it. . . . Clues should be stressed in different parts of the book, and a good clue should be given at least twice. The most important clue should sound like the wildest nonsense; in placing a cryptic clue, be sure that your reader never sees it at eye-level. This can be done by using love scenes or comic scenes.

Gardiner included her own response to Carr's advice: "Yes, Mr. Carr—you can do it. But the rest of us?"[11]

Carr said that as long as the author has planted his clues cleverly, he can include the most wildly improbable solutions. Detective fiction, Carr firmly believed, belongs in the realm of romance rather than realism. Dr. Fell was quite willing to discourse at length on this topic:

> A few people who do not like the slightly lurid insist on treating their preferences as rules. They use, as a stamp of condemnation, the word "improbable." And thereby they gull the unwary into their own belief that "improbable" simply means "bad." Now, it seems reasonable to point out that the word improbable is the very last which should ever be used to curse detective fiction in any case. A great part of our liking for detective fiction is *based* on a liking for improbability.[12]

In the 1960s in a review of a book by another writer, Carr remarked, "That I of all people should complain of improbable solutions would be like Satan rebuking sin or St. Vitus objecting to the twist."[13]

Carr disliked the hard-boiled private-eye story that emerged during the 1920s in the pages of *Black Mask* and other pulp magazines and was best represented in the novels of Dashiell Hammett and Raymond Chandler. There are exceptions, but the hard-boiled tales emphasized action rather than hoodwinking clues and misdirection, and the Golden Age writers of The Detection Club found such tales closer to thrillers than to detection as they understood it. "A clueless and featureless riot of gunplay" was how Carr in 1941 described private-eye stories.[14] Hard-boiled operatives act, Carr said, "for no reasons at all, or for no reasons that are ever explained."[15] (This is in many ways a fair criticism of Raymond Chandler, who often did not explain all elements of his mystery satisfactorily. The most famous example is his failure to tell the reader who killed the chauffeur in *The Big Sleep*.)

Carr found the hard-boiled writers to be part of the 1920s school of realistic fiction which he abhorred—and many modern scholars, who do not abhor that school, also classify Dashiell Hammett, Raymond Chandler, and their followers with F. Scott Fitzgerald and Ernest Hemingway. "My real objection to the hard-boiled school, even"—he added significantly—"among those who are grown up is that it isn't toughness at all; it is merely bad manners. And bad manners I dislike more than anything on this earth."

There are several ironies in Carr's attitude toward the hard-boiled writers. First, Carr did not understand that the private eye's tough manners were just as much a protective mask as Carr's emphasis on correct behavior. Unlike some critics, he realized that the sarcastic language of the hard-boiled sleuth was not realistic, but he saw nothing positive in being impolite in either fiction or life.

> It isn't that they don't write the English language. The trouble is that they don't write the American language. What they write is a kind of Jabberwocky, built up between the films and the cheaper magazines, which has no more relation to everyday speech than Esperanto. As for the conduct of the people concerned, do they honestly believe people act like that in real life? Or, which is more important, ought to act like that?[16]

This leads to another irony: Raymond Chandler was actually just as much a romanticist as John Dickson Carr, and his detective, Philip Marlowe, is as much a lone adventurer as any character whom Carr created or admired. But Carr disliked Chandler's novels more than those of any other writer, and Chandler hated Carr's. They depicted the world differently. Chandler wrote of streets that were not only mean but often grimy; Carr may at times during his life have seen the world in the same way, but he would not write of it like that. As early as the years when he wrote for the *Uniontown Daily News Standard*, he argued that literature should not portray the world as sordid and that there is nothing to admire in a character who does not talk courteously.

In 1950, Carr wrote a review for *The New York Times* of Raymond Chandler's *The Simple Art of Murder* in which he criticized Chandler while, unexpectedly, finding some good things to say about Dashiell Hammett. In the title essay, Chandler had attacked the British detective novel and The Detection Club for not being realistic about murder. Carr responded forthrightly, "Anything is real if it seems real," a sentence which summarizes his view of the debate on probability. Chandler's problem is that

> he can't explain why the characters acted as they did, and he can't even talk intelligibly. . . . Few writers have been more mannered (I do not say ill-mannered) or more uneven. His similes either succeed brilliantly or fall flat. He can write a scene with an almost suffocating vividness and sense of danger—if he does not add three words too many and make it funny. His virtues are all there. If, to some restraint, he could add the fatigue of construction and clues . . . then one day he may write a good novel.

Chandler was furious with the review—calling Carr a "pip-squeak" in a letter—yet Carr actually had said some complimentary things about the stories in *The Simple Art of Murder:* "Two are first-class," he admitted. But even Carr's compliments were double-edged: "When [Chandler] forgets he cannot write a true detective story, when he forgets to torture words, the muddle resolves and the action whips along like a numbered racing car." In the midst of all this, however, Carr stopped to praise Dashiell Hammett: "Mr. Hammett has never disdained clues and has always given them fairly."[17]

Carr's kind words for Hammett and a pair of Chandler's stories indicates that he was mellowing slightly in his attitude toward private-eye fiction. A few months after he wrote "The Grandest Game in the World," Carr told Frederic Dannay that "I have no objection to the hard-boiled school as such. I object to it only when it is phony or pretentious, as it nearly always is."[18] In 1949, as an advertisement for the Doubleday Mystery Guild, Carr wrote a brief essay about types of detective fiction. "Once upon a time, mind you, I didn't like [tough writers]. I didn't like them, that is, until suddenly—amid a spinning of blood, brass-knuckles, and flying bodies—I discovered that the author was calmly inserting the evidence into the bureau drawer."[19] Toward the end of his life, in his reviews for *Ellery Queen's Mystery Magazine,* Carr praised private-eye novels by Ross Macdonald and young writers, such as Bill Pronzini, who included plot construction and ingenuity in clueing.

John Dickson Carr was a major contributor to the Golden Age tradition and a major propagandist for its standards, but his stories have a different flavor from the cozy country-house mysteries of Christie, Sayers, Berkeley, and the others. More than any other writer after Poe, Carr showed in his works the connection between the gothic novel and the detective story. The Bencolin novels retain Poe's gothicism; they begin with mysteries and horrors and seemingly genuine supernaturalism. Many reviewers and critics of the 1930s saw Carr basically as "that splendid master of the macabre"[20] and often overlooked his role in the fair-play style. An article in a 1935 issue of *Publisher's Weekly,* for instance, classified mystery readers as of "two kinds: those who will read supernatural tales and those who will not. The second group is denied the pleasure of writers like ... John Dickson Carr."[21] It is not surprising that the first book-length study of Carr's works was written by S. T. Joshi, an expert on the horror writer H. P. Lovecraft. But the Bencolin novels remain by Carr's definition detective stories. They begin with horrors, but the solutions to the mysteries are material and rational, with all clues given to the reader.

Carr based the structure of his novels partly on Chesterton: Begin with a bizarre statement of the case, then investigate it not according to physical clues but according to finding the real pattern. Chesterton, writing short stories, had the unmasking of the criminal take place at the same time the true pattern is revealed. Carr, usually writing novels, made it harder on himself by having one mystery followed by another, with more than one pattern to be revealed. This technique allowed him to explain the puzzles more gradually. Perhaps about two-thirds of the way through the novel Carr usually would explain one of the most important mysteries—the locked room, or for the imposture, or the strange actions of the victim, or whatever other riddle Carr has tantalized us with—but there will then be a final stage in the novel in which the murderer is identified.

"Ingenuity" is a word often used accurately to describe Carr's books: There is ingenuity in method, normally associated with the impossible crime, and there is ingenuity in narration, as Carr sprinkles clues to the resolution of each of the mysteries. Most of his books are extraordinary accomplishments viewed merely as technical achievements; in handling a complex puzzle plot, no other detective-story author can consistently match John Dickson Carr. But Carr's stories are more than mere technique, more than challenge-to-the-reader puzzles. In order to be read generation after generation, the detective novel's story itself, not just the riddle, has to be interesting. It is here that the other weapons in Carr's armory come into play—his sense of atmosphere and hints of the supernatural, his love of color and the incongruous, his descriptions of ancient lore and past events, his ability to describe a place, and the sense of wonder and excitement of his stories.

Chapter 5

ENGLAND AND THE COMING OF SIR HENRY MERRIVALE

John and Clarice Carr arrived in England on February 14, 1933, and stayed at the Regent Palace Hotel, Piccadilly Circus. The weather was cold, with sleet and snow, but to Clarice's surprise John took to England immediately.[1] Because he had been to England on his two earlier trips overseas, he acted as tour guide for Clarice as they dashed about London. After two or three days in London, John and Clarice took a train to visit Clarice's parents, who lived in the town of Kingswood, east of Bristol on the road toward Bath. "The moment they met John," Clarice recalls, "Daddy and Mummy took him to their hearts." He also impressed Clarice's seven-year-old brother, Roy. In the 1930s, it was unusual for an American to visit the western part of England. Roy remembers that his sister's husband was reserved, but polite and very much the gentleman. He was patient with children, always ready to listen to a small boy like Roy. John seemed somewhat exotic to his young brother-in-law because he ate with a fork alone, rather than (in the English fashion) wielding a knife and fork at the same time.[2]

John and Clarice returned to London toward the end of February 1933 and took a small furnished flat on Guilford Street, which is just off Bloomsbury and a short distance from the British Museum. John went often to the British Museum seeking bits and pieces of information that he could use in his books. His contract with Harpers, guaranteeing him an income of one hundred dollars a month, meant that he had to produce typescripts at regular intervals. *Hag's Nook,* which he had completed the previous autumn, would be published in March, and Harpers planned to go to press on the second Dr. Fell novel, *The Mad Hatter Mystery,* in July, with publication in early August. *The Mad Hatter Mystery* is filled with the atmosphere of London. It begins in a bar on Great Windmill Street, near Piccadilly Circus, but quickly goes to the Tower of London, which is described in language as romantic as Carr had ever used in his college stories:

> Bugles sound before Waterloo Barracks, where once the tournaments were held, and you will hear the wheel and stamp of the Guards. In the green places under the trees, a raven comes to sit on a drinking-fountain, and looks across at the spot where men and women with bandaged eyes mounted a few steps to put their heads upon a block.[3]

Clarice was correct that living in London at that time was less expensive than living in New York City. The exchange rate was favorable for anyone with dollars, and though it was sometimes difficult to get hard cash, prices were low:

> He was writing [Clarice remembers] but we were also traipsing around at a great pace. We weren't that poor; we managed every good theater, every good movie, every sight worth seeing both in and around London. We were busy, just the two of us. The whole thing was pretty wonderful right from the beginning, but that time was particularly nice.

Mary Cleaves wanted Clarice to come home for the birth of the grandchild, and she saw no reason why John should stay in London, book or no book. In May, Clarice moved back to Bristol, and John joined her there in June. On June 20, a daughter was born; John and Clarice named her Julia. John always said that the name was taken from a favorite actress of his from the 1920s; it was not, he insisted, a gesture toward reconciliation with his mother, Julia May Lenox Kisinger Carr. Maybe not, but he did plan to give his daughter the middle name Lenox. In the event, it worked out rather differently. The birth of the child had to be registered. John planned to do it, but he was in the middle of a book and it was always difficult for him to think of anything else at those times. So Clarice went down to the registry office herself, but she decided that, if she had to go to the effort, she would choose the additional name. The daughter became officially "Yvonne Julia Carr," the first name taken from Clarice's favorite childhood doll. Julia's name would be given in different ways on various documents during her childhood, depending on whether her mother or father was recording it. Her American grandparents, however, never knew that it might be anything other than "Julia Lenox Carr."

While they looked for a place of their own, John and Clarice lived with her family for about eight months, at Sommerset Cottage, 40 Britannia Road. The Cleaveses let John have the library in the front of the house, which they fixed up as a study with a table and typewriter. Carr liked Bristol because of its large library, and he often went to the library to gather source material for his books. Living at Sommerset Cottage, John set to work on *The Eight of Swords*, the third Dr. Fell novel, this one taking place just outside Bristol. It was probably also at his father-in-law's house that he began the first Sir Henry Merrivale novel, *The Plague Court Murders*, which like *The Mad Hatter Mystery* has a London setting.

It was not easy to find a place to live, for John was used to American conveniences, then not common in England. Houses and apartments they looked at sometimes had the bathtub under the kitchen counter, or the toilet down at the end of a passageway. But around February 1934, they found a place that they loved. The Bungalow, 4 Talbot Avenue, Kingswood, was what in England is called "semidetached," and in America a "duplex." Although it had only one story, with space for storage under the roof, it was (and still is) a good-sized place. It had three bedrooms (one of which was set up as John's study overlooking the garden), a sitting room, a large hall (with oak flooring), kitchen, pantry, and bath. As Carr's books continued to appear, he became a local celebrity, and rumors spread that he had miniature skulls and skeletons hung about his study so that he could get the right atmosphere for his mystery stories. This story contained a kernel of truth, but no more. He had purchased at Woolworth's a two- or three-inch-high ashtray that was decorated as a skeleton.[4]

Neither John nor Clarice were what one might call "baby people." They loved Julia, but the daily care of an infant did not interest either of them. Clarice has always been quite frank in explaining to her daughters that she prefers children to infants. John did not like meting out discipline. He was kind to Julia and the two daughters who arrived later, and he tended to spoil them with presents, but he was not involved with fathering in the sense that he was able to think about things from a child's level. As he did with Roy Cleaves, he treated his daughters with politeness—the way he thought all children (and most adults) should be treated. Politeness, however, is an adult standard. A child might be complimented by being treated as a grownup but still hunger for the more intimate attention that John was not really capable of giving to children. Fortunately, Clarice's parents were only a ten-minute walk away from the Bungalow, and Mary Cleaves wanted to care for Julia. So Julia lived with her grandparents, whom she loved dearly, and she never felt that she had been deprived in her childhood. Her early years were shared with Roy Cleaves, who was actually her uncle but only about eight years older. Her mother spent part of each day with Julia, but her father saw her mainly on weekends. Daddy John, her grandparents would say, has to write. It was an arrangement that, with our day-care centers, strikes us as more normal than it might have seemed more than half a century ago.

John Dickson Carr was certainly working hard. During 1933, 1934, and 1935, he had twelve books published, with 1935 his most prolific year, when five of his books appeared under three different names. The normal pattern was that he began with an intriguing setting: "That would be a good place for a murder," he told himself, "now how can I fit a murder into it?"[5] Obvious examples from this period include the Tower of London in *The Mad Hatter Mystery*, Sir John Soane's Museum in *The Arabian Nights Murder* (where it was renamed the Wade Museum), and the shipboard setting of *The Blind Barber*, which was based in part on the *Capulin* which had brought John and Clarice to London. Captain Valvick of that book is an exaggerated version of the Scandinavian captain of the *Capulin*. Often, too, a book would emerge from a bit of antiquarian lore—the clocks and watches of *Death-Watch* came from the clock collections at the Guildhall and at the British Museum, and the taroc cards in *The Eight of Swords* came from Carr's increasing reading about the occult.

Several current writers who specialize in impossible crimes, including Edward D. Hoch and Bill Pronzini, have said that they sometimes begin with a situation and then attempt to invent a way to explain it. Carr approached the plotting of the first three Sir Henry Merrivale novels in that way; but in other instances, he started with a method—normally a trick drawn from a magician, such as Harry Houdini or Jasper Maskelyne—and then worked out a plot to go around it. The most important example is *The Three Coffins*, whose central impossibility is an imaginative variation of a gimmick from the popular London magic show called the Maskelyne Mysteries, with a bit added from the book *Secrets of Houdini*.[6] Throughout the 1930s and into the 1940s, Carr often developed ideas from Maskelyne tricks. In 1944, he described the Maskelyne Mysteries as having "a glaze of magic, a brilliance of invention, the glamour and romance which can be felt even now." His description of Maskelyne effects shows why they so attracted someone who loved impossible crimes:

> Would you believe that a dismembered body could put itself together and walk off the stage? Or a lady could disappear in full lights and under full sight of the audience? Or a severed hand could play dominoes? Such things could be done and were done.[7]

To make certain that a gimmick would work, Carr set up cardboard boxes on a table, with doors and windows cut out so that he could check the angles of sight for the various characters. To represent the witness who reports the seeming impossibility, he used a china statuette, about three inches in height. (Incongruously, the china figure was of the religious leader John Wesley.)

If John was deep in a book, his day would be structured around his writing. He would get up before eight in the morning and have a cup of tea and a biscuit. After showering and shaving, he had a big breakfast of scrambled eggs. Then he went to his study for the day. At lunchtime, Clarice (or in later years, their nanny, Violet Andrews) would bring him a sandwich and tea. He drank tea all day long while writing—and he smoked cigarette after cigarette. Sometimes, he would take a break late in the afternoon and go on a short walk, but then he would be back at work until dinner, which would be around seven-thirty in the evening. He rarely worked all night long as he had done at the Columbia Heights apartment, but if he were trying to complete a work, or if the words were flowing and he did not want to stop, he would stay at the typewriter until very late. A thirteen-hour day at the typewriter was not uncommon. In Kingswood, he normally allowed himself about two months to complete a book. If pressed, however, he could still produce more than five thousand words a day, as he had done with the Bencolin novels. Some books, such as *To Wake the Dead*, were written very quickly; others, especially *The Murder of Sir Edmund Godfrey*, took much longer. (*Godfrey* was eight or nine months in the writing alone, and longer in the detailed research before the writing could start.)

In the evenings, after a day at the typewriter, John would often take Clarice to the cinema. They would watch almost anything that was in town, but John preferred costume dramas and slapstick comedies, the Marx Brothers being an especial favorite.

After the Carrs first moved to Kingswood, John employed a typing bureau to make final copies of his books, but when the typescripts came back with sections left out and words muddled, Clarice decided to do the typing herself. John's work was not difficult to copy, for he never had pages to insert, or additions to be included from the margins, or sentences to be rearranged. The most he might have done was to erase a single word and replace it with another, but he did not cross sections out. If he was not satisfied with a chapter or a portion of a chapter, he tore it up, and started again. It was easy to estimate the length of a portion of the book, because John was meticulous about having the same margins on each page. Consequently, Clarice's typed copies were exactly the same in page and line count as John's originals. For the books published under his own name, John sent Clarice's typescript to Hamish Hamilton in London, who read it through, sometimes making suggestions, before forwarding it to Eugene Saxton of Harper & Brothers in New York.

About six months before publication, Harpers would ask John to send what they called "dummy material," which normally consisted of a table of contents, two chapters, and a summary of the book. In earlier publishing practice, this preliminary material would be printed and bound for salesmen to use to get advance orders. No such dummies are known of Carr's books, and it is possible that in the 1930s Harpers used the material less formally for publicity purposes, such as preparing advertisements and catalogue copy. It would be important, however, if the dummies were to show up in any form, for Carr sometimes made changes between the dummy stage and the published text. *The Murder of Sir Edmund Godfrey,* for example, was cut by about eighty pages.[8]

With a few exceptions—most notably *Devil Kinsmere* and *The Murder of Sir Edmund Godfrey*—each book was typeset in America, and two sets of proofs were posted back to England, one for Carr to correct for the American edition and one to be used as the basis for the British edition, which would have reset type. When proofs for the Hamish Hamilton edition were sent to him, Carr himself might make some additional changes, and as a result some wording differences exist between American and British printings. Normally, these are quite minor; for instance, Carr made some small changes in Dr. Fell's famous "Locked-Room Lecture" in the British edition of *The Three Coffins* (retitled *The Hollow Man*). He added the line, "I do not care to hear the hum of everyday life; I much prefer to hear the chuckle of the great Hanaud or the deadly bells of Fenchurch St. Paul." He also changed "When the cry of 'This-sort-of-thing-wouldn't-happen!' goes up, when you complain about half-faced fiends and hooded phantoms and blond hypnotic sirens" to "When the cry of 'This-sort-of-thing-wouldn't-happen!' goes up, when you complain about homicidal maniacs and killers who leave cards."[9] During this decade the Harpers edition usually was published about a month before the Hamilton.

No correspondence seems to survive between John Dickson Carr and the American and British publishers of the Carter Dickson books, so printing details are not well known. Carr sold all of the rights to *The Bowstring Murders* and the first four or five Sir Henry Merrivale books to the William Morrow Company, the American publishers. Consequently, Morrow owned British rights and made arrangements for the William Heinemann editions of those works. Around July 1936, however, Carr began to make separate contracts with Heinemann. Carr never saw proofs of *The Bowstring Murders*, and I do not know what was done about checking proofs for the other Morrow books of this period. Was it Carr or, much more likely, an editor at Heinemann who dropped the final sentence of Chapter 1 of the American edition of *The Plague Court Murders*? The sentence, "My pennies clinked in the telephone, and were gone," inaccurately describes the way British phones worked. More important are the differences between the American and British editions of *The Judas Window*. Many sections have wording changes; the map of the murder scene is not the same; and the name of the judge, a character who is important throughout the book, is changed from Justice Bodkin in the American to Justice Rankin in the British. Both editions were published in January 1938—the U.S. early in the month, the British during the third week—but we do not know why the changes in *The Judas Window* were made or who made them or in fact which version of the text is earlier. Of the ten Carr Dickson/Carter Dickson books published by Morrow and Heinemann between 1933 and 1939, seven were published first in America.

When John finished writing a book, he and Clarice would put on a Saturday-evening party at the Bungalow. Roy Cleaves remembers shopping with his mother and sister on Saturday afternoons, and then on Sunday he would help clean up, finishing off the sausage rolls and whatever else had not been consumed at the party.[10] The parties were organized around games—occasionally Murder, which John had played back in New York, but more commonly paper and pencil games. Sometimes, the guests played the game that is still popular at literary parties, in which one guest writes down the opening to a story and then folds the paper so that the writing is not visible. With no idea of what has already been written, the next guest writes another section, and so on. The result is a disjointed but often amusing story. The Carrs played a more elaborate version of this game, based on *The Plot Genie* by Wycliffe A. Hill.

John had bought a copy of *The Plot Genie* on a trip to New York during August and September 1934. His passport was up for renewal, and it was John's understanding that he had to be in America to do it. While in New York, he visited his friends Jack Reynolds and Ed and Babs Delafield, and met with his publishers. Reynolds introduced him to some editors of pulp magazines and showed him *The Plot Genie*. *The Plot Genie* included a book containing lists of plot elements and a cardboard disc called a "Genie," which had various numbers referring to plot categories and incidents in the book. Wycliffe Hill believed that there were "only thirty-one basic dramatic situations on which all drama and fiction are based." The would-be author picked one of them, then turned the disc to choose a number for the locale of the story, usual male characters, unusual male characters, usual female characters, unusual female characters, problems, obstacles, complications, predicaments, crises, and climaxes or surprise twists—each of these categories had at least 180 choices.[11] *The Plot Genie* seems absurdly mechanical, but in practice many writers used *The Plot Genie* and other competing books that had similar gimmicks.

John Dickson Carr, however, never based any of his stories on *The Plot Genie*. He did not mind taking ideas from elsewhere as long as he could do something original with them. For example, he adapted a method of fiddling with footprints from "The Sandy Peninsula Footprint Mystery" in *The Baffle Book* (1928) and used it in his novel *The White Priory Murders*.[12] But Carr had no trouble thinking up plot complications, and that's all that *The Plot Genie* provided. On the other hand, *The Plot Genie* could be used for marvelous party games; Clarice remembers:

> Lots of us would sit around and use the book to find the bones of a
> story. We'd either write our own or add to what had been suggested.
> It was a fantastic book, and some of the story plots that came out
> from guests and family members really would have been bases for a
> mystery novel.

Carr had been fascinated by table tapping, Ouija boards, and other spiritualistic phenomena and paraphernalia since the Uniontown days when he had written about Conan Doyle's lectures on the occult. Carr based his college story "The Ends of Justice" and his first Sir Henry Merrivale book, *The Plague Court Murders,* on fake spiritualists. He always professed himself skeptical about such matters, but he enjoyed spiritualist sessions at parties at Kingswood and elsewhere, and others who attended them report that he became absorbed in the attempt to contact the spirits. On one occasion in Kingswood, the table at which the Carrs and their closest Bristol friends, Garnet and Cynthia Fuge, were sitting began to make tapping sounds; then it turned and twisted. (This tale has now grown to the point that it has been asserted that the table became so enthusiastic that it chased one of the participants about the room, followed him onto a couch, and tapped the poor subject three times on his chest.) Like Houdini, whom Carr was reading at the time, John and Clarice set up a code by which one would contact the other after death, although they were less serious about it than the great magician. The living would spell out "Ouija, Ouija," and the spirit would respond with a code word. Clarice, however, has said she is too skeptical of such matters to attempt to make contact with the spirit realm.[13]

In addition to putting on parties, John and Clarice sometimes took vacations to celebrate the completion of a book. They spent one Christmas in Scotland, and they often took long weekends touring England, visiting castles and staying in small villages. They particularly enjoyed the Wiltshire village of Castle Combe just across the border from Gloucestershire. Accompanied by Clarice's mother, they also visited Wales several times, staying at the boardinghouse of a Mrs. Thomas, at Cold Knap Bay, near Barry in Glamorganshire. It was off the pebble beach at Cold Knap Bay in July 1935 that John almost drowned. An excellent swimmer, he had been warned to avoid dangerous currents by swimming parallel to the shore, but he set straight off toward the channel dividing Wales from the Gloucestershire coast. When John failed to return to the beach, Clarice and her mother became anxious, but he eventually staggered back, exhausted, and gasping, "I didn't think I was going to make it." This was one time he didn't find it necessary to dramatize an event.[14]

As sales of John's books increased during the 1930s, he and Clarice took more elaborate vacations. In September 1936, they went to Italy and Paris. In October of the next year, they vacationed on the Continent for a week, and John took Clarice on the Rhine trip that he had taken with O'Neil Kennedy seven years earlier. Their most extensive trip, however, was in September 1938 when they went on a Mediterranean cruise. They stopped at Marseilles and at the Isle of Capri to see the Blue Grotto. They went ashore at Naples and saw Herculaneum and Pompeii—in a bit of 1930s sexism, John was allowed to see the bawdy wall paintings in one of the buildings, but the guide refused to allow Clarice to enter. They then traveled north to Rome. They were back on shipboard when Adolf Hitler and Neville Chamberlain met at Munich to negotiate a treaty that would, Chamberlain was certain, bring "peace in our time." When the Carrs returned by way of Paris, however, the city was blacked out in expectation of war.[15]

After his marriage, almost all of Carr's detective novels of the 1930s feature English sleuths. Rather than trying to cover each book as he wrote it, it will be clearer if we look at the first five Carr (or Carter) Dickson volumes before going to the early Dr. Fell novels in the next chapter.

Instead of the shuddery atmospheric language of the Bencolin books, *The Bowstring Murders* begins:

> In the library at Bowstring, there is still a tall clock about which visitors are told a story. The clock is of German manufacture, and a round, smiling, yellow face used to revolve about the dial as the hours were struck. Moreover, there used to be a complicated series of chimes, and a mellow ticking; but the face ceased to turn, and the chimes to strike, on a certain night about two years ago. Not only did it mark the hours for Lord Rayle's death, but in a sense it watched over him after death—which is the reason why it is broken now. If you are a favored visitor, they may show you the bullet-holes, though the blood has been washed off long ago.

This type of opening, as though a storyteller is standing before a fire, with the cigars lighted and the port at hand, goes back to "The New Canterbury Tales," published in *The Haverfordian*, and it would become one of Carr's favorite ways of beginning a novel during the 1930s.

Like *Poison in Jest*, *The Bowstring Murders* features a detective who might have become a series sleuth but who appeared in no other book, and in both stories the detective is the most interesting part of a novel that is otherwise badly flawed. All of Carr's detectives enjoy drinking, and some of his secondary characters wander tipsily through the novels, but John Gaunt of *The Bowstring Murders* is Carr's only constantly drunk detective. Gaunt's wife died, and that tragedy has turned him into a heavy drinker. (Why Carr chose to name him after John of Gaunt, the powerful son of the fourteenth-century King Edward III, is not known.)

Several influences lay behind John Gaunt. Physically, he looks rather like Bencolin, and he has some of his theatricality and arrogance: "I knew who the murderer was," he says, "before I had been in this house an hour."[16] It may have been these Bencolin traits that made him in Carr's eyes unsatisfactory as a possible series sleuth. He differs, however, from Bencolin in that there is an air of romantic melancholy about him. He is a figure out of a romance: tall, with a short beard, "like a picture of a Cavalier." "A burnt-out man, you would have said, yet still ringed with danger; a throwback to more perilous days—polite, quiet, deadly, with a flavor of the college cloisters about him, and half asleep." One of the characters sees Gaunt at a distance walking near the ocean, "his moustache and tuft of whisker, his rakish slouch hat, and his billowing cloak. With the darkling sea to the westward, he was a royalist figure out of the Cromwellian wars—breastplate and scarlet-ribbon, beside the haunted pool where the slain cavaliers lay." The description of Gaunt as a Cavalier almost makes him D'Artagnan-as-detective, but an aging, world-weary D'Artagnan.[17]

In deductive methods, John Gaunt is Holmesian. In a scene modeled directly on Sherlock Holmes and his brother Mycroft, Gaunt makes deductions while gazing from a window at Bowstring. Like all of Carr's detectives Gaunt relies on imagination rather than science, and he objects to lie-detector tests, word associations and other modern tricks. His opposite is Inspector Tape of the local police, who brags about being a practical man. But as far as Carr was concerned, being practical does not solve murders—or, to be more precise, Carr's murders have little to do with practicality, either in execution or solution. Gaunt tells one of the characters, Frank Steyne, "You have imagination, and sympathy, and insight; you have the stuff great things are made of, and you think it's weakness."[18]

John Gaunt is sharply drawn, but the plot of *The Bowstring Murders* is unconvincing. Carr seems ready to develop a supernatural atmosphere in the novel. An empty suit of armor has apparently walked about Bowstring Castle, stolen a crossbow string and a mailed glove, and committed a murder with them. But the author does not do much with those intriguing suggestions, and the supernatural aspect simply fades away. The murder of Lord Rayle is a seemingly miraculous crime; Rayle goes into an empty room and although no one else enters or leaves and the doors are under constant observation, he is found a short while later strangled with the missing bowstring. After one character describes the impossibility of the situation, Carr adds a line that will become typical: "And, as later events proved, Tairlaine spoke the absolute truth."[19] Unfortunately, the explanation of the murder can be called, if you are generous, a creative variation of the solution in *It Walks By Night;* if you are not so generous, it is fair to say it is a bit of self-plagiarism.

The impression given by *The Bowstring Murders* is that Carr, faced with having to write a book at almost a moment's notice to get money for his move to England, chose a number of ideas and images that he had already used in other contexts, or hoped to use later, and attempted to fuse them. The solution to the watched-room problem is only one example of his borrowing from earlier works. Lord Rayle and strangulation by a bowstring are mentioned in entirely different contexts in *The Lost Gallows.* Another plot device that appears in *The Bowstring Murders* and elsewhere is the house near a waterfall. The sound of the falling water next to Bowstring Castle helps to conceal the murderer's actions, but Carr may have had a more elaborate idea in mind connected with this concept. At the beginning of *Death-Watch* (1935), one of Dr. Fell's unrecorded cases is mentioned: "the still more curious problem of the inverted room at Waterfall Manor." I confess that I am not sure exactly what this coincidence of waterfalls means, except that it further suggests that *The Bowstring Murders* is a collection of undeveloped ideas.

Carr took the names of two of the major characters in *The Bowstring Murders,* Dr. Michael Tairlaine and Sir George Anstruther, from his preparatory school and college writings—Tairlaine from "The Harp of Tairlaine" and Anstruther from "The Devil-Gun." We perhaps should not make too much of this, for Carr liked the names of the people in his apprentice work so well that he reused several of them in various books of the early and middle 1930s. For example, Von Arnheim of the *Haverfordian* stories "'And Drink the Dead . . .'" and "The New Canterbury Tales" lent his name (but not his personality) to the head of the Berlin police in *Castle Skull.* Julian Arbor of "The Shadow of the Goat" would become Julius Arbor of *The Mad Hatter Mystery* (1933); Roger Darworth of "The Ends of Justice" would be murdered a second time in *The Plague Court Murders* (1934) and Ken Blake of "The Gordon Djinn" would narrate that case; Sir Richard Bohun of "That Ye Be Not Judged" (attributed to classmate Ira B. Rutherford) would give his last name to John Bohun of *The White Priory Murders* (1934), and Septimus Depping of "The Fourth Suspect" would reappear in *The Eight of Swords* (1934).

One of the most unexpected things about *The Bowstring Murders* is how many mistakes Carr makes about England. To take two examples of many: The servants in *The Bowstring Murders* all speak a strange sort of Cockney, which is most unlikely for Suffolk, the site of Bowstring Castle; moreover,

Francis Steyne's man, Saunders, does not speak properly to a nobleman. After Lord Rayle is murdered and Steyne takes the title, Saunders does not use the new title—that is, until Carr suddenly remembers that he should have; but Carr was probably too rushed to go back and correct the earlier sections of the story. The novel has one more sign of hurried writing: Unusually for Carr, some sloppy lines appear in *The Bowstring Murders*; for example, "With one gloved hand, he dived behind the body."[20]

A characteristic of Carr's books during the 1930s was the inclusion of antiquarian information that is usually obscure to most readers but that plays an important role in the plot. Carr had done a bit of that, unconvincingly, with ancient Egyptian material in *The Lost Gallows*. His use of lore works much better in *The Bowstring Murders*, which is filled with knowledge of medieval armor and weaponry, and most readers probably found Carr's learning impressive—except, that is, for Dorothy L. Sayers, who pointed out a minor error in describing armor. She sniffed in a review to the doubtless fascinated readers of the *Sunday Times*, "I know that a vambrance is not a kind of armour-plated skirt, but a defence for the forearm."[21]

Carr called *The Bowstring Murders* "a potboiler," but it sold well for Morrow—two printings during the first month of publication, with a sale of about forty-five hundred copies. When the book was published, Carr was astonished to discover that Morrow had not bothered to tell him that they had rejected the "Christopher Street" pen name under which he had submitted the book, and chosen a new one that contradicted the entire idea of having a pseudonym. Morrow published *The Bowstring Murders* under the name of "Carr Dickson," one of the most transparent noms de plume in literary history. Carr, Eugene Saxton of Harpers, and Hamish Hamilton were irate. Thayer Hobson of William Morrow was in London early in 1934, and Carr registered his complaint personally. Hobson wished to follow the success of *The Bowstring Murders* with another book, and Carr was already working on one called *The Plague Court Murders*, but he insisted that a different pseudonym be chosen. Morrow accepted the stipulation as long as the new name were similar to "Carr Dickson," since that author already had found an audience. Carr suggested "Cartwright Dixon," and Hobson agreed. When *The Plague Court Murders* was published in 1934, however, Morrow had made another change, again without informing Carr. The book was attributed to "Carter Dickson," and so was the first British edition of the previous book, *The Bowstring Murders*, published by William Heinemann in August 1934. "I myself wasn't altogether satisfied,"

Carr explained to Hamish Hamilton a short while later, "but if that was the arrangement to which Hobson had persuaded everybody back home, I presumed they knew best."[22] All future Carr volumes published by Morrow and by Heinemann also used the Carter Dickson name.

The Plague Court Murders introduced one of Carr's greatest detectives, Sir Henry Merrivale—known to his friends as H.M., the Old Man, or the Maestro. H.M.'s name was probably taken from "Henry Merivale [sic] Trollope," to whom Michael Sadleir had dedicated his *Trollope: A Commentary,* published in 1927; Carr had a copy of this book in his library. It is also possible that Carr had in mind Sir Henry Marquis, one of several detectives invented by the American writer Melville Davisson Post.[23]

Carr always said that he based Sir Henry Merrivale on his father, and that is partly true in regards to physical appearance. Wooda Carr in his younger days was balding and portly like H.M., and photographs show him occasionally with the corners of his mouth pulled down so that he looked like Carr's description of H.M.—"as though he were smelling a bad breakfast egg." In addition, H.M.'s poker playing and his love of cigars and whiskey, possibly even his profession as a barrister (though H.M. is also a physician), may have been taken from Wooda. Otherwise, however, it is difficult to find Carr's father in H.M. The elder Carr's speech was measured, sonorous, and flowery. Sir Henry Merrivale, his own opinion to the contrary, is wildly undignified. His grammar is atrocious, his dress slovenly, and his cleanest epithets are "Burn me" and "Lord Love a duck." He addresses a jury as "my fatheads"; he describes the prime minister as "Horse-face," the commissioner of police as "old Boko," and an official of the Home Office as "Squiffy." His toasts are "honk, honk" and "here's mud in your eye." Stories later emerged that H.M. was also based on Winston Churchill, but (as Carr himself pointed out) when *The Plague Court Murders* was written, Churchill was in the political wilderness and Carr, who was never really involved in politics, had little interest in Churchill. By the time of World War II, however, as Churchill came to symbolize the dogged, never-say-die character of the English, H.M. did pick up some Churchillian characteristics,[24] and illustrations in magazines made him resemble the great prime minister.

H.M.'s literary origins can be found in Mycroft Holmes. Perhaps because he was inventing new detectives, Carr was thinking a great deal about Sherlock Holmes and the Great Detective tradition during 1933 and 1934. *The Bowstring Murders* has Holmesian references, and in *The Plague*

Court Murders Sir Henry Merrivale is nicknamed Mycroft. A character in *Plague Court* named Johnny Ireton says:

> The most interesting figure in the stories about the hawk-faced gen-
> tleman from Baker Street isn't Sherlock at all; it's his brother Mycroft.
> ... He's the one with as big or bigger deductive hat than S.H., but is
> too lazy to use it; he's big and sluggish and won't move out of his
> chair; he's a big pot in some mysterious department of the govern-
> ment, with a card-index memory, and moves only in his orbit of lodg-
> ings-club-Whitehall. ... I tell you, if our H.M. had a little more
> dignity, and would always remember to put on a necktie, and would
> refrain from humming the words to questionable songs when he
> lumbers through rooms full of lady typists, he wouldn't make a bad
> Mycroft. He's got the brain, my lad; he's got the *brain*.[25]

Like that of Mycroft Holmes, Sir Henry Merrivale's position in the government is somewhat mysterious. During World War I, H.M. was head of
counterespionage operations. Carr liked to give such romantic back-
grounds to his early sleuths; both Henri Bencolin and Gideon Fell served
as spy catchers in the same war. In 1930, when *The Plague Court Murders*
begins, H.M. is head of the Military Intelligence Department, but without
a war "its work is somewhat less dangerous than taking photographs of
the Nelson Monument." Except for references in *The Unicorn Murders, The
Punch and Judy Murders,* and *And So to Murder,* H.M. never seems to do any
work that can be called military intelligence, but in his early cases, he oc-
cupies a room at Whitehall, where he spends much of his time sleeping.
His office has a portrait of Napoleon's spy-chief, Fouché, on the wall, a
whiskey bottle in the safe (labeled "Important State Documents" in five
languages), and a secretary named Lollypop Ffolliot. In practice, he is an
unofficial adviser to Scotland Yard, but he is constantly grousing about
"that reptile," Inspector Masters, who is always trying "to do me in the
eye." H.M. wears a battered top hat and a coat with a moth-eaten collar,
and says on different occasions that they were (a) presents from Queen
Victoria or (b) trophies of victory in the first Grand Prix automobile race in
1903 or (c) the property of the actor Henry Irving. (Later in the series H.M.
replaces the top hat with an even more disreputable panama hat.) Sir
Henry Merrivale thinks it is a compliment to say to a woman, "You're a
nice lookin' nymph. Burn me, you are. I saw a girl in a film the other day,
looked just like you. About the middle of the picture she takes off her

clothes. Maybe you saw it."[26] Probably to emphasize the Great Man's eccentricity, Carr first describes him as a "fighting Socialist," but that lasts for only a few books, and H.M. ends up as Tory as his creator.

Carr later remarked that H.M.'s most obvious characteristic was orneriness, but in the early books even more important was his childlikeness. With Dr. Gideon Fell and Sir Henry Merrivale, Carr invented detectives with characteristics that he had unconvincingly hinted at in the Bencolin novels. Carr admired people who had managed to maintain the sense of wonder and wholehearted enthusiasm of children, but when he had Bencolin drunkenly sing risque songs, the reader could not easily fit that characteristic into the world of the satanic manhunter. Childlikeness fit better with Patrick Rossiter, and it works perfectly (though differently in each case) with Dr. Fell and H.M. Although we shall look at Dr. Fell in the next chapter, a few words on his own childlike nature are relevant here. Dr. Fell is genial and warmhearted, and like a child watching a stage magician he is seldom fooled by the trappings of a trick or by a mask adopted by one of the characters. H.M.'s childlikeness is somewhat different from Dr. Fell's. At least in his first three cases, this characteristic is linked to a threat of danger. He plays games but they are not harmless like the mechanical mice Dr. Fell is fond of. Sir Henry Merrivale enjoys wargames with toy soldiers and cardboard models of ships, and Carr summarizes the dual nature of the early H.M. when he describes him as having a "childlike, deadly brain."

Sir Henry Merrivale describes his method of detecting as "sittin' and thinkin'" or "imaginative common sense." Carr found pure reason cold and ultimately sterile. In H.M.'s fourth case, *The Unicorn Murders*, a French detective explains that he can offer a "logical explanation" to a crime. H.M. responds that Inspector Masters "can give you logical explanations enough to freeze your reason; and the only trouble with 'em is that they're usually wrong." H.M.'s sittin' and thinkin' solves cases by discovering what he calls in *The Red Widow Murders* a "crazy association of ideas"—which is equivalent to Father Brown's discerning the true pattern that a series of events forms.

H.M. contrasts this method, which he says is both human and humane, with "the disease of One Idea." The criminal in *The Red Widow Murders* has "the General's Disease without any army to command, and the Financier's Disease without any industries to manage." The murderer sees himself as Nietzsche's Superman, and this concept, even the philosophical discussion of it, Carr found inhuman. Logic and reason, when not

tempered with imagination and sympathy and even childlikeness, produce ruthlessness. Carr had objected to a blind worship of facts when he
edited *The Haverfordian*, and the criminal in *The Red Widow Murders* takes
that to an extreme: "He'd got accustomed to tellin' so much truth about
everybody else," explains H.M., "that he hadn't any left in himself; and
the poor fool hadn't realized that if all mankind shares a folly or an illusion, and likes to share it even knowin' what it is, then the illusion is much
more valuable and fine a thing than the ass who wants to upset it."
[****The following probably comes too close to revealing a solution, and
readers may want to skip to the next paragraph.] The murderer in *The
Red Widow Murders* is a psychologist, a profession that Carr thought almost as bad (and understood as little) as being a mathematician. The villain wants to produce an ideal state, an ordered state, a state that, as H.M.
points out, is "pretty ruthless."[27]

The first Carter Dickson books were contracted for individually, and
Carr wrote each of them without having any continuations of Sir Henry
Merrivale's adventures in mind. But they sold so well that Morrow asked
for more, and Carr obliged. *The White Priory Murders* was published in December 1934, six months after H.M.'s first case. *The Red Widow Murders*
followed in May 1935, and *The Unicorn Murders* in November. British editions were published between three and seven months after the American. Carr told Hamish Hamilton that he aimed the H.M. books at a more
popular audience than he did the novels under his own name; he explained that Carter Dickson "used hackneyed situations because people
liked them."[28] At the time, Carr was trying to assure Hamilton that the
books he was writing for Harpers and Hamilton were much better than
those he was doing for Morrow and Heinemann. We may therefore dis-
count the word "hackneyed," but it is likely that Carr meant that H.M.'s
cases were each based on a single situation that had become traditional in sensational fiction—the locked room in *The Plague Court Murders*, the body-in-a-house-surrounded-by-unmarked-snow in *The White
Priory Murders*, the-room-that-kills-anyone-who-stays-in-it in *The Red
Widow Murders*, and the contest between French sleuth and French super-
criminal in *The Unicorn Murders*.

This is not to say that the stories are any simpler than the Dr. Fell novels
being written at the same time; the twists and turns, the redirecting of
suspicion are as complex as anything in the Dr. Fell saga. But in addition
to the question of whodunit, the early Carter Dickson books focus clearly
on one problem, not on a multitude of them. In order to take this single

problem and structure a novel around it, however, Carr sometimes added an unnecessary complication that weakens the solution. In *The Plague Court Murders*, for example, the murderer commits a second killing and dresses the corpse in a certain way so that an observer will misidentify it, but he does nothing to ensure that the observer will be present at the crucial moment. In *The Red Widow Murders*, an unfair red herring is introduced when a woman testifies about the guilty actions of another suspect. It turns out that the other suspect had done nothing incriminating, but that the witness had been hypnotized into giving a false story. Carr's skill at constructing his plots, however, was so great that it takes several readings to recognize these weaknesses.

Readers familiar with all twenty-two Sir Henry Merrivale novels are apt to regard him as one of the greatest of comic detectives, whose antics frequently descend to (or rise to) slapstick. But he does not start out that way in *The Plague Court Murders*. In that novel and the other early volumes of his casebook, the humor is in H.M.'s language and in his occasional tantrums; he rarely *does* anything funny, and there is nothing comic about the mystery. The atmosphere in *The Plague Court Murders* is so thick and the creepiness so pervasive that I wouldn't be surprised if evidence were to emerge that parts of it had been written a couple of years earlier as a case for Henri Bencolin. Plague Court itself is described in language straight out of the gothic novel:

> It had almost a senile appearance, as of a brain gone, but its heavy cornices were carved with horrible gaiety in cupids and roses and grapes: a wreath on the head of an idiot. . . . In the vast fireplace burnt a very small and smoky fire. Strung along the hood of the mantelpiece were half a dozen candles burning in tall brass holders. They flickered in the damp, showing above the mantelpiece, decaying fragments of wallpaper that had once been purple and gold. There were two occupants of the room—both women. It added a sort of witch-like eeriness to the place.[29]

The Plague Court Murders is a story of the past being repeated in the present. During the final outbreak of the bubonic plague in London in 1665, a hangman's assistant named Louis Playge had killed plague-bearing rats with his awl-shaped knife, but when he himself caught the disease, no one would let him enter his family home, Plague Court. He died and was buried in the grounds. Does his ghost, however, still try to enter Plague Court? Much of this ancient background is revealed through quotations from a contemporary diary. Carr had a fine ear for the speech patterns of past ages, and "The Plague-Journal" reads as though it could have been written during the reign of Charles II. In *The Plague Court Murders*, Carr created a historical romance within the larger framework of a detective story. Most of the story occurs in 1930 when a medium named Roger Darworth plans to exorcise Louis Playge's ghost from Plague Court. But Darworth is found murdered in a locked outbuilding, the wounds having the shape of Louis Playge's knife.

The story is told by an Englishman, Kenwood Blake, but he is merely an observer, having little to do with the events except to point out how mysterious they are. To help investigate the spiritualist, Blake brings in his friend Detective Inspector Humphrey Masters, cynical and unruffled, a bit portly, his hair carefully brushed to hide the bald spot. Carr describes him as a "ghost-breaker" whose hobby is the unmasking of fraudulent spiritualists. He so dominates the early portions of the book that the William Morrow company emphasized him in its advertising blurb, and the first paperback edition (Avon, 1941) described the novel on the front cover as "A Chief Inspector Masters Mystery"; neither publisher mentioned Sir Henry Merrivale. Nevertheless, the reader who expects Masters's stolid common sense to overcome all terrors instead finds that the inspector's knowledge of mediumistic tricks is insufficient. Enter Sir Henry Merrivale, whose common sense is of the imaginative, not the stolid variety. He is without pretensions and without affectations. "His presence," as Carr says in a later H.M. novel, "was sanity and reassurance."[30] H.M.'s earthiness and his bawdiness contrast effectively, on the one hand, with the terror of apparently supernatural death and, on the other, with the unimaginative straightforward approach of Inspector Masters. Masters, whose interest in fake spiritualists is soon to be forgotten, will appear in about thirteen more of H.M.'s cases, mostly as a foil to the Great Man.[31]

The motif of adventure in what Carr called "The Grand Manner" pervades most of his books of the 1930s. The early influence of Poe had not disappeared, and never would from Carr's stories, but it became less important than the influence of Robert Louis Stevenson, particularly his book *New Arabian Nights*. Stevenson's theme was taken from the Arabian Nights tales about Caliph Haroun al-Raschid, who at night went disguised through Baghdad seeking adventures. In *New Arabian Nights*, Prince Florizel of Bohemia wanders through London finding exotic and romantic adventures in "Baghdad-on-the-Thames." Carr presented a *New*

Arabian Nights world in his books. Romance and adventure were waiting to be found in England and, in *The Unicorn Murders*, in France. The world may look commonplace on the surface, but underneath lies the realm of romance. "The Bowstring affair," recalls Dr. Michael Tairlaine in *The Red Widow Murders*, "had convinced [me] that the prosaic world had queer, terrifying holes in it."[32]

Carr's heroes during this period are usually young American visitors to England or the Continent; less commonly, they are middle-aged Americans or young Englishmen. But all of them represent John Dickson Carr in one form or another: Tad Rampole and Ken Blake are in many ways Carr himself, while the middle-aged heroes, Professors Tairlaine and Melson, express Carr's scholarly and antiquarian interests. In any event, each of them longs to escape from his unexciting life, and each finds adventure that is as fantastic as anything in *New Arabian Nights*. The most obvious example is Michael Tairlaine, who at the beginning of *The Bowstring Murders* laments that he has grown old without ever having had any adventures. His friend asks, "What do you mean by 'adventures' anyway? Do you mean in the grand manner? A slant-eyed adventuress, sables and all, who suddenly slips into this [railway] compartment, whispers, 'Six of diamonds—north tower at midnight—beware of Orloff!'" Tairlaine replies seriously, "Yes, I suppose I did mean something like that." All of the early Carter Dickson books contain similar scenes. At the opening of *The Plague Court Murders*, Dean Halliday invites Ken Blake to spend a night in a haunted house, and Ken tries "to conceal the fact that my boredom had begun to disappear; I felt an anticipatory pleasure." H.M.'s nephew, James Bennett, who is the protagonist of *The White Priory Murders*, is a sort of diplomat, but like Tairlaine and Blake, he is bored. "All I ever do," he complains, "is shake cocktails for visiting celebrities to my father's department; or else carry messages full of platitudes from the old man to the Foreign Offices of smaller governments."[33]

The connection with *New Arabian Nights* is made explicit in *The Red Widow Murders*, which (like *The Bowstring Murders*) features Dr. Michael Tairlaine. The book begins with Tairlaine, fifty years old and a distinguished professor of English, setting out to a London rendezvous with youthful excitement. He is "as hopeful as a boy playing pirate. Hopeful— it might be as well to ask himself—of what? Of adventure tapping his arm in a London mist, a shadow on a blind, a voice, a veiled woman? They did not, he thought in his muddled, kindly way, wear veils nowadays." Tairlaine's friend, Sir George Anstruther, tells him that, if he wants an adventure like the one they had shared at Bowstring, he should follow instructions to be walking along a certain street at a certain time that night, and be on the lookout "for any sort of queer thing." Tairlaine obeys, thinking of *New Arabian Nights*: "Goblin or Caliph—or what, in this muffled street where the faint hoot of a motor-horn, from the direction of Berkeley Square, came as a surprise?" A servant comes out of a house and invites him to join a gathering. Tairlaine, fully in a romantic mood, asks whether his host is Haroun al-Raschid, and a short while later the host laughingly identifies himself as Prince Florizel of Bohemia. The story centers on the selection of someone to spend a night in the Red Widow's room, where unexplained deaths have occurred in past generations. The choice is made by drawing cards, the same method used in "The Suicide Club" of *New Arabian Nights*. Tairlaine regrets that John Gaunt is not there to solve the problem, but mention is made of Gaunt's admiration of Sir Henry Merrivale.

The Unicorn Murders also emphasizes adventure in the Grand Manner, and it shows Carr's ability at juggling a fantastic series of events and suspects. The story's setting is France, and though Carr had not been there since 1930, he did not forget details and impressions:

> The mist and expectancy veiled a flat land out of which I conjured all France. Why, when you try to think of a country, must there come thronging into your head only scraps of images like a whirling carrousel? Can you build a picture from colored awnings and the beat of a slow tango-tune; from a Punch-and-Judy show on the Champs Elysees, and the firefly lights against a red sunset; from a rattle of hoofs in the street at morning, and a raucous voice crying, "Haricot verts" when you are trying to sleep; from bright eyes in a window, and the apple-blossoms of Asnieres?[34]

The novel opens with Ken Blake (who had narrated *The Plague Court Murders*) sitting at a Paris café. He had served under Sir Henry Merrivale in counterintelligence during the Great War but now is doing nothing. Evelyn Cheyne, who "in appearance . . . is the sort of thing the battalion thinks about when it is coming back from the line after three weeks under fire," suddenly shows up and quotes the opening lines of the nursery rhyme about "The Lion and the Unicorn." When she pauses, Ken courteously completes it. He has thereby inadvertently given the password identifying himself as her secret-service contact. Although he knows that he should explain that it was a mistake, the thrill of adventure is in him, and he stays silent.

The two of them discuss the great duel going on between Gasquet of the Sûreté and the picturesque thief Flamande. Carr had in mind the French love of theatrical criminals, especially Maurice LeBlanc's insouciant Arsène Lupin (who is mentioned in *The Unicorn Murders*), but an even more obvious model is the contest between Aristide Valentin and the criminal Flambeau in Chesterton's early Father Brown stories. Gasquet is based on Bencolin: "They call him 'the grinning Gasquet.' He's the sort who collars a murderer with an epigram and bows politely before he fires." Flamande, a master of disguises, challenges Gasquet to stop him from stealing something called the "Unicorn." Already a man has died with a wound in the head like that which might be inflicted by a unicorn's horn.

Evelyn and Ken set out for a rendezvous with Sir George Ramsden, a typical British amateur diplomat of fiction, who is carrying the Unicorn. Again, the theme is adventure for its own sake. Evelyn says:

> "If I didn't have that feeling . . . can't help it . . . that it's much more horribly dangerous than we ever thought . . . well, I could enjoy all this enormously. Here we go a-whizzing, nobody knows where or why or when we'll get back,"—she made a pleased gesture—"on a dark road to dark things, you see?"[35]

Our two protagonists certainly have adventures, but they are more like a comedy of errors than adventure in the Grand Manner. Ken first assaults the member of the Intelligence Department who was Evelyn's real contact; Evelyn then steals his identification card and hits him over the head with his own gun. They insult the French police and drive into a swollen river in an attempt to elude the police car following them. The occupant of the car turns out to be Sir Henry Merrivale. H.M. is insulted because Old Squiffy at the Home Office would not let him participate in the Unicorn business, so he has set out to France on his own, promising to arrest Flamande. Ken confesses to H.M. what he has done, but Evelyn is not outraged at his replacing the real secret-service man: "On the contrary, she [is] almost jubilant."

The rising river strands H.M. and the two by-now-in-love young people on an island. A plane carrying Ramsden and, probably, the diguised Gasquet and the disguised Flamande among its passengers is forced to land nearby, and all of them take refuge in the Comte d'Andrieu's chateau. There, Ken and Evelyn are faced with a problem of identities. Who is the thief and who is the policeman? Each time we think we know the answer, Carr upsets the applecart, and it reaches the point that we wonder whether Flamande is pretending to be Gasquet who is pretending to be someone else. *The Unicorn Murders* is a masterly performance in narration: Even though Carr twists the plot at the end of almost every chapter, he keeps the events clear to the reader. Eventually one of the characters is murdered with no one near him; his forehead is pierced by a hole apparently made by an invisible unicorn. In a climactic scene the secret-service officer who was insulted much earlier in the book shows up and charges Ken Blake with being Flamande. But there are yet more twists in store before the story ends with H.M.'s "sittin' and thinkin'" being victorious over Gasquet's logic. And—having announced that there is no use for a virgin except to trap a unicorn—Evelyn goes off with Ken.

After the United States publication of *The Unicorn Murders* in November 1935, Sir Henry Merrivale's career almost came to an end. On several occasions between 1933 and 1936, Harper & Brothers and Hamish Hamilton had objected to the continuing use of the name Carter Dickson as conflicting with their interests. Carr's argument that he needed the income from both names seemed to end in July 1935, when he signed a new contract with Harpers and Hamilton for three books to be published during twelve months beginning autumn 1936, for which he would be guaranteed an income of $291 each month. This replaced an earlier contract for two novels that had produced a monthly income of only one hundred dollars.[36] Having to write three novels under his own name, especially since one was to be between one hundred thousand and one hundred twenty-five thousand words in length, would make it difficult to do any Carter Dickson books. He told Morrow that his life as Carter Dickson was over, but he neglected to inform Hamilton or Eugene Saxton.

In November 1935, however, the fat began to sizzle. Heinemann released the British edition of *The Red Widow Murders* exactly one month after the publication of a Dr. Fell novel under Carr's own name. Hamilton reminded Carr that he had promised to invent a new pseudonym. The situation had become worse because Milward Kennedy, who had replaced Sayers as reviewer for the *Sunday Times,* suggested in print that he suspected a relationship between Carr and Dickson. Hamilton complained that soon Hamilton and Heinemann would be competing with each other for the Carr market.[37]

Carr himself was worried that sales of books under the Carr name might be damaged, and he was furious that Kennedy had dared speculate on the author behind the pseudonym. Carr told Hamilton that "Carter Dickson slid along without ever being connected with me"—although it's difficult to believe that no one other than Kennedy had noticed the similarity in writing style, some plot elements, and the names of the authors. Belatedly, Carr wrote to his British publisher that he had decided in July not to do any more Carter Dickson books.[38]

Morrow, however, was not willing to let one of its most successful authors go, and after several years of contracts weighted heavily in their favor, they decided in May 1936 to make Carr an attractive offer. Morrow would purchase only American rights, and Heinemann would contract separately for British rights. If Carr would guarantee them two books a year, the two publishers would together pay him somewhat more than 50 pounds, or $250, each month.[39] Together with the Harpers/Hamilton agreement, this meant Carr would be making between $500 and $600 every month, a considerable sum during the Depression. Not surprisingly, he signed the contracts and set to work on H.M.'s next case. Once again, Carr neglected to tell Harpers or Hamilton what he was doing, and the first word they received was Heinemann's announcement in *Publishers Circular* in July 1936 that a new Carter Dickson book was forthcoming. Hamilton objected again; Carr apologized but said that he could not turn down Morrow's offer; Hamilton agreed that the "offer can't be sniffed at" but a bit forlornly again suggested that a different pseudonym be used; Carr replied reasonably that neither Morrow nor Heinemann would like to start afresh with a new name.[40] From that point on, there was no question that Carr was established under two names.

Chapter 6

FELL CRIMES AND MORE MERRIVALE MURDERS

He was very stout, and walked, as a rule, with two canes. Against the light from the front windows his big mop of dark hair, streaked with a white plume, waved like a war-banner.... His face was large and round and ruddy, and had a twitching smile somewhere above several chins. But what you noticed there was the twinkle in his eye. He wore glasses on a broad black ribbon, and the small eyes twinkled over them as he bent his big head forward; he could be fiercely combative or slyly chuckling, and somehow he contrived to be both at the same time.

With these words, John Dickson Carr introduced Dr. Gideon Fell in his first case, *Hag's Nook,* written in the autumn of 1932, shortly before John and Clarice moved to England. Dr. Fell is modeled on Carr's literary idol, G. K. Chesterton. Not only his appearance, but also his speech patterns are drawn from Chesterton. Both Dr. Fell and Father Brown speak in paradoxes. "Everything is right," says the chief constable. "Yes," Dr. Fell answers. "Yes. That's what makes it wrong, you see." Like Father Brown (and Bencolin and H. M.), Dr. Fell seldom looks for physical evidence and instead finds the solution by what he calls "wool-gathering" or, more formally, "sufficient reflection," [1] a procedure that is identical with H.M.'s sittin' and thinkin'.

Dr. Fell, also like Chesterton, speaks in the formal language that we attribute to Dr. Samuel Johnson, with an occasional descent into slang. In *Hag's Nook,* his interjections are "O Lord! O Bacchus. O my ancient hat." Soon, Dr. Fell will add his famous phrase, "Archons of Athens!" It may be the Johnsonian connection that led Carr to call Dr. Fell a "lexicographer" in *Hag's Nook* even though he never does any dictionary making. Dr. Fell is in fact a historian who has lectured at Haverford College, where he taught the students to sing "the Drinking Song of Godfrey of Bouillon on the First Crusade in 1187," before his performance was interrupted by "a maniacal professor of mathematics . . . with his hands entangled in his hair." A lover of English beer—he objects to the word "ale"—Dr. Fell is working on a definitive study, *The Drinking Customs of England from the Earliest Days* (which would be fictionally published in 1946 by a firm with the murderous name of Crippen & Wainwright), and Carr would credit him with two other books, *Romances of the Seventeenth Century*[2] and an untitled study of the supernatural in English fiction. He loves to lecture on any topic that interests him, and sometimes it seems that nothing is beyond his curiosity—except, needless to say, mathematics and economics. In *Hag's Nook,* the discovery of clues hidden in an ancient verse leads him to lecture on cryptograms, but when he tries to solve it himself he finds only the word "drafghk." In one of the few instances in which Dr. Fell is ever bested, the main female character in the book, Dorothy Starberth, finds the key to the meaning of the verse.

Carr never recorded whether he took his detective's name from Dr. John Fell, Bishop of Oxford under King Charles II, or, more probably, whether he had the name first and then noticed the similarity to the bishop's. Besides the last name, Dr. Gideon Fell has nothing in common with the Restoration churchman, who was a thin, almost wasted man not famed for his sense of humor. He would be forgotten now were it not for a famous incident in which he demanded that Thomas Browne translate on the spot the famous Latin epigram of Martial beginning "Non amo te, Sabidi." Browne rendered it as:

> *I do not love thee, Dr. Fell.*
> *The reason why I cannot tell.*
> *But this I know and know full well,*
> *I do not love thee, Dr. Fell.*

Much of Carr's leisure reading at the time was on the Restoration period of British history—throughout his life he was fascinated by the character of Charles II—and he could have found the reference to Dr. John Fell in several sources. But it seems almost an afterthought toward the end of *Hag's Nook* that he quotes the opening line of Browne's verse.

Hag's Nook's plot, the atmosphere, the narrative flow, and the characters are all clearly developed and carefully integrated. The story opens with a feeling of the anglophilic warmth developed during Carr's visits to England in 1926 and 1930:

> There is something spectral about the deep and drowsy beauty of the English countryside; in the lush dark grass, the evergreens, the grey church-spire and the meandering white road. . . . Tad Rampole watched the sun through the latticed windows, and the dull red berries glistening in the yew tree, with a feeling which can haunt the traveller in the British Isles. A feeling that the earth is old and enchanted; a sense of reality conjured up by that one word "merrie." For France changes, like a fashion, and seems no older than last season's hat. In Germany even the legends have a bustling clockwork freshness, like a walking toy from Nuremberg. But this English earth seems (incredibly) even older than its ivy-bearded towers. The bells at twilight seem to be bells across the centuries; there is a great stillness, through which ghosts step, and Robin Hood has not strayed from it even yet.

Hag's Nook is told from the viewpoint of Tad Rampole, who like Jeff Marle is an American visitor to the Old World and who represents Carr's views. He is "just out of college, and he [is], therefore, desperately afraid of being thought provincial." On his way to visit Dr. Gideon Fell and his wife in Chatterham, Lincolnshire, he meets Dorothy Starberth. They travel together by train, and, just as Carr himself did with Clarice Cleaves on board the *Pennland,* Rampole falls immediately in love with Dorothy. Like the early Sir Henry Merrivale cases, *Hag's Nook* implies that events of the far-off past influence the present, that modern crimes imitate ancient ones. Dr. Fell tells Rampole that for more than a century the Starberths have died of broken necks, their bodies found near a spot called Hag's Nook. Generations earlier, Anthony Starberth was governor of a prison built near a "nook" where once witches had been hanged. Beneath his balcony is a well where bodies of the condemned were thrown. Fell gives Rampole transcripts of a diary, which indicates either that Starberth was haunted by ghosts of executed criminals—or that he was gradually becoming mad. He was found dead beneath the balcony, with his neck broken, and so were two later Starberths. Whenever a new Starberth inherits, he must spend a night in the governor's old room, obeying secret instructions once he is there.

Dorothy Starberth's brother, Martin, must go through the family ritual the night of Rampole's arrival. Rampole, the village rector, and the chief constable plan to watch with Dr. Fell at Yew Cottage. When Martin's lantern ceases being visible from the prison, they rush over and find him lying dead beneath the balcony, his neck broken. Carr expertly creates the atmosphere of unknown terror, of a curse that repeats itself, and he contrasts the fear of the supernatural with mellow descriptions of Dr. Fell's cottage and the drowsiness of the English countryside.

Dr. Fell and the chief constable assume that Martin's death is from human causes, but Dorothy Starberth points out that human agents might be worse than ghosts:

> It's either—We can't help ourselves; we're haunted; we're damned, all of us, in the blood; retribution; I never believed it, I won't believe it; or else . . . maybe it's both. How do we know what's in a person's blood? Yours or mine or anybody's? There may be a murderer's blood just as well as a ghost.[3]

Is supernatural haunting or hereditary madness more to be feared? For Carr, it is human evil, not the supernatural, that is the greater terror, and sometimes the solutions in which he finds human causes for the events are more unsettling than if he had brought in genuine ghosts.

If *Hag's Nook* had been a Bencolin novel, the conclusion would have revealed the madness that Dorothy Starberth feared, but the murderer turns out not to have been mad, merely merciless. The villain's identity is surprising because of the role he plays in the story, and even more because he seems to have a perfect alibi. When he leaves a letter confessing to the crime, however, we see not only that the murder was possible for him, but also that there were clues to his real character throughout the book. This is the kind of man, we realize, who would have committed such a crime and for such a motive. The ending is powerful: Given the opportunity by Dr. Fell to commit suicide, the murderer does not have the courage to turn the gun on himself.

Not only is the murderer's personality excellently drawn, but *Hag's Nook* has several other memorable characters. The most affectionately described is the Starberths' butler, Budge. He is meant to be an amusing character, with his fear that housemaids would leave windows open and his tolerance of the housekeeper's worries that the estate would "Get Took by Americans." Carr had been reading P. G. Wodehouse, and some of the great humorist's attitude toward servants crept in. But Budge's character is touched with nobility. Like Carr himself, Budge is addicted to movies featuring dashing heroes. On his way home from visiting friends, he lets his imagination roam:

> The sky had cleared, pale and polished and gleaming, and there was
> a bright moon. Over the lowlands hung a faint smokiness, and the
> moist air smell of hay. On such a night the soul of Mr. Budge became
> the soul of D'Artagnan Robin Hood Fairbanks Budge, the warrior,
> the adventurer, the moustache-twister—even, in mad moments,
> Budge the great lover. His soul was a balloon, a captive balloon, but
> still a balloon. He liked these long walks, where the stars were not
> merry at the antics of the other Budge; where a man could take a sav-
> age pass at a hayrick with an imaginary sword, and no housemaid
> the wiser.[4]

We see in this picture the adolescent John Dickson Carr. Budge's swash-buckling fantasy becomes real when he bravely confronts the murderer. "Budge, fat and past fifty, felt a great pain in his lungs. He did not drop behind the tree. He knew what he had to do; he was solid, with a quiet brain and a very clear eye. 'All right,' he said aloud. 'All right!' and dived for the other man." Budge is wounded, but he has proven what he was made of. Rampole tells him, "You've got plenty of nerve." And the chief constable gives the highest British praise: "As to what you did, Budge, well I don't mind telling you—well it was damned sporting, you know."

The first Dr. Fell novels have the same emphasis as H.M.'s cases on lifting the veil from the prosaic world and revealing romance, but they have an additional emphasis on incongruity, drawn from Chesterton. It is this sense of oddness—not the grotesquerie of the Bencolin novels—that dominates the six stories that follow *Hag's Nook,* beginning with *The Mad Hatter Mystery,* which was written in London shortly after John and Clarice arrived in England, and published in August 1933. The novel opens:

> It began, like most of Dr. Fell's adventures, in a bar. It dealt with the
> reason why a man was found dead on the steps of Traitors' Gate, at
> the Tower of London, and with the odd headgear of this man in the
> golf suit. That was the worst part of it. The whole case threatened for
> a time to become a nightmare of hats.

These lines are reminiscent of Chesterton's opening to a Father Brown story, "The Queer Feet," which states that there is a mystery why a member of a certain club wears a green overcoat rather than a black one. In Carr's novel, a joker has been stealing hats of prominent citizens and placing them in ridiculous spots—on a cab horse or on lampposts or atop the Nelson statue at Trafalgar Square. But the joke becomes terrifying when the humorist seems "to have created a corpse so that he could have a fitting place to hang his hat." These events become connected with the discovery of an unknown manuscript story by Edgar Allan Poe, a Dupin tale written before "The Murders in the Rue Morgue."

Tad Rampole, having married Dorothy Starberth of *Hag's Nook*, has returned to London to visit Dr. and Mrs. Fell. Dr. Fell is described more broadly than he had been in his first appearance. He calls himself "a childish old fool," and as I pointed out earlier, he is interested in children's things, such as toy mice that run across the table. He looks upon the Mad Hatter affair as a chance not merely to be a detective but, like a small boy, to play at the role. He has learned all he knows of police procedure from the cinema. When he interviews a suspect, he sets the stage with a dummy pistol and fake handcuffs. He describes himself as an "omnivorous reader" of "sensational fiction," but he also seems interested in just about everything else. At a dinner, he discusses "the origin of the Christmas cracker, Sir Richard Steele, merry-go-rounds—on which he particularly enjoyed riding—Beowulf, Buddhism, Thomas Henry Huxley, and Miss Greta Garbo,"[5] and he listens with pleasure to street organs. In short, Carr is developing the image of Dr. Fell as the Great Detective by emphasizing his eccentricities, but these eccentricities are not merely the collection of miscellaneous personality traits that many writers gave their detectives. Dr. Fell's variety of interests all point in one direction—he is without pretense; he is without hypocrisy. He can be interested in toy mice without apologizing, just as he is interested in real-life murder. "There are people before whom you instantly unbend. Dr. Fell was one of them. No constraint could exist before him; he blew it away with a superb puff; and, if you had any affectations, you forgot them immediately."[6]

The Mad Hatter Mystery introduces Chief Inspector David Hadley, who will be a major character in thirteen of the twenty-three Fell novels, and is mentioned in passing in several of the others. The role of Hadley in the Fell cases, like that of Inspector Masters in the H.M. novels, is to contrast with the brilliance of the detective, to ask the right questions, to suggest the wrong solutions, and when necessary to call in the resources of Scotland Yard. Although as the H.M. books continued Carr would tend more and more to present Masters as the stupid foil of the Great Detective, Hadley is clearly intelligent, yet he lacks Fell's childlike, scatterbrained, wool-gathering imagination, which pulls together unrelated facts to find what they mean.

The Mad Hatter Mystery is a good example of an early Fell case. It must be admitted that Hadley's refusal to arrest the murderer at the end of the story is hard to take—at the least it is out of character—but it is consistent with Carr's lifelong emphasis on justice rather than the letter of any rules. The plot is carefully constructed, with many clues to the eventual solution, and the complexities are unraveled layer by layer so that nothing is unclear to the reader; yet the final identity of the murderer comes as a surprise. And the mood of strangeness, of having stepped into a fantastic world, is maintained throughout the book.

On September 24, 1933, Dorothy L. Sayers reviewed *The Mad Hatter Mystery* in the *Sunday Times*. By the end of summer 1933, John Dickson Carr had published eight books to generally favorable reviews, and sales had gradually increased. But he had never received anything like the praise that Sayers bestowed. Carr recalled it seventeen years later as "a whopping, magnificent review."[7] It certainly was:

> If [the opening of the book] is like anybody, it is like G. K. Chesterton. And in the portrait of Dr. Fell himself one may perhaps, without being too personal, trace a certain Chestertonian exuberance of outline. . . . Chestertonian also are the touches of extravagance in character and plot, and the sensitiveness to symbolism, to historical association, to the shapes and colours of material things, to the crazy terror of the incongruous. Mr. Carr can lead us away from the small, artificial, brightly-lit stage of the ordinary detective plot into the menace of outer darkness. He can create atmosphere with an adjective, and make a picture from a wet iron railing, a dusty table, a gaslamp blurred by the fog. He can alarm with an illusion or delight with a rollicking absurdity. He can invent a passage from a lost work of Edgar Allan Poe which sounds like the real thing. In short, he can write—not merely in the negative sense of observing the rules of syntax, but in the sense that every sentence gives a thrill of positive pleasure. This is the most attractive mystery I have read for a long time.[8]

Carr told an interviewer that because of Sayers's review, "I was established overnight."[9] His acceptance by Dorothy L. Sayers (and she did have a sort of imperial attitude about which authors were and were not worthy of approval) meant a critical recognition that was important to his career, and for the next thirty years his publishers continued to quote from Sayers's review on dust jackets and publicity material.

The next two books about Dr. Gideon Fell, *The Eight of Swords* and *The Blind Barber,* are primarily comedies. *The Eight of Swords,** published in February 1934, begins with the bizarre or incongruous events that often open Dr. Fell's cases of this period, but in this instance Carr uses them for comic effect. The Bishop of Mappleham has been caught sliding down banisters, assaulting a chambermaid, and standing on a roof in his nightshirt. These strange activities turn out to be related to the bishop's hobby of criminology. Dr. Fell, himself, is here almost a slapstick version of a detective. He shows up in Hadley's office disguised as Herr Doctor Sigismund von Hornswoggle, and asks "Vot you dream?" After Hadley sees through the disguise, Dr. Fell tells him that he has just returned from America, where he was known as "Gid." While there he became an honorary fire chief, and the newspapers published his photograph sliding down a firepole. He spent the ocean trip back to London trying to construe baseball lingo into Latin.

The focal character of *The Eight of Swords* is Hugh Answell Donovan, the Bishop of Mappleham's son, who is returning from America after spending a year supposedly studying criminology at Columbia University. But, like John when he was supposedly studying at the Sorbonne, Hugh did nothing at the university. Back in England, Hugh resolves to change his life, and he thinks negatively of his wasted year in New York:

> To be shut into a hot apartment with twenty different radio programs roaring in your ear; with every light shaking to the thunder of parties on each floor; with children yelling along Christopher Street, and papers blown in gritty over-hot winds, and the rumble of the Sixth Avenue L rising montonously over the clatter of traffic. Sad. Very sad . . . . Tonight, round Sheridan Square, one poor friend would be measuring out gin drops, with the fierce concentration of a scientist, into a glass jug containing half-a-gallon of alcohol and half-a-gal-

---

*Carr took the title from Chesterton's short story "The Five of Swords" in *The Man Who Knew Too Much* (1922).

lon of water. Others would be thirstily waiting to drink it, poor devils.

In other words, Hugh spent his time in New York in much the same way as John Dickson Carr had done.

Carr then makes fun of his own romantic idealization of England when he has Hugh imagine himself "leaning on his ash stick in the twilight . . . looking with sad eyes at the brook, and musing on the villainy of those who drink alcohol-and-water in cities, and then come out and seduce poor girls all over the countryside, and make them drown themselves in brooks."[10] Hugh's thoughts are interrupted when he comes upon writer Henry Morgan and his wife, Madeleine, who immediately offer him a drink from their cottage, Hangover House. He accepts. An undercurrent—and current is the correct word—is the constant flow of alcohol throughout *The Eight of Swords.* When it is discovered that the murder victim had been a secret drinker, going on a spree in his room every other month, one character says, "Why not? Did him good, *I* say. Made him human."[11]

The character Henry Morgan also represents Carr—not Carr the failed student, but Carr the successful author. Morgan is the creator of John Zed, Diplomatist-Detective, who sleuths his way through such works as *Aconite in the Admiralty, Murder on the Woolsack, Who Shot the Prime Minister,* and *The Inland Revenue Murders.* These books, like Carr's own, are cheerfully improbable, but unlike Carr, Morgan also writes probable and realistic stories under the pseudonym. They of course please the critics, who say (according to Carr) that "you must have (1) no action, (2) no atmosphere whatever—that's very important—(3) as few interesting characters as possible, (4) absolutely no digressions, and (5) above all things, no deduction."[12]

Much of *The Eight of Swords* is a combination of P. G. Wodehouse and the Marx Brothers. Colonel Standish speaks like Wodehouse's exquisite idiots, especially Lord Emsworth of Blandings Castle, and some of the events and other bits of dialogue—for example, some remarks about the Bishop of Mappleham's ample posterior—are worthy of Groucho. Other sections of *The Eight of Swords,* however, sit uncomfortably with the comedy. The victim is found with a card from a deck of taroc (tarot) fortune-telling cards, and Dr. Fell lectures on various ways of telling the future. This occult lore is incongruously connected with yet another element, for the motive of the murder seems to hark back to the victim's gangster years in America. One character even says, "You *dirty* rat," in a colorful shoot-'em-up scene straight out of the pulps. In short, *The Eight of Swords* has too many disparate elements that never manage to come together. But as a puzzle story the novel works well, with one of Carr's most unlikely murderers being revealed at the end. Carr, moreover, includes a comment that summarizes even his weaker books of this period: "Each new development seemed to lead the case in a different direction; and each opened up like a magician's casket, to show only another box inside the last."[13] The final line of the book, however, sums up its most obvious theme: "Let's have a drink."

This bibulousness is taken to extremes in *The Blind Barber*, published in October 1934. It is one of Carr's most controversial novels. On its publication, many reviewers, including Dorothy L. Sayers, praised *The Blind Barber*. In 1962, Anthony Boucher chose the book for the Collier Mystery Classics series of reprints and provided a new introduction saying (among other things) that "death and laughter are old friends." I have defended *The Blind Barber* in print, but I must admit that, although I still find much in the novel to admire, I no longer think that it is one of Carr's best books.

Like *The Mad Hatter Mystery*, *The Blind Barber* has in the first paragraph an intriguing statement of the case: "Although he did not know it, this young man had in his luggage something more valuable than the marionettes of M. Fortinbras or the emerald elephant of Lord Sturton." Otherwise, the novel is a departure for Carr in its structure. For the first time, the detective is not present through most of the narrative. Henry Morgan, who had appeared in *The Eight of Swords*, comes to Dr. Fell's new residence at 1 Adelphi Terrace, London, which is filled with "childish things which, nevertheless, . . . formed a fitting background for his Gargantuan presence." Morgan tells Dr. Fell about the extraordinary events on board the ocean liner *Queen Victoria*. Fell acts as armchair detective; during an interlude in the tale, he lists various clues that Morgan has overlooked, and then at the end he points out more clues and identifies the murderer. The clues are delightfully Carrian, and I cannot resist giving them all:

1. The Clue of Suggestion
2. The Clue of Opportunity
3. The Clue of Fraternal Trust
4. The Clue of Invisibility
5. The Clue of Seven Razors
6. The Clue of Seven Radiograms
7. The Clue of Elimination

8. The Clue of Terse Style
9. The Clue of Wrong Rooms
10. The Clue of Lights
11. The Clue of Personal Taste
12. The Clue of Avoided Explanations
13. The Clue Direct
14. The Clue of Known Doubles
15. The Clue of Misunderstanding
16. The Clue Conclusive

The plot is so convoluted and everything (as Carr says) "so rowdy and topsy-turvy" that I will not even try to summarize the story. But to give the bare outline, Morgan is traveling with a group of tippling passengers, including a Norwegian sea captain named Valvick, who tells hilariously irrelevant stories, a young diplomat who spends much of the book in the brig, and a woman who is "devilish good-looking, and seems prim and stiffish until you realise how much devilment there is in her, or until she's had a few drinks; then she's a glittering holy terror." This group joins forces to try to retrieve a movie of an American politician giving a burlesque political speech in front of "other eminent soaks."[14] More complications arise because another passenger, Lord Sturton, has a famous jewel, the emerald elephant, which is the target for the criminal whose nickname gives the book its title. The elephant briefly ends up in the hands of Morgan and his friends; an unknown woman appears, then disappears; our heroes mistakenly—but continually—assault the captain; in fact, any kind of slapstick affair the four loonies can slosh their way into, they do.

The Blind Barber, however, has problems in its tone. One problem is the belief, which is part of the cinema and stage of the time, that drunkenness is automatically hilarious. The story, admittedly, is genuinely funny in many sections, and even when I thought that an elderly alcoholic in the book was more to be pitied than laughed at, I found myself laughing at him anyway. But, pace Sayers and Boucher, I do not think that the burlesque events sit well with the viciousness of the Blind Barber himself, whose habit is to soften the backs of his victims' skulls so that they do not die but spend the remainder of their lives as morons. Moreover, though the sixteen clues are nicely handled, and the identity of the Barber is well-concealed, events surrounding the disappearance of the unknown woman do not make much sense. She should have been able to identify the Barber as she boarded the ship, but she does not recognize him until later, thus making her a candidate for murder. She has a relative on board but he does not identify her from her description or even worry about her disappearance. Except for these problems, however, the plot (though not the tone) holds together well.

Carr was eager to know the public's response to the broad humor of *The Blind Barber;* it would, he told his British publisher, Hamish Hamilton, "govern, in part, my future detective-story writing." Hamilton wrote to Carr that *The Blind Barber* had excellent reviews, and that sales in Britain were good. About a month after publication, about fifteen hundred copies of the British edition had been sold, and that figure was better, Hamilton said, than sales for a similar period for *The Mad Hatter Mystery* and *The Eight of Swords.* We do not have direct comparisons for United States sales, but six months after publication Eugene Saxton reported sales of 2,715 copies, and that figure was apparently a bit disappointing. In short, there were mixed messages at a time when Carr was deciding what direction his writing should take.

He wanted to write comic novels, and toward the end of 1934 and the beginning of 1935, he thought of the Dr. Fell series as fitting that role; Sir Henry Merrivale was a comic character but the novels that he had so far appeared in were not comedies. Carr remarked that he had received a number of letters telling him "stick to the comedy: it's what they want, and that under all circumstances Captain Valvick and the loony young diplomat must return to another story." On the other hand, some letters urged that he drop Dr. Fell and restore Bencolin. He wrote to Hamilton: "Quien sabe, or whatever the expression is. Damned if I know."[15] In this situation, the equivocal evidence from the sales of *The Blind Barber* gave Carr no direction, and his publisher refused to advise him. Let your own muse decide, he told Carr. Meanwhile, Carr thought that some indication might come from reaction to his next Dr. Fell case, a noncomic novel entitled *Death-Watch,* which he had written in the latter months of 1934 and which would be published in March 1935 by Harper & Brothers, and in April by Hamish Hamilton.

Around 1934 and 1935, the mood of the Bencolin novels kept trying to return in Dr. Fell's and H.M.'s cases. *The Plague Court Murders* was in many ways a Bencolin novel but with Sir Henry Merrivale rather than the satanic French detective. In like manner, *Death-Watch* has Dr. Fell rather than Bencolin but in its claustrophobic atmosphere and the madness of the killer's motive it is closer to *The Corpse in the Waxworks* or to that almost-Bencolin novel *Poison in Jest* than it is to any of the preceding Fell books.

As a puzzle novel, *Death-Watch* is an extraordinary performance, with a convoluted plot and clues leading in many directions. [****Warning: A solution is coming:] As a *fair-play* novel, however, it is annoying in that Dr. Fell clears a suspect in the opening pages who ultimately turns out to be guilty. Since this scene has Fell reminiscing about the case after it has been solved, it goes beyond legitimate mystification. In addition, part of the solution has to do with the murderer moving from one place to another by means of a secret panel. In his next case, recounted in *The Three Coffins*, Dr. Fell says that "I shall not mention the low (and nowadays very rare) trick of having a secret passage to a locked room. This so puts a story beyond the pale that a self-respecting author scarcely needs even to mention that there is no such thing."[16] Although there is no locked room in *Death-Watch*, the secret panel still seems beyond the pale. Moreover, as a story (as opposed to a puzzle) *Death-Watch* is disappointing. It is a novel in which nothing much happens. A murder occurs at the very beginning; then Dr. Fell and Chief Inspector Hadley interview suspects without a break or any action for almost half the book.

Nonetheless, *Death-Watch* has several memorable sections. After an introduction by an unnamed narrator (several clues indicate that he must be Tad Rampole), we are introduced to Professor Melson, an American expert on the England of Charles II, who serves as the viewpoint character—Melson hardly does enough to be called a protagonist. The opening scene is striking both for its horror and for its hints of Baghdad-on-the-Thames. As Melson and Fell watch, a policeman goes up the steps to a nearby house—the home and shop of Johannus Carver, clockmaker—and the door opens on an amazing tableau. A man has been stabbed to death with the minute hand of a clock. The book is filled with details on the history of timekeeping—as well as some less relevant matters. Dr. Fell, for instance, lectures on the Spanish Inquisition, and seems to defend it:

> Regard it as a wrong. But don't regard it as a nightmare. Say the Inquisitors tortured and burned people, as the civil authority did in England. But they were men who believed, however wrongly, in the soul of man, and not a group of half-witted schoolboys maliciously torturing a cat.[17]

Carr's logic is hard to follow but his point seems to be that at least the Inquisitors did not engage in hypocrisy, something that he despised. He did not see the inconsistency in attacking, as he did frequently and often eloquently, modern unitary belief systems (whether Fascist or Socialist) as dehumanizing, while not understanding that older ones could be just as deadly to the soul.

Death-Watch contains some fine set pieces. Dr. Fell lists five points that must be answered to solve the murder, and for almost the first time Carr employs the false-solution-followed-by-the-true that he will use in many later novels. The intellectual razzle-dazzle in those sections is marvelous. And the characters are memorable, though like the setting they might better have suited a Bencolin case. One suspect admits to his plan to kill a stranger so that he can see how someone reacts when faced with his own imminent death. The motive for the successful murder is merely conceit, the product (Fell explains) of a "decaying brain"[18]—much like the brains of the murderers in Bencolin's cases.

In short, *Death-Watch* is an interesting but flawed book. Dorothy L. Sayers's review smugly corrected Carr's Latin—the name should be "Johannes" not "Johannus," she told the readers of the *Sunday Times*—but Sayers also accurately summarized the novel's strengths and weaknesses: "His story may be too complicated, too improbable; but between the dark and the light I am ready to listen to the voice of the enchanter and to the sinister ticking of the 'DEATH-WATCH.'"[19] Carr took Sayers's comments good-humoredly: "I saw, shining through [the review] with strong beams, the fact that Madame my Advocate detested the damn book but refrained from saying so."[20]

One more point about *Death-Watch:* Dr. Fell calls on an old French friend who "used to be associated with Bencolin at the Prefecture in Paris."[21] This statement connects the Bencolin and Fell books—despite their differences, they exist in the same world of Carr's imagination—and confirms what Carr was writing to his British publisher. His mind was on Bencolin and whether he should revive the Mephistophelean French detective.

Early in January 1935, Carr decided that, instead of producing a comic novel, he probably would give Bencolin another try, and a month later he told Hamish Hamilton that he was setting to work on a new Bencolin novel called *Vampire Tower.* "If the old man makes a return," he said, "it must be a triumphant one, and after mulling things over, I believe that I have got the most ingenious plot mechanism of a long time."[22] Carr had been thinking about an illusion involving mirrors that was used in the Maskelyne Mysteries, the famous London magic extravaganza, and he saw how the principle could be adapted into a means of having a murderer disappear from a guarded room. He and a friend in Kingswood had tested angles by moving about a table his statuette of John Wesley and a handbag-mirror, and found that the trick would work. The situation was, he believed, the best he had ever devised, and Bencolin rather than Dr. Fell was clearly the one to solve it. Unlike Sir Henry Merrivale, who was specializing in seemingly impossible crimes, Dr. Fell had not yet been faced with a locked room or similar sort of miracle problem—though several of his cases, especially *Hag's Nook*, could have been written with slight changes as impossible crime novels. Bencolin, however, had solved similar cases in the past, and Carr saw *Vampire Tower* as emphasizing the possibility of the supernatural, much as *It Walks By Night* had done.

But a major problem arose. Although Carr could without difficulty re-create the atmosphere of a Bencolin case, he found it more difficult to re-create Bencolin himself. Already by the fourth Bencolin novel, *The Corpse in the Waxworks*, he had tired of the sadistic personality he had given the Frenchman. He simply could no longer write a book with that sort of man as hero. After completing five chapters of *Vampire Tower*, he decided that

> I cannot resurrect Bencolin! I wanted to bring him back in glory with a fine impossible situation, as with his first appearance. . . . But I can't do anything with the damned detective! He's unreal, he's lifeless, he's a dummy.

If Bencolin were ever to come back to life, Carr would have to change his personality enough that he could deal with him. He threw away the unfinished typescript of *Vampire Tower*, but he did not discard the plot and the Maskelyne gimmick he had devised. Instead, he started the novel anew with Dr. Fell as the sleuth, and he changed the title from *Vampire Tower* to *The Three Coffins*. The book was published under that title by Harper & Brothers in September 1935, and as *The Hollow Man* by Hamish Hamilton in October. Exactly why the title was changed for the British edition is not recorded; Carr's original title summarizes a major part of the mystery and describes the organization of the book (which is divided into three sections, called "Coffins"). *The Hollow Man* also refers to elements within the book, but it is less precise, not even indicating that crime and mystery are involved—the title could as easily be a reference to T. S. Eliot's poem "The Hollow Men." On July 24, 1935, Hamilton was still using the American title in his correspondence, but sometimes during the succeeding week he decided that the British edition should be renamed. Carr suggested *The Hollow Man*, and then went off on his Welsh holiday at

Cold Knap Bay. Hamilton interrupted him there asking for something more effective. Carr's response, if any, is not known, but not until August 20 did Hamilton finally decide on *The Hollow Man*.[23]

In many ways, *The Three Coffins* set the pattern for the Dr. Fell series. In his sixth recorded case, Dr. Fell becomes associated with locked-room murders, so much so that Carr presents him as an expert on their use in fiction. Moreover, the experiment with raucous humor in *The Eight of Swords* and *The Blind Barber* was almost over. With one or two exceptions—especially in *The Case of the Constant Suicides*—Dr. Fell has become a serious detective investigating serious cases; comedy would be left to Sir Henry Merrivale. With its ghostly events and its emphasis on the past's influence on the present, *The Three Coffins* returns to the mood of *Hag's Nook*.

The Three Coffins is a rare example of a detective novel that can be reread with equal or even greater pleasure when the solution is known. Carr begins the book by telling us that it *is* a story; it is a romance, like (Carr thought) all good literature:

> To the murder of Professor Grimaud, and later the equally incredible crime in Cagliostro Street, many fantastic terms could be applied— with reason. . . . Thus: two murders were committed, in such fashion that the murderer must have not only have been invisible, but lighter than air. Again, according to the evidence, he killed his second victim in the middle of an empty street, with watchers at either end; yet not a soul saw him, and no footprint appeared in the snow.

Carr then goes on to warn the reader about whose evidence to accept as factual, "else there is no legitimate mystery and, in fact, no story at all." Carr had done this sort of thing before, most obviously in *The Plague Court Murders*: "It is well to be very careful of what I say," remarks Ken Blake; "not to exaggerate or mislead—at least any more than *we* were misled—so that you may have a fair opportunity to put your wits to work on a puzzle apparently impossible of solution." And he would do it again, for example in a footnote to *The Crooked Hinge*, in which he explains that "the honesty and good faith of Kennet Murray may be accepted as a fact."[24] But only in *The Three Coffins* do his characters themselves frankly explain that they are in a story. In the famous "Locked-Room Lecture," which forms Chapter 17 of *The Three Coffins*, Dr. Fell says, "We're in a detective story, and we don't fool the reader by pretending we're not. Let's not invent elaborate excuses to drag in a discussion of detective stories. Let's candidly glory in the noblest pursuits possible to characters in a book."*

In short, Carr was a teller of tales, and we in our armchairs should not fool ourselves into thinking that the story is real. But Carr believed that in most ways fiction is to be preferred over prosaic reality—the world of the *New Arabian Nights* is better than whatever our senses tell us is real or probable. Dr. Fell makes that point in "The Locked-Room Lecture": "I like some vividness of colour and imagination in my plot, since I cannot find a story enthralling solely on the grounds that it sounds as though it might really have happened."[25] *The Three Coffins* is a most improbable tale, but Carr tells us not to use standards for other (and, he thinks, worse) types of literature for judging it, and in spite of his cheerful warnings, such is his artistry that most readers suspend disbelief as they read the book. We journey wide-eyed with Tad Rampole (unaccountably, his given name has become "Ted") as the events unfold. The victim, Dr. Charles Grimaud (who has a name reminiscent of *grimoire*), is from Transylvania, and remaining from the original Bencolin version of the tale are discussions of vampires and burial alive. Although Carr carefully assures us that the seemingly impossible crimes will be explained naturally, it seems for much of the book that only a vampire or a "hollow man" could have done the deeds. Carr does not use, or need, the atmospheric language of the Bencolin novels, for the events are weird enough when they are described in ordinary terms. Grimaud has a strange history, associated with the cryptic phrases "three coffins" and "seven towers." A man named Pierre Fley, who knew Grimaud many years earlier, threatens him in veiled terms. Grimaud expects Fley to call, and he asks his assistant, Stuart Mills, carefully to watch his door. Mills receives Carr's harshest, but funniest, comment on mathematicians. "I am a mathematician, sir," he explains; "I never permit myself to think."[26] This lack of imagination—which Carr attributes to mathematicians as a group—is important as the story develops.

A mysterious figure, wearing a papier-mâché mask, enters Grimaud's house and goes upstairs. As Stuart Mills watches, the door to Grimaud's

---

*This extraordinary piece of self-knowledge on the part of a fictional character was used in a scholarly treatise, Robert Champigny's *What Will Have Happened* (1977), to illustrate a philosophical question. I'm not certain, however, what point Champigny is making in such lines as, "But what prevents us from applying this treatment of Dr. Fell's fictional cogito to the historical cogito? Cannot the imminence of the latter be similarly regarded as a grammatical mirage? Is not the inscription of the historicizing operator as a mental event in the historical field to be interpreted as a projected image of an act that transcends this field?" To quote Dr. Fell: "O my ancient hat!"

room opens. Grimaud and this hollow man stare at each other, the figure enters, and the door closes. A short while later, a shot is heard, the door is burst down, and a dying Grimaud is found on the floor. Though Mills watched the room at all times, the hollow man has vanished. To make matters more amazing, the building is surrounded by unmarked snow. The hollow man entered and left, but he made no footprints. Hadley decides to locate Pierre Fley, who it turns out is an illusionist at a cheap music hall. But Fley has been murdered in just as impossible a manner. As he walked down the center of a snow-covered street, with only his own footprints showing, he was shot in front of witnesses by an apparently invisible man. No one was near him, yet he was shot at point-blank range, and the witnesses heard a whispering voice.

In a review of a reprint of *The Three Coffins,* I complained that the solution to the murder of Dr. Grimaud is too complicated, but I now believe that I was wrong. S. T. Joshi points out that the explanation turns the whole case upside down: The truth is almost the reverse of everything that the reader thought had happened.[27] The mechanics of Grimaud's murder are indeed complex, but the emphasis on magic and illusion throughout the story prepares the ground for a variation of a Maskelyne trick, and Dr. Fell's "Locked-Room Lecture" provides direct clues to the explanation. About ten years ago, a group of mystery experts was polled to determine the greatest locked-room novels ever written. *The Three Coffins* came in first, with almost twice as many points as the second-place novel.[28] The book was also an immediate success on its publication in 1935. Hamish Hamilton told Carr that "*The Hollow Man* is moving better than any of its predecessors."

Dr. Fell's next case, *The Arabian Nights Murder,* is different in structure and approach from *The Three Coffins,* but it is just as stunning an accomplishment. Carr spent a great deal of time working on the background of the book, even learning some Arabic. Carr was enthusiastic at the resulting detective novel. "It's a beauty," he told Hamish Hamilton, and signed his name "Hassan el-Carr."[29] (In fairness, I should state here that in later life Carr came to dislike *The Arabian Nights Murder,* without ever explaining why.[30] As Carr himself knew from his research into the life of Sir Arthur Conan Doyle, an author's opinion of his own work may not be the one that critics and fans accept. Although owing to Carr's insistence, the book has never had a British paperback edition, yet it has remained one of his most popular novels in America, with at least four different publishers issuing reprints of the original Harpers edition.) This is one of the few

Carr books in which the British edition preceded the American, though not by much. The publication date of the Hamish Hamilton edition was February 13, 1936, while the Harper & Brothers printing appeared (depending on which source is acceptable) either February 20 or March 5.

By its very title, *The Arabian Nights Murder* reflects Carr's fondness for the Baghdad-on-the-Thames romances of Stevenson, and one character states the matter directly:

> He would like to imagine a world where all commonplace things had gone just a little crazy: where vicars were seen climbing the rainspouts of their churches, and the Lord Mayor of London unexpectedly said, "No" when the royal procession wanted to go past Temple Bar.

The policeman investigating the case agrees that "a thing is . . . more interesting because it is exhibited upside-down." Somewhat later, another character wonders whether he has found "some crack in the cosmos" and entered the world of the Arabian Nights.[31] This is reminiscent of Dr. Michael Tairlaine's discovery that "the prosaic world had some queer terrifying holes in it."

The *Arabian Nights Murder* begins in Dr. Fell's library at 1 Adelphi Terrace as three investigators, Detective Inspector John Carruthers, Assistant Commissioner Sir Herbert Armstrong, and Superintendent David Hadley, show their host some of the clues in a bizarre murder case: among them, two pairs of false whiskers, one white, one black; a mustache; a cookery book; and a photograph of a black mark that was made when someone threw coal against a wall. What series of events could tie together such an unlikely collection of items? As Armstrong explains in presenting the case to Dr. Fell, "It's so crazy that nobody else will understand it."[32] Each of the detectives in turn tells his story to Fell, and Carr gives each a distinctive voice—Carruthers is imaginative, Armstrong blustery, and Hadley straightforward and logical. The case itself seems to be a symphony of craziness, and each time one of the investigators explains some of the mysteries, he reveals a new layer that seems even stranger. Carruthers's story opens with a report given to him by a bobby on the beat near the Wade Museum in London*—a seemingly deranged man wearing false

---

*Carr based the Wade Museum on Sir John Soane's Museum in Lincoln's Inn Fields. An enthusiastic collector, Soane left his accumulation of various antiquities—ranging from an Egyptian sarcophagus to Hogarth paintings—and the building housing them to the nation in 1837 with instructions that nothing in it be changed.

whiskers who accused the policeman of committing murder, then vanished down the museum's coal chute. Carruthers goes to the museum and sees an attendant capering about singing of "Haroun al-Rashid's Missus." The attendant's actions may be more than high spirits, for Carruthers finds a corpse in an antique carriage; the corpse is wearing a second pair of false whiskers and holding a copy of *Mrs. Eldridge's Manual of Home Recipes.*

The second section is narrated by Sir Herbert Armstrong, but within that section is yet another voice, that of a Scottish clergyman, Dr. William Augustus Illingworth. Illingworth speaks the way many of us think a Scottish minister should—formally, a trifle pompously, but with a love of Scotland's heroic and tragic past. He is also naive. On his way to London to visit the Wade Museum at the request of its owner, he picks up a book called *The Dagger of Doom,* about a super-criminal named Dr. Chianti. Illingworth thinks that the novel is a manual of police procedure, and when he enters the museum that evening he believes that it has been taken over by gangs—one member of the supposed gang is wearing the inevitable false whiskers and another is dressed as a Persian potentate. Illingworth does not realize that his leg is being pulled when he is addressed as "Wallace Beery" and when one of the characters is called "Clark Gable." Thinking that he is breaking up a fiendish plot led by Dr. Gable, he calls himself "Beery of the Yard." This section comes close to being the funniest that Carr ever wrote. With its elaborate misunderstandings and exaggerations of language, it is directly out of P. G. Wodehouse, whose great character, Jeeves, is mentioned in Chapter 12. At times, Illingworth's exploits threaten to become slapstick, but they never descend to that level, and his tale is the funnier for that relative restraint.

Hadley's section is a closely reasoned explanation of the crime, which identifies a murderer whom we did not think was even near the museum. But for various reasons, he cannot be tried for the crime, and the three sleuths therefore take the case to Dr. Fell for his advice. Dr. Fell shows that Hadley had everything correct but the murderer, and he follows this false solution with the truth—which is even more unexpected.

In all of his earlier novels, Carr had felt the need for a focal character who might not do much but who could express Carr's views and provide someone with whom the reader could identify; with a couple of exceptions (Henry Morgan and Ken Blake) these viewpoint characters were Americans visiting England or the Continent. But after living in England almost four years, Carr had become so acclimated that in *The Arabian*

Nights Murder he no longer needed to include the viewpoint of an American, and he was sure enough of his craft that he could tell a story through various narrators.

Carr's next book under his own name was *The Murder of Sir Edmund Godfrey,* which is an important culmination of another line of development in Carr's writing—so important that I hope the reader will forgive me for delaying a discussion of it until a later chapter. Meanwhile, we should follow the development of the Merrivale and Fell novels of the later 1930s.

During this period, the cases of Sir Henry Merrivale appeared at almost the promised rate of two a year: *The Magic Lantern Murders* was published in Britain in November 1936 and in the United States, as *The Punch and Judy Murders,* in January 1937; next came *The Peacock Feather Murders* (British title, *The Ten Teacups*) in July 1937, *The Judas Window* in January 1938, and *Death in Five Boxes* in September 1938. There was then a delay before *The Reader Is Warned* was published in July 1939. Together these five books form an important stage in H.M.'s career. As Carr tended more and more to make Dr. Fell a formal, even dignified figure and to present his cases as serious investigations rather than slapstick romps, he made Sir Henry Merrivale more comic. His bad grammar, his informality (he addresses young women as "my wench"), his malevolent expressions, his regrettable taste in clothing—all receive more emphasis. In *The Magic Lantern Murders,* his panama hat is first mentioned: Ken Blake remarks, "The effect of that festive Panama, its down-turned brim giving it the look of a bowl, and the malignant face blinking under it as he sat motionless, with his hand folded on his stomach, was not one that could be seen with gravity."[33]

Carr said later that Sir Henry enters cases "with a rush and crash, heels in the air."[34] This type of comic entry is done fairly mildly in *The Peacock Feather Murders:* H.M. is introduced dictating a letter to the *Times.* It begins "Dear Stinker" and the subject matter concerns "the leprous and hyena-souled b. b.'s who have the dishonour to compose our present government" and their failure to install a lift to his office.[35] The humor is broader in *The Judas Window,* in which the Old Man acts as barrister for the defense: "He rose majestically," says Ken Blake, "an effect which was somewhat marred by the fact that his gown caught on something, probably himself. It tore with a ripping noise so exactly like a raspberry that for one terrible second I thought he had given one." Only with the greatest effort does he stop himself from addressing the jury as "fatheads."[36] This, however, is mild in comparison with his first appearance in his next case, *Death in Five Boxes*. In an attempt to lose weight, he borrows a fruit-barrow and, dressed only in his underwear and a bathrobe, he pushes it up a steep street in Hampstead—at which point Chief Inspector Masters drives smack-dab into the barrow, sending the fruit in a majestic shower and Sir Henry Merrivale into a ditch. "What the goddamholyblazes do you think you're doing," howls H.M. "You tried to murder me, that's what you did! Oh, gimme breath! Just gimme the goddam strength to get my hands round your neck—"[37] It is in this book that we learn that H.M. loves having his photograph taken; he poses like a stuffed dignitary, top hat in one arm, fist on his hip, and glares at the camera. *The Reader Is Warned* mentions briefly some of the Old Man's past exploits—his driving a train and hitting a cow, his launching a ship and hitting the mayor with the champagne bottle, and so on. In this book he fights the government's attempts to relegate him to the House of Lords, a fight that will continue during later cases.

In short, whether you like the H.M. novels depends in part on whether you like broad humor and think it can belong in a detective novel. S. T. Joshi finds the comedy for the most part overdrawn. On the other hand, LeRoy Lad Panek praises the humor of the Merrivale novels, and the mystery scholar Howard Haycraft, writing in 1941, said that H.M. was "the present writer's admitted favorite among contemporary fictional sleuths."[38] Carr himself came to prefer Sir Henry Merrivale to Dr. Gideon Fell; certainly he had more fun writing the books. Clarice Carr recalls John roaring with laughter in his study as he invented new scrapes for H.M. My own opinion is that, although in some instances—especially in the Great Man's final books—the humor does not work, most of the time H.M.'s antics are hilarious, and that H.M. is the best and funniest comic sleuth in fiction.

The Carter Dickson books of the late 1930s are topsy-turvy affairs, with convoluted plots, ingenious murder methods, multiple solutions, and cleverly hidden least-likely miscreants. Unlike most writers of the period, Carr rarely reused a solution; even when elements of it are familiar, Carr put them in a new mix so that the reader does not realize until too late which way the evidence points. Sometimes Carr's solutions, especially his explanations of the locked room and other impossible crimes, take so much close reasoning that some readers think there must be a hole there somewhere. And it is true that sometimes there is. Like solutions and gimmicks in some novels of Agatha Christie, Dorothy L. Sayers, and Ellery

Queen, the mechanisms of Carr's books from this period have been subjected to exhaustive analysis; it is fair to do so, since Carr himself emphasized the fair-play nature of his puzzles. Therefore, I shall on several occasions have to give solutions in order to discuss criticism leveled against the books. On each occasion, you will have fair warning.

The Magic Lantern Murders appeared in the United States under the title *The Punch and Judy Murders.* Neither title says much about the book, though at least the American does reflect the novel's comic mayhem. Like the immediately preceding book in the Sir Henry Merrivale series, *The Unicorn Murders,* it is constructed so that every time the reader thinks he knows what's going on, Carr gives the plot another twist. Also like *The Unicorn Murders,* the book has some secret-service background, based on Sir Henry's role as head of the Military Intelligence Department, but it is fundamentally a murder mystery. Heinemann called it "a thriller with detection,"[39] and although Carr disliked the term "thriller," for once a publisher's blurb got it right. For the first time, H.M. is not faced with an impossible crime, but the book has some of the same feeling: The victim is trying an experiment in astral projection, and for a while it seems as though a noncorporeal visitation was responsible for the murder.

What follows is a simplified version of the novel's complex plot. On the eve of his wedding to Evelyn Cheyne, Ken Blake receives a telegram from H.M. demanding his help. A former German espionage agent named Paul Hogenauer wants to sell the government some information about a mysterious super-spy called "L." H.M. orders Ken to burgle Hogenauer's house to check him out. Evelyn Cheyne, described by H.M. as "your *petit morceau de* fluff," decides to keep track of Ken, and she too gets involved.[40] After Ken heads off toward Hogenauer's house, he is arrested by the local police on the instructions of the Old Man himself. Justifiably annoyed with H.M.'s perfidy and afraid that he will be late for his wedding the next day, he escapes in a constable's uniform and enters Hogenauer's house. There he finds the German agent dead with, bizarrely, a Turkish fez on his head. Still trying to stay one step ahead of the police, Evelyn and Ken head toward Bristol. Ken is now disguised as a clergyman, but manages to have a real minister of the cloth arrested. In Bristol, they find another corpse, killed in the same way as Hogenauer. Eventually, after five different solutions are given, H.M. sorts everything out, and Ken and Evelyn dash off to their wedding. Unfortunately, the clergyman who was to hear their vows turns out to have been the one whom Ken had arrested. . . .

The Peacock Feather Murders (or *The Ten Teacups*) has elements drawn from both Robert Louis Stevenson and G. K. Chesterton. *New Arabian Nights* and the Suicide Club are mentioned by name, and through much of the book the reader wants to discover "what secrets may have crept out of Lisbon or Milan or Toledo four hundred years ago, to turn up in holes and corners of modern London."[41] The phrase "Ten Teacups" is from Chesterton's *The Club of Queer Trades;* Carr was fascinated by Chesterton's tantalizing line, "Of the Ten Teacups, of course I dare not say a word."[42] At the time that the book opens, Inspector Masters has worried for two years about the meaning of "The Ten Teacups." Scotland Yard had received a message that "there will be Ten Teacups" at a certain location. They found there a man murdered next to a table with a tea service for ten carefully laid out. The case was never solved, but now Masters receives a similar message concluding, "The presence of the Metropolitan Police is respectfully requested." Masters sends Sergeant Pollard to the house where the Ten Teacups will be. Outside, Pollard sees a professional adventurer named Vance Keating, incongruously wearing a hat that is so large that it bends the tops of his ears; later, we find that Keating told his friends that he was wearing the outsize hat because it had magic power. Keating enters the house, followed a bit later by Pollard. The sergeant is outside a room in the house when he hears two pistol shots. He breaks down the door and finds Keating shot twice with a hair-trigger .45 revolver, which is lying next to a body. Both bullets were fired at point-blank range, as judged by powder burns, and in fact the cloth around one of the bullet holes is still smoking. But the murderer has vanished.

[****The explanation is one of Carr's most ingenious.] The murderer was in a room across the street. He fired at Keating, who had a burned place on the back of his head (covered earlier by the hat) made the previous day by the powder wad of a blank cartridge. After shooting him, the murderer threw the gun across the street through a very large window—the dimensions are carefully given—aiming at Keating's body. When the gun landed, the hair-trigger caused it to fire again, and this second bullet also hit Keating. In 1982, the great mystery scholar E. F. Bleiler wrote a detailed article about *The Peacock Feather Murders* taking Carr to task for "sloppy gimmicking, loose-end plotting, and careless presentation." What this amounts to is that Carr made several errors. First, he had Keating push the window *up* rather than *out*, thus showing that it must have been a sash window, not a casement window, which would open to the side. The top part of the window, therefore, must still have been covered with glass when Keating was shot, and Carr's detailed measurements have to be cut in half. According to Bleiler, it was nearly impossible for the murderer, good cricket-bowler though he was, to have thrown the gun through the small space that was open. Second, for various mathematical reasons the murderer would have been unable to see Keating's body, and therefore he could not have thrown the gun at the corpse. (Unfortunately, Bleiler weakened his arguments by misstating how a cricketer throws the ball—he throws overhand rather than underhand as Bleiler thought.) The murderer had tried to make the existence of a secret society called the Ten Teacups believable by including a vague comment on it in a travel book he had recently published. Bleiler said, "As Carr well knew, publishing a book from MS. to finished product usually takes a year or so," and no murderer would have laid a false clue so far in advance. In Carr's experience, however, it never took a year for a book to be published. Usually only six months—sometimes fewer—elapsed between the time he sat down to start a book and the time it was published.[43]

It's not surprising that Carr came a cropper with mathematics—Bleiler even does some trigonometric calculations to prove his point about the murderer's line of sight. But I think that most readers will find the objections to *The Peacock Feather Murders* to be picking at nits. Let's simply assume (a) that Carr really had a casement window in mind and (b) that, as in fact was the case, the murderer did not need to see Keating's body when he threw the gun. Indeed, it is a tribute to Carr that someone exercised so much care and effort to check on his ingenuity.

Robert Adey, the greatest expert on the history of impossible crimes in fiction, calls H.M.'s next case, *The Judas Window,* "perhaps the best locked room novel ever written," and S. T. Joshi praises it as "a narrative *tour de force.*"[44] I don't think that either expert has overstated the case, though again we might nitpick about the mechanics of the locked room. The first part of the story is narrated from the viewpoint of James Caplon Answell, who has been invited to meet his future father-in-law, Avery Hume. Hume is an expert on archery, and his study has prize-winning arrows attached to the wall. Answell drinks a convivial whiskey and soda with Hume, but then his head begins to swirl and he collapses. When he wakes, he finds his host lying dead with an arrow embedded in his chest. All the doors are locked from the inside. Answell is clearly the only person who could have committed the murder, but Sir Henry Merrivale believes in his innocence and undertakes the defense. The rest of the book is told by Ken Blake, and it consists primarily of Answell's trial for murder.

The book is based on the intriguing premise that, no matter how hermetically sealed a room might be, it still has a "Judas window" for a murderer to enter. A Judas Window is a peephole in the door of a jail cell, but Carr also uses the term to refer to any method of entering a locked room. H.M. explains to Ken Blake:

> The door really was tight and solid and bolted; and the windows really were tight and solid and bolted. Nobody monkeyed with a fastening to lock or unlock either. Also, you heard the architect say there wasn't a chink or crevice or rat-hole in the walls anywhere; also true. No, I'm tellin' you: the murderer got in and out through the Judas window.

Ken leaves H.M.'s office with "a confused idea of thousands of houses and millions of rooms, piled into the rabbit-warren of London: each respectable and lamp-lit in its long lines of streets: and yet each containing a Judas window which only a murderer could see."[45]

The wonder of *The Judas Window* is not only the exceptional impossible situation but also the strength of the narration. Most of the story is about the trial of James Answell, yet Carr so carefully and progressively reveals clues to the truth that tension is created with very little action. He distinguishes the personalities of the witnesses through varying speech patterns and different gestures. As the trial continues, Sir Henry proves that Hume was killed by an arrow shot by a crossbow, but that does not seem to help matters since there is no such weapon in the locked room. In the climax, the Old Man introduces the door as evidence and demonstrates the "Judas window." But even with the murder method revealed, we still do not know the identity of the murderer until the very end.

[****The explanation of the mechanics of the crime follows.] The Judas window in Hume's room is the hole where the spindle of the door-knob passes through the door. The murderer removed the knob on the outside of the door, and tied a string through a hole in the spindle. She then pushed the spindle through the door so that it was hanging on the room side. After placing the arrow through the opening, she nocked it in the crossbow, attracted Hume's attention, and shot him. After that, the murderer pulled the string, drawing the spindle back into place, and reattached the knob. The question is: Is this method practical? I have never seen objections in print, but several scrupulous Carrr fans have told me that they cannot believe that the spindle could indeed have been pulled back. Clarice Carr, however, recalls that John and a friend spent many hours at Kingswood removing the doorknobs and spindles from the doors of the Bungalow; the result was that the method did in fact work. Clarice believes that the British spindles of the 1930s were larger than modern ones; I am not qualified to resolve that question.[46] There is, however, another difficulty in the solution that has never been pointed out. The murderer had no certainty that Hume would stand in such a way that the arrow would hit him in a lethal place, especially since the murderer could not see the victim; even if there were a sight-line, the thickness of the door would have prevented her from aiming the arrow. The problem could have been handled by making Hume a collector of exotic arrows, and adding a dab of poison (curare?) to the death weapon.

I feel somewhat guilty about debating the mechanics of Carr's locked rooms. He always spent a great deal of time testing the methods—non-lethally, of course—that produced seemingly miraculous murders. The mystery writer Christianna Brand, who knew Carr a decade later, remembered that "I mentioned a very minor plot of mine to him. In a moment he was up, tying bits of string to light switches, measuring distance, ensuring that the trick would actually have worked."[47] In each case where he made an error—the sash window in *The Peacock Feather Murders*, the impossibility of aiming in *The Judas Window*—the problem could have been corrected with a few changes (casement window, poison-tipped arrow), and in any event is not noticeable without several close readings. Even E. F. Bleiler, Carr's harshest critic on mechanical matters, recalled that when he first read *The Peacock Feather Murders* he found it "a clever, ingenious mystery."[48] I think that's more the point than trigonometric quibbles.

The Judas Window was followed by *Death in Five Boxes,* a good, but not major, case for Sir Henry Merrivale, though my view may be based on the fact that this is one of the few Carr books to which I worked out the solution before the detective—the explanation of the miracle problem, that is, not the identity of the murderer, who is so well masked that at least one expert has complained that the guilty party plays too small a role in the book.[49] The main mystery is how the drinks of four people* could have been poisoned when it was impossible to tamper with the liquor, the shaker, and the glasses. The answer depends on British drinking habits, but Carr liked the gimmick so much that he would reuse it in later radio plays. A more interesting problem is why the victims had a strange con-

---

*One of the victims is Bonita Sinclair, a name that (as we shall see) Carr liked.

glomeration of apparently unrelated items in their pockets—one man has four watches, another has the innards of an alarm clock, a woman has phosphorus. As in *The Arabian Nights Murder,* the challenge is to discover what connection of events can satisfactorily explain such an incongruous lot of clues. To make matters more mystifying, one of the victims left five boxes in his solicitors' office, but after the crime they were stolen.

H.M.'s next case, *The Reader Is Warned,* is a model of authorial dexterity. As the title indicates, Carr challenges the reader to guess the solution at every step of the way, and he even includes footnotes ostensibly to guide the reader but in fact forming part of the misdirection. Moreover, though Sir Henry Merrivale continually tells us that the solution will turn out to be material, Carr so emphasizes the impossibility and creates such a feeling of the occult that the reader does not always trust H.M.'s assertions. A man named Herman Pennik announces that not only can he read minds but by a principle called "teleforce" he can control things to the point that by thought power alone he can kill a man. When challenged by a Colonel Blimp type named Sam Constable, Pennik says that dinner need not be prepared for Constable, because he will be dead by eight o'clock. A few moments before that time, Constable's wife, Mina, begins screaming. Dr. John Sanders, who plays the Ken Blake role in *The Reader Is Warned,* runs out and sees Constable swaying against a banister. He collapses, twitches, and Sanders feels his pulse stop. An autopsy finds no physical cause of death. (It might be pointed out here that Carr got the idea for Constable's death when two people in Bristol died in a similar manner, and he confirmed the medical details through a book that he used almost as a bible during the 1930s, *Taylor's Principles and Practice of Medical Jurisprudence*—which also provided some of his better poisoning ideas.)

Pennik takes credit for the killing, but points out that a legal case cannot be made against him. Mina Constable responds by challenging him to kill her. He accepts, and she dies in much the same way her husband died. Witnesses swear that at the time of the second murder Pennik is at a pub, but Sanders believes that he has seen Pennik's head floating outside a window. By this time the press has gotten hold of the sensational story—abetted, for what seems an obscure reason, by H.M. himself—and suggestions are made that Hitler and Mussolini might be dispatched by teleforce. Pennik has become a celebrity, but Sanders cannot stand his posturing and issues a challenge to make him his next victim.

The Reader Is Warned has much of interest. It turns out that Pennik is a South African mulatto who grew up knowing about the Bantu fetishism of his grandfather. A brilliant man who was later educated in England, Pennik tried to explain African magic scientifically as teleforce. Had other authors been writing this book, some racist statements might appear here, and in fact the true murderer, who has been manipulating Pennik, does make such comments. But H.M. and Carr himself, though still having some stereotypes about the genetic holdover of primitivism ("reverted to type"), have a grudging respect for Pennik: "He really has got a remarkable brain," says H.M., "a stunnin' penetration, an ability to read thoughts in the sense of reading people." Masters is not sympathetic: "I've not got much pity for *that* gentleman, Sir Henry, even though you seem to have." The Old Man explains that African fetishism is no different from medieval European witch beliefs. In short, Carr seems to be saying that whatever evil beliefs and practices exist, they are not racial; they are human.[50]

Chapter 7

WITCHCRAFT

"Crime and the occult," says a character in one of John Dickson Carr's books, "these are the only hobbies for a man of taste." In his books of the early and middle 1930s, Carr had often obtained his literary effects by suggesting through atmosphere and seemingly impossible events that occult powers were responsible for the crimes. Nightwalkers and deadly rooms, vampires and hollow men, séances and returning spirits, crawling hands and invisible unicorns—all these had already appeared (or seemed to appear) in Carr's mystery stories. Probably, however, witchcraft most perfectly combined Carr's interests in the occult, the past, and mysterious death. He was fascinated by witch beliefs. A decade later, he purchased two Devil tapestries, each about seven feet by two feet, showing various demons and gargoyles in red on a cream background. Carr liked to pretend, at least, that they had been used by a witch cult in a Black Mass. This chapter will discuss the six novels published under Carr's own name between 1937 and 1939; of these books, two (*The Burning Court* and *The Crooked Hinge*) are based on organized groups of witches, or at least the possibility of their existence.

Scholars have long differed about whether witchcraft was actually practiced, what beliefs it had, and whether witches formed organized groups. The historical sources are often tainted—confessions drawn from tortured prisoners and accusations made by theologians who searched for evidence to confirm their preconceptions—and thus scholarly judgments have run the gamut from the most skeptical (no one even tried to practice black magic) to the most credulous (witches were able to do what they were charged with doing). The problem is to distinguish between what was actually going on and what people believed was happening. Most modern students of medieval and Renaissance witchcraft argue that black magic was indeed practiced. The evidence is overwhelming that people *believed* they could cause harm through certain magical practices. In this, European and American witchcraft differed little from practices in many cultures; Carr was correct in *The Reader Is Warned* in finding similarities between African and European magic. What gives witchcraft in Western culture a special flavor is the perceptions of it by theologians and jurists. They tried to fit the primarily folkloric practices, some of which were pre-Christian, of uneducated villagers into a Christian worldview. The only way, they believed, that magic could be practiced (except for the miracle of the Christian Mass) was through a pact with the Devil. The intellectuals created an image of devil worshipers who were organized as a conscious anti-Christian group, performing perverse reversals of Christian rites— the Black Mass or Devil's Sabbat, and so on. Outside the image created by theologians and inquisitors, however, there is no good evidence of the reality of pacts, organizations or covens of witches, or even of the Black Mass during the Middle Ages. But by the later seventeenth century, some court aristocrats, who had no connection with the folkloric witch practices of the countryside, had accepted the intellectuals' arguments and formed groups that performed such rites as they believed to be genuine. Thus perceptions had begun to influence reality.

During the 1920s and the 1930s, studies of witchcraft were dominated by the anthropologist Margaret Murray and the occultist Montague Summers, both of whom are mentioned in Carr's books.[1] Summers, a defrocked priest who was also an expert on two of Carr's other interests, Restoration plays and gothic novels, actually believed that witches could accomplish what they were charged with. If inquisitors and others said that witches could murder people magically at long distance, Summers accepted those claims without hesitation. And because he thought that the charges against witches were true, Summers argued that the persecution of them was justified. Carr's odd statement about the Inquisition in *Death-Watch* may have been based on Summers's *History of Witchcraft* and *Geography of Witchcraft*, but Summers's main influence on Carr came from the many colorful details he gave on witch practices, at least as charged in law courts.

Margaret Murray's theories, given in her *The Witch-Cult in Western Europe*, sound more plausible than Summers's, and, because she wrote the article on the subject in the *Encyclopedia Britannica*, her views were once widely accepted. Basically she argued that witchcraft was an elaborately organized pre-Christian religion that had survived in spite of all churchly attempts to suppress it. "The Old Religion," as she labeled it, had covens, Black Masses, and all the rest, but unlike Summers she did not believe that witches really caused harm through magic. Instead, she thought that witches' salves and similar things gave the worshipers the sense of night flying and so on. Dr. Fell expresses Murray's view succinctly in *The Crooked Hinge:*

> We can't deny, as a matter of history, that the Satanist cult really existed and was a powerful force from the Middle Ages to the seventeenth century. It had an organization as carefully arranged and managed as the Church itself.[2]

Few current scholars agree with Margaret Murray and Gideon Fell about a genuine satanist cult. Murray's conclusions sometimes were, to put it mildly, against what we know of the past. For example, she argued that the foundation of the Order of the Garter was associated with witch beliefs, and even that some English monarchs were conscious leaders of the Old Religion. In short, Murray showed a thoroughgoing disregard for sources, choosing only those that seemed to support her position, and using those in the wrong contexts. But whether correct or (much more likely) not, Murray's and Summers's works provided a great deal of material for the mystery novelist.

The Burning Court, published in April 1937, came in the middle of an extremely productive period in Carr's career, when he was writing some of his finest books. I may open myself to howls from fans of Dr. Fell and Sir Henry Merrivale in saying that *The Burning Court,* which features neither of Carr's great detectives, surpasses even such achievements as *The Three Coffins, The Arabian Nights Murder, The Judas Window,* and *The Crooked Hinge.* These Fell and H.M. novels are among the most ingenious detective stories ever written. Yet, although ingenuity of the highest order is also present in *The Burning Court,* the distinctiveness of that book lies elsewhere—in its startling combination of fair-play puzzle making and witchery.

In later years, Carr said that he wrote *The Burning Court* to answer a critic who said that no really terrifying supernatural story could have an American setting,[3] but the immediate impetus was to reply to pressure from his British publisher. Almost every time he received a typescript from Carr, Hamish Hamilton would praise the novel, perhaps suggest eliminating some Americanisms, then rather sorrowfully state that Carr's plots were too far removed from everyday reality. For example, about *The Three Coffins*, he said, "My only criticism, a mild one, is that the crime and explanation are perhaps almost too ingenious for the ordinary reader, though no doubt the connoisseur in detective fiction will relish this."[4] But in spite of Hamilton's (relative) diffidence in making the suggestion, it was clear that as a publisher he was less interested in appealing to the relatively few connoisseurs of detective fiction than to the larger number of casual readers. When *The Arabian Nights Murder* was published, Hamilton suggested that Carr's works might be too grotesque in both character and setting:

> There is a large section of the public which fights shy of anything which is so grotesque as to seem unreal, or perhaps I should say, unlikely to happen in ordinary life. Why not try the experiment some time of taking a perfectly usual situation and exercising your ingenuity on that? Waxworks, museums, hermetically sealed rooms, eccentric clubs, etc., are all fine and dandy, but the ordinary chap like myself spends comparatively little time in them.

This was hitting Carr pretty hard, for he had no interest in writing about "usual situations" and "ordinary life." And Hamilton did realize that "it . . . would mean such a complete change of style that you may not even consider it."[5]

Carr responded rather mildly, pointing out that, since he had stopped writing about Bencolin, he had already eliminated some of what he called "the fantastic coloring of my stories." "Of course," he continued, "I shall never be able to eliminate this quality altogether . . . and a completely commonplace story would send me to sleep." It is instructive to see what Carr thought might make "a commonplace theme not handled in a commonplace manner." He sent the following plot outline to his publisher:

> A fairly commonplace young man, married, comfortable, not well off but with a decent job; living in a suburb in New York or London or Bristol or anywhere you like; making his daily round and half wishful that something will happen. Nothing has happened, except the

death of a next-door neighbor from commonplace causes. *But*, right in the middle of the humdrum, he secretly discovers that his quiet, demure wife, with whom he is very much in love, is a famous and absolutely unscrupulous poisoner. He keeps quiet—but what does he think about and how do things go in the home? That's the beginning of the story. It's commonplace enough, but I think I see a way to make it rather a terrible business in the development.[6]

Not even the repetition of the word "commonplace" makes Carr's plot sound like the usual, everyday thing that Hamilton had in mind, but it led to an important development in Carr's writing. Instead of beginning with the bizarre or the terrible, Carr realized that it might be more effective to open with ordinary events into which the extraordinary would then intrude. The tension and the terror would then be greater. The plot idea that Carr outlined to his publisher would develop into a most noncommonplace novel, *The Burning Court,* and some of its elements—especially a spouse suspected of murder—would reappear in such later books as *Seeing Is Believing* and *Till Death Do Us Part.*

Almost as soon as Carr wrote that he was "keeping carefully to the this-might-happen-to-you-or-me idea," he came up with an extremely nonstraightforward device, based on the Maskelyne Mysteries, and enthusiastically sent a description of it to Hamish Hamilton. The Maskelyne magic show featured a mysterious box that various people would enter and then vanish. This gave Carr an idea for an exceptional gimmick—the disappearance of a body from within a private vault that was sealed with concrete. Hamilton, perhaps shaking his head over what had happened to his request for a straightforward mystery, wrote to Carr, "You are a most ingenious cove."[7]

As Carr continued to develop the plot, it became clear that in its use of supernatural elements *The Burning Court* would be quite unlike any of his previous books. Carr therefore suggested that it might be time that he adopt another pseudonym, and Harpers and Hamilton could advertise the book as written by someone whom Carr called "a new writer of promise."[8] Hamilton liked the idea, but he pointed out that with any book under the John Dickson Carr name, he could guarantee advance orders in Britain of about one thousand copies, but with a novel by a new author, he could expect to place only around four hundred copies. Eventually, it was decided to publish *The Burning Court* under Carr's own name. After completing about half the manuscript by April 1936, Carr laid it aside for five or six months. When he picked it up again early in October, he was not pleased. "I am rewriting it," he said, "and putting the scene in England." Nonetheless, he promised Hamilton to do all the revising and complete the final half of the book before the end of the month. By the middle of October, however, he had changed his mind again and restored the American setting. From then on, the writing went smoothly. "It is something new in mysteries," he told his publisher.[9] He was quite right.

Carr was willing to go some distance to satisfy Hamilton's oft-stated preference for a commonplace mystery. *The Burning Court* opens in an ordinary setting with ordinary people, but it doesn't remain ordinary for long. The contrast between our settled, protected life and the terrors that may be just outside it is indicated by one of the characters in *The Burning Court*:

> We huddle together in cities, we make bonfires of a million lights, we can get a voice from across the ocean to sing to us so that we needn't feel lonely; it's a sort of charmed circle, with no heaths to walk at night in the wind. But suppose you . . . in your apartment in New York; or you . . . in your flat in London; or John Smith in his house anywhere in the world—suppose you went home at night, and opened the ordinary door, and heard another kind of voice. Suppose you didn't want to look behind the umbrella-stand, or go down to attend to the furnace at night, because you might see something climbing up?[10]

The Burning Court takes place in spring 1929 in the small Pennsylvania town of Crispen, an invented locale that Carr placed between Haverford and Bryn Mawr. This connection with Haverford made Carr recall his college days, at least to the extent of choosing three names from that period for the book. One character is named Partington, though he seems to have no other connection with Carr's friend James Partington. Also mentioned are two of his pseudonyms: C. G. Baker appears as "Dr. Baker" and Caliban shows up in the "Caliban Club." Ted Stevens, an editor with the publishing house of "Herald & Sons" (i.e., Harper & Brothers), is traveling by train to his weekend home at Crispen to join his wife, Marie. Probably in deference to Hamish Hamilton's wishes, Carr keeps emphasizing how commonplace everything seems:

> [Stevens] was not much different from you or me. . . . It must be emphasized, too, that there was nothing unusual about the day or the

evening. He was not stepping across a borderland, any more than
you or I step across; he was simply going home.

On the train, however, the door to another world opens. Stevens begins to
read the typescript of a new book about female poisoners, written by true-
crime expert Gaudan Cross, and he sees a photograph of his wife. It is
captioned "Marie D'Aubray: Guillotined for Murder, 1861."[11]

Meanwhile, it seems that a rash of poisoning has been occurring at
Crispen, and all the signs point to some sort of witchcraft. A neighbor,
Miles Despard, had died a short while earlier; though the cause is diag-
nosed as gastroenteritis, his nephew Mark suspects it is really arsenic. The
housekeeper saw a mysterious woman, who was dressed in old-fashioned
costume, in Miles Despard's room before his death, but the woman was
opening, and walking through, a door that had been bricked up for more
than two hundred years. Mark hopes to solve some of the mystery by un-
officially opening the Despard vault and having a friend of his, a former
medical doctor, test his uncle's body for arsenic. But when he and Stevens
open the coffin, they find it empty. The evidence is absolute that the body
was deposited in the crypt; there is no other way in or out; yet the body
has disappeared.

> It wasn't only a locked room. It was worse. It was a crypt built of
> granite, without even the advantage of a window; and closed up not
> by a door, but by a stone slab weighing nearly half a ton, six inches of
> soil and gravel, and a concrete-sealed pavement which one witness is
> willing to swear has not been disturbed.[12]

The presence of the supernatural seems overwhelming, and indications
accumulate that Marie Stevens is a witch. Drawing from Margaret Murray, Carr creates the image of a cult of witches who are compelled to use
poison, but he adds to that the idea that when each one dies, he or she
will eventually return as the "nondead." Not only does Ted's wife look exactly like the photograph of her nineteenth-century namesake, but a seventeenth-century portrait of a poisoner in Louis XIV's court, though
damaged, is also clearly of Marie Stevens. Signs of witchcraft were left on
Miles Despard's deathbed, and even Marie's quirks add confirmatory evidence. Her dislike of ordinary funnels, for example, is associated with
a famous torture, in which water was poured through a funnel into
the mouths of suspected witches. Other characters, too, may have had
past lives as nondead: A Despard was involved in prosecuting the

seventeenth-century poisoner, and an ancestor of the author Gaudan Cross was the poisoner's associate.

But just as the reader is certain that Carr has finally broken from his pattern of finding a rational explanation to the eerie events of his novels, Gaudan Cross appears. He is one of Carr's most interesting detectives— simian in appearance, cynical in langauge, he admits that years ago he himself committed murder—but (he claims) it was a justifiable murder. He says that the events surrounding Miles Despard's death are not super- natural, and he provides detailed and persuasive explanations of the van- ishing corpse and of the woman who walked through a nonexistent door. But as he finishes his evidence, he suddenly dies from poison himself— poison obviously administered by the guilty person. This is a shocking conclusion, for rarely had authors killed their detectives at the denoue- ment—but at least the reader could return safely to his or her tidy world. The supernatural had again been shown to be an illusion, a trick like those of the Maskelynes to make us believe what is obviously impossible.

[****The importance of *The Burning Court* cannot be discussed with- out revealing the solution.] The novel has an epilogue in which we enter Marie Stevens's mind and discover that she is a witch after all. She mur- dered Miles Despard through supernatural means, and stole his body from the crypt so that he would join the nondead. She muses that "it was clever of [Gaudan Cross] to pluck a physical explanation, a thing of sizes and dimensions and stone walls, out of all those things which had no ex- planation I was prepared to give them." But Cross wished her to come back to him as a lover, so she was forced to murder him. "He will return to flesh and bone presently, but I have the better of him now." Meanwhile, Marie plans to make her husband one of the nondead. She then hears Ted returning from work, and "her face became the face of a pretty wife."[13]

The Burning Court is extraordinary. It is a bold departure from anything John Dickson Carr or indeed anyone else had done before. In his previous books, Carr had always shut the supernatural horrors back in their box, and he often pointed out that the human horrors can be infinitely worse than anything produced by ghosts or vampires. In those books, the world remained ordered, and I think that Carr found it important to make that the case. Only in *The Burning Court* did he indicate that fundamentally there is no material order in creation. I might add here that Carr included some clues that may be read to indicate that there might be yet a further epilogue to *The Burning Court*, but these are so vague that I leave them to an appendix. Meanwhile, *The Burning Court* is probably John Dickson Carr's most powerful book.

Carr never wrote another novel with a supernatural ending, despite the urging of some friends and correspondents. The young writer and critic William A. P. White, who used the pen name Anthony Boucher, was a great admirer of Carr's novels. The two men became acquainted when Boucher wrote to Carr in 1939 to beg for another novel in the style of *The Burning Court*, and he repeated the request on several later occasions. Carr responded that if he wrote such a book "it is to be feared that the faithful customers would murder me. I got into enough hot water over that *Burning Court* one, with letters ranging from mildly shocked disapproval to puzzled wrath." (As late as 1969, Carr remarked that "occasionally I still get a letter asking me what the hell I meant.") Moreover, the serial market in Britain, where his stories were starting to find success, was primarily in the women's magazines, and editors would not consider supernatural novels—short ghost stories for Christmas, yes; detective novels that end up as horror stories, never. Nonetheless, Carr promised Boucher to think about writing another novel of witchery. He expressed approval of Boucher's using the name of the American murderer H. H. Holmes as a second pseudonym, and said that he would call himself "Neill Cream" (a famous English poisoner) if he ever did another supernatural novel.[14]

Carr would return to witchcraft as a background for a novel in *The Crooked Hinge*, published some eighteen months after *The Burning Court*. But a year and a half was a long time for Carr during the 1930s, and between his two witchcraft novels he published two other detective novels under his own name. Both books, *The Four False Weapons* and *To Wake the Dead*, seem in a sense to mark time; neither points toward the emotional intensity that Carr was developing in his novels beginning with *The Burning Court*. *The Four False Weapons*, published in the United States in October 1937, is somewhat reminiscent of Chesterton's "The Three Tools of Death"; in both the problem is to explain why so many murder weapons are at the scene of the crime. The plots of the stories and the explanations for the multitude of weapons, however, are quite different. In John Dickson Carr's works, *The Four False Weapons* looks backward in two ways. On the one hand, like the work of earlier detective novelists, it is filled with physical clues. It is Carr's commentary on the Great Detective who picks up a matchstick or examines a heel mark and deduces the identity of the murderer. As the title indicates, however, the weapons left at the scene of the crime are all false, and the case is solved through entirely different means.

The Four False Weapons looks backward in another way—it revives Monsieur Henri Bencolin. After the false start in *Vampire Tower* (which he had rewritten as *The Three Coffins*), Carr realized that he could not bring back the satanic Bencolin who had enjoyed tormenting his prey. The original Bencolin of Carr's college stories, however, had been gentle, amiable, and even a bit shambling. If Bencolin were to come back to life, he would have to be that original Bencolin. In *The Four False Weapons*, Carr set out to prove that Bencolin's personality in, say, *The Lost Gallows* had been only a mask to exhibit to criminals. As Carr remarked as he neared completion of the typescript of *The Four False Weapons*, "He is not merely a bogey-man now: he is a real character and a human being."[15] Rather than the immaculately dressed manhunter we had come to expect, the Bencolin of *The Four False Weapons* is described as looking like a scarecrow. Now retired from the Sûreté, he wears a worn corduroy coat and a questionable hat and smokes a foul-smelling pipe. He speaks genially and has a "spark of devilment." Bencolin admits that in earlier years he had played a part to scare the Parisian underworld but now he is tired of that role. Once or twice the Bencolin of the earlier novels seems to return—"Possibly old habits are asserting themselves," he says, "and I show my teeth for the salutary moral effect on suspects."[16] The Bencolin who solves *The Four False Weapons*, however, is an amalgam—a bit of the old *juge d'instruction*, more of the kindly Bencolin of the college stories, and even some of Dr. Gideon Fell (in his occasionally pedantic speech) and Sir Henry Merrivale (in his taste for rank tobacco and disreputable clothes).

The Four False Weapons has some memorable sections. The book begins with a restatement of the possibility of romantic adventure in the workaday world. A young and bored lawyer named Richard Curtis dreams of someone saying to him (in words reminiscent of those used in *The Bowstring Murders*):

> Here are three passports and an automatic pistol. You will proceed at once to Cairo, in whatever disguise you think fit; but take care that you are not followed by a man whose cufflinks take the form of a small black cross. Arrived in Cairo, you will proceed to the Street of the Seven Cobras, to a house which you will identify by—

Curtis's fantasy seems to come true when a superior calls him in and says, "I have a mission for you to undertake."[17] The book also has an excellent concluding scene, as Bencolin, Curtis, and the suspects play a card game called "Trente-et-le-va" from Louis XIV's court. Tension mounts with the increasing stakes on the table. But between these two sections, the book is a letdown. Coincidences abound, not only to explain the various false weapons but also to justify the number of suspects who unaccountably descend on the murder site. People act in ways unseen in heaven or earth, and rarely in fiction.

Like *The Four False Weapons,* the next Carr novel, *To Wake the Dead,* has a stunning opening but a disappointing center. For John Dickson Carr, the most important part of writing a book was the detailed working out of plot and characters before setting anything down on paper. In the case of *To Wake the Dead,* it seems that he had not spent enough time dovetailing everything; more specifically, he had not yet worked out where the opening was to lead. The reason for Carr's failure has to do with agents, serial publication, and book publishers. Before Carr chose the British firm of Pearn, Pollinger and Higham early in 1937 as his agents, he had usually negotiated his contracts himself, not always with the best results. David Higham, and the firm's American representative, the Ann Watkins Company, obtained much better deals for Carr, including retaining serial rights for his novels. Watkins was never able to find magazines to serialize his works in the United States, which eventually soured Carr on the Watkins Company*—but David Higham did very well for him in England. He placed *The Peacock Feather Murders* (*The Ten Teacups*) with the weekly *The Passing Show* and *The Four False Weapons* with the monthly *Woman's Journal.* For the latter, Carr received three hundred pounds, a considerable amount above his monthly guarantee from Harpers and Hamilton. But there was a problem with the serial publication of *The Four False Weapons.* The editors of *Woman's Journal* insisted that their serialization appear before publication of the British edition of the book. Consequently, Carr asked Hamish Hamilton to delay the book from its tentative publication date of November 1937. The publisher, however, was not pleased, for he would still be contributing to Carr's monthly guarantee without a new book to bring in money. Carr resolved the problem by promising to write a different book for autumn publication in Britain. The result was that *The Four False Weapons* was published in fall 1937 in the United States, and in

---

*Carr believed that Ann Watkins never worked very hard in his behalf, but the more likely reason for the agent's failure to sell his books to American magazines is that the so-called slicks had a rigid formula preferring easy-to-follow stories. Carr's novels were anything but straightforward.

March 1938 in Great Britain. The book to appear for the autumn trade in Britain was *To Wake the Dead,* and author and publisher had to rush to get it into print. The book was finished early in October 1937, and Hamilton managed to get printed and bound copies to the bookstores a little more than a month later. *To Wake the Dead* was published in March 1938 in America.[18]

To Wake the Dead begins with Christopher Kent's showing up penniless in London. A thriller writer who was stung by a cousin's statement that he had never done an honest day's work, he wagered that he could work his way from Johannesburg to London in ten weeks. He has made it back to England but now he had no money for breakfast. He decides to cheat the Royal Scarlet Hotel in Piccadilly (based on the Regent Palace where John and Clarice had stayed in 1933) by ordering breakfast and charging the bill to room 707, occupied by someone he does not know. The scheme works, but then a hotel employee asks him to accompany him to room 707 to search for a lost bracelet. On the door, he finds the words "Dead Woman" scrawled on the "Do Not Disturb" sign. Turning the sign around so that the hotelman does not see it, Kent enters and finds a woman's body. After this intriguing beginning, the reader expects (or at least I do) that Christopher Kent will be charged with the crime, and that the book will be built around his attempts to free himself from suspicion. But no: Kent sneaks out through another door, calls on Dr. Fell and Superintendent Hadley, and is immediately cleared.

In addition to the opening scene, the novel has some other clever bits, especially the appearance of someone dressed in a hotelman's livery in the middle of the night in a country house where another murder has been committed. It is clear, however, that Carr had not worked out what he was going to do with the story. Kent's bet leads nowhere; most of the book is taken up with elaborate alibis rather than action; and the conclusion, involving (astonishingly for Carr) a secret passage, is unsatisfactory.

In March 1938, Carr announced to Hamish Hamilton that he was working on a new novel to be called *The Crooked Hinge,* and he asked whether the title was attractive. Hamilton replied that the title was fine, except that he was mystified as to the nature of a *straight* hinge. Carr kept the title, but added a line in the typescript: "What was a crooked hinge? Or, for that matter, a straight hinge?"[19] The plot elements of *The Crooked Hinge* came from several sources: The witchcraft references are from Margaret Murray and Montague Summers; the emphasis on stage magic is again from the Maskelynes, specifically in this instance from their development in the nineteenth century of a card-playing automaton called Zoe; also included are references to the *Titanic* disaster and to the famous case of the Tichborne claimant. In short, *The Crooked Hinge* is a novel rich in supernatural, magical, and historical lore.

It begins with a direct challenge to the reader. The first section is headed with a quotation from a turn-of-the-century book of parlor magic:

> The first rule to be borne in mind by the aspirant is this: Never tell your audience beforehand what you are going to do. If you do so, you at once give their vigilance the direction which it is most necessary to avoid, and increase tenfold the chances of detection. We will give an illustration.

The Crooked Hinge, of course, is the illustration of the principle of misdirection. This statement could summarize Carr's entire technique, but rarely did he begin by so openly admitting that he was out to bamboozle the reader. In this way, the book is similar to *The Three Coffins,* which also sets out the challenge at the opening, but *The Crooked Hinge* is a more intense book. The intensity comes not from the viewpoint character—Brian Page, like Tad Rampole and Michael Tairlaine, is only an observer, not a genuine participant—but from the problem that besets two of the characters. Sir John Farnleigh, of Farnleigh Close in the Kentish town of Mallingford, was rescued many years earlier from the *Titanic.* He has been plagued by a recurring dream—an image comes to him of a crooked hinge. Arriving in Mallingford is a man using the name Patrick Gore who claims that he is the genuine John Farnleigh, and he promises proof that the holder of the title is an impostor. With great dexterity, Carr guides the reader's sympathies from the man we know as Farnleigh to the claimant and back again, and each time we think we're sure who has the legitimate claim to the title, he twists the story once more. Gradually, Carr also introduces other elements. The Golden Hag, a seventeenth-century automaton, is hidden in a small room at Farnleigh Close. A mystery attaches to it, apparently involved with the Farnleigh claimant, and the Golden Hag seems to be able to move about at will. Evidence mounts that a small group at Mallingford is attempting to practice witchcraft: This is not a genuine witch group as in *The Burning Court* but some jaded moderns seeking thrills. An old tutor of the real John Farnleigh has returned to identify the genuine claimant, and Carr artfully leads us to believe that the schoolmaster is a candidate for murder. But it is the current holder of the title who is murdered, apparently alone in an area surrounded by low hedges. The detection is handled by Dr. Gideon Fell. Since by this time Carr had decided that Sir Henry Merrivale rather than Dr. Fell would be his comic sleuth, Dr. Fell is more formal and less exuberant than in his early novels.

[****Carr's explanation of the seemingly impossible murder of Sir John Farnleigh has been questioned.] *The Crooked Hinge* has the plot device of a false solution followed by the true one. Dr. Fell makes a persuasive case demonstrating how Sir John Farnleigh's wife, Molly, murdered her husband using a particularly diabolical method, a gypsy throwing ball covered with fish hooks. Many writers would have been satisfied with this solution, but Carr had a more spectacular one up his sleeve. It turns out that Gore is the genuine Farnleigh, and since his boyhood he has been in love with Molly. He and Molly flee, and in a letter Gore reveals how he committed the crime. He had lost his legs, apparently just above the knees, in the *Titanic* sinking. Living as a circus performer, illusionist, and spiritualist, he used different pairs of artificial legs to vary his height. He killed the so-called John Farnleigh by removing his artificial legs and moving along below the level of the hedge on the padded stumps of his real legs. All this is well-clued, as Carr emphasizes Gore's clumsy walking.

In 1981, however, James Kingman published an article claiming that it is impossible for someone without genuine knees to climb stairs or rise from a sitting position without his disability being obvious. He asserts that even to walk on the level, Gore would have needed a cane: "Carr has no explanation for the miracles Gore has to perform, for no artificial leg then or now could manage them."[20] Although some of this may be true, Kingman overstates his case. Derek Smith, an expert on Carr's writings and the author of a classic locked-room novel, *Whistle Up the Devil,* has prepared an unpublished analysis of *The Crooked Hinge* and the artificial leg matter. He points out that Sir Douglas Bader, a British flying ace of World War II, lost both his legs, but by sheer determination learned to walk with artificial limbs. Bader never used a cane, but he had a clumsy rolling gate. Whether this was like Gore's clumsy walk, I do not know, for Carr never specifically describes it. Leaving aside such matters, *The Crooked Hinge* is one of Carr's great successes simply as a story. Carr himself pointed to it in later years as one of the best (or "least bad," as he put it) of his books, and it influenced at least one other writer, Edmund Crispin, to try his hand at detective fiction.[21]

Carr's two Dr. Fell novels for 1939 were *The Problem of the Green Capsule,* published in the United States in May and in Britain as *The Black Spectacles* in September, and *The Problem of the Wire Cage,* published in the United

States in October but not until May 1940 in Britain. Though neither reaches the level of two of Carr's 1938 books, *The Judas Window* and *The Crooked Hinge,* they are accomplished performances, with fine puzzles, clever clueing, and distinctive characters. Both demonstrate one of Carr's main strengths as a storyteller: He could differentiate characters by giving each of them different rhythms of speech. Personalities are vivid rather than, as in his first novels, grotesque. We meet people whom we have known in the real world, and this makes the incredible events they are involved in the more compelling.

Carr's original title for *The Problem of the Green Capsule* was *The Black Spectacles,* based on the spectacles that the murderer wore while committing the crime. One of the themes of the story, moreover, is that "all witnesses, metaphorically, wear black spectacles." Harpers, however, objected that the title was not particularly intriguing for a novel of crime and mystery. Carr then suggested *The Problem of the Green Capsule,* and Harpers agreed.[22] I shall, however, refer to the book by Carr's first choice of title.

The book begins in Pompeii, with a carefully evoked description of the ruins based on the Carrs' own Mediterranean trip in 1938. Detective Inspector Andrew MacAndrew Elliot (who had played a role in *The Crooked Hinge*) overhears the conversation of a group of English tourists. Marcus Chesney is arguing that no observer ever reports things accurately; most of his companions disagree. Elliot especially notices Chesney's niece, Marjorie Wills, who has "not only beauty but intelligence." "Never had he met a person of whose presence he was so intensely *aware,* like a physical touch."[23] This is enough: Like many of Carr's heroes, Elliot falls immediately in love, even before meeting the object of his affections. A short time goes by, then the scene shifts to Sodbury Cross, where Chesney and his family live. Elliot has been brought in to investigate a seemingly motiveless poisoning at a candy store, which resulted in one death. The local residents suspect Marjorie Wills. (Carr based the candy murder and other details of the Sodbury Cross poisonings on the case of Christiana Edmunds, who in 1871 filled some chocolates with strychnine, killing a four-year-old boy.)

The most important action in *The Black Spectacles* occurs offstage. Elliot is rarely on hand for any of the events, but he is told about them by the other characters. Shortly after he arrives at Sodbury Cross, he hears that Marcus Chesney has been murdered. To prove his point about the unreliability of witnesses, Chesney had tried an experiment. He told his family and guests that he would do certain things while they were watching, and that a "cine camera" would record what happened. He would then challenge the witnesses to report what they had seen, and their memories would be compared to the moving picture. But the murderer took advantage of Chesney's scheme. Disguised and wearing black spectacles (masks again) the murderer entered and forced a green capsule filled with poison down Chesney's throat—all this in spite of the fact that the camera was running. At first glance, Chesney's death seems to be a relatively simple matter. The film should provide enough clues to identify the murderer. But matters are not that straightforward. While waiting for the film to be developed, Elliot questions the witnesses—all of whom disagree about key points—Chesney was right, at least on that matter. Moreover, the motion picture film does not clear up much of anything, except to reveal that Chesney had laid traps for the witnesses. Eventually, Elliot finds that all the possible suspects have alibis: It seems that the Green Capsule puzzle is not a whodunit but a nobody-dunit. As Elliot says, "The case is too funny and queer and fishy to be taken at one swoop. It's a box of tricks right from the start." Fell agrees. When asked whether he believes his own eyes, he responds: "Certainly not. Definitely not. Observe the mess in which we have already landed by believing our own eyes. We are travelling in a house of illusions, a box of tricks, a particularly devious sort of ghost-train."[24]

In short, The Black Spectacles is a book about illusions, some created by the victim himself, some by the murderer, and some (unnecessarily) by Dr. Fell. Carr was so eager to fool the reader that sometimes he did not allow the events of the novel themselves to carry the mystery. In Death-Watch, he had had Dr. Fell make an out-and-out misstatement (indeed, "lie" is not too strong a word) to direct the reader's attention away from the guilty person. In The Black Spectacles, Fell also tells an untruth that seems to clear the murderer. Carr so often proclaimed his adherence to the fair-play rule that it is unexpected when he engages in a bit of misdirection that few readers would consider fair. Carr's plots are puzzling enough without having the additional challenge of trying to discover when to believe the sleuth.

The role played by the detective in The Black Spectacles is an important development in Carr's work. Dr. Fell does not appear until almost halfway through the book, though early on we learn that he is in nearby Bath "taking the cure." In most of his earlier novels, the detective was present throughout the story. The major exceptions are The Blind Barber and *The Arabian Nights Murder,* in which the story begins and ends with the detective, and the remainder of the novel consists of witnesses' telling him of the events. After Dr. Fell shows up in *The Black Spectacles,* he becomes the center of events, but in several later books Dr. Fell remains in the background until the conclusion. Instead of helping Dr. Fell or at least tagging along after him, the viewpoint character acts independently of the sleuth.

The emotional involvement of the main characters is what separates Dr. Fell's next case, *The Problem of the Wire Cage,* from the stories that preceded it. In Carr's novels during the 1930s, the protagonist often falls in love with the female lead—Jeff Marle with Sharon Grey, Tad Rampole with Dorothy Starberth, Ken Blake with Evelyn Cheyne, and so on. In *The Black Spectacles,* Detective Inspector Elliot is in love with the main suspect, but that fact plays almost no part in the story. There is no tension built up over her guilt or innocence or any danger to her, and none over possible conflicts in Elliot's loyalties. In *The Black Spectacles* as well as in two of Sir Henry Merrivale's cases from the end of the decade, *Death in Five Boxes* and *The Reader Is Warned,* Carr sets up the opportunity to make such a relationship integral to the mystery, but instead he lets the love affair remain a peripheral matter. Even in *The Burning Court,* Ted Stevens's concern about his wife and his growing fear that she is a witch never become as emotionally compelling as the reader expects. Carr's decision in most of his early novels to keep the focal character as a disinterested observer, his refusal (most obviously in *To Wake the Dead)* to place the hero in any real danger, and his occasional admissions within his novels that they are fiction, his emphasis on their storytelling framework—all this indicates that Carr still saw fiction as removed from involvement with real life, and real life, he thought, was the purview of the naturalistic and realistic writers whom he despised. But though he never came to like such writers and though he always saw novels as at their best incorporating the wonder of *New Arabian Nights,* his works were changing. Instead of being detached from the events, his main characters will become desperately concerned with the outcome of the mystery, for their happiness, perhaps even their lives, are in the balance. Although *The Problem of the Wire Cage* is not one of Carr's best novels, it is one of his most important, for it clearly marks this change.

Unlike the relaxed, I-will-challenge-you-with-a-puzzle mood that Carr had employed right through *The Crooked Hinge, The Problem of the Wire Cage* begins with emotions already stretched to the breaking point: "Possibly because the day was sultry," Carr says in the third paragraph, "emotions were growing sultry, too." And, somewhat later: "Nerves and heat had been strung to too high a pitch."[25] The tension is based partly on financial issues that divide the protagonists, partly on personality conflicts, but above all it is sexual. Hugh Rowland is in love with Brenda White, and she is willing to kiss him passionately but not to marry him. She is engaged to Frank Dorrance, and unless she goes through with this marriage, she will not receive her inheritance. Carr mentions over and over the threatening thunderstorm and the heat of the evening to symbolize the nervous strain that is about to snap. The "wire cage" of the title is a tennis court surrounded by a metal fence. It is there that Hugh discovers the body of Frank Dorrance, who has been strangled—and next to the body is Brenda White, with only her footprints leading across the sand that makes up the surface of the court. Brenda swears that when she first saw Frank's body, there were no footprints at all, and Hugh believes her. Unlike previous heroes, who act almost as acolytes to Dr. Fell and the police, Hugh immediately decides that Brenda's only hope is for both of them to lie about the tracks.

In these circumstances, Dr. Fell and Superintendent Hadley do not seem allies to Hugh and Brenda. Fell is the same physically, but even his Rabelaisian aspects have now become a bit sinister: "Old King Cole and Father Christmas present a terrifying aspect when they appear in the guise of a detective."*[26] Other characters in The Problem of the Wire Cage are as vividly described as Dr. Fell, especially the middle-aged Dr. Nicholas Young, a hail-fellow-well-met sort who enjoys having young people about him and being the genial and generous host. But his nickname, "Old Nick," reveals his real personality. Despite appearing generous, he is really mean and he manipulates those around him.

The Problem of the Wire Cage is strikingly ingenious. Carr eventually gives five possible explanations for the body surrounded by unmarked sand. Two of the explanations are, in fact, more persuasive than the ultimate solution produced by Dr. Fell, which depends on an overcomplicated gimmick and requires the victim unconvincingly to have assisted in his own demise. Another weakness in the book is a second murder that seems tossed in for no particular reason except to keep the story moving.

*The Problem of the Wire Cage contains, for the last time for almost twenty-five years, reference to that nebulous woman Mrs. Fell. By 1950, Carr seemed to have temporarily forgotten that there had ever been a Mrs. Fell; he did not mention her in a Who's Who entry about Dr. Fell that he contributed to Anthony Boucher's anthology, Four-&-Twenty Bloodhounds.

It was common in Golden Age detective novels to begin with one mysterious death, then, about three-quarters of the way through the story, to introduce another murder to stop the plot from dragging. But the second murder in *The Problem of the Wire Cage* is unsatisfactory because it assumes completely silly behavior on the part of the killer and blindness on the part of witnesses. Carr himself was not pleased with what he had done. When Anthony Boucher wrote to him that "I find the second murder in *Problem of the Wire Cage* markedly unconvincing," Carr responded, "I admit heartily that the second murder in *The Problem of the Wire Cage,* was not only bad, but unethical and lousy. That book should have been a novelette; instead I had to lug in more gore in order to get the proper length."[27] Besides length requirements from book publishers, Carr was faced with the demands of magazine editors, who wanted some kind of major event in the latter part of the story to keep the interest of readers in the serial. (He received 315 pounds from *Modern Woman* for the serialization of *The Problem of the Wire Cage* under the title "The Cage.")

The 1930s was John Dickson Carr's most prolific period. Under his own name and his Carr/Carter Dickson pseudonym, he wrote twenty-eight full-length detective novels—five about Henri Bencolin, eleven about Dr. Gideon Fell, nine about Sir Henry Merrivale, and three about one-shot detectives (Patrick Rossiter, Sir John Gaunt, and Gaudan Cross). Twenty-three of these books were published between 1933 and 1939. But these figures, as impressive as they are, do not include everything that Carr published during this amazingly productive decade, when he was tossing off one ingenious mystery idea after another. The next two chapters will discuss his historical reconstructions and his short fiction, as well as a collaborative novel. So we shall return to 1934 and another pen name.

Chapter 8

THE LURE OF HISTORY, THE DETECTION CLUB, AND A COLLABORATION

In many ways, John Dickson Carr was a historian manqué. "To write good history," he said in 1936, "is the noblest work of man."[1] But he did not think that all types of historical writing produced "good history." Not for him the analysis of economic and social trends, or how geography and demography affect a people. He preferred narrative history, the sort of thing that Thomas Babington Macaulay had written some eighty years earlier and that Winston Churchill continued to write. History to Carr, as it was to his father, was a mighty, romantic collection of adventures, a sweeping panorama of swordplay, and kings, and battles, and fair damsels, and mystery:

> Let there be a spice of terror, of dark skies and evil things—a pond by a blasted tree, and horsemen galloping by night. Let there be drums behind a great stage—of a nation caught with panic, of kings playing at chess, or fiddles in the drawing-room, and of ladies more fair than any this side of the grave.[2]

He was fascinated by the idea that behind the formal portraits and the dry, yellowing papers of the past were real humans with lusty emotions—"sizzlers long dust," he called them.[3] Carr mentioned his feelings briefly in the semiautobiographical first chapter of one of his last novels, *Deadly*

Hall. The book was published in 1971, but the events take place in 1927, when John Dickson Carr was in Paris attempting to write a historical novel. The hero, Jeff Caldwell (who has two of Carr's initials), is a successful historical novelist, who began his writing in Paris. "I want to write historical romances . . . ," he says, "swashbuckling stuff, not altogether free of gadzookses or the like, but at least historically accurate. . . . I think I can write readable English, and I'm game for all necessary research."[4] Carr inserted short historical romances into some of his contemporary novels of the middle 1930s—*Hag's Nook, The Plague Court Murders, The Red Widow Murders*—but he also wanted to create full-length historical novels.

Above all, he was interested in Restoration England and King Charles II, who reigned between 1660 and 1685. The king's cynicism, his wenching, his lively mind, his years of wandering after the execution of Charles I—all these were attractive to a young romanticist like John Dickson Carr. During the Kingswood years, he read voraciously accounts of the Restoration in the Bristol library. Toward the end of that decade, he listed five types of books he read, including detective novels, ghost stories, the works of Chesterton, Shaw, and J. B. Priestley, books of criminology, and "the literature of the later seventeenth century, particularly of the reign of Charles II."[5]

Throughout the Victorian period, King Charles II had been described as morally reprehensible and politically backward-looking. The great Whig historians, including Macaulay, saw English history as moving inevitably toward the dominance of the House of Commons, and thus the Whig school dismissed Charles II, who fought to maintain royal prerogatives, as standing in the way of progress. Some historians of the period after World War I, however, interpreted Charles's reign entirely differently. Arthur Bryant and C. H. Hartmann were strongly influenced by Macaulay's narrative approach to history, but they thought that Charles understood more clearly than his Parliament the true interests of England. These so-called Stuart apologists, living in a period of international tensions, believed that Charles's support of the English navy against what they perceived as the interference of his penny-pinching Parliament made him a "patriot king." It may be added here that neither the Whigs nor the Stuart apologists were particularly interested in appraising Charles's reign according to the standards of his own era; reality, as usual, lies somewhere between the two extremes, with neither Parliament so progressive as the Whig historians thought nor the king so patriotic as the Stuart apologists believed.

Carr was unabashedly of the Stuart-apologist school. Whether it was closer to the truth than were the Whigs is debatable, but the Stuart position was certainly the more romantic. Carr criticized what he called "the Whig schoolbooks,"[6] and he accepted Bryant's and Hartmann's view of the characters of the Restoration era. Charles, Carr wrote, "understood foreign affairs better than all his counsellors put together," and the opposition led by the Earl of Shaftesbury was "crooked." He compared Shaftesbury's party with the American "gangsters" of the 1930s.[7]

Carr's interpretations of Shaftesbury's motives and actions were misleading, but he never could sympathize with views based on idealism. He had long thought that people who commit themselves to a theoretical view of human behavior end up dehumanizing all of us. His hatred of seventeenth-century Puritanism, like his opposition to Hitler and, for that matter, his portrayal of the nasty crook in *The Red Widow Murders*, was based on hatred of all schemes to control people or modify human behavior. But Carr was unfair in constantly depicting the Puritans as hypo–crites who sought pleasure themselves while denying it to others—"sour enough fellows," he called them.[8] Having no strong religious faith himself, he did not understand the power of religion over others. His heroes are free and easy where drinking and sexual relations are concerned, and when they marry they do so out of love. Shaftesbury, like others of Carr's villains (who, it must be added, are not necessarily his murderers), "never took a bottle too many, or made a fool of himself over a woman," and he married not for love but for money and power. Thus when Carr described him as "of liberal views and great virtue" he was not praising Shaftesbury but criticizing his sort of liberality and his type of virtue.[9]

John Dickson Carr's fascination with Charles II's era and his research at the Bristol library resulted in *Devil Kinsmere*, a novel set in the year 1670. It is possible that *Devil Kinsmere* is a version of the novel that Carr began and then destroyed in Paris in 1927, but that is no more than speculation. Carr completed *Devil Kinsmere* in December 1933 and sent it to Hamish Hamilton in London. Already publishing two books a year under Carr's own name, Hamilton decided that *Kinsmere* had to appear pseudonymously. Hamilton chose the name "Roger Fairbairn" with, as a possible alternate, "Piers Henderson." "Being myself of Scots descent," Carr recalled almost forty years later, "I couldn't or at least didn't object."[10] Hamilton published the book under the Fairbairn name in September or October 1934. Eugene Saxton of Harpers was willing to issue the novel in the United States, but without enthusiasm. *Devil Kinsmere* was, he feared, too British in subject matter for the American market. He therefore decided to save money and not have the book typeset and printed in the United States. Instead, he had Hamilton print and bind an extra supply of pages, with the Harper rather than the Hamilton imprint on the title page and spine, even though he knew that the American copyright might be lost by such a procedure. Although the Harper & Brothers edition of *Devil Kinsmere* had the British date on the back of the title page, it was not published until February 6, 1935.

Hamilton told Carr that Saxton's decision to publish the book through sheet importations was a bad sign; it showed that Saxton didn't have enough confidence in its success to invest much money, and in fact *Devil Kinsmere* received very little advertising. Some of the small amount of publicity may have been written by Carr himself. We may see, for instance, Carr's hand in Harpers' claim that the book was a successor to *The Three Musketeers*. Although reviewers were unwilling to let that assertion pass without challenge, their comments about the book as a whole were generally favorable. Nevertheless, sales in the United States could not be called brisk. Almost two months after publication, 566 copies of *Devil Kinsmere* had been sold compared with 2,715 for *The Blind Barber* during a similar period.[11] Hamilton's sales figures do not survive, but the book seems to have done better in Britain. It was reprinted in February 1935, and the *Cumulative Book Index* indicates that Hamilton did a total of three printings. Nonetheless, no matter how one looks at it, *Devil Kinsmere* was a great disappointment for the author and his publishers. If it eventually sold one thousand copies in the United States, Carr would have earned royalties of only two hundred dollars.

Devil Kinsmere is one of Carr's rarest books, but most fans know its plot. Some thirty years later, under very different circumstances, he revised the book and published it under his own name as *Most Secret*. The rewritten version is interesting on its own, but it belongs to a later phase of his writing career. At this point, we should look at *Devil Kinsmere* as a young man's work. Carr approached the task of re-creating the past more diffidently than he would in his later historical mysteries. In the preface to *Devil Kinsmere*, he points out anachronisms in the narrative and adds that "these lusty men and women can hardly be said to talk in the style of the seventeenth century." Carr excuses the presence of anachronisms by stating that the tale was told in 1815 by Devil Kinsmere's grandson, Major R. B. Kinsmere, to divert the attention of his grandnieces as the Battle of Waterloo was about to occur, and therefore that the language is closer to the nineteenth than to the seventeenth century. Major Kinsmere was, Carr explains, "one of the most genial old liars who ever glorified the family name."

In short, as in *The Three Coffins* and other early works, Carr is cheerfully willing to admit that he is writing fiction, but he still claims "some of [Major Kinsmere's] more outrageous anecdotes are entirely true, whereas some of the more plausible items are pure invention."[12] *Devil Kinsmere* concludes with a section called L'Envoi, which tells what happened after the narrative left off, and quotes from an (invented) Victorian account of the Kinsmere family, which describes the rowdy hero as "given to study and good works." "Awesome as it seems," Carr concludes, "this is what they call the Verdict of History. . . . In its own tuppenny way, it might serve as a symbol for the verdict of history in general." In other words, historians too often ignore the humanity, the passions, and the rowdiness of our ancestors, even in this instance in which a fictional historian writes about a fictional ancestor.

With its youthful exuberance, *Devil Kinsmere* clearly belongs with Carr's other writings of 1933 and 1934. Its hero, Roderick or "Devil" Kinsmere, travels from Somerset (near Bristol) to London to claim an inheritance, and thus he plays the role of Jeff Marle and Tad Rampole of the young visitor to the old world—in 1670, Somerset was as remote from London as America was from Europe in the 1930s. Carr includes descriptions of drinking habits that would have interested Dr. Fell for his definitive study, *The Drinking Customs of England from the Earliest Days*, and he depicts London as almost awash in liquor. In this emphasis on drinking, *Devil Kinsmere* is similar to *The Blind Barber*, which was written around the same time.

On his arrival in London, Kinsmere is wearing a ring given him by his father. One of the king's agents, Bygones Abraham, notices the ring and reveals to Kinsmere that it is now the sign of a royal messenger. Abraham is a well-drawn character: With his old-fashioned Cavalier loyalties and his constant insertion of badly pronounced French phrases into his conversation, he wants to be recognized as a gentleman—and that he can never be. Kinsmere falls in love with Dolly Landis, an actress in the Nell Gwynn mold who is the brutal Ratty Harker's mistress, and secretly another agent of Charles II. Kinsmere gets into a swordfight with Harker, and then murder occurs. The unconscious Harker is mysteriously knifed to death. Even in a historical novel, Carr seemed to have felt the necessity of providing a crime puzzle as well. He eventually reveals that the killer is a Puritan cleric named Jeremiah Gaines, who while committing murder piously urges people to repent; but the murder is not the most important mystery. The book hinges on the puzzle of who is attempting to undermine Charles's policy. Who is Gaines's employer who wanted Harker eliminated?

Within the drinking and the wenching and the swordplay, *Devil Kinsmere* has a major theme: the value of loyalty to things that are real, including traditions and people, rather than to ideas and ideals:

> All he was beginning to realise was that you had to choose a side. It seemed to him that Rights generally meant somebody else's rights, not your own. They were apt to vary according to the views of the new orator who was persuading you to do something, or to the new dictator who was forcing you to do it. Whereas Traditions and Loyalties might be muddle-headed things also, but you could count on them.

In other words, people who speak of "Rights" generally are hiding self-interest. Carr's heroes seldom pay attention to self-interest, and this is something that his villains cannot understand. Jeremiah Gaines says to Kinsmere, "To be candid, I detest you and everything you stand for. You will not see reason—logic—sense—self-interest. Christ! . . . Why can't I understand you?"[13]

Devil Kinsmere is an exciting story, filled with action, mystery, and colorful characters. Chapter 2, a panoramic description of Charles II's London, is one of Carr's finest pieces of writing: "It was a noisy time, a posturing time; a time of jigs and of bludgeoning wit; a cruel, swaggering, credulous, clever time, for smoky London on its mud-flats." The only problem for readers of historical novels is that the story is occasionally too cerebral. Carr slows down the action to explain in detail the varying schemes hatched by the king and the opposition. He spends time making certain that the reader realizes that the clues to the solution of the mysteries are all given fairly. But the major reason that the book did not sell is that it was the first novel by an unknown writer, whose American publisher had few expectations for the book and did not bother to publicize it.

Carr was not unduly discouraged by the failure of *Devil Kinsmere* to find a wide audience. He was full of ideas for other historical novels. Throughout 1934 and 1935, he gathered material for a novel, probably also to be attributed to Roger Fairbairn, about Judge George Jeffreys. Jeffreys was infamous in English history for leading the Bloody Assizes by which the government of James II executed the Monmouth rebels in 1685.

Carr hoped to have the book published during the 250th anniversary of the rebellion. He envisioned a book of about five hundred pages, covering only the years from 1677 to 1685, just before the Assizes began. This limitation seems to miss the drama of Jeffreys's life, but Carr thought the earlier period to contain:

> His most picturesque years . . . his bribes and his love-affairs. . . . The last scene in the book will be Jeffreys getting into his coach, with the trumpets blowing and the guard on the march, and rolling away "to the Bloody Assizes and eternal infamy." That's the sort of thing.

Carr planned to call the book either *Bloody Jeffreys* or *The Seat of the Scornful*. "Ever since I was a kid I've wanted to write a book (about anything) called *The Seat of the Scornful*. It has such a roll and thunder."[14]

On his visit to New York in the summer of 1934, Carr discussed ideas for the Jeffreys novel with Eugene Saxton, who was not enthusiastic. Instead, he suggested that Carr choose a topic that would be easier to push in the American market. Carr said that he was also interested in writing a novel about the American Revolution from the viewpoint of a British officer. After he returned to England, Carr asked Hamilton for advice about which historical theme to try first. Hamilton was not very helpful: He said that the American Revolution novel would do better in the States, and the Jeffreys better in England. The decision about which novel to write he left to Carr. Carr, however, was already beginning to wonder "whether these historical novels are profitable enough (or ever would be profitable enough) for all the work that goes into them."[15] Consequently, the book about Jeffreys was put aside.

Meanwhile, Carr's trip to the United States had given him another idea for a novel—and, incidentally, reintroduced him to baseball. He brought a baseball mitt, bat, and ball back to Kingswood, and tried without much success to teach his young brother-in-law, Roy Cleaves, and the neighborhood children America's national pastime. In Bristol, Carr became involved in cricket for the first time since the matches at Haverford, and he found that the techniques used for the British sport were entirely different from those for baseball. He tried to hold the cricket bat pointed toward the ground in the correct English fashion, but he could not hit the ball. Frustrated, he told the bowler to throw the ball in baseball fashion, and he held the bat just off his shoulder like an American ballplayer. Clarice Carr still remembers that he hit the ball "over the horizon."[16] Carr thought that this experience might be incorporated into a book. "I've got a good idea for a comic novel, which ought not to be a detective story," Carr said in January 1935. "It concerns an International Peace Conference in London, and the efforts of the higher diplomacy to promote international good feeling by sending an American baseball team over to play cricket, while the Test Team meets them at baseball." Hamish Hamilton poured cold water on this idea, suggesting that Carr stick to two genres, historical and detective, and not add a third.[17] Though Hamilton did not say so, Carr's proposed book probably would have bemused both Americans who did not understand cricket and British who knew nothing of baseball.

Neither Eugene Saxton nor Hamish Hamilton had responded positively to some of Carr's suggestions for new novels, but they agreed to have Carr write a nonfiction historical work. In July 1935, Harpers gave him a contract for three books, two of which were to be detective novels (as it turned out, *The Arabian Nights Murder* and *The Burning Court)*, while "the third book is to be one of from 100,000 to 125,000 words in length dealing with an historical event." Clarice Carr recalls that Harpers demanded that he produce three books rather than two in a year, and that is certainly the implication of the contract, even though it turned out that only two of his books were published by Harpers and Hamilton in 1936 and two in 1937. The new contract was much more generous than the previous agreement. Instead of a guarantee of $100 a month as had been the case in 1934 and early 1935, Harpers and Hamilton together paid him a bit more than $290 a month. Carr professed himself "thoroughly pleased" with the agreement, and it was one reason he felt that he could drop Carter Dickson for a while;[18] the other reason was that his new historical work was more ambitious than any work he had previously undertaken.

While reading about the reign of King Charles II, Carr had come upon material related to the strange death of Sir Edmund Godfrey in 1678. Godfrey, a well-known Protestant magistrate of London, had been found strangled and stabbed with his own sword on Primrose Hill north of London. England, whose politics had long been dominated by anti-Catholicism, was already tense with rumors that "Papists" planned to assassinate the king and place his Catholic brother James, Duke of York, on the throne. Titus Oates, who had revealed this so-called Popish Plot, had sworn to the truth of his testimony before Godfrey, and consequently Godfrey's death seemed to confirm the truth of the plot. The Whig opposition to the king, led by the Earl of Shaftesbury, took advantage of

Oates's claims and tried to weaken the monarch's authority and to exclude his brother from succession to the throne. Eventually, Charles defeated the Whigs, but three innocent Catholics were executed for Godfrey's murder. The truth about Godfrey's death has never been finally determined.

Carr seems to have become interested in the episode when he read an article by J. G. Muddiman, "The Mystery of Sir E. B. Godfrey," in *National Review*, September 1924. Muddiman identified a previously unsuspected nobleman as the murderer. Muddiman's case was undetailed—the article is only seven pages long—but Carr became convinced that Muddiman was correct. Gathering material at the Bristol Library, he found more and more evidence to support Muddiman's theory. Carr enjoyed working on the book; it was, Clarice Carr recalls, "his joy and delight."[19]

Carr saw the work as historical detection; in fact, his working title was *The Murder of Sir Edmund Godfrey: A Detective Story*. It would be a narrative of the case, with all events and speeches taken from contemporary sources, but as he explained in August 1935 to Hamish Hamilton, he would structure it "exactly like a detective story, with clues planted and a surprise (but I think true) solution." For a while, Carr and his publishers debated whether to use the Roger Fairbairn pseudonym for *The Murder of Sir Edmund Godfrey*, but the sales of *Devil Kinsmere* did not indicate that a Fairbairn book would get much attention. Carr told Saxton that he preferred to use his own name on the book because it "would then be bound to receive at least the attention that is given to the regular detective stories." Saxton agreed.[20]

Carr first planned the book to be in ten parts, with the first two being an overview of the characters and the politics of Restoration England. Carr thought that the printed book would have more than four hundred pages. He put aside work on *The Burning Court* in order to complete *The Murder of Sir Edmund Godfrey*, and by early May 1936 he had sent Hamilton the first six parts in 243 pages. But the publisher was not pleased. He advised "drastic cutting" so that the reader's interest would not be lost in details that had nothing to do with the murder mystery. Carr agreed to replace the first two chapters—some eighty pages—with a brief "Preface for Connoisseurs in Murder" of about 19 pages, and he estimated that the entire book could be shortened to around 360 pages. He completed the book, which was now in eight parts, on June 9. "I'm glad it's finished," he said, "and I'm a little woozy in the head."[21] It was published in London on October 9, 1936, and in New York about a month later.

Carr described *The Murder of Sir Edmund Godfrey* as a "really good work." "It has," he went on, "what I think is known as a wallop."[22] In this instance, Carr was a perceptive self-critic. The book belongs with such novels as *The Three Coffins, The Burning Court, The Crooked Hinge, The Judas Window,* and one or two others at the very top of his writings of the 1930s. It is, wrote Jacques Barzun and Weldell Hertig Taylor, "a classic in the best sense—i. e., rereadable indefinitely."[23] It is certainly one of Carr's most innovative books. Although books had long been written presenting new solutions to classic murder cases, Carr was the first in the field to construct the work in the form of a detective story:

> Let the evidence not all be thrown at us in a lump; but let it grow up as the story unfolds, so that each new turn is a surprise to us as it was to those who saw it happen. Let the real murderer walk and talk unsuspected throughout the story; let there be no nods or elbow-joggings from the author, no hints to watch his gait, no speculations as to what went on in his mind. But let the clues to his identity be scattered shrewdly, for the reader to find if he cares to do so. Let there be half a dozen persons who might have committed the murder, each suspected in turn, and each in turn proved innocent. . . . And at intervals, over our pipes and glasses, let us discuss the evidence in a certain long library where we shall sit as the Society of Connoisseurs in Murder.[24]

It is probably the narrative flow of *The Murder of Sir Edmund Godfrey* that most impresses the modern reader: It is history told with the techniques of a novelist. Following the short Preface, the events unfold as a colorful story, with political intrigue balanced against the story of a murder. About halfway through the book, Carr inserts "An Interlude for Connoisseurs in Murder"—the phrase is taken from Thomas de Quincey, who in his essay "Murder Considered as One of the Fine Arts" mentioned a club in London that "may be denominated a Society for the Encouragement of Murder, but . . . [which] is styled—The Society of Connoisseurs in Murder."[25] Carr's Interlude discusses twelve possible solutions for the murder of Sir Edmund Godfrey. This section is followed by further narrative chapters on the trial of the three innocent Catholics who were eventually executed for the murder. After a chapter about political developments culminating in Charles II's defeat of Shaftesbury's Whigs, *The Murder of Sir Edmund Godfrey* concludes with "An Ending for Connoisseurs of Murder," in which the previous solutions are discussed and dismissed, and a new solution is proposed. Carr produces far more evidence than Muddiman had found supporting the guilt of a previously unsuspected character.

Carr's techniques as a fiction writer produce both the strengths and the weaknesses of *The Murder of Sir Edmund Godfrey*. The writing is often brilliant, with telling details and memorable turns of phrase. The book is infused with a sense of drama, of great events across a vast stage. Part of the effect of the book comes from Carr's determinedly pro-Stuart bias. His love of Charles II comes through on almost every page, and so does his hatred of the Whigs. The passion of the book may not really recapture the passion of the times, but the reader is caught up.

In order to create this drama, however, Carr sometimes goes further than the evidence will allow. He has been deservedly praised, for example, for his poignant description of the treatment of Samuel Atkins, clerk to Samuel Pepys, the secretary of the Admiralty, who was temporarily accused of participation in the Popish Plot. Atkins was imprisoned in the hope that he might incriminate his master:

> It was not that he much minded, one way or the other, but he would not be put upon. It was the mere bigness and overbearing calm cheat of this business, as though a tapster should swear you had not paid a reckoning when you had paid it, that determined him to fight: the calm fashion in which they told you you had better swear away your master's life, and no nonsense about it. God rot'em anyhow! thought the mouse, and began to nibble at his bonds. . . . Samuel Atkins stopped writhing in his manacles. . . . He saw a cabin with wine-bottles on the table, and the laughing faces of women half-boozy, and the captain a-chuckle.[26]

This is compelling writing, but there is no documentary evidence for Atkins's reactions, which, with their opposition to "bigness and overbearing calm cheat," sound more like those of John Dickson Carr than of a seventeenth-century clerk. In various instances, moreover, Carr describes glances and gestures that are not in the records, and he takes conversations from one context and puts them into another—thus he describes a meeting between Charles and Shaftesbury at a time when in historical fact Shaftesbury was out of London. While Carr's technique of re-creating history may not be accurate, however, it is marvelously effective in presenting Godfrey's death as a detective story.

Of course, the major issue is whether Carr, following Muddiman, correctly fingered Godfrey's murderer. I have analyzed the solution in detail in an Afterword to the most recent edition of *The Murder of Sir Edmund Godfrey* (International Polygonics, 1989). To summarize, in recent years there has been reexamination of the medical evidence, which indicates that some of Carr's assumptions must be modified, but no one has suggested a better candidate for the murderer. The Muddiman-Carr theory was confirmed and amplified in a recent book by Stephen Knight, *The Killing of Justice Godfrey* (London: Granada, 1984), but Knight unfairly denigrates the investigations of his predecessors. Although Carr believed that the culprit's motive was personal, Knight suggests that the murder was part of an elaborate political conspiracy, for which (I might add) there is precious little evidence.

"I feel it in my bones," Carr wrote in July 1936, "that *Godfrey* is going to be a success." But there was already a bad sign. As they had done with *Devil Kinsmere*, Harpers decided to purchase sheets from Hamilton's British edition rather than to typeset and print the book themselves. Cass Canfield and Hamish Hamilton discussed mentioning the matter "casually" to Carr to see whether he would notice that he could lose United States copyright if the book were not produced on that side of the Atlantic. Carr apparently did not catch on, for the first U.S. issue of the book contains pages printed in Britain in a U.S. binding. The number of British-produced sheets must have been quite small, for the book quickly sold out in America, and a second printing was produced in New York to handle the back orders. Reviews of *The Murder of Sir Edmund Godfrey* were generally positive, but as was the case with *Devil Kinsmere*, Harpers did not promote the book: Instead of the full-page advertisement that Harpers usually purchased in *Publishers' Weekly* for a new Carr book, they merely listed *The Murder of Sir Edmund Godfrey* in a "Checklist of Harper Fall Books."[27]

Despite having the book go into a second printing, Harpers reported that *The Murder of Sir Edmund Godfrey* faced "initial sales resistance." Some figures predicting royalties are included in 1937 correspondence, but they are not detailed enough to estimate total sales of *Godfrey*. The figures, however, are of some interest. In February 1937, Cass Canfield of Harper & Brothers estimated that *The Burning Court*, to be published in spring 1937, would earn a royalty of about $550 during 1937, a figure that indicates a projected sale of 2,750 copies at a list of $2; the numbers would be higher if succeeding years were considered, but there was no estimate of those figures. Canfield thought *Godfrey* would earn royalties of $200 during 1937. *Godfrey* was a longer and more elaborately produced book than

The Burning Court, with gold lettering on the front cover and spine and photographic reproductions of contemporary illustrations; so its list price was $2.50. Canfield's figures for *Godfrey* indicate projected sales of about 800 copies for the year 1937, but that figure does not include November and December 1936 sales. When sales in successive years were added in, Canfield thought that "the total earnings of *The Murder of Sir Edmund Godfrey* will probably not exceed $600," or around 2,400 copies. What all this amounted to was that Carr's detective novels outsold his historical works by more than three to one. One further point can be derived from Canfield's estimates: About two-thirds of Carr's income under his own name came from United States sales, one-third from British. It is likely that the ratio was similar for Carter Dickson books.[28]

Canfield recorded these figures to make a simple point. Carr's books were not earning the $291 a month guaranteed in the July 1936 contract, and as a result he proposed to lower the payment to the level of the previous contract, that is, $100 a month. In February 1937, Canfield explained to Carr why he had to cut payments by 65 percent. "Carr was depressed by this," Canfield reported to Hamilton in what must have been an understatement, but he promised Carr to try to do better if sales picked up. They apparently did improve, for in the contract signed in May 1937, Harpers increased the guarantee to $150 a month. Canfield also held out the carrot of a larger monthly payment if Carr would produce three books a year for them, one of which might be a historical novel. He suggested that Carr write "a *Godfrey* type of book in time for publication before the autumn of 1938," and Carr responded by reviving the idea of a novel about Judge Jeffreys.[29] But for a person making a living with his typewriter, the money earned on *The Murder of Sir Edmund Godfrey* was not enough for the time he had spent on the book, and it was not until 1950 that he tried another historical novel, and that one was quite different from *Godfrey.* To fellow writer Lillian de la Torre, Carr explained why he never attempted another book to solve a genuine murder mystery. After reading *The Murder of Sir Edmund Godfrey,* de la Torre had written two books of what she called "histo-detection"—*Elizabeth Is Missing* and *The Heir of Douglas*—one of which was dedicated to John Dickson Carr. Many years later, de la Torre recounted the following conversation, which took place in the 1950s:

He said to me: "I'd give a lot to write the books you write." "Why John," I protested, "that's ridiculous! You wrote the best one ever, and I only imitated it." "I know," he replied, "but I can't afford to any more. I have two daughters in college, and it takes two of my mystery novels a year to keep them there."[30]

In spite of the unsatisfactory sales of *The Murder of Sir Edmund Godfrey*, the middle 1930s were good years for Carr's career. The sales of his detective novels continued to increase, and critical recognition continued to come. Powys Mathers, the critic who signed his work "Torquemada," called him one of the "Big Five" of mystery writers. Probably the most gratifying recognition was his election as the first (and during his lifetime the only) American member of London's exclusive Detection Club in 1936. The initial contact between Carr and the club is not recorded; perhaps it was through Hamish Hamilton, who had earlier attended a meeting as a guest. Hamilton told Carr that the club represented "all the swells in your own game." Among the swells that Carr hoped to meet was The Detection Club's honorary president, G. K. Chesterton, Carr's literary idol and the model for Dr. Fell. "My spies informed me," Carr said many years later, "that Chesterton was not at all displeased" about being Dr. Fell's inspiration. Sadly, Chesterton died shortly before Carr was to be inducted. The new president was E. C. Bentley, author of the classic *Trent's Last Case*. Carr's sponsors were the club's founder, Anthony Berkeley, and its most active member, Dorothy L. Sayers. The initiation ceremony was an elaborate bit of mumbo-jumbo, which was (Carr recalled) written by Sayers.[31] When she succeeded Bentley as honorary president in 1949, she insisted on the performance of the ceremony with the solemn punctiliousness of a religious liturgy. The ceremony was not a secret; it was described first by Chesterton himself in the May 1933 issue of *The Strand*. With his hand on "Eric the Skull"—because of the technical wizardry of writer John Rhode, Eric's eyes lit brightly—the candidate for membership was asked to swear to the following:

> Do you promise that your detectives shall well and truly detect the crimes presented to them, using those wits which it may please you to bestow upon them, and not placing reliance on nor making use of Divine Revelation, Feminine Intuition, Mumbo-Jumbo, Jiggery-Pokery, Coincidence or Act of God? Do you promise never to conceal a vital clue from the reader? Do you promise to observe a seemly moderation in the use of Gangs, Conspiracies, Death-Rays, Ghosts, Hypnotism, Trap-Doors, Chinamen, Super-Criminals and Lunatics; and utterly and for ever to forswear Mysterious Poisons unknown to

Science? Will you honour the King's English? All this I do solemnly
swear. And I do furthermore promise and undertake to be loyal to
the Club, neither purloining nor disclosing any plot or secret com-
municated to me before publication by any Member, whether under
the influence of drink or otherwise.

The "ruler" then said to the candidate:

You are duly elected a Member of The Detection Club, and if you fail
to keep your promise, may other writers anticipate your plots, may
your publishers do you down in your contracts, may strangers sue
you for libel, may your pages swarm with misprints and may your
sales continually diminish. Amen.

I might add here that the prohibition of Chinamen was in response to the
Fu-Manchu books and imitators that presented any Asiatic as ipso facto
bent on dominating the world. Chesterton explained that "the incessant
and reckless propagation of wicked Chinamen, to do the dirty work of
Europeans in their sensational novels, has been one of the most servile
and anti-social forms of the employment of Chinese labour," and he
praised Earl Derr Biggers for inventing Charlie Chan and making him the
policeman rather than a supercriminal.

Carr later recalled that The Detection Club's rules were "amusing and
rather impressive when spoken with resonance." There was usually, he
said, considerable debate before a candidate received the invitation for
membership; no matter who might be proposed for membership, someone would object that he or she either did not write the king's English or
did not play fair with the clues.[32] All of which was rather odd for a club
that was basically a social gathering, with members chosen at least as
much for their conviviality as for any other quality.

In 1981, I asked Gladys Mitchell, who had become a member of The
Detection Club in 1933, for her memories of John Dickson Carr's participation in the club. She wrote:

I remember him as a most pleasant and friendly member, always
alert and cheerful, very active and sociable and greatly liked by all. In
those days, we met every second month to dine and then to go to the
Club rooms for a talk and often to hear a guest from Scotland Yard or
the world of forensic medicine and so forth. At two of the meetings,
members were allowed to bring one guest each and it would have
been at such gatherings that Mrs. Dickson Carr was present, apart

from the annual dinner to which any number of guests could be invited. When John first joined he did attempt to introduce dreadful paper and pencil games which the lazy and replete (the dinners at L'Escargot Bienvenu in Soho were cheap but filling) English did not want to play, so we soon persuaded him that this form of mental torture was not for us. At that time we had a couple of sleazy rooms in Gerrard Street, just off Leicester Square, and if there was no guest speaker we sat about on members' discarded and disreputable furniture, chatted and drank beer which was provided out of the Club funds. John, bless his heart!—true to his Scottish forebears and mine!—used to augment this with a splendid bottle of whiskey. Apart from this and the renown he brought us by his brilliant and popular books, I think his chief contribution to the Club was a certain informality of approach to his fellow members and this, I think, led to a breakdown of the stiffness and what I felt was the snobbishness of some members before he joined us.[33]

With the death of Gladys Mitchell in 1983, Clarice Carr is the only living person who often attended Detection Club meetings during the 1930s. She was always present at the annual banquet, and occasionally at some of the bimonthly meetings as well. Oddly enough, no one has written a full history of The Detection Club, so (unless another source is given) the following descriptions of the members are taken from Clarice's memories.[34] She was a welcome guest because she was interested in things other than shop talk and because, at the age of twenty-seven, she had a youthful vivacity that pleased the older members. The only uncomfortable moments she had at the meetings were with Dorothy L. Sayers. Sayers tended to be, if not exactly condescending, at least impatient with those she felt did not have the education she had, or who were a bit flippant at things she thought important—such as the club's ritual. Clarice thinks that her appearance was against her in Sayers's eyes: She is a petite woman while, except for Gladys Mitchell, most of the female members of The Detection Club during the 1930s were large—"foursquare," Clarice calls them. When Sayers put on an aloofly impatient attitude, Clarice and others were annoyed, but now Clarice recalls, "I got a feeling that wasn't Dorothy; I think of herself she was actually a kindly person." On the other hand, though he admitted that she had a "somewhat formidable public manner," John was tremendously impressed with the woman who not only created Lord Peter Wimsey but also had been instrumental through her *Sunday Times* reviews in promoting his work. He described her as "the Club's moving spirit . . . [who] guarded the gate against those who neither played fair with the clues nor wrote good English." In later years, an occasional grumble arose among some Detection Club members that John Dickson Carr could be counted on to support whatever Dorothy L. Sayers proposed, and Clarice told some of the disaffected that she agreed with them. John remembered one occasion when Sayers was not so toplofty: "I alone (with John Rhode) was present when Dorothy Sayers, after making some inroads on a bottle of Scotch, arose like one addressing a Sunday School and recited the limerick about the young girl from Madras."[35]

Margery Allingham, the creator of an elegant series of mysteries featuring Albert Campion, was uncomfortable around Sayers. Allingham told Clarice Carr that Sayers "absolutely frightened her to death," but when Sayers was not physically in the same room, Allingham was very entertaining. Clarice remembers her as erudite and likeable, and her husband Youngman "Pip" Carter as a total charmer. John, whose memories of friends at The Detection Club tended to be rather bibulous, wrote:

> Well I remember a somewhat drunken weekend with Margery and Pip Carter at their home in Essex, when she handed me one of her books inscribed thus:

> For John Dickson Carr,
> The world's best detective-story writer
> EXCEPT ME—
> Margery Allingham[36]

Agatha Christie, who was very shy, hated any kind of bickering, even when—as was usually the case at The Detection Club—the participants were enjoying the argument mightily. She would then disappear into another room until the dispute was over. When she succeeded Sayers as honorary president of The Detection Club, she would not perform the public functions, so Lord Gorell (the author of some traditional but forgettable detective stories) became copresident. He led the rituals and was called by the disrespectful title "Lord Sheep." Christie was friendly to everyone, and even though she and her husband, the archaeologist Max Mallowan, were not intimate friends of the Carrs, they sometimes visited socially.

Clarice recalls Gladys Mitchell as gentle, fair-haired, and slightly built, with "a school mistressy manner"—and she was in fact a school mistress in private life. She was an independent and capable person, whose special talent was watching over the business side of The Detection Club.

Anthony Berkeley was the founder of The Detection Club, and one of its most active members during the 1930s and 1940s. He was known as First Freeman, probably because two of the other charter members were Freeman Wills Crofts and R. Austin Freeman. Carr remembered Berkeley declaring, "With Freemans to the right, Freemans to the left, Freemans on every side, the founder of this club is damn well going to be First Freeman, and don't you forget it."[37] A man of independent wealth, Berkeley was legendary for his stinginess. Christianna Brand, who became a member in 1946, said that he would invite himself to her house so that he could drink free gins-and-tonic, and then—perhaps feeling a bit guilty—pay for the tonic he had consumed but not the gin.[38] Clarice says that one day she asked him to autograph one of his Roger Sheringham detective novels, which she had brought with her to a Detection Club meeting. Berkeley did not notice that she had the book in her hand, and suggested, "My dear girl, if you go out and pay, oh, I think the cheap one is 3s 9d, and bring it to me, I might autograph it." She answered, "Anthony Berkeley, I've got your wretched 7s 6d copy, and I don't want it autographed." But he was not like that all the time. He could be an urbane and witty conversationalist, and Clarice remembers him as very good-looking in an English-film-star sort of way.

In 1969, Carr wrote that "following the death of A. E. W. Mason just over twenty years ago, I have always ranked [Anthony Berkeley] second only to Ellery Queen, and should have ranked them equal if Tony hadn't stopped turning out novels of any kind in 1939."[39] Considering that Dorothy L. Sayers and Margery Allingham died long after Mason, and that Agatha Christie and Ngaio Marsh were still active in 1969, Carr's praise of Berkeley's novels was high indeed.

Clarice Carr never met the Baroness Orczy, author of the classic Old Man in the Corner mysteries from the opening years of the century, but John did and was impressed, describing her as "a small, vivacious old lady with white hair and flashing dark eyes."[40] They sat next to each other at a Detection Club dinner, and as he told Clarice when he returned home that evening, the baroness turned to him and said, "Oh, Mr. Carr, no one would ever guess, you know, that you're an American." She clearly considered this a compliment, and John was most amused, especially since it came from someone who was born in Hungary and still spoke with a slight accent.

Like the Baroness Orczy, Dr. R. Austin Freeman began writing detective stories shortly after the turn of the century. When Carr joined The Detection Club, Freeman was in his middle seventies, but he still published a novel each year. Clarice saw him at meetings but they did not have any conversations. John, however, later recalled that he "would escort Dr. Austin Freeman up and down the stairs to the Club rooms in Gerrard Street, hoping he wouldn't die of a heart attack on the way to dinner."[41]

Unlike some other members of The Detection Club, E. C. Bentley was a reserved man. Carr described him as "burly, quiet-voiced, always with a twinkle in his eye."[42] Clarice recalls that when she met Bentley his current interest was the Napoleonic Wars, and since she had recently been reading about the same era, they got along splendidly. Another undemonstrative man was Freeman Wills Crofts, the author of the Inspector French novels and the master of the complicated alibi. Crofts was only fifty-seven years old in 1936, but with his white mustache he appeared elderly to Clarice. Although he was polite, he always gave the impression that his thoughts were elsewhere, perhaps turning over another method of breaking an alibi.

Both John and Clarice enjoyed meeting A. A. Milne, the creator of Winnie the Pooh and (more to the point) the author of the classic comedy-of-manners detective novel *The Red House Mystery*, which John had read some fourteen years earlier but found too slow-moving. Later, he admired the book, writing that in his early opinion "I couldn't have been more mistaken. . . . It was a fine achievement then; it remains a fine achievement today."[43] Milne did not regularly attend The Detection Club, but Clarice's memories of him are vivid:

> He was there just once at one of the affairs. He fascinated me. He was a purely English type, nice-looking, almost film-starish, slim and small-boned, not short but not very tall either, with light brown hair. Apparently he was in his quiet mood. He'd take himself to a corner, and just sit there, talking to no one, looking at no one. And I said to John Rhode, "You know that's terrible; it looks as though everyone is ignoring him. Do you think I should sort of go over and have a little chit-chat, bring him back into the company?" He said, "Oh, no, he's thoroughly enjoying himself. You know, that's his social mannerism."

The Detection Club had a few members whose contributions to the genre were small. Ianthe Jerrold, for example, has been almost entirely forgotten. Her two books about a dilettante named John Christmas were imitations of Sayers, but with Anthony Berkeley's sponsorship, she became one of the charter members of 1930. But then she stopped writing detective novels, and Berkeley spent much effort trying in vain to persuade her to try another. Somewhat more important, but little-known today, was Milward Kennedy, author of two series of detective novels, one featuring Sir George Bull, the other featuring Inspector Cornford. Before joining The Detection Club, Carr was by turns amused and annoyed with Kennedy. In the anthology *A Century of Detective Fiction*, each contributor wrote the blurb that preceded his story. Carr was amused when Kennedy described himself as ranking "with the giants in this field of fiction." We have already seen, on the other hand, how much Carr and his publisher disliked some of Kennedy's reviews in the *Sunday Times*—but even this could lead to amusement on Carr's part. In his reviews, Kennedy often begged authors to include more maps and plans in their mystery stories. "I don't see," Carr remarked in 1935, "how he can carry his own copy to the newspaper office without a large-scale diagram of Fleet Street. That man could get lost in a telephone-box, and a journey by Underground would kill him. I don't think there is any harm in him. He means well."[44] Clarice describes him as "an enormous man; he was well built and tall, broad-shouldered and slightly thick through the body."

John Dickson Carr's closest friend in The Detection Club was Major C. J. C. Street, who wrote novels under the pseudonyms John Rhode and Miles Burton and who was generally known at the club under his Rhode name. Both Carr and Rhode considered the fair-play rule sacrosanct, but otherwise their works were quite different. Rhode's detective, Dr. Priestley, was a scientist—or, as we would now make the distinction, a technologist. Rhode's writing style tended toward the stodgy, with little emphasis on atmosphere, characterization, and setting. But his plots were solidly constructed, with Priestley using his knowledge of scientific principles (and gadgets) to elucidate the crime. In spite of their literary differences, however, Rhode became what Carr described as:

> my greatest friend in the flourishing years of the London Detection Club. . . . He once boasted of being the Detection Club's heaviest member, always excepting G. K. Chesterton. I have watched him polish off ten pints of beer before lunch, and more than that after dinner.[45]

Unexpectedly, for someone whose books are rather flat, Rhode was in person a great storyteller with entertaining accounts of his army experiences. Clarice's memory of him is that "he was fun," and the Carrs often visited John Rhode and his wife, Eileen, at their home in Laddingford, Kent.

John Dickson Carr was an extremely active member of The Detection Club, and for the rest of his life he remembered the bimonthly meetings as some of his happiest times. Unlike Christie, he reveled in the spirited give-and-take at the club. In 1937, he told Sayers that "at the last Club meeting, we did not get in quite as thoroughly late an argument-session as I (who love 'em) would have liked."[46] Four years later, when the club had suspended its meetings because of the war, Carr wrote to Frederic Dannay:

> In happier times you would probably have been interested to attend a dinner of our Detection Club. We used to meet every other month to talk shop, and our conversations froze the waiter's blood. "Don't shoot him, old man; you'll get into difficulties later. Strangle him." "She must definitely die in convulsions; I'm using strychnine."[47]

John and Clarice Carr were the unofficial photographers of The Detection Club. They had dabbled in photography in Kingswood. Even though John was a chain smoker of cigarettes and rarely touched a pipe, he insisted on Clarice's taking a photograph of him pensively smoking one. The picture gave him, he believed, a Holmesian look,[48] and it appeared on the dust jackets of his books for a number of years. By the end of 1936, he and Clarice were busily taking photographs of club members and various displays of books and prints owned by the club, and John displayed some of the pictures over his desk for the rest of his life.[49]

Shortly after his installation as a member, Carr became the club's honorary secretary. One of his duties was to take the place of the president whenever he could not be present, but Gladys Mitchell recalled that E. C. Bentley faithfully attended, and she did not think that Carr ever took the chair in Bentley's place. But he did send out the notices of meetings and invite guests to address the gathering. On one occasion, he gleefully wrote to Sayers that he had unearthed "a genuine Viennese psychoanalyst to talk to The Detection Club on murder." His greatest success, however, was persuading the eminent barrister Norman Birkett, who was famous for representing those whom Carr called "the defenseless and even the indefensible," to speak at a meeting in May 1939. Neither John nor Clarice knew what Birkett looked like, but John had the idea that all eminent barristers were barrel-shaped, rather like Sir Henry Merrivale and, in his younger days, Wooda Carr, and Clarice spent some time accosting various stout gentlemen outside the club trying to locate Birkett. At last the barrister introduced himself, and he turned out to be tall and thin. Birkett delighted the gathering with some indiscreet anecdotes about obviously guilty clients of whose innocence he had persuaded juries.[50]

As secretary, Carr was also expected to represent the views of The Detection Club before the public. For example, he expressed the club's outrage about Howard Spring's review in *The Evening Standard* of Agatha Christie's *Hercule Poirot's Christmas* (1938). The reviewer had shocked the club by revealing the solution to the mystery, and the next day an irate Anthony Berkeley telephoned Carr and demanded that he write to the *Standard*. This Carr did, but the reviewer responded that detective fiction was trash. Sayers entered the fray by pointing out that the issue was not taste in fiction but whether the book's conclusion should have been revealed in a review. Others then crossed swords. John found the entire affair hilarious, and used a version of it as the opening of *The Case of the Constant Suicides* (1941). More than thirty years later, when he had himself become a reviewer, Carr cited Spring's comments as an example of what a critic should *not* do. Masking him under the name of "Richmond Fall," he expressed the hope that "since then he has been eaten by bears, like those children who mocked the prophet."[51]

Three years after Carr joined The Detection Club, he and a number of others met at the home of the writer F. Tennyson Jesse to form an organization to be called The Black Maria Club, as a forum for the discussion of true-life murders. Mrs. Belloc Lowndes read a paper on Lizzie Borden; among the other club members were the novelist Hugh Walpole, the mystery writer A. E. W. Mason, and Harry Hodge, publisher of *Notable British Trials*. The Black Maria Club agreed to accept judges as members "if they behaved," but there was no opportunity to admit them or indeed any other new members. The Black Maria met only once before World War II intervened. But Carr memorialized it under the name of The Murder Club in *He Who Whispers* (1946) and *In Spite of Thunder* (1960).[52]

Carr had a lively curiosity about unsolved crimes. He read many accounts of true crimes and often referred to them in his novels. Dr. James E. Keirans has noted seventy-two instances in the Fell and Merrivale mysteries alone where Carr mentioned genuine criminals. Moreover, some of these real-life murders provided the plots of several of his novels and short stories, but in most cases it is uncertain whether he thought that his fictional solution was in fact the answer to the actual murder. For example, "Blind Man's Hood," a short story published in 1937, is based on the death of Rose Harsent in the Peasenhall Case in 1902. Similarly, the murder in *Below Suspicion* (1949) has resemblances to the mysterious death of Charles Bravo in 1876—a case that Carr thought "has few rivals in the history of crime"—but with its witchcraft elements the book could not have given Carr's solution to the real murder. Although he wrote about the Bravo mystery on two other occasions, he refused to name his choice of culprit. In 1945, he wrote a dramatic version of the case for BBC radio, without suggesting a solution. It ends, "You have heard the evidence. Who killed Charles Bravo?" Almost a decade later, he contributed an introduction to John Williams's account of the case, *Suddenly at the Priory,* but he announced that "to theorize is none of my business."[53]

Theorizing, however, about unsolved crimes was one of Carr's favorite games at Christmastime. His daughter, Bonita, remembers that he would recount a famous case and ask his family or guests to suggest possible answers. His interest in true crime was primarily in how it could be made to fit a fictional pattern. When he presented his ideas, he carefully distinguished between fact and theory; he rarely suggested that such-and-such an answer solved the mystery. He said that it was *an* explanation, but not necessarily *the* only one, of the known facts. He often speculated about the identity of Jack the Ripper, who committed the "Whitechapel Murders" of prostitutes in 1888 and 1889. Although he gave a brief outline of the case in print, and even asked rhetorically "Who was Jack the Ripper?" he did not publish his solution.[54] His family, however, recalls that he was fond of the "Jane the Ripper" theory, that the murderer was a midwife who was such a fixture in the neighborhood that witnesses did not notice her presence. Carr knew of no evidence of the motive, but he thought that in a work of fiction the midwife would have a daughter who had become a prostitute and died of a botched abortion. Her mother then would have avenged her daughter's death by carving up others who had the same profession.[55]

Another of Carr's favorite cases was the murder of Julia Wallace in 1931. He described it as "a real sizzler, a knockout, a wow of a problem." Julia and William Wallace were a quiet married couple, with few friends but with several interests in common, including music—he had taken violin lessons, she piano. One evening, Wallace received a message to meet a man named Qualtrough on a business matter. The address he was given, however, was nonexistent, and when he returned home he found his wife brutally murdered. That, at least, was his story. The police believed that Wallace killed his wife and set up a crude alibi based on the imaginary

Qualtrough. Wallace was tried and convicted, but the jury's verdict was overturned on appeal.

Carr discussed the case on several occasions at The Detection Club with Dorothy L. Sayers, who had written an excellent account of the mystery for the 1936 Detection Club volume called *The Anatomy of Murder*. He followed up with two letters to Sayers about William Wallace's trial. "I don't believe Wallace was guilty," he said, "for real reasons as well as artistic ones." In the second letter, he wrote that "I don't believe that the crime was committed for money." But he refused to come out and say who he believed was guilty: "With this mysterious to-be-continued-in-our-next, I fold my cloak over my head and slink away." If there was an "our next," it has not been preserved. But he gave some hints both to Sayers and, in some of his Christmastime sessions, to his family. Julia Wallace had been murdered in the seldom-used front sitting room, where a gas fire had been lit. From that evidence, Carr assumed that she had been expecting the murderer, and the only people who seemed to fit that requirement were the Wallaces' music teachers. In 1937, Carr hinted to Sayers that it was the violin master, who in fact had been out of his house at the time of the murder: "I have a firm belief in the guilt of a certain person not unconnected with violin-playing." Later, he revised his opinion and told his family that he thought the murderer was Mrs. Wallace's piano teacher. He had, however, no suggestion about the motive.*[56]

Besides the murder of Sir Edmund Godfrey, on only two occasions did Carr suggest in print his solution to an unsolved murder. In 1937, the London newspaper *The Star* ran a contest called "Unsolved Mysteries of Real Life." In a series of short articles, each about a notorious case, a reporter gave the details of a murder, and then a "well-known thriller author" presented an original solution to the mystery. Readers were invited to compete for a prize of five guineas for presenting another solution to the crime. Among the writers who participated were John Rhode and John Dickson Carr. Carr proposed an explanation of the mystery surrounding the shooting of Caesar Young in 1904, for which his lover, Nan Patterson, was twice tried and twice released when the juries could not reach a unanimous verdict. Carr suggested that Young, who was trying to per-

*In the now-standard study of this case, *The Killing of Julia Wallace* (1969), true-crime scholar Jonathan Goodman gave overwhelming evidence that Wallace was innocent, but unlike Carr he believed that the motive was money. Goodman attributed the crime to one of Wallace's business associates, whom he called "Mr. X." In a 1981 radio broadcast, he identified the suspect as Richard Gordon Parry.

suade Patterson not to cause trouble when he returned to his wife, drew out a gun and pretended to commit suicide. Patterson in a panic grabbed the gun, and it accidentally discharged.[57] The other time that he suggested a solution to an unsolved murder was in a brief passage in the Sir Henry Merrivale novel *Seeing Is Believing*. In 1862, Jessie M'Lachlan was arrested and convicted for the murder of a servant girl named Jessie M'Pherson. In company with other experts, Carr—or at least H.M.—suggested that the real murderer was a vile old man named James Fleming.[*58]

John Dickson Carr's connection with The Detection Club, and the friends he made there, was one of several reasons why the Carrs moved to London at the end of 1937. Clarice loved the Bungalow in Bristol, and at one time she and John tried to buy it, but his publishers and agents were in London, and they found it convenient for Carr to be on the spot. At least that was the reason he generally gave for the move, but, in addition, ever since he had left Uniontown he felt drawn to cities. He told Dorothy L. Sayers, "I found I had to get closer to town, which is my favourite stamping-ground anyway."[59] Carr especially liked the northwestern area of London around Hampstead Heath. (Tony Medawar, who has done much important work on Carr's life and writings, has pointed out to me how many of his books, including those written before Carr moved to London, mention Hampstead and the names of its pubs.)

For six months Carr looked for a home near Hampstead, until one day he noticed a block of new flats being erected, and the Carrs moved there in December 1937. Though he reported to Hamish Hamilton that the apartment building was in Hampstead, it was actually on Haverstock Hill, near the Chalk Farm underground station, that is, about midway between Hampstead Heath and Camden Town. The Carrs' address was 90, Eton Rise, Haverstock Hill, London N.W.3. The building is still standing. It climbs Eton Rise, and depending whether you are referring to the lower or upper end, it is between five and seven stories in height. From the lower end, the Carrs' flat was on the third floor. The outside of Eton Rise is rather drab, and the flats were smaller than the Bungalow in Kingswood, but the Carrs converted their hallway into a dining room and they had a balcony that looked out over a courtyard. Carr told Hamilton that the flat

---

*The most thorough study of this case, Christianna Brand's *Heaven Knows Who* (1960), also tends to make Fleming the murderer, but as the book's title indicates, the crime remains unsolved.

had "all the conveniences," and for an American that was an important consideration. Julia Carr, then four and a half years old, stayed with her grandparents in Bristol, but Clarice returned there often, and John visited as well.[60]

The Carrs often entertained at their new flat. The Detection Club might object to party games, but at their own apartment, John and Clarice always had pen-and-pencil challenges and they often played the Murder Game. Among the guests at the Carrs' parties were Powys Mathers ("Torquemada"), the famed Yorkshire novelist J. B. Priestley, Agatha Christie, and Dorothy L. Sayers. The first time Christie came to one of their parties, she and Priestley were stuck for more than half an hour in the lift. "Over Mr. Prestley's language," Carr said, "it is best to draw a veil, but the creatrix of Hercule Poirot was only amused." In the Murder Game that evening, Priestley played a chief inspector from Scotland Yard and Agatha Christie one of the suspects. When she claimed an alibi at Westminster Bridge with the Archbishop of Canterbury, Priestley accused her of having done in the cleric.[61]

Carr considered club life an important part of London. Though occasionally imitated in other countries, gentlemen's clubs are a fundamentally English institution. Their history can be traced back to eighteenth-century coffee houses, but they did not take form until the early nineteenth century, during the regency of George IV, and their heyday was in the high Victorian period. In part they seem to have been created as a way to keep the male-only public-school life going into adulthood; the presence of women was normally permitted only at an annual Ladies' Night. Most clubs had and still have certain themes: Their members were supposed to share the same political outlook, or to be members of the same professions. Carr liked the image of English clubs with their deferential servants and leather chairs occupied, according to tradition, by somnolent colonels. The English detective stories that Carr had read as a boy and young man often mentioned clubs: Mycroft Holmes, for example, spent much of his life at the Diogenes Club, and Lord Peter Wimsey solved his fourth case at the Bellona Club. Carr had first used a club as a setting for one of his books in *The Lost Gallows,* when he created the grotesquely exaggerated Brimstone Club. On his frequent trips to London his publishers and other friends had taken him as a guest to their clubs, and as a result the much more believable Noughts-and-Crosses Club appears at the opening of *The Plague Court Murders.* H.M., like Mycroft Holmes, was a member of the Diogenes Club.

Carr himself became a clubman when he was elected a member of the Savage Club on July 27, 1939. The Savage had been founded in 1857 by the novelist George Augustus Sala as a meeting ground for novelists, journalists, and artists, and throughout its history it numbered many distinguished people among its ranks: W. S. Gilbert, Henry Irving, Tom Hood, W. Somerset Maugham, Beerbohm Tree, Sir Edward Elgar, and the most famous thriller writer of the 1920s and the early 1930s, Edgar Wallace. In 1936, three Savages were kings of England: George V, Edward VIII, and George VI. The club had long been resident at Adelphi Terrace (near Dr. Fell's home), but in 1936 it moved to Carlton House Terrace. During his early years as a member, John Dickson Carr went to the Savage only every two or three months, but he enjoyed taking people there as his guests, and he often made contacts with publishers and editors at the club.[62]

At The Detection Club and at the Savage, John Dickson Carr sometimes spoke with friends about the possibility of collaborating on a book. In practice, however, John's method of writing, especially his careful construction of plots with the solution to the mystery puzzle dependent on a pattern of interlocking clues, made it difficult for him to work with other writers. But on one occasion, he devised an impossible crime on which he needed technical advice, and he turned to his friend John Rhode. Carr had an idea about a murder committed in a closed elevator: A man would enter an otherwise empty elevator; it would descend without stopping until it reached its destination; the door would open and the victim would be found alone shot at close range. Carr had worked out several methods to accomplish this trick, but he was not satisfied with them. (These are probably the four false solutions presented in the novel.) He already had in mind yet another gimmick, this one involving the firing of a bullet twice, but he could not make the trick work in a closed elevator. I cannot say anything more without revealing the solution, but the point is that, needing some scientific advice, he went to John Rhode, and the two decided to write the novel together, with the authors' names given as John Rhode and Carter Dickson.

Carr and Rhode agreed that the American edition would be published by Rhode's publishers, Dodd, Mead, and the British by William Heinemann, who had issued the Carter Dickson books. The American contract for the book was signed on March 22, 1938. At that time the book was untitled, but about three weeks later, when the British contract was signed, the novel was called *Dropped to His Death*. The contract itself was later altered by hand to give the final British title, *Drop to His Death*.[63] Both the

British and the American editions were published in January 1939, the U.S. edition under a new title, *Fatal Descent*.

It is difficult to know why Rhode received top billing in the book, for, Clarice Carr recalls, almost all of it was written by Carr. On several occasions he went down to Rhode's home in Laddingford, Kent, to work on the book, but their joint efforts were on plot details, not on the actual writing.[64] Except for a few pages of technical explanation that were certainly provided by Rhode, *Drop to His Death* is entirely in Carr's writing style.

Unlike most of Carr's books, nevertheless, *Drop to His Death* has few atmospheric sections. The collaborative novel is made up primarily of dialogue and brief character descriptions without the descriptive passages typical of Carr's works. It is possible that after the two men plotted the book together, Carr did a draft that was mostly dialogue and brought it to Rhode for revision. Rhode added the technical descriptions, but he probably did little else. It is at least clear that the two detectives, who work in friendly competition to solve the crime, represent Carr's and Rhode's different approaches to fictional sleuthing. Dr. Horatio Glass, police surgeon to Scotland Yard's A Division, is the Carrian detective par excellence. He is less interested in routine police work than in finding an imaginative solution of the case:

> "In that Lauriston case," pursued Patricia, in a thrilled voice, "you supplied the police with sixteen separate explanations of the mystery—every one of 'em convincing, and not one of 'em right—and nearly drove the chief inspector mad. In the Bayswater case, you demonstrated the only possible way by which Slug McGinnis could have stolen Lady Maynge's pearls. And *he* hadn't done it like that; but somebody else thought of it, when they read your explanation, and stole a sackful of diamonds from the Duchess of—"
>
> Dr. Glass waved his hand with dignity.
>
> "A detail," he said. "It's the principle of the thing that counts."[65]

Inspector Hornbeam is on the whole typical of John Rhode's detectives. "His knowledge was the practical knowledge picked up by experience." He had "extraordinarily cautious and methodical habits." Like Rhode's Dr. Priestley, he is interested in physical clues. Glass complains:

> If that fellow sees a matchstick on the floor . . . he measures the match to see how much of it remains unburnt. He finds out the brand of match and buys a similar box. He then carries out a lurid se-

ries of experiments to see how long one of these will burn till it gets to the length of the original.

Hornbeam spends much of the time in the book trying to keep Glass's flights of fancy within practical realms, but even Hornbeam expresses some of Carr's views. He has, for example, "the impression that psychologists must be a trifle madder than the people they tried to cure."[66]

The publisher who fatally descends in *Drop to His Death/Fatal Descent* is Sir Ernest Tallant, widely hated by Tallant Publications' editors. At the opening of the story, Sir Ernest's niece Patricia is editing *Tallant's Golden Key to French,* and like many of Carr's heroines is fed up with everything that is prim and proper. She is trying to include a French version of "My friend is paralyzed drunk; kindly help me to assist him into the taxi." A bit later she asks help on whether, when a student goes to Montmartre with his professor, their purpose is to see "de femmes nues" or "des femmes nues." Like the French friend who is paralyzed drunk, the characters in *Drop to His Death* are fond of alcohol. Indeed, when one of them hides a whiskey bottle in his office so that he can have sustenance while engaged in editorial chores, Glass explains that it is "the most innocent and natural of all human actions." The reviewer and crossword-puzzle creator "Torquemada" even told Carr that the novel should have been called "A Drop Too Much."[67]

Within all this rowdiness is an excellently plotted detective story. The first mystery is who is stealing an oddly assorted group of items—a traveling clock, a toy airplane, a revolver, and a first edition of Joseph Addison's essays. This is reminiscent of *The Arabian Nights Murder* and other of Carr's novels with their bizarre Chestertonian clues. The second mystery is how Sir Ernest could have been impossibly murdered in the sealed lift, and the solution demonstrates that all the strange thefts have a direct bearing on the murder. Inspector Hornbeam, with his interest in mechanics, rather than the overly ingenious Dr. Glass, solves the crime: It is, Hornbeam explains to Glass, "a popular-mechanics crime all the way through."[68]

Drop to His Death/Fatal Descent sold well, and the contracts indicate that Carr and Rhode considered collaborating on future novels. (The outbreak of World War II was probably responsible for ending those plans.) Reviews were also good, but perhaps the most striking was one that appeared in the January 15, 1939, *Los Angeles Times*. The reviewer, one "W.N.," was curious about writers and pseudonyms (he or she had previously speculated that "John Dickson Carr" was the pseudonym of P. G. Wodehouse). In regard to *Fatal Descent*, W.N. decided that both Carter Dickson and John Rhode were pseudonyms of Carr, "who is himself someone else again, maybe the Rev. Montague Summers." Anthony Boucher sent Carr a copy of the review.

> It has [Carr wrote to Boucher] caused much hilarity in this family. However, to be accused of being P. G. Wodehouse, John Rhode, and Montague Summers tends to make my brain reel. The idea is certainly ingenious: write under two names and then collaborate with yourself. There is a fourth dimensional quality about it that I like.[69]

Chapter 9

MINIATURE MURDERS

Throughout the 1930s, John Dickson Carr sought new topics and new markets for his fiction. During his visit to New York in 1934, he not only tried out some ideas for novels with Eugene Saxton of Harper & Brothers, but he also made another contact—one that would result in his first short stories as a professional writer. It was probably during this trip that he arranged to submit material to Popular Publications, one of the major publishers of pulp magazines. Founded in 1929–30 by Harry Steeger and Harold Goldsmith, the firm eventually became one of the most successful pulp publishers in the country, with more than forty-five magazines in its stable. Popular published standard types of pulps in the early 1930s—private-eye, western, and so on—but Steeger envisioned a new subject area for a magazine, a particular type of horror tale that differed from the stories featured in *Weird Tales*. He had attended performances of the Grand Guignol in Paris and thought that the murders and tortures and other sorts of depravities that so attracted theatergoers could be transferred from the stage to the printed page. The reader, Steeger believed, wanted to feel menaced by something horrible, something deformed and drooling and slimy. Thus began the pulp genre called "weird menace." The stories were written as though they were supernatural, but they usually ended with rational explanations of the horrors, no matter how unconvincing—mad scientists and laboratory mutations were quite popular in the weird menace magazines.

The weird menace style began when Steeger took his existing magazine *Dime Mystery* and added horrors in the October 1933 issue. It was so successful that he followed it with new magazines, *Terror Tales* (September 1934) and *Horror Stories* (January 1935), and other publishers also jumped into the new market. Eventually, the magazines would come to emphasize slobbering cretins torturing—or threatening to torture—scantily clad women, but that development remained a few years in the future.[1]

How John Dickson Carr became involved with Popular Publications is not certain. When Steeger talked with me almost sixty years later, he remembered that Carr wrote for him but no longer recalled the circumstances. The most likely explanation is that Carr's friend John Murray Reynolds, who produced stories for Popular Publications, took Carr to his editor in the summer of 1934. Nevertheless, Reynolds has no recollection of such an event, although he thinks that it may well have happened.[2] Carr, already drawn to the Grand Guignol approach, would have found the new strain of pulps an attractive market. After he returned to Kingswood, he sent two stories to Popular Publications, "The Visitor" (which the publisher retitled "The Man Who Was Dead") and "The Door to Doom." He may have written a few more. Ryerson Johnson, who was a copyeditor at Popular in 1935, believes that Carr submitted more stories, but if so they were published under pseudonyms that have not been identified. Johnson wrote to me:

> It was always a special day for us when a Carr story landed in the office. We all scurried around to be the one to edit it and prepare it for the magazine, because it came in such clean copy, styled and expertly presented. The way that some copy came in, you wouldn't believe: sloppy typing and a half-baked plot that we had to struggle with. Not John Dickson Carr's. Actually, we couldn't imagine why we were lucky enough to be on the receiving end of his stories. We knew his both-sides-of-the-Atlantic reputation. His stories were so sound that we felt they could have been sold to the slick [magazine] market, with just a little nod in their direction.[3]

Johnson is correct that Popular felt that Carr's name was worth something, for they featured it on the covers of *Dime Mystery* and *Horror Stories*. But they misspelled his middle name "Dixon." In later years, Carr described the spelling as "an editorial howler. The editor [Rogers Terrill] had got it stuck in his head that this was, or ought to be, the spelling of my middle name."[4] One canceled check survives from Popular Publications to John "Dixon" Carr. It indicates that he was paid at the rate of a penny and a quarter a word. According to Steeger, that rate was a bit higher than usual, but not the amount an established pulp writer could command, which might be as high as five cents a word.[5]

Carr wrote "The Man Who Was Dead" and "The Door to Doom" with the requirements of the weird menace pulps in mind. The plots of both stories are based on a growing threat to the narrator from a terrifying but undefined presence, and they are filled with the language that the market expected. In "The Man Who Was Dead," for example, we find: "The grin grew wider, although you could see no teeth. It lifted one hand and removed the black spectacles. Then we could see the cobwebs in the eye sockets." And in "The Door to Doom":

> But—for just one second—he thought that he had seen another face reflected in that dark mirror as well as his own. The imaginary face had been flabby and pinkish in color. The white eyeballs were upturned, the mouth hung open, and a thin trickle of blood ran down from one corner of the mouth.[6]

Both stories, however, differ from the usual weird menace fare in that the violence is mostly offstage and that the supernatural turns out to be real. In short, they are Carr's first genuine ghost stories since his college writings. Indeed, the two weird menace stories have a close relationship to *Haverfordian* tales. "The Man Who Was Dead" is an expansion of a plot first used in "The Legend of the Cane in the Dark" in *The Haverfordian*'s "New Canterbury Tales," and "The Door to Doom" recaptures the mood of "The Devil-Gun."

Like *The Plague Court Murders*, "The Man Who Was Dead" (*Dime Mystery*, May 1935) begins in the Noughts-and-Crosses Club. The narrator, Nicholas Lessing, explains that while traveling home on the London underground he read of his own death in a newspaper. Lessing feared that he had become separated from the real, physical world. Something, blind and tapping a cane, was following him. Was it one of the malevolent "undead"? The explanation of almost everything, including the narrator's own reported death, is material. The story ends, however, with no explanation of the ghostly pursuer.

"The Door to Doom" (*Horror Stories*, June 1935), like *The Red Widow Murders*, which was written about the same time, is about a murderous room. Both tales ultimately derive from Wilkie Collins's "A Terribly Strange Bed," in which the canopy on a bed descends to smother the sleeper. Carr's story is similar in that the scheme was also devised by French innkeepers as a method of killing travelers and stealing their money. But the explanation of the deadly room in "The Door to Doom" is entirely different and includes a large dollop of the uncanny. The Inn of the Twisted Doors was built on the foundations of the château of a nobleman who had practiced the Black Arts. During the French Revolution, a mob had tortured him to death. The innkeeper's wife muses, "It must have been a pretty sight. Everywhere there were bits of bone sticking up through the blood and silk and ruffles."[7] An American named Peter Maynard stays in a chamber in the inn where others have died and thinks that he sees the ghost of the devil-worshiping count. Carr builds up the tension through atmospheric language reminiscent of the Bencolin books. The story ends with the innkeeper and his wife being forced by what seems to be the ghost—or is it an illusion?—to fall victim of their own trap.

Both pulp stories can be described kindly as "overwritten," but they are ingenious and within their weird menace world they are effective. What may be most interesting is the role that the supernatural plays within them. Carr seems to have been intent on retaining an ordered universe; even when it is populated by dark powers, these forces help the hero escape from human menace. The figure following the narrator in "The Man Who Was Dead" and the ghostly count in "The Door to Doom" are malevolent, but their hatred is directed against evil humans. It is also interesting that in "The Door to Doom" Carr allows at least the possibility of material explanations even for the supernatural. He said this clearly in a letter to his friend Frederic Dannay:

> I tried to combine a formula of mine: that every apparently supernatural event should be explained, and yet at the end a real enigma of the supernatural should remain. You see, Fred, I *can't* write a straight ghost story. For my own soul's comfort I must have an explanation. It seems untidy, it seems dodging a writer's real responsibility, to say, "Oh, that was a ghost." I know (when we consider the work of M. R. James, for instance) that this attitude is irrational and would even spoil the literary effect of the story. Let others do it, and I shall read and admire. But to write it, no. Hence the compromise by which the difficult problem is explained naturally, but the easy problem—that

which a child might explain in half a dozen ways—is allowed to be supernatural.[8]

Carr explained the phrase "For my own soul's comfort" by the reference to a writer's responsibility to his audience, but I think that in fact it has a deeper meaning. Carr included mysteries and their solutions in almost all of his work—not just in his detective stories but also in his historical novel, *Devil Kinsmere,* and in his ghost stories. He needed these explanations; he needed to believe that the world is ordered, that things somehow do make sense. Even his ghosts support order. It is this consideration that makes *The Burning Court* so unusual in his oeuvre and that may explain more fully than references to magazine market and similar matters why he never wrote another story of this kind.

(In March 1935, Carr planned to write a series of what he called "short terror-stories" for an English periodical syndicate, but they seem never to have been published. About the same time Carr suggested to Hamish Hamilton that he write "a book of six stories about apparent supernatural happenings, in which three should be plain ghost stories and three should have material explanations—the reader to be challenged which was which." Hamilton wasn't interested.)[9]

In the middle of 1935, Carr's association with Popular Publications resulted in a near breakdown of his relationship with Harper & Brothers and Hamish Hamilton. Details of this episode remain obscure, but the broad outlines can be reconstructed. In January 1935, Popular Publications had decided to form a subsidiary, the Hartney Press, to publish books primarily aimed at the lending-library trade. Hartney planned to emphasize genre publishing—romances, westerns, and thrillers, as well as what the publisher called "moderns," that is sensationalism (*Tough Little Trollop* was one of their first publications). During the firm's short life—it went out of business in November 1935—it seems to have issued only seven books, but they were attractively produced, and one of them, Q. Patrick's *The Grindle Nightmare,* is an early volume by a pair of authors who would go on to write some extremely successful novels under the pseudonym Patrick Quentin.[10] When Hartney still looked like a going concern, Harold Goldsmith of Popular Publications asked Carr for a book. He agreed to write a detective novel entitled *The Mystery of Four Faces.* But with a fine disregard for business matters, he did not consider his contractual obligations to Harper & Brothers. On September 6, 1934, a day or two before he returned to Britain after his United States trip, Carr had signed a contract with Harpers granting the publisher an option on his next two books.[11] His earlier understanding with Saxton meant that the contract did not affect his work as Carter Dickson for William Morrow, but it certainly did not extend to writing books for yet another publisher.

On June 20, 1935, Hamish Hamilton heard from Harpers that the Hartney Press would become Carr's publisher; he then wrote to Carr that there must be some mistake. Carr's response is not recorded, and the next surviving note is dated two weeks later. Cass Canfield of Harpers had met with a Hartney representative, who said that Carr had definitely promised them *The Mystery of Four Faces*. By this time, either Harpers or Hamilton had explained forcefully to Carr what his contract required of him: If he wrote *The Mystery of Four Faces*, Harpers had an option on it. But in that case, Hartney might have some claims on Carr for any expenses they had incurred over the projected book. Realizing at last that he was on shaky ground, Carr agreed to let Canfield or Saxton handle negotiations with Hartney. Meanwhile, Harold Goldsmith wired Carr and then telephoned him, trying, as Carr wrote, "to see whether anything could be saved from the wreck." Carr simply kept repeating, "All this must be settled in New York," and directed Goldsmith to write to Saxton.[12]

The actual agreement ending the dispute with Hartney is not recorded, but Carr never wrote a novel called *The Mystery of Four Faces*. Some of the plot of that lost story, however, is preserved in a novelette that Carr wrote for one of Popular Publications' detective rather than weird menace pulps. The story is called "Terror's Dark Tower," and its publication in the October 1935 issue of *Detective Tales* must have been part of an agreement to let Carr off the hook. At least the proposed title of the novel is explained, if rather vaguely. An ancient and horrific legend is told as a background to the story. In 1621, Rupert Henley had courted Vivian Mortlake, who lived in Moat Hall, a towered brick house near Bristol. When she rejected him, he gravely informed her, "Madam, love has four faces like a compass; and I am the needle to be drawn wherever you are." So, to settle the matter, she murdered him by tying him to a pole for the carrion crows to feed on. His last words are a vow to return to her: "And she will find that death has four faces too." Just before Vivian Mortlake was to be married:

A dead Rupert Henley [rode] up that road on a dead horse, with his blind eye sockets fixed on this tower; and . . . the cloud of crows left his head to fly up here through this window and covered Vivian Mortlake's face as though with moving black fur.[13]

Twice in later years, Mortlake women have had their eyes torn out as though by crows, and each victim has been alone in a tower with its doors locked and windows barred. Death is accompanied by the sound of "a great beating of wings." An explanation is finally provided by the detective Sir James Fenwick, late of the Indian Police.

The affair of *The Mystery of Four Faces* should be understood in light of Carr's attempt to open another writing front. He was producing four novels a year—generally two about Dr. Fell and two about Sir Henry Merrivale—but he still wished to write other things as well. As part of the expansion of his writings, early in 1935, he wrote "The Other Hangman," his first historical short story since his college days. The publisher, Hutchinson & Company, asked him for a contribution to the anthology *A Century of Detective Stories*. Since the introduction was to be written by Carr's literary idol, G. K. Chesterton, he "shot in one of my best plots which I should have been sensible enough to reserve for a novel." In it Carr explains how a man can legally kill someone whom he knows to be innocent, and get paid for doing so—and he makes all this seem justifiable to the reader. The small-town setting with country lawyers is reminiscent of some of the tales of Melville Davisson Post. (Anthony Boucher wrote to Carr some years later that "I'm sure that 'The Other Hangman' brought gleams of rejoicing to [Post's] spirit eye.") Although the story has neither detection nor much mystery, it has a fine O. Henry twist ending. As S. T. Joshi points out, however, "The Other Hangman" fails in its attempts to use colloquial dialogue.[14] Nevertheless, it is interesting to compare its purposefully unsensational tone with the pulp stories that Carr wrote at the same time.

One result of Carr's participation in The Detection Club was the first short story about Dr. Gideon Fell. A London newspaper, *The Evening Standard*, asked Dorothy L. Sayers to arrange for a series of "great detective stories," and she turned to her Detection Club friends. Carr's "The Wrong Problem," published on August 14, 1936, begins with a graceful tribute, under a slightly different name, to the club: "At the Detectives' Club it is still told how Dr. Fell went down into the valley in Somerset that evening and of the man with whom he talked in the twilight by the lake, and of murder that came up as though from the lake itself." "The Wrong Problem" has a plot similar to the pulp tale "Terror's Dark Tower," published only in the United States, and it has the same solution; but the tone is quite different. Instead of the suspense and terrors of the earlier story, "The Wrong Problem" is filled with brooding sadness.

[****To understand what Carr does in "The Wrong Problem," it is necessary to give away the solution.] The events surrounding the impossible murder in the tower are recounted by a man named Brownrigg, whom Fell and Hadley meet by chance. Brownrigg explains that he has "been trying to find the real answer for thirty years," but at the end Fell identifies Brownrigg himself as the murderer. He had left in the tower room a pair of binoculars, which, when focused, sent sharp blades through the eyes of the victim. Who did it is "the wrong problem"; the real problem for Brownrigg is, "Why did I do it, all those years ago? Why? Is there no rational scheme of things, and no answer to the bedeviled of the earth?"[15]

"The Wrong Problem" is reminiscent in its title of G. K. Chesterton's "The Wrong Shape," and it is Chestertonian in its telling. "You may well believe," Carr said about this story, "that the recent demise of my literary idol had me well under his influence at the time."[16] But Father Brown would have had little hesitation in suggesting an answer to the bedeviled of the earth. Carr's refusal to explain Brownrigg's actions makes his story tremendously effective, and for his biographer it introduces once again Carr's equivocal position on whether the universe is rational and ordered. Much of the time he argued that creation is indeed rational, and he concluded most of his novels and short stories with detailed material explanations of the seeming impossibilities; but occasionally, as in "The Wrong Problem," he seemed to say that although "how" can be explained, there is not always an answer to "why." That may explain the fact that in his books Carr so often shied away from the question of "why" in favor of "who" and "how."

Less significant a matter than Carr's worldview, but worth pointing out to those who argue that all of Carr's solutions are impossible, is the fact that Scotland Yard's Black Museum has a pair of binoculars rigged up like the ones in "The Wrong Problem" and "Terror's Dark Tower." The mystery writer Anthony Lejeune, who was a friend of Carr's some twenty years later, reports that the binoculars are so clumsily constructed that the father of the intended victim detected the threat immediately. Carr himself did not know of them until sometime in the 1950s when his friend R. L. Jackson, assistant commissioner, Criminal Investigation Department of Scotland Yard, took him through the Black Museum, and Carr saw the binoculars "bristling up from one table of exhibits." No one at the museum professed any knowledge of how and when Scotland Yard obtained them. "If they landed there before the year 1936," Carr said, "well and good. I should hate to think I inspired any dirty work of a practical sort."[17]

Many of the British weekly magazines published ghost stories in their special Christmas issues, and during the later 1930s Carr aimed some tales at this market. He read a great number of ghost stories at this time, and in an article called ". . . And Things that Go Bump in the Night" (*Woman's Journal*, December 1938), he praised "our Christmas ghost stories," especially those written by Dr. Montague Rhodes James. "These are no sensations in crude colours," Carr wrote. "They are for the sophisticates. Dr. James never 'cracks the whip or goads the adjective,' but terror comes as lightly as a face poked suddenly round a corner."[18] Influenced by James's *Ghost Stories of an Antiquary* and other books, Carr's ghost tales no longer had the Poe-esque atmosphere of his college stories or the weird menace tone that he had employed for the American pulps. (On the more mundane level, Clarice Carr recalls that payments for these stories always came just in time for the family's purchase of Christmas gifts.)

Carr's first Christmas ghost story, "Blind Man's Hood," appeared in the Christmas 1937 number of *The Sketch*. In this smoothly told tale, detective-story author Rodney Hunter and his wife, Muriel, arrive for the Christmas holidays at a Jacobean manor house. Instead of the welcoming party they had expected, the Hunters meet only a young woman, who (seemingly irrelevantly) explains why no one living there today plays the game blind-man's buff.[19] Many years ago, an impossible crime had been committed in that house: a young woman had been killed—her throat slit and her body set on fire—and the murderer escaped through snow without leaving any footprints. Some years after the murder, the young woman continues, a Christmas house party played blindman's buff. A woman with a hood over her head began to follow a guest, who (we discover a bit later) was the murderer. The hooded figure, moving jerkily and smelling of burned cloth "or something worse," followed her victim behind a curtain. When the other guests looked behind the curtain, the mysterious figure had disappeared and the man she had followed was dead. The young woman with Rodney and Muriel then explains how the original murder had been committed, and then she too vanishes. In this story, as in "The Door to Doom" and "The Man Who Was Dead," the mysterious crime is explained rationally, but an element of the supernatural remains. In all three cases, the ghost intervenes to punish the murderer.

For the 1938 Christmas issue of *The Sketch*, Carr wrote another ghost story, "Persons or Things Unknown," which he later described as "a great favorite of mine."[20] In this tale a party gathers to celebrate at a seventeenth-century manor house, and again a seemingly supernatural episode of the past is told, based on the diary of "Mr. Everard Poynter"—a name taken from M. R. James's story "The Diary of Mr. Poynter."[21] The host entertains his guests with a story about Richard Oakley, who in the year of Charles II's return to the throne was suspected of consorting with Dark Powers. When he was found stabbed over and over again with no visible weapon, it seemed obvious that he had called up some fell creature he could not control. Carr's explanation of the disappearing weapon is superb. "Persons or Things Unknown" concludes, however, with no one quite certain that the material solution is sufficient:

> "These are natural explanations [said the host]. Everything is natural. There's nothing wrong with that little room at the head of the stairs. It's been turned into a bedroom now; I assure you it's comfortable; and anyone who cares to sleep there is free to do so. But at the same time—" "Quite," we said.

We can pass quickly over Carr's final Christmas ghost story, "New Murders for Old," published in *The Illustrated London News*, Christmas number, 1939, for it is a rewritten version of the pulp story "The Man Who Was Dead," which was in turn a retelling of the college story "The Legend of the Cane in the Dark." The 1939 version does not seem to me so successful as the pulp story, whose references to spiderwebs in eye sockets and other horrific images are suited to the growing terror of the story. On the other hand, "New Murders for Old" is the more effective in its emphasis on the hero's feeling of separation from the ordinary world.

Two of Carr's short stories published in 1939, "Harem-Scarem" and "The Diamond Pentacle," are lighthearted tales with no hint of ghosts. Neither was reprinted during Carr's lifetime, and in fact all knowledge of them was lost until they were recently discovered by the British researcher Tony Medawar. "Harem-Scarem," published in *The Daily Mail* on March 24, 1939, is an entertaining short-short of about one thousand words. Like *The Plague Court Murders* and "The Man Who Was Dead," "Harem-Scarem" begins in Carr's favorite fictional club, the Noughts-and-Crosses. "Bah, you stay-at-homers, you umbrella-carriers and pursuers of the 9:15!" a man named Ives says to his clubland audience, "what do you know of adventure?" The tale he recounts is almost the same as the one Patrick O'Riordan had told Bencolin and others twenty years earlier in *The Haverfordian*'s "New Canterbury Tales."

Published under his Carter Dickson pseudonym in the weekly edition of the *Times*, November 15, 1939, "The Diamond Pentacle" tells of a challenge to enter a locked bedroom to steal a piece of jewelry. The method for the impossible theft is so clever that Carr reused it in the 1941 novel, *The Case of the Constant Suicides*—a fact that may explain why Carr did not include "The Diamond Pentacle" in his short-story collections. It was not reprinted until it appeared in an omnibus collection, *Merrivale, March and Murder,* published fourteen years after the author's death.

Before we discuss the series of short stories that Carr wrote for *The Strand Magazine,* we should look at *The Third Bullet,* a novella written under the Carter Dickson name for a short-lived paperback series called "New-at-Ninepence," published in 1937. In this story, as in others that he wrote at the time, Carr begins with a bizarre statement of the case. Mr. Justice Mortlake* has been murdered, apparently by Gabriel White, who is in love with one of the judge's daughters. Inspector Page tells Colonel Marquis, assistant commissioner of Scotland Yard, that:

> Mortlake was alone—with White—in a sort of pavilion on the grounds of his house. It is absolutely impossible for anyone else to have reached him, let alone shot him. So, if White didn't kill him, the case is a monstrosity. But that's just the trouble. For if White did kill him—well, it's still a monstrosity.

Page explains that he was watching one window of the pavilion as White ran in and locked the single door. The other window was nailed closed. Page heard two shots, and when he broke in, he found Mortlake lying dead, and White staring with a dazed expression at the corpse. White was holding a gun from which only one bullet had been fired. He admitted that he shot at Mortlake, but claimed that he missed and that someone else actually fired the fatal shot. Another gun was found in a vase, and it too had been recently fired. The situation is bad enough with a disappearing murderer, but matters soon become even more inexplicable. The post-mortem shows that the fatal bullet was fired neither by the gun in the vase nor by the one that White was holding. Where did this third bullet come from? Besides White, were two more people in the room, one to fire the gun found in the vase, and the other to do the actual killing?

The Third Bullet contains some of Carr's most strident comments against those who believe that abstract causes are more important than individuals. Gabriel White explains his membership in a radical society called the Utopians in these words: "I believe in a new world, an enlightened world,

*Justice Mortlake has no known connection to the Mortlake family in "Terror's Dark Tower."

a world free from the muddle we have made of this. I want a world of light and progress, that a man can breathe decently in; a world without violence or war." Marquis asks him how he will introduce such a world. White answers:

> First, all capitalists would be taken out and hanged. Those who opposed us, of course, would merely be shot. But capitalists would be hanged, because they have brought about this muddle and made us their tools. I say it again: we are tools, tools, tools, TOOLS.[22]

Carr probably meant this statement to be ironic, since it is later discovered that White is actually the son of an earl, but it is so exaggerated that it ends up being silly.

After the original paperback publication of *The Third Bullet*, it was almost completely forgotten, and the 1937 book rivals *Devil Kinsmere* as Carr's rarest volume. In 1946, Frederic Dannay found a reference to the novella and made arrangements with Carr to print it in the January 1948 issue of *Ellery Queen's Mystery Magazine*. But Carr, who no longer even had a copy of the original paperback, not only gave Dannay permission to abridge *The Third Bullet* but positively begged him to do so. "Look here," he said, "don't you think you had better do a lot of cutting in *The Third Bullet*? I haven't seen the story since I wrote it; but I remember being uncomfortably verbose in those days." Dannay abridged the twenty-five-thousand-word story by about 20 percent, but he did not wield the blue pencil very subtly, and some of the character descriptions, red herrings, and even clues were dropped. No wonder that, reading only the shortened text, S. T. Joshi concluded that Marquis "remains nebulous throughout the work," and Jacques Barzun and W. H. Taylor judged the story as "told without vim."[23]

Dannay not only did not say in *Ellery Queen's Mystery Magazine* that his version of *The Third Bullet* was abridged; he went so far as to announce that the Carr story began the magazine's new policy of publishing "detective novels complete in one issue."[24] This version of *The Third Bullet* could hardly be described as complete, but in 1954, when Carr was ill and his publisher assembled a collection called *The Third Bullet and Other Stories*, only the abridgment was available. All reprints in anthologies and magazines have relied on the short version, and the original 1937 text was not restored until the posthumous collection, *Fell and Foul Play* (1991).

Carr described Colonel Marquis as "probably a mental forerunner of Colonel March,"[25] who was shortly to appear in a series of short detective stories for *The Strand Magazine* credited to Carter Dickson. However, the only similarity between Marquis and March is their name. Marquis is "a long stringy man," and March has "something of the look of a stout colonel in a comic paper." Carr based the personality and physical appearance of Colonel March on his friend, the detective-story writer John Rhode. March is "a large amiable man (weight seventeen stone) with a speckled face, an interested blue eye, and a very short pipe projecting from under a cropped mustache which might be sandy or grey." He is fond of working out all sorts of puzzles, and he has a fund of useless information; therefore Scotland Yard has put him in charge of Department D-3, popularly called the Department of Queer Complaints. It is to Colonel March that Scotland Yard assigns problems that "do not seem to bear the light of day or reason." March himself explains, "If somebody comes in and reports (say) that the Borough of Stepney is being terrorized by a blue pig, I've got to decide whether it's a piece of lunacy, or a mistake, or a hoax, or a serious crime." March also mentions cases involving "a walking corpse" and a "curious thief who steals only green candlesticks."[26] Like some of Sherlock Holmes's adventures mentioned briefly by Watson, these particular D-3 investigations remain unrecorded.

The name of March's department may have been inspired by G. K. Chesterton's otherwise unrelated book *The Club of Queer Trades*, for the stories have some Chestertonian echoes. In Chesterton's "The Honour of Israel Gow," for example, Father Brown suggests explanation after explanation connecting a series of strange clues, and he concludes that "ten false philosophies will fit the universe; ten false theories will fit Glengyle Castle. But we want the real explanation of the castle and the universe." Similarly, Colonel March says in the final *Queer Complaints* story, "I can think of a half a dozen theories. But they don't explain the main difficulty. Suppose any lurid theory you like." These two quotations illustrate an important difference between Chesterton and Carr. Chesterton's style is mannered, and his detective metaphysical. Both Carr's style and his sleuth are sturdy, and Colonel March has a no-nonsense attitude: "His mind is so obvious that he hits [the explanation] every time."[27]

Carr wrote the first Colonel March stories in 1937—a busy year, in which he published four novels, a novella, and the first of his Christmas ghost stories—but they did not begin to appear in *The Strand* until the next year. In all, nine of the Colonel's cases were published between April 1938 and February 1941. Seven of these were collected in the Carter Dickson book *The Department of Queer Complaints*, published in England in September 1940 and three months later in the United States. Also included in the book were four stories first published under Carr's own name, "The Other Hangman" and the three ghost stories from *The Sketch* and *The Illustrated London News*. Of the two *Queer Complaints* stories that remained uncollected for many years, "William Wilson's Racket" (February 1941) appeared in *The Strand* four months after the book was published, and "The Empty Flat" has a central gimmick that Carr had already reused in *The Reader Is Warned*.

If it were not for the silly "William Wilson's Racket," I would say that the entire Colonel March series achieves a high standard of ingenuity and readability. Even "William Wilson" begins with a good situation. How can a man vanish while leaving his clothes behind? But the explanation—that the vanisher donned an extra suit of clothes and "simply slipped out when [a witness's] back was turned"—cannot be called clever. The other tales offer good storytelling, stunning problems usually involving impossible crimes, and solutions that not only explain the apparent miracle but also point the finger at the least-likely suspect. The series began with "The New Invisible Man" (April 1938), which explains how disembodied hands can fire a gun. The solution, like others Carr based on magic tricks, is taken from the Maskelyne Mysteries, in this instance from Colonel Stodare's famous Sphinx illusion. "The Crime in Nobody's Room" (June 1938) is a gem of a tale. An inebriated young man returns to what he thinks is his flat, but the room is unfamiliar; the objects in it, even including the picture on the wall, are different. After the young man finds a corpse in the strange flat, he is knocked out. When he regains consciousness, both the corpse and the room have vanished. In "Error at Daybreak" (July 1938), a man sees an old friend alone on the beach. The friend waves, then collapses. A doctor arrives, examines the corpse, and finds a stab wound—which no one was near enough to inflict. The story provides two answers to this miracle problem.

"The Hiding Place" (February 1939) was submitted to *The Strand* under the title "The Elusive Wallet" and then received its third title, "Hot Money" when it was reprinted in *The Department of Queer Complaints*. It is a lesser problem involved with figuring out where a person could have hidden a suitcase full of banknotes in a room that is thoroughly searched by police. "Death in the Dressing-Room" (March 1939) is the only *Queer Complaints* story without an impossible crime, but it is an engrossing story, reminiscent of Agatha Christie. A young policeman is investigating a blackmail scheme centered on the Orient Club, whose exotic atmosphere

Carr captures convincingly. Blackmail leads to murder when the club's lead dancer is stabbed to death with a pair of scissors. Carr got the idea for the next story, "The Empty Flat" (May 1939), from the thinness of the walls between the apartments on Haverstock Hill. Unbeknownst to each other, two young scholars living in the same building are competing in research on Charles II's England. When they hear a radio blaring in an empty flat, which is rumored to be haunted, they investigate and find the body of a man apparently frightened to death.

The setting of "The Silver Curtain" (August 1939) is based on the town of Touques in Normandy, where the Carrs had vacationed a short while earlier. Having found it boring to watch people gamble in the casino, they hired a carriage to drive about the countryside. Carr was particularly impressed by the fairytale charm of the buildings. He wrote in "The Silver Curtain" that the town "is full of flat-roofed and queerly painted houses which give it the look of a town in a Walt Disney film."[28] The story begins in a casino, reminiscent of scenes of E. Phillips Oppenheim novels that Carr had read as a teenager, but the scene moves to the end of a street, a cul-de-sac where a man has been mysteriously stabbed to death. Only one person could have approached the victim, and he is innocent. Colonel March solves the case in association with M. Goron, prefect of the local police. Some eighteen months later, Carr remarked that it was his favorite of the Colonel March stories.[29]

"Clue in the Snow" (January 1940) is better known as "The Footprint in the Sky," by which title it was reprinted in *The Department of Queer Complaints*. A young woman, who has walked in her sleep in the past, wakes to discover that only her footprints lead to the home of an old lady who has been battered to death. A footprint, however, is found in a remarkable location—on the top of an archway through a snow-covered hedge.

Internal evidence indicates that the second Dr. Fell short story, "The Proverbial Murder," was written at the same time as the *Queer Complaints* cases, but its earliest known publication was in the July 1943 issue of *Ellery Queen's Mystery Magazine*. The story is filled with worries about the forthcoming (or possibly just begun) war with Germany. Dr. Ludwig Meyer, a German living in England, has been charged with espionage by his young English wife. The story opens with police officers watching Meyer's study window. They hear a shot and rush into the study and find Meyer murdered. Clues to the crime include the discovery of a bit of moss and the disappearance of a stuffed wildcat. Dr. Fell shows up, makes cryptic remarks about proverbs, and solves the murder in short order. Except that the solution requires technical knowledge—it is similar to a trick involving a bullet in *Drop to His Death*—"The Proverbial Murder" is one of Carr's finest short stories.

Whenever Carr looked back at his spurt of short-story writing during the late 1930s and early 1940s, he said that he was "a little uneasy" about the stories because he had had to produce them quickly and construct them according to magazine formulas.[30] But even when he made such comments, he almost always pointed toward at least one story as an exception. The oddity is that on each occasion he mentioned a different story. All of which leads me to think that Carr did not enjoy the experience of short-story writing, but on the whole he deemed the results acceptable, and this conclusion has been confirmed by the constant reprinting of his shorter works in magazines and anthologies.

In 1938, John Dickson Carr attempted another type of writing, though only briefly. Many authors—among them F. Scott Fitzgerald, Raymond Chandler, William Faulkner, and Ellery Queen—had found that writing screenplays could be lucrative; many of them also found that the demands put on them by studio executives could be unbearable. Carr became involved with screenwriting through his good friend the novelist J. B. Priestley, who lived in nearby Highgate. The Carrs were guests at Priestley's home for a New Year's Eve party, 1938–39, and the two often discussed various writing projects.[31] On July 7, 1938, they signed a contract with London Films, a subsidiary of Korda Films, to write a filmscript called *Q Planes*, which would include "a central character to be portrayed by Ralph Richardson." The production company was Harefield Productions Ltd.[32] Nothing went right with Carr's involvement with the film. At the best of times, he had trouble collaborating—*Drop to His Death*, which he was working on about the same time, was completed only because Carr did almost all the actual writing. Clarice remembers that John hated "with complete loathing" the time he spent at Korda.[33] Carr himself described the whole project as "thrice-accursed." A character in *And So to Murder*, written shortly after Carr's Korda experiences, remarks, "I am only one of the writers, the lowest of crawling creatures about a film-studio."

About this time, Carr was corresponding with Clayton Rawson, a magician and detective-story writer whose first book, *Death from a Top Hat*, was a locked-room novel full of Carrian references. Rawson was also doing some work for the movies, and Carr wrote to him:

I hope your experiences with the film barons keeps you saner than mine did. They are lunatics, every damned one of them; madder than a crate-load of coots; and why I still preserve some vestige of my reason remains a mystery. I never used to believe those tales about Hollywood, but now I could believe anything. If Sam Goldwyn has anything on Korda, I should be interested to hear it.[34]

After Carr quit working, the Korda studios replaced *Q Planes* with another film written for Richardson, *Clouds Over Europe*. This movie, released in 1939, was credited to "a screenplay by Ian Dalrymple, based on a story by Brock Williams, Jack Whittingham, and Arthur Wimperis," but the outline of the plot given in *The New York Times* makes it sound as though some of Carr's ideas may have survived:

> [*Clouds Over Europe* is] about a slightly potty Scotland Yard man who, alone in the United Kingdom, believes there is something more than coincidence in the disappearance, over a year's span, of four bombing planes on trial flights to test secret War Department apparatus. . . . *Clouds Over Europe* is far more comedy than a spy thriller.[35]

If we can say little with certainty about the fate of *Q Planes*, we can say even less about a second Carr-Priestley collaboration. In December 1938, they agreed to write a serial story entitled *The Dancing Men*, to be published in the British magazine *Answers*. The story was apparently completed, for the two men were paid three hundred pounds for it in April 1939, and a book edition was announced under the name *The Dancing Postman*.[36] But *Answers* never published it, no book under that or a similar title appeared during the late 1930s or early 1940s, and no typescript is known to survive. It is possible that another magazine published the serial, perhaps under a pseudonym and with a different title, but searchers have found nothing.

Carr claimed that his work with Priestley at the Korda studios kept him in England in June 1938 while his wife and daughter took a trip to Uniontown,[37] but the most important reason was his dislike of his mother. Clarice had done her best to keep contacts with Uniontown open. On John's thirtieth birthday in 1936, Clarice had sent his parents photographs of both of them—the one of John was his preferred Holmseian depiction with a pipe. O'Neil Kennedy had the photographs published in the *News Standard*, and Kennedy sailed to England and visited the Carrs in

Kingswood around 1937. With the ground prepared, Clarice decided that Wooda and Julia Carr should meet their grandchild. John, however, was not ready to see his mother again, and Clarice went on the *Queen Mary* without him. She and her daughter arrived in Pennsylvania in June 1938 and stayed for about a month.*

At first the visit went well: Clarice was charmed by her father-in-law, or Gramps, as she and "little Julia" called him. He was an easygoing man, and he was delighted with John's family. Clarice's mother-in-law seemed initially to accept her, introducing her to friends and taking her to visit the aunts in Brownsville. Soon, however, she began to pick at everything Clarice did. She said that Clarice's hair style was wrong, and so were her clothes, and Clarice should not have taught little Julia to eat in the English way with a knife and fork, and on and on. Yet Grandma treated little Julia entirely differently. The contrast was so great that Clarice decided that the real problem between John and his mother was that she had always wanted him to be a girl.[38]

A year later, John finally agreed to travel home to reestablish relations with his parents. Leaving their daughter at the home of Clarice's parents, John and Clarice left Southhampton on August 23, 1939, on the *Aquitania*. On shipboard, they heard the news that Germany and Russia had signed a ten-year nonaggression treaty that removed Germany's fear of invasion from the east. The Carrs landed in America about August 30 and stayed overnight with Jack Reynolds in Bloomfield, New Jersey. John told Reynolds that, since war seemed imminent, they might not stay in Uniontown for the full three weeks they had planned. The next day, they arrived in Uniontown, and Kennedy published a front-page article about their arrival: "John Carr Home for Three Weeks' Visit," read the headline. Kennedy knew, however, that John was worried about the situation in Europe, and he explained that the Carrs planned to stay in America until September 23, but "whether or not this schedule will be adhered to . . . will be decided for him by Herr Hitler."

On September 1, Hitler and Stalin invaded Poland, and shortly thereafter Britain and France declared war on Germany. Instead of spending three weeks in America, John and Clarice turned around, booked passage on the *Georgic*, and sailed for England about September 8. "Our alleged 'holiday' in America," Carr told Sayers, "was too hot, too full of argument and too confused by rumors; so I am rather glad it had to be curtailed by a

---

*In 1934, Wooda Carr had been appointed Uniontown's postmaster, a position he would hold until 1947.

fortnight. But I managed to instill a strong dose of propaganda in a very brief time." He described the return voyage as "a happy ten days, of dodging submarines."[39]

John Dickson Carr's stories from this period are filled with both the fear that war was inevitable and the confidence that Britain would prevail. In "The Proverbial Murder," for example, he affirms his belief in individual loyalty and his distrust of ideologies and, especially, such unitary systems as fascism. Thus, he had some respect for individual Germans who supported their country but he could not abide anyone who consciously chose to be a Nazi. At the conclusion of "The Proverbial Murder," Dr. Fell points at a patriotic German who lives in England and tells him, "Sir, I know nothing against you. I believe you to be an honest man." He contrasts this honest man with an English citizen who is an undercover Nazi:

> There goes a portent and a warning. The alien we can deal with. But the hypnotized zealot among ourselves, the bat and the owl and the mole who would ruin us with the best intentions, is another thing. It has happened before. It may happen again. It is what we have to fear; and, by the grace of God, *all* we have to fear![40]

John had written *The Reader Is Warned* around January 1939, shortly after he and Clarice returned from their Mediterranean vacation, when Munich was the main topic of conversation. In it, he compares fear of the Nazis' power with the terror created by the supposedly supernatural "Teleforce." Sir Henry Merrivale looks toward Whitehall and reflects on the familiar Carrian theme of masks:

> Don't let the outside alarmers scare you. The trident's still on the coin. They don't speak Esperanto in Billingsgate yet. When you hear about these super-planes, these super-gasses, these super-weaknesses on our side, think of Teleforce too. This tendency to believe anything puts a leerin' face on people. It's a face made a little larger than life; but it's still rubber that can be pulled about to look more hideous than it really is. Most of it's Voodoo, son; and, d'ye know, there never was much room for Voodoo here.[41]

In 1940, Val Gielgud of the British Broadcasting Corporation wrote in his diary that Carr's decision to see the war through in the country he loved was "a gallant and quite uncalled-for gesture on his part."[42] It would be through Gielgud and the BBC that Carr made his contributions to the war.

Chapter 10

WAR AND THE SOUND OF MYSTERY

During the 1940s, John Dickson Carr was almost as well known as an author of radio drama as he was as a detective novelist. His British mystery series, *Appointment with Fear*, was so popular that the title became a catchphrase in political cartoons throughout the war, and it was sometimes used as a punchline in the music halls.[1] Today, with television ever present, it is difficult to re-create the atmosphere that surrounded popular radio drama. Television presents us visually with the setting, the actions and expressions of the characters, and in a detective program, even the physical clues. Radio, on the other hand, has to suggest everything through sound. Val Gielgud, the prime force behind British radio drama, argued that it may be the most demanding medium. It takes what Frederic Dannay, who himself wrote for radio, called "different muscles" from those used for prose or television fiction. Though radio may seem one-dimensional, the scriptwriter has to be in some ways more sophisticated, more in control of his medium, than the stage, screen, or television author who is able to appeal to several senses. Narration, sound effects, and above all dialogue must create images for the listener, so that he or she can "see" what the writer is suggesting. A radio writer can, moreover, set the play wherever he or she wishes through the use of sound. In short, when it is most creative, radio offers fewer limits than other forms of drama; it can range as far as the imagination of the listener.

Many writers of detective novels tried their hands at radio scripts, among them Dorothy L. Sayers, Agatha Christie, Anthony Boucher, Freeman Wills Crofts, Ellery Queen, Cornell Woolrich, and Nicholas Blake. It is, however, no exaggeration to say that John Dickson Carr's plays were probably the best mystery dramas ever created for the radio. He had an ear for the rhythm of language; to return to Sayers's famous remark, he could "create atmosphere with an adjective." His combination of creepy atmosphere with rational solutions, his sense of pace, his gift for creating vivid characters with a few deft descriptions—all were perfectly suited for a listening audience. Carr not only knew how far an audience's imagination could range; he counted on it. Many of his plays, in fact, depend on listeners' fooling themselves by means of their own imagination.

Carr planned every element of his radio scripts to produce a precise effect, and thus he expected much from the actors to put the play over. His stage directions and descriptions of characters are highly specific, and he fretted when an actor did not interpret a character exactly as he had intended. We can sympathize, however, with the actor told by Carr to have a "fat" voice, or the one directed to sound querulous but nonetheless deserving of our respect. Carr's friend from the Columbia Heights days, John Murray Reynolds, was a naval commander stationed in London during the war. He recalls:

> I several times sat with John in the booth while episodes of [*Appointment with Fear*] were being broadcast. He certainly put himself into it. His lips moved with the words spoken by any of the actors as if he knew them by heart, as he undoubtedly did, and his facial expression matched the part. He said nothing audible, but he went through the entire episode. He worked as hard as the actors did.[2]

By 1944, Carr was beginning to "produce" (that is, direct) some of his own plays, and his frustrations grew with trying to have an actor give precisely the author's interpretation of a character. Carr explained the matter in a letter to Dannay:

> I wonder whether the good compassionate God has endowed me with enough patience with actors. What you want to say, through clenched teeth, is this: "Listen. Couldn't a little golden-haired child

understand THAT THAT LINE IS TO BE DELIVERED *LIKE THIS?* HAVEN'T YOU GOT ANY BRAINS AT ALL IN YOUR ENTIRE GOD-DAMNED HEAD?" Instead you say, "Now just try it again, old man. Try it again." All the same, I wouldn't have any other work.[3]

Fortunately, most of Carr's radio scripts survive. Around seventy-five are in the British Broadcasting Corporation's Play Library, and another twenty-four have been deposited at the Library of Congress by the Columbia Broadcasting System. In addition, more than twenty of his scripts have been printed. But no matter how important these typescripts are, Carr's radio work can best be appreciated by listening to performances of the plays, with their timing and sound effects and tension-raising "knife chords." In this respect John Dickson Carr's biographer has been lucky. Recordings exist of almost all of the shows Carr wrote for the famous CBS program *Suspense,* and a few of his programs for the BBC and the later CBS series *Cabin B-13* are also preserved on tape.

Only a few of Carr's radio dramas feature a detective or any kind of investigation, but except for his propaganda broadcasts, almost all of his plays are fair-play puzzle stories. He explained to his British audience: "Not all the shows are detective stories, though most of them aim at presenting the evidence fairly and upsetting the apple-cart at the end. And all deal with *diablerie* in one form or other."[4]

For more than twenty years, beginning in 1929, British radio drama was dominated by Val Gielgud, the handsome, goateed brother of the actor Sir John Gielgud. Friends remember Val Gielgud, who was an actor himself, as a supremely theatrical character in his public life, often wearing a cloak and carrying a sword-cane[5]—in short, the kind of man who would appeal to John Dickson Carr. As both a writer and an actor, Gielgud saw the problems of the medium from several viewpoints. He was sensitive to the intentions of the playwright. He preferred radio plays to be between forty minutes and an hour in length, but he did not insist on a predetermined format. Although, as correspondence with Carr demonstrates, he might well suggest changes—sometimes asking for several additional pages of dialogue—he wanted the author to be in control of, and responsible for, the final script. He encouraged the scriptwriter to be present at the preliminary reading by the cast, to explain his intentions, and, whenever necessary, to revise narration and dialogue. Unlike the situation that Carr had faced at the Korda studio, even if the final script did not match all of the original ideas of the writer, it was still *his* script.

In addition to his work at the BBC, Gielgud was the author of some competent detective novels, notably *Death at Broadcasting House* (1934), and Carr invited him to attend the May 10, 1939, meeting of The Detection Club as his guest.[6] At about the same time, Moray McLaren, who was temporarily in charge of Gielgud's BBC drama department, had received an idea for a contest play from an actor named Anthony Melrose. Surviving correspondence is vague, but it implies that Melrose's idea was to have a serialized play: After one of the episodes, the radio audience would vote on which suspect was guilty of murder, and the result of the vote would be revealed in a trial scene. The title was to be "Consider Your Verdict." Gielgud and McLaren decided to ask Carr to turn Melrose's idea into a radio play. Melrose received five guineas for the idea, and Carr 125 pounds for writing the three-part script, which he decided would feature Dr. Fell.[7] The play went through a number of drafts and title changes— the next choice was "What Say Ye?" followed by "Whodunnit"—until "Who Killed Matthew Corbin?" was finally accepted. Ironically, among the many changes in the script was the eventual decision to eliminate Melrose's scheme of an audience contest.

The play was broadcast in three parts, on December 27, 1939, and January 7 and 14, 1940. It begins with a BBC interviewer discussing unsolved crimes with Dr. Fell. Carr included the following instructions about Dr. Fell for the benefit of director and actor: "He has a huge, rich, Dr. Johnsonesque kind of voice. You picture him as rearing up like Dr. Johnson with immense dignity each time he speaks." Fell decides to talk about the murder of Matthew Corbin seven years earlier:

> Dr. Fell: And I can tell you in three words what I think about
> the Corbin case. (*Impressively*) Everybody was wrong.
> Interviewer: I don't think I understand.
> Dr. Fell: The judge was wrong. The jury was wrong, the prose-
> cution was wrong. The defense was wrong.
> Interviewer: But, doctor, *everybody* couldn't be wrong.
> Dr. Fell: Sir, you do not know your own countrymen.[8]

Although "Who Killed Matthew Corbin?" was Carr's first attempt to write for the radio, the script shows that he had already mastered the craft. An innocent woman is arrested for the murder of Matthew Corbin, tried and convicted. The listener suffers with her through her seemingly hopeless attempt to have the verdict overturned. Each time Carr revised the play, he made certain that he was absolutely fair with the clues, and in fact the main clue—that the bullet went on a straight line through Corbin's coat, waistcoat, and chest—is emphasized again and again. [****The solution is an adroit use of the least-likely-person gambit.]* The BBC interviewer himself turns out to have been one of the suspects seven years earlier, and Fell had tricked him into doing the interview to force him to reveal his guilt. The play ends with his arrest by Superintendent Hadley.

"Who Killed Matthew Corbin?" was a great success. After the first installment, Cheatle wrote to Carr that the actor Gordon MacLeod had played Dr. Fell, wheezes and all, so convincingly that a number of people had called to offer their sympathy to him and to suggest a few remedies. Carr was delighted with MacLeod's performance and with that of Valentine Dyall, who played a slightly sinister character in the mystery. Visiting Clarice's family in Kingswood, Carr asked about eighteen people to listen to the broadcast in various homes and pubs. He was pleased that most of them tumbled into a trap that he had laid and identified an innocent person as guilty of the murder. Although the listeners debated about the point of the bullet hole in the waistcoat, none of them correctly interpreted the clue.[9]

In the glow of the success of "Who Killed Matthew Corbin?" he wrote John Cheatle, "I have been bitten by the bug. In O. Henry's words, I have ate the lettuce. I am going to write more radio plays."[10] His next two scripts, "The Black Minute" (February 13, 1940) and "The Devil in the Summer-House" (October 15, 1940), again feature Dr. Fell. In February 1940, Carr went up to Manchester, where the BBC's drama department had been moved during the war, to watch the production of "The Black Minute." He promised not "to interfere or hang about or make a nuisance of myself in any way," but he did want to see how the sound effects were produced.[11]

"The Black Minute" has one of Carr's finest solutions to a miracle problem—the death by stabbing of a medium named Riven during a séance while all the possible suspects are grasping each other's hands; there are no fingerprints on the knife and no smudges from a glove. Did a ghost wield the knife? Carr expertly builds up the atmosphere until Dr. Fell explains that the impossible is only too possible. The only weakness with this radio script is something that also occurs in Carr's novels of the period. Even though the murderer has previously killed his wife and has now dispatched the medium who had been blackmailing him, Fell tells

---

*The producer, John Cheatle, suggested the final twist to Carr.

him how to cover up the second crime: "If you killed your wife, you deserve to be hanged. But you don't deserve this. You have been a great man, and I will not see you shamed. . . . I am no policeman. Let them find out who killed Riven if they can."[12] Carr disliked most authority figures, but helping a cold-blooded murderer escape the consequences of his crimes so that he won't be shamed is a bit much, even for Dr. Fell. It certainly makes one wonder why Scotland Yard continually called him into its cases.

"The Devil in the Summer-House" was written as part of a series of radio plays by members of The Detection Club. Carr proposed the idea to the BBC, and with John Cheatle's approval, he made the arrangements with the club. During 1940 the BBC broadcast six Detection Club plays by Anthony Gilbert, Anthony Berkeley, John Rhode, Nicholas Blake, Gladys Mitchell, and G. D. H. and M. Cole.[13] Carr's first draft of "The Devil in the Summer-House" envisioned a two-part broadcast, like the other Detection Club plays, but he shortened it to an hour, and when it was aired, there was no mention of the club. Carr, like the other authors of The Detection Club series, was offered seventy-five pounds for the script. Nancy Pearn, of his agents, Pearn, Pollinger & Higham, objected and she was supported by Cheatle and McLaren, who argued that Carr's script was outstanding and that, because of the trouble he had taken over the series, his payment should be increased. Cheatle and McLaren won, and Carr's payment was increased.[14]

Like "Who Killed Matthew Corbin?" "The Devil in the Summer-House" begins with Dr. Fell being interviewed in his study. The interviewer is, of course, different from the one in the earlier play, but here too he turns out to be involved in a murder case. The interviewer is a lawyer who was in love with the victim's wife when murder took place in a summer-house twenty-four years ago. Carr experimented with radio techniques by having the various suspects, most of whom are long dead, speak to the interviewer-cum-lawyer by whispering in his mind. At the end, Fell explains the case to Superintendent Hadley—who presumably hasn't heard how the doctor had played with justice in "The Black Minute" (or perhaps Hadley recalled his own tinkering with the law in *The Mad Hatter Mystery*). The explanation, which is more than three pages in the printed version of the script, may be a bit too long and involved for radio, and a major clue—how an army officer wears his cap—has lost its fairness in the passing years.

There was a gap of some eight months between "The Black Minute" and "The Devil in the Summer-House" because Carr was working on his most ambitious project for the radio, an eight-part historical mystery called "Speak of the Devil." As broadcast in February and March 1941, each episode took twenty minutes, for which Carr was paid a total of 160 guineas for Home and Forces programs, plus an additional 40 guineas for overseas transmission.[15] This play, Carr's first historical romance since he had been disappointed by the sales of *Devil Kinsmere* and *The Murder of Sir Edmund Godfrey*, takes place in Regency England. The narrator explains:

> This was the age of the bucks and the dandies, of the gamesters and the duellists, of the coaching-road and the prize-ring. It was an age of fine manners and boisterous drinking, when Boney had been beaten at Waterloo only a year before. When gentlemen in tall hats sauntered down St. James's Street, or lounged in the bow-window at White's. When ladies in poke-bonnets ate ices at Vauxhall Gardens, or danced the waltz at Almack's, or gossiped of the fall of Beau Brummell and the scandal of Lord Byron. When Tom Cribb was champion of England. When that new miracle, gas-light, had begun to flicker in the cobblestoned streets. When already the balloon and the steamboat were commonplace sights. When, in short, progress was carrying us straight to the devil.[16]

"Speak of the Devil" is the story of Captain Hugh Austen, who is seeking a young woman whom he met at a ball three nights before the Battle of Waterloo. She has disappeared, and though he has a miniature portrait of her, everyone denies that she exists. A man dressed entirely in black, who was with the mysterious woman at the ball, has also disappeared. This seeking of a lost, perhaps unreachable, love is reminiscent of some of Carr's *Haverfordian* tales, but in "Speak of the Devil" the quest is a practical one, and the woman is not *la belle dame sans merci*. At last, Austen finds her, only to have her vanish once again, and a lawyer explains that "she is not alive.... I saw her cut down from the scaffold myself. She was hanged for murder more than a year ago."[17]

"Speak of the Devil" was popular on the radio. Carr himself was proud of it. He was in Devon during the broadcasts, and he wrote to his friends at the BBC:

> Down here in this neglected spot, they queue up to hear it. One formidable maiden lady passed the comment: "It's odd how you seem to be

seeing it as well as hearing it." I stifled my impulse to reply: "Madam, if you knew how hard the producer and the author worked to achieve that effect, you wouldn't think it was so bloody odd after all."[18]

Carr asked his American correspondents to listen to the program on shortwave.[19] His agents even received an inquiry from a film producer about rights to the story. Typically, Carr had kept no copy of the script, but the BBC was willing to supply one. Unfortunately, as with most requests for cinema options, nothing came of this proposal.[20]

Carr's next two radio plays, "Never Tell Parents the Truth" (July 6, 1941) and "Lord of the Witch Doctors" (September 13, 1941), are minor works. The first is a comedy about an elderly Shakespearean actor, his dithering wife, and their son, who (much to his father's horror) wants to act in avant-garde plays. Many of us would sympathize with the son, but Carr admires the father, who tricks the lad into giving up his dreams. Gielgud, who was sometimes criticized for refusing to broadcast experimental drama, must have been pleased by Carr's conservative attitude. "Lord of the Witch Doctors," broadcast for some reason under the nom-de-air Robert Southwell, is a thriller set in late-nineteenth-century Zanzibar, then the subject of colonial dispute between Britain and Germany. The play amusingly features a Cockney slight-of-hand performer as a double agent who has persuaded the natives that he is a witch doctor. "Lord of the Witch Doctors" tries to make the point that Germans are too rigid to succeed, either in colonial wars or, by extension, in the Battle of Britain, which was raging when the play was broadcast. Unfortunately, the play has some dull moments, especially in the center, where nothing happens.

These two forgettable efforts were followed by Carr's most effective use of radio creepiness, "The Dead Sleep Lightly," a Dr. Fell play that Carr wrote in September 1941. The story features a coldhearted publisher named George Pendleton, who had deserted his lover, Mary Ellen Kimball, and an unacknowledged child many years earlier. Mary Ellen had told him that she would come back to him whenever he called for her. But she is now dead, and at Kensal Green cemetery, Pendleton happens on her grave. With slight regrets for the past he mechanically notes the number of the tombstone, "Kensal Green 1-9-3-3." He cannot get the number out of his mind, and that evening when he is making a telephone call he mistakenly tells the operator that he wants Kensal Green 1-9-3-3. She says that she will connect him; then Mary Ellen's plaintive voice is heard on the telephone:

Voice: I knew you'd call me sooner or later, dear. But I've waited *ever* so long. . . . (*Eagerly*) And of course I'll come if you want me. I'll be there just as soon as I can.

Pendleton: I tell you—!

Voice: I'll be there by seven o'clock, truly I will. But you mustn't be frightened at how I look now.

Pendleton: You're not Mary Ellen! This is a trick! *Mary Ellen is dead!*

Voice: Yes, dear. But the dead sleep lightly. And they can be lonely too.

Pendleton: Don't talk to me! You can't talk to me! I won't listen to you! I . . . .

Voice: I'll wear a veil, dear. Because I'm not very pretty now. But I won't hurt you, my darling. Truly I won't![21]

And if this were not enough, it turns out that the telephone that Pendleton has been using has been disconnected from the wall. Pendleton asks Dr. Fell for help, but (because his taxi has engine trouble) Fell arrives at Pendleton's house after seven o'clock. He finds Pendleton unconscious, his body marked with smudges of graveyard clay.

As S. T. Joshi points out, the theme of a ghostly lover is common to supernatural stories,[22] but it is handled in "The Dead Sleep Lightly" in a fundamentally Carrian way. After creating a situation for which an otherworldly explanation is almost inevitable, Carr proves again that all the tricks were created by humans for human motives, and at the end Dr. Fell protects the hoaxer from discovery by Superintendent Hadley. In this instance, however, the listener agrees completely with Fell's actions.

With "The Man in the Iron Mask," broadcast on January 5, 1942, Carr returned to historical mystery, this one set in the England of Charles II and the France of Louis XIV and based on the genuine mystery of the famous prisoner who wore (depending on the sources) either a velvet or an iron mask. The play is interesting for its references to Carr's theme of masks, and as a piece of fiction it is quite successful. Its explanation that the masked prisoner was Charles II's Jesuit son, however, no longer holds water, for the simple reason that—as historians are now certain—Charles had no such son.

Carr's final play aimed solely at entertainment during this stage of his radio work was "Inspector Silence Takes the Underground" (March 25, 1942). Val Gielgud and Francis Durbridge had invented the character of

Inspector Silence for a serial called "Death Comes to Hibiscus," broadcast during the later months of 1941 and the beginning of 1942.[23] It featured the famous radio actor Leon M. Lion as Silence. Carr's play, which also starred Lion, tells the story of the British police officer's visit to New York, where he and others are trapped on a subway car with a serial killer called False Face (masks again). Despite this promising premise, the story is lightweight and the clue to the identity of the murderer obvious. But "Inspector Silence Takes the Underground" does not survive on audiotape, and it is possible that the broadcast version was more impressive than the written script, for people who heard it in 1942 still remember it as an effective program.

John Dickson Carr's contributions to the war effort were primarily in the form of propaganda plays for the BBC. In September 1941, Stephen Potter of the BBC sent him a script written by Robert Westerby called "Black Market," which had a good idea but was not satisfactory for broadcasting.[24] Carr revised it into a thriller about a young man who aspires to become "Public Enemy Number One" by making a fortune dealing in black-market eggs. The play ends with the young crook being injured in a car chase, and a policeman says, "His suit's messed up, and there's blood on his hands." Another character responds, "There's blood on all their hands, man. *There's blood on all their hands.*"[25] Broadcast on October 7, 1941, this play is typical of Carr's propaganda writing; he took a wartime theme that might have been presented heavyhandedly and made it entertaining.

Carr wrote twelve propaganda plays during 1941 and 1942. "Britain Shall Not Burn" (December 12, 1941), for example, tells of the destruction of an imaginary town that did not heed the government's advice about watching for air raids. However, even Carr's use of Poe's poem "The Bells" to increase tension cannot make this play readable for modern fans of his works. "You're Not Behind the Plow" (February 15, 1942) was beamed at the United States to explain British military structure to GIs and to persuade them that the army was not organized along class lines. "Black Market" (March 6, 1942), which had no relation to the earlier broadcast with the same title, showed Britons the danger of buying chocolate from unauthorized sources. "Four Smart Girls" (November 12, 1941) encouraged British women to volunteer for military duty. Revised, this play became "Women on the Guns" (February 27, 1942) to explain that women can act as spotters of enemy planes but—thank heavens!—do not actually fire the guns. Some eight years later, Carr told Robert Lewis Taylor that this program got him into trouble with his superiors. During air raids, he crawled from gunsight to gunsight copying down the colorful code that the female plane spotters used. He did not know, however, that the code was filled with profanity, and when he began the program with some exceptionally steamy code words, many listeners who knew the code were upset.[26] Unfortunately, the surviving script does not confirm this excellent anecdote, but the coded profanities may have been added during the cast's read-through of the play.

Carr was too imaginative a writer to be limited to the rigidities of writing straight propaganda. The factual material for his plays came from the British government and from embassies of the various occupied nations, but he used the information for storytelling purposes. More and more, he began to add surprise endings to his plays. For instance, in "Starvation in Greece" (February 6, 1942), a kindhearted but seemingly slow-witted scissors grinder turns out to be a British agent. In "Men of Sparta" (April 11, 1942), a Greek woman tricks her own people into killing her in order to help her brothers escape to freedom.

All of Carr's propaganda plays reflect Carr's values. He despised the Nazis for putting an abstract ideal above human values and for their creation of a rigid, humorless, and brutal system that cared nothing for human beings. A freedom fighter in an occupied country explains it this way in one of Carr's plays: "They coolly say that we shall die—that human beings shall die—because it was planned in someone's notebook or drawn in diagrams on a chart. . . . I hate their cold faces and their governed minds."[27] In "Black Gallery No. 4: Heinrich Himmler" (June 4, 1942), Carr presents a horrifying portrait of a Nazi who has given up all humanity in his desire for power. "If you hurt a man enough, he'll behave himself afterwards," Carr has Himmler say, "surely that's only good sense." Himmler cynically builds his career not by accepting but by exploiting human weakness. Although this play is straight propaganda, it is well constructed, with a trio of "Yes-Men" encouraging Himmler's self-praise, while a ghost voice whispers to him the truth: "You're afraid the robots will turn on you one day, and wreck you." The play ends, "I am Heinrich Himmler. Let me shake your hand. Wouldn't you like to be ruled by me?"[28]

Carr believed that the Nazis, like all fanatics, have a weakness: They can understand no viewpoint but their own. This point was made most clearly in one of Carr's best propaganda plays, "Denmark Occupied" (March 16, 1942), which makes the Germans seem ridiculous rather than terrifying. The play features Baron Von Renke, the inflexible German minister to Copenhagen, who is hornswoggled by the Danish minister of justice and by Detective Inspector Vinterburg. Vinterburg is described as "like Sherlock Holmes in England," but with his wheezing and his love of drink, he is clearly out of the same mold as Dr. Gideon Fell and Sir Henry Merrivale. Von Renke wants to discover why the Danish underground has been able to sabotage German facilities without interference from the police. He demands to know why there have been no arrests: "We Germans always believe in encouraging the police to make arrests, and long ago we started practicing on ourselves." As the German minister gradually turns purple in rage, Vinterburg blandly explains, "The only conclusion I can come to—and I say this, mind, with all my experience to back me up—is that maybe the whole business is a series of accidents." "*Accidents?*" Von Renke screams, and throws his papers about the room so that they resemble a snowstorm. But Von Renke can do little because "we Germans are great psychologists; we never make a mistake in judging the character of a people," and he is certain that "in the Danish character there is none of that detestable, anti-social quality which the English call a sense of humor."[29]

In other plays about events within the occupied countries, Carr expressed a theme that he had used in his short stories for *The Haverfordian*, written some seventeen years earlier. The thrust of these plays is that it is important to resist, to fight for a human cause even when the fight is futile. His characters now are willing to die for something as simple as self-respect, and something as mighty as a belief in one's country. But both in Carr's college stories and in some of his propaganda scripts, the theme is lost causes—"lost" at least in the immediate situation. This is best expressed in "They Strike at Night" (January 6, 1942), when a Frenchman named Marcel, only eighteen years old, explains why he will die to oppose the German occupiers of his country:

> Probably I'm not very wise. But it seems to me there are certain things we must do; and all you leave us, messieurs—the only little rag of self-respect—is the self-respect of defiance. You, as Germans, pride yourselves on your feats of arms. (*Fiercely*) Well! I have heard of a day when all Europe shook in its shoes at mere mention of Bonaparte and the Grand Army, and when greater eagles than yours flew from the Danube to the Nile. Many of my countrymen have forgot-

ten it, now. The Great War was a cruel war. They are tired, and they have fallen upon sleep. But one day, soon, they may remember it. And then, perhaps, we shall see. God speed that day![30]

With that, he is taken away to face the firing squad.

"To me the London of World War Two, with all its dangers and difficulties," John Dickson Carr wrote in 1968, "will always remain, next to that same city in the late nineteen-thirties, the place I remember with most pleasure."[31] He faced the war with public and private confidence in the ultimate result. The seemingly lost causes that he wrote about for the radio would, despite all odds, eventually prevail. He often contrasted such normal activities as reading mystery novels with the disruptions of war. On February 28, 1941, at the height of the Battle of Britain, Carr wrote to Clayton Rawson:

> At the moment we are awaiting invasion without any noticeable agitation, being convinced that any Nazi who tries to land here will wish to hell he hadn't. There is, further, the pleasurable feeling that Churchill is no gentleman and in good time will pay back every bomb with knobs on. However, no more about the war. Let me know if you have encountered any good detective stories.

One of the normal things that the dangers of London put a temporary end to was meetings of The Detection Club. Most of the members, including Sayers, who was its heart and soul, had left London for the country.[32]

The United States government, still officially neutral in the war, announced toward the middle of 1940 that American citizens should leave the areas of combat. Carr feared that, if he left England, he would not be allowed to return, but both his and Clarice's parents argued that it was unwise to keep seven-year-old Julia in England. In late summer 1940, therefore, Clarice, then some five months pregnant with their second child, sailed for America with Julia. They boarded the American ship *Washington* from a port on the west coast of Ireland. To let the Germans know that the ship was not British, it was painted with stripes all over its decks and sides and brightly lit with spotlights shining on the American flag at the masthead. Jack Reynolds met them in New York, and John's parents came and took Julia to Uniontown in time for school there. Clarice stayed a few days with the Carrs' old friends Ed and Babs Delafield before going for a short time to Uniontown herself. She took a British ship back across the Atlantic: It was carrying airplane parts bolted to the upper deck, so the ship was a prime target for German submarines. Just as in 1939 when the Carrs had hurried back to England shortly after the declaration of war, Clarice's ship zig-zagged safely across the Atlantic.[33]

After Clarice returned, she and John made final arrangements to purchase their first house—a brave decision considering that German planes bombed London almost every day. They chose a property at 118A Maida Vale, southeast of their flat at Haverstock Hill but still in the northwestern part of London. Renting with an option to purchase, they moved in early in September 1940. It was, Clarice recalls, a lovely house set in its own grounds, with an orchard and garden walls. It had a maple tree and a birdbath or sundial in the front garden.[34] But none of this lasted long. On September 18, 1940, the house was almost completely destroyed by a German bomb. Carr wrote apologizing to Anthony Boucher for not having acknowledged receiving a copy of Boucher's *Nine Times Nine*, which was dedicated to Carr: "I was just finishing the book when continuity was somewhat interrupted by a thousand-pound bomb which totally demolished my house without so much as scratching either my wife or myself, who were in the house at the time."

In his interview with Robert Lewis Taylor, Carr said that he and Clarice were reading in their living room when they heard a whistle, followed by a hiss and a series of concussions. They were knocked to the floor, and when the dust cleared they noticed that there was no longer any wall to impede their view of the garden. Val Gielgud heard that the Carrs' escape had been "miraculous," which indeed it had been, and John told him that he managed to dig out of the debris the five parts he had completed of "Speak of the Devil." His books, however, were entirely destroyed. "Most of them were so disreputable," he wrote to Fred Dannay, "that my wife wouldn't have them downstairs. But they had been accumulated through years of browsing, and they suited me."[35] Some of their furniture, however, survived, and they sent it back to Clarice's parents in Bristol, where it was stored in a small shed or pavilion. With a child due in two months, Clarice herself settled for the time being in Kingswood, which (or so it seemed) was safer than London.

John meanwhile took up residence at the Savage Club, but the Luftwaffe seemed to be zeroing in on him. Another thousand-pound bomb took off the club's back wall. He later recalled that he was sitting at the bar, and after the bomb landed he and the other drinkers were left staring off into space. Once again, some of his papers had to be rescued from the ruins, in this case the proofs for a novel, *The Man Who Could Not Shudder*.[36]

At this point, John decided to join Clarice (and his furniture) in the West Country. Almost immediately, Bristol too came under attack, and the Cleaveses' home lost its windows, doors, and roof. The reason that the damage was not even more extensive was that the shed containing the remains of the Carrs' furniture took a direct hit. Carr explained to Harper & Brothers:

> Jerry's score was complete. I can imagine the triumphant German airman hurrying back to Goering and saying, "I have busted der resten den furniture von Carr!" and Goering swelling under his medals and saying, "Gut! Sie wilst der iron cross getten! Heil Hitler!"[37]

The loss of the furniture was accompanied—almost at the same moment—by an addition to the family. John and Clarice's second daughter was born on November 29, 1940, during the height of a blitz. "She seems," John remarked, "not to have suffered from such a pyrotechnic entrance." The new daughter's name came from a trip that John and Clarice had made to Scotland just after she had returned from taking Julia to America. Throughout the Scottish trip, they kept coming across the phrase "Bonnie Mary" in reference to Mary, Queen of Scots. When the baby was born, Clarice told John that she would not name the child "Bonnie Mary" but would choose "Bonita Marie." John beamed and said that Bonita was the name of one of his favorite characters, Bonita Sinclair, the art expert drugged in *Death in Five Boxes*. To help Clarice care for Bonita (or Bonnie, as she was inevitably called), the Carrs hired a nurse named Violet Andrews. Andy, a large Englishwoman from Dover, remained with the family for many years. She was, Julia recalls, a great force in all of their lives. She was a combination nurse, nanny, and housekeeper; not only did she help Clarice manage the children's growing up, she also was called upon to rescue John when alcohol became more than he could handle.[38]

By early 1941, John and Clarice had seen the Blitz in several different places. "The thing had become monotonous," he said, "and both Clarice and I were growing a little bit fed up with living constantly in a series of residences bearing some resemblance to a doll's house with the front off." The Germans had indeed finished with the Carrs. Not willing to risk another "permanent" residence, however, they moved from place to place for about a year. They stayed with Clarice's family until January 1941, then John moved to an inn in Devonshire where he caught up on his book obligations (which had suffered while he was preparing scripts for the BBC) by writing about two hundred thousand words in just over two months.[39] In March he rejoined Clarice in Bristol, renting a furnished house next to the Bungalow where they had lived from 1933 to 1937. It belonged, Carr told Gielgud,

> to a wealthy paper-manufacturer with a passion for gadgets which won't work. Its interior decoration resembles a cross between a film-set and an American whore-house. Its conservatory contains a trick fountain with which, by pressing a hidden switch, you can make a dozen jets of water shoot up into the face of any mug who can be persuaded to bend over and look at the goldfish. (The owner is addicted to this highly subtle form of humour; and it surprises me that he has not been murdered with a curious Eastern dagger.)[40]

It is understandable why Clarice and John stayed in this house of surprises for only two months. From May until October, they rented a furnished house at Elstree in Hertfordshire, then moved to the Inverness Court Hotel in London, where they stayed until January 1942. Between these moves, they were often back in Bristol, but in the middle of January John seemed to have found a permanent spot in which to settle. He wanted to be in London, but Clarice preferred staying with her parents in Bristol. He rented a flat at 93 Eton Place, just below their old flat in Haverstock Hill. It had not, Carr noted, been touched by bombs, and he expressed the hope that, unlike his residences during the last four months of 1940, it would stay in one piece.[41]

Meanwhile, Carr's position as an American resident in England was becoming difficult. The United States entered the war in December 1941, and the government was expected to call all relatively young men to register for the draft—including the thirty-five-year-old John Dickson Carr. It was unlikely that he would be called for active duty, but the Americans might find some other war-related assignment for him. Carr believed that he could contribute most to the war effort by remaining in England, and he was sarcastic in his writings about those who bailed out and found safety in another country.[42]

Along with almost every other resident of England, he participated in the fire watch, going to rooftops in Bristol and London—often on the BBC building itself—with buckets of sand to put out fires caused by German bombs, but his main contribution was through the propaganda plays for the BBC. There is no doubt that his work was effective. One play, "Starvation in Greece," was so moving that the Foreign Office objected to using it on the Home Service. They told the BBC, "The effect upon the listener would be that the situation was so appalling that something must be done instantly without counting the pros and cons. This would produce the sort of atmosphere which would make right decisions more difficult."[43] In other words, John Dickson Carr might cause an invasion of Axis territory before the British were able to undertake one successfully.

The BBC put in a request with the United States embassy to allow Carr to remain in London to continue his propaganda work, but in August 1942, he was ordered to return to America and register for military service. Bonnie was less than two years old, and the Carrs decided to leave her with Clarice's parents in Bristol when they sailed to the United States. Nine-year-old Julia was already in America, living with John's parents in Uniontown, and because of schooling she did not join her mother and father until January 1943. Their friends Ed and Babs Delafield had a summer home on Mt. Airy Road, Croton-on-Hudson, Westchester County, New York, and the Carrs rented a small, three-bedroom house next door. It was in Croton that their third daughter was born on December 29, 1942. The baby was named Mary Bright, after Clarice's mother.[44]

During this sojourn in the United States, Carr met one of his correspondents, Frederic Dannay, who was half of "Ellery Queen." With his cousin, Manfred B. Lee, Dannay wrote some of the most popular (and complicated) detective stories in the fair-play school. Not surprisingly, Carr's favorite Queen novel was the ingenious locked-room mystery *The Chinese Orange Mystery* (1934). He wrote to Dannay in 1941 that it has a "brilliantly bizarre situation," but, he continued, "*The Greek Coffin Mystery* . . . pushes it hard for honours, with *The Door Between* as a runner-up."[45] As editor of *Ellery Queen's Mystery Magazine,* which he had founded in 1941, Dannay became the leading influence in America on the detective short story. An intellectual who wrote poetry in his spare moments, he was one of the few people who could match and, in some instances, surpass Carr's knowledge of detective fiction. The two men often stayed up until late into the night discussing obscure books and authors and arguing about the fine points of plot and character. Dannay was eager to include Carr's uncollected short stories in his magazine. In July 1942, he printed "The Wrong Problem," and between July of the next year and December 1948, he published six additional Carr short stories, an abridged version of *The Third Bullet,* and four radio scripts.

It may have been through Dannay that John Dickson Carr became associated with the Columbia Broadcasting System and its classic anthology series *Suspense*. Dannay was coauthor of *The Adventures of Ellery Queen,* which had made its debut on CBS radio in 1939. In January 1942, the series shifted to NBC, but Dannay retained contacts with CBS.[46] On June 17, 1942—two months before Carr returned to the United States—*Suspense* had begun its long run with an excellent adaptation of *The Burning Court* by Harold Medford. In a program lasting only thirty minutes, the *Suspense* broadcast nonetheless retained most of the plot and all of the fire-and-brimstone atmosphere of Carr's novel. At the end of October, Carr became a writer for *Suspense*. His stories, a CBS press release announced, "are to be melodramas with a surprise ending, virtually all stories of crime."[47]

Suspense was one of the great programs in the history of American radio, lasting more than twenty years and airing some of the most terrifying mysteries ever broadcast. CBS looked upon it as one of its prestige shows. While Carr wrote for it, it was a "sustaining program"; in other words, CBS paid for it without sponsors. *Suspense*'s director, William Spier, was a master of timing and effect; the series had a full radio orchestra, with music composed and directed by Bernard Herrmann, who would gain fame from his film scores; and its guest stars were major actors and actresses. Some of the actors who were featured in Carr's plays during 1942 and 1943 were Martin Gabel, Geraldine Fitzgerald, Ralph Bellamy, Roland Young, Susan Hayward, Paul Lukas, George Zucco, and Wendy Barrie. Peter Lorre, whose caressingly sinister voice was perfect for the mood of Carr's plays, was the main character in three of Carr's *Suspense* mysteries. Just as effective was Sydney Greenstreet, who made a perfect Dr. Fell in "The Hangman Won't Wait." Each story was introduced by eerie music and the hollow bonging of bells, over which the narrator, the Man in Black (played by Joseph Kearns), intoned the following words:

> Suspense. The hushed voice. The prowling step in the dead of night. The crime that is almost committed. The stir of nerves at the ticking of the clock. The rescue that might be too late, or the murderer that might get away. Mystery and intrigue and dangerous adventure. We invite you to enjoy stories that keep you in . . . suspense.[48]

American radio drama tended to be more histrionic and atmospheric than British. Carr preferred the American approach; as early as "Who Killed Matthew Corbin?" British directors had asked Carr to tone down his effects. Nothing was toned down on *Suspense,* which was filled with sound effects, eerie music, and "knife-chords" to emphasize the nail-biting tension that author and director worked to create. Carr wrote his plays at the Croton house, normally allowing two days for a thirty-minute script, but he usually went into Manhattan once a week—often, despite the distance, by taxi—to attend the rehearsals. His daughter Julia sometimes accompanied him and watched the actors put the finishing touches on the performance.[49]

During a period of thirty-five weeks, from October 27, 1942, through June 22, 1943, *Suspense* broadcast twenty-two John Dickson Carr radio plays. Three of them were revised versions of BBC scripts: "Lord of the Witch Doctors," "The Devil in the Summer-House" (this American version without Dr. Fell), and "The Dead Sleep Lightly" (also without Dr. Fell). Two of the *Suspense* programs recycled gimmicks from BBC plays but placed them within new plots. "The Hangman Won't Wait," the only Dr. Fell play for *Suspense,* has the same major clue as "Who Killed Matthew Corbin?" and "The Moment of Darkness," which features Ken Blake from H.M.'s cases, is similar to "The Black Minute." Two of the plays are dramatized versions of Colonel March's investigations, though the colonel himself does not appear. Another play uses the solution to the impossible crimes in "Terror's Dark Tower" and "The Wrong Problem." Fifteen of Carr's plays, however, were entirely new, and they are probably the finest products of the radio mystery. A leading scholar of mysteries, Francis M. Nevins, Jr., says that Carr led "us into outer darkness as skillfully with pure sound as with the written word."[50]

Rather than analyze all of Carr's plays for *Suspense,* I shall focus on seven representative examples. "Will You Make a Bet with Death" (November 10, 1942) has a stunning situation. John Destry has made a wager with his impoverished stepson, Robert Penderel, that he will be able to murder Penderel within six months. The play begins in the crazy atmosphere of a funhouse, the Old Haunted Mill at Coney Island, as Penderel is trying to stay alive for the last few hours of the bet. "Menace in Wax" (November 17, 1942) is set in England during the Blitz. A young reporter named Bert Rogers finds himself teamed up with Suzy Dubois, who speaks a strange combination of French and Cockney English. Suzy frequently fractures English clichés, saying such things as "they have not got the chance of a snowshoe in heaven." The play begins with the rumor that wax gamblers at Madame Tussaud's actually play card games during the night. Suzy points out that no matter what game the inanimate figures are playing, one of them is cheating. That clue provides evidence that German Junkers are about to bomb the British "Q Factory."

Because of its improbably happy ending, "The Bride Vanishes" (December 1, 1942) is a lesser story, but Carr handles the Capri setting very well, and the impossible situation is compelling. Some three years earlier, a woman who was about to be married disappeared from the balcony of the Villa Borghese. As the play begins, young newlyweds rent the villa, and the bride again disappears. The solution, which Carr borrowed—probably unconsciously—from Chesterton's Father Brown story "The Miracle of Moon Crescent," is incredible, and the killer's motivation must be heard to be believed.[51] "The Pit and the Pendulum" (January 12, 1943) was one of Carr's own favorites of his radio work. He told Spier that he wanted to adapt the Poe terror tale, but the director was not certain it would work on the radio, since many of the events occur in the narrator's mind. Carr's script, however, was so successful that it was broadcast four times on *Suspense*, with Henry Hull, Jose Ferrer, Vincent Price, and Raymond Burr successively taking the lead role.

"The Devil's Saint" (January 19, 1943) is a small masterpiece. It begins with the unreal gaiety of a fancy-dress ball in Paris in 1927. Lord Edward Whitehead attends with a mysterious young woman named Ileana, whom he had met four days earlier but already plans to marry. Ileana's uncle, Count Stephen Kohary—wonderfully played by Peter Lorre—will not permit the marriage. Instead, he invites Whitehead to his home, the Château d'Azay, and challenges him to spend the night in the Tapestry Room. Like those who spend the night in the Widow's Chamber in *The Red Widow Murders* or at the Inn of the Beautiful Prospect in "The Door to Doom," all who sleep in the Tapestry Room are found dead in the morning without a sign of what killed them. Kohary tells Whitehead that a night in the room will cure him "permanently" of his infatuation with Ileana. The explanation of the murderous room is entirely different from Carr's earlier use of the theme, and the solution is more than merely surprising; it is so unexpected as to be shocking. The play is filled with Carrian motifs—past deaths repeated in the present, a society of witches, and an emphasis on masks. What we truly are, Carr says, is often more terrifying than whatever disguises we adopt. The following dialogue occurs at the masked ball:

> Kohary: Look all about us! Crowds of our fellow-guests, pouring down the main staircase. Shapes of nightmare. Shapes of delirium. Great goblin masks where only the eyes move. Mightn't you be terrified if you could look inside those painted masks to the real faces they hide?

> Whitehead: No, I don't think so. They're only ordinary people like ourselves.
>
> Kohary (*amused*): That, sir, is where you make your mistake. I shall expect you for the weekend. Good night.[52]

"Will You Walk into My Parlor?" (February 23, 1943) is another masterpiece of suspense, fair-play clueing, and a totally unexpected upsetting of the apple cart at the conclusion. The narrator begins: "Just how far does any man trust his wife? Or his fiancée either?"[53] At a village fete, Philip Lester is told by Inspector Brandon—who is posing as a fortuneteller—that his fiancée, Mary Sherwood, is a compulsive poisoner. The problem is that no one has been able to discover how she or anyone else could have administered the poison. Brandon warns Philip that Mary Sherwood will make him the next victim. The method of poisoning is the same as that in *Death in Five Boxes*, but even *Suspense*'s listeners who were familiar with Carter Dickson's books probably did not foresee the final twist in the plot.

The most famous play that John Dickson Carr wrote for *Suspense* is "Cabin B-13," first broadcast on March 16, 1943, and repeated on several later occasions. As Frederic Dannay pointed out when he printed the script in *Ellery Queen's Mystery Magazine*, Carr's tale is a variant of the situation in the classic Paris Exposition story: A young woman leaves her mother in a hotel, but when she returns, her mother has disappeared and the hotel claims that she never existed. (The original story concludes that the mother had bubonic plague and the hotel therefore hushed up her presence there.)

In "Cabin B-13," Richard and Anne Brewster, married so recently that Anne is still using a passport in her maiden name, board the *Maurevania*, being assigned Cabin B-13. Anne leaves the cabin, but when she comes back she cannot find the correct cabin number on any door. The stewardess whom she asks for help says that there is no such cabin on the *Maurevania*. Her husband has vanished with the room, and witnesses say that Anne boarded alone. No one believes Anne's frantic story except Paul Hardwick, the ship's doctor. The solution is entirely different from that in the Paris Exposition story. It is surprising that Carr never turned "Cabin B-13" into a novel, but it was adapted for television, and "Cabin B-13" became the basis for a 1953 feature movie, *Dangerous Crossing*, starring Jeanne Crain and Michael Rennie. Unfortunately, the screenplay by Leo Townsend ignores the radio play's feeling of strangeness, of having stepped into another dimension, and it reveals the solution too early. The result is no better and no worse than a typical damsel-in-distress film.*

Carr's *Suspense* plays have only one recurring weakness, one that was encouraged by the medium itself and that is more obvious to the reader of the scripts than to the listener to the broadcasts. Not only the story but also the setting and the actions of the characters had to be relayed solely by sound. Because it would be intrusive to have the narrator always explain to the listeners what was going on, Carr and other radio dramatists had the characters themselves indicate actions through dialogue. Sometimes, however, the characters provide plot background or describe what they are doing in an unnatural manner. Years later, Val Gielgud remarked that Carr did very well with what he called "purely descriptive dialogue, i.e. speeches deliberately designed to effect substitution for visuality," but he complained that occasionally such lines in Carr's plays stand out artificially.[54]

Taking one play at random—"Till Death Do Us Part" (December 15, 1942)—let's see how Carr conveys action through dialogue. The sinister German professor Erwin Krafft, played by Peter Lorre, is talking to his long-suffering wife, Cynthia. He says such things as, "I put two tumblers on the coffee-table, so . . . then, lemon juice, hot water to the top," and (to her suspected lover, the American Jim Craig) Krafft says, "But you're still securely tied up, I'm glad to say, roped, sealed, and delivered." When Krafft, who like all Nazis "leaves nothing to chance," nonetheless mistakenly poisons himself rather than Cynthia, Craig says, "You're staggering into the cupboard! Into the cupboard."[55] No one, needless to say, would in real life tell his enemy where he is staggering, and then repeat it. Although these lines seem unnatural when seen as print, they are less obviously awkward when heard.

It is difficult to believe that Carr could write such brilliant radio plays at a time when his drinking was getting out of control, but that was the situation. In his early days in Brooklyn Heights and during his first years of marriage, he did not drink while at the typewriter, and his sprees re-

---

*While this book was in typescript, another film version of "Cabin B-13" was produced. On April 8, 1992, the USA cable network broadcast a "world premier movie" called *Treacherous Crossing* starring Lindsay Wagner, Angie Dickinson, and Jeffrey de Munn. The story, taking place in 1947 and filmed on the *Queen Mary*, perfectly captured the late 1940s atmosphere, and Elisa Bell's script emphasized the strangeness of the situation. Unfortunately, the film played down the impossible crime, and the revelation of the criminal came as a letdown. Nevertheless, it is probably the best film adaptation of a Carr story.

sulted in nothing worse than hangovers. By the time the Carrs moved to Croton, however, he had persuaded himself that he could write while he was drinking, and as far as the quality of his writing indicates, he was correct.

But the brief sprees and hangovers of earlier years had become at times prolonged benders. At the beginning of one of these binges, Carr was a delightful companion, and throughout its course he usually remained gentle and courteous. If he ran out of liquor, however, he might become edgy around people and go off without a word. Unlike many alcoholics, Carr could control his drinking. He drank when he wanted to and stopped when he did not want to drink. Indeed, if a visitor showed up unexpectedly when John was in one of these spells, he could become sober almost immediately, and then after the visitor left, collapse in a near stupor. Doctors sometimes explained to his family that it was impossible to become sober so quickly, but several witnesses have told me that it happened.

When a binge was particularly severe, Carr might leave home for a while, ringing up friends in the middle of the night, and occasionally finding some seedy characters to share a bottle. Frequently he did not recall what he had done during the drinking spell. In a novel that he wrote about this time, *Seeing Is Believing*, Sir Henry Merrivale asks, "Did you ever go on a binge? And have too much to drink? And then wake up the next morning, without an earthly notion of what you had been doing; and feeling ghastly and thinking of all the dreadful things you *might* have done?"[56] Carr might even reach the stage of having hallucinations— demons were after him, he would explain. But the bender had to run its course; only then could Clarice pick up the pieces and bring him around. In later days, she sometimes came from a distance to rescue him, announcing that "the marines have arrived." And he would reply, "Oh, baby, I'm so glad to see you."[57]

Dealing with John at such times showed Clarice's fiber. Some of their friends even thought that she did too much for John during his drinking bouts. If she had left some of the grisly details of life for him to handle, if she had let him clean up after himself, he might have been less likely to go off on what she sometimes called a "toot." But there is no indication that John would have changed, whether or not Clarice was there to depend on. Moreover, at this time, people did not let such matters become public knowledge. They kept alcoholism hidden; they never admitted it to friends, and often never acknowledged it to the alcoholic himself. In the event, everyone who knew John knew about his drinking—and almost always liked him anyway. It was not something that could be kept hidden in the small world of mystery writers and radio dramatists in London and New York, especially since John often became publicly flamboyant while hitting the bottle.

When the binge had reached a crisis point, a large dose of chloral hydrate would sedate Carr for about twenty-four hours. When he woke, he would be weak, but the spell had passed and he would start work on a new book. But the chloral hydrate was itself a problem. It is what a standard pharmacology textbook calls a "sedative-hypnotic drug" whose main medical use "is to produce drowsiness and promote sleep." At this period, doctors often prescribed it as a mild, all-purpose sedative. Combined with ethanol it is much stronger and becomes what is popularly called a "Mickey Finn" or "knock-out drops."[58] John had trouble sleeping while he was working on a book, and sometime before the war he went to a doctor, who explained to him that chloral hydrate was so mild that doses could be given to babies to soothe toothaches. (Dr. James Keirans, who has studied references to drugs and poisons in Carr's novels, has found several passages about chloral hydrate, usually as a remedy for sleeplessness, starting with *The Four False Weapons* in 1937, and that may be when he began taking the drug.) More recent medical opinion, however, recognizes how dangerous chloral hydrate can be—it is an extremely addictive depressant. Calling the drug "mother's medicine," Carr took it in large quantities. With the alcohol and the chloral hydrate, the situation in 1942 and 1943 had reached the point that Clarice decided that something had to be done. She sought professional treatment for John, and it seemed to work, but before any cure could be permanent, the United States government at last decided what to do with him.[59]

In spring 1943, the BBC sent a representative to New York City. He tried to find out whether the American authorities would allow John Dickson Carr to return to London to write propaganda scripts, and whether Carr himself wanted to leave America. Carr went to see him at his hotel and expressed his willingness to return. These preliminaries out of the way, the BBC asked the American embassy in London to intervene with the Selective Service Board to allow Carr to return to England. Around May 1943 the United States government decided that Carr could work in London to help in the British propaganda effort. Although American radio paid considerably more than he could earn from the BBC, Carr was somewhat relieved to sever his ties with CBS. The network was, he thought, too sensitive when it told him to avoid using members of certain ethnic groups—especially Italians—as villains. Moreover, *Suspense* was going to take on an advertiser, and he feared that he would have to tailor his scripts to fit the sponsor's demands.

Carr had completed his *Suspense* scripts through June, the final one being "The Man Without a Body" (broadcast on June 22, 1943) which has a typically imaginative plot about how a man can be hurled from a church tower with no one near him. Carr hoped that he could persuade Gielgud to use some of his *Suspense* plays on British radio, but his main purpose in returning to England was to contribute to the war effort through propaganda scripts. Clarice was unhappy about the situation. Julia had dual citizenship and could return to England at any time, but Mary had been born in the United States and, as Clarice recalls, "the authorities didn't take too kindly about taking underage Americans to a war zone." Clarice told John that she wanted him to wait until she and both children could go with him, but he feared that any delay would result in his being stuck in the United States. "Baby," he said, "I've got to go back."[60] He was in England by the end of May 1943.

Chapter 11

WAR AND THE PUZZLE TALE

By the beginning of World War II, John Dickson Carr had become a very successful writer. Most of his books appeared in edition after edition both in Britain and in the United States. In the United States, Grosset & Dunlap reprinted all but three or four of Carr's novels in a format similar to the first editions, and during the 1940s, these versions were sometimes followed by more cheaply produced reprints by companies with such imprints as Tower Books and Books Inc. Moreover, these years saw the flowering of twenty-five-cent paperbacks, often with press runs of more than one hundred thousand copies. Although the royalty earned on each copy was tiny, the increase of readership was so great that authors were eager for paperback reprints. Between 1940 and 1943, fifteen of Carr's books appeared in American paperbacks, some in pocket-size format from the most important publishers in this market (Pocket Books, Avon, Dell, and Popular Library), and a few in larger digest-size form published by Lawrence E. Spivak under names like Bestseller Mysteries and Mercury Mysteries.

In Great Britain, the general pattern was for Hamish Hamilton and William Heinemann to reissue Carr's books in 3/6 and 2/6 editions in cloth. In addition, between 1938 and 1940, Penguin Books published three Carr novels in paperback and Guild issued another in 1941. Another indication of the popularity of his books was the increasing number of translations into various languages. Besides a German edition of *It Walks By Night* and a French of *Poison in Jest*, both published in 1931, there seems to have been no interest in foreign editions of Carr's works until 1936. But then the flood began. During the next five years, at least thirty translations of his books were published in Dutch, French, German, Italian, Norwegian, and Swedish.[1]

Despite spending a great deal of time preparing scripts for the BBC and CBS, Carr continued to be a prolific writer of detective stories. This chapter will discuss Carr's short stories and novels written between the outbreak of the war in September 1939 and May 1943, when he left Croton to return to London. We have, however, already looked at four short stories published during this period—two Christmas stories and two Colonel March cases. The remaining stories include two that feature Dr. Fell.

"The Locked Room" (July 1940), which Carr sold to *The Strand* under the cumbersome title "How Dr. Fell Solved the Mystery of the Locked Door," is an entertaining story that is, however, weakened by too much misdirection. A man is beaten over the head by an attacker who seems to have vanished from a locked room. His secretary, working in another room, says that she heard thuds "like the sound of a butcher's cleaver across meat on the chopping block." When the victim recovers consciousness, he confirms that he was hit over the head and that he heard the footsteps of his attacker. **[****Warning: Part of the solution follows.]** In fact, however, the cleaver sounds were objects falling off a table, and the victim lied about having heard footsteps. Carr's central gimmick in "The Locked Room" is clever enough and his trickiness about the time of the attack is convincing enough that it was unnecessary to misstate the so-called cleaver sounds and to have the victim tell the lie. We have already seen this tendency toward unnecessary misstatements in some of Carr's earlier books, and it will increase in his novels of the early 1940s.

"A Guest in the House" (*The Strand*, October 1940), which also features Dr. Fell, shows that Carr could tell a story straightforwardly—or at least relatively so—and still make the reader look in the wrong direction. In a manor house filled with valuable paintings, a burglar is found stabbed to death. When his mask is removed, the guests discover that the thief is the owner of the house himself. Why would a man dress up as a burglar in order to break into his own home? The pictures are uninsured, so fiddling with an insurance company cannot be the motive. This fine story twists and turns several times before Dr. Fell shows us the correct way to look at the case. It is interesting to note, incidentally, that Chief Inspector Ames, who is a subsidiary character in the Colonel March stories, also plays a small role in "A Guest in the House," one of the rare occasions in which a John Dickson Carr work overlaps with stories by Carter Dickson. This may indicate that Carr first wrote "A Guest in the House" as a Colonel March story.

The other two stories from this period do not feature any of Carr's recurring characters. "Strictly Diplomatic" (*The Strand*, December 1939) is one of his few secret-service stories, but it contains Carr's trademark, an impossible crime. A young woman—who turns out to be a British intelligence agent—vanishes from within a tunnel through an arbor. The solution is a variant of the one Carr had used at Haverford in "The Shadow of a Goat"—a story that, of course, readers of *The Strand* would have been unaware of.

"The Clue of the Red Wig" (December 1940), which Carr sent to *The Strand* under the title "The Turkish Bath Mystery," is told with such high spirits that the reader overlooks the fact that the plot is dependent on too many coincidences. As in "A Guest in the House," the challenge of this story is to explain a bizarre situation. A weight-control expert named Hazel Loring has told readers of her magazine column that they can eat anything they want as long as they follow her exercises for three minutes each morning. In the middle of winter, she is found dead in a garden, wearing only her underwear and a red wig. Her outer clothes are neatly folded beside her, in such a manner as to prove that she must have undressed herself in spite of the weather. The detecting is shared by Inspector Adam Bell, who admits to himself that he behaves "like a good deal of a stuffed shirt," and Jacqueline Dubois, a young newspaper reporter who has come to London from Paris "when things over there went to blazes."

During the four years from 1940 to 1943, John Dickson Carr published nine novels and a short-story collection, *The Department of Queer Complaints*. The novels include three featuring Dr. Fell, five about Sir Henry Merrivale, and one nonseries volume that, I suspect, was originally planned as the first Colonel March novel. Although Carr was already known for his mastery of locked rooms and other impossible crimes, only five of his novels written during this period have miracle problems. At least two of the others could have had a locked-room murder with only slight changes in the plot, but at this point in his writing career, Carr did not feel compelled to have an impossible crime in every story.

Several elements connect the nine novels of this period. Carr backdated the time period of five of them to shortly before the war. This is a significant development, but it is easy to exaggerate its extent. S. T. Joshi, for example, has written about what he calls Carr's "failure to make use of World War II." "The fact is," he continues, "that Carr's puzzle-stories are not adaptable to a war setting, and so he chose the simple expedient of avoiding the conflict while it was occurring."[2] There is, however, nothing that prevents a puzzle story from having a wartime setting, and in fact three of Carr's novels published between 1940 and 1943, *And So to Murder, Nine—and Death Makes Ten,* and *She Died a Lady,* depend on the war for their plot development. In addition, although *He Wouldn't Kill Patience* (1944) was written after the period under discussion, it is permeated with wartime references, and its solution is related directly to the Battle of Britain.

In short, Carr's stories are clearly adaptable to a war setting, and it is therefore even more noteworthy that he consciously chose a prewar setting for the majority of his novels published during these years. This decision was based partly on his understanding of the market for his works. Carr's description of his nonpropaganda radio plays is also true for his novels:

> Now these plays are, frankly, forms of escapism. The present war is seldom or never mentioned; the action takes place against a peacetime security. That, we felt, was the only atmosphere in which a listener can bother about being scared by shadows.[3]

He told American correspondents, however, that once the war was over he would be able to use some of his experiences as a basis for fiction: "I have had various adventures at dodging high explosives which will no doubt be useful for future stories."[4] But the fact is that after 1945, he did not use events of the Blitz for any novels, and he continued to choose the 1930s as the setting for some of his stories. He increasingly saw the contemporary age, whether wartime or peacetime, as unsatisfactory, and he used his fiction to reflect what he considered a happier time.

Some of Carr's novels from these four years continue the occasional weaknesses that we saw in his short stories and radio plays of the same period. Dr. Fell sometimes seems more interested in thumbing his nose at authority than in finding an ethical resolution of the crime and mystery. This tendency is mild in *The Case of the Constant Suicides.* Dr. Fell refuses to confide in the police because "my present purpose (between ourselves) is to swindle the insurance companies so that Colin Campbell can bask in good cigars and fire water for the rest of his life."[5] He does in fact allow the murderer to escape so that the insurance will be paid. In *The Man Who*

Could Not Shudder, he burns down a Jacobean manor house to save the murderer, though in this case the crime was committed accidentally. Yet nothing can justify Fell's actions at the conclusion of *The Seat of the Scornful.* He forces the killer to confess to a coldhearted murder, but then astonishingly lets him go with the warning, "Don't be so cocksure about your judgment in the future."[6] This rivals the conclusion of the radio play "The Black Minute" in making no ethical sense whatever.

Moreover, Carr continued to engage in authorial lies, or had the characters make such blatant misstatements that his dedication to the fair-play rule can be called into question. A minor example is in *The Man Who Could Not Shudder:* An innocent person announces that something has tried to seize her by the ankle. This turns out to be an unmotivated (or at least weakly motivated) lie; Carr's main purpose in including it was to prepare the ground for a supernatural legend of an ankle-grabbing ghost. More serious is Sir Henry Merrivale's statement in *And So to Murder* absolving one character of suspicion of guilt. That character turns out to be guilty, as H.M. knew at the very time he was clearing him. Carr does provide an explanation for H.M.'s misstatement—that H.M. did not want the murderer to know that he was under suspicion—but Carr comes close to breaking one of the guidelines he himself set up for fair-play detection: "The essence of the detective story is that the one guilty man shall fool the seven innocent; not that the one innocent shall be fooled by the seven guilty."[7] "It must be assumed," Carr says in *The Three Coffins,* "that *somebody* is telling the truth—else there is no legitimate mystery, and, in fact, no story at all.[8]

[****The most notorious example of Carr's questionable fairness is the first lines of *Seeing Is Believing:* "One night in midsummer, at Cheltenham in Gloucestershire, Arthur Fane murdered a nineteen-year-old girl named Polly Allen. That was the admitted fact."] This "admitted fact" governs much of the book, and Carr does a superb job using it to create human drama, but at the conclusion H.M. reveals that Arthur Fane did *not* murder Polly Fane. Whoa, says the reader, I thought the author told us that this was a fact. H.M.'s explanation is not satisfactory: "Y'see, ma'am, your knowledge that your husband was a murderer was the 'admitted' fact. Sure. But who admitted it?"[9] The person who "admitted it," says H.M., was the real murderer. To put that another way, H.M. claims that it may have been an *admitted* fact, but it wasn't a *genuine* fact. The fair-minded reader feels swindled. Anthony Boucher sent a steaming letter to Carr about this deception:

> May I step down for a moment from my position as your most loyal
> admirer and raise hell about *Seeing Is Believing?*. . . This opus, sir, is
> the goddamnedest piece of weaseling jiggerypokery ever put over
> on an unsuspecting public.

Carr responded in temperate tones:

> You are, probably with justice, a bit rough on *Seeing Is Believing;* but,
> though I admit weaseling and jiggerypokery, I remain unrepentant.
> One wrong word in that first chapter would have spilled the beans
> on the very first page.[10]

It may be noted, however, despite Carr's refusal to repent, that he never
again so questionably stretched the limits of fair play. If Carr himself did
not make an icon of playing fair with the reader—in his later book reviews, he mentions the theme in almost every column—I would not
spend so much time pointing out his failure to obey his own rules. But
these occasional flumdiddles do not seriously damage the novels of
1940–43. Among these books are some that are equal (or nearly so) to
Carr's best, including *The Case of the Constant Suicides, Nine—and Death
Makes Ten,* and *She Died a Lady,* and even the ones that cheat the reader are
often compelling in the human emotions they evoke.

Carr's novels of the early 1940s continue a pattern that began with *The
Problem of the Wire Cage.* Rarely does he use the plot device that had dominated his works of the middle and later 1930s—adventure lurking behind
prosaic doorways in the fashion of *New Arabian Nights.* The short story
"Strictly Diplomatic" is almost the final example of that theme in Carr's
works, although there is a bit of it in *The Case of the Constant Suicides* (and
even in a book of almost thirty years later, *Deadly Hall*). Nor does he often
include antiquarian and similar lore—quotations from ancient diaries, descriptions of curious objects, and the like—to produce atmosphere. In the
few instances that he does engage in antiquarianism, as with Napoleon's
snuff-box in *The Emperor's Snuff-Box* or the antique pistols in *The Man Who
Could Not Shudder,* a key plot device depends on those particular objects.
The occasional discursiveness of the earlier books has been replaced with
a tightness in plot whose main energy is produced by a combination of
the puzzle and the tension among the main characters—usually between
the male and female leads. Indeed, from this point onward it is a rare John
Dickson Carr book that does not have the heroine bickering with the
hero; the conclusion of the novel not only solves the puzzle but also ends
all the misunderstandings that were behind the tensions.

Sometimes, as in *The Case of the Constant Suicides,* the sexual tension is handled in a comic fashion, but more often it is serious—even deadly serious. In *Seeing Is Believing,* a wife is certain that her husband has committed murder. In *The Emperor's Snuff-Box,* the heroine is harassed by her brutal former husband, who thinks that he can get her back whenever he wishes. A good summary of the sexual war in Carr's books is in *Nine—and Death Makes Ten:*

> Their conversation in the bar the night before had been a kind of skirmish, an affair of outposts, in which each gauged the other's strength by maneuvering. He saw it in her fierce, snappish eyes. Each remained undecided. Each said, in effect, "I can't make up my mind about you." They parted almost on a note of hostility.[11]

In these books, nerves seem always near the snapping point. As Carr puts it in *The Seat of the Scornful,* "If emotion had been sound, the room would have been full of wash like the noise of the sea."

Of the three Fell novels published between 1940 and 1943, one (*The Case of the Constant Suicides*) ranks with Carr's finest books, and the other two (*The Man Who Could Not Shudder* and *The Seat of the Scornful*) are solid performances filled with ingenious ideas. Carr took the title of *The Man Who Could Not Shudder,* published in May 1940, from "The Boy Who Could Not Shudder," G. K. Chesterton's favorite Grimms' fairy tale. Carr's novel is a haunted-house story based on locations he knew well. It begins in 1937 at London's "Congo Club" with a discussion of ghosts and hauntings. The Congo Club is a thinly disguised version of the Savage Club, and one of the participants in the discussion is "the editor of *The Fleet Street Magazine,*" that is, Reeves Shaw, editor of *The Strand Magazine.* As a result of the discussion, a retired businessman named B. Martin Clarke purchases the seventeenth-century Longwood House, which is reputed to be haunted. Some fifteen years earlier, an octogenerian butler had been killed when, or so it seemed, he was attacked by a crawling spook that tried to seize his feet, and to save himself he leaped and grabbed a metal chandelier. The chandelier fell and crushed him. Whether one is terrified by the image of something snapping at the ankles, or ironically amused by an ancient butler swinging from a chandelier, the picture is reminiscent of Carr's early emphasis on the grotesque. Longwood House itself is based on J. B. Priestley's holiday home, Billingham Manor, on the Isle of Wight. It was purported to have a ghost or two, and Priestley invited Carr to spend a night in a haunted room. Carr accepted, spent the night there, and was dreadfully disappointed when nothing spectral showed up.[12]

But a great deal that seems ghostly shows up at Longwood House in *The Man Who Could Not Shudder*. Martin Clarke invites visitors to the house and tells them a story of a corpse with a scratched face that has a penchant for grabbing at ankles. As the plot of the novel develops, ankles are indeed grabbed, and a gun leaps off the wall and, without anyone being near it, fires and kills a man. The clues to explain the impossibility are fairly given, and Carr's device of having at least one false solution followed by the true is excellently handled (*The Man Who Could Not Shudder* has three separate solutions). Nevertheless, as Eugene Saxton of Harpers wrote to Carr when he received the typescript in March 1940, the actual method to have the gun fire produces a major problem: Anyone could have accidentally set it off and given the whole show away. The possibility of accident was necessary in order to justify the third and final solution to the puzzle, but (without revealing too much) I should add that the third solution was not necessary and that, as Saxton also said, it plays too many games with the reader's sympathies. Saxton asked Carr to consider making last-minute changes in the typescript based on his comments, but though Carr's reply does not survive, it is clear that he made no changes. There probably was no time anyway, since the book was to be published two months later.[13]

Carr followed this slightly flawed exercise in creepiness with one of his great successes, *The Case of the Constant Suicides*, published in June 1941. The novel was inspired by a holiday that John and Clarice had spent in Scotland in the early autumn of 1940, and at least one of the characters, a newspaperman named Swan, was based on someone they had met during that trip.[14] The book itself begins on September 1, 1940. *The Case of the Constant Suicides* is entirely different in tone from any of Dr. Fell's cases since *The Blind Barber*. Like *The Blind Barber*, *The Case of the Constant Suicides* has some amazing drinking scenes, but they work much better in the latter book, perhaps because tipsiness does not dominate the entire story. The book has a rich array of comic characters. The bawdy, alcoholic Dr. Colin Campbell, the Bible-quoting Aunt Elspat Campbell, the Canadian newspaperman, Swan, who represents a London scandal sheet—all these are comic masterpieces. Only Dr. Fell remains a serious (though, needless to say, eccentric) character; the shenanigans of his earlier years, as recounted especially in *The Eight of Swords*, no longer appear even in such extravaganzas as *The Case of the Constant Suicides*—such things are left for Sir Henry Merrivale.

The main characters are two argumentative young scholars, Alan Campbell and his cousin Kathryn, who fall under the spell of Scotland. After sharing a bottle of the Doom of the Campbells, Alan fences drunkenly with Colin Campbell. Kathryn, who witnessed it all, tells Alan the next morning that Colin announced, "'Alan Oig, there is dirty work to be done this night. Let us hence and look for Stewarts.' You thought that would be a perfectly splendid idea." Kathryn recalls that Alan and Colin spied Swan the newspaperman in the moonlight, took after him, and stuck him in the behind with a claymore. "Don't you think," Kathryn asks Alan, "we'd better get out of Scotland before it corrupts us altogether?"[15]

The comedy of *The Case of the Constant Suicides* is placed within an excellent puzzle plot with two of Carr's finest locked rooms. Old Angus Campbell had apparently committed suicide by leaping from the sixty-foot tower of Shira Castle. Murder seemed out of the question: No one could have gotten near him. Was a Highland ghost involved, and what had been in the empty suitcase (with airholes) that was found under Angus's bed? Later in the book, Alec Forbes, one of the suspects who may have brought the suitcase to Angus's room, is murdered in a locked cottage, and Colin, who decides to sleep at the top of the tower, is seemingly thrown out the window by an invisible intruder. The solutions to these locked rooms are excellent (one of them is taken from Carr's short story "The Diamond Pentacle"). I could go on about the structure of the story— for example, Carr's cleverness in having Dr. Fell solve the mystery of Angus's death just when he is entirely mystified by Alec's murder—but suffice it to say that *The Case of the Constant Suicides* is a constant delight.

Constant Suicides was Dr. Fell's final involvement in a case filled with slapstick. Some six months before the book was published Carr had already completed his next detective novel, and it was a serious, even somber work. In January 1941, Carr summarized the plot: "It is all about a hanging judge who maintains that circumstantial evidence can never convict an innocent man, and himself gets caught in the same trap where it appears that he must have done the dirty work."[16] As the title, Carr chose the nearly perfect *The Seat of the Scornful*, which he had previously planned for his never-written novel about the seventeenth-century Judge Jeffreys. The jurist in the new Dr. Fell case is named "Ireton," after one of Cromwell's generals during the English Civil War.

The Seat of the Scornful focuses on a man who, as judge, has never found weakness an excuse, or motive a justification, for committing a crime. Like Heinrich Himmler of Carr's "Black Gallery" radio script, Justice Ireton cannot be bothered with people: "There is hardly anything," Ireton says, "of less value than relationships based on mere feeling."[17] On the bench, he has always said that circumstantial evidence was sufficient. How would such a man act when circumstantial evidence seems to show that he himself is guilty of murder? The victim is a man named Tony Morell, who has approached Justice Ireton in a seeming attempt to extract money in exchange for breaking off his engagement to the judge's daughter. Carr does not treat Morell with much sympathy, even after it becomes clear that he is not in fact a gigolo—but Morell announces proudly that "I never use tobacco or spirits," and no one with such ideas can be a hero in a Carr book.[18] When Morell is murdered, Ireton is found with the murder weapon, and circumstances have conspired to point to his guilt.

Harpers did not get the point of Carr's title, *The Seat of the Scornful*, which did not seem to them right for a detective novel, and before even seeing Carr's typescript asked for an alternate. Carr apparently did not send an acceptable suggestion, for Harpers devised the American title, *Death Turns the Tables*,[19] which does describe a part of the book but misses Carr's theme. The American edition was published in December 1941, the British in April 1942.

The Emperor's Snuff-Box, published in August 1942, is Carr's only novel of the 1940s not to feature either Dr. Gideon Fell or Sir Henry Merrivale. The story is associated with the Colonel March case "The Silver Curtain." Both take place in La Bandelette at Touques on the Normandy coast, and a major character in both is Aristide Goron, prefect of police. It's possible that Carr first planned to have Colonel March solve *The Emperor's Snuff-Box*,[20] but as the story developed it emphasized the issue of a witness's perceptions, and Carr decided to replace March with a psychologist, Dr. Dermot Kinross. In true Carr fashion Kinross falls in love with the heroine, Eve Neill. In the only instance in which Carr came close to successfully adopting a woman's viewpoint, the early sections of the book are seen through Eve's eyes. Eve was married to Ned Atwood, a thorough cad who not only had an affair with a famous woman tennis player, but also physically abused Eve. Not wanting to bring her personal life before the court, Eve has obtained a divorce from Ned on the grounds of adultery. Nevertheless, the world blames her for the collapse of her marriage.

When the novel opens Eve in a muddled sort of way has agreed to

Above: Wooda Nicholas
Carr about the time he
ran for Congress.
Right: John D. Carr III
with his father, 1911–12.
*(Courtesy of Wooda N.
Carr II)*

The Hill School, autumn 1924. The editorial board of *Snooze*, a humor magazine. John Dickson Carr is standing at the far right. *(Courtesy of the Honorable Herbert S. MacDonald)*

Above: Photo postcard sent to Haverford classmate James Partington, Jr., Amsterdam, October 1927. On the back Carr identified himself as a "distinguished criminal" sought by M. Henri Bencolin. *(Courtesy of James Partington, Jr.)*
Right: William O'Neil Kennedy and Carr, Paris, 1930.

The first-edition dust jacket of John Dickson Carr's first book. *(Courtesy of Otto Penzler)*

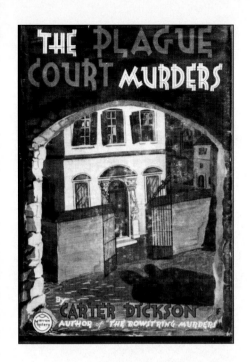

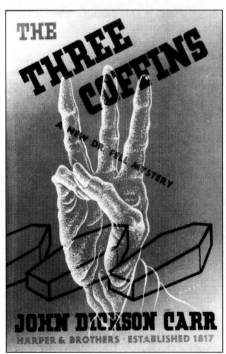

First-edition dust jackets. *Above left:* the first Sir Henry Merrivale book (U.S. edition). *Above right:* the first case for Dr. Gideon Fell (U.S. edition). *Below left:* the sixth Dr. Fell book. *Below right:* a Chestertonian portrayal of Dr. Fell on his ninth book (British edition). *(First three photos courtesy of Otto Penzler)*

Photographs taken by Clarice
Carr at The Detection Club,
autumn 1936. John Dickson
Carr had the photographs
framed, and they hung on the
wall in his various studies
for the rest of his life.
Top: Anthony Berkeley,
founder of The Detection
Club. *Left:* E. C. Bentley,
president 1936–49.

Top: Dorothy L. Sayers. *Right:* John Rhode (Major C. J. C. Street), the Carrs' closest friend in The Detection Club. Both Sayers and Rhode are holding Eric the Skull.

Snapshots, 1935–40. *Top, left and right:* John and Clarice, The Bungalow, Kingswood, Bristol, 1935–36. *Bottom:* John in his favorite pose, holding a pipe that he didn't smoke, 1936.

Opposite, top left: Versailles, 1938. *Top right:* Marseilles, 1938. *Bottom left:* Clarice, John, Julia Kisinger, Wooda Carr, Uniontown, 1939. *Bottom right:* Remains of the Carrs' house, Maida Vale, after German bombs, 1940.

Above: Val Gielgud at a BBC control panel. *Left:* David Higham, John Dickson Carr's agent beginning in 1937. *(Courtesy of David Higham Associates; photograph by Mark Gerson)*

John Dickson Carr presents Edgars for 1947 at the Mystery Writers of America award ceremonies held the next year. *Top:* with Frederick Dannay. *Bottom:* with Clayton Rawson. *(Courtesy of Hugh Rawson)*

Clarice and John Carr in the living room of Clayton and Kate Rawson, Mamaroneck, New York.

John Dickson Carr with Adrian Conan Doyle at the Sherlock Holmes exhibition, New York, 1952. The publicity release with the photograph stated that the two men were plotting a story in the *Exploits of Sherlock Holmes* series. (UPI/Bettmann)

Above, clockwise from top left: Violet Andrews (the Carrs' housekeeper-nanny), John, Clarice, Mary, and Bonita Carr. *Below:* Julia McNiven, Clarice, and Mary. Reproduced from slides taken in the winter of 1960.

John and Clarice in the Indian summer of their marriage. *Above:* Mamaroneck, August 1958. *Below:* Greenville, summer or autumn, 1965 *(Courtesy of Edna Seaman)*

John Dickson Carr after his stroke and his first bout with cancer. Photographs of a Christmas visit to Mamaroneck, 1971, taken by Carr's son-in-law, James Cron.

marry a stuffed shirt named Toby Lawes, but Ned is certain that he can re-
claim her. He forces his way into her apartment and threatens to rape her,
believing that doing so will bring her back to him: "There's only one thing
I ought to do. . . . Your sex-appeal, especially in those pajamas, would
make an anchorite forget himself. . . . *You'll* enjoy it."[21] Carr, who sometimes seemed to believe that sexual intercourse can solve all male/female
disagreements, also knew that it must be with the consent of both parties,
and Ned Atwood is one of the most abhorrent characters in his books.
This scene is, however, not only evidence of Ned's caddishness (to put it
mildly), it also is an integral part of Carr's detective plot. Carr wants us to
sense Eve's fear both at Ned's specific threat and at the loss of her reputation; she does not want Toby's father, Sir Maurice Lawes, who is examining a rare Napoleonic snuff-box in a room across the street, to see her and
Ned together. Despite her entreaties, Ned looks out the window and describes seeing a murderous attack on Sir Maurice. Eve joins Ned at the window and sees a hand withdrawing from the door of Sir Maurice's room.

[****To show that *The Emperor's Snuff-Box* is about the fallibility of
human perceptions and human memory the solution will be revealed.]
In fact, Ned murdered Sir Maurice before going to Eve's apartment, but
he impresses on her that she has seen not only the mysterious hand but
the attack as well. This is why Dermot Kinross comes into the story. Carr
had become more open to the tenets of psychology since his early sarcastic references to Viennese doctors, but he saw its role as explaining the *how*
rather than the *why* of human behavior. Thus *The Problem of the Green Capsule* was subtitled "Being the Psychologists' Murder Case" not because it
had to do with inhibitions or obsessions or Oedipal complexes, but because the clues involved how witnesses saw things. In *The Emperor's Snuff-
Box*, Carr tells us that Eve "was more susceptible than most persons to the
power of suggestion."[22] Carr was trying a double trick, one in a sense on
his characters, and the other on the readers: Eve is persuaded that she
saw what did not in fact happen, and she repeats her faulty statement
with enough conviction that the reader is also persuaded of her story.
Carr remarked that he was playing a "low-down and dastardly dirty trick
[on] the reader. This is as mean and filthy a swindle as has been devised,
but I believe it is new and I claim it is fair."[23]

The Emperor's Snuff-Box sold well in its American edition; according to
records in the files of Carr's American agent, the Ann Watkins Company,
6,405 copies at $2.00 each were sold from the end of October through De-
cember 31, 1942, and the book had gone through five printings by March

1943. By the end of 1943, total sales were almost 9,000 copies. On June 30, 1944, Harpers sold hardback reprint rights to Grosset & Dunlap, which immediately printed another 5,000 copies at $1 each. This was followed in September by an even cheaper hardback edition from Books, Inc.—20,000 copies at 49 cents—and the same month a paperback edition from Pocket Books, of 150,000 copies at 25 cents.[24] The goal that since the middle 1930s his publishers had dangled in front of John Dickson Carr of making him one of the most widely recognized names in the mystery field was clearly being met.

Between 1940 and 1943, Carr wrote five Sir Henry Merrivale books, beginning with *And So to Murder* (published in the United States in May 1940). The title is taken from a repeated phrase in the diary of Samuel Pepys, who often ended an entry "and so to. . . . The setting, however, is not Pepys's seventeenth-century England, but a very modern film studio. Pineham Studios, being rented by Albion Films, is based on Carr's experiences with the Korda company in 1938. One of the major characters in the book is an author of detective stories named Bill Cartwright—the name taken from "Cartwright Dickson," which Carr had suggested around 1934 as his pseudonym for the H.M. stories. Among the films Albion is working on is something called *Spies at Sea*, which in spite of being based on the navy rather than the air force is related to *Q Planes*, on which Carr had been briefly engaged for Korda. Carr breaks up the puzzle plot of *And So to Murder* with interludes featuring an American film producer who is working on a costume drama about the Battle of Waterloo. He livens up history by having the Duke of Wellington saved by a surgeon from Oshkosh or Peoria.

Like *The Emperor's Snuff-Box*, *And So to Murder* has a major section told from the viewpoint of a woman—Monica Stanton, who, though inexperienced in the ways of the world, has written some steamy romances about an adventuress named Eve D'Aubray.* But instead of being assigned her own novels to make into films, she has to work on Cartwright's detective stories—and he in turn must write the scripts for her romances. This of course opens the way for male-female bickering, but it will not surprise readers of Carr's books that Monica and Bill fall in love. Meanwhile, evidence emerges that Nazi spies have infiltrated the studio, and someone seems to be trying to kill Monica for an unknown reason. She is trapped in a house on the set, enticed to put a speaking tube to her ear, and barely

---

*A cousin, I assume, of the Marie D'Aubray of *The Burning Court*.

escapes when acid is poured down the tube. The murderer must have read Bill's detective novels, for Bill had used the acid-down-the-tube trick in one of his mysteries. H.M., assisted for the last time by Ken Blake, is in a more serious mood than usual; he is again head of Military Intelligence as Britain gears up for war. The only mild humor about H.M. in this book is his physical description ("on his face was an expression which would not have been out of place in the Chamber of Horrors at Madame Tussaud's"), his fear that he will be sent to pasture in the House of Lords, and his desire to dress up for a screen test as Richard III. Unlike some of his other cases this one does not involve his actually *doing* anything outrageous.

The next Carter Dickson book, *Nine—and Death Makes Ten,* is probably the most somber of H.M.'s books since the middle 1930s. As Carr points out in a brief preface, the setting of the story is based on John and Clarice's shipboard experiences when they returned to England from New York in September 1939. Carr changed the name of the ship from the *Georgic* to the *Edwardic,* and he increased the tension by having his fictional vessel carry munitions, but the blackout, the zigzag journey to avoid German submarines, and the growing claustrophobic atmosphere were all part of the Carrs' trip back to England. William Heinemann, the British publisher of Sir Henry Merrivale's cases, thought that a mystery on a blacked-out ship was a good sales gimmick and rushed the book into print. Heinemann decided to delay the publication of *And So to Murder* until March 1941, and published *Nine—and Death Makes Ten* in August 1940, two months before the United States edition. The British printing was titled *Murder in the Submarine Zone.*

Nine—and Death Makes Ten is one of Carr's best books of the early 1940s, and it rivals the most challenging of H.M.'s cases of any period. The impossibility and its explanation are superb; the wartime suspense is carefully integrated into the puzzle plot; and there is absolutely no fat in the book. The main character is a newspaperman named Max Matthews. The murder is especially bloody—Mrs. Zia Bey's throat was slit, and the murderer has left two bloody thumbprints on her white gown. Identifying the murderer seems easy; All that need be done is to take the fingerprints of everyone on the *Edwardic* and compare them with the prints left by the murderer. Fingerprints of all the passengers and crew are taken, but none match the ones left by the murderer. The situation is clearly impossible— the fingerprints on the dress are not faked; the prints of everyone on board were taken without "flummery or mistake"; and yet no one's prints match those of the killer. As he had done in earlier books, Carr adds a footnote that all these statements are perfectly correct. Meanwhile, it seems as though there may be a Nazi spy on board, probably a woman, who plans to signal German submarines about the location of the *Edwardic*. More mysteries appear as—in one of Carr's more colorful use of his mask theme—one passenger seems always to be wandering about with his face covered with a gas mask.

Sir Henry Merrivale is on the *Edwardic*, but perhaps because he is in the submarine zone, he is unexpectedly subdued. The sole comedy in the book is in the Great Man's attempts to have a shave while the barber suggests that he purchase some bottles of hair restorer. This scene, incidentally, provides a clue to the murderer's identity. Two of the other clues, one involving the gas mask, another the naval uniform of a certain nationality, are directly related to the war, but there are enough other clues, including some explaining the fingerprints of a nonexistent person, that the book remains a fair-play triumph.

Carr's original title for the succeeding H.M. book was the rather dull *X Marks the Spot*,[25] but when it was published in August 1941 the title was changed to the not-much-more-interesting *Seeing Is Believing*. The events of the story take place in 1938, and without the horrors of war as the background, Carr allows H.M. to engage in broad farce. In this book, Philip Courtney is ghost-writing H.M.'s memoirs, which the Great Man plans as a way of gaining revenge on his real and imagined enemies—especially his uncle George Merrivale, "who may with moderation be described as a bounder and a louse." Meanwhile, Vicky Fane, believing that her husband is a murderer, finds herself in a potentially deadly parlor game. Dr. Rich, a hypnotist, explains that no one will act under hypnosis in a way contrary to his or her own character or desires. He allows Vicky to overhear him explaining that he is setting out two weapons, a loaded gun and a realistic-looking rubber knife. When she is hypnotized, she is ordered to kill her husband. She is expected, of course, to choose the harmless knife—and in fact, despite fearing and hating her husband, that's what she does. But somehow the knife has been switched for a real one, and Arthur Fane dies. The problem is that no one could have come near the knife.

Carr took the explanation of the impossible crime in *Seeing Is Believing* from a trick used by the fake spiritualists the Davenport Brothers, who had been exposed by John Nevil Maskelyne. The method, however, strikes me as too risky for a murderer to stake his life upon. The identity of the killer is excellently hidden; Carr had in an unexpected way blackened his name to make him appear innocent. As one of the characters remarks, "It would be rather awful, wouldn't it, if somebody we thought figured in one role really figured in exactly the opposite role?"[26] That's exactly what Carr makes the reader think in *Seeing Is Believing.*

The Gilded Man, published in June 1942, is an expansion of the main plotline of the short story "A Guest in the House," about someone who burglarizes his own house, but with Sir Henry Merrivale replacing Dr. Fell as the detective. Typical of the H.M. books of this period, the Great Man does not enter *The Gilded Man* until about one-third of it has been told, and just as typically, he enters in an uproarious scene. The story takes place on December 30 and 31, 1938. The male and female leads, mistaking H.M.'s battered top hat as a castoff left on top of a wall, hit it with a snowball. When H.M. rises in anger, he is the recipient of a second snowball, which Carr specifies as rather squishy. Later in the book, H.M. appears as the Great Kafoozalum, the magician in a New Year's Eve fete put on for local children.

As a detective novel, *The Gilded Man* has several flaws. Even more obviously than in *The Problem of the Wire Cage,* the murder at the end of the book is unnecessary, and in this case it is a genuine tragedy that sits oddly with the comic scenes that occur at the same time. Moreover, a section in the middle of the novel, having to do with an El Greco painting and a scheme to empty a South American lake of its sacrificial gold, has even less to do with the story than Carr's usual red herrings. In addition, after several readings of the book I still do not know why the activities of the murderer should not have been immediately evident in the footprints left in the frost; if Carr did not make an error about the murderer's wanderings, the book needs a sketchmap to show the reader how he could have left the house without leaving footprints pointing outward.

Partly because so much of his time and ingenuity were taken up planning and writing radio dramas, Carr published only one book in 1943, the first time since 1930 that he had not written two or more detective novels in a single year. *She Died a Lady,* published in the United States in January 1943, was probably written at Croton-on-Hudson, but it is filled with the background of war in Britain. The story takes place from May to July 1940, with an epilogue in February of the next year. The setting is Lyncombe on the north cost of Devon, based on Lynton, where Carr had stayed in the early months of 1941. "Those were bewildered days," Carr wrote in *She Died a Lady* about May and June 1940:

Nazi tanks were loose like blackbeetles across a map. You could almost smell the smoke of destruction from the other side. We puzzled our wits as to what was wrong; in a daze we saw the fall of Paris and the collapse of all ordered things. It was as though you had found that the very schoolbooks of your youth had been telling you lies.[27]

She Died a Lady is a book of carefully drawn contrasts. Sometimes they are minor, as in Carr's recollection that as almost all of Europe was falling to Hitler, everyone that summer was whistling "Over the Rainbow."[28] More often, they are important insights, as Carr contrasts the reality of war with the ordered life of an English village. Perhaps because, as was the case with *Hag's Nook*, *She Died a Lady* was written in America, Carr invests English life with a romantic haze. He creates a world that never quite existed and makes it wonderfully attractive.

She Died a Lady has a clever plot with many twists and a baffling impossible situation. The identity of the murderer is well concealed, and the conclusion is poignant in a way that is unusual in Carr's works. Like the war itself, the identity of the murderer is a tragedy; except for a sheer chance, caused ironically by the war, the revelation of the killer would have shaken the tranquil assumptions of the characters as much as the war did.

In *She Died a Lady*, Carr uses a narrative voice that is unusual for him. The story is told by Luke Croxley, a sixty-five-year-old country doctor, and (with only minor inconsistencies) Carr maintains Croxley's viewpoint and tone throughout the book. Carr probably took the idea of having a doctor tell the story from Agatha Christie's *The Murder of Roger Ackroyd*, and the surname of Paul Ferrars, who adds the epilogue to the novel, is also taken from Christie's novel. But these hints and parallels to Christie are red herrings to mislead the reader familiar with mystery fiction, and anyone who predicts that Carr's novel will have the same solution as *Roger Ackroyd* will be fooled.

She Died a Lady is a story of adultery. The sultry Rita Wainright, supposedly thirty-eight years old (but actually in her forties) is married to Alec Wainright, a mathematics professor who is two decades her senior. She falls in love with a twenty-five-year-old actor named Barry Sullivan, who is handsome but (Carr tells us) "somewhat weak of jaw." (Carr obviously thought that all mathematicians are imperceptive; Alec seems not to notice that "emotions had been strung to so high a pitch,"[29] and instead spends his time listening to war news on the radio.) Dr. Croxley attends a card party with the Wainrights and Sullivan, and after Rita and Barry leave together, he finds their footprints leading to a cliff overlooking the Atlantic. No other prints, coming or going, are there. It seems to be a clear case of double suicide, and all that's left is to wait for the bodies to wash ashore.

H.M. enters at this stage with "an expression of almost inhuman malignancy." He has broken his big toe, and has confined himself to a wheelchair in an attempt to obtain sympathy. The chair is motorized, and as he drives it imperially up the middle of the street, he is attacked by the village dogs and ends up crashing through the door of a pub. "I'm a mild-mannered bloke," H.M. complains, "known far and wide for the urbanity of my temper and the ease of my bearing. I love animals like St. Francis of Assisi, blast their ears."[30] Despite his success in counterespionage in *And So to Murder,* his help is no longer wanted at the War Office and the government is still trying to force him into the House of Lords. He is in Lyncombe having his portrait painted in a Roman toga. Later in the book, dressed in his toga but with a vile cigar in the center of his mouth, he rides about Lyncombe in his wheelchair.

H.M. suspects that the suicide may have been faked and suggests a possible way for the footprints to have been made by one person walking forward and backward. Then Rita Wainright's and Barry Sullivan's bodies are found, shot at close quarters rather than drowned, and the evidence shows that the victims could not have killed themselves:

> Two persons were shot as they stood on the very edge of a cliff. The murderer couldn't have climbed up or down that cliff. Presumably he couldn't fly. Yet he approached them and got away without leaving a footprint on that whole expanse of soil.

A second false explanation is offered, this one having to do with parachutes, before Dr. Croxley uncovers the true way that the footprints were produced. It is up to H.M., however, to identify the murderer in the epilogue.

By the time the British edition of *She Died a Lady* was published (August 1943), Carr had been back in England for several months working at the BBC and experiencing firsthand the effect of war on his adopted country.

Chapter 12

DRAMA—STAGE, RADIO, AND LIFE

On his return to London around May 1943, John Dickson Carr took a top-floor flat at 115 Eton Rise, Haverstock Hill, in a companion building to the apartment house where the Carrs had lived during the late 1930s. Twenty years later, Carr explained how he was able to find the flat so quickly:

> Despite an acute housing shortage, I had obtained that flat for reasons quite apart from my Scottish luck. When I moved into it in 1943, Adolf Hitler still walked the earth. He had yet to unleash the Little Blitz, the flying bombs, the rockets, and other drolleries from his inexhaustible sense of humor. But we were all expecting something of the sort. And nobody except your obedient servant was stupid enough to want a flat on the top floor.[1]

The Little Blitz came soon enough. In 1944, Carr sent a letter to Frederic Dannay describing what was going on:

> We have been having tolerably exciting days and nights here, with doodle-bugs littering the place. They're pretty wicked, especially when they roar so close over the roof you imagine you could reach up and field 'em; but in my own opinion they're not nearly as bad as stuff in the old blitz days. For one thing, there isn't the incessant gun-

fire. On the other hand, the blitzes always stopped at dawn; you could turn over and go to sleep soundly again; but dawn is just the time that the first of these damned things start doing their aerial-motor-car act. Civilization, 1944.[2]

Doodle-bugs were just one problem that Carr had to contend with; another and, in the event, a more personally serious one was of his own making. He was living with another woman in the Haverstock Hill flat, and with Clarice trying to obtain permission to return to England, he was likely to face a crisis.

Friends of the Carrs who knew how much John doted on Clarice wondered why he was not always a faithful husband. No other woman ever replaced Clarice in his affections, but he seems to have needed to have a woman around. Clarice is philosophical about this trait in John's character. "I knew my John," she says; "he wasn't the sort of person to go for a year or so in the blameless way."[3] Carr treated women with a courtly attentiveness that some found hard to resist. Indeed, when he presented flowers to female acquaintances with a few words of graceful compliment, he may have meant little by it—such behavior was the image of a gentleman he cultivated, the mask he presented to the world—but some women, especially those who were unaccustomed to male admiration, read into his attentions more than he had in mind. (One member of The Detection Club, who was in middle life, formed an extravagant passion for him and became very difficult when he showed the same gentlemanly attentions to other women.)[4]

Despite being a kind and civilized man, Carr never thought that he was acting in a cruel manner by taking a mistress when Clarice was away from him. He sometimes rationalized his actions (and those of the male sex in general) by saying that infidelity should be blamed on the damnable attractiveness of women. Especially in his later books, he referred to women as "charmers," and in a radio play written in 1948, a character remarks about a sexual affair, "I'm not even sure I liked her. But she hypnotized me with an attractiveness that—now do you understand?"[5] Like many men, Carr expected his wife to turn a blind eye toward her husband's affairs. Many of the female characters in his later books, most of which are historical mysteries, accept what he called their husbands' "drunkenness and duels and infidelities." Dr. Fell is just as broadminded in In Spite of Thunder, published in 1960; he says that adultery is something that "old-fashioned people still consider an offence."[6]

Carr had had several brief affairs—"encounters" might be a more accurate word—but only when he was alone in London during 1943 and 1944 did he form a serious extramarital liaison, and even this seems not to have been a fundamental challenge to his marriage. Because his mistress is still alive, her name will not be revealed here. I shall call her "Maureen" for the simple reason that the name is in no way similar to hers. She was connected with the BBC, and contemporary rumors suggested that she had been introduced to Carr by friends at Broadcasting House in the hope of starting some sort of relationship. Perhaps the motive was to have someone watching out for him at a time when he had again begun to drink. According to BBC gossip, although the alcohol did not damage his writing, sometimes he did no work on those days he was drinking, and then had to catch up later by putting in extra hours.[7] Whatever the BBC's motivation, John and Maureen did begin an affair. Jack Reynolds, who was stationed in London with the United States Navy, knew about the woman who had moved in with John, and he attributed it to the wartime atmosphere. Carr, he admits, was susceptible, but so were many people who in other situations would not have been. Long-term relationships, even marriages, seemed insignificant when you could not be certain that you would survive the next air raid.[8]

After many frustrating months of trying to obtain permission to return to England with Julia and Mary, Clarice Carr at last received the proper authority, embarking in late April 1944. When she arrived about May 5, she went to her parents' home in Bristol, where Bonnie was staying. Suspecting what might be going on ("I knew my John"), she got in touch with Violet Andrews, who had been supposed to help John at his north London flat. Andy told Clarice, "I couldn't do for Mr. Carr. I was going to set up a meal, keep the place clean, but then I found some female clothes there and I knew they weren't yours."[9]

Meanwhile, the Cleaveses had wired John that Clarice had arrived, and when he came to Bristol a day later, she told him, "John, I know all about it, but I'm not French and the *ménage à trois* is not my cup of tea." He replied, "I know, baby; I'll do something about it." John, who had believed that Maureen was a secret from Clarice, first thought that Jack Reynolds had revealed the whole affair. He eventually realized that Reynolds had not blown the whistle on him, but meanwhile he had to straighten out the situation. Maureen solved the problem. John disliked fuss, and when she threatened suicide as a way of keeping his affections, the issue was decided. Clarice knew that faced with hysteria, John would give a sad look and end the relationship, and that's what happened.

On May 24, 1944, he wrote to Dannay that Clarice's "welcome home was terrific; I am myself again." He was glossing over a great deal with that simple comment, but it was basically true.[10] By that time, Maureen had reconsidered her suicide threat, packed her belongings, and moved out. Carr remained in London to continue his work for the BBC, while Clarice lived with her parents in Bristol, primarily so that the children could go to school there. John wrote to Dannay that "Clarice and the children, I am glad to say, are in the country with her people. They should be quite all right even if Jerry develops one of these weird Tom Swift rockets that are being so much talked about."[11] Clarice often came to London for long weekends, and John was occasionally in Bristol, so their living arrangements did not in any way indicate a formal separation.

The importance of this interlude with Maureen for Carr's writing is its effect on the female characters of Carr's later books—or, to be more precise, how the males respond to the females. I have already discussed Carr's handling of fictional characters in various novels and short stories, but some generalizations about the entire issue should be made here.

Probably nothing about Carr's writing has received more varying comments than his characterizations. It has sometimes been said that flat, wooden, or mechanical people fill his novels; yet for many readers the personalities of Bencolin, Fell, and Merrivale, along with some of the lesser characters, are memorable. In *John Dickson Carr, a Critical Study*, S. T. Joshi encapsulates the difficulties of a balanced approach to the issue. Throughout his discussion of individual novels, Joshi praises Carr's handling of his characters: "A miracle of character portrayal"; and "Carr's brooding intensity and portrayal of character . . . reach perhaps their heights here"; and "All characters stand out vividly." He remarks that one of Carr's novels provides "evidence to refute the claims of critics that Carr could not draw character." Nonetheless, it is revealed later in Joshi's book that he is himself one of those critics: "The issue of Carr's characterisation can be dealt with very simply: he could not draw character at all."[12] These quotations are from a perceptive critic, and they have an important observation. When we read a Carr book, we are struck by the lively characterizations; the actors in his detective dramas are anything but cardboard. When we look at his work as a whole, however, we recall the larger-than-life sleuths, but many of the other figures fade in our memories.

The problem with characterizations in Carr's books is not that they are unrealistic but rather that Carr does not vary them enough. The same people appear and reappear with their names but not their natures changed. For example, all of his young visitors to the Continent or England seem alike, and the naive but passionate female lead is repeated in book after book. Carr himself recognized the problem. "I wish I could enlarge my range of character types," he said years later, "since I find myself writing about the same old people under different names."[13]

Another point must be kept in mind. In a detective story, the reader cannot know everything about a character or there is no mystery. In understanding the works of John Dickson Carr and in fact almost all masters of detective fiction, the point is not so much *comprehending* a character as *believing* in him or her and in the role he or she plays in the story.

Moreover, Carr sometimes uses the reader's expectations that he *is* dealing merely in character types as a tool to misdirect suspicion. He knew that people are complicated, that their motives are ambiguous. He used human ambiguities—and the fact that masks may not be the same as what they hide. An experienced reader of Carr's books is wary of people whom he describes as "good-natured" or "kindly"; under the right (or wrong) circumstances they might also be killers. The charming rogue who seems to be included in the story merely for comic relief, the fussy lawyer whose role appears to be to supply evidence, the young policeman who is a friend of the narrator—each of these might turn out to be a murderer in John Dickson Carr's books.

Most of the above comments, however, are limited to Carr's male characters. With only a few exceptions—especially Eve Neill in *The Emperor's Snuff-Box*—his women are described from the viewpoint of men, and much more obviously than the male protagonists they are types rather than individuals. Carr's stories written at Haverford show him attracted to but afraid of women. Over and over he had used the image of the seductive woman who lures men to their destruction, but coupled with this was a misty romanticized view of the female sex. Realists, he complained in "The New Canterbury Tales," "would take the Lorelei off the rocks and substitute Margaret Sangers and Carrie Chapman Catts."[14] He objected to anyone, including Margaret Sanger (the feminist and advocate of birth control), who seemed to take the romance and mystery out of sex. In the Bencolin short story "The Murder in Number Four," he included a bitter portrait of a fictional feminist who had written *Woman, The Dominant Sex*.

No matter what changes occurred over the years in Carr's attitudes, his objection to—and perhaps fear of—dominant women remained.

Presumably by the time that he wrote the Bencolin books, Carr had some experience with women, but it hardly affected his attitude toward them in his books; he still found them attractive, terrifying, and ultimately unfathomable. Sharon Grey in *It Walks By Night* is remote and, at the same time, a destroyer of men. In *The Lost Gallows*, she is "Sharon of iced flesh, who mocked."[15]

Destructive women never entirely disappear from Carr's works. Both *The Plague Court Murders* and *The Reader Is Warned*, for example, feature a woman who manipulates a man to kill for her, and in fact fear of female sexuality is implicit throughout Carr's literary career. But a major change occurred in the books that Carr wrote around the time that he met Clarice Cleaves. He realized that the dim woman of romance, whom he had once called the "Guinevere who dreamed lonely," was not only unrealistic but rather silly. He made fun of Professor Michael Tairlaine's attitude in *The Bowstring Murders*:

> Tairlaine . . . liked fragility in women as much as he disliked strong-mindedness; thus had been the tenor of whatever rusty bachelor dreams lay behind him. . . . It was unimportant that few thoughts would ever mar the serenity of that forehead; thoughts would only frighten her.[16]

The typical women at this stage of his writing career are not fragile, serene, Wordsworthian ideals; they are natural, energetic, sexy young things and eminently approachable.

Compared to the repressed Victorian and Edwardian types that still appeared in so much fiction of the period, Carr's female characters seem in some ways modern. They are as interested in sex as are the men, and as willing to take the lead in forming attachments; and they do not have to wait for the formality of marriage. Men do not *take* women in Carr's books; sex is consensual. But these women are in no sense liberated from the male world. During most of the 1930s, Carr's ideal was Patricia Standish in *The Eight of Swords*:

> She was not cool-headed or strong-minded. She could no more have accompanied the detectives with a gun than she could have brought down the villain with a flying tackle. Quite to the contrary, she was content to leave that sort of thing to the proper people; to beam up at

you as though she were saying, "What a Man!"—and you threw out your chest and felt about nine feet tall.

Patricia complains to Hugh Donovan that "I suppose you're one of those nasty people who think women are toys, and oughtn't to have careers and do some good in the world." Hugh answers:

Right you are. . . . The idea of you having a career is unthinkable. Preposterous. If you became a doctor, your patients would wake up out of the strongest anaesthetic the moment you felt their pulses. If you became a barrister, you would probably throw the inkstand at the judge when he ruled against you.[17]

Patricia, for some reason, finds all of this quite charming.

Some of Carr's most extreme statements about the role of women appear in his books written around 1933–35. In *The Unicorn Murders,* Ken Blake says of Evelyn Cheyne, "She would never admit her true *metier.* She said she wished to be valued for her Brain—and, like a fool, I believed it." Even more annoying are H.M.'s comments: "She's a member of the Intelligence Department; oh, far from intelligent, I admit! Her purpose is merely to be charming."[18] Many of the women in Carr's books of the mid-1930s spend their time burbling and saying "oooo" and "eeee." In fact, one of the chapters in *The Mad Hatter Mystery* is entitled "Miss Bitten Burbles." Yet Carr considered her the very model of a modern woman:

There were no inhibitions whatever about Sheila Bitten. After one question to her, a psychoanalyst would have pulled out a handful of his whiskers and slunk back to Vienna in baffled humiliation. It would have embittered his life.[19]

Carr even invented the revealing term "ginch" to refer to this sort of woman. A portmanteau word, it combines "girl" and "wench"—child and seductress. Carr was able to handle his fear of destructive women by making them children rather than adults and thus nonthreatening to manhood. Indeed, like Patricia Standish and others who think "What a man!" most of Carr's women are proud of their men and accepting of their faults. When Tad Rampole decides to go out on the town with Dr. Fell in *The Mad Hatter Mystery,* his wife leaves him a note telling him to have his address pinned to him so that, however intoxicated he becomes, the cabman can take him back to the hotel. "There," thinks Rampole, "was a *wife.*"[20]

By the late 1930s, however, Carr's depiction of women had changed again: The empty-headed, sexy ginch began to disappear from his books, to be replaced by a series of intelligent adults who seldom burble. Even Evelyn Cheyne, whom H.M. had hired shortly before *The Unicorn Murders* simply because of her decorativeness, is described in *The Judas Window* as "intelligent." An important development came with *The Problem of the Wire Cage*—from here on the female leads are often at loggerheads with the male protagonists. The male-female bickering reaches such a point and the hero becomes so frustrated at having to deal with such a stubborn creature that he expresses a desire to shake her, or slap her, or even (to get back to the child-woman of earlier novels) spank her. But though sorely tempted, Carr's protagonists are not women-beaters; only in *The Emperor's Snuff-Box* are we presented with a man who physically attacks his wife, and Carr uses that fact to reveal the character as a thoroughgoing louse. In other words, Carr did not advocate beating women; he expressed what he considered a normal male frustration at how women treat their men.

Added to the edginess created by these misunderstandings and frustrations is the fact that, starting with his 1944 Dr. Fell novel, *Till Death Do Us Part*, Carr's books often show the hero's affections and loyalties divided between two women. He deeply loves one of them, but he is physically attracted to the other. *Till Death Do Us Part* (which has nothing to do with the *Suspense* script of the same name) was published in August 1944, but written during the months while Carr was living with Maureen. Although the situation in *Till Death Do Us Part* reflected Carr's own feelings, the-man-torn-between-two-women was also a convenient plot device, and he would use and reuse it long after the Maureen days had passed.

Till Death Do Us Part is a fine book. It has a clever locked-room puzzle, good characters, many twists and turns of suspicion, and a well-concealed murderer. Carr took the central idea of the book from his CBS radio script "Will You Walk into My Parlor" (February 23, 1943), which he rewrote for the BBC under the title "Vampire Tower" (May 11, 1944). (Carr had wanted to call *something* "Vampire Tower" at least since it had been the working title for *The Three Coffins* a decade earlier.) A young playwright named Dick Markham is in love with Lesley Grant, who looks "about eighteen years old, in contrast to the twenty-eight she admitted." She goes to a fortune-telling tent occupied, Dick is told, by Sir Harvey Gillman, a Home Office pathologist, and "one of the greatest living authorities on crime."[21] With Major Price—who, like Colonel March, is based on Carr's friend John Rhode—Dick sees Lesley's shadow as the fake swami talks to her. Sir Harvey seemingly says something shocking to Lesley, and she dashes out of the tent. After he is shot and wounded by Lesley, in an apparent accident, Sir Harvey tells Dick that his fiancée is actually forty-one years old and that she has perfected a method of poisoning people in locked rooms. Whether or not she really loves Dick, she can no longer help herself and will be compelled to poison him. Sir Harvey asks Dick to help him set a trap for her so that he can find out how she accomplishes the locked-room trick.

Dick watches the house where Sir Harvey is waiting in a locked room, hears a shot ring out, sees a bullet hole in a window, and rushes in. Sir Harvey, however, is not shot but poisoned. About halfway through the novel, Dr. Fell arrives and almost immediately reveals part of the truth, and we begin to see how in typical Carrian fashion a murderer has entered another person's schemes and turned them against the victim. At the conclusion, Carr provides a clever and, probably, practical solution to the locked-room problem. Carr himself later said that it was his favorite gimmick, "if we confine matters strictly to getting out of locked rooms rather than the general field of the impossible situation."[22]

The real power of *Till Death Do Us Part* is the situation facing Dick Markham. He is in love with Lesley Grant, but he does not know whether she is an innocent victim or a psychotic killer. Should he protect her or fear her? In chapter after chapter Carr teases the reader with the mystery of Lesley Grant; it is, Dick knows, "the eternal, torturing riddle . . . of Lesley herself." Meanwhile, Dick is attracted to the sturdy and unmysterious Cynthia Drew, and he is bedeviled by what he believes to be her feminine unreasonableness: "He took her by the arms, with something in his mind between kindly reasoning and an impulse to shake her until her teeth rattled." But, as much as they might like to, Carr's heroes rarely rattle women's teeth. "Then, he could never afterwards remember how, Cynthia was in his arms." The intensity of this book, and of many of Carr's later mysteries, is dependent on which of the two women is to be trusted. It is worth quoting Carr at length as he describes Dick's emotions:

> The whole damned business was too close! Too personal! Too entwined with emotion! It seemed to resolve itself into a balance of what you believed between Lesley Grant on the one hand and Cynthia Drew on the other. And the balance weight wouldn't stay still.
> One of these girls, reading the matter like that, was clear-eyed and honest, telling the truth with sincere purpose. The other hid many

ugly thoughts behind a pretty face, which might wear a very different expression if you caught it off guard.

Both of these girls you know well. Both you have recently held in
your arms—though Cynthia only for the purpose of consoling her, of
course. . . .

Not that he wavered in his loyalty to Lesley. He was in love with
Lesley.

But suppose, just suppose after all?. . .

Nonsense! She couldn't have had any motive!

Couldn't she?[23]

All of this is a far cry from the addle-pated ginches who populated Carr's
novels of a decade earlier.

Carr sets this tense novel against the background of a seemingly
changeless England before the war, a time that Carr would more and
more look back upon as a golden era. (The year is never given, but the
dates fit for 1937.)[24] The book opens with the description of the fete and
the tents where the swami was telling fortunes.

It was a scene which, four or five years later, would come back to
Dick Markham with a nostalgia like anguish. A lush green, burning
England; an England of white flannels and lazy afternoons; an England which, please God, we shall never lose for any nonsense about a
better world.[25]

Till Death Do Us Part was a commercial success. About a month after its
August 1944 publication some 10,000 copies of the American edition had
been shipped to fill library and bookstore orders, an impressive figure,
especially compared with the 6,000 copies of *The Emperor's Snuff-Box*
shipped during a similar period. Harpers had not expected such a demand, and two printings were ordered before the publication date, and
by the end of 1944, *Till Death Do Us Part* had sold 12,829 copies.[26]

(This may be the place to mention that around September 1943, Carr
wrote a serial about the BBC entitled *Death at Broadcasting House*—a surprising choice of title, since in collaboration with Holt Marvell, Val Gielgud had written a detective novel with the same title nine years earlier.
The records of Carr's British agents, Pearn, Pollinger & Higham, indicate
that it was sold to a magazine or newspaper, and Harpers announced a
book edition, but as far as is known the story was never published—unless it became the basis for the later novel *The 9 Wrong Answers* (1952),
which takes place in part at Broadcasting House.)[27]

Carr's 1944 book about Sir Henry Merrivale, *He Wouldn't Kill Patience*, was written probably shortly after he returned to London from Croton-on-Hudson. The hero, Carey Quint, is not torn between two women, but a good deal of the book is based on male frustration at dealing with the strange creature called "woman." The story opens on September 6, 1940, at the height of the Blitz, and the wartime setting is important for providing the atmosphere and the mechanics of the locked room. Carey is at the Reptile House of the Royal Albert Zoological Gardens (based on the London Zoo, Regent's Park) when Madge Palliser arrives. They are the last representatives of two great families of magicians that have been feuding for three generations over who invented a whist-playing automaton called Fatima in 1874 (based on the Maskelynes' automaton, Zoe).

Merely "as a result of nervousness," Carey manages to insult Madge: "I'd seen your photographs, of course. But I thought they were touched up for publicity purposes. I expected you to be rather a mess, actually." Madge: "How foul you are." This conflict gives Carr a chance to make a sweeping generalization about the way women act, something that he indulged in with some frequency: "A woman, especially a woman in Miss Palliser's state of mind, seldom hears what is actually said: she hears what she expects to hear."[28]

In *He Wouldn't Kill Patience*, Carr also presents another type of woman—one whose main way of getting through life is to put men on the defensive. Loud, pretending to a slight deafness, Agnes Noble looks upon events, even murder, as a discourtesy to her, and she forces others to do so as well. When she does not want to answer questions, she accuses those around her of bad manners. In some ways, she is an exaggerated version of Carr's mother; in other ways Agnes Noble, who is a hardheaded businesswoman, is Carr's comment on women who enter a man's profession. But whomever she may represent in Carr's life, in the story she is simply a nasty person, and H.M. gives her a comeuppance.

The zoo setting in *He Wouldn't Kill Patience* is effective; the characters are sharply drawn; and the locked room is spectacular. Toward the end of 1940, Clayton Rawson had written to Carr that he had figured out a method to dispatch a victim in a room whose doors and windows are sealed on the inside with gummed tape. Carr responded, "Your gummed-paper murder interests me; I am having a go, now, at complete disappearance out of a room similarly guarded. If only Hitler would go and do likewise, we could all take a rest."[29] It took three years for Carr's solution to the problem (changed from a disappearance to murder) to appear in print in *He Wouldn't Kill Patience,* and another four for Rawson to publish his solution, in a short story called "Out of This World" (*Ellery Queen's Mystery Magazine,* June 1948). Their approaches are entirely different, but equally ingenious. Carr's main clue is the *absence* of a German plane over London. The story ends with Carey and Madge in each other's arms, and H.M. grousing, "If anyone starts any canoodlin' in this place, I'm goin' to stick straws in the hair I ain't got. I hate canoodlin'! I'm always runnin' into it, and I hate it."[30]

When *He Wouldn't Kill Patience* and *Till Death Do Us Part* were published, John Dickson Carr was a member of what the BBC called "the Unestablished Staff," with an office at Broadcasting House in London. The playwright and mystery novelist Ernest Dudley, who also worked for the BBC during these years, recalls that by "Unestablished" the BBC meant that it did not guarantee a salary but did pay for, and have the rights to, any radio work that the author produced. On the surface, it seems odd that despite being called back to London to help with the British propaganda effort, Carr did not in fact write any propaganda shows for the radio until February 1944, but all along he was editing and rewriting scripts by other writers—on only one of which, Robert Barr's "The French Fight On" (July 14, 1943), did he receive credit as coauthor. He also prepared for broadcasting entertainment scripts, including an adaptation of Sir Arthur Conan Doyle's *The Lost World,* during rehearsals of which he became a close friend of Doyle's son Adrian. Carr's name also appeared as editor of *Corner in Crime,* which broadcast dramatizations of true crimes. In addition, he directed some drama programs. He seems to have enjoyed most of all working with sound effects:

> To mess about with effects [he wrote to Dannay] to bang bells and blow horns and make rocks fall down the side of a mountain, is a pleasure I haven't had since I used to catch hell for doing the very same thing at home. It's very mysterious to think that the things which get themselves condemned as foolishness when you are a kid are rewarded . . . as you grow older. Remind me to philosophize about this in a book some time.[31]

As a BBC staff member, Carr appeared as a frequent guest on various shows, sometimes explaining to listeners how radio drama was written—it is perhaps not a surprise that he emphasized the use of sound effects. He also participated in detective quizzes on the radio. During 1945 he edited a program of such quizzes and appeared himself sometimes as contestant, sometimes as quizmaster.

John Dickson Carr's main work for the BBC, however, was as a scriptwriter. Almost as soon as he returned to England from Croton-on-Hudson, he talked with Val Gielgud about using his *Suspense* plays on the BBC. CBS and the BBC had a working arrangement by which they could use each other's scripts without payment, a situation that, as Carr remarked, "pleases everybody except the author." Gielgud, two years later, recalled that Carr

> suggested to me that there might be a place in English programmes for a series of thrillers handled in the American manner, with all the trimmings of atmospheric bass-voiced narrator, knife-chords and other specially composed musical effects, and a regular length of half an hour timed to the split second. My slight experience of American methods made the temptation to compete "on the home ground" irresistible.[32]

The British series was named *Appointment with Fear*, and Valentine Dyall, whose cadaverous appearance (though of course not visible to radio listeners) exactly matched his wonderfully sinister voice, became the Man in Black, narrator of the stories.[33] Gielgud and Martyn Webster produced the program.

Appointment with Fear was originally planned as a short series, running for eleven weeks from September to the middle of November 1943. Carr chose what he considered the best of his *Suspense* plays, beginning ("inevitably, I suppose," he said at the time) with "Cabin B-13" starring Constance Cummings as the bride whose husband has vanished. This was followed by Carr's extraordinary adaptation of "The Pit and the Pendulum." He took a boyish delight in trying to get the proper sound for the pendulum, which during the last part of the play sweeps closer and closer to the helpless victim. Carr wrote to Dannay that "a conscientious soundman had nearly worn himself out swinging a damned golf-club in front of a microphone, hoping to get the proper *whush*. But we shall have to use the air-hose after all."[34] Unlike the *Suspense* broadcasts, almost all of which survive on tape, only three *Appointment with Fear* dramas are preserved on sound recordings, but they indicate that Gielgud had indeed mastered American radio drama. All the atmospheric sound effects, the knife-chords to emphasize moments of suspense, and the split-second timing are present.

At first the BBC was uncertain how the public would respond to *Appointment with Fear*. According to Gielgud, "The unabashed histrionicism of the presentation proved something of a shock to the domestic hearth. We were told that we would scarify the children. We were rebuked for treating horror with levity." A BBC memorandum, moreover, indicated that some listeners were confused by Carr's complex solutions to the mysteries. But the BBC discounted this problem and instead emphasized Carr's "mastery of touch" and his ability to "build up quite a complicated story from start to finish within the limits of half an hour"—which is an understatement considering how many times Carr could twist the plot in a thirty-minute play. In fact, despite such worries, *Appointment with Fear* was extremely popular. As the series continued, the Man in Black, who introduced each program, became the "most famous of all characters in radio thrillers," and Gielgud wrote that

> Valentine Dyall as "The Man in Black" became a particular favourite among schoolboys, and . . . children seemed to beg to be allowed to stay up to hear the plays rather than have nightmares as the result of them, [so] we were allowed to persist. A large number of grown-ups proved that they retained the lovable childishness of their youngers and betters.[35]

While waiting for the BBC to decide whether to schedule a second series of *Appointment with Fear*, Carr worked on several other projects for the air. Most interesting were his contributions to *Here's Wishing You Well Again*, a variety series for members of the armed forces in hospitals and convalescent homes. Each program featured a six-minute mystery playlet, which was introduced by the author and ended with a challenge to the listeners to deduce the solution. The four best answers would receive a prize of ten shillings, sixpence. The plays all took place during an inquest, and they were solved by the coroner, Dr. Carteret. Among the distinguished detective-story writers who contributed to the series were Margery Allingham, E. C. Bentley, Freeman Wills Croft, and John Dickson Carr. Carr's first playlet, broadcast in November 1943, was a neat little problem called "The Riddle of the Cabin Cruiser," whose solution lay in the fact that you cannot read a pennant on a boat when there is no wind. His second, broadcast a month later, was "The Riddle of the Poisoned Cocktail," which uses the same gimmick as *Death in Five Boxes* and the *Suspense* play "Will You Walk into My Parlor?"[36]

After some bureaucratic mulling over the matter, the BBC asked Carr not only to write another series of *Appointment with Fear* but eventually to prepare a total of five series, with the final drama broadcast in October 1945. Carr replaced Val Gielgud as Martyn Webster's coproducer of the series, though the BBC decided that it would be "excessive" to mention him as more than the author.[37] Carr continued to reuse his *Suspense* scripts—some of them considerably revised—but he had to come up with about nineteen new scripts. Of these, three were retellings of Carr's own short stories. "Death Has Four Faces" (a title that he had previously planned to use for the novel promised in 1935 to the Hartney Company) is an excellent version of Carr's favorite Colonel March story, "The Silver Curtain." Almost as good is "The Gong Cried Murder," based on another of March's queer complaints, "Clue in the Snow." In neither radio case, however, does the colonel himself appear.

"The Man with Two Heads," which has perhaps the worst title that Carr ever invented, is yet another version of the story of the man who reads about his own death, which Carr had already used as the basis of three short stories ("The Legend of the Cane in the Dark," "The Man Who Was Dead," and "New Murders for Old"). In some ways, the radio play has the best structure of the four versions of the tale. It begins with a man meeting the protagonist on the upper deck of a London bus, and Carr does an excellent job contrasting the ordinariness of a double-decker bus with the weirdness of the story, which is told, radio-fashion, in flashbacks. The tale is filled with the aura of strangeness, especially the protagonist's feeling that he has somehow become two people. Carr, of course, uses the image of masks. "I went out on deck, among the moving crowd, in that weird light that made faces look like masks. Everything seemed *unreal,* as though I were no longer part of myself." And later:

> That was when I first had the feeling of two separate entities, two separate persons, and both of them were myself. One was the self I knew. The other was a kind of horrible soul, what the Germans call a *doppelgänger,* that put on human flesh and moved in my image.[38]

Carr based five of his new *Appointment with Fear* scripts on stories by other writers. His adaptations of G. K. Chesterton's Father Brown story "The Purple Wig" and Melville Davisson Post's "The Great Cipher" follow the plotlines of the originals closely. Neither story is among its author's best-known works, but both contain the type of bizarre situation that fascinated Carr. The Chesterton tale explains why a nobleman would spend his life wearing a wig of a distinct purple hue; the Post provides a material explanation of the description of a fabulous monster in a diary seemingly written in cipher.

Carr's other adaptations take a great deal more liberty with the originals. Robert Louis Stevenson's "The Sire de Maletrot's Door" appeared in one of Carr's favorite books, *New Arabian Nights*. In Stevenson's story, Denis de Beaulieu in 1429 has to escape from enemy soldiers. He finds Maletrot's door strangely open, and stumbles in to save himself. Maletrot had left it open as a trap for his niece's lover, or for whatever other man might enter. The man has the choice of marrying the niece or being hanged. In revising the story for the radio, Carr added a lady friend for Beaulieu, made his brother into a main character, inserted a swordfight, and had Beaulieu unknowingly kill the niece's lover. More important, Carr changed the atmosphere and motivations to fit his own ideas. Indeed, much of the story is a throwback to the historical romances that he had written at Haverford with their sometimes overly atmospheric language and emphasis on unreasoning codes of love and honor.

Beaulieu is willing to give up his life rather than marry Maletrot's niece for a reson that was typical of Carr's adolescent writings. "Because," he explains, "in the language of the troubadours, I have the honour to have fallen in love with you. . . . We live by a strange code, mademoiselle, which permits us every liberty except that of being sensible."[39] Stevenson would have been astonished at the changes in his story, but they reveal that within thirty-eight-year-old John Dickson Carr the young romanticist still lived.

Carr's versions of Edgar Allan Poe's tale of madness "The Tell-Tale Heart" and Ambrose Bierce's horror story "The Suitable Surroundings" (which Carr retitled "The Devil's Manuscript") are so altered that they are essentially his own stories. Carr took a single part of each of the plots—from the Poe story, the heart whose beating only the murderer can hear; from the Bierce, the manuscript that kills anyone who reads it—and wrote a new plot around it. In both instances, Carr replaced the elements of insanity or the supernatural of the original stories with material explanations. In the case of the Bierce story, Carr's explanation is a good one. On the other hand, Carr's explanation for the incessant beating of the heart of the victim in "The Tell-Tale Heart" cannot compete with Poe's for critical acceptance. Poe simply has us accept the growing insanity of the murderer, while Carr unsatisfactorily suggests that the murderer suffers from a physical disease that made him hear the beating of his own heart.

Carr's original stories for *Appointment with Fear*, written during 1944 and 1945, do not have the sustained excellence of his *Suspense* scripts, but the British series includes several gems, and even the lesser plays have points of interest. "The Oath of Rolling Thunder" is Carr's attempt to write about cowboys and Indians—fortunately, he did not try again. He simply could not write in an uneducated manner. Here's a sample of the language put in the mouth of a western mayor:

> My daughter says I hadn't ought to crack up the fixin's this way. And Ellen's educated; she ought to know. So I'll just say, fellow-citizens, that Ellen and me are travellin' with our guests as far as Forge City. And in honour of this being a peace-and-goodwill trip, I hereby un-buckle my belt with the shootin'-irons.[40]

Three of the plays, "I Never Suspected," "The Room of the Suicides," and "The Man Who Was Afraid of Dentists," are about catching nasty Nazi spies, and they tend to preach too much. One of them, however, has a memorable opening. "I Never Suspected" is set in an empty movie theater at two o'clock in the morning. Without anyone apparently being present, a movie—discordantly, one about Tarzan—is being shown on the screen. Then a body is discovered bathed in a ghostly light. The solution involves a clever scheme for sending messages to enemy airplanes.

The best plays written directly for *Appointment with Fear* are "The Dragon in the Pool," "Lair of the Devil-Fish," "He Who Whispers," and "The Curse of the Bronze Lamp." "The Dragon in the Pool" is filled with improbabilities but it is told with such intensity that the script still packs a wallop. The main gimmick is taken from the short story "Persons or Things Unknown," but the plot of the radio play is entirely different. Narrated by Mary Prentice, it tells of the stabbing death of her father. The death appears to be murder rather than accident or suicide because the knife cannot be found. Mary goes on to explain how Prentice's stepson, Tony, had persuaded him to commit suicide in a seemingly foolproof way, and in an unexpectedly chilling conclusion Mary uses a similar method to kill Tony as he dives into a swimming pool. The story, says the Man in Black, "has caused me many a chuckle as I ponder on the ways of women."[41]

"Lair of the Devil-Fish" takes place in a Cuban bay shortly before the war, and it is based on Carr's memories of his own trip to Cuba in 1930. Divers want to recover bullion that went down with a cabin cruiser many years ago—according to local legend the boat was pulled under by a giant squid. When a diver locates the wreck, he is attacked by the devil-fish, which is seemingly protecting its lair. But the criminal turns out to be all too human.

"He Who Whispers" is an early version of some of the plot elements that Carr would use in the Sir Henry Merrivale novelette "Ministry of Miracles" (also known as "The Man Who Explained Miracles" and "All in a Maze"). In Victorian London, David Venner is uncertain whether he is going mad or is surrounded by ghosts who want to kill him. In the Whispering Gallery at St. Paul's Cathedral—where whispers carry distinctly even from great distances—he hears insidiously threatening words:

> I shall be with you, night and day, David Venner. I shall pass through walls of stone, and walls of brick, and walls of wood; and no lock can keep me out. And then, presently, I shall kill you. Pleasant, isn't it? How do you like me for a companion?[42]

Not only is no one near when these awful words are spoken, but it is proved impossible that someone could have used the strange qualities of the Whispering Gallery from a distance. That evening, David is almost asphyxiated when someone turns on the gas in his locked bedroom.

"The Curse of the Bronze Lamp" also became the basis for a later Carr story, in this instance the Sir Henry Merrivale novel also called *The Curse of the Bronze Lamp*. In the radio play, British archaeologists led by the Earl of Wexham and Professor Gilray have discovered the tomb of Herihor, High Priest of Ammon, but Gilray dies mysteriously, seemingly as a result of an ancient curse. When the earl's daughter, Lady Helen Loring, tells the press that she will take Herihor's bronze lamp back to England, an Egyptian named Alim Bey warns her that she will be "blown to dust as though she never existed." Vowing to defeat the curse, she returns to London with the lamp and joins Kit Farrell, who is in love with her. Kit and Helen drive to Wexham Hall; she enters Wexham Hall ahead of him; when he arrives a moment or two later, Helen has vanished without a trace, leaving behind only the bronze lamp and her mackintosh. The servants heard nothing except her footsteps, which stopped suddenly. Alim Bey shows up in England and announces:

> The corpse-priest [Herihor], defiled, arose in his grave-clothes; his spell struck in white fire, as a lightning-bolt strikes; and the pretty face that defied him is now dust on the floor of a tomb. . . . Don't you believe *now* that the dark arts are not mocked? Don't you believe *now*

that your ordered world is laid in ruins and that you have seen a
deed of magic outside the laws of nature?

But at the conclusion we find that Lady Helen's disappearance is not outside the laws of nature: "The Curse of the Bronze Lamp" contains Carr's
most cunning use of a method of impossible disappearance, which he had
been experimenting with since his college days, and which he had used
most recently in the short story "Strictly Diplomatic" and the radio play
"Cabin B-13." The play closes with the Man in Black ridiculing those who
would believe the Alim Beys of this world: "And so ends the story, 'The
Curse of the Bronze Lamp,' which makes us think twice when the terror-
mongers whisper direly behind turnip-ghosts."[43]

I have saved "Vex Not His Ghost" for the last play to be discussed from
the 1944–45 *Appointment with Fear*, not because it is one of John Dickson
Carr's best plays—it is hardly that—but because it is one of his most interesting for its depiction of an innocent man who has been condemned to
death. Dorothy Lake is a reporter, a woman with a profession whom Carr
(who has changed a great deal since he praised ginches) treats seriously.
She is going to Sing Sing to interview Harry North, who is to be executed
that evening for a murder that he did not commit. On the way, she picks
up a hitchhiker, who, improbably, turns out to be the executioner, Butcher
Riley. Interviewing Harry, she admits that she had admired him from a
distance when they were in school, and in a poignant scene they reminisce about their college life, before Harry breaks down: "Oh, God, Dolly,
I don't want to die." Carr contrasts these emotions with callous descriptions of death by electrocution: "It's the way their bodies jerk against the
straps. It's the smoke that comes up from them—a little bit of singeing—
where the electrodes meet the flesh."[44] The play concludes with the executioner, Butcher Riley, being himself identified as the murderer.

"Vex Not His Ghost" is best read as a tract against capital punishment.
It may come as a surprise to readers who know of Carr's conservative political and social positions to discover that he opposed capital punishment, but that is the fact. Apparently the only interviewer who thought to
ask Carr about his attitude toward executing criminals was a Swedish reporter in 1955. Carr responded that he was very much against it, and
when asked about the execution of Ruth Ellis, the last woman to be
hanged in England, in July 1955, Carr responded simply, "I felt sick."[45]

In fact, however, Carr's opinion should not have been unexpected. He
was willing to use the threat of execution as a plot device, even to the

point of having his detectives express no regrets about hanging a particularly distasteful criminal—"You'll hang, my lad, you'll hang by the neck until you are dead," says Colonel Marquis in *The Third Bullet*, "and if the hangman kicks your behind all the way to the gallows, I can't say it will ever weigh very heavily on my conscience."[46] But Carr always distrusted authority, and even more important, he was too aware of how chance can make the innocent seem guilty—of what H.M. called "the blinkin' awful cussedness of things in general"—to accept such a final solution as the death penalty. Perhaps Dr. Fell and Inspector Masters were justified in letting some murderers go free.

Before looking at Carr's later propaganda plays, we should mention briefly a few of his nonseries scripts. In 1945, he wrote a fine adaptation of "The Adventure of the Speckled Band," which followed Sir Arthur Conan Doyle's story very closely. This show was quite popular, being rebroadcast by the BBC several times during the next eleven years. "New Judgment: John Dickson Carr on Edgar Allan Poe," broadcast in May 1944, is based on Hervey Allen's biography of Poe entitled *Israfel*. Carr shows Poe as a brooding figure of romance, "a man hounded to death by his own imagination."[47] In July 1944, Carr wrote about his fascination with stage magic in "Magicians' Progress," which emphasized the contributions of Robert-Houdin and John Nevil Maskelyne. A month later the BBC broadcast Carr's story of France shortly before the Revolution. He wrote to Dannay that "The Scandalous Affair of the Queen's Necklace" will be done "with the grand manner and the big bass drum." The play re-creates the famous scandal involving a diamond necklace, Marie Antoinette, the Cardinal de Rohan, and the mountebank the Count Cagliostro—who Carr says in the stage directions "might have borne a striking resemblance to Benito Mussolini." One of Carr's best lines occurs in this play. When Rohan thinks of how much he might give to become the queen's lover, he remarks that "to sell one's soul to the devil would never do; it would not be well-bred."[48]

Carr's signed propaganda work during these years was limited to a series called *The Silent Battle*, six plays broadcast during February and March 1944 about the underground front in Europe. The emphasis in these plays is on the emotions of those trying to free their homelands from the Nazis. Supposedly, all the stories were based on genuine events in occupied Europe, and it is certainly true that Carr obtained at least the bare bones of his plots from the governments in exile in London. "They Saw Him Die" is a frightening story about the killing of a Polish wedding party by the German occupiers and the underground's unexpected revenge: The Germans are tried in a kangaroo court, then freed to be ridiculed by their own high command. "Secret Radio" has Carr's specialty, a miracle problem. Why can't the radio of the Polish Resistance be found even after several searches by the Gestapo? The answer is that it is hidden in the false hunchback of a hurdy-gurdy man.

"Army of Shadows" is similar to "Denmark iOccupied," which Carr had written before he returned to America. Both plays make the Nazis appear silly rather than sinister. "Army of Shadows" concerns the successful efforts of patriotic Belgian journalists to produce an imitation of the collaborationist newspaper, *Le Soir*. The fake articles are Carr at his most outrageously funny. Not even some of Sir Henry Merrivale's pratfalls can outdo the following:

THE BERLIN CONFERENCE
Unconditional Surrender
(From our Special Correspondent in Berlin)

Fascist trains always arrive punctually, so that Monsieur Mussolini's train was ahead of its timetable when it shot into Anhalt Station. The trumpet sounded. The Duce alighted.

"Duce!" cried the Führer. "Führer!" cried the Duce. And their voices were strangled with emotion. The band then struck up the Führer's favorite piece, "Ich hatt' einen Kamaraden"—"I had a Friend"— which drew tears from the guard of honor.

Acknowledging the "vivats" of the crowd ranked on the pavements, the great men entered the shelter of honor at the Wilhelmstrasse, where they were joined by the Tenno, the Japanese Ambassador.

"Take the trouble of sitting down," said the Führer. "Unnecessary," screamed the Duce; "we're in agreement." "In agreement," said the Tenno. "In agreement! In agreement!" The Berlin Conference ended.[49]

At the same time that Carr was working for the BBC as writer, director, editor, and even radio personality, as well as trying to keep his contractual commitments as a novelist under two names, he also attempted to have yet another writing career, this time as a playwright. It was probably his hopes for success with theatrical writing that led him to join the Garrick Club on April 27, 1944. Named for the eighteenth-century actor David Garrick, the club had a long history of eminent actors as members, but it also accepted publishers, authors, and others. Carr was proposed by a friend, the novelist J. B. Priestley, and seconded by his publisher Hamish Hamilton. Others who recommended his candidacy included his friend from The Detection Club, A. A. Milne, and Valentine Dyall's father, Franklin Dyall, who sometimes was himself the voice of the Man in Black when Valentine had other commitments. Official Garrick Club records erroneously indicate that Carr never paid his subscription; in later years, he certainly paid the two guineas membership dues.[50] Nonetheless, the Savage remained his favorite association with what is sometimes called clubland.

Carr's association with the British stage began about three years before he became a member of the Garrick Club, and about half a year before he was called back to the United States. Val Gielgud had already written several stage plays, and late in 1941 the two men decided to collaborate on a three-act play, around two hours in length, called *Murder Takes the Air*. It would feature Inspector Silence, who had been created by Gielgud and Francis Durbridge but whom Carr would soon use in a radio play, "Inspector Silence Takes the Underground." By early January 1942, most of the script was completed, and the two men were approached by Amalgamated Press about turning it into a serial for the magazine *Answers*, but it seems not to have appeared there and there is no evidence that Carr and Gielgud ever did a novel or novelette version of the story.[51]

Leon M. Lion, who played Inspector Silence on the radio, took the same part in the stage play, and the rest of the cast were members of the BBC repertory company. Everyone connected with the play seems to have been optimistic that, under its new title, *Inspector Silence Takes the Air*, the drama would be a great success. It was originally scheduled to open the first week of April 1942, but because of what Carr called vaguely "the singular ability of everything to go wrong," it was delayed until April 25. The first performances took place at the Pier Pavilion in Llandudno, which Carr described uncharitably (but only to an American correspondent) as "some God-forsaken town in Wales." After fine-tuning the play in the provinces, Carr, Gielgud, and Lion planned to have it at St. Martin's Theatre in London in May.[52]

Inspector Silence Takes the Air takes place in the cellar of a stately home that has been set up as a BBC broadcasting studio. Retired Inspector Silence is present to introduce a series of true-crime reenactments, beginning with the murder of an adulterous wife. The three actors playing the main parts for the radio are in fact in a triangular relationship, and during the rehearsal, when the prop gun loaded with blanks is fired, one of the actors falls dead of a bullet wound. This idea of a play within a play is very well done, and the mystery is as well. All the suspects seem to have been in clear view at the time of the murder, and in addition, the gun that fired the fatal shot has vanished. The room is searched. The actors and technicians are searched. Carr and Gielgud even have two of the young women characters take off their dresses on stage revealing (according to the stage directions) "charming set[s] of underclothes and delightful fig-ure[s]" but no gun. Eventually, Silence says that "the evidence shows" that no one could have done the killing. "I know he's dead," Silence says, "all I say is that by police regulations he oughtn't to be."[53] There is no in-dication in the script which sections were written by Gielgud and which by Carr, but Carr must have contributed the ending in which Silence al-lows the murderer to get away.

The reviews of *Inspector Silence* were on the whole favorable. It is, said *The Stage,* "a capital evening's entertainment."[54] But the play was not a success. It was soon at the Grand in Blackpool, and only a month after it opened it had its final performance on May 25, 1942, at another Grand Theatre, this one in Leeds. It is impossible to tell from the surviving script how good the actual performances were, but reading it, as well as three later Carr stage dramas, indicates some weaknesses. All of Carr's plays tend to have a great deal of talk and little action. When the dialogue is taut, this works satisfactorily, especially in some sections of *Inspector Si-lence,* which has the male-female tension that Carr was so expert at pro-ducing. But too often the characters simply stand around and exchange information, and the complexities of the who-and-howdunit plots require too much explanation at the conclusion.

By July 1942, Carr and Gielgud had started working on their second play, *Thirteen to the Gallows, or Out of Town Tonight,* but Carr's return to the United States delayed its completion until the end of 1943. Once again, the play was written for Leon M. Lion, who not only starred in it but also was its director, and with its BBC setting and inclusion of some characters from the earlier Carr-Gielgud play, it may be that it was planned as an-other adventure of Inspector Silence. By the time that it was produced, however, the detection was done by a new character, one Colonel Sir Henry Bryce, late of the Indian Police. This play had a brief run beginning on April 17, 1944, at the Royal Theatre in Leicester, and as with *Inspector Silence Takes the Air* a London run was planned. For some reason, how-ever, it was taken off the boards for almost a year and a half. It reopened at the Royal Theatre in Brighton on September 17, 1945, and appeared with some success around the country until it closed on October 27, 1945, without ever having made it to London. The final performance was at the Alhambra in Glasgow.[55] Reviews were kind—"The play is very well written and superbly cast," said *The Stage*[56]—but the short run of *Thirteen to the Gallows* must have been disappointing to both Carr and Gielgud.

Judging only from the script, *Thirteen to the Gallows* is an improvement over *Inspector Silence Takes the Air*, although it also is too chatty. Again, the story takes place in a temporary BBC studio rigged up outside London, but some of the action is broad farce. The BBC is getting ready for a program called "Out of Town Tonight," and Carr and Gielgud have great fun with an array of eccentric guests: James Whitehead, "the oldest bell-ringer in England," who plays "My Bonnie Lies Over the Ocean" on the air; Penelope Squire, "the youngest munition factory beauty queen in England," who recites Oscar Wilde's "Ballad of Reading Gaol"; and an exiled Austrian policeman named Sandoz, who makes a living exhibiting sea lions. Unfortunately, he cannot bring his pets to the makeshift studio, but, no matter, he can sound like them: "You have just heard my imitation of the sea lion how she call when she mate."[57] The puzzle plot in *Thirteen to the Gallows* is taken from Carr's radio script "The Man Without a Body," one of the few *Suspense* plays that Carr did not reuse on *Appointment With Fear*.

By the final months of 1944, *Appointment With Fear* had become so popular on the radio that the decision was made—probably by Carr and director Martyn Webster—to adapt it for the stage. Under the same title, the theatrical production was made up of three one-act plays. The show began with a mystery by Carr called *Intruding Shadow*, followed by *Prize Onions*, a farce by E. Eynon Evans. The show concluded with Carr's historical romance *She Slept Lightly*. The recorded voice of Valentine Dyall as the Man in Black introduced each playlet. *Appointment With Fear* was Carr's most successful experience with the theater. The show opened on April 2, 1945, at the Palace Theatre, Westcliffe. After three weeks, *Prize Onions* was dropped, but Carr's plays remained throughout the show's four-month run. It closed on July 30, 1945, at the Princess Theatre in Bradford. Part of the reason for the success was the performance in *She Slept Lightly* of the well-known actress Dame Irene Vanbrugh ("She has grace of carriage and that undefinable method of bringing power to her every scene," said a review),[58] but credit also belongs to Carr, whose short plays have a focused intensity lacking in his longer work for the theater.

In its expert manipulation of the viewer's expectations and in its careful masking of the murderous schemes, *Intruding Shadow* will remind modern theatergoers of *Sleuth* and *Catch Me if You Can*. The theme of *Intruding Shadow* is taken from the title of a book that is left lying about: "Murder Considered as One of the Fine Arts"—obviously the Thomas de Quincey essay that Carr had used in *The Murder of Sir Edmund Godfrey*. A mystery writer named Richard Marlowe tells his butler that he plans to kill Bruce Renfield. His motive, like that of a suspect in *Death-Watch*, is to note the reactions of a man threatened with death—but Marlowe is going to go one better by bringing in a witness, Anne Corbin, and recording her reactions. But is that really his motive? At various points in the play, we are certain that Marlowe will not take the plan to the point of murder, or that his genuine scheme is simply to tie up Renfield—who turns out to be a slimy blackmailer—and force him to hand over incriminating letters written by Anne Corbin. But when Renfield actually arrives, he collapses in front of Marlowe and Anne Corbin with a crushed skull. As they wonder what to do with the body, the doorbell rings and Inspector Stephen Sowerby enters.

Suspicion goes back and forth among the various characters, until the murderer admits how and why he killed Renfield (the method is similar to that for the second murder in *The Peacock Feather Murders*). The surviving script has two different conclusions, and it is not certain which was used in the theater. In the first, the play ends with justification for the murder, and the killer prepares his story for the police. In the second (which has internal indications of having been written later), Sowerby solves the crime but then allows the murderer to escape. As he tears up the blackmailing letters, he says:

> That's right, ma'am. Never tamper with evidence. You may think, for instance, a rather decent young fellow was only trying to protect his girl. You may think a swine of a blackmailer got just what was coming to him. You may think, for once, the police might turn a blind eye. But never tamper with evidence, ma'am. It's against the law. Good night.[59]

As mystery scholar Tony Medawar says, this conclusion "is a clear statement of Carr's personal and controversial beliefs about the means of justice and might."[60] It also reflects Carr's extraordinary view that a professional policeman might risk his career by releasing a murderer.

She Slept Lightly, the third play in *Appointment With Fear*, is a stage version of the radio serial *Speak of the Devil*, including the ghostly manifestations of a young woman who had been hanged for murder.[61] Benefiting from what was for Carr a brief explanation of the impossibility, *She Slept Lightly* is a taut play with an effective ending: The curtain falls as the murderer is about to be stabbed to death.

This was Carr's final work for the stage. On various later occasions when the suggestion arose to dramatize his books, he always said that others should do the adaptation. In 1946, Gielgud wrote to him that another scheme to dramatize *Appointment With Fear* was under discussion.* This time it would be a single play called simply *The Man in Black,* starring Valentine Dyall. Gielgud was certain that Carr would not be interested in writing the script, and Carr confirmed that he was now putting his efforts in other directions.[62] A film entitled *The Man in Black* starring Dyall was released in 1950, but although the credits stated that it was based on *Appointment With Fear* by John Dickson Carr, the script was not related to any of Carr's stories. As late as 1955, however, Carr was involved, apparently as the proposed author, in a stage play again called *The Man in Black*—the title indicating how popular Dyall's part remained. Contracts were signed and a West End run foreseen, but the play was never produced.[63] Carr, nevertheless, remained fascinated by the theater, and his experiences influenced several of his later books.

John Dickson Carr had what used to be called "a good war." He had contributed to the Allied cause, especially to his adopted country, through his propaganda work. Yet he realized that the England he had loved was never to return. On the day of German surrender, he wrote to Frederic Dannay from his office at the BBC:

> I am writing this on a day whose significance I can't realize even yet. The office is practically empty . . . and I'm sitting here because there's nothing I particularly want to do. I don't want to celebrate; in fact, I never felt less like having a drink in my life. Instead of whooping elation, which ought to be the case, I feel gloomy and a little irritated. Let-down? I sat by the window last night, and tried to think about five and a half years, and all I could think of was the picture made by anti-aircraft guns in the sky on the night my house was destroyed. The odd part is that I feel the loss of house and possessions more than I did long ago when it happened.[64]

*The French film expert Roland Lacourbe reports that a three-part film called *Appointment With Fear,* narrated by Valentine Dyall, was produced by British Foundation Pictures in 1946 and distributed by Twentieth Century-Fox. All three parts were adapted from Carr's radio scripts. No Carr fan of my acquaintance has seen this film, and Lacourbe says that the British Film Institute does not have a print of it.

Chapter 13

THE POSTWAR
WORLD AND
THE LIFE OF DOYLE

The period after World War II was a time of increasing dissatisfaction, dis-
illusionment, and restlessness for John Dickson Carr. The kind of world
he admired seemed irrelevant; it was difficult for him to pretend that it
had anything to do with modern life. Carr must have realized that there
never was an age when adventure in the grand manner was just around
the corner. In the 1930s and the early 1940s, however, he had created such
worlds in his fiction and was able to make them seem real in the present
age. He could no longer do that after the war. Joan Kahn, who became his
editor at Harper & Brothers in 1946, summarized her impression of his attitudes in the following words:

> John Carr probably never should have lived in the 20th century. All
> his instincts were for a less scientific world, a less mechanized one, a
> more romantic one. I think he would have been happier in the 18th
> century, with sword play and sudden personal dramas, with cos-
> tumes and carriages, and beaus and belles, with the long talks over
> mugs of wine near the fireplace and if any crimes had been commit-
> ted, they were fashionably done, with eclat, and solved by witty, ele-
> gant experts, not plodding patrolmen. He put up with the present
> world, but grudgingly.[1]

Although Carr was not opposed to science or mechanics—he liked such modern developments as television—Miss Kahn's memories are basically correct. The world he preferred did not have rationing and socialist regulations; it was romantic and filled with sudden drama.

John Dickson Carr continued working for the BBC through 1945, but he spent part of that time in the United States. The United States Treasury asked the BBC to allow Carr to tour with various other authors—an oddly assorted group that included Bennett Cerf, Lillian Hellman, and Kathleen Winsor—to promote Victory Bonds. The British Ministry of Information sponsored and paid for Carr's trip, and during the third week of October 1945, he sailed to the United States on the *Queen Elizabeth*.[2] All went well with the tour at first. The schedule was flexible enough that he was able to visit old friends like Ed Delafield and Fred Dannay. Dannay introduced him to mystery writers and critics in the New York area, including Howard Haycraft, who in his 1941 history of detective fiction, *Murder for Pleasure*, had written a laudatory account of Carr's work. For the occasion of meeting Haycraft, Carr smoked a pipe—the image he preferred—rather than his usual cigarettes. A few months later, Haycraft wrote a brief sketch of the creator of Dr. Gideon Fell and Sir Henry Merrivale: "Carr is short, slight, mustached, pipe-smoking, witty, reserved but affable; doesn't look his 40 years. Favorite conversational topic: detective stories."[3] Dannay reported in *Ellery Queen's Mystery Magazine* that he and Carr "attended literary luncheons, 'tec teas, and detective dinners."

A bibliophile who had one of the finest collections of detective fiction in America, Dannay took Carr to various antiquarian bookshops, including the House of El Dieff in New York City. Nostalgic for the books of his youth, he bought the complete detective novels of Carolyn Wells—some 150 volumes—and arranged to have them boxed and shipped to London. He also signed a contract with Dannay to write six short stories for *Ellery Queen's Mystery Magazine*, and the two men talked shop constantly, filling the room with tobacco smoke. They spent one "memorable evening in [Dannay's] study when we killed imaginary characters by the carload and between us killed a bottle of Burdon's prewar sherry." Dannay recalled this episode with amusement, especially the fact that the sherry affected them both to the extent that on three separate occasions Dannay looked at his watch and reported that it was ten o'clock without either of them realizing that his watch had stopped.[4]

But the sherry and similar episodes happened with such frequency that from the viewpoint of the Treasury Department the trip became a disaster. Traveling and speaking for Victory Bonds quickly became boring, and when Carr was bored he would be hit by what some friends called "his down-beats"; he would drink heavily, and then take chloral hydrate, which in turn resulted in an edginess that made it difficult for him to be around people for long periods. As part of this pattern, he disappeared when the tour reached Buffalo, causing the Treasury Department frantically to search for him without success. He showed up briefly at Ed Delafield's apartment in New York City, before going off again.

Meanwhile, Dannay had arranged that Carr would be the guest of honor on November 29, 1945, at a dinner meeting of the newly formed Mystery Writers of America. Carr arrived early at the Gotham Hotel where the meeting was to be held, but found that he could not face attending it. He hurriedly wrote Dannay a note:

> The guest of honor arrived about an hour and a half early; we Carrs were always too quickly off the mark. However, I did want to show that my intentions were good, and that I damned well did want to get there. Believe me, it was an effort as you can judge by this scrawl.

He followed with an apologetic telegram, and then disappeared again. Finally, he turned up at the Bronx apartment of an Englishwoman who had helped to care for his daughter Mary three years earlier at Croton-on-Hudson, and he asked her to help in contacting Clarice, who was the only one who could put the pieces together when John was in this condition. She telephoned Clarice and enlisted the help of the British embassy in booking return passage. On December 10, 1945, John Dickson Carr left for England. Clarice did help him recover, and as usually happened after such episodes he immediately hit the typewriter to begin a new book. Around January 6, he called on his British agents; Clarice's ministrations had done wonders, for they reported to their American associates that Carr looked rested and that he was going full steam on novels and on the short stories that he had promised Dannay.[5]

There was still the matter of repairing things with Dannay, and Carr did so gracefully in a letter written in early January. "I was ashamed to face you," he said. "Those spells don't take me very often—sometimes as little as once a year—but, while they last, they are so stupefying that I *must* keep away from company." Except for not mentioning the cause of the spells, Carr's summary of the situation was honest and factual. Meanwhile, he promised to complete the short stories for *Ellery Queen's Mystery Magazine*—"if you still want them." Friendship was reestablished. Dannay did want the stories, and by June, Carr was outlining some plot ideas to him—a story about a man who could not be photographed; one about a reporter who mistakenly drops in at the shop of Sweeney Todd (the Demon Barber of Fleet Street) for a haircut; and the tale of "the haunted execution-shed at Pentecost Prison, where (apparently) the earth-bound influence of murderers bumped off there had such power that it provoked a prison-riot." But although Carr used these ideas in other contexts, the stories themselves were never written. He completed only one tale covered by his contract with *Ellery Queen's Mystery Magazine,* and oddly enough it was not one of those he had outlined to Dannay. Even the story that he did finish, "The House in Goblin Wood," took him almost three months to write. "I have got this morbid idea now," he said, "that nothing must be released until it is at top-level."[6]

"The House in Goblin Wood" is the only short story about Sir Henry Merrivale, and it is certainly top level in every respect. Carr began it in August 1946. He tore up one draft as being no more than "all right" and finally posted the finished version to Dannay in the middle of October. "The best way to arrange the punch-ending," Carr explained, "was what gave me trouble. I discovered to my surprise that the Old Man himself is easier to handle in a short story than he is in a novel." Dannay was delighted. He invented a new category for his magazine's second annual short-story contest—"Special Award of Merit"—just for "The House in Goblin Wood," although he later admitted that most readers thought that it deserved the first prize in the contest.

When Dannay published it he included his own analysis of the tale as "almost a complete manual of detective-story theory and practice."[7] Part of its power is the contrast between its slapstick opening and its grisly conclusion. Two young people, Eve Drayton and Bill Sage, are waiting outside the Senior Conservatives' Club for Sir Henry Merrivale—who, obviously, has given up his earlier socialism. (His conversion to Toryism, incidentally, must have been sudden, since Carr backdated the story to 1936.) By this time in Carr's writing career, H.M. almost always enters a story in some kind of comic disaster or uproar. In "The House in Goblin Wood," H.M. descends the steps of the Conservative Club "with [a] lordly sneer," but he slips on a banana peel and lands on his posterior. Carr suggests that stepping on such an object probably accounted

for what Mr. Gladstone said in 1882. In any case, it accounted for what Sir Henry Merrivale said now. From the pavement, where H.M.

landed in a seated position, arose in H.M.'s bellowing voice such a torrent of profanity, such a flood of invective and vile obscenities as has seldom before blasted the holy calm of Pall Mall.

To Eve's solicitous inquiry, H.M. replies, "My behind's out of joint."[8]

Eve and Bill persuade the Great Man to go on a picnic with them near a house in Goblin Wood—which may be related to the Goblin Wood mentioned briefly in *Till Death Do Us Part*.[9] Twenty years before, a girl named Vicky Adams had disappeared from the locked house, only to reappear a week later with a tale about being stolen by fairies. The puzzle was never explained, and now Vicky may be planning to do the same thing during the picnic. Despite H.M's presence, and the locked doors and windows, Vicky does disappear. It is interesting to note that most of the essential clues are given during the comic opening scene of the story. As Carr explained, "once we think an author is only skylarking, a whole bandwagon of clues can go past unnoticed."[10] Despite a minor problem in the solution (of which I will say only that Carr may not have calculated the distribution of weight),[11] the conclusion is brilliant. Dannay's prediction that the story "would become one of the anthological favorites of all time" has come true.[12]

Probably during his trip to the United States at the end of 1945, Carr had made an agreement with his old friend Edward Delafield of Crown Publishers to edit a massive anthology to be called *The Ten Best Detective Novels*—a title Carr disliked, preferring to think of it as "ten of the best." He chose Sir Arthur Conan Doyle's *The Valley of Fear*, Gaston Leroux's *The Mystery of the Yellow Room*, A. E. W. Mason's *At the Villa Rose*, Agatha Christie's *Death on the Nile*, Anthony Berkeley's *The Poisoned Chocolates Case*, S. S. Van Dine's *The Greene Murder Case*, Philip MacDonald's *Murder Gone Mad*, Rex Stout's *The League of Frightened Men*, and Dorothy L. Sayers's *Strong Poison*. At Dannay's suggestion, Ellery Queen was represented by a novella, *The Lamp of God*. As Dannay pointed out, however, there was one notable omission: Carr decided not to include one of his own novels. He explained the decision to Dannay:

> As regards including a book of my own, brr! No! This question came up with Crown when we first planned the anthology and I vetoed it then. Let me try to be honest about this: it isn't a matter of modesty, false or otherwise; but I'm hanged if I know what it is. . . . I might, if pressed to tell the whole truth and nothing but the truth, say I thought one of mine might slip through into the first ten; that's only

human vanity. But it's only a thing I could say in private; I could no more proclaim it publicly than I-don't-know-what. If first you write a long introduction on how such stories ought to be written, and then you shove in one of your own as though you were saying, "Look there, boys; that's the way to do it,"—no, the idea makes my flesh creep.

Dannay was not persuaded, and in his introduction to *Dr. Fell, Detective* (a collection of Carr's short stories that he assembled in 1947) he said, "If Ellery Queen had been asked to choose the ten best detective novels, you can bet all the deductions in Detectiviana . . . that one of those ten would be a story by John Dickson Carr or Carter Dickson." The anthology, however, was never published: Three publishers adamantly refused to let their authors appear in the collection. Carr put the situation in these words: "If it had been a question of the publisher saying, 'Look here, we want you to use this writer's The Blood-Bolstered Pincushion instead of The Case of the Candid Monkey,' that would have been different. But they were against the whole project."[13]

Carr had completed his lengthy introduction—fifty-eight pages in typescript—to the anthology. Dannay made arrangements to print it in *Ellery Queen's Mystery Magazine* in 1946, but after the anthology had been canceled, he held the typescript for some seventeen years before publishing it in the March 1963 issue of his magazine, and (probably simultaneously) as a separate pamphlet edition limited to three hundred copies. Dannay made two major changes in Carr's essay. First, he took Carr's final words in the introduction and made them the title for the entire essay, "The Grandest Game in the World"—by which it has been known ever since. Second, he omitted about seventy-five hundred words from the essay, that is, the sections that explained Carr's choices of novels to include in the anthology. It is this shortened version of "The Grandest Game in the World" that has been widely reprinted; the complete essay was not published until 1991 when it appeared in the revised edition of *The Door to Doom*.

With the end of the war, Carr was eager for The Detection Club to resume its prewar activities. In the early months of 1945, the club met for the first time in five years: "The brethren shocked me," Carr mourned, "by looking so much greyer and more worn, though it's only to be expected. The fire seems to have gone even out of D. L. S[ayers], who is now devoting herself entirely to translating Dante." During his trip to America a few months later, he told Dannay that not only Sayers but other older members had become inactive in the field, and that there were so few new British mystery writers that the club was having trouble filling vacancies.[14] During 1946, however, The Detection Club did welcome four new members, two of whom—Cyril Hare and Christianna Brand—were experts of the first water. In later years, Brand remembered Carr as "thoughtful and generous, full of laughter and fun." He enjoyed telling tales about himself, some of which were true, some made up, but all were dramatic, and he was unfailingly generous about helping his friends.[15]

Despite welcoming some new members, Carr reported to Dannay at the end of October 1946 that The Detection Club had ceased to function officially. During 1947, however, the club became more active. Dorothy L. Sayers, who was a leader of the High Church movement in England, had found the club a rather dingy meeting room in a house owned by the Church of England at Kingly Street, which runs parallel to Regent Street. The club met there once a month (later every other month), then went to dinner, often at Sayers's favorite restaurant, L'Escargot Bienvenu. Brand recalled that after the club's meetings and dinners, Carr would hire a large automobile and drive the members to their homes. Indeed, according to Brand, Carr would often go further:

> Nothing would deflect him, when he was set on having one's company. He would ring up, one would refuse an invitation and the next thing was that a huge hired car with or without John in it, would arrive at one's door. For very weariness in argument, one usually gave in.[16]

The two new Detection Club members chosen in 1947 were Carr's old friend Val Gielgud and a much newer friend, Robert Bruce Montgomery, who used the pseudonym Edmund Crispin. Montgomery was a composer and schoolteacher who, while studying at Oxford in the early 1940s, had read *The Crooked Hinge* and decided then and there to write detective novels. (For convenience, I shall refer to him as Crispin.) His first book, *The Case of the Gilded Fly,* featured a locked-room problem whose solution was almost the exact reversal of the one Carr had devised in *The Peacock Feather Murders.* Probably not coincidentally, Crispin's detective, Gervase Fen, has the same initials as Gideon Fell, and in *The Case of the Gilded Fly* Fen refers to Fell as though he is a real person.

Crispin was an early member of the Carr Society, which had been formed in December 1944 by Michael Self, Peter Self, and Geoffrey Bush during a convivial meeting at a pub near Oxford. The inspiration was Carr's *Appointment with Fear* radio plays, and as a diversion the four men invented and narrated on the spot short mystery stories as an homage to Carr. Bush recalls that "we appointed as our patron (without permission) John Dickson Carr." The experiment was so successful that the meetings became a semiregular affair. Each participant would tell an original detective story, with proper clues and so on. The other members would propose solutions to the mystery, and then the real solution (if different) would be given by the narrator and analyzed by the members. Meetings of the Carr Society continue to this day. Crispin's novel *Love Lies Bleeding*, published in 1948, originated as one of the tales told to the Carr Society, and it is dedicated to the "Carr Club," as he invariably called the group. A year or so earlier, the society had invited John Dickson Carr himself to attend. Clarice Carr recalls that John received a mysterious letter (penned by Crispin) inviting him to face danger, and daring him to go by train to the meeting at the King's Arms pub in the village of Ockley, Surrey. He was delighted to accept. Geoffrey Bush has written to me:

> I remember that there were seven stories, though Carr's was more of
> a personal reminiscence than a real detective story. I remember him
> as being exceedingly friendly, unpretentious, convivial—he seemed
> to enter fully into the spirit of the occasion, making an attentive lis-
> tener to the contributions of others.[17]

It was shortly after this that Carr, as honorary secretary of The Detection Club, wrote to Crispin asking whether he would like to become a member. At the initiation ceremony, Carr proposed Crispin's membership, and Agatha Christie seconded him.[18]

For a year or so after the end of World War II, John remained in London while his wife and daughters lived in Kingswood. Julia has written of her father's arriving on Christmas Eve 1945:

> In he strode out of the cold, looking as merry as the ghost of Christ-
> mas present. He was hung all about with packages and parcels,
> which I knew instinctively were black-market toys for my sisters, and
> equally forbidden and treasured bottles of sherry for the adults. Be-
> fore we could greet him properly, out he dashed into the snow again,
> and came back carrying (with some difficulty) a large and extremely
> battered suitcase. "Here, Skeezix," he said. "This is for you." And
> looking at me closely, "It's too big to wrap. Why don't you open it

now?" Defying all our Christmas traditions, which dictated a Christmas-morning opening time for presents, I dropped to the hearth rug and opened the disreputable suitcase, releasing a splendid smell of old leather and dust. Inside were lots of books. How can I explain that, in those days of bitter shortages, there were never lots of anything. My first joy was in the sheer number of volumes, rose-red and gentle to the touch. "Read this one first, and see how you get on with it," my father said. The book he handed me was entitled *The Three Musketeers*.[19]

Around October 1946, John and Clarice Carr purchased a three-story, brick Victorian house at 22 Frognal Lane, Hampstead. It was big enough, he said, for his collection of books—sadly depleted during the early days of the Blitz—and his growing collection of seventeenth-century rapiers and daggers, which he had been purchasing at Sotheby's auctions and from dealers. But then infuriating problems with the house arose. The building had sustained bomb damage during the war, and Carr had to get permits from the Hampstead Council to make repairs. His friend Adrian Doyle thought that Carr had obtained the permits without difficulty, but Carr himself was not pleased, especially when the builders' charges turned out to be twice as much as they had originally estimated. In December, after two months of dealing with local authorities, work began and he confidentally expected that the family would be able to move in by the middle of January 1947. In the dead of winter, however, the workmen turned the water on to make tea, and left it on. When John and Clarice arrived the next morning, the water had seemingly gone everywhere, and then frozen; icicles were on the ceiling. With the additional water and ice damage, work had to start over again. The months crept on, and Carr remained at his flat at Haverstock Hill. It was not until the end of May or the beginning of June that the Carrs were able to occupy their house. Julia stayed in Bristol where she was going to school, but Mary and Bonnie, along with their housekeeper-nannie, Andy, lived with John and Clarice at Frognal Lane. Within a few months, however, John had become so frustrated by the situation in England that he was considering pulling up stakes and returning to the United States.[20]

England after the war was a country of shortages and rationing. Clarice recalls that it was difficult to purchase things as simple as soap, sugar, and cigarettes. Money for clothing went for school uniforms for the girls, so Clarice and Andy had to make underwear and night clothes for her and their daughters from bright orange nylon once used for parachutes. John's view of the shortages was that England had become "a dreary country bereft of booze and turkeys." The bitterness of winter of 1946–47 was exacerbated by the shortage of fuel and by government-ordered power cuts. He remembered that he "sat at the typewriter in an overcoat beside a window as grey inside as it was outside, and tried to see the keyboard." Moreover, the taxes were, from John's viewpoint, equivalent to expropriation. He told Frederic Dannay that his income taxes for 1945 and 1946 were well over three thousand pounds each year, even though most of his earnings were coming from America. The situation reached the point that he asked Dannay not to send money until further notice for Carr stories published in *Ellery Queen's Mystery Magazine;* otherwise "Mr. Bloodsucker the income-tax collector" would take most of it.[21]

John Dickson Carr generally paid little attention to the ins and outs of political debate. When politicians of any persuasion appear in his early stories, they are often figures of fun—Boko or Squiffy, as H.M. calls them—or pompous stuffed shirts like Francis Hale in "William Wilson's Racket," who (Carr suggests) ought to go on the "razzle-dazzle" in order to become human. After the war, however, Carr's dislike of the situation in England quickly evolved into dislike of the Labour party. Not only did Labour's socialist policies go into effect at the same time as the shortages in England, but the party's dependence on government regulation fed Carr's long-standing opposition to anyone who tries to control anyone else. His wartime anger at the Nazis was now transferred to the Labourites. Carr personalized these feelings, his particular bête noire being Sir Stafford Cripps, who as chancellor of the exchequer from 1947 to 1950 was a convenient target for everyone who hated shortages and taxes. Carr referred to "the grisly and gristly dial of Sir Stafford Cripps" and recorded his hopes for a victory of the Conservative party in the general election of 1950—"with Labour ministers being quite literally booted out of their office-windows, a public service in which I should be happy to help."[22]

These feelings came to a head with the difficulty of getting permits for the Frognal Lane House and with the problems in importing the Carolyn Wells books that Carr had purchased in New York toward the end of 1945. Some six months later, Carr was able to report:

> I finally got permission—ie, licence to import—the Carolyn Wells
> books, after an incredible amount of wrangling and a stern letter say-
> ing it is not customary to allow importation of fiction. The regula-

tions in this country grow more and more damnable. One more war for liberty, and we shall all be slaves.

Incidentally, after reading many of the Wells books, he discovered that he could not recapture his youthful admiration for her work:

I never want to see the lady's literary face again. . . . But the earlier stories now afford such whoops of delight that I should be a hound to complain. I am thinking of having framed the coloured frontispiece of the dramatic-looking girl lifting a knife with the words: "Stop looking daggers at me, Justin, or I will return your glance thus!" As they used to say at about the same period: Hot ziggety dam![23]

During most of 1947, John and Clarice Carr thought only vaguely about leaving England for the United States. John was gathering material for a major work, a biography of Sir Arthur Conan Doyle, and most of the documents were in England. The impetus behind this book was the desire of Doyle's eldest surviving son, Adrian, for an authorized biography to replace Hesketh Pearson's *Conan Doyle: His Life and Art*, published in 1943. Although Pearson had the general cooperation of Doyle's family, the book was in no way authorized, and in fact Adrian was enraged when he read it. He always referred to Pearson's work as "fakeography," for in Adrian's eyes Pearson committed two major sins. First, he had portrayed Conan Doyle as an average man and consequently had attributed Doyle's popularity to a simplicity that was the same as his audience's. Adrian, on the other hand, thought that his father was anything but average. According to Adrian, Sir Arthur was the scion of Plantagenet nobility and one of the great men of this or any age. Even if we avoid Adrian's hyperbole, it is easy to sympathize with his objection to Pearson's tone, which was decidedly uncomplimentary. Second, Pearson accepted Sir Arthur's own statement that he based Sherlock Holmes's deductive abilities on those of Doyle's old teacher, Joseph Bell. From this Pearson made Holmes a fictional version of Bell. If this was going too far, Adrian's own view in another direction was even less defensible. He believed that his father and Holmes were the same.

Adrian Conan Doyle was a flamboyant man; everything about him seemed larger than life. He was kindhearted, but he could fly into a tizzy at the smallest provocation. Even his arm gestures were more sweeping than most men's. His defense of his father (or of his image of his father) was in some ways a defense of himself. Adrian saw himself as out of place in the crassness of modern time. His book *Heaven Has Claws* shows that, like his father, he had a colorful writing style and an eye for detail. Unlike his father's works, however, it also shows a supercilious attitude toward those he considered beneath him. Unfortunately, he never developed his talents as a writer. His real profession was being the son of Sir Arthur Conan Doyle, and with his brother, Denis, he ran the Doyle estate. He took personally any disparagement of the Doyle myth that he so assiduously fostered. He was constantly threatening lawsuits to protect his beloved father's reputation and the estate's rights, as he understood them.[24]

It may have been from Adrian's reputation of having a short fuse that a legend emerged about John Dickson Carr and Adrian Conan Doyle. According to this story, Carr first planned to write a biography of Sir Arthur without clearing the matter with the estate; when he announced his intentions publicly, Adrian Doyle threatened to sue him. Somehow, Carr and Doyle compromised their differences, and Carr's work became the authorized life of Sir Arthur.[25] This account is consistent with Adrian's character and has appeared several times in print, but the letters from Adrian to his brother, Denis, now in the collection of Richard Lancelyn Green, show that it is untrue.

Carr, of course, had long admired the Holmes stories, and he had attended a meeting of the Baker Street Irregulars in January 1943 when he was living at Croton-on-Hudson.[26] In 1944, he worked with Adrian Doyle on BBC radio versions of Sir Arthur's Professor Challenger novels, and about this time Carr gave Doyle a copy of Frederic Dannay's recently published anthology, *The Misadventures of Sherlock Holmes*. Carr thought that Adrian was "quite pleased" with the book, but if that was the case it was only a first reaction. The book contains pastiches and parodies of Holmes, and Adrian thought that poking fun at his father's writings was akin to sacrilege. Through some complex legal maneuvers, he forced the suppression of the book,[27] and he let it be known that anyone publishing any unauthorized Holmes stories in the future could expect similar treatment.

In 1945 and 1946, Adrian Conan Doyle was filled with schemes to promote his father's works. He tried to persuade the German writer Emil Ludwig, then well known for his biography of Beethoven, to write what Adrian called "the great biography" of Sir Arthur. The book, Adrian wrote to his brother, Denis, would be the finest biography of the past hundred years because the subject was unique. While gathering together the tremendous quantity of Doyle manuscripts at the family home at Bignell

Wood in Hampshire, Adrian arranged with Carr to edit what he naturally described as "the great anthology" of his father's best work. In April 1946, Adrian came to London and stayed with Carr to discuss the anthology, and in December of that year, Carr went down to Bignell Wood to make final plans.[28]

Meanwhile, Ludwig was not showing as much interest in his unique opportunity as Adrian had expected, and consequently Adrian decided that Ludwig was not the best choice. Adrian wrote to his brother that Ludwig knew nothing about Sir Arthur, or about his works, and, besides, the book would not be written in English—something, one would think, that Adrian might have worried about earlier. Just as Carr arrived at Bignell Wood to work on the anthology, Adrian was coming to the realization that there were plenty of other possible writers for the project, and within a few days he decided that John Dickson Carr was the best choice, "because of his unique knowledge of Daddy's works, his deep personal love for Daddy and his life; because he is an exceedingly painstaking writer; and finally because he is the leading crime novelist today on both sides of the Atlantic." He delayed asking Carr to write the book until he got some material returned from Ludwig, but by the middle of January "the great anthology" had been put on hold, and Carr had agreed to write "the great biography." Adrian announced that Carr had dropped all of his other work and his contracts—not entirely true, as John assured Morrow when the word got out—in order to concentrate on the biography. With typical exaggeration, Adrian said that Carr considered the biography "a sacred work" and that "he looks upon Daddy as the No. 1 man of the world."[29]

During the spring and summer of 1947, Carr and Adrian Doyle were in frequent contact. Adrian and his wife, Anna, visited John and Clarice at Frognal Lane. John had his collection of seventeenth-century rapiers on the walls of the hallway, and the two men, both of whom were in a sense lost Cavaliers, fenced enthusiastically, with unbuttoned foils, much to the annoyance of the women. John was often at Bignell Wood, sometimes accompanied by Clarice. Probably the most difficult thing for John to handle, both in his friendship with the Doyles and in the biography, was the issue of spiritualism, which Sir Arthur and his children embraced wholeheartedly. Clarice still recalls that whenever there was an unexpected sound—a bump or some rustling—at Bignell Wood, Adrian would say, "Oh, that's Daddy prowling around in the library," and then he would continue with whatever he had been discussing. Fortunately, Adrian did not expect John to become a spiritualist, and in the rather static Chapter

21 of the completed biography, Carr was able to discuss the matter without making any judgments at all. "The writer of this biography," he said, "is not a Spiritualist. Spiritualism is not a subject on which he yet feels qualified to pass an opinion."[30] That was, of course, not the whole story. He had been a skeptic as a teenager writing about Doyle for the Uniontown paper, and he remained a skeptic.

As a biographer, Carr was fortunate with his written sources. Sir Arthur Conan Doyle was a prodigious correspondent, as well as a prodigious packrat when it came to anything on paper. Included in the material preserved at Bignell Wood were Doyle's diaries, notebooks, and scrapbooks—some eighteen of them—as well as copies of his own letters, including fifteen hundred letters to his mother. All of this was piled into large tin boxes, about the size of small trunks. For early material, Carr had to assist in the identifying and cross-checking undated letters, but as he reported to Dannay, after about 1903, Doyle had become such a public figure that, had Carr wished, he could have produced a daily account of his life.[31]

Except for a short notice in the *Times Literary Supplement*, Carr did not announce that he was working on the biography because, he said, "I didn't know whether I was equal to the task; if I had to give it up, I wanted it to remain a secret." The first person outside his family whom Carr informed was Frederic Dannay, in June 1947, and he asked him to keep the news confidential. The situation changed early in July when Adrian and Denis Conan Doyle discovered a hatbox that Sir Arthur had placed in a bank strongroom. It contained several papers relating to Sherlock Holmes, including an unknown Holmes play. Adrian immediately rang Carr up and the two men sorted through the material. Always aware of the value of publicity, Adrian broke the news to London newspapers, and Carr was interviewed about the biography. As publicity increased, so did Adrian's optimism about the success of the book—the biography could mean a million dollars a year to the estate; Sir Arthur's books would become, as Adrian put it, "à la mode to the last degree"; new films would be made of Doyle's works; just as Walt Disney marketed his cartoon characters, so the biography would help in the marketing of Sherlock Holmes; and so on.[32]

In his letters Adrian took almost a proprietary interest in the biography, even though as the contracts make clear Carr did the writing and received all royalties. Nonetheless, Adrian went over Carr's work line by line, even asking (and obtaining) an entire rewrite of one chapter that did not satisfy him. Adrian said that "I would not attempt to dictate to John," but (he went on) Carr was very intelligent and therefore valued the points he raised. This must have been a trying experience for Carr. He completed the first eight chapters in four months—a slow rate for him—but then things picked up and by the middle of June 1947 he told Dannay that he had written about half the biography. In August, he was sure enough of his work to say that it would be completed that autumn.[33]

The Life of Sir Arthur Conan Doyle was published in Britain by John Murray and in the United States by Harper & Brothers. On September 16, 1947, Carr signed the contract with Murray, who guaranteed the generous royalty rate of 15 percent for the first 2,500 copies, 17.5 percent for the next 5,500, and 20 percent on all sales above 8,000 copies. The contract for the American edition was not signed for another six months (March 18, 1948); Harpers' royalty rate was good, but not so generous as Murray's—12.5 percent for the first 5,000 copies, 15 percent thereafter—but the American market was much larger than the British. The biography was originally scheduled to be published by both Murray and Harpers in August 1948.[34] Murray's proofs were ready toward the end of May, and Adrian Doyle was on hand to check over the indexes and to make sure that nothing untoward had crept into the text. Without conferring with Carr, he made at least one change, and not unexpectedly it was in regard to his father's aristocratic ancestry: He changed the phrase "descended from feudal nobility" to "descended from the House of Plantagenet." The new wording appears in the British edition, but not in the American.[35]

Plans for 1948 publication, however, became impossible because of the paper shortage in Britain. At John Murray's request Harpers agreed to delay until January 1949. There is some confusion about the actual publication date of *The Life of Sir Arthur Conan Doyle.* In November 1948, Adrian Conan Doyle said that "the huge debut in America" would be January 21; some reviews of the book, however, date the publication of the Harpers edition as February 2, which was the publication date of the British edition.[36] Despite attempts to publish the American and British editions simultaneously, the American was certainly available at the end of January, perhaps a week before the Murray edition was published in London.

For John Dickson Carr, the purpose of biography, like the purpose of fiction, was not to engage in psychological speculations about what made the characters what they are, but to show them as human beings through describing their actions. Above all, a biography should be a story. "This is a story of adventure, sometimes even of melodrama," Carr wrote in *The Life of Sir Arthur Conan Doyle*; "to paint in dull colours, to check the gallop,

would be to misrepresent the man himself."[37] On the whole, Carr succeeds in showing Conan Doyle as a romantic hero—a man of honor and
ideals who was willing to challenge the world for his beliefs. Carr had an
unerring eye for picking out those points in Conan Doyle's life that were
most dramatic and presented his subject as a larger-than-life hero. His
ability to find the colorful, telling detail never falters. The first chapter, for
example, begins: "At Edinburgh, one summer afternoon in the year 1869, a
gentleman approaching middle age sat at his water-color painting in the
small, scrubbed dining-room off the kitchen." The "small, scrubbed" room
perfectly creates the image of Arthur Conan Doyle's father, Charles. The
chapter then goes on as a kind of flashback, as Carr has Doyle—"his
clothes, shabby-genteel"—thinking about the past twenty years of his life.
Carr describes the London of Conan Doyle's boyhood in evocative language: "its lamps glimmering through brown fog and its curtained mys-
tery-haunted streets."[38] Another example of his ability to create a setting
through precise details occurs at the beginning of Chapter 17 (entitled, in
Carr fashion, "Fantasia: Sports, Beards, and Murder"):

> They lined up the motor-cars at Homburg in Hesse-Nassau, fifty
> British entries against fifty German, for a grand parade before the
> start of the race called Prince Henry's tour. Among the cars could be
> seen Sir A. Conan Doyle's twenty h. p. Dietrich-Lorraine, with a
> horseshoe stuck on the front as a mascot.

In a biography that has Carr's narrative drive and colorful style stamped
everywhere, it is astonishing how much the story is "told" by Arthur
Conan Doyle himself. One of Carr's strengths is his controlled use of quotations, and he tells us in the foreword that every quotation, indeed every
description, is taken directly from diaries, letters, notebooks, and other direct sources. Nevertheless, he uses the quotations and other pieces of primary evidence in a daring, and, some might say, not always legitimate
way. He takes quotations from Doyle's correspondence, but often
arranges them as "conversations." In short, *The Life of Sir Arthur Conan
Doyle* resembles *The Murder of Sir Edmund Godfrey* in its method of manipulating the source material. As we saw in *Godfrey*, this can be dangerous
when the quotations are placed out of context, or when they are combined in a way that gives them new meanings. In a valuable and detailed
study of Carr's biography, Doyle expert Howard Lachtman points out
that the effect of Carr's narrative method is to give both intimacy and
vividness to the narrative, but it also raises questions about what was

omitted from the quotations and about what the original context of the quotation may have been.[39]

But all biographers pick and choose their material and use it to illustrate points about their subjects. Carr knew in his own mind who Sir Arthur Conan Doyle was—in Lachtman's words, he presents Doyle as "The Ideal Storybook Hero." Doyle's creed, Carr says, "could be expressed in two words: knightly honour."[40] And it is obvious that he not only idolized Doyle, but also saw in Doyle some aspects of himself. This is clear in small points that Carr picks up on—Doyle's dislike of mathematics, his love of romantic history, his desire for his novels to be judged for story rather than theme, his admiration for the works of Stevenson, and so on.[41] Both authors valued the romanticized ideals of the past—represented in Sir Nigel of Doyle's *The White Company* and by Roderick Kinsmere in Carr's *Devil Kinsmere*—and, in a way, both tried to preserve what never really existed. Lachtman says that for both men "modernity was a curse and ordeal. . . . It was a case of *en garde* against the ravages of the twentieth century."

Doyle's biographer was an American who in his early years could not decide whether he was genuinely Irish or Scottish (or simply a devotee of lost causes), but who by the late 1940s was considered by most readers to be English. It was this man who wrote a biography of another writer who was Irish in descent and Scottish in upbringing, but who, at least according to Adrian Conan Doyle, was fundamentally "an English gentleman."[42] What could be more fitting than that John Dickson Carr write the authorized biography of Arthur Conan Doyle?

It is for this reason that the image of Adrian Doyle checking over every one of John's chapters, and even changing the proofs of the biography, no longer seems so incongruous. Carr was not simply producing the portrait of Arthur Conan Doyle that the family wanted; he was producing one that he himself wanted, and there is no evidence that the book would have been fundamentally different in its conclusions had Adrian not been so closely involved. But what about the points that had so infuriated Adrian about Pearson's biography, the enraging ones that made him turn to Carr for the authorized biography? In the case of Doyle's aristocratic, indeed royal Plantagenet, ancestry, Carr could not bring himself to credit the heritage instead of the man. Despite his romantic tendencies, Carr believed too much in individualism, and he remained too much an American to believe that Plantagenet blood produces better human beings. Carr handled the problem by arguing, probably correctly, that Arthur Conan

Doyle's mother's constant emphasis on ancestry had strongly influenced the boy. But he went on almost sardonically to point out that "lineage, however, was small help to a young married couple." Later, when Doyle made up his mind to refuse a knighthood, Carr says that the decision came from "black ancestral pride."[43] Surprisingly, Adrian left these passages intact.

The other issue important for Adrian's filial pride was whether Sir Arthur Conan Doyle himself was Sherlock Holmes. Adrian had an uphill battle persuading anyone of this contention, for his father said over and over that he had based Holmes on Dr. Bell. There is, however, some evidence to support Adrian's claim, especially Sir Arthur's own detective ability as demonstrated in his interventions in the Edalji and Slater cases,* and some scattered hints in the Holmes stories themselves—for example, Holmes's calling himself "Altamont," a Doyle family name, in "His Last Bow." Pierre Nordon, the only scholar after Carr to have access to Doyle's papers, refers to Sir Arthur's self-identification with Holmes as "semiserious," and I doubt that it was more than that. Most experts probably agree that Holmes was not based on only one person: His deductive abilities and some of his physical characteristics came from Bell; some of his attitudes (especially his chivalry) came from Doyle; his misogyny, his cocaine addiction, his tobacco-in-the-Persian-slipper, and much else that we consider typically Holmesian came from Doyle's imagination and his attempt to create a genius detective with identifiable eccentricities. This kind of subtlety, however, could not appeal to Adrian Doyle. He announced in August 1948 that the forthcoming book would end all talk that Bell was the model of Holmes.[45]

In *The Life of Sir Arthur Conan Doyle*, Carr gives fully the claims for Joseph Bell as the model for Holmes, but on the other hand, he even more completely offers Adrian's case for his father, and what's more, appears to accept it. I think, however, that he was too close to the documents, and too honest, to believe that a simple identification would suffice. In some

---

*George Edalji was convicted in 1903 of mutilating a pony, the conviction based more on racial prejudice (his father was a Parsi from India) than on the evidence. In 1906, Doyle examined the evidence and determined that Edalji's "astigmatic myopia" meant that he could not see well enough to do the things the police claimed he had done. The Slater case, which took place in 1908, involved the murder of an old woman, apparently for her jewelry. Oscar Slater, whose German-Jewish background was against him, was tried and convicted of the crime. Doyle, after many years of fighting the matter, showed that the old woman must have been killed by someone who knew her rather than by a stranger like Slater. Carr pointed out that Doyle hated "colour prejudice as much as racial or religious prejudice,"[44] a statement that (except for some odd remarks in his final novels) describes Carr as well.

places in *The Life of Sir Arthur Conan Doyle*, Carr presents the case and leaves it as a question, even though he adds that "the answer will be self-evident." After describing Doyle's work on the Edalji case, for instance, he concludes the chapter by asking "Who was Sherlock Holmes?" In discussing the Altamont reference in "His Last Bow," Carr says that "Conan Doyle at last identified Holmes with himself,"[46] which is rather different from saying that "Conan Doyle said that he was Sherlock Holmes" or "was the model for Sherlock Holmes." But in spite of Carr's careful wording in these and other instances, the book as a whole presents as persuasively as possible Adrian Conan Doyle's convictions about his father as Sherlock Holmes.

Taking all the arguments about Carr's use of evidence, about his presentation of biography-as-adventure-story, about his role as Adrian's coworker, the main question must be: Did he get it right? Is the Conan Doyle presented in the biography the genuine man? Lachtman says that Carr will be "remembered as the creator of Sir Arthur Conan Doyle—not the real Conan Doyle, perhaps, but an ideal one whom many readers have preferred to believe was a storybook character in his own right, a man as heroic as Holmes and as lovable as Watson."[47] Of course, in one sense, every biographer creates his or her subject, but the question is whether Carr's creation of Doyle is true to the person himself. Sir Arthur's only surviving child, Dame Jean Conan Doyle, who was eighteen years old when her father died, remains of the opinion that Carr's depiction captured her father. "Of all the books, it conveys most clearly the personality, the nature of the man. It is the most accurate portrait in words."[48]

The Life of Sir Arthur Conan Doyle was published with much fanfare. Harpers took out advertisements in major newspapers throughout the country, and a portion of Carr's chapter about Doyle's involvement in the Edalji case appeared in the January 1949 issues of *Harper's Magazine* and *The Strand*. *The American Weekly*, a Sunday supplement carried by many American newspapers, ran an illustrated article about the book based on an interview with Carr.[49] Vincent Starrett, the great bookman and expert on Sherlock Holmes, retold anecdotes from the book in a series of weekly columns in the *Chicago Tribune*. Carr, who was in New York when the book was published, spoke to various groups and was interviewed on the radio about Doyle. He gleefully wrote to Adrian, however, that one radio appearance had to be canceled. Carr was to be a guest on *Author Meets Critic*, in which various critics launched literary attacks on the author, but, he said, the affair did not come off because no one could find any critic willing to attack *The Life of Sir Arthur Conan Doyle*.[50]

Carr was also the featured speaker at the annual dinner of the Baker Street Irregulars, who had long playfully claimed that Watson was the real author of the Holmes stories and Doyle merely his literary agent. The Irregulars had, moreover, considerable animus toward Adrian Doyle because of his zealous guarding of his father's estate, especially in regard to the suppression of *The Misadventures of Sherlock Holmes*. According to a printed account, Carr began his speech by saying that he "would deal only with fictitious people—like Sir Arthur Conan Doyle." In a letter to Adrian, however, Carr gave a different version of his address:

> When I lectured to the Baker Street Irregulars, I made a deliberately challenging beginning with, "Let us just imagine, for once, that there really *was* a man named Sir Arthur Conan Doyle"—result, uproar. But it quietened, and all the Irregulars have given the most royal and enthusiastic support.[51]

Carr was correct. In *The Baker Street Journal*, for example, Edgar W. Smith unreservedly praised what he called "John Dickson Carr's authoritative biography of Sherlock Holmes's great and good friend Sir Arthur Conan Doyle":

> There is no cluttering of the account with gratuitous psychological twists of the author's own contriving; there is a happy absence of the heavy overtones and turgid undertows too often thrown between the subject and the reader to satisfy the biographer's fetishes and fancies.[52]

For the most part, other reviews of *The Life of Sir Arthur Conan Doyle* were also positive, sometimes overwhelmingly so. Both the *Chicago Tribune* and the *San Francisco Chronicle* devoted the first page of their magazine sections to Carr's work. Many of the reviews emphasized the picture of Doyle that Carr was at pains to paint. Joseph Henry Jackson in the *San Francisco Chronicle* called Doyle "the Last of the Knights." The headline over the review in the *New York Herald Tribune* described him as the "Parfit Gentil Knight." The *St. Louis Globe-Democrat* headline was "Conan Doyle's Life Delightful as Romance," and Dorothy L. Sayers's review in the London *Sunday Times* called him "Conan Doyle: Crusader." Several of the reviews praised Carr's writing style. The *Providence Journal* called him "one of the masters of effective English today," and *The New Republic* said that

"The Life of Sir Arthur Conan Doyle . . . gives further support to the often expressed theory that some of the best contemporary writing is being done by detective-story writers, like, for example, John Dickson Carr."[53]

There were, of course, a few negative reviews, mostly focusing on Carr's idolization of Doyle, which, according to some critics, made the book too close to hagiography. Unlike most other critics, Dorothy L. Sayers in an otherwise sympathetic review objected to Carr's writing style: "It suffers somewhat by a determined brightness of style, reminiscent of a radio feature-programme, whereby every episode is remorselessly dramatized, every chapter begins with a tableau and a flash-back, and rhetorical questions abound." Whether one finds this a positive or negative characteristic, Sayers was correct in finding the hand of the radio dramatist in *The Life of Sir Arthur Conan Doyle,* and (as we shall see) the same influence was also increasingly evident in Carr's novels.

Adrian Doyle was enraged whenever a negative review appeared, charging that the reviewers were absolute scoundrels who hated his father. On one occasion, he asked John Murray not to advertise in a journal that presumed to criticize the biography.[54] In Adrian's defense, he did have reason to object to Hugh Kingsmill's comments in *New English Review.* Kingsmill, a friend and occasional collaborator of Hesketh Pearson, spent most of his review praising Pearson's biography of Doyle. Carr's work, he said, will not be preferred by those who want "a credible biography rather than a panegyric which would stagger even a court poet to an Oriental tyrant." Adrian dashed off a letter to Carr asking him to send a strong reply to the magazine. It would have been wiser to let Kingsmill's review pass without notice, and in fact that is what Carr almost invariably did whenever his novels received less than favorable comments in the press. But whether he was fired by Adrian's enthusiasm, or he felt committed to support his friend, who was himself writing to *New English Review,* Carr sent an intemperate letter to the editor. Carr told the editor that Kingsmill's "place in the literary world—if he has one—I am unable to identify." He then took Kingsmill's comment about "panegyric" as somehow implying that either John Dickson Carr or Adrian Conan Doyle or both were liars. He concluded by challenging Kingsmill to point out where he had exaggerated any of Sir Arthur's accomplishments. Once Kingsmill had done so, Carr would reply defending his interpretation. To make the matter worthwhile, Carr went on, he and Kingsmill should each put up a stake of one hundred pounds, and the editor of *The Strand Magazine* would judge who had told the truth.[55] (It may have been a trifle disingenuous of Carr to suggest *The Strand's* editor as judge, for he had recently printed an excerpt from *The Life of Sir Arthur Conan Doyle* and could be expected to be in Carr's corner.) Carr's letter may be charitably described as silly, and it was probably fortunate that *New English Review* did not publish it.

A more serious challenge resulted from a review by Harold Nicolson in the *Daily Telegraph*. He praised Carr's "taste and cunning" in making an interesting book out of "someone whose fame was wholly out of proportion to his intrinsic merit." Sir Arthur Conan Doyle, Nicolson said, was "a dull and worthy gentleman" who had "an uninteresting mind." He concluded the review by pointing out that Doyle's mother was responsible for inculcating in her son the values of chivalry. That was in fact exactly what Carr had said, but Adrian saw that statement as an insult to his grandmother, especially when the reviewer added, "It is this silken thread which explains much of [Sir Arthur's] foolishness and gives colour and originality to a biography which in other circumstances might be dull indeed." Adrian, believing (as he wrote to John Murray) that most critics are mere literary tradesmen, was particularly incensed because he had considered Nicolson a gentleman, with all the attributes of class and behavior that word implies. Therefore, he decided that no mere letter would suffice to avenge the insults to his father and grandmother. He challenged Nicolson to meet him in France, with weapons of his choosing, and prove his manhood.[56] This whole affair ended with neither a bang nor a whimper; Nicolson simply ignored Adrian Conan Doyle.

On March 13, 1949, *The Life of Sir Arthur Conan Doyle* first appeared on *The New York Times* bestseller list, and it remained there for six weeks. Six months later, Carr reported that the biography was "coining money." On April 20, 1950, the Mystery Writers of American awarded him a special Edgar (the MWA's equivalent of an Oscar) for the biography.[57] John Dickson Carr was able to accept the award in person. By this time he had been living in the United States for more than two years.

Chapter 14

MAMARONECK

By autumn 1947, John and Clarice Carr had decided to return to the United States with their three daughters. Clarice recalls that the main reason was the continuing shortages and rationing in England. She told her husband that, because he had retained his American citizenship, there was nothing to prevent their pulling up stakes and returning to the United States. John, however, always said that the decision was not based on economic considerations. "We didn't leave England because of shortages," he wrote to Val Gielgud, "but simply because of the Labour government." He was more blunt to Frederic Dannay: "We can't stand this bloody government any longer."[1] John had to stay in England for a while for business reasons—among other matters, he was arranging with the BBC for the broadcast of some scripts by members of The Detection Club. While his family sailed to New York, he stayed at his favorite London hotel, Claridge's. Around Christmas 1947, Clarice, Violet Andrews, three children, six enormous packing cases of John's books and collection of rapiers, and Clarice's Pekinese, Nicodemus, arrived at New York Harbor during a heavy snowstorm.

After staying for a few days with a friend in the Bronx, the ménage went off to Uniontown to visit John's parents. Leaving Andy to help Wooda and Julia Carr care for the children, Clarice returned to New York to meet John and to begin looking for a house. They chose Mamaroneck in Westchester County because it was near Larchmont where Fred Dannay and his wife, Bill, lived, and it was on the railroad commuter line to New York City. They found a lovely large house at 118 Beach Avenue—at least it seemed to be lovely and large. When they first saw it, it was covered with snow, but they bought it anyway and waited for a thaw so that they could move in. The spring revealed a Dutch Colonial house with a front porch, green shutters, and a large attic where John could have his study. It was set in about an acre of grounds. Carr hung his devil tapestries and collection of swords, rapiers, and daggers on the walls of the living room and study, and according to Robert Lewis Taylor's *New Yorker* interview, "He is forever handling them with a peculiarly wistful look." The Caruso Studios photographed Carr with a steely look in his eye as he thrust a sword toward some person or object just off-camera, and the photograph appeared on the dust jacket of the Harpers edition of *Below Suspicion,* published in 1949. While he wrote in his attic study, Carr smoked continuously and tossed the cigarette butts on uncarpeted parts of the floor, which by 1951 was covered with burns. Taylor said that "despite his air-conditioner, [the attic] is fragrant with the invigorating smell of scorched pine." One wall of the attic was filled with Carr's collection of reference works on crime, including his multivolume *Complete Newgate Calendar* (the classic account of seventeenth- and eighteenth-century criminality), Hans Gross's *Criminal Investigation,* and the *English Coroner's Official Handbook to Poisons* (the only copy, Carr told Taylor, in the hands of a nongovernment employee).[2]

Despite having his books and swords about him, Carr told his English correspondents that he was not happy in Mamaroneck. "I hate it," he wrote some fifteen months later to Gielgud. "This, I think, is because about six times a day I hear from some fellow-American a quite innocent statement which sends my blood-pressure to the danger mark." He said that he was waiting only for a victory by the Conservative party in the next election so that he might return to England; indeed, he went on, perhaps he would come back even if the despised Labour government were still in power.[3] Some of this was merely grousing, a reflection of his general dissatisfaction, which was associated less with Mamaroneck than with the world of the late 1940s. That point becomes clear in *A Graveyard to Let,* a Sir Henry Merrivale novel written in Mamaroneck in 1948. The story takes place in "Maralarch," an obvious combination of Mamaroneck and Larchmont. The hero is Cy Norton, an American reporter who had lived in England for eighteen years.

He was, however, fired from the New York newspaper that had published his articles from London, because he hated the Labour party. Crystal Manning, one of the female characters in the story, recognizes what is gnawing at Cy Norton—and at John Dickson Carr:

> You're not actually happy here in America. . . . You want Europe, and especially England, as England was before the war. But those old days are gone forever. You know that, you hate it, and it's poisoning your life. . . . You want a life of graciousness, and dignity, and a "decent reserve."

Cy is not the only character in *A Graveyard to Let* who represents Carr's views; that erstwhile socialist, Sir Henry Merrivale, finds it a deadly insult to suggest that he might shake hands with Sir Stafford Cripps. H.M. even levels the term "bastard" at the British "Minister of Muddle."[4]

In short, although he might have said otherwise, John Dickson Carr was as happy during the three and a half years he lived in Mamaroneck as he could have been anywhere at that time. After child-care from grandparents, trips back and forth across the Atlantic during the war, and separate residences in London and Bristol, the Mamaroneck years were the first time that the Carrs had ever lived together as a family.[5] Once again, John's attitude can be seen in *A Graveyard to Let*, which is in several ways an exceptionally revealing work. Frederick Manning tells his children:

> Has it ever occurred to you that a really happy marriage can be not spoiled but badly hurt by these intruders called children? No, it hasn't occurred to you! The sugary sentiment of our age won't permit it. In the sort of marriage I mean, husband and wife are all in all to each other. . . . If they need to have children to "bind them together," they were never happy in the first place.

But Manning's children have now grown, and "whether he swore it or not—he was so obviously fond [of them] now."[6]

To the Carrs' surprise and pleasure, Clayton and Catherine (Kate) Rawson lived only a block away in Mamaroneck. John had corresponded with Clayton since the late 1930s, and the two men had challenged each other over solutions to impossible crimes. Kate Rawson still remembers meeting the Carrs at Fred Dannay's house in Larchmont, and being impressed with the quiet politeness of a well-brought-up English child like Julia. The two families became good friends. Several times a week, John, Clayt, and sometimes Fred Dannay would meet for an evening's session to discuss true crime, detective fiction, and how to trick readers.[7] The Rawsons' oldest son, Hugh, who was around eleven years old when the Carrs came to Mamaroneck, recalls:

> I sometimes hung around on the fringes of many conversations. John was not a formidable or unapproachable person. He was a fascinating conversationalist. He was very theatrical; he'd talk parts. He would for long periods be social and outgoing, in part of the world so to speak; but I think during this time, he would be plotting his next book. When it came time to write, as I recall, he would just sort of disappear for about six weeks or two months. He'd go up into the attic of their house, and I don't even think his family saw much of him during this period.

The Carrs and the Rawsons became so close that when Clayton Rawson, Jr., was baptized in 1948, John and Clarice were his godparents.[8] The next year, Carr dedicated the Carter Dickson book *A Graveyard to Let* to Clayton Rawson "in honor of those two fine arts, friendship and magic."

Besides being an author and editor, Rawson was a professional magician who enjoyed putting on magic parties for his friends, and although (as he admitted) Carr was not clever at prestidigitation himself, he often helped Rawson set up the tricks. Some of the parties were held in the Rawsons' backyard, where Clayt had a small stage complete with curtains and a trap door; he was even able to perform levitations (of his children) in the backyard. In addition, Carr and Rawson spent many hours planning a haunted-house party, which was given in the Carr's attic. The guests were led through a small chamber of horrors and were entertained by various spiritualistlike stunts. Carr especially enjoyed a trick involving the classic story about a one-armed brakeman whose hand becomes severed and takes on a life of its own. Hugh Rawson describes it this way: "I remember John in his best theatrical form, telling the story and as he's approaching the climax, a hand skitters out from underneath the couch where everybody is sitting."[9]

Mystery writer Lillian de la Torre and her husband, Professor George McCue, visited the Carrs one evening in 1948 when the Rawsons were also guests. Influenced by *The Murder of Sir Edmund Godfrey,* de la Torre had dedicated her first book of "histo-detection," *Elizabeth Is Missing,* to John Dickson Carr. She remembers that "my first impression [of Carr] was of open-hearted sweetness and romantic good looks, a little like Poe perhaps, regular features, smooth dark hair, haunted dark eyes." That evening, she taught the Carrs and Rawsons to play a game called Receptions. One player was chosen to leave the room while the other players devised a "reception" for him or her—a little play in which, when the player returns, he or she is treated as the central character and must guess what part he or she is playing. "John was a wonderful actor," de la Torre says. "The solemn nobility of his bearing was excruciatingly funny as he personated Robert E. Lee giving up his sword (a real one, of course) to Clayt, who soon divined he was U. S. Grant." In another skit, de la Torre had to leave the room. On her return, Rawson and Carr played thugs ("What thugs Clayt and John made!") who proceeded to abduct her. De la Torre failed to guess that she was the title character of her own book, *Elizabeth Is Missing*. On other occasions, the Carrs revived the table-tapping sessions that they had had back in the Kingswood days. John, de la Torre recalls, was skeptical but willing, and one evening they did indeed receive tapped-out messages—but whether from the spirit world or a more earthly source never became clear.[10]

Another person who sometimes was present at such gatherings was Dorothy Salisbury Davis, now a doyenne of American mystery writers but then new to the field and, she remembers, very much in awe of the great figures in the profession, such as John Dickson Carr. She attended a dinner party given by Rawson for Lillian de la Torre, and the Carrs were there along with Fred Dannay and Edward Radin, who had recently devised a new theory about the Lizzie Borden case. Carr and the others reenacted the crucial scene in the Fall River murder on Rawson's staircase.[11]

Rawson put on an annual magic party for members of the Mystery Writers of America, among whose active members was John Dickson Carr. Minutes of April 1948 record Carr's attendance at board of directors meetings, and he was chosen along with Hugh Pentecost to present the Edgars at the annual awards dinner for that year. In February 1949, he became president of the MWA, a ceremonial position having no executive or administrative duties. Harold Q. Masur, who joined the MWA in 1948 and has since become well known for his series of novels and short stories about lawyer Scott Jordan, says that Carr was "courtly, unassuming and friendly," but when an issue arose on which he felt strongly, he became "forceful and assertive . . . and because of the high perch he inhabited as a major figure in the field, few board members took issue with him. No reason they should. As a gifted logician his opinions were generally sound."[12]

Edward D. Hoch, then an unpublished writer but in later years one of

Carr's most important followers in the locked-room story, sometimes sat in on the open board meetings. Hoch met Carr in the spring of 1950, when he was no longer president but still a member of the board of directors.

> The thing I remember most about him was his voice. I was surprised that he had such a powerful, commanding voice for his slight stature. I can still remember one board meeting when a well-known television producer appeared to ask for the use of the MWA name on a proposed anthology series. This was in the early days of TV, of course, and the rest of the board seemed willing to grant permission for little or no advance payment. Carr, virtually alone, led the opposition, beating down the TV producer with his powerful voice until terms much more favorable to MWA were agreed upon.[13]

Between 1948 and 1952, the MWA produced a series of skits at their dinners under the generic title "The March of Crime." Both John and Clarice sometimes acted in these performances. In Clayton Rawson's "The Unsuspecting," Clarice was hilarious in a burlesque of the "Had-I-But-Known" type of story written by Mary Roberts Rinehart and others. John starred as Wendell St. John in Kelley Roos's "The Great Locked Room Mystery," which (as the title indicates) was a take-off on the type of books John wrote. The room is so completely locked that it takes the police three days to blast their way in, and when it is discovered that the room has no windows, Inspector Trout deduces an "architect's blunder." "JDC was the quintessential ham," Masur says of Carr's performance, "posturing and proclaiming to marvelously ludicrous effect."[14]

Carr wrote two MWA playlets, both broadly humorous parodies of Sherlock Holmes. In "The Adventure of the Conk-Singleton Papers," performed at the April 1948 Edgar Awards Dinner, Queen Victoria is accused of having sent Prime Minister Gladstone a case of poisoned whiskey as a Christmas present. Clayton Rawson played Holmes, and Carr gave himself the role of the mysterious visitor who turns out to be the villain. Rawson was again Holmes and Carr assigned himself the part of the French ambassador in "The Adventure of the Paradol Chamber," featured at the April 1949 Awards Dinner. In that play, Holmes alone notices the key clue—that lord Matchlock left Buckingham Palace wearing no trousers. "Scotland Yard," Holmes explains, "observed nothing."[15]

When Carr resigned from his position at the BBC, he had expressed relief that he would no longer have to grind out scripts, but that is exactly what he decided to do shortly after he moved to Mamaroneck. Sometime during the spring of 1948, Carr and CBS reached an agreement for a new radio mystery program written solely by Carr, and on June 23, 1948, the network began a press release with the words "Mysteries Circle the Globe: *Cabin B-13* New Series by John Dickson Carr." The director was John Dietz, and original music was by Merle Kendrick. *Cabin B-13* had only the slightest relationship with Carr's *Suspense* play also called "Cabin B-13." The idea behind the new series was that the S.S. *Maurevania* was on a round-the-world cruise. At each port or city—or at least, as Carr wrote to Val Gielgud, at each one "of which I could remember enough"—the ship's surgeon, Dr. Fabian, would tell a mysterious story related to that city. The announcer described Fabian as "world traveller and collector of strange and incredible tales of mystery and terror."[16] Occasionally, Fabian was more than a storyteller; he sometimes acted as detective in unravelling the mystery. Fabian was played by radio and movie actor Arnold Moss. When Moss had to fulfill a screen contract in Hollywood, the role of Dr. Fabian was taken by Arnold Hewitt.

Each episode began with three hollow booms of the ship's horn, followed by an announcement of the evening's story, some atmospheric music, then an opening statement from Dr. Fabian. The following, from the first story, is typical: "As I sit here in my Cabin [pause] B-13, I am reminded how the tides and storms of a thousand voyages have wrought nothing more strange, more sinister than man's desire for adventure in the strange ports and lands we touch."[17]

For many years, all that was known of *Cabin B-13* was the titles of some of the stories as listed in newspaper broadcast schedules. As time passed, it gradually became almost a fabled program, with aficionadoes who recalled the original broadcasts describing it as "among radio's very best mystery series."[18] Within the past decade, however, tapes of three of the tales have been discovered, and even more recently British researcher Tony Medawar located the scripts to the entire series among the CBS material at the Library of Congress. Medawar and James E. Keirans have published a detailed account of the scripts entitled "Suspense on the High Seas" in *The Armchair Detective*. What follows is a briefer evaluation. The most obvious impression left after reading the scripts is of Carr's fertility of invention. During the first four months of the series, from July 5 through November 7, 1948, the scripts were all original, with one minor exception: "Footprint in the Sky" is a thoroughly revised version of the BBC "The Gong Cried Murder," which in turn was based on the Colonel March story "Clue in the Snow." Only one other of the fifteen scripts broadcast during this period is an adaptation of a Carr story. "No Useless Coffin" is based on "The House in Goblin Wood," but with Fabian replacing Sir Henry Merrivale as the detective and with another important change: The victim was a Nazi spy, and therefore the murder, which was chillingly heartless in the short story, is justified in the radio play. Another broadcast, "The Street of the Seven Daggers," uses a variation of the gimmick from the short story "The Silver Curtain," but the plot of the radio play is entirely different.

Cabin B-13 began with "A Razor in Fleet Street," based on an idea that three years earlier Carr had planned as a short story for *Ellery Queen's Mystery Magazine.* In reading the script, I was struck by how unconvincing is Carr's use of doppelgängers and how extraordinary is the foolishness of the main character, Bill Leslie, but in its broadcast version (this is one of the shows that survives on tape), these weaknesses are not apparent. Leslie is an exact double of a killer named Flash Morgan. Despite being warned that Morgan wants to murder him for his identification papers, Leslie leaves his hotel room and enters a barber shop. Shortly thereafter, Morgan's body is found, but both Leslie and the barber swear that neither was out of the other's sight while the crime was committed. The second play, "The Man Who Couldn't Be Photographed," is also based on an idea that Carr originally hoped to use in a short story. (The gimmick explaining why a man cannot be photographed was first suggested many years earlier by George Bernard Shaw, but Carr more likely found it in Gross's *Criminal Investigation.*)[19] A vain actor named Bruce Ransom is cursed by a descendant of a witch: "I offer my life, I offer my soul, if this man can never face a camera again. And this I swear by the reversed cross of Satan."[20] The curse seems to come true: Whenever Ransom has his picture taken, the photographer tells him that the picture cannot be developed. The solution, based on some obscure medical knowledge (or, at least, assertions), is a letdown.

The remaining plays range from good to superb, with imaginative treatments of impossible crimes. "The Blindfolded Knife-Thrower" and "A Most Respectable Murder" have original locked-room gimmicks. In "The Count of Monte Carlo," a woman is thrown from a balcony with no one near her. In "The Man with the Iron Chest," a large metal chest as well as a fortune in diamonds vanish. In "Below Suspicion," a woman is strangled on a beach, her body surrounded by unmarked sand. Each of these plays provided the basis for one of Carr's later novels or short stories, but he never reused one of his best impossible situations from *Cabin B-13.* In

"The Power of Darkness," Carr inverted a famous impossible crime gambit—the disappearing house. In this play, the house does not vanish, but everything surrounding it does. A young American historian, Alan, and his fiancée, Ruth, visit a villa near Rome, which is reputed to be haunted by the ghost of a sadistic nobleman who was murdered three hundred years before. He died as he dragged his horribly broken body through the fields trying to get back to the villa. Carr makes the listener feel the presence of terrifying things from the past, and then almost before Alan's and Ruth's eyes, the noisy suburbs of modern Rome disappear to be replaced by the empty fields of the seventeenth century. As the frightened couple watches, the nobleman's ghost seems to be crawling toward the window. At the conclusion to this excellent play, Dr. Fabian produces a rational explanation for the specter and for the vanishing surroundings of the villa.

The remaining plays include "The Nine Black Reasons," about nine black pearls and an extraordinary reason for producing a corpse, and "Island of Coffins," about a woman who has tried to preserve the past by turning the calendar back twenty-five years. Mrs. Almack explains to Dr. Fabian that she brought her grandchildren to an island off Abyssinia to shield them from the modern world. "It was to live again—even in imagination—through the only years that were worth living." Carr, who was himself increasingly estranged from the modern world, must in some ways have sympathized with Mrs. Almack's position. Having lived through Hitler's years, however, and having found the British Labour government's regulations unbearable, he could not accept Mrs. Almack's control of the children. He describes her as a tyrant, and Dr. Fabian says, "Tyrants aren't always so powerful as they think." Unusually for any of Carr's works, "Island of Coffins" is memorable for its ambivalence.

By the end of October 1948, Carr was finding it increasingly difficult to keep up with his deadlines for *Cabin B-13*. A year later, he wrote to Val Gielgud:

> What happened was what always happens. I overestimated my stamina in keeping going indefinitely. (No booze whatever; there couldn't be.) And I did pretty well, keeping up a new story a week . . . squarely to the two-week-ahead deadline. But I was down for the count.[21]

The pressure on Carr may be responsible for the fact that sometimes the titles of the plays that CBS announced as to be broadcast the succeeding week were replaced by other titles. "The Witch of the Low-Tide" was replaced by "The Blindfolded Knife-Thrower," "Last Night in Ghostland" by "The Power of Darkness," "The Eyes of the Blind" by "The Man with the Iron Chest," "Four Ways to Danger" by "Death in the Desert," and "The Man Eaters" by a rebroadcast of "The Man Who Couldn't Be Photographed." How many of these were simply alternative titles for the same scripts, and how many represent stories that were never written, is not known, but Carr was obviously writing so close to his deadline that announcements of forthcoming shows were made before he had finished writing them.

For the rest of the run of *Cabin B-13*, from November 14, 1948, through January 2, 1949, Carr reused old scripts—three from *Suspense*, three from *Appointment with Fear*, and one that had already been broadcast three months earlier on *Cabin B-13*. Although CBS continued to publicize the stories as "baffling originals,"[22] only one play from the final months of the program has any claim to originality: "The Dead Man's Knock" is a thoroughly revised version of the BBC "Room of the Suicides." CBS was not pleased that *Cabin B-13* was no longer broadcasting entirely original plays. Carr reported:

> There were a number of "conferences," which means that people tear their hair and bang the table. I pointed out that I was willing to go on, but the story-quality would drop, the rating follow it, and the sponsor follow that. . . . They said it was all right if I agreed to return the following Autumn, with perhaps some help in the matter of a ghost when things grew too difficult.[23]

The series planned for the next autumn, whether by Carr alone or assisted by a ghostwriter, never materialized, though in July 1949, Carr made an unofficial inquiry of the BBC whether he might be able to use the *Appointment with Fear* title for a new American program. Permission, again unofficial, was granted, but apparently the plans fell through. Gielgud, however, asked Carr for copies of the *Cabin B-13* scripts for possible use on the BBC. Carr obliged, but the BBC decided against doing a British version of the series.[24]

Carr's final association with American radio began in June 1949. The Mutual Broadcasting System produced a new anthology series called *Murder by Experts*, the gimmick being that each show was chosen by an important mystery writer. Although Carr wrote none of the scripts, he introduced each program during the first part of its run. Almost a dozen of the shows survive on audiotape. It is not surprising that after having spent almost fourteen years in England, Carr spoke with a slight British accent. His broadcast tones were clear, precise, and resonant—and a bit deeper than his normal speaking voice. Clarice attended one of the recording sessions and was amused to hear John consciously lowering his voice as he spoke into the microphone.

Early in April 1949, Clarice had received a letter from Bristol that her mother, Mary Cleaves, was ill from what John described as "paralysis and wandering mind." Clarice got a plane to England, leaving her husband and three children with Violet Andrews. Mary Cleaves died in May, but Clarice had to stay to help her father and her brother Roy settle the estate. Meanwhile, Andy had become ill, and John asked Julia, not quite sixteen years old, to take over caring for Bonnie and Mary (aged nine and seven) and keeping the house together. Julia was both optimistic and mature for her age—in the autumn she would enter Wellesley College, two years younger than her classmates—so she agreed, and in fact everything worked out.[25]

John Dickson Carr was busy during the late 1940s. "The brain-pan boils with ideas," he said.[26] In addition to radio scripts and the Doyle biography, Carr wrote eight detective novels about Sir Henry Merrivale and Dr. Gideon Fell between 1945 and 1950.* Even though one of his finest books, *He Who Whispers*, appeared during this period, it seems that Carr had become so concerned with the puzzle element that he did not always pay enough attention to the requirements of storytelling. This point can be overstated, for all eight novels are good, and three or four must be rated highly against another of Carr's standards, ingenuity. Nonetheless, a tiredness in narration and construction occasionally appears, and at times Carr seems to be trying almost too hard to give the reader all the clues.

In August 1946, he wrote to Dannay that

> I find myself, as I get older and craftier at the game, taking more and more pains with every detail rather than relaxing. It has got almost to a point where every speech in the book has got to bear some interpretable relation to the solution.[27]

Once in a while, Carr's craftiness got in the way of clear narration. Carr remarked, "The first essential of style [in a detective story] is clarity, clarity, and still again clarity,"[28] but he did not always follow his own precept.

---

*Also published during these years was a slim paperback, *Dr. Fell, Detective, and Other Stories*, edited by Frederic Dannay under the Ellery Queen pseudonym. It contains six short stories and two radio scripts, all of which have also appeared in later Carr collections.

Perhaps the best example is a line in *The Sleeping Sphinx,* published in 1947. One of the main characters says, "She would have been thirty-six years old in January; she was so fond of young people." The second part of the sentence is so obviously a non sequitur that Hamish Hamilton queried it in the galleys. When he had read further and found that it contained an important clue, he asked Carr "to consider introducing it in a rather more natural way. At present, it sticks out like a sore thumb." Carr, however, refused to make any changes. The structure of the sentence, he said,

> was very, very deliberate. I wanted it to stick out a mile. I wanted the reader to trip over it, so that he would remember it. Nothing is easier than to slip in a clue unobtrusively. I always do this when the clue is dangerous: that is, when a single clue might give the whole show away; and then, in the interests of fairness, I repeat the unobtrusive clue somewhere else. But in the "young people" matter, it is not at all dangerous to say this at the time, even though it is important; so I walloped out with it in a loud voice.[29]

All of which is reasonable, but the lines makes for herky-jerky reading, and the dialogue is needlessly obscure.

Carr's novels of this period are characterized by nostalgia for the past, a sense of loss, a knowledge that prewar England would never return. The novels are filled with increasingly strident complaints about the present. *He Who Whispers,* published in 1946, is set a year earlier, and Carr described in almost aching clarity the feelings of people who had been numbed by five years of war:

> People didn't celebrate that victory hysterically. . . . Most people were a little apathetic because they could not yet think of it as real. But something awoke, deep down inside human beings' hearts, when the cricket results crept back into the papers, and the bunks began to disappear from the Underground.

Already in this book, however, Carr had emphasized the continuing difficulties in living in London after the war—the shortages, the queues, the pubs without any liquor—"but," he continued, London was "a place free at last from the intolerable weight of threats."

This caveat does not appear in Carr's later books written during the immediate postwar years. In *My Late Wives,* published in 1947, Carr remarks that people's "nerves [have been] scratched by so many small annoyances that at times life becomes unendurable." In *The Sleeping Sphinx*, also published in 1947, Dr. Fell says that "in this free England today you have only got to sound official, act officiously, or behave in general as though you were snooping to get the goods on somebody, and you will be accepted everywhere without question." *The Skeleton in the Clock* (1948), which Carr wrote shortly before moving to Mamaroneck, presents a situation that is, in some ways, even worse for someone like Carr, who had once thought of London as Baghdad-on-the-Thames: The chief character in that book believes the life in postwar England has become "dull and intolerably frustrating." *Below Suspicion* (1949) is almost a litany of complaints about the England Carr had left and about the regimenting of the people that Carr believed was a policy of the socialist Labour government. "Once, when the individualist had been a national pride, England had stood alone in her glory; and her lightest breath shook the world. Now the man was subjugated by the mass." People in England have "a grey life." They are "stifled in crowds, hammered to docility by queues, entangled in bureaucratic red tape, snubbed by tradesmen with whom [they] must deal."[30] A major element of the plot of *Below Suspicion* is the existence of a genuine witch cult, and Carr suggests that the dismal life in postwar England is enough explanation for why people have joined such a cult.

He Who Whispers, published in spring 1946 in both the United States and Britain, is Carr's best novel of the later 1940s. It almost perfectly combines the eeriness of some of his great books of the previous decade with the nerves-on-edge tension that characterized his more recent productions. The story begins with a young historian named Miles Hammond attending the Murder Club as Dr. Fell's guest. He hears the tale of the impossible murder: A few years before the war a man had been stabbed to death alone in a tower, and rumors had spread that the crime was committed by a vampire. The marks of a vampire were found on a boy in the village, and a mysterious woman named Fay Seton was rumored to be able to change herself into this bloodsucking creature.* Throughout the novel, Carr focuses the reader's fears and suspicions on Fay. Is she a creature of supernatural evil? Is she a more mundane murderer? In any case,

---

*This plot seems perfect for a title that he had been playing with for more than a decade, "Vampire Tower." He chose, however, to call it *He Who Whispers*, a title that he had used in 1944 for an unrelated *Appointment With Fear* radio script, but one that describes the novel almost as well as "Vampire Tower" and is even more atmospheric.

her presence seems the center of growing terror.

Shortly after hearing the story of the vampire, Miles meets and falls in love with Fay herself. He romantically sees her as the image of a long-dead eighteenth-century charmer, though Miles's sister, Marion, warns him against her. Alone in her bedroom, Marion almost dies of fright, and she claims that some *thing* she did not see whispered softly to her. The terrifying image of something whispering in the dark is worthy of Montague Rhodes James, who was second only to Poe in influencing Carr as a horror-story writer. Dr. Fell explains that "the vampire, in folk-lore, whispered softly to her victim at the beginning of the influence that threw the victim into a trance."[31] Eventually, Dr. Fell explains the impossibilities, banishes the vampire to folklore, and shows how Fay has been a constant victim of human malevolence. Carr's misdirection about the identity of who is behind the murder on the tower and the whispering is extraordinarily subtle; we are misled by what we expect. [****Here I shall reveal a small portion of the solution, though not the identity of the murderer.] Fay, a genuinely good person, suffers from nymphomania. Carr does not treat this subject leeringly but as a tragedy:

> She is no more to be blamed for it [says Dr. Fell] than for the heart-weakness which accompanied it. . . . Her outward puritanism, her fastidiousness, her delicacy, her gentle manners, were *not* assumed. They are real. To have relations with casual strangers was and is torture to her.[32]

Fay, meanwhile, has suffered a heart attack and lies in a hospital with only a few months to live. Although another character tries to persuade Miles that he does not love Fay but rather "a dust-image out of old books, a dream you've created in your own mind,"[33] he goes to her, and the novel ends.

The next Dr. Fell novel, *The Sleeping Sphinx* (published February 1947 in the United States; July 1947 in Britain), has many good elements, but it is ultimately unsatisfactory. It has an intriguing opening scene: Sir Donald Holden returns from the war, having reportedly been killed in battle. Now he must reintroduce himself to the young woman whom he loved before the war but had not dared ask to marry him. She is now engaged to a young and priggish member of Parliament named Derek Hurst-Gore. The book has some excellent scenes, especially the playing of the party game Murder, with each of the participants wearing the mask of a famous murderer. Moreover, *The Sleeping Sphinx* has an interesting narrative structure. Very little of it happens in the reader's presence, and very little is told by the author as omniscient narrator. Much of the story is related in flashbacks, and various characters come, in a sense, on stage and describe events through dialogue. Holden, for example, is told by his commanding officer such things as "The war's been over a year and three months. You're out of the army; out of MI 5; out of everything."[34] Holden doesn't need to be told how long the war has been over; the reader, however, does not have that knowledge, so it must be conveyed somehow. That Carr chooses to introduce these facts in a conversation rather than simply to relate them through narration may be a result of his experience writing for the radio, where dialogue is the main way of conveying information.

Unfortunately, portions of the plot of *The Sleeping Sphinx* come close to being ludicrous. One example is the way Carr handles the issue of wife beating in the solution to the puzzle. The victim, Margot Marsh, had been attacked on several occasions by her husband, Thorley. He hit her with a razor strap and started to strangle her. Carr, who found wife beating abhorrent, has one female character say:

> It sounds almost funny, doesn't it, when you read about it in the newspapers? "My husband hit me about," like a brawl in a cheap pub. It isn't funny; it's horrible. But some women are so dreadfully respectable, and have such a horror of what people will say, that they'll go on and on and put up with anything, rather than have a soul know it isn't a happy marriage.[35]

[****Once again, I shall give away a portion of the solution.] Carr weakens this sympathetic view by revealing that Thorley was not in fact a wife beater. Margot had exactly the opposite of Fay Seton's problem: She was sexually frigid and sometimes went into hysterics when her husband even touched her. Thorley's actions were only attempts to stop her hysterics. Nonetheless, Margot's frigidity suddenly ended when she fell in love with the man who eventually murdered her. Whether it is really possible that Margot could have changed so completely I do not know, but it is too convenient for the requirements of this plot to be convincing.

A minor matter, but also indicating how Carr was bending plot to fit the convenience of the puzzle, is Dr. Fell's activities. When he reveals the solution to the mystery, he has to explain how he knew certain facts that Holden and Thorley Marsh had discussed privately. Rather than having someone tell Dr. Fell—which might have revealed too much too early—

Carr has the gargantuan detective successfully eavesdrop and even shadow Holden. The image is difficult to contemplate with a straight face.

The next Dr. Fell novel, *Below Suspicion* (published in August 1949 in the United States, but not until March 1950 in Britain), is a fascinating experiment in misdirection. Some readers do not approve—"unfair tricks," thunder Jacques Barzun and Wendell Hertig Taylor[36]—and I admit that I find the trickery based too much on the manner of telling rather than the events and the clues themselves. The story begins with a barrister named Patrick Butler visiting Holloway Prison where Joyce Ellis is awaiting trial for murder. We follow some of Joyce's thoughts: "She was quite innocent; she really hadn't killed Mrs. Taylor. . . . She had raged and screamed against the filthy injustice of it." During the trial, we again read her thoughts: "And she wasn't guilty! She wasn't guilty!"[37] The jury finds her not guilty, and for the rest of the book the reader tries to interpret the clues to determine who really killed Mrs. Taylor and, a bit later, Richard Renshaw. Dr. Fell discovers that Renshaw had led, and that Mrs. Taylor had been a member of, a witch cult that not only worshiped Satan but acted as hired poisoners. Who then has replaced Renshaw as leader of the cult?

[****For the third time in a few pages, I am going to reveal much of the solution.] With Dr. Fell's help, Butler discovers that Joyce Ellis is the new head of the witch cult and that she indeed was the killer of Mrs. Taylor and Richard Renshaw. How then could we have followed her innocent thoughts? She believed that the poison had been removed by someone else, and (as Butler says to her):

> The consciousness of guilt never touched your mind. You could rave inwardly about irony and filthy injustice. . . . Someone could have written down your thoughts, up to and during the trial, and it would have been quite fair in the detective-story sense.

"Quite fair" seems a bit too strong for the trick that Carr just pulled, especially considering that one of the rules for detective fiction that Carr included in "The Grandest Game in the World" is that "the criminal shall never turn out to be . . . any character whose thoughts we have been allowed to share."[38]

Carr scholar Geoffrey Webster has suggested to me that Carr planned *Below Suspicion* as Dr. Fell's swan song, and that he hoped to begin a new series featuring Butler alone. Although nothing is known to survive in Carr's correspondence to confirm this speculation, it is not unlikely. Dr.

Fell did not reappear in another novel for nine years, and in *Below Suspicion* Butler is the most vivid character. Carr took the name Patrick Butler from a barrister in G. K. Chesterton's Father Brown story "The Man in the Passage," but he told his family that he based Butler's personality on Adrian Conan Doyle.[39] Even though (or perhaps because) the barrister is a fictional version of Doyle, he is a fantasy figure, similar to such early Carr characters as Patrick O'Riordan. Carr describes Butler over and over as a figure from the eighteenth century. To give but two examples, Butler has "a very real streak of eighteenth-century gallantry," and when he rises in court, "his black gown [sweeps] round him like the cloak of a Regency duellist."[40] Butler is, moreover, bombastic, egotistical, arrogant, opinionated, and occasionally pompous. His statement, "I am never wrong," makes such conceited detectives as Agatha Christie's Hercule Poirot and Rex Stout's Nero Wolfe (as well as Bencolin and John Gaunt) seem the soul of modesty in comparison.

The five Sir Henry Merrivale novels published between 1945 and 1950 follow the same basic pattern as Dr. Fell's cases. None of the books are to be dismissed, and several of them have considerable ingenuity, but their narrative drive occasionally flags. Clarice Carr remembers that for John Dickson Carr, H.M. was a representative of happier days, and it became more and more difficult to continue writing about him. The scrapes that H.M. gets into in these later novels are more overdrawn, and less funny, than in books written only a few years earlier. In *The Curse of the Bronze Lamp* (1945), he argues about the fare with a Cairo taxi driver and ends by gluing a five-pound note over the driver's face. Nowadays, the Arab stereotypes in this chapter are difficult to find amusing. *My Late Wives* (1946) includes a Scotsman named Donald Fergus MacFergus—more related to the music hall than to any genuine resident of Scotland—who teaches H.M. how to play golf. H.M.'s malevolence toward the golf ball, and his attempts to circumvent the rules despite MacFergus's watchful eye, are genuinely funny. (Carr himself did not play golf, but he was amused by those who did: For example, his Uniontown idol, O'Neil Kennedy, had been an avid golfer.) In *The Skeleton in the Clock* (1948), Sir Henry is at "Willaby's" to attend an auction of rapiers, daggers, swords, and other weapons. (Willaby's is, as Carr told Dannay, a barely disguised Sotheby's, where he had purchased many of the weapons in his collection.)[41] H.M. believes that he is the reincarnation of a seventeenth-century Cavalier poet, but as he marches into the auction rooms, his hand resting negligently on an imaginary sword, he is bopped in the face by a shield held by an imperious lady. She blames him for the accident, and H.M. gains revenge by sticking her in the behind with a halberd. In *A Graveyard to Let* (1949), the Great Man causes a riot in the New York subway system, and later demonstrates his ability to play baseball. *Night at the Mocking Widow* (1950) is, like *She Died a Lady,* one of Carr's few attempts to write an English village mystery, and H.M.'s arrival is similar to the wheelchair chase of the earlier novel, even to the participation of the neighborhood dogs. After handing out cigars to the local preteenage boys, H.M. sees his wheeled suitcase head down a hill and run into a man painting a water-color picture. In several of these books, Carr follows his own advice of hiding the most important clues in comic scenes, but H.M. has gotten so close to being a buffoon that it is difficult to believe that he can actually solve cases.

Let's look more closely at the plots of the H.M. novels of this period. *The Curse of the Bronze Lamp* is an expansion of the radio script of the same name. Carr began writing the book at his BBC office in London, probably even before the broadcast of the radio play in November 1944. He com-pleted it in January 1945 while on a holiday at the Bull Hotel, Gerrard's Cross. It was published in the United States in June 1945, and in Britain early the next year under the title *Lord of the Sorcerers.* It was one of Carr's favorite books, probably for two reasons. First, it used a setting he was fond of. He had visited Egypt on one of his early trips abroad (either 1927–28 or 1930) and loved Cairo's colorful atmosphere. (When he was writing the book, Carr conceived of the action as beginning in spring 1935, but he forgot that Sir Henry was in France solving *The Unicorn Mur-ders* at almost the same time. When one of his fans, Francis Wilford-Smith, wrote him about the chronological problems, he cheerfully agreed that the events of *Bronze Lamp* must actually have occurred in 1936.)[42] Second, like the radio script, it contains one of his favorite miracle problems, an impossible disappearance. In the dedication of the book to Ellery Queen, Carr said that "the particular form of the 'miracle' problem set forth here—*not* the locked room, be it said—is perhaps the most fascinating gambit in detective-fiction." In a letter, Carr challenged Dannay to solve the mystery before H.M., but Dannay—somewhat to Carr's chagrin—wrote back that he had done so.[43]

Carr's positive judgment on the book seems to me justified. He ex-panded the radio play's plot primarily by having another character inter-vene in the vanisher's scheme, so that the case becomes one of attempted murder. Nonetheless, as had become typical, H.M. allows the would-be murderer to go free. Perhaps the most interesting part of the book is its depiction of a thoroughgoing cad. In earlier books a cad was someone who beat women; in *The Curse of the Bronze Lamp,* the definition is expanded to include fortune hunters—men who pretend to be in love with women for financial gain.

Carr's next Sir Henry Merrivale novel, *My Late Wives,* was published in October 1946 in the United States but, because of the paper shortage, not until September 1947 in Britain. The story is based on the matrimonial and murderous career of Henri Landru, who married and killed at least ten women between 1915 and 1919. Landru's technique was to have the women disappear—later it was discovered that he had burned their bodies in his oven.[44] Roger Bewlay, Carr's Bluebeard in *My Late Wives,* worked out a different method of disposing of his wives' bodies. In 1934, eleven years before the book begins, Bewlay's last wife had vanished—and so had he. Failure to catch Bewlay is still galling to Inspector Masters. Now, someone has anonymously mailed the actor Bruce Ransom* a play based on Bewlay's career, and containing information known only to the police.

Did Bewlay write the play? To test the play's conclusion that Bewlay could be living as a respected resident of a small village, Ransom decides to go to the village where the packet was postmarked and hint that he is himself Bewlay. Shortly after he arrives, a murder occurs, and it seems obvious that Bewlay is living there under a respectable mask. Ransom has done such a good job of acting that the townspeople think he is Bewlay, and Carr hints that they may be right. The explanation of Bewlay's method of making the bodies disappear is painfully obvious, and many readers will beat H.M. to the punch (and wonder why Masters had not caught on years before); but the identity of the murderer is a surprise. Carr used almost the same method of misdirecting the reader that he had chosen in *He Who Whispers,* but even with that knowledge most readers will choose the wrong least-likely suspect.

The Skeleton in the Clock (published in October 1948 in the United States, and almost a year later in Britain) is in several ways an unsatisfactory detective novel, despite some memorable moments. Much of the book is based on one of Carr's most deeply held beliefs: Women can be so damned frustrating. During the war, Martin Drake fell in love at first sight

---

*Carr seems to have associated the name Bruce Ransom with an actor, for he used the same name in the *Cabin B-13* play "The Man Who Couldn't Be Photographed."

with a young woman wearing a WREN's uniform; therefore (or so it seemed) she called herself Jenny. They became separated at the inevitable train station, but Martin has continued to look for her ever since. When at last he finds her—at Willaby's where H.M. causes such havoc—it turns out that his friend Ruth Callice had known Jenny's whereabouts but said nothing. Moreover, Jenny, who could easily have found Martin but felt the next move was up to him, has gotten engaged to someone else. And even worse is Jenny's grandmother Lady Brayle, representing the domineering woman due for a comeuppance every time she appears in a Carr book: She "meant to get her own way, always got her own way, and accepted this as naturally as she expected a lamp to light at the click of a switch. Whether you liked her, or didn't like her, simply didn't matter."[45]

The story line of *The Skeleton in the Clock* involves the death twenty years before of Sir George Fleet. With no one near him, he was thrown off a flat roof. "It was an accident, of course. Or else . . . It was supernatural murder."[46] Both H.M. and Lady Brayle are eager to gain possession of a macabre item—a case clock with its works replaced by a skeleton. The skeleton turns out (though in a not very persuasive way) to provide evidence explaining Fleet's death. The book, however, has two excellent sections. Carr had toyed with the idea of writing a short story based on the idea that the souls of murderers hanged at a prison might haunt the execution shed. In *The Skeleton in the Clock*, two of the characters challenge malign spirits by spending the night in the execution shed of "Pentecost Prison." Carr creates the eerie atmosphere beautifully, and the scene ends with the discovery of a corpse. Even more effective is the unmasking of the murderer in the "Mammoth Mirror Maze" during a fete held on Lady Brayle's property.

The Skeleton in the Clock was followed by Carr's first novel in twelve years to be set in America, *A Graveyard to Let* (November 1949 in the United States, October 1950 in Britain). This book is a favorite among many readers for its exceptional impossibility. Frederick Manning, fully clothed, dives into a swimming pool in the presence of witnesses. As they watch, his clothes float to the surface, but Manning himself does not appear. When the pool is drained, his body is not there. The problem of a disappearance from a swimming pool had been tried before by S. S. Van Dine in a book called *The Dragon Murder Case* (1933), but Carr's explanation is much more satisfactory. It is an imaginative variation of the method that Carr had already used in several stories, most recently in *The Curse of the Bronze Lamp*. Unfortunately, Manning's motive for vanishing from the swimming pool is unbelievable, and portions of the plot, especially those involving Manning's wife, are ridiculous. Indeed, a key element of the story was already used in Mrs. Henry Wood's well-known Victorian melodrama *East Lynne* (1861), and it is just as unbelievable in Carr's book. And to top things off, H.M. lies to the reader, as he (and Dr. Fell) had done earlier in the decade. But, still, the swimming-pool gimmick is beautifully handled.

Night at the Mocking Widow was published in the United States in June 1950, but (despite a 1951 date in the book itself) not until January 1952 in Great Britain. Although the book has much to praise in it, neither the solution nor the character of H.M. is entirely acceptable. Carr allows him to succumb to the flamboyant charms of his landlady, Virtue Conklin—who spends a good deal of her time advising other women about sex tricks they can use to catch men[47] These discussions are, to put it mildly, a bit heavy-handed. The book also features a mud fight involving a bishop, a vicar, and a young woman wearing only a slip.

Night at the Mocking Widow takes place in 1938 in the small village of Stoke Druid, between Wells and Glastonbury. The geography of the area is dominated by a prehistoric megalith, called the Mocking Widow. H.M. enters the tale when he is asked by an old friend to investigate a nasty case of poison-pen letters, which are signed by someone taking the name of the Mocking Widow. In his essay "The Grandest Game in the World," Carr had praised Dorothy L. Sayers's book *Gaudy Night* for its "overpowering sense of menace," and the "malignant mind" behind the anonymous letters that almost destroyed the cohesiveness of an Oxford college.[48] Carr succeeds in creating a similar air of menace in *Night at the Mocking Widow*. In fact there is no murder until almost the end of the book, and it is not really necessary for the plot. Other parts of the story are also praiseworthy. For almost the first time, Carr depicts a clergyman—the Reverend J. Cadman ("Jimmy") Hunter—in a favorable manner, though he does make him more naive than most men of the cloth would have been. (Chesterton understood that the clergy must know about life, a fact showed in his characterization of Father Brown.)

Night at the Mocking Widow has a fine impossible situation: A young woman sees the Mocking Widow herself in her bedroom, but when the witnesses who are watching the doors and windows break in, they find that the woman is alone. (The solution is taken from the *Cabin B-13* play "The Blindfolded Knife-Thrower.") It is difficult, however, to believe that this locked room was practical. To make the Mocking Widow miraculously appear in the bedroom, the perpetrator had to take extraordinary chances—including asking a witness to disarm another witness but counting on his refusal to do so: "You made your request to take the gun away from Cordy a boys-will-be-boys suggestion. You intimated West wasn't to take it very serious. And West didn't take the gun." Depending on someone's disobeying your request seems chancy even for one of Carr's murderers. Moreover, the criminal has the help of two innocent witnesses—one of whom tells an untruth because she is hysterical and the other because he is nervous.[49]

It is perhaps too easy to exaggerate the weaknesses in the Fell and Merrivale novels of this period. None of them commit what Carr called the "one unforgiveable sin [of] being dull."[50] Yet Carr himself seems to have found some of these books unsatisfactory. He did not write another Dr. Fell novel for a number of years, and he wrote only three more Sir Henry Merrivale novels and one novelette before retiring the Old Man. Carr's objections to life in the later half of the twentieth century were turning his interest toward writing historical fiction.

Chapter 15

RESTORATION RAKES, REGENCY BUCKS, AND SHERLOCKIAN EXPLOITS

Looking back on the early 1950s, Carr told the Swedish mystery critic Jan Broberg that he had decided to write historical romances because he was "in danger of going stale" and needed to write something that would "renew the author":

> It's hard to care who stabbed Sir Oswald in a locked library or to imagine the reader will care either. But a writer *must* enjoy what he is doing, or he can't expect to communicate enthusiasm. If his secondary interest has always been history, it occurs to him that he may generate enthusiasm by combining the two techniques.[1]

It is not an overstatement that Carr was renewed by living in the past with his fictional characters. Three of his historical novels, *The Devil in Velvet*, *Fire, Burn!*, and *Fear Is the Same*, are direct wish fulfillments: The hero of each of them is transported from the twentieth century to an earlier, more romantic era where adventure was possible and gentlemanly values were respected. In *The Devil in Velvet*, for example, Mary Grenville says to Nick Fenton, "You must many times have wished, before this, to be carried back into the past?" Fenton replies in words that express Carr's own longings: "'Wished' is a mild word. God! How I longed for it! How I writhed on a bed of nettles, as men scarify themselves for money or women for social position!"[2]

In 1955, Carr summarized the novels that he was writing at the time:

> The hero is always a gentleman, both by birth and manners. He is highly cultured and cares nothing for the mob. He never wants to own a garage, or explore the wilderness, or fight his way to the presidency of Amalgamated Cookies, Inc. Indeed, he would laugh at such things. . . . When the hero goes into action, he uses his brains and not his fists completely to shatter and destroy the villain: who, in turn, is usually the tough-guy type who has now become almost an American hero. . . . I invariably assume I am writing for people of intelligence and at least decent education; I don't hesitate to make a man speak French or quote Latin.[3]

Besides the fact that Carr's historical novels have more action, whether swordplay or pistol duels or fisticuffs, than he implies, this is a good assessment of many of his later books. The strengths of his historical fiction resemble those of his puzzle novels—strong plotting, vivid though not detailed characterizations, and a colorful sense of setting. Normally, each of his historical romances has one spectacular scene in a place that somehow typifies the period—the Italian opera in *The Bride of Newgate*, the Alhambra music hall in *Scandal at High Chimneys*, Vulcan's gambling den in *Fire, Burn!*, the field of hydrogen-filled balloons in *Captain Cut-Throat*, and so on. The problems in narrative drive in some of his books written a few years earlier—which will reoccur in some of his nonhistoricals of the 1950s—are absent from the historical romances. Carr's pace seldom falters; the tension increases; and the books conclude in slam-bang fashion, with the hero winning the fair charmer, defeating and usually humbling the sneering villain, and resolving the mystery. The first three historicals of the 1950s, *The Bride of Newgate*, *The Devil in Velvet*, and *Captain Cut-Throat*, have strong whodunit problems, and two of them have a seemingly impossible crime, although the clueing tends to be less elaborate than in his detective novels set in the modern world. His publishers and Carr himself looked at the historicals as quite distinct from his detective stories. They were promoted differently, and they were not always thought to be covered by Carr's typical three-book contracts, which specified the publication of detective novels.

Carr was fascinated by what he called in *The Devil in Velvet* the "minutiae" of the past.[4] Before beginning a book, Carr would immerse himself in material about the sights, sounds, and even smells of the age, and in Mamaroneck and elsewhere the details that he had unearthed were often the subjects of his conversations with his friends and family. With only a few exceptions, Carr included an afterword (usually called "Notes for the Curious") in each historical novel explaining "how much is imagination, and how much true." Carr paid a great deal of attention to the language of the past. It is noteworthy how many different speech patterns Carr reproduced. In *The Bride of Newgate,* which takes place in 1815 (the England of the prince regent), the aristocratic characters speak formally when they greet each other ("Your servant, sir"), but in a more lively idiom on other occasions. The arrogance of Sir John Buckland comes out in his language: "Went to see Bedlam once. Watched all the madmen dance and howl. Damme, that was sport! This ain't. Is the demnition convict a deaf-mute? Why don't he speak? Or can't he?" The foppish Jemmy Fletcher speaks like this: "Damme, old boy, but you're ten minutes late. Deuced sorry, you know too . . . The bow window, damme! The famous bow window above the door! Only a very select few can sit in that window. Or they glare daggers at you until you go away. Here! Dash it! Stop!" Blazes, the turnkey at Newgate, has a lower-class dialect: "W'y, bless your innercence. I've seen old Brunskill—afore Langley come in—so full-up o' brandy-and-water he tried to put the halter round the parson's neck 'stead of the coffin meat's. And that's no word of a lie either." For a novel taking place in an earlier period, Carr could write in still a different dialect. *The Devil in Velvet,* set in the England of Charles II, contains such language as: "Hold your clack! God's body! Must you skreek out like a carted dell if a man but use you with court civility?"[5]

The Bride of Newgate (published in March 1950 in the United States and seven months later in Britain) was such a personal book that John Dickson Carr dedicated it to his wife with a graceful quotation from Robert Louis Stevenson: "If this the least be good . . . the praise be thine." His working title for the book had been *The Power of Darkness*[6]—a title taken from one of the *Cabin B-13* radio plays—and it effectively describes both the mood and one of the main events of the novel. But the ultimate choice, *The Bride of Newgate,* is even more effective. The story begins in 1815 with Dick Darwent waiting in Newgate Prison to be hanged for the murder of Sir Francis Orford, whom he apparently killed in a duel. Caroline Ross, accompanied by the brutal and arrogant Sir John Buckstone, comes to the prison to present Dick with a proposition. Caroline will inherit an estate if she marries by the time she is twenty-five. She will do so only if she can immediately become a widow. She finds the idea of going to bed with a man "rather ridiculous and faintly revolting," and probably just as important she objects to the subsidiary position of a woman in marriage. "We are taught to simper, and swoon, and tap coquettishly with a fan, and cry 'Fie!' at some mildly bawdy jest. For what purpose? To 'catch,' dear me, a husband who is not worth the trouble to catch!"[7] In exchange for fifty pounds that he can send to his mistress, Dolly Spencer, Dick agrees to marry Caroline. When, however, Dick remarks that Buckstone's manners are bad, the rake whips him for impudence, thus creating an enmity that will dominate much of the remainder of the novel.

Caroline's plans go awry when word comes that Dick's conviction was illegal. At the time that he was tried, it was not known that his cousin had been killed at Waterloo, and that, consequently, Dick had become a peer of the realm, the Marquess of Darwent. A nobleman could be tried only by the House of Lords. When Dick is retried before the Lords, the nobles find him not guilty, and Dick is freed to enjoy his marriage to Caroline. He is, however, more interested in moving Dolly Spencer into his new establishment.

The Bride of Newgate plunges from adventure to adventure, but within the swashbuckling framework the question remains: Who killed Orford and framed Dick? Carr makes expert use of the technique of gradually revealing the solution, so that small mysteries are solved while the larger ones remain—or are sometimes even made more mystifying, until the final twist comes at the conclusion. In prison, Dick has told the Reverend Horace Cotton what he remembered of the murder. He had been kidnapped and bundled into a "ghost coach" by a strange coachman, later described as wearing a coat covered with graveyard mold. He is carried to a room in a country house where he sees Orford's body. After viewing the room, he is knocked unconscious, and then awakes elsewhere with Orford's corpse nearby and the setting arranged to suggest a duel. Later, however, when he demands to see the room where he was previously taken, he finds that the room is covered with cobwebs and has not been occupied for at least two years.

This plot gimmick originated in a conversation between Carr and Clayton Rawson sometime in 1948 in Frederic Dannay's parlor in Westchester. Rawson said that he had long dreamed of a plot involving the disappearance of all the furniture from a room. Dannay reported to readers of *Ellery Queen's Mystery Magazine* that Carr casually remarked that he saw the way to make the furniture vanish. When *The Bride of Newgate* appeared two years later, Carr told Rawson that the novel contained his solution to the problem.[8] Carr, however, was not satisfied with the way he had worked the trick—in part because in *The Bride of Newgate* the room changes but the furniture stays there—and off and on for the rest of his life he mentioned to various correspondents that he was continuing to work on the problem. As late as August 1975, in answer to a query about the disappearing furniture, he replied, "Though I swear I can solve this one, I never have; and, at so late a date, it's unlikely I ever shall."[9]

Perhaps the most interesting part of *The Bride of Newgate* is the relationship between Caroline Ross and Dick Darwent. She has married for convenience, and maintains her contempt for men and for the marriage market that women must endure. But, as so often happens with Carr's characters, she also falls madly in love with the hero almost at first sight. His standing up to the bullying Buckland in prison catches her interest, and then when he breaks in on her in her milk bath she is completely captivated. But Carr does not let this attraction completely change her character. She remains haughty and continues to believe that women should not be controlled by men. She explains to Dick that she had hated men because "the wife must remain his slave, his servant, the worshipful admirer of his idiocies, until death do them part." Even being in love with Dick does not alter her opinion of what society has done to women: "I would free women from being bond slaves," she says, "yes, and give them rights equal to men!"[10] Caroline tells Dick that they are both rebels against their society, she by believing that women have rights, he by accepting the opening phrases of the United States Declaration of Independence.

In *The Bride of Newgate* we see most clearly Carr's belief in what we can call "aristocratic egalitarianism." He admired gentlemanly conduct and values, and his heroes are often connected with the aristocracy. But like Lafayette, whose life had impressed Carr ever since he heard about his visit to Uniontown, Carr's heroes fight for a fundamental equality of treatment, a respect for the individual. "All men," says Dick Darwent, "are, or should be, equal in their rights before the law." Carr connects this belief, rather oddly, with the fallen House of Stuart, which had been replaced with "dolts . . . of the Hanoverian stock." (That statement is best understood as a reflection of Carr's romanticism and his fondness for lost but noble causes.) Carr did not object to the class system, at least not consistently, but he did despise those who treated their social inferiors arrogantly. Much of *The Bride of Newgate* is built around that issue. Buckland whips Dick when he is helpless. Unlike a man of fashion, who "never even noticed servants, let alone thought of them as human beings," Dick is almost worshiped by his servants because he treats them with consideration. The motive for the murder is related to the same issue: Orford cheated a tradesman simply because he was not his social equal. "Let us suppose, for the sake of argument," says Dick, "there is a hell. Do you know why Frank Orford's soul rots deep in it? ... It was not because Frank cheated a poor devil. ... It was because Frank thought he had a *right* to cheat him."[11] Carr thought of his novels as entertainments, and for him that was enough; still, a strong sense of ethical values comes through. His values, especially when he tried to combine them with admiration for aristocracy, may have been impractical; they may have been primarily a love of a romanticized past; but they are, in the nonclassist sense, noble, and they infuse Carr's best historical novels.

Carr's next foray into historical fiction was a short story, "The Gentleman from Paris," written to fulfill a promise to Dannay to submit another story to the annual contest in *Ellery Queen's Mystery Magazine*. It won the two-thousand-dollar first prize and was published in the April 1950 issue. Carr always considered "The Gentleman from Paris" and "The House in Goblin Wood" his two best short stories. "The Gentleman from Paris" is told in the form of a letter, dated April 14, 1849, from Armand de Lafayette, who has just arrived in New York City. Carr took the careful descriptions of mid-nineteenth-century New York from Charles Dickens's *American Notes*.[12] In a tavern, Lafayette brings a problem to a tipsy gentleman calling himself Thaddeus Perley. An old woman has had a stroke shortly after writing a will in favor of Claudine Thevenet. The will has disappeared, and the old woman cannot speak, but before she dies she tries to indicate the location of the will by moving her eyes toward a stuffed rabbit and a barometer. Carr almost lovingly describes the search for the will. It seems that every place is examined or taken apart, but the will has vanished.

The story has a double punch. First is the solution to the mystery, which turns out to be a bit disappointing. It is difficult to believe that the searchers would not have located the will's hiding place, which is much the same as one in Anna Katherine Green's *The Leavenworth Case* (1878), a book that Carr knew well. Second is the revelation at the conclusion of the real identity of Thaddeus Perley. It was probably this kicker at the end that interested Metro-Goldwyn-Mayer in turning Carr's story into a movie.

Carr was visiting Adrian Conan Doyle at the time the film people showed interest, so his wife handled the negotiations, selling the film rights for about five thousand dollars.[13] The movie, entitled *The Man with a Cloak,* was released by MGM in 1951. Hollywood changed Carr's story in many ways: The dying old woman becomes a dying old man, with a raven on his shoulder; almost as soon as the will is lost, it is rediscovered; and the real identity of the tavern detective is obvious almost as soon as he appears. But the acting, by Joseph Cotten, Barbara Stanwyck, Leslie Caron, and Jim Backus, was good, and the movie makes for an entertaining evening. According to a family story, Carr did not see the movie until it appeared on television, and then he missed the opening credits, which acknowledged that it was based on his story. As the story progressed, he became more and more agitated, finally exploding, "They stole my plot; they stole my words; they stole everything." But he did not think that the film script did a good job of stealing, and a few years after *The Man with a Cloak* was released, he said that it had been "most appallingly filmed."[14] Though it was not appalling, it wasn't as good as the short story it was based on.

Before beginning his next historical novel, *The Devil in Velvet,* Carr accepted an invitation to spend part of the summer of 1950 in Morocco as the guest of Adrian and Anna Doyle. The Doyles had recently moved into a large house on New Mountain outside Tangier. By international agreement Tangier was a free city allowing citizens of all countries that had signed the Algeciras Treaty of 1924 to live there without hindrance. The advantage of all this was a low cost of living and no income tax, and unlike the situation in England servants were easy to find. The disadvantage from Doyle's viewpoint was that after the war Tangier was full of displaced persons, many of whom were financial adventurers and social climbers who falsely claimed royal or aristocratic connections. In his book *Heaven Has Claws,* Doyle sniffed that "dishonor and ingratitude are synonymous with the flow of displaced humanity."[15] Carr, on the other hand, was fascinated by the presence of adventurers and parvenus. He described Tangier in these words:

> It was the air, the very feel and texture of the air, entwining the languor of the Mediterranean with the harshness of North Africa. It was a leopard's skin, all claws removed. It was bright, timeless, proud, yielding. You drank the air, and were at one with the pagan.[16]

Carr, however, was ailing during his Tangier holiday. He had experienced some eye trouble in the early months of 1950, and around the same time had suffered from a fistula that threatened to lead to an abscess. In Mamaroneck, he had had a painful but not serious operation for the fistula, but it failed to solve the problem. In Tangier, he needed the operation done again by Dr. Fraser Anderson, an expatriate Scot from Aberdeen. Carr set part of *Behind the Crimson Blind* next to Anderson's nursing home. The surgeon himself is an offstage character under the name of "Dr. MacPhail"; he is described as having "a head like a respectable Caesar" with "the twinkle in his eyes" and "the competence of his manner."[17] Neither the twinkle nor the manner, however, turned out to be sufficient to cure the fistula. Back in the United States in the autumn, Carr was on light medication to keep the discomfort down, and with Dr. William Barrett, a close friend in Mamaroneck, hovering about to make certain he was recovering, Carr wrote *The Devil in Velvet* in his dressing gown and slippers.[18]

The Devil in Velvet, published in April 1951, was Carr's favorite of his historical novels. At some 123,000 words, the book was one of his longest works, but even though he was not well when he wrote it, the writing went quickly, and he became so involved in the characters and the events that he sometimes came down from his attic office around dinner and acted out some of the scenes. It was during one of these sessions that Carr outlined an idea for the conclusion of the book in which the hero actually changed history. Clarice, however, proposed a different way of handling that question, and it was her suggestion that ended up in the published book.[19]

The Devil in Velvet is Carr's first novel to depend on the reality of the supernatural for its plot. He had often suggested the possibility of a supernatural explanation of the impossible events in his earlier novels, but he always provided a rational explanation. *The Burning Court* is something of an exception to this generalization, but in that book the supernatural epilogue is not a necessary part of the plot. *The Devil in Velvet*, however, begins with Professor Nicholas Fenton quite literally selling his soul to Satan, and toward the conclusion we discover that one of the female characters had done the same thing seven years earlier "because she found the world insufferably dull and she was overfond of men." Fenton's agreement with Satan is that in exchange for his soul, the Devil will transport him back to 1675 and place him in the body of his namesake, Sir Nicholas Fenton, a "wencher, rakehelly, gamester" of the court of King Charles II. The Devil is one of the most convincing characters that Carr ever created. He speaks like a gentleman, but he is no gentleman. Fenton tells him, "You are history's greatest cheat. . . . You would not give fair play to a sick dog."[20] The bargaining concludes as the Devil issues Fenton a warning:

He will retain his own identity within Sir Nicholas's body, but if he should lose control of his temper, Sir Nicholas will take over.

Although the Devil tells him that it is impossible to change history, Fenton plans to try. He has a seventeenth-century manuscript that describes the events leading up to the murder of Sir Nicholas's wife, Lydia, on June 10, 1675, and the modern Fenton will do everything in his power to prevent it. Carr ratchets the tension tighter and tighter as June 10 approaches. The solution revealing who has been scheming against Lydia is dependent on some unfair statements made early in the novel, but the strength of the book is not closely related to its detective elements. The novel has terrifying undertones that go beyond historical reconstruction.

Though he probably never would have admitted it, Carr made a psychological point in *The Devil in Velvet*: Professor Fenton's struggle to keep Sir Nicholas at bay can be read as an attempt to control the beast within all of us. When Fenton almost loses his temper, Carr says, "Professor Fenton, as though fighting to shut down a coffin lid with some rolling horror inside, felt the struggle cease and the lid click shut."[21] In many of his novels, Carr had controlled his fear that the universe may indeed be chaotic by providing human, material, and rational explanations for seemingly impossible events. In some books, however, especially *The Burning Court*, human rationality was not enough, and chaos threatened to burst through. In *The Devil in Velvet* we see that the chaos, the irrationality, may not only be part of the universe but also be within us as humans. What keeps it under control is a code of behavior; when anger takes over, the coffin lid rises and the monster emerges. Earlier in this biography, I quoted Bencolin's comment touching on the same matter: "To examine one's own mind and heart, and explore them fully, is a poisoned doctrine." It is in part this understanding that we are not entirely what we appear on the surface that explains Carr's constant mask imagery.

On January 7, 1952, *Westinghouse Studio One*, a CBS series, broadcast a live dramatization of *The Devil in Velvet*, starring Whit Bissell and Phyllis Kirk. The program, which survives on kinescope (and has recently become available on videotape), was well acted and imaginatively staged, with elaborate sets and costumes, and trickier camera work than usual for early television. Unfortunately, the adaptation did not follow Carr's novel closely, and Nicholas Fenton's attempt to change the past was resolved entirely differently.[22]

Unlike Nicholas Fenton, John Dickson Carr had to live in his own age. No matter where he took up residence during the 1950s, however, he could not be happy and he would soon pull up stakes to try somewhere else. Sometimes he would simply tell Clarice and the children that it was time to move, and he would go to London or Tangier and expect her to sell the house and pack up the belongings. She believes that her husband's unhappiness was based on more than his dislike of the postwar world. She thinks that he was somehow running away from himself, but can make no suggestion about what he found wrong with being John Dickson Carr except, possibly, his physical size.[23] Perhaps the coffin that he sensed within all of us occasionally seemed to open in him; he never said, however, what he saw within it. Whatever the explanation for his restlessness, if we say that Carr had a "home" when he lived in a place for at least two months, he had at least eight different homes between 1951 and 1954. Clarice was often but not always with him during these peregrinations. Bonnie and Mary needed regular schooling, so after Clarice's father died in 1952 and she inherited property in Kingswood, she often resided there while John was elsewhere. As was the case during the middle 1940s, however, they did not consider themselves separated, and when they were on the same continent, stayed with each other over long weekends.

When he returned to Mamaroneck from Tangier in the summer of 1950, Carr was already considering leaving the United States and again taking up residence in England. The Labour party had almost lost its parliamentary majority in the February election, and Churchill was talking as though the return of the Tories to power was inevitable—as indeed happened some twenty months later. In March 1951, Carr cabled his British agents that he would return to London in the late spring and declare permanent residence.[24] But plans were delayed because John and Clarice's oldest daughter, Julia, left Wellesley and planned to get married. She had fallen in love with a young man named Richard McNiven who lived across the street from the Carrs in Mamaroneck. Dick was an avid mystery fan, but he soon learned not to praise the works of Hammett and Chandler in front of his future father-in-law. It says something for his commitment to Julia that Dick switched his allegiance to the classical fair-play writers. At the time of their marriage, Julia was only eighteen years old, but they had been dating for two years, and Dick had two jobs—he was an instructor at New York University and he had a full-time position on Wall Street. They were married on July 14, 1951, after (Dick remembers) Clarice rummaged through John's desk drawer in search of uncashed checks.[25]

Almost immediately following the wedding, John and Clarice Carr with Bonnie and Mary headed off to London, having arranged to have their Mamaroneck house sold in their absence. They stayed at Duke's Hotel in St. James's Place. In *The 9 Wrong Answers*, published the next year, Carr recorded his feelings on returning to London: "It isn't beautiful, like the New York skyline. It doesn't turn your head, as Paris does. It's only a great mass of dingy brick and stone, yet you dream about it. There must be magic; but where's the magic?" As he had done about Tangier, Carr summarized his feelings by finding the magic in the air of London: "The very air seemed old, yet clean and fresh to breathe."[26] London was celebrating the Festival of Britain, and everything was floodlit at night. The Carrs felt certain that the fuel shortage that had made the winter of 1946–47 so miserable was at last over. They went out to look for a house in London and discovered that it was a buyers' market. "Eager house-agents," Carr reported, "stood ready at the door to jerk you in." They soon found, however, why buyers were sought so eagerly. The fuel shortage was in fact not over: It was difficult to get coal, and nearly impossible to get gas and electricity.[27] Carr eventually decided that he could not go through another winter without heat. It would be better, he decided, to take the family to Tangier. They stayed in London for about three months—long enough for John to reestablish his connections with the BBC and to accept Val Gielgud's request that he write a series of twelve radio scripts based on the Sherlock Holmes stories. Gielgud thought Carr was the only person who could get around the obstacles that Adrian Doyle often threw up when it came to adapting his father's work.[28]

Toward the end of October 1952, Carr flew to Morocco and stayed with Adrian Doyle while he looked for a house for the family. Within a short time he had rented a former hotel called the Villa Mimosa. With eight rooms and a garden, it overlooked the Mediterranean. Clarice, Bonnie, Mary, and their housekeeper-nannie, Violet Andrews, soon joined him. Villa Mimosa had two Spanish-speaking caretakers; Carr wrote from Tangier that he and the caretakers "mutually misunderstood each other."

> Since Clarice and I speak only English and French there have been some scenes with electricians, plumbers and telephone officials, to say nothing of a water-rate collector who was looking for a defaulting previous tenant.

Clarice enjoyed the four months they lived there, especially the seafront and the native sections around the Kasbah, but she hated the treatment of animals as beasts of burden and the way that live poultry was carried bundled together by the feet. John spent time with Bonnie and Mary, reading to them stories by Chesterton and Dickens and other favorite authors. Mary, who had found John a distant father, discovered to her surprise that he could be a good companion.[29]

While he was in Tangier, Carr's seemingly constant problems with the fistula flared up again. He had already had two operations, but the difficulty had not been solved, and an abscess threatened. On December 23, 1951, Dr. Anderson, whom Carr called the "guid Scots surgeon," operated on him once again. The operation appeared to be successful, but he came out of the ordeal quite weak, and the surgeon ordered him not to work for about two months. Carr, however, reported to Gielgud that "I fooled 'em," and went ahead with his writing anyway, some of which he was doing in his head.[30] Despite his fragile health during the winter and early spring of 1952, Carr worked on the Sherlock Holmes scripts for the BBC, and he continued to write detective novels. He completed *The 9 Wrong Answers* and dedicated it to Gielgud in January 1952, with a reference to the planned radio series.

The Carrs returned to London in April 1952, staying again at Duke's Hotel, and within a week or two, John called on Gielgud to discuss the Holmes series. "With," said Gielgud, "a humility as surprising as it was unexpected in any author," Carr told him that he did not like the three plays that he had already sent to the BBC. He asked for their return and promised to start again on the series. Gielgud agreed and in a BBC memorandum expressed concern for Carr's health.[31] There were already signs that the most recent operation had not been a success, but Carr was determined to ignore his health problems.

Around June or early July 1952, John Carr decided to return to the United States, staying at the Gramercy Park Hotel, while Clarice and the two daughters went back to Bristol. His purpose in going to New York was to join Adrian Doyle, who was bringing a Sherlock Holmes exhibit that he had put together in London the previous year. Doyle had sponsored a re-creation of the sitting room at 221B Baker Street. The room captured the somewhat cluttered, claustrophobic atmosphere of the late Victorian and Edwardian age, and it included the famous bust of Holmes that played a pivotal role in "The Adventure of the Empty House" as well as mementoes of other Holmesian cases, from Violet Smith's bicycle to the Giant Rat of Sumatra. The Carrs had visited the exhibit in London, and John used it for the climactic scene in *The 9 Wrong Answers*. He was a guest at the opening of the American version of the exhibit in July 1952, and it was at that time that he and Adrian Doyle decided to write a new series of Holmes stories based on cases mentioned but never recorded in the original stories.

Carr and Doyle told mystery writer Herbert Brean, who wrote about the collaboration for *Life* magazine, that they had first thought about creating new Holmes cases while Carr was gathering material for *The Life of Sir Arthur Conan Doyle,* but nothing came of the idea at that time. Sometime in July 1952, according to Carr,

> We were having coffee late one night in Adrian's suite at the Gladstone, and got to talking about Doyle's penchant for introducing American characters into his stories. Once again the project we had long discussed came up and Adrian said, "Well, why don't we get down to it?" I said that for some time I had had an idea involving seven clocks, and began outlining it.

Brean reported that the two men prepared themselves by studying the minute points of Sir Arthur Conan Doyle's style—his use of commas, the length of his sentences, and so on. The actual method of collaboration as reported by Brean sounds like a publicity release, but it is worth quoting:

> The usual method was for each to pour out his ideas for plot points, phrases or bits of dialog [sic], and the other to criticize or improve. As the story developed, either would scrawl sentences on sheets of paper as they were jointly agreed on; Carr would make notes on a typewriter when one was at hand. Says Doyle, "Some of it is written line by line alternately: we cannot tell, nor can anyone else, who wrote which phrase. When we write, our brains are each a half, forming one whole." Usually the halves became a whole with both men lounging and leaping up by turns to pace, argue or gesticulate. Doing dialog one often took the part of Holmes and the other of Watson. . . . Arguments about fine points were not infrequent. . . . They found that this intense joint concentration was best continued for two hours at a time at most.[32]

By the end of July, after the two men had completed "The Adventure of the Seven Clocks" and begun "The Adventure of the Gold Hunter," Adrian undertook to persuade his brother, Denis, and sister, Jean, to support the project. It was not an easy task. He himself had always opposed pastiches of his father's works when done by others, even to the point of threatening legal action, and Denis believed that no one, not even Adrian, should add to the canon. Adrian argued that the earlier pastiches had been bad, but that the new ones would be in the true Holmesian style. These, he continued, would have large sales because the name of Conan Doyle would be on the cover. Moreover, Adrian predicted confidently that with serial rights, films, radio, television, and so on, their father's books would also increase in sales. He suggested that the estate receive one-third of the profits, Carr one-third, and himself one-third. Jean Conan Doyle never consented, and Denis would only agree not to oppose publicly the new stories (but vociferously expressed in private his dislike of the entire project). Although Adrian never officially received the permission of his father's estate, he nonetheless included what he admitted was a "perfectly fictitious" authorization notice when the first story was printed at the end of 1952.[33]

In August 1952, Adrian Conan Doyle, who was always a good publicist, announced the projected series in the press, and David Higham, Carr's British agent (who had heard nothing about the plans), sent Carr an urgent letter asking what was going on. Meanwhile, Doyle had introduced Carr to his American agent, Rene de Chochor of James O. Brown Associates. Carr had had no United States representation since he had left the Ann Watkins Company around 1946, and he found Chochor a congenial person. The problem with all this was that Adrian insisted that his British agent, John Farquharson, act for both Carr and Doyle for British and non-English-language rights. From a distance of forty years, the squabbling over who would represent whom is amusing, but it was a serious matter at the time since a great deal of money was expected to be involved. The situation must have been a strain on Carr. Both sides wrote to him in Tangier, where he had gone with Adrian to work on more of the Holmes pastiches, and finally in early November 1952 he settled the matter in typically generous fashion by saying that he would pay both Higham and Farquharson from his share of the proceeds.[34]

The episode of the competing agents was only one problem that Carr had to deal with in Tangier that would result in his failure to complete his part of the new Holmes short stories. Before discussing the pastiches any further, we shall look at the various crises that emerged late in 1952 and early in 1953. Although he wrote to his wife in Bristol that he was in good health, Carr was in fact not well. In August, David Higham had told Val Gielgud that Carr's "general condition is giving cause for the greatest anxiety." Late that month, still claiming that his health was good, he told

Clarice that, since the fistula was giving no trouble, he planned to enter a hospital and have the whole thing "tidied up once and for all." What he meant was that, despite the failure of the two operations he had in Tangier, he planned to enter Dr. Fraser Anderson's nursing home for treatment. He moved into the nursing home early in September 1952 and began a treatment of what he described as "injections with some brand-new chemical discovery." He did not describe what the chemical might have been, or how it was supposed to stop a fistula from developing into an abscess. Within a month, however, he announced that he had been cured. "I can scarcely believe it," he said.[35] His skepticism, such as it was, was justified. Soon the difficulty returned.

Meanwhile, yet another problem arose. Since 1949, Carr had been dissatisfied with both Harper & Brothers' and Hamish Hamilton's efforts in promoting his books. He felt he was being taken for granted, but (or so he said three years later) he did not do anything about it because of the distractions of his health problems. His contract with Hamish Hamilton, Ltd., signed in 1947, had called for extremely favorable royalty rates—15 percent to 6,000 copies, 20 percent thereafter. In 1950 and 1951, Hamilton asked for a lower royalty on *The Bride of Newgate* and *The Devil in Velvet* on the grounds that they were substantially longer than his usual books and that the paper shortage in England was increasing the production costs. The new royalty, agreed to by Carr's agents, for *The Devil in Velvet* was 15 percent to 10,000 copies, 20 percent thereafter. At about the same time, Harpers also requested and received a lower royalty. The old royalty had been 12.5 percent to 5,000 copies and 15 percent thereafter; the new was 10 percent to 5,000, rising then to 15 percent.[36] Carr's unhappiness increased when Hamish Hamilton wrote to him in the middle of November 1952 that his contemporary mystery novel, *The 9 Wrong Answers,* had an advance sale of more than a thousand copies fewer than *The Devil in Velvet.* Hamilton complained that the book was too long for "a modern mystery novel." Harpers' advance sales on the book were also disappointing, although numbers do not survive in the correspondence. All of this made Carr question whether Harper & Brothers and Hamish Hamilton were the best publishers to handle his books. "In all likelihood," he wrote to Hamilton, "no other publisher can do better with my books than you have done in England and Harpers in America, but I feel it is time someone else had the opportunity to try."[37]

At the end of 1952 in Tangier, Carr was working not only on the Sherlock Holmes stories, but also on two books—a Sir Henry Merrivale novel that would become *The Cavalier's Cup* and a new historical set in Napoleonic France to be called *Captain Cut-Throat*. He was confident that *Captain Cut-Throat* would outdo the sales of his previous historicals, but certain as well that neither Harpers nor Hamilton would promote it vigorously. Since he owed Harpers one more book on his contract, he told them that they could not have *Captain Cut-Throat* but instead "a detective novel, which I can write in a month." He added, in a letter to Hamilton, that it would be "of an acceptably short length."

As Carr told David Higham, he was furious when he wrote to Hamilton, but "this in itself is of no importance, since I sometimes am furious." He was, however, sincere that he wanted to find new publishers. Hamilton's four-book contract, of course, was a problem, but Higham thought that since the contract specified "detective novels" there was no requirement that Hamilton be offered a historical like *Captain Cut-Throat*. Whatever Carr had believed, the consternation in the offices of Harpers and Hamilton showed that he was not taken for granted, or to be more precise *would* not be taken for granted. Hamilton immediately wrote a four-page letter to Carr asking for further explanation and announcing his attention to fly to Tangier to continue the discussion. Soon cooler heads prevailed, and Hamilton did not set off for Morocco. Although Carr had not initiated the dispute merely as a ploy to screw better terms out of Hamilton and Harpers, that is what happened. Cass Canfield of Harpers told Carr that if his firm were allowed to publish *Captain Cut-Throat*, he would restore the old royalty rate. Moreover, he offered a bet of one thousand dollars that Harpers could promote the book so well that it would outsell his most recent books. If he failed, he promised to release Carr from all remaining contractual obligations. Carr had calmed down by this time, and he agreed. A similar arrangement was made with Hamilton.[38]

While all this was going on, Carr and Doyle were continuing to work on the Sherlock Holmes pastiches. Carr was never happy collaborating with another writer, and after writing "The Adventure of the Seven Clocks" and "The Adventure of the Gold Hunter" together, the two men agreed that each would have primary responsibility for individual stories. By early October, Carr had written "The Adventure of the Highgate Miracle" and "The Adventure of the Wax Gamblers," and he had devised plots for the next two stories, "The Adventure of the Black Baronet" (for which Doyle would do most of the writing) and "The Adventure of the Sealed Room" (for which Carr planned to do the writing). It was important that the series, now called *The Exploits of Sherlock Holmes*, be completed, for contracts were being prepared. Chochor sold "The Adventure of the Seven Clocks" to *Life* magazine for ten thousand dollars, and *Collier's* magazine bought rights in the successor stories for forty thousand dollars. A total of twelve stories was planned.[39]

By the end of December 1952, Carr could no longer take the pressure. Not only was Doyle demanding more stories, but Carr's health was breaking down; he was having difficulties with agents and publishers; and the BBC was exerting pressure on Carr to complete the Sherlock Holmes radio plays for which he had already received partial payment. Carr's British agents confidently told Gielgud that "John has come to life again," but in fact the collapse was near. Doyle had just completed "The Adventure of the Black Baronet"—he told his brother that he had done about 90 percent of the writing of that story—and Carr had begun the next one, "The Adventure of the Sealed Room." He had written only three pages when, on January 2, 1953, he began a two-month drinking binge. He did not stop until Clarice Carr flew from England to Tangier to rescue him. With the fistula, the drinking, and the chloral hydrate, he was in bad shape, weighing only about ninety pounds. Clarice took him back to the United States where he began to recover from some of his health problems. The fistula, however, was still there.[40]

Doyle meanwhile was in a tizzy. Furious at Carr, he had no choice but to complete the final six stories himself, and *Collier's* magazine published them under his name alone. Before Carr's spell began, Doyle and Carr had been considering a contract for American rights to a book edition of the stories. Random House offered six thousand dollars advance—a surprisingly small sum considering the amount paid for serial publication—but Doyle was certain the book would be a bestseller and make up in royalties what it hadn't gotten in advances. Unfortunately, his frequently expressed prediction that there would be a television series based on the book did not come true. Only one of the stories was dramatized: "The Adventure of the Black Baronet," starring Basil Rathbone as Holmes and Martyn Green as Watson, appeared on CBS's television version of *Suspense* on May 26, 1953. It was, moreover, disappointing that in spite of Doyle's great hopes that a major British magazine would publish the stories, they were eventually sold to a newspaper, *The Evening Standard*, which printed all but one of them in the autumn and winter of 1953–54. The newspaper publicized the stories heavily, using sandwichboard men in ulsters and deerstalkers to announce the series, and even having a hansom cab clip-clop along the London streets with representations of

Holmes and Watson seated inside. One result, however, was that Val Gielgud, who did not know that Carr was again very sick, wrote a grumbling
memorandum wondering how Carr could find time to write these stories
and yet ignore his agreement for the Holmes radio series.[41]

The United States edition of *The Exploits of Sherlock Holmes* was published by Random House at the end of March 1954, and the British about a
month later, by John Murray. Both editions begin with a publisher's note
stating that Carr could not complete his part of the project because of illness. Sales, though acceptable, did not come close to fulfilling Doyle's optimistic predictions; only some fifty-five hundred advance orders were
recorded in the United States, and eight thousand copies had been sold
by early June.[42] (The book, however, has had staying power, going
through several printings of the original editions and being reprinted in
paperback in both Britain and the United States.)

Even before the stories began to appear in *Life* and *Collier's*, some Sherlock Holmes enthusiasts condemned them. Considering that Adrian
Conan Doyle had himself opposed attempts by other writers to continue
the Holmes adventures, this reaction is not surprising. On the whole, the
reviews were divided between those of the general literary world, which
praised the stories, and those from the Holmes specialists, who picked
holes in them. On the positive side, *Time* magazine said that "by sticking
strictly to the original ingredients and prose style, authors Carr and Doyle
handle the job very well. . . . Only Sir Arthur's ghost is likely to be really
critical of this loving attempt to relight the master's dottles." On the negative, the gentlemanly Vincent Starrett wrote that "inevitably they lack the
old magic, the divine spark, as I suppose the two authors would be the
first to admit." Anthony Boucher said, "It is an agreeable and entertaining
collection, containing some of the best (largely by Carr) and a few of the
worst (chiefly by Doyle) of such imitations to date." The most intemperate
comments came from Earle F. Waldridge writing under the name "Jabez
Wilson" in *The Baker Street Journal*:

> On the 30th of March—a day that will live in infamy—a volume
> dubbed *The Exploits of Sherlock Holmes* heaved itself over the Baker
> Street horizon. (It might better have been named *Sherlock Holmes Ex-
> ploited*). . . . Mr. Carr was then smitten with a mysterious illness—
> probably the curse of the Conans—and Adrian alone was left to
> concoct the rest of this witch's brew, which he did with right good
> will but dubious results.[43]

In evaluating *The Exploits of Sherlock Holmes* after forty years, the most obvious point is that the stories plotted by Carr are extremely imaginative. In several of them, Carr took gimmicks from his earlier writings but put them into new contexts. Carr took the murder method in "The Gold Hunter" from his *Suspense* radio script "The Devil's Saint." "The Wax Gamblers" is a version of another of Carr's scripts, "Menace in Wax." "The Highgate Miracle" has the method for an impossible disappearance that Carr had used several times, most recently in *A Graveyard to Let*. The deathtrap in "Black Baronet" goes back to one of Carr's earliest stories— "'As Drink the Dead . . .'" from *The Haverfordian*. "The Sealed Room," the final story plotted before Carr collapsed, is a straight locked-room puzzle. The gimmick is original, but Carr would use it again in his final novel, *The Hungry Goblin*. Some of Carr's phrases, however, do not remind the reader of Sir Arthur Conan Doyle. For example, the sentiment "he is by no means a swaggering figure of the imagination; too many such men lived in our grandfather's time" in "The Wax Gamblers" is pure John Dickson Carr.[44] The six stories by Adrian Doyle alone are closer to the original Sherlock Holmes stories in their language. Less happily, they are also closer in plot; each of the tales has borrowed its main story line from one of the Holmes adventures written by Sir Arthur Conan Doyle. But writing exact pastiches of another author's work is impossible, and even with the inevitable flaws, Carr and Doyle produced an enjoyable collection.

John Dickson Carr's health improved briefly after Clarice brought him from Tangier to New York City, but then the fistula finally turned into the long-threatened abscess. By the summer of 1953 his condition was serious. John was living in a hotel in New York City when Clarice flew in from England in July to stay with Julia for the birth of their first grandchild. As soon as she saw John, she realized that something would have to be done immediately. She still says she "kidnapped" him, though perhaps "strongly persuaded" would be the better description. Early in July, she took him out to Mamaroneck, where Dr. William Barrett did the surgery. When Julia entered the hospital to have her baby—a daughter named Lynn Clarice, born on July 23, 1953—her father was still in the hospital recovering from his operation.[45] At long last, medical treatment proved successful, but the recuperation period lasted more than six months.

After he had fully recovered, Carr wrote to Anthony Boucher that he had had "all sorts of unpleasant fears—the sort everyone gets." He had genuinely thought that he might die, and somewhat later a physician confirmed that he had waited almost too long for the surgery. Carr reported that, "shorn of profanity," the doctor said:

> You bloody fool, it's a wonder you didn't bloody well so-and-so die. I still don't bloody well this-and-that see how you lived. Having lived, however, you will be better than ever. Your bloody adjectival trouble was that you wanted to be well too soon, and that was impossible.[46]

Shortly before Christmas 1953, Carr was well enough to join Clarice, Bonnie, and Mary in Kingswood. In early February 1954 he had a final checkup by an English surgeon, with the verdict that his healing was complete: "I can now jump out of a window and land on my stern without danger to it, if I should feel inclined for such an unusual exercise."[47]

His health and enthusiasm restored, Carr looked back over what he had written during his illnesses. He was not pleased. He summarized the situation to Boucher: "Like a fool I *would* write during this time, against all advice. There was no necessity to write; I didn't need the money; but, for some nonsensical reason, not to write seemed like giving in to something or other, and almost a sin." The result, he said, was that he had published "several indifferent novels."[48] Besides the collaborative Sherlock Holmes pastiches, Carr had written one short story and three novels during these years. The word "indifferent" describes the story, "The Black Cabinet"—a historical romance set in 1858 Paris—quite adequately. It first appeared in the 1952 Mystery Writers of America anthology, *Twenty Great Tales of Murder*, but I do not know if Carr wrote it directly for the MWA or submitted it first to a magazine, which then rejected it. (A number of years later, Frederic Dannay decided that it was not good enough to reprint in *Ellery Queen's Mystery Magazine*.)

Carr's judgment of "indifferent" was too negative about one of his novels during this period, *The 9 Wrong Answers*, but overly generous about the other two—*Behind the Crimson Blind* and *The Cavalier's Cup*. *The 9 Wrong Answers* was written primarily in Tangier in the later months of 1951, and it was published almost simultaneously in Britain and the United States in October 1952. Anthony Boucher, who almost always praised Carr's novels, wrote in *The New York Times* that it was "below Mr. Carr's standards," and he echoed an opinion that Carr had already received from Hamish Hamilton: The book, Boucher said, is of "inordinate length."[49] Most readers would agree with Boucher that the novel does not belong at the top of Carr's works primarily because it takes almost one hundred pages for the story really to begin. As an example of plot dexterity, however, *The 9 Wrong Answers* is difficult to equal. In common with most of his other nonhistorical novels written during the 1950s, it is based on a radio script, in this case "Will You Make a Bet with Death?" written for *Suspense* in 1942. Bill Dawson, like earlier Carr heroes, looks for Adventure in the Grand Manner. He agrees to take the place of Larry Hurst, who is terrified of his sadistic uncle, Gaylord Hurst. As in the radio script, the old man traps the younger one into a wager. Gay bets that he can kill Bill-as-Larry within three months. (One of the attacks on Dawson is made at the BBC, where Carr introduces some of his old colleagues under assumed names. Val Dyall, for example, appears as Del Durrand.) At the climax Carr proposes the solution that he had used in "Will You Make a Bet with Death?" then withdraws it as not being properly matched to the criminal's character. The ultimate solution is a superb job of misdirection—although it does have some similarities with an Agatha Christie short story called "The Dream," published in *The Strand* in 1938 when Carr was also contributing stories to that magazine.

The 9 Wrong Answers shows how Carr could play with the form in order to make it "the grandest game in the world." Within the book, Carr included footnotes for the experienced reader of detective novels. Every time the reader thinks that he or she has figured out the twist Carr will put on events, Carr explains that the reader's guess is another wrong answer. Unfortunately, the final footnote giving the ninth wrong answer is itself wrong. (In that note, Carr claims not to have misdescribed a character, merely misled the reader in a legitimate way. In fact, he does directly misdescribe him in several instances.) I suspect that Carr would have done some rewriting had he not had one of the fistula operations just as he was completing the book. In addition, Hamish Hamilton and Anthony Boucher were correct that the novel is wordy. About a year after the dispute with Hamilton about publishing future Carr books, Carr agreed with the British publisher that "the book is too long anyway." When Bantam Books published a paperback edition of the book in 1955, the publisher obtained Carr's permission to abridge it by around 15 percent.[50] Since that time, all American and British paperbacks have used the shortened text, though not all of them admit it.

The final two Sir Henry Merrivale novels, both written during this period, reflect more clearly than *The 9 Wrong Answers* the pain of John Dickson Carr's illnesses, and I shall discuss them together. During the early months of 1951 while he was ill and often sedated, he worked on a book setting H.M. in Tangier. The novel was first called *The Mystery of the Crimson Blind,* but soon after its completion in May 1951, he changed the title to the more effective *Behind the Crimson Blind.* The book was published in January 1952 in the United States, and in October 1952 in Britain. Carr's working title for the next and, as it turned out, final H.M. novel was *The Unreasonable Doubt.* Although he wrote to Clarice from New York in September 1952 that he had completed the book, he decided to do some further work on it that autumn in Tangier. By November, he had retitled it *The Cavalier's Cup,* but he left a phrase in the final chapter that justifies the original title.[51] The United States edition of the book was published in May 1953, the British in January 1954.

Both books pay much more attention to comedy than to plot, but H.M.'s antics do not seem to arise spontaneously from his character—they are simply tossed in without much regard to the story line. In *Behind the Crimson Blind,* the Old Man is welcomed in Tangier with a band and a red carpet, and he pompously struts across accompanied by two women whom the Arabs think are his mistresses—"con tetas grandes," as one of them puts it.[52] He also disguises himself as a Moslem holy man and unbelievably fools the natives into accepting him. In *The Cavalier's Cup,* he takes singing lessons from "Signor Ravioli," who speaks in an accent reminiscent of Chico Marx. Moreover, especially in *Behind the Crimson Blind,* H.M.'s character almost seems to be disintegrating. For instance, he visits a brothel and is disappointed that he is supposed to bring in a woman rather than have one waiting for him. Later, he plans to take an Arab woman as his mistress.[53] Even more deplorably, when he is attacked in the Kasbah by a knife-wielding thief, he calmly kills him without compunction.

Behind the Crimson Blind is more violent than any other H.M. novel. One of the heroes actually plans to murder another character after first challenging him to turn around and face him. That consideration, according to Sir Henry Merrivale, makes it "a fair duel . . . a sportin' proposition and a straight one. Cor! I'd like to wring the scrawny neck of the red-robed mummy of a judge who said it wasn't." And there's worse: An accomplice of the criminal tries to escape, but the Tangier police shoot him down with a barrage of bullets. Not only is the graphic description of this scene quite unlike Carr, but from the viewpoint of the story it is foolish, since the police action effectively removes the one person who can identify the main criminal. One of the heroines comments, "Oh, I didn't mind the bullets so much. In fact, I rather liked them."[54]

As this line indicates, Carr's attitude toward the women in *Behind the*

Crimson Blind and *The Cavalier's Cup* is embarrassing. After the intelligent and strong (though often frustrating) women in his books of the 1940s, it is distressing to find that empty-headed ginches return in H.M.'s final novels—indeed, a new term appears, "ginchlet."[55] H.M.'s favorite type of woman is "breathless but not much inhibited." The female characters in these two books want men to be "silly-wonderful," and they look at them admiringly, even when they admit to consorting with women of the street. Above all, these women want sex. Carr's women were always refreshingly open about sex, but in *Behind the Crimson Blind* and *The Cavalier's Cup* they "smile dreamily" and nearly swoon every time they think about it.[56] Carr clearly wanted to be modern and sophisticated in describing sexual relations, but he ended up being merely awkward and a bit jejune. In *The Cavalier's Cup*, for example, Congressman William Harvey seduces Elaine Cheeseman, a Labour member of Parliament, by saying, "The hell with your intellect! You're the most beautiful thing I ever saw." This approach may not be suave, but subtlety is unnecessary for the congressman. He simply overwhelms her protests and takes her into the library. After a few hours there, they are in "an exalted mood" when her (soon to be former) fiancé, a Labour radical named Hereward Wake, shows up. With Miss Cheeseman dressed only in her underwear, they chase Wake while shooting at his posterior with a bow and arrow. In both books, moreover, Carr expresses sweeping generalizations about women, what sort of sexual techniques they like, and their penchant for lying: "She had as much taste and indeed natural preference for telling lies as any other normal woman."[57] And somehow Carr is quite certain that women enjoy seeing other women dancing naked: "All women like to see these exhibitions," a female lead says, "if they tell the truth about it. It's natural, somehow."[58]

Behind the Crimson Blind is an expansion of the *Cabin B-13* script "The Man with the Iron Chest," with the setting changed from Athens in 1939 to Tangier in 1950. H.M. is inveigled into trying to capture a daring jewel robber who always carries a heavy iron chest. On one occasion, the robber is completely surrounded on a street, but vanishes. On another, one of the heroines sees the robber's accomplice with the chest and a pile of uncut diamonds, but when the police break in, both the chest and the diamonds have disappeared. The solution to the robber's disappearance is flimsy, and the explanation of (and vanishing of) the iron chest is dependent on the mistaken testimony of a witness; all of this was handled more persuasively in the radio play.

More interesting is Carr's attitude toward the romantic thief. In *The*

Unicorn Murders he had waxed eloquent against the Raffles and Arsene Lupin type of thief who believed that he could take anything without earning it. In *Behind the Crimson Blind,* however, Carr praises "Iron Chest" for being a sportsman. Carr now saw romantic thieves as symbolizing the struggle of the individual who has traditional values of fair play against the oppressive power of the state. Communism and the Soviet Union, for instance, have nothing to do with the plot of *Behind the Crimson Blind,* but Carr brings them in anyway, primarily so that Russians can be described as "Soviet insects."[59] One of the characters, Juan Alvarez, is a throwback to the impractical romantic heroes like Retif in Carr's college story "The Dim Queen." Alvarez is a Spanish royalist, and in his foolish pride he is compared by H.M. to the Spanish conquistadores. Unlike the conquistadores, however, Alvarez believes in fair play and sportsmanship; he describes sportsmanship as his "god," and H.M. agrees. At the conclusion the Old Man not only allows "Iron Chest" to escape, but even diverts the authorities' attention by blowing up a ship in Tangier harbor. "Iron Chest," in H.M.'s eyes, "was the only real sportsman of a criminal, if you can call him a criminal at all." H.M., like his creator, has lost faith that justice can be found in modern life: "Don't come any moralist nonsense over me," says H.M. "Don't try any blatter about 'law' or 'justice'; we both know they don't exist, unless we go out and get 'em for ourselves."[60]

John Dickson Carr dedicated *The Cavalier's Cup* to "my daughter Julia and her husband, Richard, but not forgetting Gramp." He wrote all three dedicatees into the book, Gramp (that is, Wooda N. Carr) is—for the most part, anyway—Congressman William T. Harvey, and Julia and Dick McNiven appear as Virginia and Tom Brace. The physical description of Ginny Brace matches Julia: "Even wearing her heels she was only about five feet tall. Her soft and silky light-brown hair fell to her shoulders and curled out a little in artless, young-girl fashion. Her eyes were large and grey, with luminous whites." Still, considering that Ginny was depicted as an empty-headed ginch, it is not surprising that, when her father gave Julia a copy of *The Cavalier's Cup* and told her that Ginny was based on her, she was not altogether delighted.[61] It was odd, moreover, that Carr depicted his father as an amorous and amoral roustabout. With his sense of dignity, Wooda Carr would probably have been offended, but he was too ill to read the book when it was published.*

---

*Wooda Nicholas Carr died on June 28, 1953, at the age of eighty-two—about two months after *The Cavalier's Cup* was published. John was in New York at the time, very ill from the recurring fistula problem, and did not attend the funeral.

Unusually for one of his contemporary novels of the 1950s and early 1960s, *The Cavalier's Cup* is not based on a radio script, but the main gimmick is an interesting variation of a locked-room possibility that H.M. had mentioned briefly in *The White Priory Murders*.[62] The problem is how a seventeenth-century cup could have been moved within a locked room. Although the cup is not stolen, H.M. does not blame anyone for trying.

> In my philosophy, if somebody swindles or cheats or acts too sharp in a business deal, it's the lowest trick on earth and deserves years in prison. But to pinch a book or a painting or an *objet d'art* out of a public institution—where, like heavy-game huntin', the odds are even—that's all right. It shows the fine spark of individualism still burns in a brutish mass.[63]

It is perhaps best to put this extraordinary statement aside along with the rest of *The Cavalier's Cup* and *Behind the Crimson Blind* as the product of Carr's illness. Both books are unfortunate aberrations.

To avoid ending this chapter on a negative note, let me anticipate a point I shall make shortly. Sir Henry Merrivale will have one final appearance, in a novelette, and it will be a return to his great days.

Chapter 16

RETURN TO LONDON

John Dickson Carr's recovery from three years of illness left him buoyant with plans for future projects, and with a resolution to stop moving from country to country. "I am in England," he said, "and, by all the Gods, I like it."[1] He told friends that he would stay there the rest of his life. It did not work out that way, but he lived there almost five years, which for John Dickson Carr during this period of his life was a long time. Around July 1954, he sent his British agents some autobiographical notes, which included the comments, "Great Britain only country on earth which really suited me," and "lived in England 1931 [sic]–1948; feel ashamed to state reason, but loved the place; can't be happy anywhere else." He was even cheerful enough to accept the Labour party, because "moderate Labourites—good men—seem in control now."[2] On March 8, 1954, he went to London to look for a flat, and within a short time he found a fairly new five-story apartment building at 40 Greenhill, just off the Hampstead High Street.[3] Clarice and their two younger daughters were usually in Kingswood, though Clarice often stayed with John in London and John holidayed with his family in Kingswood. According to Christianna Brand, Carr sometimes used this living arrangement as a way of dramatizing things. On one occasion, he rang Brand up in an apparent panic to announce that his wife had left him. She had in fact gone back to Kingswood having written him a note that might be interpreted in various ways. It said something like, "I can't wait any longer—I'm leaving." Brand later recalled that Carr

> knew perfectly well—as I did not—that she was merely leaving the London flat and going to their home in the country. We went through some hours of trauma during which he enjoyed himself tremendously and I did not. Of course next day, everything was all right.[4]

Carr became active again in The Detection Club. At the annual dinner held in October 1955, the members performed one of the playlets that he had written for the Mystery Writers of America, "The Adventure of the Paradol Chamber," with Cyril Hare as Holmes, Richard Hull as Watson, Dorothy L. Sayers as Mrs. Hudson, and Carr as the French ambassador. [5] The most vivid memories of Carr's life during this period come from fellow Detection Club member Christianna Brand. Unfortunately, Brand and others who recorded their recollections generally saw Carr between books and other writing projects, and this meant that, as Brand put it, he was usually "tight as a tick"—something that by the 1950s was never true when he was writing. At this time, Carr sometimes halfheartedly tried to stop drinking. In a recent interview with Tony Medawar, Alan Wykes, who knew Carr as a member of the Savage Club, said that on one occasion when Carr refused a drink he explained that he had in the past drunk too much, but now he was giving it up. The novelist Sir Kingsley Amis recalls something similar. In 1955, Edmund Crispin arranged for him to meet Carr, who had read and enjoyed Amis's first novel, *Lucky Jim*, a fact that, Amis says, "made me feel like a fledgling composer patted on the head by Beethoven." They met at the International Musician's Association, a place where the liquor flowed freely. As soon as he realized the ambience of the place, Carr announced, "This is where I fall off the wagon with a resounding crash."[6]

Christianna Brand liked to retell an episode that occurred on August 15, 1955. I have read three versions of the story written by Brand, each differing in details, and the mystery writer, Michael Avallone, who heard it from Brand, has sent me yet another version, which has further differences. Nevertheless, the general pattern is clear. About half past ten at night after returning from a party, Carr called Brand's husband, Roland Lewis, who was a surgeon, with a desperate plea: "Doc, doc, come at once, I'm in agonizing pain. It feels as if an arrow were being twisted into my vitals—not just the modern everyday arrow, doc, but the fourteenth-century arrow with the barbs bent forward." According to Avallone, Brand told him that such telephone calls from Carr were not uncommon, with Sayers also being the recipient of some of them—but the weapon in the intestines would change, sometimes being a sixteenth-century spear, sometimes an Italian stiletto, a Turkish scimitar, and so on. Whatever the case, Lewis reacted gloomily to Carr's entreaties. "Your damned writing friends," he told his wife, "they even know the date of the arrow that is harrowing their intestines." Christianna Brand and her husband toiled up to Hampstead and rang Carr's bell, and Carr opened the door in pajamas and dressing gown. He had forgotten about his telephone call, but was delighted to welcome guests. "Do come in," he said. "Has your pain subsided then," asked Lewis. "What pain?" said Carr.

For many years before this occasion, Carr had regaled his friends with the story that as a student at Haverford, he had needed emergency surgery for a burst appendix, so a friend had whipped out a penknife and successfully operated on him. Lewis took this opportunity to confirm this tale. Removing Carr to another room, he insisted that the writer strip for an examination. When they reemerged, he announced that "I don't think there is anything seriously wrong," then whispered to his wife, "no sign whatsoever of the famous operation with the pen-knife by the heroic friend; not a scar in sight." When Carr told them that his doctor prescribed sleeping medicine—probably chloral hydrate—Lewis advised him to take it and go to bed. Brand fetched the medicine for him; then they left.

The next morning, London newspapers reported that Carr had been found unconscious from a drug overdose and that "doctors were fighting for [his] life." That evening, after it was known that he was out of danger, The Detection Club met and Dorothy L. Sayers was in full spate trying to protect the name of the club. "Not our John Dickson Carr at all," she declared. "I've been in touch with everyone concerned: it was some other person with the same name—just a coincidence." "But Miss Sayers," Brand said, "I put the bottle in his hand myself."

When Clarice heard the news, she dashed back to London and found John already out of the hospital, giving interviews to reporters. Brand either telephoned him or visited him at his Hampstead flat—her story is not consistent on this point—but John had by this time forgotten about her late-night visit with him, and asked whether she also wanted an interview. Carr typed and signed a brief account of the episode, which was published in the evening newspapers. He explained that his writing had left him exhausted: "I was tired. I was bored. So I went to the party. It was a pretty good party. If I had too much whiskey, who doesn't occasionally? Anyway, when I woke up the doctor was taking charge of me." Scotland Yard announced that "his condition is no concern of ours." Carr told the reporters that he was giving up whiskey "temporarily."[7]

During 1954 and 1955, Carr was indeed writing a great deal. As soon as he was certain that the problem with the fistula was over, he came up with idea after idea for novels and tales, but among his first tasks was the repairing of his damaged relationships with old friends. He wrote to Adrian Doyle, whose anger evaporated almost immediately. Doyle told Rene de Chochor that he kept Carr's letter in his study so that it would be in sight at all times—which sounds like an exaggeration, but it is consistent with Doyle's character. By the end of 1954, Doyle had invited Carr to meet with him: "Nothing would give me greater joy than to be with . . . dear old John again. His temporary absence has caused a break in my life that nothing can fill except his return. He is a true brother-in-arms."[8]

More serious were Carr's problems with Val Gielgud. In 1952, he had been paid 150 pounds for three plays in the abortive Sherlock Holmes radio series. He had withdrawn the scripts but not returned the money. In October 1954, Carr called on Gielgud to make amends. He suggested that for no additional payment he supply six scripts for a new *Appointment with Fear* program. Gielgud was excited about the possibility, for *Appointment with Fear* had almost legendary status with radio listeners, and a revival was certain to be popular. Carr, however, then had cold feet: "It was not that the old scripts were particularly good. But people all over the country are firmly convinced they were. We built up a legend; and it's damned hard to live up to a legend no matter what you do." In *The 9 Wrong Answers*, Carr had claimed with justification that the "most famous line in British radio" was Valentine Dyall's introduction to *Appointment with Fear*: "This is your storyteller, The Man in Black." Carr was afraid that the scripts he had offered to the BBC, which were primarily from *Cabin B-13*, "were anything but a necklace of masterpieces." Gielgud, however, was pleased with the plays.[9]

Appointment with Fear was broadcast on Tuesday evenings, July 26 through August 30, 1955, with David H. Godfrey as the director and Valentine Dyall re-creating his role as the Man in Black. The final series contained only two *Cabin B-13* scripts, each slightly revised: "The Man Who Couldn't Be Photographed" and "The Power of Darkness," retitled

"The Villa of the Damned." The other scripts were entirely original. "White Tiger Passage" is a rarity: a comedy about a serial killer. A young reporter is tired of doing lighthearted features under the name of Willie Whiskers and insists on investigating the "Slasher of the Boulevards." Helped by his girlfriend, and fighting off the advances of his editor's wife, he tracks down the Slasher to a Brighton hotel. One of the several clever clues in the play is the interpretation of a limerick. An even better play is "The Sleuth of Seven Dials" in which a young solicitor named Hugh Prentice longs for something to break the monotony of his life. Adventure comes in the person of Hassan el Moulk, who is murdered alone in Prentice's office, and Prentice and his partner Jim Vaughan swear that nobody else entered. Hassan el Moulk's last words are "your gloves." Unless Prentice is guilty, the death seems an utter impossibility.

The other two scripts of the 1955 *Appointment with Fear*, "The Dead Man's Knock" and "Till the Great Armadas Come," are no better than average. The first, which is not related to the *Cabin B-13* script of the same name, is about a middle-aged historian so interested in the past that his wife plans to leave him. The story is interesting because it is the only time that Carr wrote anything about the afterlife, and it is not surprising that when he dies the historian goes back to the era that fascinates him, late-eighteenth-century England. The final play, "Till the Great Armadas Come," is based on what must have seemed at the time a good idea, but now seems silly. Hitler plans to have a final air raid of Britain in 1944, and Colonel Fielding is certain that it will be a spectacular symbol of the Nazi cause. His investigation turns up the fact that the fifth columnists have placed incendiary devices in the center of London that will be set off at the same time and, from the air, be in the shape of a blazing swastika. He easily defeats the Führer's scheme.

With the broadcast of these six plays ended the greatest mystery and suspense series on British radio, though there would be attempts to bring it back. Nine years later, for example, Carr lunched with Richard Imison, script editor for BBC drama, and suggested that *Appointment with Fear* might return. Imison thought the program had become "old hat," so Carr countered with a program to be called either *S.S. Suspense* or *M.V. Suspense*. It would feature a ship's purser who would tell stories about the various ports the ship visits. In other words, he wanted to try the format of *Cabin B-13* again. Imison was interested, but nothing came of the idea.[10] Since that time, the BBC has occasionally attempted new programs under the *Appointment with Fear* name, and recently the BBC used the character of the Man in Black for a series called *Fear on Four*, but none of these revivals has been successful.[11]

The 1955 series of *Appointment with Fear* was one of several projects that Carr was involved in, or at least considered, after he regained his health. For example, in March 1954 he agreed without much enthusiasm to write an essay giving his solution to Charles Dickens's unfinished *The Mystery of Edwin Drood* for a French publisher, Editions Gerard, which would translate it into French and use it as an epilogue to their edition of Dickens's novel. Gerard wanted five to ten thousand words, but was willing to pay only one hundred dollars. The idea was discussed between Carr and his British agents off and on for two more years, until May 17, 1956, when, according to a memorandum in the files of the agents, Carr decided to leave the matter alone "till he feels like it." Carr had recorded the basic outline of his *Drood* theory in a long letter to Lillian de la Torre some years earlier. He had worked out an elaborately twisting plot, which strikes most readers as more typical of John Dickson Carr than of Charles Dickens. Carr believed that Drood was murdered by Helena Landless dressed as a man, and that John Jasper, mistakenly believing he had killed Drood, acted as an accessory in disposing of the body. Carr discussed these ideas with a friend, the scriptwriter John Keir Cross. With Carr's permission, Cross used Carr's solution for a television serialization of *The Mystery of Edwin Drood*, shown on British television in 1960.[12]

Carr also considered and rejected some other writing projects during 1954. Harry Allen Towers, an independent producer who often worked with the BBC, asked Carr to write adaptations of twenty-six Sherlock Holmes stories for a series to star John Gielgud as Holmes and Ralph Richardson as Dr. Watson. After writing one script and beginning a second, Carr decided not to do the project because "it seems futile to deal forever with somebody else's characters instead of my own." To replace Carr, Towers hired John Keir Cross. Carr's objection to using another author's characters resulted in the failure of still another project. Dorothy L. Sayers was asked to work on a television series featuring Lord Peter Wimsey. Sayers replied that she could not do the scriptwriting required, unless she had the assistance of John Dickson Carr.

> You know [Carr mused] I don't seem to have a life of my own. They all want me to be somebody else. . . . So far nobody has suggested that I have a crack at imitating Shakespeare or finishing Dr. Johnson's Dictionary, but I feel these spectral selves are just round the corner.

Rene de Chochor, Carr's American agent, advised him not to commit himself to write about someone else's creation. Instead, he said, Carr should work on some scripts about Sir Henry Merrivale, and in fact there was at this time considerable interest in an H.M. series for television. Carr took Chochor's advice and rejected the offer to write Wimsey scripts,[13] but he also decided not to work on any H.M. scripts. He was never happy with the idea of writing for television, a fact which indicates why he was not involved in a series called *Colonel March of Scotland Yard*, which was broadcast in 1954.

On June 27, 1952, Laurence Pollinger of Carr's British agents, Pearn, Pollinger and Higham, had sold options of the film rights to *The Department of Queer Complaints* to an American firm called Atlas Productions. After several extensions, the company, now calling itself Panda Films (later, Fountain Films), exercised its option for a total payment of two thousand pounds, a surprisingly small sum, as Carr's American agent complained. The producers had already hired veteran actor Boris Karloff, then nearing seventy years of age, to play a Colonel March who, thin and with an eyepatch, did not physically resemble Carr's character. Although the series was filmed in England, it was aimed from the first at the American market. For British audiences, however, three of the episodes were cobbled together into an episodic feature called *Colonel March Investigates*, released by Criterion Films.

Carr did not know of the movie, and until the syndicated feature *Colonel March of Scotland Yard* showed up on various American stations beginning on January 6, 1954, he was unaware that the stories had been filmed. The first he heard about the series was in early February 1954 when his mother wrote to him that she had been enjoying his stories on television. Even then he had no idea what was going on: "With the deepest of bows, I was compelled to assure *ma mere* that she must have been looking at the wrong programme or imagining things, because *I* don't know anything about it." In June, however, Carr realized that there was indeed a *Queer Complaints* television series. He read in London newspapers that Karloff had appeared at the Crime Book Exhibition in London and announced that "I have reverted to my old ways of crime; I am now playing the part of Colonel March in the John Dickson Carr stories for American television."[14]

Panda Productions filmed twenty-six half-hour episodes of *Colonel March of Scotland Yard*, only about half a dozen of which were based directly on Carr's *Queer Complaints* stories. The program was first broadcast from January through June 1954 and remained available for local stations throughout the 1950s. Recently, it has appeared on cable television in the United States, and several of the episodes have been for sale through video dealers. As *TV Guide* pointed out when *Colonel March* was originally broadcast, the series had a tightly budgeted look; the sets were inexpensive and showed little variety, and the supporting actors were usually young and little-known. On the other hand, the producer, Donald Ginsberg, and the director, Cyril Endfield, had good eyes for talent, and the series had convincing performances by such young actors as Antony [sic] Newley and Arthur Hill. Karloff himself did a smooth and entertaining job, and the stories remained true to the world of *The Department of Queer Complaints*. *TV Guide* said that Karloff's portrayal of Colonel March should win him "almost as many fans as did his grotesque movie roles." The program, the magazine went on to say, "spins a strange yarn each week, making for good viewing even though some tales lack credibility." Historians of early television also find much to praise in *Colonel March of Scotland Yard*. Richard Meyers, for instance, compares it to similar programs of the period that tried to be realistic: "Far more florid, thereby making it far more entertaining, was . . . *Colonel March of Scotland Yard*. . . . [Karloff] brought style and class to the inexpensive proceedings."[15]

As soon as he realized that Colonel March was appearing on television, Carr asked his American agents to find out whether a magazine might be interested in a new series of *Queer Complaints*. "On my oath, mon vieux," he wrote to Chochor, "an assignment like this would be pie for me. I could do it in my head—*if* there is a market." A potential market was easy to find. *This Week* magazine, a Sunday supplement for newspapers, had done well with short-shorts by popular authors, including Ellery Queen, Q. Patrick, and Mignon G. Eberhart, and its editor, Stewart Beach, asked to see a Colonel March tale of around thirty-five hundred words. If it was acceptable, he would pay a dollar a word. Chochor was certain that Beach would commit himself to buying an entire series of March stories. Carr agreed to send some stories to *This Week*, but despite telephone calls from Beach to Chochor, and letters from Chochor to Carr, no stories were written, and the matter simply faded away with no explanation by the end of October 1954.[16]

One of John Dickson Carr's undertakings that did result in publication was his participation in a round-robin mystery novella. The London *News Chronicle* asked Jean LeRoy, who ran the newspaper and magazine side of Pearn, Pollinger and Higham, to arrange for the writing of a thriller called

Crime on the Coast to which six mystery writers would contribute succes-
sive chapters. LeRoy persuaded Carr, Valerie White, Laurence Meynell,
Michael Cronin, Joan Fleming, and Elizabeth Ferrars to write the book,
and they all met on July 13, 1954, for lunch at the Savoy's Gondoliers
Room to make plans. Elizabeth Ferrars, who already knew Carr through
The Detection Club, remembers:

> We discussed the project over the meal, but only in so far as we de-
> cided the order in which we were to write, the length of each contri-
> bution, payment and so on. Nothing at all was decided about the
> story itself. I was the one who really suffered through this later on, as
> I was chosen to write the final instalment. One of my memories of
> John is his saying he thought this was a very good arrangement, be-
> cause after he had read my last book—I think it was the one called
> *The Lying Voices*—he had come to the conclusion that I could solve
> anything.

Although *Crime on the Coast* was to begin in the *News Chronicle* only three
weeks later, Carr agreed to write the first two brief chapters. They introduce Phil Courtney,* a typical Carrian hero, who "was not really a stuffed
shirt" and who longs for adventure. At the Fun Fair at "Breston," a woman
whom he has never met suddenly claims acquaintance with him and begs
that he take her into Ye Olde Haunted Mill. (The setting comes from the
Suspense play "Will You Make a Bet with Death?" and it was the only part
of the play that Carr had not incorporated into *The 9 Wrong Answers*.) With
this request, "Phil Courtney stepped right into the Arabian Nights." As
they float in a boat through the Haunted Mill, the woman tells Phil that
someone in her family is trying to kill her. Carr's section ends as the boat
suddenly stops moving, and they hear someone heading toward them.
Elizabeth Ferrars recalls:

> I read each instalment, as it was sent to me, with utter dismay, won-
> dering how on earth I was going to tie it all up together in the end.
> Then Joan Fleming wrote her part and sorted out things wonder-
> fully, so after that I was not so alarmed. By the time my turn came I
> decided that about the only thing we had left out was an atomic sci-
> entist, so I brought one in.[17]

---

*Courtney had a previous incarnation as Sir Henry Merrivale's biographer in *Seeing Is
Believing*.

Because of Carr's ill health during 1953, he did not submit a new novel to Harper & Brothers for 1954 publication. Harpers, therefore, decided to publish a book of his short stories, under the title *The Third Bullet and Other Stories*; an editor at Harpers chose the stories to be included. The book was published at the beginning of June 1954 in the United States and at the end of the month in Britain. Harpers did not know that there were two versions of the title story, and they used the readily available, but unsatisfactory, abridgment from *Ellery Queen's Mystery Magazine*. Otherwise, however, the collection is excellent. It contains what Carr said were his two best short tales, "The House in Goblin Wood" and "The Gentleman from Paris," as well as two Dr. Fell shorts ("The Wrong Problem" and "The Proverbial Murder") and the nonseries "The Clue of the Red Wig." On reading the book, however, Carr was not happy with the title story (at least in its abridged version) and one or two of the others, and feared that, especially after he had published two or three below-average novels, critics would "quite justifiably play hell with it." In fact, however, the reviews were almost entirely positive. He was especially pleased with Anthony Boucher's comments in *The New York Times*, and he wrote a lengthy letter to Boucher to express his gratitude.[18]

Whenever Carr invented a title he liked, he stored it away for a time that he had a plot in mind that would fit it; we have seen several titles that Carr tried in various places—*Vampire Tower, The Seat of the Scornful, Till Death Do Us Part, The Dead Man's Knock,* and others. The title *Captain Cut-Throat* first appeared as the name of a play mentioned in passing in *My Late Wives*, and when he got the idea for a Napoleonic novel, he decided to use it again. Carr had begun the book in August 1952, and in November he said that it was moving toward completion. It was this book that Carr had briefly planned to offer to new publishers, but that Harpers and Hamish Hamilton retained by wagering Carr that they could increase sales. When he turned back to *Captain Cut-Throat* in spring 1954, he did not like what he had written:

> I suddenly saw where it went wrong. I scrapped every word I had written except most of the first chapter. I altered the whole character of the hero and the heroine. I set out to make it less a detective story than a story of human conflict, in which the pressure on the reader's nerves should be tightened page by page until it could be tightened no longer. [19]

Carr traveled to France in the middle of 1954 to get the topography correct, and he completed the typescript early in October 1954. This time he was pleased. He wrote to Boucher that what he called "the ancient hand did not seem to shake any longer. I was not stumbling about in bad construction, as God knows I had been doing when I did so much of my writing for more than three years." *Captain Cut-Throat*, he said, had no unnecessary words, unlike *The 9 Wrong Answers*, which he now admitted was "sprawling."[20]

Carr's assessment of *Captain Cut-Throat* was accurate. It is a tightly controlled novel whose emphasis is less on solving the detective puzzle than on seeing whether the hero will be able to survive. The story, which is set in France in 1805, is about a deadly contest of wits between an English spy named Alan Hepburn, who attempts to discover whether Napoleon is planning to invade England, and Joseph Fouché, Napoleon's minister of police—whose portrait, incidentally, hung in Sir Henry Merrivale's office in Whitehall. Fouché, whom Carr calls "puppet-master" and "father of lies," has captured Hepburn but gives him the chance of saving his life if he can identify a murderer calling himself Captain Cut-Throat. This mysterious man or woman had been killing soldiers at Napoleon's Boulogne camp, but no one can see the killer. To force Hepburn to agree, Fouché threatens to charge his wife, Madeleine, with spying for England. Alan had left Madeleine because he believed she was a French spy, but he still loves her. If that is not enough of what Carr calls "emotional gunpowder," Alan has made Ida de Sainte-Elme his mistress in order to obtain important information to send to England. The first third of the book takes place in a nerve-wracking coach ride between Paris and Boulogne, with Alan, Madeleine, and Ida all traveling together.

Alan must do his job as a spy, save himself and Madeleine, identify Captain Cut-Throat, protect himself from a sneering villain, Lieutenant Hans Schneider, and defeat Fouché's schemes—and all within a week. The identity of Captain Cut-Throat and the explanation of his vanishing (a variation of a method for an invisible knife in a *Cabin B-13* play, "The Street of the Seven Daggers") are somewhat disappointing, but this is a minor matter compared with the growing suspense about the fate of the heroes. It is not until the final two paragraphs that we discover whether Hepburn has outdueled Fouché.

Carr was eager that Harper get *Captain Cut-Throat* into print so that his audience would forget the quality of the books he had written during his illness. Cass Canfield of Harpers was also anxious to show that he could indeed promote Carr successfully and thereby win the bet that he had made with him two years earlier and keep Carr with the firm. Harpers took out advertisements in major newspapers, and by the time the book was published at the end of March 1955, the advance sale was around 11,500 copies. The final sales figures for the Harper edition of *Captain Cut-Throat* are not available, but clearly Canfield won his bet. By the end of April, Carr wrote that he would never dream of leaving Harpers after what they had been able to do for the book.[21]

Immediately after he completed writing *Captain Cut-Throat,* Carr made plans for two books to be published in 1956. One was to be a new novel about Sir Henry Merrivale, which would rescue him from the caricature that had appeared in *Behind the Crimson Blind* and *The Cavalier's Cup.* H.M. would have, Carr promised, "a come-back in a strong detective-thriller story where he appears as his real self and not a complete buffoon."[22] The other would be a historical mystery novel based, like *The Devil in Velvet,* on time travel. Carr worked on the two stories at the same time, but we shall look first at the H.M. tale.

Sir Henry Merrivale's final case, "Ministry of Miracles," was based on the 1944 *Appointment With Fear* play "He Who Whispers." Carr used this plot for what he called a "tourist murder-story" taking place at St. Paul's Cathedral and Hampton Court. In October 1954 he still planned to write the H.M. story as a novel. A month later, however, he decided that "Ministry of Miracles" was to be a novelette of about fifteen thousand words. I don't know why Carr changed his mind; certainly there is enough *story* in the old radio script to expand into a novel. Whatever the case, Alan Wykes, fiction editor of *The Housewife* (and a friend from the Savage Club), purchased the novelette sight unseen for 750 guineas—well over two thousand dollars. Carr completed "Ministry of Miracles" in April 1955,[23] and it was published serially in *The Housewife* from January through March 1956. After failing to sell the novelette to *Collier's,* Carr's American agents followed his advice and sent it to Frederic Dannay, who immediately bought it for six hundred dollars. Knowing his friend's penchant to make changes in typescripts, Carr dropped Dannay a note that "it mustn't be cut; there is not an unnecessary word." Dannay, however, was not happy with Carr's title. He believed that to Americans the word "ministry" suggested the church, so for *Ellery Queen's Mystery Magazine* he changed the title to "The Man Who Explained Miracles."[24] Carr approved the change, and in fact used a slight variation of it as the title of his 1963 short story collection, *The Men Who Explained Miracles*. For this book, the H.M. novelette was renamed "All in a Maze," by which title it is now most commonly known.

By whatever name, "Ministry of Miracles" is a meaty story, tightly plotted, with (despite some improbabilities in the actions of one character) a genuinely mystifying puzzle. Sir Henry Merrivale, himself, is in fine form. The main humor in the tale, H.M.'s taking on the role of tour guide at Hampton Court, comes naturally out of his character, and it is an important part of the plot. Instead of being clownish, he uses his historical lectures as he guides a party through the maze as a way to catch the criminal. Unlike *Behind the Crimson Blind* and *The Cavalier's Cup*, "Ministry of Miracles" has no misguided attempt to bring it up to date by including heavy sexual byplay and irrelevant attacks on communism. Instead, H.M. is back in his old haunts at Whitehall, with the portrait of Fouché still on the wall and the bottle of whiskey in the safe. The Old Man had gotten in trouble with the British government by having bank accounts in New York, Paris, Tangier, and Milan, and he had spent more money abroad than he could account for. When he returned to England, "They hoicked me up on the carpet before an old friend of mine. I won't say who this louse is, except to tell you he's the Attorney-General." H.M. was let off with a fine on condition that he take charge of "Central Office Eight of the Metropolitan Police," to which Scotland Yard sends "any loony case that doesn't make sense."[25] In other words, Carr revived Scotland Yard's Department of Queer Complaints under a new name.

"Ministry of Miracles" begins when Jenny Holden runs in terror from St. Paul's Cathedral right into the arms of Tom Lockwood. She has heard a voice on the Whispering Gallery threaten her life. Tom takes Jenny to a teashop, and she explains that her aunt, Hester Harpenden, is forcing her to marry Armand de Sennevillle, who wants to obtain her dowry. As is obvious from her name, the aunt is one of the domineering women whom Carr hated all his life. The episode at St. Paul's is not the first seemingly impossible threat to Jenny's life. The previous night, she was almost asphyxiated when someone turned the gas on in her bedroom, but all the doors were locked and no one else was in the room. Tom suggests that she see Sir Henry Merrivale, whose office is now "humorously called The Ministry of Miracles." "He can explain miracles," Tom says; "that's his purpose in life nowadays." H.M. sympathizes with Jenny when she explains that she is marrying only because "people are so determined." He replies: "Yes, I know, but that's what causes so much unhappiness in this world, especially for gals."[26]

Carr did not plan "Ministry of Miracles" to be Sir Henry Merrivale's swan song. Although it will take us forward several years, let's follow Carr's attempts to continue H.M.'s saga. Two months after "Ministry of Miracles" was published, he told his British agent, David Higham, that he was working on a book to be called *Commander Sir Henry Merrivale*. By November 1, 1956, he had changed the title to *Enter Three Poisoners*. For a considerable length of time, he assured both his British and American agents that he would soon complete it. In June 1957, he promised it within a month, but nothing happened. By January 1959, Carr had given up, with the explanation that "I can't expect to be the king-pin of two detective-lists, so I prefer to stick with Harper where I remain top dog." Further pressure, especially the reminder that he was contracted to Morrow for another book to take care of already-paid advances, led to his announcement in February 1960 that he would "buckle down to it and revive H.M." But he found it difficult to create a satisfactory H.M., and for a while he considered hiring a collaborator to help.

> Then I withdrew the idea [he told Higham]. I don't mean that it's dishonest. I do mean that the books, bad though they may be, are still mine. I've got to do them myself, down to every damned comma, or I couldn't meet my conscience on the stairs at night.

In February 1961, Carr said that he would do no more Carter Dickson novels, and he had moved so far from his earlier desire to preserve the Carter Dickson name that he asked his American agents to find out whether Morrow would mind having the Sir Henry Merrivale books reissued by another publisher under Carr's own name. Morrow, of course, objected.[27]

Carr's attitude changed once again a few months later. Morrow had told him that no one would agree to reissuing the Carter Dickson books in paperback unless a new Sir Henry Merrivale novel appeared.* Consequently, Carr decided again to try a novel about H.M.—and this one came near to completion. In September 1961, he told David Higham that it was now to be called *The Six Black Reasons*.[28] Probably the novel was to be based on a radio script, "The Nine Black Reasons," broadcast on *Cabin B-13* in August 1948. The play was about black pearls, and it is likely that

---

*This turned out not to be true. The Berkley Publishing Company would reissue almost all the Carter Dicksons in paperback beginning in 1963.

pearls were also to be the "reasons" in the H.M. case. Otherwise, it is difficult to see how the play could have been expanded to novel length. But Carr still found that he could not revive H.M.:

> By the end of November [1961], I had written eight chapters (out of the customary twenty chapters in each H.M. story). I had a strong plot; this much I was sure of. Then, rightly or wrongly, I began to be uncertain of the central character. When H.M. makes his return after ten years' [sic] absence, it's got to be a properly triumphant one. I don't mean so far as the critics are concerned; be damned to those gentlemen, since two generations of them have now been sniping at me in anything from a tone of modest nausea to a kind of fury reaching, "What, isn't he dead yet?" I mean it must be done to my own satisfaction. The doubts (which may be groundless) arose from the wonder as to whether H.M. himself might belong so entirely to a different world—the nineteen thirties and the nineteen forties—that the story might better be done as a period piece.[29]

He therefore put the typescript aside until he could finish a book that he had promised Harpers. Dwye Evans of William Heinemann, Ltd., was in New York in March 1962, and Carr talked with him about the difficulties he was having with reviving Sir Henry Merrivale. Evans suggested that *The Six Black Reasons* be rewritten to feature Colonel March rather than H.M.—a perfectly feasible idea since both H.M. and the colonel had handled queer complaints for Scotland Yard. Carr agreed enthusiastically, and Heinemann went as far as to advertise the book as forthcoming. In August 1963, however, Higham had to tell Heinemann that nothing was likely to come from Carr on this project in the near future.[30] *The Six Black Reasons* was never completed, and the typescript of the eight chapters has disappeared.

In 1954, while Carr was working on what turned out to be the last Sir Henry Merrivale story, he was also making plans for a historical mystery, which would become *Fear Is the Same*. At first, this was to be issued under his own name, but when he decided that "Ministry of Miracles" would be a novella rather than a novel, he decided to publish *Fear Is the Same* under the Carter Dickson name primarily to keep the pseudonym before the public. Thayer Hobson of Morrow and Dwye Evans of Heinemann were willing to publish the historical mystery rather than a new H.M. book, but then Carr had second thoughts. Morrow's sales had never been as good as Harpers', so he asked his American agent whether it was ethical to submit a Carter Dickson book to a new publisher. The agent scrawled on Carr's letter, "No, of course not," but his reply to Carr was diplomatic, pointing out that he was contractually obliged to offer the next Carter Dickson novel to Morrow. "You are absolutely right," Carr replied; "pay no attention to my occasional brain-waves."[31]

Carr began work on what became *Fear Is the Same* in October 1954, and, after a five-day holiday in Denmark in November, he wrote to his American agent Rene de Chochor that "I am immersed in a novel which, completely worked out in my head, has so got me by the throat that I can think, eat, and even dream nothing else. This should be a Carter Dickson. But it is not an H.M., and not even a mystery in the accepted sense."[32] His first plan was to feature a distinguished present-day actor who would be transported back to the mid-Victorian period.* When *Fear Is the Same* was published, however, Carr had changed the plot radically from his original idea. Carr's story now has as its hero a young impoverished aristocrat who makes his living in contemporary England as a prizefighter under an assumed name, and he and the heroine are transported not to the 1860s but to 1795, the England of the prince regent.

It is tempting to argue that Carr actually wrote at least part of *Fear Is the Same* ten years earlier. The year 1795 is given over and over in the book; the contemporary world they left is clearly the middle 1950s; but on at least six different occasions, the hero or the heroine says that they have been transported 150 years into the past.[33] In other words, 1945 rather than 1955 must be the year when the story opens. Carr's grip on mathematics was never strong, but this discrepancy of a decade is striking. Was the book or a portion of it written in 1945, but not completed until Carr found that his mid-Victorian plot was not coming together? In that case, *Fear Is the Same* rather than *The Devil in Velvet* would be Carr's first attempt to widen the limits of the detective novel by including time travel.

A kernel of the plot of *Fear Is the Same* had appeared in Carr's *Appointment With Fear* play "The Dead Man's Knock," broadcast on August 9, 1955. In the radio play, a man suffering from heart disease dies and returns to the 1790s, where he briefly investigates a murder. The surprise at the end is that he has not died of a heart attack but has been murdered; the events of his killing are identical with those of the one that took place 160 years earlier. In *Fear Is the Same*, the hero, Lord Philip Clavering, has not been killed, but he is the main suspect in a modern murder, and when

---

*Appendix 5 prints the outline of the original plot, as sent to Anthony Boucher.

he finds himself in 1795, the same murder is about to be repeated. In the novel, Carr reverses in an extraordinary way a pattern that had frequently appeared in his books. Carr's plots had often been based on past murders being repeated in the present; in *Fear Is the Same*, a twentieth-century murder will soon be reenacted in the past.

The story opens when Philip Clavering and Jennifer Baird wake up in 1795, with only confused memories of their other lives. In *The Devil in Velvet*, Carr had the Devil transport the hero to the past, but in *Fear Is the Same*, Carr did not want such fire and brimstone. He wrote to his friend Tony Boucher, who was then editing *The Magazine of Fantasy and Science Fiction*, asking for "a logical (so to speak) fantastic explanation of what carries [the hero] back." He added, however, that he was not sure that he needed an explanation, and certainly he did not want a scientific or pseudoscientific gadget. "I love fantasy, but by a Chestertonian paradox dislike gadgets in fantastic stories almost as much as I have been accused of liking them in detective stories." Boucher was not able to answer for six months, and then wrote to suggest that Carr might mention flaws or holes in time. Carr had, however, already decided not to suggest any explanation at all. As Jennifer strives to regain her memory, she recalls only that she and Philip had been running in a rainstorm and she cried out, "Oh, if only we would be out of this! If only we could go back a hundred and fifty years in time, and forget it!" Then she heard a voice in her head whispering, "Would it be any different if you did go back?" There was a thunderclap, and she found herself in the past.[34]

Fear Is the Same is a powerful story. Philip and Jennifer know only that they had been in deadly danger when the thunderclap came, and that the same events are being repeated, but they cannot remember what the danger was—and will be. When Philip finds himself a nobleman in the England of the prince regent, he discovers that he is married to the scheming Chloris, who is contemptuous of him. Soon he realizes that he is actually in love with Jennifer. He cannot, however, keep away from his wife. Finally, he tells Chloris: "Every man on earth has had at least once the same experience. There is one woman he loves. There is another he desires. In youth, in stupidity, he thinks these qualities may never exist in the same woman." A rarity in a Carr book, the hero actually strikes a woman. When Chloris calls Jennifer "Your mopsy. Your light-Jane. Your whore," Philip hits her. Carr says, however, that he "never . . . would have dreamed of doing" such a thing in his other life.[35] I should add, too, that this scene was necessary for the plot, for it provides evidence that Philip has a murderous rage against Chloris. When a maid who resembles Chloris is found murdered, Philip is suspected of having killed her by mistake.

Jennifer and Philip, assisted by the bibulous playwright Richard Brinsley Sheridan, desperately try to prove his innocence in the face of the enmity of Colonel Toby Thornton, one of Carr's typical sneering, bullying villains. Eventually, Philip is forced to fight a duel against two opponents, both of whom are armed with swords while he has only boxing gloves. As S. T. Joshi points out, the book achieves great poignancy when Jennifer prays:

> "O, Thou," it was a trembling through her, "bid us go from this cage in which we are held. Lead us back to our own space and time. Set us free from this dirt, and cruelty, and snobbishness. Was it not marked, only a moment ago, how the worst of men was called worthy because he was the grandson of a duke, and no man laughed, or even smiled?
>
> "Is my lover, my husband, forever to be beaten to his knees? He stands up again; he defeats them, and I am glad. But there is much blood on his head; he is changing every hour before my eyes, and I am afraid. Let him go! And, if I be considered worthy, let me go too."[36]

Carr loved the past, but he was not blind to its dirt and cruelty and snobbishness.

This scene is followed by Philip's despairing comment that summarizes the book: "'Tell you something,' he muttered in that low, groping voice. 'In all ages, everything changes. Manners, customs, speech, views on life, even morals—all change. But fear is the same. Only fear is the same.'"[37] As a statement of our human insecurity, and even as justification for writing about the past, there have been worse statements than Lord Philip Clavering's anguished remark.

Philip and Jennifer are then rescued by the Prince of Wales, whose beliefs about justice and fair play are similar to Sir Henry Merrivale's in *Behind the Crimson Blind*. But somehow such sentiments are more persuasive coming in 1795 than in the early 1950s:

> "That man," [the prince] said, "has been tricked and cheated by all save a few. Whether he is innocent I know not and at the moment I care not. But fairly he has met his enemies, and fairly he has beaten

them all. And now, when he is wounded and alone, shall he be pulled down by a pack of yapping curs? No! I think not."

The Prince of Wales leads a group of friends who help Jennifer and Philip: "Ahead of them all, drunken, untrustworthy, selfish though he might be, marched one who was still the First Gentleman of Europe."[38]

But this rescue is not the end of the story, as Carr tightens the screws a bit more on the reader's nerves. Philip proves his innocence to an unofficial court headed by the prince, but the physical evidence is then destroyed, and his witnesses die in a carriage accident. When King George III issues a warrant for Philip's arrest, the prince can no longer protect him. Philip and Jennifer dash out in a thunderstorm, and with another loud crash they find themselves running through the streets of modern London. Detective Inspector Somers approaches them, and Philip cries, "It's no good running, Jenny. It's no good at all, in this age or any other. They always catch up."[39] Whether he is arrested for the twentieth-century murder, I shall leave the reader to discover. It is worth doing so, for *Fear Is the Same* is probably John Dickson Carr's best historical novel.

Fear Is the Same was published in February 1956 in the United States and two months later in Britain. The Morrow edition officially revealed for the first time the real identity of Carter Dickson.* On the back of the dust jacket, Morrow published a photo of Carr, and beneath it, a blurb writer said that "Carter Dickson (alias John Dickson Carr) needs no introduction to the cloak-and-dagger set." Morrow, however, did little to publicize the book, and in spite of good reviews it did not sell. Five years later, Carr remembered that "good, bad, or indifferent, it was as good as any I have turned out for the other firm. And it was a dud for Morrow. This may have been my fault or theirs or nobody's, but it's not encouraging."[40] As late as 1967, eleven years after the book was published, Morrow was still selling copies of the first printing of *Fear Is the Same*.[41]

After Carr had decided that *Fear Is the Same* would be a Carter Dickson book and (eventually) that it would go to Morrow, he had to determine what sort of book he would write for Harpers. He first planned to write a sea novel set in the reign of Queen Elizabeth I. Its tentative title was ini-

---

*Frederic Dannay also revealed Carter Dickson's identity when he printed "The Man Who Explained Miracles" in the March 1956 *Ellery Queen's Mystery Magazine:* He gave the authorship as "Carter Dickson (John Dickson Carr)." The magazine probably reached the newsstands about the same time as the publication of *Fear Is the Same*. In any event, the pseudonym had not been a secret for many years.

tially *The Sea Stingers*; then a short while later he called it *Health and Gloriana*. Carr said in April 1955:

> If I can only handle the plot I have in mind, it should have a sensational effect. Its pattern appears old and obvious: an Elizabethan sea-story, but the pattern is very different from what it appears, because I think I have got hold of something which, for some reason, the historians have missed. . . . It will be ready about the end of October. [42]

Before beginning the new book, John and Clarice Carr took a two-week holiday in Sweden during July 1955. Their hosts in Stockholm were representatives of the Albert Bonniers Company, who had published translations of his books. Unfortunately, not knowing that many Swedes take vacations in July, the Carrs found the city almost deserted—and as emergency cablegrams to David Higham indicated, their hotel was dreadful. Nonetheless, they both enjoyed the holiday, being especially fascinated with the old parts of Stockholm. The newspapers ran extensive articles about Carr. *Expressen* described him as "a small man with a coquette moustache, who reminds you quite a bit of Agatha Christie's sleuth Hercule Poirot. But where Poirot is Belgian in every inch, Mr. Carr is unbelievably English; a gentleman right out of London City . . . with dark red braces." Some years later, Carr erroneously recalled that the reporter had written that "I looked and talked exactly like Bertie Wooster in the Jeeves stories: a rank libel." The description was at least kinder than one printed a few days earlier that saw him as having "a thin moustache, a thin brown face and rather big ears."

Carr told reporters that he planned to write a book with a Swedish setting, and he spent at least one day traveling about Stockholm with the Swedish mystery writer Sune Lundqvist (who used the pseudonym Vic Senuson). In the company of a reporter for *Expressen*, the two writers traveled about checking various possible locales. Among the photographs published the next day in the newspaper is a wonderfully contrived one showing Carr and Lundqvist finding a "corpse" on a stairway as the perpetrator runs off.[43]

Carr was serious about writing a Swedish novel, and he returned to Stockholm in September to gather more material. He told Ake Runnquist of the Albert Bonniers firm that the book was to be published under his own name, but he was not yet certain whether it would feature Dr. Fell.[44] Carr may have been thinking of it as a historical mystery, since during his first trip he had asked many questions about the Stockholm Massacre of 1520, when King Kristian II of Denmark butchered a goodly number of Swedish noblemen. But whatever Carr had in mind, he never wrote a novel about Sweden.

Nor, in fact, did he write the Elizabethan novel that he had outlined earlier in 1955. When Cass Canfield came to London in April, Carr mentioned the project to him at a party, but then he began to wonder whether it was a good idea to have another historical published a year after *Captain Cut-Throat* and at the same time as *Fear Is the Same*. Surviving correspondence is incomplete, but it seems that he decided while on his first visit to Stockholm that it might be better to delay *The Sea Stingers* and instead write a book featuring both Dr. Fell and Patrick Butler, neither of whom had appeared since *Below Suspicion* was published in 1949. He wrote to Canfield with the suggestion, and Canfield agreed with alacrity that it would be better to go with a contemporary detective novel. Carr therefore began work on what would be called *Patrick Butler for the Defence*. He decided, however, to omit Dr. Fell entirely (except for a passing remark or two in the book) and allow Butler to do all the sleuthing. Carr completed the book by the end of 1955, and it was published in the United States early in July 1956 and the next month in Britain.[45]

Patrick Butler for the Defence is an expansion of "The Sleuth of the Seven Dials," a radio script that was broadcast in August 1955 as a part of the revived *Appointment With Fear*, and it has the many virtues of that script, above all a *New Arabian Nights* feeling that the door to adventure can open on anyone's stodgy world. The book is reminiscent of the beginning of *The Four False Weapons*, written twenty years earlier. In both cases a young lawyer dreams of adventure. In *Patrick Butler for the Defence*, Helen Dean tells Hugh Prentice:

> You'd dearly love to walk straight into some roaring adventure ... and pit your wits against the crafty villain. . . . Up out of the fog would slip a mysterious dark-skinned stranger with a foreign accent. "I am Omar of Ispahan," he'd say. And he'd tell you about a corpse in a sealed room.[46]

And this, of course, is almost exactly what happens. "Abu of Ispahan" is murdered in Hugh's office; as in the radio play, Abu dies with the cryptic words "your gloves" on his lips.

Even more successfully than in "The Sleuth of the Seven Dials," Carr works the plot around the fact that Hugh seems to be the only one who could have committed the murder. In this way, the book has affinities with another twenty-year-old novel, *To Wake the Dead,* in which the protagonist also comes under immediate suspicion, but Carr uses the plot device more effectively in *Patrick Butler for the Defence.* He expanded the radio play by inserting his usual subplot of having one man attracted to two women, and in Lady Pamela de Saxe, whom Hugh falls for even though he is engaged to Helen Dean, Carr created one of his most interesting women. She begins as a featherheaded ginch, but gradually we understand that she has only put on what she herself calls "a mask" to face the world. Her father wanted her to act in a certain way and so she does.[47]

Other expansions of the radio play, however, are not successful. A nearly pointless scene occurs on a foggy night at an antique store, when Prentice and Butler see a sign announcing "Dead Men's Gloves." It turns out that a character who has very little to do with the story has decided for very little reason to trick the two men into the store, knowing that in spite of "the fog-barrier," Butler would see the sign, succumb to his curiosity, and enter. Fatuous though it is, this scheme works. The book is in fact filled with events and characters that have little to do with anything, but Carr's writing skill makes this problem obvious only on a second reading. What stands out on the first reading is the character of Patrick Butler, who is as arrogant and insufferable as ever.

But John Dickson Carr liked Patrick Butler, and for the next few years planned to write more books about him. In June 1956, he telephoned Hamish Hamilton to say that he had another novel in the works about the barrister, this one to be entitled *Look Upon the Prisoner,* and he promised to complete the typescript in August.[48]

Meanwhile, Carr was working on another project that he never completed. Around January 1956 he had suggested to David Higham that he write a thirty- to forty-thousand-word nonfiction work called *How to Write a Detective Story*; the book, he promised, would be written in an "amusing" manner. His fifteen-thousand-word essay "The Grandest Game in the World" was still in typescript, and Carr probably planned to expand some of the material from it into a treatise of moderate length. Higham immediately called several British publishers, and all expressed interest, especially his regular publisher, Hamish Hamilton, who sight unseen offered an advance of 150 pounds, and a 15 percent royalty on a published price of ten shillings, sixpence. Harpers also agreed to publish it, and a contract dated July 24, 1956, signed by Carr's British agent, survives in the Hamish Hamilton files. But already there were signs that Carr no longer was interested in the project. An internal memorandum in the David Higham papers, written a month before the contract, summarizes Carr as saying "Hamilton terms will be all right if and when he does the book."[49] The "when" never happened.

It seems to have been during his summer holidays in the middle 1950s that John Dickson Carr made final decisions about what book he would write each autumn. In Stockholm in 1955, he had decided to replace *The Sea Stingers* with *Patrick Butler for the Defence*. In June 1956, he went to Geneva to stay with his friend and former agent Rene de Chochor, the only person who ever represented him in America whom he completed trusted. He enjoyed the holiday so much that he returned in July and again in September.[50] It was around the time of his first Geneva holiday that Carr decided to delay his Patrick Butler novel *Look Upon the Prisoner* for a year; that is, it would become his 1958 novel for Harpers. For 1957 publication, he would write a historical detective story, set in 1829, about the founding of Scotland Yard.

Carr completed writing *Fire Burn and Cauldron Bubble*—another title that he liked, having already used it for a *Suspense* radio script—toward the end of October 1956. The title was shortened to *Fire, Burn!* when Harpers' salesmen told Carr's editor, Joan Kahn, that the original title was too long.[51] Meanwhile, his American agent, James Oliver Brown, was trying once again to do what had so long seemed impossible, find an American magazine to publish the novel before it appeared in book form. British magazines usually published Carr's books serially, but American magazines had rarely even shown interest—a fact which had led on several occasions to Carr's expressing dissatisfaction with every one of his American representatives except Chochor. This time, however, Carr was more hopeful:

> For some time [he wrote to Brown] I have been feeling a trend away from the bash-'em-and-heavy-sex-make-no-sense style of writing, and towards my own type: which certainly does not lack action or a love story, but makes all these depend on the deductive problem with all clues presented.

Brown sent the typescript of *Fire, Burn!* to *Collier's* magazine, which liked the story very much but requested that it be abridged from 90,000 to around 22,000 words. If that were possible, they would pay between $7,000 and $10,000 for rights. Carr agreed to allow *Collier's* to cut the novel, but then disaster struck. In December, *Collier's* announced that it was suspending publication. Never again would Carr get so close to a major American magazine sale of one of his novels.[52]

The Harpers edition of *Fire, Burn!* was printed in April 1957, but not officially published until June. It is possible that the Hamish Hamilton edition preceded the American, for it was announced for May 30. Nonetheless, British reviews did not begin until July.

Carr was pleased with his work in *Fire, Burn!* In 1963, in answer to a request from the Swedish mystery critic and editor Jan Broberg for a list of his personal favorites from among his impossible-crime novels, Carr included *Fire, Burn!** Four years later, I wrote Carr a fan letter and received a gracious reply in which he said, among other things, that *Fire, Burn!* was a book "I particularly enjoyed." His British agent, David Higham, was as enthusiastic in an internal memorandum as he was in letters to Carr. "This is an extremely good Carr," he noted, "much better than any he has done in a long while." Higham was correct; *Fire, Burn!* rivals the Carter Dickson book *Fear Is the Same* among his novels of the middle and later 1950s.[53]

Fire, Burn! has similarities to *The Devil in Velvet* and *Fear Is the Same.* All three are time-travel novels. In *Fire, Burn!*, Detective Superintendent John Cheviot steps into a taxi and directs it to Scotland Yard; when he alights, the cab has become a horse-drawn carriage, and the year is 1829. Cheviot thinks that going back in time is one of "the secret dreams all men hide and cherish." Carr even makes a hesitant bow toward Boucher's suggestion that scientific explanations of time travel are possible: "Even in time-trickeries there must be a how and why," he says in *Fire, Burn!*, but he neglects to tell us what the how and why are.[54] Not only is Cheviot transported to the past, but, as in the two earlier time-travel novels, the heroine turns out to live in both the past and the present. Both the positive and negative characters in *Fire, Burn!* conform to Carr's traditional types in the historicals, and they express familiar attitudes. Cheviot, like Philip Clavering and Jennifer Baird in *Fear Is the Same,* dislikes the snobbery and unfairness of the past. He hates the easy way of referring to people as "vulgar," and he recognizes that Flora Drayton's exaggerated femininity is a product of the age: "You have no rights, little freedoms, no privileges. What other weapons can you use?"[55] The villain is Captain Hogben, lisping,

---

*The other three on the list were *Till Death Do Us Part*, *He Who Whispers*, and *The Curse of the Bronze Lamp*.

condescending, an aristocrat with no aristocratic virtues who "never gives fair play."

But the similarities between *Fire, Burn!* and Carr's other time-travel mystery novels are superficial, setting the frame of the story rather than its substance. Probably because Cheviot is from Scotland Yard, detection is emphasized over the elements of historical romance. When Cheviot finds himself in 1829, Scotland Yard is just being established, and it is in part through his efforts that it gains an early respect. Cheviot is attracted to Flora Drayton, but this time Carr does not make his hero choose between two women. Flora thinks that Cheviot is in love with either Margaret Renfrew or Louise Tremayne, but even though Louise is the typical ginch of Carr's earlier books, Cheviot is interested only in Flora.

Cheviot's first case in 1829 seems trivial; he has to investigate the disappearance of birdseed from a canary cage. But the matter quickly becomes more serious when Margaret Renfrew is shot dead. She is in a passage, faced only by Cheviot, Flora, and Cheviot's assistant, Alan Henley. The only person to have a pistol is Flora Drayton, and she is innocent—at least of the murder. "We are left," Cheviot remarks, "with a belief in miracles or deviltry or witchcraft."[56] Without the resources of modern Scotland Yard, Cheviot must solve the case by his own wits at a time when the "Peelers" get scant respect.

Fire, Burn! has an almost pell-mell pace. Carr usually included one highly colorful scene in his historicals; in this instance it is a gambling den called Vulcan's. Vulcan, himself, is reminiscent of the grotesque characters from the Bencolin books:

> The man was too cat-footed of step, his neck too thick and firm in carrying the immense bald head. He had scarcely any eyebrows. The glass eye was his right; it gave the only staring, rather sinister touch to a manner of charm and grace.

Carr, however, makes Vulcan human and sympathetic by a sensitive description of his love for a lower-class doxie; and unlike Captain Hogben, Vulcan "in his own twisted way is a sportsman."[57]

Carr handles the puzzle dexterously, carefully directing the reader away from the murderer by misleading but entirely fair character descriptions. The solution to the apparent impossibility, though based too much on technical knowledge, is fairly clued. Perhaps most interesting is that it is related to three very early Carr stories: "The Ruby of Rameses," "The Marked Bullet," and "The Fourth Suspect." Each of those tales had a flaw that made the solutions even more impossible than the locked room they supposedly explained. In *Fire, Burn!* the situation is similar—but I cannot say more without revealing the murderer.

In December 1956, about two months after completing the typescript of *Fire, Burn!*, Carr began plans for his 1958 book for Harpers and Hamilton. Since 1948, Carr had been trying to find a plot to go with an evocative title, *The Witch of the Low-Tide*, and at the end of 1956 he decided that he would use the title for a novel featuring Patrick Butler.[58] When he actually began to write his book for 1958, however, he had changed his mind. In June 1957, he told Higham that his new book would be *Scandal at High Chimneys*. Nevertheless, he dropped, or delayed, this book as well. What actually did appear as the book for 1958 was a contemporary mystery, *The Dead Man's Knock*, featuring for the first time in almost a decade Dr. Gideon Fell. It was published around August 1958.* Nothing is recorded to explain why Carr changed his mind twice on what book to write, but it seems likely that Harpers' desire for a contemporary detective novel was involved, and Harpers may have asked for a return of Dr. Fell as well. Carr's books with contemporary settings generally sold better than the historicals. At about this time, Carr said that he would alternate historical mysteries with contemporary ones,[59] and it is true that the seven novels from *Captain Cut-Throat* (1955) through *The Witch of the Low-Tide* (1961) do follow that pattern.

Carr took the plot of *The Dead Man's Knock* from two radio scripts. Like the 1955 *Appointment With Fear* play of the same name, the book begins with a scholar (Mark Ruthven in the novel) about to lose his wife (Brenda Ruthven) to a young cad. Brenda genuinely loves Mark, but cannot stand the fact that sometimes he is more attentive to books than to her. The locked-room gimmick and the relationships among the characters are taken from another radio script, "A Most Respectable Murder," broadcast in 1948 on *Cabin B-13*. The title of the novel is from one of Carr's favorite books, R. H. Barham's *Ingoldsby's Legends*: "Fly open, lock, to the dead man's knock, fly bolt, and bar, and band."

The Dead Man's Knock has some intriguing plot elements. Mark is writing a book about the Victorian novelist Wilkie Collins, and he has discov-

---

*Carr's correspondence indicates one date for the British publication, but official records show another. Carr's agents wrote to him on May 22, 1958, that the Hamish Hamilton edition of *The Dead Man's Knock* was to be published that day, but other records put it in July, and reviews began in August. The American edition was printed in July and published in August.

ered a letter in which Collins suggested a locked-room murder as a plot of a novel. When a locked-room murder occurs in *The Dead Man's Knock*, it seems identical with the situation described in Collins's letter. Carr centers the book on the destructive female who sometimes appeared in his earlier novels, but rarely in such a major role. The book is divided into four sections, the first three of which are entitled "Wayward Woman," "Clever Woman," and "Strange Woman." Rose Lestrange is the type of femme fatale whom Carr had been both attracted to and repelled by, at least in his writings, since Haverford. She wants to control men, primarily through sex; but since Carr often makes the act of physical love equivalent to a depth of feeling, he says that Rose is actually frigid. Whether one accepts or rejects Carr's view of women, or at least of some women, his portrayal of Rose Lestrange is powerful.

In spite of some interesting elements—and its being Dr. Fell's first case solved in America—*The Dead Man's Knock* is a book written by a tired man. Looking back at these years (but not naming this particular book), Carr said that "I seemed to be losing the zest and drive that had carried me hitherto. Writing, once a breeze, became hard work except for certain moments in books I particularly enjoyed." He himself blamed his illnesses of the early 1950s,[60] but also involved was his increasing disaffection with a world that he neither liked nor understood. He could be enthusiastic in most of his historical novels written in the 1950s, but he found it difficult to put life into a novel like *The Dead Man's Knock*, which, although he backdated it to 1948, was still set in the modern world.

His weariness appears in *The Dead Man's Knock* in the too-convoluted relationships among the main characters, in which everyone seems to be bedding, or hoping to bed, almost everyone else. This of course produces an "emotional heat ... so high that it hissed." But it hisses too often, and many things that seem mysterious actually have no significance. Moreover, the main characters avoid having normal conversations; they lecture and posture and speak (as Carr admits) "in phrases deliberately cryptic."[61]

In *The Dead Man's Knock* and other books at this time, Carr was developing a new narrative technique. Instead of having linear accounts of events, he often ended a section with some mystery or a twist of the plot, then began the next section some hours later. We discover what happened in the interval through the conversations of the main characters. Carr did this to tease the reader by delaying the explanations, but the result is oddly stop-and-start. This technique, nonetheless, can be compelling. Almost like a Greek tragedy in which the horrifying scenes occur offstage, the attention is on the characters' emotions rather than on the sensational happenings. This two-steps-forward-one-step-back storytelling works very well in Carr's next three books. It is less successful in *The Dead Man's Knock*, which in spite of the hissing heat of emotions is a static novel.

In 1957, while Carr was working on *The Dead Man's Knock*, he wrote his final short stories. The market for short mystery fiction had been contracting for many years; *Collier's* and other glossy paper magazines in the United States were disappearing, and similar journals in England, such as *The Strand*, were gone. Remaining were intellectual journals, which rarely published detective fiction, some men's magazines, and digests like *Ellery Queen's Mystery Magazine*, whose pay scale was low. Carr, however, accepted a commission from *Lilliput*, an English men's magazine, to write a short story, "King Arthur's Chair," for its August 1957 issue. Although the story features Dr. Fell, it was published as by Carter Dickson, probably because Carr was still hoping to maintain the name's currency. Frederic Dannay printed it in the April 1958 *Ellery Queen's Mystery Magazine* under the title "Death by Invisible Hands." He made many minor editorial changes in the story, and they have been retained in all later reprints, published under the abbreviated title "Invisible Hands."

Like most of Carr's work at this time, "King Arthur's Chair" is an adaptation of an old radio script—"Below Suspicion" from *Cabin B-13*. It is the story of Brenda Lestrange (names that, in different combination, he also used in *The Dead Man's Knock*), who is found strangled in a stone outcropping (the titular "chair") surrounded by unmarked sand. Dr. Fell's solution to this traditional impossible crime gambit is nothing short of brilliant.

Carr's other short story of 1957, the thirty-two-hundred-word "Detective's Day Off" (submitted under the title "Scotland Yard's Christmas"), however, falls considerably short of brilliant. It was published in *Weekend*, December 25–29, 1957. The tale is so poorly told that, when I first read it, I had to wonder whether Carr wrote it. It does, however, have a number of Carrian touches, including an attempt to solve a puzzle propounded to him years earlier by Clayton Rawson—how can a person disappear from a telephone booth that is constantly under observation? I suspect that the publisher cut Carr's typescript drastically, especially the solution, which (most unlike Carr's work) is short and unclear. The story has been reprinted only twice since its first appearance—by Jack Adrian in *Crime at Christmas* (1988) and by me in *Merrivale, March and Murder* (1991), where it appeared under Carr's original title. Both Adrian and I had to add paragraphs to the original printed story to clear up the solution. But even so, Carr's explanation of the vanishing is clumsy—and he realized it. In 1963, he said that "I have yet to write" a solution of the telephone booth problem.[62]

Something else that John Dickson Carr could not yet find a solution to was his restlessness during the 1950s. In 1954, he had said that he could be happy only in England; by 1958, however, he was thinking about returning once again to the United States.

Chapter 17

RETURN TO MAMARONECK— AND ELSEWHERE

John Dickson Carr's decision to leave England in 1958 came as a surprise to many of his friends. Two years earlier he had announced to the press that he was at long last going to become a British subject, with Val Gielgud, Dorothy L. Sayers, and R. L. Jackson, assistant commissioner of Scotland Yard and chief of the Criminal Investigation Department, as his sponsors. "I have been here 26 years," Carr (who was never good with numbers) told an interviewer, "and the country suits me."[1] When Julia McNiven read about her father's announcement in the American press, she was not pleased. Julia has dual British and United States citizenship, but she was at that time in her life a staunch American, and she dashed off a note to her father "saying that I was the only one who remembered the Alamo." Clarice told John that the decision was up to him, but she doubted that he would go through with it since he sometimes had what she calls "a kind of American reverse snobbery." As royalist as he showed himself to be in some of his historical novels, he could nonetheless never admit that by birth a king or queen was anyone special. In the middle 1940s, for example, he had been invited to a royal audience because of his radio work, and he absolutely refused to attend—a decision that led to a brief estrangement with Gielgud. In any event, he decided not to apply for British citizenship, and the reason that he gave was financial. "There were such difficulties over tax," he explained, "I decided to drop it."[2]

Carr also said that taxes were the reason he made up his mind to leave England again. That, however, could not have been the main explanation. Although from an American's viewpoint, British tax rates could be considered confiscatory, Carr had earlier returned to England when they were just as high, and in comparison with the United States during the 1950s, living expenses were generally low. The most important reason was his general unhappiness and restlessness during these years. These feelings of malaise were related to the fact that he was tired of living alone. When he went to Kingswood to celebrate his fiftieth birthday, November 30, 1956, with Clarice and their two younger daughters, he had trouble persuading himself to return to London: "It was so pleasant after this lonely bachelor existence in London that I stayed over ten days instead of the two or three I had intended."[3] In March and April 1957, Julia McNiven and her two children* visited her mother and sisters in Kingswood, and toward the end of the trip stayed with her father at Hampstead. She told her mother that if they wanted to return to the United States, she could provide a home for her sisters until a house could be located. Clarice, meanwhile, agreed with her husband that the family should live together. Around September 1957, Carr gave up the lease on the flat at 40 Greenhill and joined by his wife and two daughters, rented a house at 16 Church Row, also in Hampstead. This, however, was not enough. Shortly after renting the house, Carr decided that they would return to the United States. Early in 1958, he told his friend Edmund Crispin that he was considering moving to northern Virginia, which he had just used as the setting for *The Dead Man's Knock*. The Carrs decided, however, to live again in the New York area, and Clarice wrote to Julia taking her up on the offer to house her sisters. Bonnie, almost eighteen years old, and Mary, then fifteen, set off some weeks before their parents, who first had to settle their affairs in England.[4]

On June 24, 1958, John and Clarice Carr embarked on the liner *Caronia*. John told a reporter in London that he would stay in America at least a year. On arriving in New York City on July 1, however, he said that he planned to stay permanently in the United States.[5] They wanted to live near their friends in the Mamaroneck and Larchmont area and rented an

---

*Lynn Clarice, born in July 1953, and Michelle Mary, born in August 1955.

apartment in Mamaroneck for a month or so, until John found a house he liked at 211 Beach Avenue. It was a rambling, gabled house, with large porches, a captain's walk on the roof, and an attic room that he could turn into a study. The house was in shocking disrepair, but it was what Carr wanted, and he bought it with cash—something that astonished the realtor. The house was fixed up, and mother, father, and two daughters, along with Violet Andrews to keep house, moved in. Immediately, Carr had shelves built in his study and the living room for his voluminous collection of books, and he had his devil tapestries and sword collection mounted on the walls.

As John settled back into the routine of writing, Clarice for the first time since their marriage took a job. She earned her real estate license, and (she recalls proudly) actually sold a house.[6]

Otherwise, the Carrs spent their second period in Mamaroneck rather quietly. Although an accomplished hostess, Clarice never enjoyed entertaining, and—probably as part of his increasing retreat from mid-twentieth-century life—John no longer sought new social contacts. The contrast is marked between the first and second Mamaroneck periods. In the late 1940s, the Carrs often had guests at their house, including members of the Mystery Writers of America and Mamaroneck neighbors; in the late 1950s, however, only old friends such as Kate and Clayt Rawson were regular visitors. Carr had by no means become a recluse and he accepted invitations from others, but his day was usually spent in his study, writing and reading, especially history—and smoking copious numbers of cigarettes.[7]

One such invitation came from his friend the novelist William Lindsay Gresham. In summer 1959, Gresham invited Carr for lunch to meet his editor and his wife. The small gathering became a discussion of detective fiction and true crime. Mary Cantwell, the wife of Gresham's editor, recalls, "We talked all afternoon, he, elderly and small as a jockey; I, young and big with my first child—and our words tumbled over one another's." They talked about methods of scattering clues, murder means, and their mutual favorite true-crime case, the murder of Julia Wallace. "He was especially pleased by my love of *The Burning Court*," Cantwell says. "I suppose I remember the day as well as I do because I was so touched by it." Gresham was living under severe financial difficulties at this time, and "one knew it really strained Gresham's purse to entertain, even with ground beef, but he had the air of a Spanish don. Carr behaved like he was dining in the grandest of London Clubs." After lunch, Carr insisted that the Cantwells come to Mamaroneck. He showed them a portrait of Gideon Fell painted by a friend, and source materials that he used for researching his historical novels—volumes of *The Newgate Calendar* and old London street maps ("he was very proud of his geographical accuracy," Cantwell remembers).[8] There were other social occasions during this period of Carr's life, but like his meeting with Gresham and the Cantwells, he rarely initiated such contacts.

But no matter how grim his mood might become, Carr loved Christmastime and buying gifts for his grandchildren. When he was living in Mamaroneck, or in later years when he was visiting for the holidays, he would go to two stores on the main street. The first stop was the toy store, from which he would emerge with an armload of gifts for children under about fifteen years of age. Then he'd go to the jewelry store, where he would buy presents for everyone older than fifteen. No matter that Julia McNiven had refused to buy an expensive present for one of her children; they could prevail upon their grandfather to get it. As he had indicated in *A Graveyard to Let*, Carr had never quite known what to make of his own children, but he was a wonderful Santa to his grandchildren. He had a Sir Henry Merrivale streak that allowed him to relate to children, at least when he did not have to be a father to them. On one occasion, when Julia returned from an errand she found that he had attached fake bullet holes to her windows. He had also brought with him collapsing spoons, dribble glasses, and whoopie cushions—the last of the sort that requires tremendous determination in sitting to obtain any sort of sound at all. He also loved fairs. He enjoyed gathering up a batch of children to take to Mamaroneck's Firemen Carnivals and to the Lollypop Fair at the Methodist church where they had a spook house. John Dickson Carr together with the children would go on every ride over and over again.[9]

Carr had changed residences so often that he was able to speak authoritatively of the effect pulling up stakes had on him: "As often happens when you move from one country to another," he remarked in January 1959, "I am in the midst of a strong creative streak." He planned to go back to a schedule of two books every year, something that he had accomplished only once during the past six years.[10] In addition, he agreed to select the best stories by Sir Arthur Conan Doyle, to be published in a volume commemorating the centennial of Doyle's birth. Carr's introduction to this volume, published as *Great Stories* in 1959, is filled with heartfelt praise of Doyle and criticism of the "pseudo-intellectual" who can't tell the difference between great storytelling (Carr named Kipling,

Dumas, Dickens, and Stevenson along with Doyle) and the psychoanalytic modern writers who tell us "that we are all dull and damned as well as being damned dull."[11]

In the event, however, Carr could no longer write two novels a year. His 1959 novel was *Scandal at High Chimneys* set in the London of 1865. This is another Carr novel from the 1950s that may have been published first in England. The Harpers edition was printed in June, but not officially published until August 1959, though copies were probably available earlier; the Hamish Hamilton edition was published in the middle of July. Unusually for one of Carr's historicals, his publishers managed a book-club sale: The Detective Book Club included *Scandal at High Chimneys* in one of its triple volumes.

Scandal at High Chimneys shares some of the problems of the previous year's *The Dead Man's Knock*. As in the earlier book, Carr artificially creates what he calls an "atmosphere of tension and hysterics"[12] by overusing his trick of saying obscure things, and by beginning to explain a mystery only to have the revelation interrupted. I counted thirteen separate instances in *Scandal at High Chimneys* in which someone, for insufficient reasons, refuses to reveal something.[13] It is easy to sympathize with the protagonist when he moans that although two people say they know who the murderer is, and two more certainly do, "no one will say a word."[14]

On the other hand, Carr superbly handles the Victorian setting of *Scandal at High Chimneys,* and effectively integrates the background of the time with the people and events:

> A boisterous autumn night, blowing all the waste-paper which is as thick as grit in London streets, whooped outside. Though the windows might be sealed with thick dingy-green curtains as all their lives (they hoped) were shrouded and sealed from view, the wind found loose frames; draughts carried away most scents except the pervasiveness of the damp greatcoats and the boiled mutton.[15]

Surrounding everything is a feeling that the proper behavior of the Victorians masks depravity.

The puzzle facing the hero, Clive Strickland, is which child of Matthew Damon, master of a house named High Chimneys, is really the offspring of a murderess. As in *The Third Bullet* (as well as many genuine Victorian novels), the contrast between Damon's two daughters is that one is fair and the other dark. And also as in *The Third Bullet,* Carr uses this contrast to play tricks with the reader's assumptions. Before he can reveal the truth, Matthew Damon is killed, seemingly by a ghost wearing patterned trousers—in its gruesome use of the ordinary, this image is reminiscent of the man tapping his cane in "The Man Who Was Dead" and the head held at an odd angle in *The Plague Court Murders*. The case is solved by a genuine detective of the time, Sergeant Whicher, who had identified the murderer in the sensational Constance Kent case of 1860.

Carr followed *Scandal at High Chimneys* with *In Spite of Thunder*, a Dr. Fell novel set in Geneva in 1956—when Carr himself was vacationing in that city. In honor of the thirtieth anniversary of Carr's first book, Harpers hoped to publish the new novel in the same month as *It Walks By Night*, that is, during February 1960.[16] Unfortunately, although he promised to complete the typescript by autumn 1959, he did not submit it until December, and by that time it was too late to publish the book the next February. Harpers, however, did in a sense honor the anniversary by briefly reviving the 1930s gimmick of having the final pages of the novel sealed. The United States edition appeared in June, the British at the end of September 1960.

The book has many of the characteristics of Carr's late style. For example, people often speak like no one living in the twentieth century. Some of the dialogue resembles a radio script, with conversation providing stage directions: "Then if you will glance where I am pointing—so!—you may get something of a surprise," and, "Stand just where you are, here at the foot of the stairs!" Not only Dr. Fell but many of the other characters pose and speak portentously and pretentiously. When one character simply asks, "Do you agree?" another responds, "In candour and honesty: very well. Yes!" In candor and honesty, only the last word was necessary. Yet Carr himself was aware of this growing tendency in his writing, and so were the characters in his novels, who say such things as "confound your pompousness."[17]

As stilted as all this is, it nonetheless works much of the time. In *In Spite of Thunder*, Carr creates a world in which people protect themselves through formal speech and behavior, but Carr—who tended to protect himself in the same way—invests these scenes with intensity. He does this partly through the forward-backward narrative technique that I have already discussed, which stretches the reader's curiosity almost to the breaking point. In addition, Carr uses the threatening weather, indicated in the title, to symbolize the emotions of the characters. This technique is, of course, old and almost hackneyed, but few other mystery writers have so effectively dramatized a background of "thick overcast air, a hollow of thundery heat."[18]

As with many of Carr's novels at this time, the plot of *In Spite of Thunder* is based on who is sexually attracted to whom. In this book the older characters, both male and female, want to bed younger ones. The hero, Brian Innes, aged forty-six, is in love with Audrey Page, who is nineteen years younger. Audrey, in turn, is engaged to Phil Ferrier. In other words, Carr puts a new twist on the familiar triangular relationships of his main characters. Instead of the expected situation in which a man is attracted to two women, the heroine in *In Spite of Thunder* must choose between two men. Phil is the son of Desmond Ferrier, an aging actor, who is married to an actress whose stage name was actually Eve Eden. A mystery surrounds Eve. A Nazi sympathizer, she had been in Germany in July 1939 with her elderly lover. With no one near him, the old man had fallen to his death from a terrace of Eagle's Nest, Hitler's retreat high above Berchtesgaden. "Then nothing moved on the terrace except a big flag, a black swastika on a red-and-white ground, curling out above them and throwing shadows."[19] Had Eve murdered him? If so, how did she do it? To end rumors that she was a murderer, she invites the surviving witnesses to her villa at Geneva, but—again with no one near—she is killed when she falls from a terrace.

Carr took the explanation for his impossible murder from a *Cabin B-13* script, "The Count of Monte Carlo," but he improved it by also providing two persuasive, but false, solutions. Moreover, he revived a plot device that he had used in early novels, including *Castle Skull*, *The Unicorn Murders*, and *Fatal Descent*: Two detectives compete to unearth the truth. Sir Gerald Hathaway, a methodical criminologist, is certain that he knows the truth of the 1939 death, but Dr. Fell seems to be working in a different direction. "Unlike Gerald Hathaway, who never does anything by accident," Brian Innes remarks, "Gideon Fell seldom does anything by design."[20] Although not one of Carr's great novels, *In Spite of Thunder* is a successful exercise in ingenuity and suspense.

After his initial enthusiasm in returning to the United States, Carr began to feel more and more out of touch. A year after leaving England, he wrote back to London that he was homesick and asked his agents to subscribe to *The Spectator* and *Punch* for him. His letters from this period are filled with depressed comments, especially about his age. Some of his remarks are jocular—"My whiskers are as long as a Chelsea pensioner's," and, "I tell myself firmly that I will do more work in the future and that

even a person of my age and decrepitude can manage it." Some of the remarks, however, are serious. When he decided no longer to have an
American agent and to make arrangements with Harpers himself, he
wrote: "life grows grimmer . . . I am in my middle fifties; I *ought* in all conscience to be able to manage this out of whatever common sense has accumulated in me."[21]

As usually happened when he was unhappy, Carr thought of moving
to another country. His younger daughters were leaving home, and although the Carrs had the inevitable worries connected with those events,
there were also fewer ties holding them in one place. Bonita attended Vas-
sar in the autumn of 1959, but after only about six weeks, she quit and to
the entire family's astonishment enlisted in the Marines. Her father was
suspicious of almost any sort of authority, but he did not oppose her decision. Soon, in fact, he was sending Bonnie amusing letters about the "string
of hieroglyphics" that the Marines attached to her name, and expressing
pride in her plans to join Military Intelligence. He wrote her a mock letter
as though he were "formerly Chief of all the French Secret Service":

> One applauds. One lifts the hat. . . . Perhaps they will not really allow
> you to use the cloak and the dagger, or to wear wigs and hiss outside
> windows after the fashion of us in France. And yet why not? I ask
> myself again: why not?[22]

In 1960, Bonnie announced that she was going to marry a Marine named
Charles Harrison. John and Clarice were not certain of their daughter's
choice of husband, but the decision was hers, and she did marry. Her son,
Stephen Harrison, was born in July 1961.

In the spring of 1960, Mary told her parents that she wanted to attend a
British university. Carr replied that he had been thinking of leaving
Mamaroneck anyway, although he was uncertain where he wanted to re-
side. His first thought was that he and Clarice would take up residence
again in England, but more as a headquarters than as a permanent domi-
cile. Taxes remained high there, and as he wrote to his cousin Nick Carr,
"The old days are gone and our friends scattered, and there's not much to
draw us back." Instead, they would spend most of their time traveling. A
short while later, however, he considered moving to Ireland, which was
tax-free to writers and other artists. Oddly enough, in spite of his early
love for Ireland and his proximity to the island for many years, he had
never been there. Mary decided to apply to Trinity College in Dublin. She
was accepted, but meanwhile her father changed his mind again. As Mary

got ready to go to Dublin, her parents prepared to return to Tangier, where, they had heard, it was even less expensive to live than in Ireland.[23]

Richard and Julia McNiven were looking for a large house for themselves and their three children (Wooda Howard McNiven had been born in March 1958), so they purchased 211 Beach Avenue from her parents. John and Clarice usually cleaned out all their papers before their moves, but this time they decided that they would have no room to take John's books and collections of daggers and rapiers to Tangier. They left the books behind, and gave Dick the rapier collection; the McNivens still have the collection as well as many of the books.

The Carrs arrived in Tangier on September 2, 1960, and took rooms at a hotel—or, as Carr described it, a "glorified boardinghouse"—called L'Ermitage on the rue de Grenade. In January 1961, they rented an apartment at 18 Inmueble San Francisco, which was in the Spanish quarter at the Plaza de Navarra.[24] Living in Tangier was indeed extremely inexpensive but Carr was frequently dispirited. He had problems with his teeth, resulting in the extraction of most of his upper teeth. He was at first sensitive about this, so in an odd move, but probably a psychologically sound one, he shaved off the mustache he had had for thirty years. He reasoned that his friends would notice the lack of the mustache rather than the lack of teeth. He grew a mustache again in 1965, but kept it only briefly. During the early months living in Tangier, the Carrs did some traveling—to Paris the last ten days of September 1960, then for two weeks to Dublin to visit Mary in November. But when his agent David Higham wanted him to visit London to discuss business, Carr refused:

> I daren't afford much pleasure these days. ... A trip to London would entail more expense than at the moment I feel justified in undertaking. Am I becoming too dour and cautious with increasing years? I may be growing old, it's true, or I may only be growing up.[25]

Low spirits, which were often part of Carr's life at this time, had set in again. Carr said that, after thirty years of writing mystery novels, he now wanted to write only nonfiction.

This admission came because a proposal from NBC television offered the possibility of freeing Carr from doing an annual novel. The NBC anthology series *Dow Great Mysteries* had televised a dramatization of *The Burning Court* on April 24, 1960. Carr pronounced the adaptation "an admirable job,"[26] and he was pleased when NBC asked about rights to the character of Dr. Fell for either an hour or a half-hour television series.

There was nothing unusual about such a request. Carr was used to television networks—as well as film and radio companies—inquiring about rights to his stories, and sometimes options had been granted. Only rarely had anything resulted. Still, television prospects looked good toward the end of 1960, at a time when Carr was eager to free himself from publishers' deadlines. He immediately accepted NBC's terms, agreeing that the network could write its own stories or use any of Carr's plots. The point, he told his agent, "is that for years—my God, how many years!—I have dreamed of a time when perhaps for a twelvemonth or even two years I could sit back without the necessity of doing a damned thing during that time except a biography or a historical study I really want to write." But, he continued, "I'm not getting golden illusions. We both know how chancy these television projects can be."[27] Unfortunately, as with similar proposals in the past, the network's initial enthusiasm faded; comments about a Dr. Fell series in Carr's correspondence became rarer and rarer until they finally disappeared.

Let's take a moment here to look at the film adaptations of Carr's work that I have not previously mentioned. Besides the Colonel March film (which was cobbled together from three television episodes), very few feature-length movies have been made from Carr's stories, and two of these (*The Man with a Cloak* and *Dangerous Passage*) have already been discussed. Also filmed was a version of *The Emperor's Snuff-Box*, starring Petula Clark, Dan O'Herlihy, and Wilfrid Hyde-White. It was released to generally unenthusiastic reviews in Britain as *That Woman Opposite* in 1957, and two years later in the United States as *City After Midnight*. Correspondents who remember it report that it was a lackluster production— "without tension and rhythm," says French film expert Roland Lacourbe, "and very bad photography." There was soon to be another film based on Carr's works, a French version of *The Burning Court*. Negotiations for cinema rights for this book began in November 1960, while Carr was in Tangier. Directed by Julian Duvivier and starring Nadja Tiller and Jean-Claude Brialy, *La Chambre Ardente* was released in France in 1961, and with English-language dubbing, it appeared in the United States in 1963. Prints do not seem to be available, but Roland Lacourbe has sent me a summary. Except for Marie D'Aubray, the names of the characters were changed, and the setting was moved from Pennsylvania to France. Lacourbe writes:

> I remember some very good scenes in the old castle in the center of
> the Forêt Noires, with ghostly apparitions, long shadows over the

walls, and so on. A very gothic atmosphere. The first part of the film was very close to the book, but the middle and the end were completely different, and the adaptors didn't respect the two solutions of the book.[28]

When a television series about Dr. Fell did not come through, Carr could not indulge his dream of taking a year off from writing fiction. While in Tangier in 1960 and 1961, he completed a new historical novel, *The Witch of the Low-Tide* (which I shall discuss shortly), and he made plans to write mystery novels set in Tangier. One of them would combine the comic with the sensational in modern Tangier; the other would be set in the seventeenth century, apparently during the British occupation of Tangier under King Charles II. Carr did some research for the historical novel in archives at the British Consulate, but neither idea for a Tangier novel ever got past the planning, or perhaps musing, stage. [29]

Once Carr had finished *The Witch of the Low-Tide*, he decided that it was time to return to the United States. The restlessness that had afflicted him since the late 1940s had reached the point that he was rarely willing to stay in any place for more than seven or eight months. At the end of April 1961, with the lease on the apartment coming up, the Carrs booked passage on the *Leonardo da Vinci* and left for New York from Gibraltar on May 1. They stayed in Mamaroneck from May through July, but not surprisingly almost immediately John regretted returning to the United States. By June he was grumbling about "the beginning of a murderously hot summer. I am beginning to wish myself back in North Africa, where at least it is reasonably cool." In July and August, while Clarice remained in Mamaroneck, he went to London for three weeks, and on August 10 he was back in Tangier, renting the same apartment in the Spanish quarter for two months. But before the lease had expired, he decided to go back to London for another two weeks, then return directly to Mamaroneck at the end of September 1961.[30]

At the beginning of this third period in Mamaroneck, John and Clarice Carr rented a small apartment over a laundry on Mamaroneck Avenue, but they both preferred living in a house. A few months later, they purchased (with cash again) a small home at 326 Melbourne Avenue, one street over from the Beach Avenue house that they had sold to Julia and Dick. Clarice remembers the Melbourne residence as "a lovely little house." Still standing, it has two stories, a porch on the front, but no attic study for John. Because of his grandchildren, he spent much time at the

McNivens'. Almost every Wednesday, he showed up, allowed himself to be persuaded to have dinner, then watched television with his grandchildren the rest of the evening.[31] He liked mystery dramas, especially a few years later *The Man from U.N.C.L.E.*, but if a favorite program wasn't on, he would still find something to watch.

This time, Carr did not complain about where he was living. As had happened some years earlier, he felt the creative juices flowing after the change in residences. "I have been writing like hell since my return to this country," he said in February 1962, "and scarcely leaving the house."[32] He began one abortive project that we have already discussed—the eight chapters of an H.M. book entitled *The Six Black Reasons*—and he made tentative plans to collaborate on a book with Clayton Rawson. The project had begun when Rawson tried to pin down a legend that Poe did some of his drinking at a Mamaroneck tavern. Biographies of Poe do not mention any visit to Mamaroneck, but it made an intriguing background for a novel or short story. As in *The Mad Hatter Mystery*, the plot would have involved the discovery of a Poe manuscript—this time, in one of the tombs in the local cemetery—but nothing came of the idea.[33] Meanwhile, Carr worked on what he now called "my customary yearly Harper-Hamilton book."

In the midst of all these moves from 1960 to 1962 and possible writing projects (ideas for Tangier novels, a possibility for one featuring Poe, and hopes of reviving H.M.), Carr completed two books, both of them historicals—thereby breaking his recent pattern of alternating historical with contemporary novels—and both involving in a general way the development of the London police. In "Notes for the Curious," which appears in the British but not the American edition of *The Witch of the Low-Tide*, Carr wrote that "this is the third and last of three detective novels designed to have their background at Scotland Yard from the founding of the Metropolitan Police to the opening decade of the twentieth century." The first was *Fire, Burn!*, which took place in 1829. Carr asserted that the second was the mid-Victorian *Scandal at High Chimneys*, though including it as a Scotland Yard novel may have been an afterthought, since the detective was a private investigator who had been forced to resign from the Metropolitan Police. *The Witch of the Low-Tide* takes place in 1907, when Edward VII was on the throne, and one of the major characters is Inspector George Alfred Twigg of the Yard. Carr, however, was typically uninterested in police procedure, and the emphasis of the book is upon a duel of wits between the hero, David Garth, and Inspector Twigg. *The Demoniacs*, published a year after *The Witch of the Low-Tide*, might be called, using a recent term, a "prequel" to the Scotland Yard series. The events occur in 1757, and a major character is Blind Justice Fielding, head of London's Bow Street Runners for a quarter of a century.

Carr had wanted to call some work "The Witch of the Low-Tide" for a considerable number of years. The phrase first showed up in 1948 as an unused title for one of the *Cabin B-13* scripts, and almost a decade later Carr planned a Patrick Butler novel with the same title. Published in both the United States and Britain in October 1961, *The Witch of the Low-Tide* is an impressive performance, both as a detective novel and as a historical re-creation. It has, however, some of the writing quirks that occasionally weaken Carr's novels of this period. Carr sometimes keeps the mystery going by interrupting important conversations and by refusing to explain things; in one instance, David Garth stops the heroine, Betty Calder, from revealing to him what she had done, because he is short of time and, anyway, he already knows the truth. The reader, however, doesn't know, and is more frustrated than intrigued.[34] But these matters do not dominate the book.

Carr's characters in *The Witch of the Low-Tide* occasionally employ florid speech, and people address each other anachronistically as "your servant, sir." When he received the typescript, David Higham (who was twelve years old in 1907) told Carr, "I don't believe anyone in my boyhood would have said 'Your servant, sir' as one man to another; nor I believe for a long time before that."[35] For the most part, however, people speak normally without undue formality, and Carr distinguishes the characters by the rhythms of their speech. Inspector Twigg, for example, talks in a slang that is quite different from David Garth's educated tones. In his historical novels, Carr did well with period details—of which there are many in *The Witch of the Low-Tide*, including smells: "Afterward he never forgot the air or the texture of the evening: the tarry smell of wood-paving after a day's heat."[36] But he was not always so successful with period attitudes. The characters usually reflect Carr's own views, no matter the era of the events.

Most interesting in *The Witch of the Low-Tide* is Carr's discussion of the importance of writing historical novels. As he had said in *Fear Is the Same*, the point is our common humanity, no matter the age. He remarks in *The Witch of the Low-Tide*:

> If you stood motionless in the stream of time, listening to crying voices out of the past, you might presently believe that your feelings or your neighbour's were of puny significance because they had

been experienced so often before and would be experienced again when you had gone. Whereas they did matter; they were the only reality; there was no shame in feeling the hurt.[37]

And we hear Carr's own sadness about the changing world. Garth remarks, "Nothing ever remains the same. We can't expect it to." Another character responds, "I don't expect it really. But, my God, Garth, how I dislike it!" Garth: "Perhaps, in my own heart, I like it no better than you. That doesn't alter the fact that the child grows into the adult, and everything changes."[38]

David Garth, even more obviously than most Carr heroes, is a stand-in for the author. He is a Harley Street physician, but a bit more than halfway through the book, Garth admits that he also writes impossible-crime detective novels under the pseudonym "Phantom." The book has brief discussions of two of the authors who strongly influenced Carr, Gaston Leroux and Jacques Futrelle. A woman even has the name Mrs. Hanshew, but any connection to the author of the Hamilton Cleek stories is not revealed. Garth explains that the purpose of detective novels is not to scare the public:

> Great Scott, no! That's only the excuse for the story; we don't really meet ghosts in Piccadilly Circus. It's the exercise of one's ingenuity, the setting of the trap and the double-trap, the game you play chapter after chapter against a quick-witted reader.[39]

The Witch of the Low-Tide is indeed an exercise in ingenuity. The main mystery is a murder in a bathing pavilion surrounded by sand marked with footprints only of Garth and Betty Calder, both of whom arrive after the murder. Carr had always enjoyed working out solutions to the problem of the body surrounded by snow or sand; the situation in *The Witch of the Low-Tide* is similar to that in *The White Priory Murders*, *The Problem of the Wire Cage*, "Error at Daybreak," "King Arthur's Chair," and less directly, *She Died a Lady*. The explanation in *The Witch of the Low-Tide* is a cunning variation of the one given almost thirty years earlier in *The White Priory Murders*.

Carr handles the verbal battle between Garth and Twigg with great facility. The reader doesn't know what Garth knows; the reader doesn't know what Twigg knows; but the reader does know that Garth must prevail or Betty Calder is in jeopardy. It takes all of Carr's narrative skill to keep the story clear by revealing solutions to early mysteries as the story develops while keeping the impossible situation and the identity of the murderer unexplained until the climax of the story.

Carr completed his next book, *The Demoniacs,* in the middle of April 1962.[40] It was published in October in the United States, and a month later in Britain. His books written shortly after his recovery from three years of illness a decade earlier had generally been of high quality. Some from the middle 1950s, especially *Fire, Burn!* and *Fear Is the Same,* compare favorably with any of his earlier books, but it cannot be denied that there was a falling off in his work toward the end of the decade and the beginning of the next. But this decline was not steady. For example, both *Scandal at High Chimneys* and *In Spite of Thunder* are far better than *The Dead Man's Knock,* which immediately preceded those books. Carr's lessening powers as a writer, however, are obvious in *The Demoniacs.*

Before we look closely at *The Demoniacs,* I should point out that the title is irrelevant. The hero, Jeffrey Wynne, explains that the Demoniacs are a society like the genuine Medmenham Monks (or Hellfire Club) of the eighteenth century, but they do not appear in the book at all. On one occasion, Blind Justice Fielding says, "I am a human soul like yourself, prone at times to behaviour I can't justify." Jeffrey responds, "Yes, we are all demoniacs."[41] This hardly seems enough justification for the title of the book.

The Demoniacs has some vividly realized scenes. The book opens on old London Bridge, where the houses are being torn down, then proceeds to Mrs. Salmon's Waxworks and Ranelagh Gardens, where trysts are made and woman walk about almost naked. Some of the characters, too, are interesting, especially the Reverend Laurence Stern, a drunken clergyman (and later novelist) who acts as the comic relief. The impossible crime is the death, apparently by fright, of an old woman named Grace Delight who is still occupying a house on London Bridge. The situation is similar to the deaths in *The Reader Is Warned,* but the solution is different.

Jeffrey Wynne, a Bow Street Runner in the year 1757, has gone to France at the order of Sir Mortimor Ralston to bring back his niece, Mary Margaret ("Peg") Ralston, who has run off to escape being imprisoned as a common bawd—in fact, however, she has been a "bawd" only to Jeffrey. Jeffrey's loyalty to Peg is constant, though his behavior might lead rational people to think otherwise. He turns Peg over to her uncle and threatens to throttle her. Jeffrey is in many ways the least attractive of Carr's heroes—he tends toward violence to women (though he never actually strikes one), and later in the book, the reader discovers that he had considered robbing and murdering an old woman. Though Carr seems to like him, most judicious readers will probably decide that his predicaments—as well as Peg's—are his fault partly because he always seems to be riding off on his high horse, and partly because (like most of the characters) he will not say clearly what he means.

As in *The Witch of the Low-Tide* and *Captain Cut-Throat*, the plot has to do with a duel of wits among the principal characters. The problem in *The Demoniacs* is that there are too many duels going on. In *The Witch of the Low-Tide*, Carr was able to keep the story line clear; in *The Demoniacs*, he fails. Everyone has secrets, most talk in riddles, and they hide their meaning when a few plain words would help. If Carr had explained things as he went along and not been so concerned about having every revelation hinted about in earlier sections, the book would be easier to follow. At the end, some of the actions seem not to have been sufficiently motivated, or at least explained with enough clarity that the reader knows why people acted as they did. The result is that everything is mysterious, even when it needn't be—though the ultimate mystery may be why so many characters act like idiots.

Even the clueing is less fair than usual. Jeffrey finds evidence in certain documents without revealing it to the reader, and an important clue is simply wrong. On publication of the book, Anthony Boucher wrote to Carr that a key line on page 26 of the United States first edition is flatly contradicted on page 128. (I can't say more without revealing a major point of the solution.) In some embarrassment, Carr replied:

> Your objection to *The Demoniacs* . . . is entirely valid. . . . Invariably, in writing the end, I leaf back through to see the precise words that were used: as a rule it is necessary to quote dialogue. I did so in this book—except, stupidly, at that particular point, because only the author had been speaking and I imagined I remembered. A blunder like that has not occurred in a quarter of a century; it must not occur again. However indifferent the books may be, at least I take pains with them.

Boucher suggested that the mistake be corrected in reprints, and though the alterations would have been easy to make, the erroneous wording has remained.[42]

Chapter 18

THE LAST WANDERINGS

It was early spring in 1963 at Mamaroneck. John Dickson Carr, sipping tea in his study in the Melbourne Avenue house, was writing a new detective novel. Lynn, Michelle, and Wooda McNiven* had come to have tea with their grandmother in the garden. When Clarice Carr went inside to ask John whether he wanted more tea, she found him lying on the floor unable to move. She remembers that she knew that her husband must have had a stroke. Uncertain what to do, she called her good friend Kate Rawson, who lived only one block away. She and Kate telephoned the police for help, and they tried to contact Dr. William Barrett, who had done so much a decade earlier during John's serious bouts with the fistula and the abscess. Barrett was on his way to New York City to take a flight to a medical convention, but when he got the message, he turned around and headed back to Mamaroneck. The police arrived, and so did an ambulance, but Barrett decided that it would be better to treat Carr at home. He did not expect that Carr would be able to walk again.[1]

Looking back at the situation, Clarice Carr thinks that her husband was, in a sense, working up to the stroke during the previous year. Dr.

*By this time, the McNivens also had a fourth child, a girl named Russell Hope, born in January 1963.

Barrett had warned him that something like a stroke might happen if he did not get his drinking under control, and Carr had been sick off and on in 1962. He often dozed off while he was with others, and when family problems came up he simply was not well enough to handle them.

John's mother, Julia Kisinger Carr, was a particular worry at that time. Following the death of Wooda Nicholas Carr nineteen years earlier, Julia Carr had sold the old house on Ben Lomond Street and moved into an apartment near her sisters in Brownsville, Pennsylvania. In the spring of 1962, when she was eighty-four years old, she fell and was unable to care for herself. John and Clarice were notified that Julia Carr should be put into a nursing home. John was unwell at that time, so Clarice went by herself to Uniontown, feeling very guilty about sending an unwilling old woman to institutional care. Almost as soon as Clarice placed her mother-in-law in the home, however, Julia Carr left it and returned to Brownsville. John's old friend Edward Dumbauld, who had become a federal judge, helped in the situation, and eventually she did return to the nursing home. John not only paid for her care but visited her there on several occasions. She died in 1966.[2]

Carr's letters during 1962 and the early part of 1963 are not merely grumpy; they are depressed. Shortly after Christmas 1962, he asked his British agent, David Higham, for "anything pleasant you can tell me." "This," he continued, "is a rather grim season of year." In February, he wrote to several people about his increasing age, although he was only fifty-six years old.

> I have reached that stage of antiquity at which people murmur, "Good God, is *he* still alive?" Perhaps I had better shut up before some public-spirited friend (or enemy) remedies the oversight with a pinch of cyanide or a well-directed bullet from a window on 42nd Street. No doubt he would be doing the world a good turn.

"I am not the young and enthusiastic slogger I once was," he told his agent. "I must not expect eternal productivity, any more than I must expect eternal life." As usual when he was unhappy, he thought about changing countries. As early as May 1962, he had made plans to return to England. Prices were too high in the United States, he complained, "where the price even of a ham sandwich is out of all proportion to the value of the ham or the bread."[3] His British agents continued to expect him in London, but he explained that there were tax matters to work out.

"Though my health continues to be good, *Dei gratia*," Carr said about two months before the stroke, "there are intimations of mortality for everybody."[4] The stroke was apparently of the form called "cerebral hemorrhage"; it affected his speech and paralyzed his left side. As he slowly recovered, he was at first withdrawn, and he brooded. Although perfectly amiable, he did not want to hold a conversation with anyone. His mental processes were not affected, but in Clarice's words, "He wouldn't speak any more than he absolutely had to. But he was still writing." Although he remained withdrawn for some months, he was determined to overcome the physical affects of the stroke. He had almost no use of his left hand, and his left leg dragged when he walked. He did exercises to strengthen the hand, and every morning, even in the worst weather, he hobbled around and around the block. He even forced his body to play tennis.[5] But in spite of everything, he never entirely recovered. He walked with a limp for the rest of his life, and his left hand remained so weak that he could not eat or type with it.

One result of the stroke was to limit Carr's drinking. Dr. Barrett had wanted him to give up alcohol entirely, but that solution was not in the cards. Carr, however, knew that his body could not take the abuse that he had been giving it for years, and he limited his drinking, except on rare occasions, almost entirely to beer, and he usually avoided even that until around ten o'clock at night. He very much looked forward to the evening when he could down three or four cans in rapid succession, but the old days of binge drinking were over.[6]

Carr had been writing a new novel at the time he was stricken, and as soon as he could he tried to get back to work. The result, Carr said, was "so feeble that I put it aside and fell back on a book of short stories."[7] In short, the situation was much as it had been ten years earlier when, because Carr found himself unable to write, Harpers had published a short-story collection. The new short-story volume, *The Men Who Explained Miracles,* was assembled quickly in July 1963 and printed in August for autumn publication in the United States. The British edition did not appear until March 1964. The book contained almost all of Carr's uncollected short stories written during his career as a professional writer. The exceptions were primarily tales of which Carr himself probably no longer had copies—the three pulp stories from 1935, and the two newspaper stories ("The Diamond Pentacle" and "Harem-Scarem") from 1939. The other uncollected story that was omitted from *The Men Who Explained Miracles* was the relatively recent "Detective's Day Off"; Harpers or Carr himself may have rejected it as not up to Carr's usual standard—as, indeed, it wasn't.

The Men Who Explained Miracles contains two excellent tales, the Dr. Fell case entitled "Invisible Hands" (originally, "King Arthur's Chair"), and the Sir Henry Merrivale novelette "All in a Maze" (originally, "Ministry of Miracles"). Also included were a good Colonel March tale, "The Empty Flat," and a bad one, "William Wilson's Racket." Two stories, with no connection to each other, were put in one section as "Secret Service Stories"— the fine contemporary story "Strictly Diplomatic," and the rather dull historical romance "The Black Cabinet." Finally, the book has "The Incautious Burglar" (originally, "A Guest in the House"), an ingenious Dr. Fell story that became the basis for the H.M. novel *The Gilded Man*. In short, *The Men Who Explained Miracles* is a mixed bag, but with enough good stories to make it worthwhile.

In early May 1962, about a month after the stroke, Barrett told Clarice Carr that medical attention had done as much as possible. She was then very worried about her husband. He was, she recalls, "very stiff, and he felt like a walking corpse." Moreover, he continued to brood. She knew that when John moved to different surroundings, his mood usually improved, so she suggested that they spend part of the summer in Dublin, where Mary was attending Trinity College, and then decide whether to move back to England. After selling the Melbourne Avenue house, they left the United States the second week of May. They took an apartment at 166 Pearse Street, in a crumbling district just behind the college. John got a library card for the Dublin Municipal Library and he haunted the used-book stores, especially the shilling and sixpenny bins. He bought Clarice a secondhand car (whose gear lever would not stay in place), and they took day trips throughout Ireland.

At Drogheda, where Oliver Cromwell had slaughtered the Catholic defenders three centuries earlier, Carr drew comparisons between the Puritan leader and the current leader of the Labour party: "And the old so-and-so seems to have been more sure of God's will," he said in a letter, "God's will being what O. C. wanted, than anybody has been until the time of Mr. Harold Wilson and the present-day opposition." Clarice remembers that, even though he was interested in what was going on around him,

> John still talked as little as possible even to me at pretty short intervals. When he did talk, it surprised me that he had a tremendous amount of knowledge of the history of Ireland, not just the occasional battles but the church history. It was like having a guide book.

After giving Mary the car with the questionable gearshift, they went to London early in September, staying at Duke's Hotel, and they decided that they would remain in England through the end of the year.[8]

During the autumn and early winter of 1963, John and Clarice sublet an apartment from Dwye Evans of Heinemann publishers on the coast of the southern county of Hampshire; the address was Flat 4, Lepe House, Lepe, Nr. Exbury. The area is described in Carr's 1965 novel, *The House at Satan's Elbow:*

> The road, after dipping into a hollow, climbed to the left up a low headland bowered in trees. Past that headland, past squat entrance-pillars with a sign reading "Lepe House—Private," they saw water at last. On their right and well below them, following the curve of Lepe Beach, the Solent threw out faint gleams against a darkening sky. The breeze was fresh and westerly; waves showed white. . . . They could hear the surf slap at a shingle beach.[9]

The Carrs' flat looked out over the Solent and toward the Isle of Wight only three miles away. In these surroundings, Carr's outlook gradually began to improve. Once again, he told his friends that he wanted to settle permanently in England and become a British subject, "If they will have me." He toyed with this idea for about five months before he gave his usual reason for remaining an American citizen: "I am not [in England] permanently; there are too many tax problems."[10]

Meanwhile, Carr's British agent, David Higham, broached a project to him. In October 1963, the Colston Leigh Lecture Bureau in New York asked Higham whether Carr would be willing to go on a lecture tour during the early months of 1965. Over the past few years, Carr had turned down several ideas that Higham has suggested—doing television scripts, writing a book on the history of dueling, and so on—and because of Carr's recent illness, Higham was certain that he would reject Leigh's suggestion out of hand. But the invitation came just at the time that Carr wanted to prove to himself that he had recovered from the stroke, and to his surprise, Higham received a letter back from Carr almost immediately:

> With regard to the suggestion of lecturing: if these people are interested, I *am* interested. . . . Aside from writing . . . it is the one thing on earth I can do well. My old man taught me all the tricks; also I enjoy it.

Speaking to audiences was nothing new for Carr. In Britain in the late 1930s he had spoken to public gatherings as a representative of The Detection Club, and in the United States, he had occasionally lectured at colleges "to oblige academic friends." In 1956 and 1957, at the request of his friend and fellow Savage Club member Alan Wykes, he had given talks on detective fiction at the Writers' Summer School held at Swanswick.[11]

The Colston Leigh Lecture Bureau offered Carr a guarantee of five hundred dollars a week for ten weeks, with any moneys earned above that amount to be divided equally between Carr and the bureau. Leigh would handle publicity and travel expenses in the United States. Carr agreed to prepare three lectures—on detective fiction, on historical romances, and on real-life murders. "Each must be full of meat," Carr said, "each must be entertaining, and each, by the terms of the contract must be an hour and fifteen minutes long."[12] Since, however, the tour would not begin until a year later, Carr had more than enough time to put them together.

Because of the tax situation, Carr said that he could afford to live in England only three or four months each year, and he decided to spend January through April 1964 with the McNivens in the United States, while Clarice (who still owned property in Kingswood) remained in England. She wanted to be near her daughters, Bonita and Mary. Bonnie was now divorced from Charles Harrison, and she had moved to a flat in West Hampstead with her son, Stephen—in his letters to Bonnie, Carr affectionately called him "the sausage."[13] In late 1963, Bonnie began working for the London office of Harper & Brothers. Mary, who would shortly graduate from Trinity College, planned to share her sister's flat.

Carr arrived in the United States on January 17, 1964, and Julia and Dick McNiven gave him his old attic study in the house at 211 Beach Avenue. Harpers expected a new novel from him, but Carr could not seem to put one together. The book he had begun before the stroke was going nowhere, and he discarded what he had written. He had tried again in the flat at Lepe, but again nothing publishable resulted. As a writer, he said in October 1963, "I am seriously beginning to doubt myself." At first things went no better at Mamaroneck. One evening when Frederic Dannay was visiting, Carr said that he seemed to have no new idea at all for a new novel. Dannay responded, "If you can't write a good new book, write a good old book."[14] Dannay may have been thinking that Carr might once again find a usable plot in one of his radio plays, but the suggestion sent his thoughts in a different direction. He decided to do a thorough revision of *Devil Kinsmere*, the historical novel he had written thirty years before.

Carr spent most of the winter and spring of 1964 in the McNivens' attic rewriting *Devil Kinsmere*. He carefully hid the fact that he had the use only of his right hand, and not until the book was completed did Julia realize that her father had typed it one-handed. He delivered the completed typescript of a book he now called *Most Secret* to Harpers in April; it was printed in August but apparently not officially published until November.[15] The Hamish Hamilton edition appeared in London a few weeks later. The dust jacket of the British edition, by B. S. Biro, was one of the best to grace a Carr book; it shows King Charles II looking out over a swordfight.

Carr himself was not pleased with *Most Secret*. He described it as a "not very successful piece of swashbuckling," and in a letter to me written seven years later he criticized both *Devil Kinsmere* and *Most Secret*. The earlier book he called "crude, immature stuff" containing unauthorized changes by the publisher. As for the latter: "I am not even pleased with the revised version, *Most Secret*, though there I can blame nobody but myself."[16] I suspect that the difficulty he had in writing *Most Secret* affected his judgment of it. Although it is not among his best books, its pace and sense of adventure make it an enjoyable tale.

In *John Dickson Carr, a Critical Study*, S. T. Joshi gives some specific examples of how Carr rewrote various paragraphs and sections to make *Devil Kinsmere* into *Most Secret*.[17] Joshi has important insights into the development of Carr's style over thirty years, but I would like to approach the changes more generally. Carr retained the plot and most of the incidents of *Devil Kinsmere*, though he did divide the book differently. He kept the eighteen chapters of *Devil Kinsmere*, but put them into three sections: "The Raree-Show," "The Grand Design," and "The Puppet-Master." The title of the first section is inspired. Seventeenth-century puppet shows were called "Raree Shows," from the cry *"rares choses à voir,"* and the theme of *Most Secret* is King Charles II as a puppet-master.

Carr, moreover, made alterations in almost every sentence. Some of the changes are minor: "Devil" Kinsmere becomes "Rowdy" Kinsmere; Dolly Landis's name is changed from "Dorothea" to "Dorothy"; the birth dates of Kinsmere's children are altered. Carr made other revisions intended to make the story more true to the seventeenth century. In *Devil Kinsmere*, Carr had been careful not to claim historical accuracy for everything in the novel, and his Editor's Note at the opening goes so far as to point out anachronisms, concluding that "these lusty men and women can hardly be said to talk in the style of the seventeenth century." By the time that he wrote *Most Secret,* however, Carr had become proud of his ability to get facts and language right, and the Editor's Note in the later book points out the author's accuracy: "Colonel Kinsmere's characters talk so entirely in the style of the seventeenth century."[18] Among many other changes between the two books, we might point out that in the earlier version, Kinsmere inherited five hundred thousand pounds, an impossibility three hundred years ago, so Carr changed the sum to the still impressive ninety thousand pounds. To give another example, in *Devil Kinsmere* the hero strolls about with "his hands in his pockets"; Carr altered the line to "thumbs in his sword belt."[19] Most significant of all the changes, however, was that Carr rewrote every conversation, lengthening the speeches and making the language closer to that of the seventeenth century.

But with all the changes, *Most Secret* remains at heart the work of the young man who had read Dumas and Stevenson, rather than that of an ill, aging author who often found life grim. It is an Adventure story in the Grand Manner.

Soon after completing the typescript of *Most Secret,* Carr decided to rejoin Clarice in England. John arrived on April 24, and they again sublet Flat 4 in Lepe House on the Hampshire coast. In June they decided that they wanted more room, so from June to December they rented a house a short distance away, at 4 Old Farm Walk in Lymington. It was called "Samolo," a name that amused Carr: "I don't know who invents such outlandish names for houses. At least we have been spared 'Bide-a-Wee' or 'Kozy Korner,' but 'Samolo' is almost as bad. It sounds like a corruption out of *Pickwick.*"[20]

Carr remained physically frail during 1964, but he was determined to resume his active career as a writer. Nineteen sixty-four was the first year in almost a decade during which Carr wrote two novels—*Most Secret,* finished in the spring, and *The House at Satan's Elbow,* written at Lymington and completed at the end of September. It was, however, not published until almost a year later. I should mention for those interested in bibliographical minutiae that there are slight differences between the American and the British editions. When Carr's agent, David Higham, read the British proofs, he hurriedly wrote to Carr that he had misspelled "Deirdre" as "Deidre" throughout the book. It was, Carr replied, "my own stupid mistake; never having known a woman of that name, I really thought it was spelled like that." By the time Higham noticed the error, however, it was too late to make any corrections. But two minor problems ("shoes" for "boots" on page 5 of the American printing and "whistle" for "hoot" on page 50) were corrected in the Hamish Hamilton printing (on pages 11 and 57, respectively).[21]

Before discussing *The House at Satan's Elbow,* let's look at the general characteristics of John Dickson Carr's final novels. Several people who knew Carr well have told me that the spark that had driven him as a writer was extinguished by the stroke, that his books became increasingly mechanical. I think that judgment is basically correct, except that the spark had already flickered less brightly for several years. The sense of mystery and adventure that he had seen in Baghdad-on-the-Thames during the 1930s was gone—or, more accurately, could be found, he believed, only in the past. As he grew older and faced severe health problems, he found it more and more difficult to find joy even in writing historical novels. *The Demoniacs,* completed some months before the stroke, was as mechanical and labored as any of his books that came later.

I have already discussed in various places in this book characteristics of Carr's late style, but it would probably be helpful to pull together the major points here. Carr had become so fascinated by the techniques of mystifying the reader that he sometimes paid too little attention to telling a good story. Instead of a straightforward narrative, he had characters constantly speak in riddles. He felt that he had to have each new plot development hinted at in enigmatic dialogue, or a pregnant but unexplained pause, or a mysterious change of expression. Everything had to be clued; everything had to be a challenge-to-the-reader. As a result, instead of the clear story line that characterized even the most complicated plots of his earlier books (and some recent ones, like *The Witch of the Low-Tide),* Carr's final books too often exist in a sort of narrative haze. No one speaks straightforwardly. The odd point is that Carr realized this problem; in almost every one of his later books, one character begs another to stop making unnecessary riddles. Even Dr. Fell, no slouch at being enigmatic himself, becomes fed up: "When the Sphinx propounds a riddle, we have a right to demand just what the devil the riddle is."[22] Carr had always reveled in cryptic comments, but until his final books, they never obscured the narrative.

"Everybody," to quote Garret Anderson in *The House at Satan's Elbow,* ". . . has been posturing and dramatizing things into high tragedy."[23] Anderson is correct—everyone does posture and pontificate in Carr's last novels. Carr, who had once been able to give his characters markedly different "voices," now had them talking in the same manner. They "strike a pose" and orate; they speak in a formal language that would surprise even Dr. Johnson; and they tell the story through dialogue rather than narration. I previously indicated that Carr's later language comes from two sources—from the use of dialogue to reveal information in radio plays and from the formal language of polite discourse in historical novels. But use of language was more fundamental to Carr than mere technique. He had always looked upon language as powerful, as a means of control—hence the verbal battles in several of his historicals. The one who could, in a sense, out-talk the opponent would win the day. In addition, language was one of the masks that Carr thought protects someone from the world. The people in Carr's books express this view as early as the Bencolin novels, but by the later 1950s and, especially, after his stroke in 1963, most of his characters face their world with posturing and stilted speech. And again, Carr's characters seem aware of what's going on. In exasperation, one of them says, "Look, sir, I'm begging you! Say what you want to say; say what you've got to say; just don't *orate* at me."[24] The reader, tired of speeches, agrees.

The result is just as unfortunate when Carr attempted to write contemporary slang in his later books. Such lines as "it leads us straight to the nut-house. Dig?" are awkwardly self-conscious. Carr has an American police officer use such terms and phrases as "kook," "goofed," and "get your can over."[25] He is no more successful in having his characters speak the American tongue called "Southern":

> You reckon *you're* no Southern girl, Madge Maynard? . . . Now don't you start talkin' foolishness, honey! . . . f that makes you any kind of damnyankee, then my name's Tecumseh Sherman. . . . Like to be twenty years 'fore I get a partnership, if then. Who'd pay any mind to the likes of me, anyway?

A South Carolina policeman speaks like this: "It's a hard job and a thankless job and it don't pay hardly anything, but we're not such a bad bunch in the long run; you hear?"[26]

Beginning with Jeff Marle in *It Walks By Night*, almost all of Carr's heroes have been stand-ins for Carr, but this pattern is exaggerated in his final books. Already in *The Witch of the Low-Tide*, the hero-detective has Carr's profession as author of impossible-crime detective novels. Written shortly after the time that he expressed his desire to write biographies, *The House at Satan's Elbow* has a biographer as protagonist. *The Ghosts' High*

Noon features an author of espionage novels, and *Deadly Hall* has an author of historical romances. But except for the focal character, the people in Carr's later novels tend to be uninteresting and insufficiently delineated. It is difficult to become concerned about men and women whose main role is to make enigmatic utterances. The women, especially, are dull. We have seen them too often before—they exist solely to frustrate the hero. It's odd that Carr, who knew that a love interest was unnecessary in a detective or mystery novel, had almost the same one in book after book. In the later novels, the hero usually has lost the heroine before the book begins—they both said things they shouldn't have—but he regains her in the course of the story. Carr's heroes still fall in love immediately, and they quickly express their feelings physically: "It was not so much what she said or did; such things can be counterfeited; in the delirium of intimacy there were unmistakable physical signs that she shared his own emotions to the full."[27]

An oddity about his later books is that the characters tend to call each other by supposedly amusing nicknames. A lawyer is addressed as "Blackstone" or "Solon"; Dr. Fell is "Gargantua," "Magister," or "Grand Goblin"; an adventure-story writer is called "Sabatini," and on and on. The most extreme case is the nicknames given to Captain Josephus Ashcroft in *Dark of the Moon*. Because Ashcroft has a biblical-sounding first name, various characters address him as "Hezekiah," "Judas Maccabaeus," "The Prophet Ezekiel," "Caiaphas," and "the Lion of Judah." Carr realized that these nicknames did not always work. He admitted that such labeling is at best "heavy facetiousness" that "wasn't very funny in the first place."[28] In short, Carr clearly understood why his later books could not stand up against those of even a few years earlier. He not only understood, but his characters often complained about the posturing, the overuse of cryptic remarks, even such minor matters as the heavy-handed nicknames. For some reason, nevertheless, Carr could not make himself write differently.

After itemizing these problems, it would be easy to conclude that John Dickson Carr's final books are unreadable. That judgment would be far from the truth. His ability to construct a complex and mystifying plot remained unrivaled among all mystery writers. He was still a puppet-master whose creatures responded to his commands. Moreover, Carr's use of atmosphere remained persuasive; indeed, he recaptured much of his earlier mastery of the supernatural. In many of his books during the late 1940s and the 1950s, the impossible crime had been presented with-

out any hint that a ghost or a witch or a demon might have been responsible. But in his later books, especially *The House at Satan's Elbow* and *Dark of
the Moon*, the suggestion that some supernatural agency might have been
responsible is effective. In both of these books, as well as in *Deadly Hall*
and (to a lesser extent) *Panic in Box C*, the modern crime seems to repeat
an ancient one. Carr could still arouse the reader's fear of the unknown,
or of human reason collapsing in the face of evil.

When *The House at Satan's Elbow* was published, Anthony Boucher
praised it in *The New York Times* as "a brilliantly constructed locked-room
problem. . . . A happy return to the Golden Age of detection." Although
the novel has many of the weaknesses of Carr's later books, it succeeds on
the strength of its plot. Boucher did not exaggerate when he wrote that it
was brilliantly constructed, and the locked-room puzzle is one of Carr's
finest. Garret Anderson, a historical biographer, has become wealthy because his book about Thomas Babington Macaulay had been turned into a
Broadway musical called *Uncle Tom's Mansion.* An obvious Carr stand-in
who lives in Hampstead and is a member of the Thespis (i.e., Garrick)
Club, Garret is invited by his old friend Nick Barclay to visit his home
called Greengrove at Satan's Elbow, near the Lepe-Lymington area of
Hampshire. Nick, incidentally, attended a prep school, "the American
Harrow at Gottsburg, Pennsylvania" (that is, The Hill at Pottstown), so he
too represents Carr in some ways. On the train, Nick tells Garret about
the ghost of the eighteenth-century justice Horace Wildfare, who before
his death wore a black silk veil to hide the ravages of a loathsome skin disease. His ghost has reappeared periodically at Greengrove, and other
mysterious events have been occurring—"Mysterious women, flesh-and-
blood women, appearing for a time and then vanishing as though they'd
never existed."[29]

Shortly after they arrive, Garret and Nick hear reports that Justice
Wildfare's ghost is again walking, and Nick's uncle Pennington Barclay
asserts that a figure wearing a black veil fired a gun at him and then vanished from a locked library. Dr. Fell and Inspector Elliot come to
Greengrove, but their presence has no effect on the supposed ghost. Another revolver shot is heard, and Uncle Pen is found badly wounded in
the locked room.

A portion of the solution to the eerie events in this haunted-house
novel is drawn from *The Peacock Feather Murders*, but the most important
part, the explanation of the locked room, is brilliantly simple and brilliantly practical. Because of what Carr called their "mutual interest in

tricks and impossibilities," he dedicated *The House at Satan's Elbow* to Clayton Rawson.

Clarice Carr did not believe that her husband was healthy enough to go on the lecture tour scheduled for the early months of 1965, and she herself preferred to stay at Lymington rather than face the hazards of bus, train, and air travel in America during the dead of winter.[30] But John could rarely be dissuaded from something he especially wanted to do, and he sailed for the United States on December 16, 1964, on the *Queen Mary*. Between lectures, he stayed in Mamaroneck with Julia and Dick McNiven. In the back of his mind was the thought that he might find some place to live in the United States. Neither John nor Clarice had been delighted when, in October 1964, Harold Wilson became prime minister in a Labour government. "My wife and I decided to depart those shores," he said, "when ... they elected *another* damned Socialist government of the sort which so nearly ruined the country between '45 and '51." To friends in England he wrote, "If the political climate should change and bring in a government less intent on murdering the taxpayer, I may be able to indulge my hope of living here [in England] after all."[31]

In spite of Clarice's worries about his physical condition, the lecture tour was a great success. Holly and Arthur Magill, who were his hosts at Greenville, South Carolina, recall that he was an excellent speaker, with a rapid-fire style. "When John was making a speech," says Mrs. Magill, "he would stand sort of sideways to the audience and his arm flung out, and these sentences would come out like they were shot out of a gun, almost." Her husband called him "machine-gun Carr."[32] Carr's schedule took him primarily to meetings of library groups and to college campuses. No complete list of the cities on the tour seems to survive, but from notes in Carr's agent's files and a few postcards he wrote on the tour, an incomplete itinerary can be constructed:

> January 1965: Evanston, Illinois
> January 1965: Fort Wayne, Indiana
> February 2: Little Rock, Arkansas
> March 3: Pottstown, Pennsylvania
> March 8: Cleveland, Ohio
> March 15: Baltimore, Maryland
> March 16: Pelham, New York
> March 17: Hartford, Connecticut
> March 23: Greenville, South Carolina

After completing his tour, Carr wrote a book sending Dr. Fell on a similar series of lectures, and he had Fell talk about the experiences Carr himself had had:

> Despite an itinerary carefully prepared by the lecture-bureau, you will find yourself pushed aboard planes at unholy early hours of the morning. Please accept the fact that no commercial aircraft ever takes off on time, even when the weather is good. When the weather is bad, and you are obliged to use trains or buses, these develop similarly erratic habits. . . . In February, when they are likely to send you through the Middle West, a blizzard will paralyze whatever city you happen to be performing in. With all planes grounded, and every jam-packed train running six to ten hours late out of Chicago, you will land back in New York, if you land back at all, towards four o'-clock in the morning.[33]

On the personal level, the most important stop on the lecture tour was in Greenville, South Carolina. Arthur Magill, president of the Friends of the Greenville County Library, had organized lectures by a number of popular authors in order to obtain money to build a new library. Erskine Caldwell, for example, spoke at Greenville in February, and John Dickson Carr delivered his lecture a month later. He talked to newspaper, radio, and television reporters at a luncheon at the Greenville Country Club, organized by Edna Seaman, promotion manager of a local television station; and that evening at Greenville High School he addressed the Friends of the Library on the topic "Famous Murders and Scotland Yard."[34]

Carr liked the people he had met in Greenville. At the luncheon, Edna Seaman suggested that he consider moving there, and Arthur Magill remembers that after Carr's lecture, the possibility of living in Greenville came up on the following fashion:

> I asked him, "How do you like England?" Well, he was fed up with it because of the socialistic tendencies. So I said facetiously, "Why don't you move back to America?" And he said, "I've been thinking of doing that." I said, "Move to Greenville." He replied, "Well, I might do that," and I said, "if you're seriously thinking of it, come on down here and I'll put you up for a couple of weeks while you look for a house or apartment."[35]

A short while later, Carr returned to the McNivens in Mamaroneck and prepared to rejoin Clarice at Lymington. But, without telling his daughter, he changed his mind and telegrammed Magill that he would accept his offer to stay with him a short while in Greenville. While Julia thought her father was on shipboard heading for England, he had in fact returned to Greenville. The Magills showed Carr about the community and investigated the availability of apartments. Arthur Magill located a one-story duplex with a covered carport on a tree-shaded cul-de-sac at 33 Knoxbury Terrace. John cabled Clarice that he had found a place that he thought she would like. Much to Julia's surprise, a week after he had supposedly left for England, her father showed up at her front door in Mamaroneck. She recalls that with little explanation Carr made himself at home. Clayton Rawson dropped by and the two men chatted all afternoon. On April 15, 1965, Carr boarded the Cunard liner *Sylvania* and arrived in England a week later.[36]

Fearing having to pay British taxes, Carr told David Higham that he was not "officially" in England at all. He and Clarice spent nearly a month packing their goods and arranging for their shipment at the end of May from Southampton to Norfolk, Virginia—where their furniture remained for almost two months until Carr could persuade the shipping company to send it on to Greenville. John and Clarice sailed to the United States around the first week in June 1965. He told his friends in England that he hoped to return every year.[37] In fact, he never returned. His almost two decades of wanderings were over.

Chapter 19

GREENVILLE INDIAN SUMMER

Whenever John Dickson Carr's friends asked him why he chose to live in Greenville, South Carolina, his answer was always, "I like its people and its easy-going ways." Occasionally, he would be a bit more elaborate: "As Charles the Second said of the Vicar of Bishop's Stortford, my nonsense suited their nonsense."[1] In moving to Greenville, Carr had, in a sense, returned to Uniontown. As a boy he had dreamed of the larger world outside small-town life; as a young man he had moved from Uniontown to New York City, and later from Kingswood to London. (Though Bristol was large, it was provincial compared with London.) Even in his middle years, when he had settled in Mamaroneck, he told friends that he liked the town because it was next door to New York. One of the reasons John and Clarice had so often lived separately was John's desire to be in a city. But in 1965, almost sixty years old, John moved back to a relatively small town. Greenville, with a population of more than fifty thousand, was larger than Uniontown, but in its geographical distance from big cities, its pace, and its sense of community it was much like his hometown. That may be what Carr meant when he said that his nonsense suited their nonsense.

John and Clarice Carr were happy to get away from the rigors of

Mamaroneck winters and the dampness of London ones. "The summer climate [of Greenville] might be improved," he admitted in September 1965:

> But then everything is air-conditioned as a matter of course. It can
> get just as hot in New York, where everything is not air-conditioned.
> Also when winter winds are whistling along Fifth Avenue and down
> Regent Street, I am unlikely to wish myself in New York or London
> either.[2]

Carr's health meant that he preferred a mild climate. He never completely recovered from the stroke, and he no longer had the energy he once had. But Carr would rarely admit that anything was wrong. "I enjoy good health," he told his friends and correspondents over and over again. He sometimes even denied that the stroke had affected him at all. When, for example, a reporter asked him about his pronounced limp, Carr responded that it was only a temporary condition brought on by playing roughhouse football with one of his grandchildren.[3]

Carr liked the very idea of living in the South, away from New York, which he was finding almost as socialist-liberal as England. "I am an archconservative," he explained. Besides his general abhorrence of taxes, his claim of conservatism, not unexpectedly, was involved with history: "Like myself," he said of a correspondent, "he's a wholehearted Confederate supporter."[4] He thought of the South as combining pre–Civil War elegance with the modern friendliness and easy pace he found in Greenville. South Carolina was not, he told his British friends, a region of decaying families and racial tensions:

> Both Clarice and I are very fond of the territory below the Mason-
> Dixon Line, which—in South Carolina at least—is very different from
> the South as pictured by Tennessee Williams, William Faulkner, et al.
> No fat ogre of a *pater familias* sits in a pillared house roaring out or-
> ders to a drunken son and a nymphomaniac daughter, or swills mint
> juleps as he plots the lynching of every Negro in sight. I sometimes
> wish our more advanced writers would go and look at the South
> they profess to be writing about.[5]

This judgment, like the judgments Carr had been making about "advanced writers" for forty years, was hardly fair; Tennessee Williams and William Faulkner not only looked at the South, they were native Southerners. Carr's statement on racial problems misses the point, but I shall have occasion a bit later to examine his attitude toward race relations as expressed in his later books.

John Dickson Carr was a celebrity in Greenville. He was interviewed several times in local newspapers, and he was a guest on midday television shows. Holly and Arthur Magill had a large party for the Carrs on their arrival, and it was there that Clarice Carr met Edna Seaman, who would become their best friend in Greenville, and to whom Carr would dedicate his novel *The Ghosts' High Noon*. Edna worked for the local NBC television affiliate, and brought the Carrs to meet national television executives who flew down from New York. John did not initiate these contacts; he still spent most of his day reading or writing in his study, and often Edna Seaman and Clarice would go to the theater without him. He was quiet but friendly at parties. Edna Seaman puts it this way:

> He was very cordial and very nice, but not an outgoing person at all. But I liked him. When you talked to him, he was brilliant. He could quote English history, and he was never wrong. Now if you said something that was wrong, he didn't correct you immediately, he'd say, "Well, now, I thought it was so and so."[6]

Edna Seaman recalls that Carr's conversations were urbane, witty, and kindly, but his longheld attitudes had become so much a part of him that there was no room for debate. He had written in 1962, "A man should always be willing to defend his prejudices. As he gets on in years, those prejudices may constitute the most satisfactory sum total of all the things that he has—or is."[7] In an odd way there is something noble about Carr's self-knowledge, but as Holly Magill remarked, it limits conversation: "He was pretty conservative on all counts as far as I could see. But this thing that sticks with me about him was how positive he was—he had very definite views about a lot of things. And he made no excuses about them. That's what he believed and that was it."[8] Besides dislike of leftwingers and all that they had wrought, Carr's most common topics of conversations in interviews were his work for the BBC during World War II— despite wartime hardships, he looked back at those years with fondness— and the great detective-story writers he had known in London's Detection Club. He could (and often did) recite The Detection Club's oath from memory, and he emphasized the importance of fair play as the *sine qua non* of a good detective story.

The Carrs rented the duplex at Knoxbury Terrace until December 1968, when they bought a single-story house at 102 Jones Avenue. In both residences, Carr turned a bedroom into a study. He bought a functional steel desk on which he placed his old Underwood typewriter. He had never regained full use of his left hand, and he briefly experimented with dictating his novels. He was, however, the sort of writer who had to see his words on the paper, so he continued to type his books and letters with one hand. On the walls of the study he hung mementoes and photographs. The photographs included one taken of Carr with other Detection Club members at their High Table in 1936; one of Carr with Peter Lorre during the *Suspense* days, and at least two from the early days of the Mystery Writers of America with Fred Dannay. Also on the study walls were caricatures of Chesterton and other favorites, a drawing of H.M. prepared for a magazine publication of *The Curse of the Bronze Lamp,* a portrait of Sherlock Holmes from *The Exploits of Sherlock Holmes,* a charcoal drawing of Sir Arthur Conan Doyle signed by Doyle and the artist and given to Carr by Adrian Doyle, a sketch of Carr himself with his four important detectives in the background, and at least four framed wartime political cartoons that used the phrase "Appointment with Fear." In other rooms Carr hung a photograph of Haverford College and a fine portrait of Dr. Fell seated next to a skull. Next to the Fell picture Carr placed the two Devil tapestries that he had taken with him from residence to residence for more than twenty years. He also had a set of toby jugs in the shape of Devil's heads.[9]

Until illness struck again, the Carrs' life at Greenville resembled an Indian Summer. They generally flew up north two times a year, always including Christmas when John could descend on his grandchildren like Santa Claus. Not only did Julia and Dick McNiven still live in Mamaroneck, but Bonnie and her son, Steve, had returned to New York in January 1966, where she worked for Harper & Row. In 1969, she joined the publishing house Appleton-Century-Crofts. Mary married Lawrence Howes in 1965 and returned to New York where she entered New York University to study psychology and earned master's and doctoral degrees.*

Shortly after John and Clarice Carr moved to Greenville, they bought a Ford Mustang, a small car but with a powerful V-8 engine and sporty

*Mary Howes has a son, Nicholas, born in 1984. She is an Associate Professor of Psychology at the State University of New York at Oneonta and the author of *Psychology of Human Cognition* (Pergamum Press).

looks—it was black with red leather interior.[10] Clarice, who almost always did the driving, liked powerful cars, and she fell in love with this one. They often took off on weekend trips to visit the great cities and towns of the old South—Williamsburg, Richmond, Charleston, New Orleans, and Savannah—as well as other localities that were new to them, including the mountains around Asheville, North Carolina, and Sullivan's Island, the setting of Poe's tale "The Gold Bug." John of course looked for settings that he might use in his detective novels. They enjoyed Williamsburg, but unlike Charleston and New Orleans, it produced no sparks in either John or Clarice. "No authentic atmosphere," Clarice recalls. John remarked, "Williamsburg is restored; Charleston is the real thing," and he wrote the final Dr. Fell novel, *Dark of the Moon*, as "a tribute to Charleston." Savannah, which John and Clarice visited in the spring of 1968, was also "a great 'story,' city," and he considered writing about it, but he was most fascinated with New Orleans. He and Clarice visited New Orleans, and he returned on several occasions to do research in the New Orleans Public Library and the library of Tulane University. He did additional research at the Greenville County Library, which provided him with microfilm of New Orleans newspapers. The result would be three novels set in different periods of New Orleans history.[11]

Carr had no financial worries. He often told his correspondents that he no longer needed to write a book a year, because he had done well on investments. What he actually meant, of course, was that Clarice had been handling their finances for years, including investments—which were mainly in the form of savings accounts and conservative securities. In addition, Carr pointed out that he had a large backlog of titles that continued to produce income. Most of his books were in print as paperbacks in both Britain and the United States. In England, Penguin kept many Carr and Dickson books available, and Pan usually picked up what Penguin didn't want. In the United States, Berkley was regularly reprinting the cases of Sir Henry Merrivale—an especially lucrative arrangement for Carr. Because of pressure placed on Morrow by David Higham, Carr's British agent, Carr received 70 percent of the proceeds from the Berkley royalties instead of the usual 50 percent. During the 1960s, Collier Books reprinted many of Carr's early novels published under his own name, and Bantam kept in print many of his books from the 1940s through the early 1960s. Various other publishers—Signet, Pyramid, Berkley—purchased paperback rights to the books published between 1963 and 1967. Carr's books were also published in many foreign editions. In addition to the languages mentioned earlier, his books were also translated into Danish, Finnish, Greek, Hebrew, Hungarian, Japanese, Polish, Portuguese, Russian, Serbo-Croatian, Spanish, and Turkish. With all of this, Carr was able to remark in 1969 that "my wife and I contrive to live very comfortably."[12]

During the 1960s and 1970s, John Dickson Carr received increasing recognition as a great writer of detective fiction. In 1962 the Mystery Writers of America had awarded him its highest honor by designating him "Grand Master," and on May 1, 1970, he received special recognition from the MWA, in the form of a tiny pistol and cannon, of his fortieth anniversary as a detective-story writer. He could not attend the ceremony, so his daughter Mary accepted the honor for him. Carr was touched by the recognition. In a statement to be read at the ceremony, he said that the Edgars he had won were important, but that:

> This pistol and this cannon, symbols of death in miniature, are marks of a personal regard that are nearer the heart. Whether or not readers have enjoyed my books, my wife and I have enjoyed every one of them. If the strength of the flesh equalled that of the spirit, we could promise forty years more. But at least the omens are propitious, the sky looks serene, and we can go rejoicing, bringing in the sheaves.[13]

In 1970, when mystery writers were only beginning to receive scholarly attention, Roger Herzel wrote what is still one of the best analyses of Carr's work as a chapter in Charles Alva Hoyt's book *Minor American Novelists*, published by Southern Illinois University Press. Four years earlier, a Carr fan named Rick Sneary had produced the first published attempt to do a complete checklist of Carr's books. The four-page mimeographed publication was called *The John Dickson Carr Bibliophile, No. 1*, but Sneary never attempted another issue. Anthony Boucher announced it in *The New York Times* on September 4, 1966, and within a few weeks some 250 people had written to Sneary for copies.

Another form of recognition that came to Carr was in the "sincerest form of flattery"—parodies and pastiches of his stories and characters. This type of tribute had begun some years earlier with the publication in the August 15, 1951, issue of *Punch* of Alex Atkinson's "Chapter the Last, Merriman Explains." This tale is not only a marvelous take-off on Carr's style, but also a sharply focused parody of the summing-up scene that concludes many fair-play detective novels:

Merriman frowned. "You really are the dumbest crew I ever struck," he snarled. His gay wit was so infectious that the tension eased at once.... "Haven't you realized yet that the Mrs. Ogilvie who flung the grandfather clock over the banisters was in reality her own step-mother—Eleanor's sister's aunt by marriage? Even by the light of the single candle you should have noticed the blonde wig, the false hands, or the papier-mache mask—the very mask which was found later up the chimney in Simon's bedroom!"[14]

In 1965, the young writer Norma Schier, who was a friend of Julia Mc-Niven's, met John Dickson Carr in Mamaroneck and wrote a pastiche of Sir Henry Merrivale for a series of "anagram mysteries." "Hocus-Pocus at the Drumis Tree" (the final two words are an anagram of "Murder Site"), which was published in the April 1966 issue of *Ellery Queen's Mystery Magazine*, can stand on its own as a clever mystery, but it also does a fine job capturing Carr's style. In this tale, Henry Merrivale appears anagrammatically as "Marvin Rhyerlee," Masters appears as "Starmes," and the story itself is credited to "Handon C. Jorricks," a wonderful rearrangement of the letters in "John Dickson Carr." Schier asked Carr to read a typescript of her pastiche during one of his visits to Mamaroneck. She recalls that "he chuckled as he read and told me that I was a good writer."[15] Jon L. Breen's "The House of the Shrill Whispers," *Ellery Queen's Mystery Magazine*, August 1972, is a hilariously perceptive parody of Carr's narrative style, characters, and attitudes. The hero, Millard Carstairs, had "a conservative lower upper-class upbringing," and the characters give the background through dialogue. The detective is a combination of H.M. and Dr. Fell, under the name of Sir Gideon Merrimac. He solves the case of the "invisible-lighter-than-air-killer-with-wings-who-can-walk-through-walls-and-leaves-no-footprints," who haunts the House of Shrill Whispers on July 12 of the last year of every decade.[16]

Since the 1930s, Carr had regularly received fan letters, but it was particularly gratifying for him in his sixties that young enthusiasts contacted him. "It was a great pleasure," he replied to one fan, "to hear from some intelligent and articulate member of the younger generation who does not think that, as a writer at least, your correspondent is limping his way towards senility and the grave."[17] Carr's letters to enthusiasts such as Nelson Bond, Richard Clark, John Curran, Allen J. Hubin, Francis M. Nevins, Jr., Otto Penzler, Peter and Paula Sperling, Francis Wilford-Smith, Donald Yates, and others during the Greenville years are filled with praise of

South Carolina, criticism of socialist politics, occasionally truculent nostalgia, and reminiscences of his life—most of which have been incorporated in relevant places in this biography. His daughter Bonnie, who worked for the international department of Harper & Row during the late 1960s, was impressed at the amount of fan mail he received from around the world, which she forwarded to him.[18] Most interesting was the attempt of *Punch* cartoonist Francis Wilford-Smith to treat Sir Henry Merrivale as the Baker Street Irregulars treat Sherlock Holmes—that is, to sort through inconsistencies and to work out a chronology of his adventures. Wilford-Smith sent the chronology to Carr in 1967. He replied that he accepted the chronology as official and would "defend it against challenges."[19]

It may have been the contact with Wilford-Smith that turned Carr's thoughts toward reviving Sir Henry Merrivale, whom he had ignored since his unsuccessful attempt to write *The Six Black Reasons* in 1961. In November 1967, he said that he was "aware . . . that the Old Man must be roaring at me beyond whatever door he finds himself confined," but he added that he would continue to ignore H.M.'s bellows. By December, however, he had begun toying with the idea of writing again about H.M. The problem, he told several correspondents, was the Old Maestro's age. Carr had once stated that H.M. had been born in 1871, which would make him ninety-six years old in 1967. His great age would eliminate the slapstick elements of the novels that Carr so enjoyed: "Even I can't see him doing this at so venerable a time of life." The problem, he thought, might be handled by simply ignoring H.M.'s age, or setting a new novel back into the period of World War II. After mulling over the matter, however, he rejected both solutions. He decided that, having given the Old Man's birthdate, he was stuck with it, and that, on the other hand, modern readers would not accept a detective novel set a quarter-century earlier: "They would squirm and hoot at an adventure from what they consider the remote past."[20]

Carr told people that his move to South Carolina had made it fun again to write detective novels. "All the original joy returned with a whoop just over two years ago," he said in 1967, and he claimed to be pleased with the novels written during the late 1960s. "I enjoyed writing [*Panic in Box C*] more than any book in decades." *Dark of the Moon* "rolled out as though to orchestral music." *Papa Là-Bas* "almost seemed to write itself." As for *The Ghosts' High Noon*, "I enjoyed writing that book more than any I have written for a very long time; or, rather, it seemed to write itself with very little help from me."[21] None of this was true. More honestly, he admitted that "you lose some of the roaring joy and zest, but you pick up a few tricks along the way."[22]

Carr wrote *Panic in Box C* during the autumn of 1965, shortly after he had moved to Greenville, and dedicated it to Holly and Arthur Magill. It was published about September 1966 in the United States, and two months later in Britain. *Panic in Box C* is a theatrical novel in both senses of the word—the characters' emotions are theatrical, and much of the action occurs in a theater, unsurprisingly named the Mask. Like Garret Anderson in *The House at Satan's Elbow*, Philip Knox of *Panic in Box C* has lived a life much like Carr's: now in his fifties, he is an American who has resided in England since 1933; his father was a Presbyterian lawyer; he is a historian with Carr's attitude toward history; his hobby is fencing; he is in the United States on a lecture tour; in politics he is an eighteenth-century conservative; and he stays at the Gramercy, a New York hotel where Carr often stayed. Most of the events of *Panic in Box C* take place in Richbell, a fictitious town next door to Mamaroneck. Almost forty years ago, an actor had died at the Mask Theater, and now his widow, who has become a *grande dame* of the stage, plans to reopen the theater. She is, however, murdered with a crossbow bolt while sitting alone in a locked theater box. Dr. Fell's solution is good, but not original for Carr fans. It combines elements from the short story "The Silver Curtain" and the radio play "The Phantom Archer."

More intriguing are some asides Carr makes in the novel. He had obviously been thinking about some of his earlier books as he constructed *Panic in Box C*, for included are mentions of Dr. Fell's wife, of Edward Stevens from *The Burning Court*, and of Miles and Fay Hammond from *He Who Whispers*.[23] Stevens by implication and Fay Hammond by direct statement should not have long survived their novels, but it is interesting to know that Carr reprieved them. It is also pleasant to hear that Dr. Fell once lectured "at a fashionable Eastern preparatory school," which Carr described in such exact language that it is obviously The Hill.[24] The best part of the book is the climactic scene in which the murderer is tracked down in the Old Haunted Mill at an amusement park. Carr had previously used the mill in the radio play "Will You Make a Bet with Death?" and the round-robin novella *Crime on the Coast*, but it is most effective in *Panic in Box C*.

The reviews of *Panic in Box C* were mixed. Some papers, including the *Los Angeles Times*, praised the book: "No one can possibly convey what richness it is to come again upon a story like this." But others took Carr to

task, especially for his attempts at humor. In his *New York Times* review column Anthony Boucher said that some parts of the book were tasteless—
not surprising since Carr thought it amusing to have a male character
affectionately address his lady friend as "my fornicator." Carr wrote to
Francis Wilford-Smith:

> I hope you enjoyed [*Panic in Box C*], which is more than the American
> critics did. In accents stern, almost heartbroken, most of them told
> me I have a low mind and a crude sense of humour, as though the
> creator of Sir Henry Merrivale could have anything else.[25]

The problem, however, was less whether Carr's humor was low or crude
than that it seems forced and ultimately rather sad. He no longer found
the world amusing, and it showed.

For his 1967 book, Carr considered writing a historical novel whose
events would take place exactly a century earlier in a London publishing
house. He planned to base it on the famous firm of John Murray, which
he knew well from his associations with Sir John Murray during the publication of *The Life of Sir Arthur Conan Doyle*.[26] Carr never developed his
ideas for this book, because in spring 1967, he visited Charleston, South
Carolina, and decided to have Dr. Fell solve a case in that city. Critics who
had disliked *Panic in Box C* were even less enthusiastic about Carr's
Charleston novel, *Dark of the Moon*, published in November 1967 in the
United States and April 1968 in Britain.

Boucher suggested that readers would do better to buy several of
Carr's books from the 1930s in the Collier paperback editions. Despite the
fact that the critics were basically correct *Darl of the Moon* is more than a
pale shadow of what Carr had once been able to produce. Carr's love of
history and sensationalism come through in an excellent telling of an invented late-seventeenth-century legend about a murder apparently committed by the ghost of an old pirate named Nat Skeene. The body was
found surrounded by unmarked sand. A similar murder took place in
1867, and now, in May 1965, the past is again repeated when the body of
Henry Maynard is discovered surrounded by fine, unmarked oyster
shells. The novel contains other good elements reminiscent of Carr's early
use of the incongruous. Why were a scarecrow and a tomahawk stolen? Is
the ghost of Nat Skeene leaving the messages signed "N.S." that mysteriously appear on a blackboard? But, though the tricks are present in abun-
dance in *Dark of the Moon*, the zest is gone. Not much happens in the book,
and none of the characters are very interesting. The women continue to

frustrate the hero, but are passionate withal. The men are uniformly childish, showing off to the women by trying to outdo each other playing baseball.[27] John Dickson Carr at sixty years old seems to have almost despairingly grasped at youth by praising childish behavior. As readers, we find it acceptable that Sir Henry Merrivale and to a lesser extent Dr. Fell could be childish; we are distressed when every character acts like an adolescent and Carr thinks that such behavior is admirable.

Carr's reaction to the reviewers after the judgment was in on *Dark of the Moon* was mild:

> At their hands, in general, I have fared far better than I deserved. Since my first book was published in 1930, a second generation of critics now polishes up its knives for dissection. If some go on griping that the old bastard's later books aren't up to the earlier ones, their fathers or uncles were saying the same thing a good twenty years ago.[28]

He had great hopes that his next book, *Papa Là-Bas*, a historical detective novel set in pre–Civil War New Orleans, would "confound" the critics. He completed it on his sixty-first birthday, November 30, 1967,[29] and it was published almost a year later in the United States and in the late spring or early summer of 1969 in Britain.

In many ways *Papa Là-Bas* did confound the critics. Although the novel comes nowhere close to Carr's greatest works, it is so much more readable than his previous two books that it briefly seemed almost a revival in his career. Allen J. Hubin, who on the death of Anthony Boucher in 1968 had become mystery critic for *The New York Times*, wrote that the book is "vividly constructed out of diligent research. . . . On his stage [Carr] has put murder and concealed the killer with devilish cleverness." *Book World* succinctly summarized the book's strengths and weaknesses: "[Carr's] sorcery is at work again in this beautifully detailed historical puzzler. . . . A trio of principals in the lively cast exchange the most excruciating Tom Swiftian dialogue."[30] (In this recapturing-youth period of his writing, Carr did have the main characters speak in a falsely hearty teenaged way—and they act like adolescents too.) But it's at least true that all of the cleverness and at least some of the joy are back in *Papa Là-Bas*. And, unlike *Dark of the Moon*, things happen in the book.

The story develops out of a genuine scandal that occurred in New Orleans in 1834. Delphine Lalaurie was charged with sadistically chaining and whipping her slaves, and a mob destroyed her house. *Papa Là-Bas* takes place twenty-four years later, and it seems that Madame Lalaurie's son has returned and is systematically murdering those who had persecuted his mother. Carr expertly combines this plot with tales of a Voodoo Queen—"Papa Là-Bas" is the Voodoo name for Satan—and magic does seem to be the only explanation for some of the events. A young woman is seen entering a carriage; she is followed home, and witnesses swear that she never left the carriage; yet when it arrives, she has totally vanished. A short while later, a distinguished jurist who, like most of Carr's characters in his final books, "seems to strike a dramatic attitude whenever he can"[31] is killed when he appears to be thrown from the top of a flight of stairs. No one is near him.

The detection is handled by Senator Judah P. Benjamin, who was later secretary of state in the Confederacy. No anti-Semite himself, Carr was well aware of such prejudices in the modern South, and even had the police detective realistically express those attitudes in a line of *Dark of the Moon* when people call him by biblical names—"if it goes on this way, they'll be callin' me a Jewish so-and-so." Carr told his correspondents, however, that anti-Semitism was not part of the pre–Civil War South, and adduced Benjamin's career as evidence.[32] Benjamin's revelation of the murderous son of Madame Lalaurie is dramatic. Carr borrowed a device from "Death in the Desert," a *Cabin B-13* radio play, to misdirect the reader from identifying the murderer.

S. T. Joshi has rightly taken Carr to task for his distressing comments on slavery in *Papa Là-Bas*.[33] Dick Macrae, the British consul in New Orleans, says that people who oppose slavery are singing "pious hymns"—by "pious" Carr seems to mean "hypocritical." Another British visitor says, "I can't be as shocked by slavery as people at home think I ought to be." No character even mentions that slavery was a moral issue. Senator Benjamin, it is true, objects to it, but only because it is not economically sound. But the point to keep in mind is this: Carr almost never objected to a social structure. Although in his Restoration and Regency historical novels he suggested that aristocrats should somehow be more egalitarian, he did not want the system that created them to be overthrown. In several of Carr's historicals, the male lead becomes a hero to his servants because he treats them as human beings, but Carr never even hinted that there might be anything wrong with a system that has one person serve another. Similarly, in *Papa Là-Bas* part of the plot of the story is that slaves must be treated with consideration, and when one character calls a black man a "nigger," Macrae objects while "restraining his own wrath"—not because it is a racist comment but because it is bad manners.[34] Carr was always interested in individual human beings, not social or ideological systems.

Carr returned to New Orleans for the setting of his next two novels, *The Ghosts' High Noon* (1969) and *Deadly Hall* (1971). Both take place in years that Carr remembered vividly—*The Ghosts' High Noon* begins in Washington in 1912, before proceeding to New Orleans. When Carr wrote to Cass Canfield of Harper & Row about the novel, he explained that "though only a small boy at the time, I well remember Washington during the first Wilson administration."[35] *Deadly Hall* takes place in April 1927, when Carr was attending Haverford. Perhaps just as important, *Deadly Hall* takes place only four days before the events of Carr's first novel, *It Walks By Night*. Both *The Ghosts' High Noon* and *Deadly Hall* have sections of what can only be described as literary nostalgia. The first impossible occurrence in *The Ghosts' High Noon*—the disappearance of a man from the corridor of a railway car—is almost exactly the same as in one of Carr's *Haverfordian* stories, "The Murder in Number Four," and the explanation is the same as well. *The Ghosts' High Noon* and *Deadly Hall* have several references to Stevenson's *New Arabian Nights*,[36] though they have no genuine relevance to the stories. *Deadly Hall* opens with a semiautobiographical chapter. Jeff Caldwell has spent two years in college before deciding to become a writer, traveling to London and Paris, where (like Carr) he refused to become part of the Left Bank. In the late 1920s, Carr had been torn between finding his career writing historical novels or detective stories. Caldwell had the same dilemma, but chose historicals.[37] One of Caldwell's novels has a title from a Carr radio-play, "Till the Great Armadas Come." Caldwell also wrote a novel called *The Inn of the Seven Swords*, a title reminiscent of several of Carr's works.[38]

In spite of setting *The Ghosts' High Noon* and *Deadly Hall* in periods that he recalled vividly, Carr could not recapture the feelings of his youth. He could bring to life in a romanticized way pre–Civil War New Orleans in *Papa Là-Bas* much more successfully than the times that he had actually lived through. Both books, however, contain some ingenious bits. *The Ghosts' High Noon* offers a good impossible situation: A man drives a car into an unoccupied barn, a revolver shot is heard, and the body of the driver is found in the car—all entrances are under observation, but the murderer and the weapon have vanished. The solution is simple and effective, though the motive in creating the situation is not to be believed. *Deadly Hall* is set in a Tudor manor house that has been moved and reconstructed brick by brick near New Orleans. Shortly before the Civil War,

Commodore Hobart had found the treasure of a fleet of Spanish galleons and hidden it in Delys Hall so cleverly that his descendants have never been able to find it. Soon after Jeff Caldwell arrives at Delys Hall, one of the heirs is seemingly thrown out of the window from a locked room. The explanation for the defenestration was suggested to Carr by his boyhood friend Macon Fry, who had since become an electrical engineer and to whom Carr dedicated *Deadly Hall*. The use of electricity and other elements in *Deadly Hall* is reminiscent of *The Man Who Could Not Shudder*.

The reviews of *The Ghosts' High Noon* and *Deadly Hall* were generally bad. *Saturday Review* summarized what had gone wrong with Carr's books: "I hate myself for saying this about a man whose books once had me chewing fingernails late into the night, the pace is so maddeningly tedious [in *Deadly Hall*] and the writing so stilted that I found the novel as deadly as the hall."[39] Carr's books, however, did come to the attention of William F. Buckley's conservative magazine *National Review*, which, in one of the most perceptive reviews of Carr's work since the days of Dorothy L. Sayers, noted that Carr's stories look back toward a more orderly world. *National Review* said that Carr

> is the nearest thing to a moralist practicing the noble art of literary detection. . . . Carr hates all Puritans and bluenoses. What he is, instead, is an unapologetic Tory—an old-fashioned champion of gentility, taste, standards and romance.[40]

Late in his life, Carr was better represented as a writer by his book-review column than by his novels. He had been writing reviews since the late 1940s, primarily for *The New York Times*. During the middle 1960s he had done an annual column called "Murder-Fancier Recommends" for *Harper's Magazine*. After the death of Anthony Boucher, who had reviewed books for both *The New York Times* and *Ellery Queen's Mystery Magazine*, Frederic Dannay asked Carr to take over his EQMM column. Carr said that he agreed because of the free books rather than the pay, which was tiny. Beginning with the January 1969 issue he enjoyed "fulminating every month rather than once a year as in *Harper's*."[41] Each column took him only two days to write, and he normally wrote them three months before the cover date on the issue in which they were to appear. Frederic Dannay and his managing editors (successively, Clayton Rawson and Eleanor Sullivan) were extraordinarily flexible in allowing Carr to write what he wanted. If he couldn't find four new books worthy of review, he reviewed an old book and suggested that readers haunt used-book stores until they found a copy. At other times, he dedicated entire columns to reminiscences about The Detection Club and analyses of important writers of the past—S. S. Van Dine, Baroness Orczy, Margery Allingham, Anthony Berkeley, Sax Rohmer, R. Austin Freeman, Melville Davisson Post, and others. The result was some of the best writing that John Dickson Carr had done in years.

Carr's policy was set at the opening of his first review for *Ellery Queen's Mystery Magazine:*

> Permit an old devotee of blood and thunder to introduce himself. Having been improving my mind with sensational fiction for fifty years, I step in the critic's pulpit with few qualms and little diffidence. . . . As a reader of this magazine, you are more than devoted to blood and thunder; you want the best blood and thunder on the market.[42]

James E. Keirans has published an analysis of Carr's book reviews, which shows that during the eight years of the column, he reviewed 314 books by 208 authors.[43] It is not surprising that traditional mysteries, especially books by Emma Lathen, Agatha Christie, Ellery Queen, and Peter Lovesey, received the most attention in Carr's reviews, but it is surprising how often he praised thrillers. Carr often reviewed spy novels, and he praised five books each by Dick Francis and Jack Higgins. It is, to me at least, unexpected that Carr found Donald Hamilton's Matt Helm to be "my favorite secret agent," since at first glance Hamilton's books have little in common with Carr's. The explanation may lie in Carr's comment that in espionage novels he preferred Matt Helm's "cloud-cuckooland" world.[44] Carr never valued realism in fiction.

Even contemporary writers of private-eye novels came in for a share of praise, though often Carr expressed surprise that their detectives were not as unlikable as Spade and Marlowe. Of Ross Macdonald's private-eye, Carr wrote "unlike the sneering, snarling heroes from Hammett and Chandler, Lew Archer is a decent sort who does not make bad manners the guiding principle of his life."[45] Carr made the same point about the novels featuring "Nameless," by a young writer named Bill Pronzini, who has since become a major private-eye novelist: "Though he professes admiration for the ancient pulp fiction of Hammett and Chandler, this unnamed sleuth bears no resemblance to dull, swollen-headed snarlers like Spade or Marlowe."[46]

Above all, Carr praised sound construction and fair play in detective novels. A quick count finds that in about fifty-five of his ninety-two columns, Carr praised, often at length, the construction of clues or the fairness to the reader of various novels, and on several occasions he held up The Detection Club's oath as the standard by which to judge any detective story. This predilection could lead to some oddities in criticism. For example, unlike most critics who admired Ross Macdonald's power of description, his sensitive delineation of human relationships, and his understanding of California society, Carr said that Macdonald "writes a true detective story, full of snares and traps."[47] For Carr, the point of a detective story was the same as it had been since he had first started to write almost half a century earlier—it must mystify the reader.

In some ways, Carr's most impressive review was of A Catalogue of Crime by Jacques Barzun and Wendell Hertig Taylor, a well-informed but supremely quirky book. Like Carr, Barzun and Taylor preferred formal detective stories, but unlike Carr they admired what they called "straightforward tales." This preference resulted in criticism of writers who excelled in ingenuity and who liked bizarre touches—for example, Clayton Rawson and Anthony Boucher. Above all, they disliked the books of John Dickson Carr. Carr, however, was generous about A Catalogue of Crime. In his review, Carr said that Barzun and Taylor discuss authors, "each of us, with strengths examined as well as faults or blunders too. If the critics' judgment sometimes grows pompous, it is fair, honest, and sympathetic. Cherish this book; it deserves an honored place on your shelves."[48]

In a minor aside, written about August 1969, Carr used his review column to defend "us sinful, but unrepentant heavy smokers" from the "television blast" of health warnings. Two years earlier, he had told a Charlotte, North Carolina, newspaper reporter that he would continue to be a heavy smoker "cancer warnings, or no."[49] Carr's addiction to cigarettes was already having an effect on his health. Julia McNiven thought that he had emphysema, though her mother says that no formal diagnosis was made.[50] He may have developed the smoker's bronchitis that often comes after years of chain-smoking. Whatever the case, Carr had no inkling that anything was seriously wrong. At the end of September 1970, he started a new novel, untitled at this stage but eventually to be called The Hungry Goblin.[51] When he had completed around half of it, probably toward the middle of November, he had a routine physical examination, and an X-ray revealed cloudiness in a lung. Tests found a mass that was determined to be malignant. John and Clarice hesitated about accepting the diagnosis until they went up to Mamaroneck and Carr's old friend, Dr. William Barrett, confirmed what the Greenville physicians had said.

Carr did not tell anyone that he had lung cancer. His daughters simply gradually came to understand that the condition was serious, but they were never certain whether Carr even admitted to himself that cancer was involved. Back in Greenville, he submitted to chemotherapy and radiation. His system reacted well to the treatment; though chemotherapy left him weak and he lost weight, he did not lose his hair or have other outward signs about what was going on. The therapy appeared to be successful, as X-rays showed that the cancerous mass had disappeared. "I have been through a rather bad time," Carr said some months later, "but the worst is past now; and with anything like luck, there should be no further trouble."[52]

As had happened during his previous illnesses, Carr became determined not to stop writing. He continued to write his column for *Ellery Queen's Mystery Magazine*, missing only one issue—March 1971, for which he had been supposed to submit his typed copy the previous November.[53] Meanwhile, in spite of his continuing weakness, he worked on *The Hungry Goblin*. "Though the latter part was written under some difficulties," he recalled about two years later, "it had been so carefully planned that impetus carried me through."[54].

As far as most readers are concerned, nevertheless, *The Hungry Goblin* doesn't have much impetus. The story is set in London of 1869, and its main character is Kit Farrell.* Though British, Farrell had been a newspaper reporter in the United States during the Civil War—sympathetic with the Southern cause, of course. Now back in London, he hopes to find Patricia Denbigh, with whom he had had a whirlwind affair, and his old friend, the African explorer Nigel Seagrave. Nigel has his own problems: He suspects that his wife has been replaced by someone else who looks exactly like the woman he married. His current wife, however, has more bedroom knowledge than his earlier one. Before this situation can be sorted out, Nigel is wounded with a bullet just over the heart, in a locked conservatory. Nonetheless, a few hours later, he is out of bed and (like the rest of the characters) rushing about purposelessly. Indeed, much of the book is taken up by the characters getting together and trying to straighten out who was dashing where and when—none of which turns

---

*An ancestor, perhaps, of the Kit Farrell in *The Curse of the Bronze Lamp*.

out to have anything to do with the solution of the mystery. Soon we are faced with some elaborate and unbelievable wife-swapping, which also has nothing to do with the solution. The detective in all this is the great Victorian novelist Wilkie Collins. He is lucky that he solves the crime, because every time Nigel tries to explain about the person who shot him, he is interrupted. (As a detective story, the book would have worked better if Nigel had been killed, but that might have damaged the wife-swapping sections.) The explanation of the near-murder in the locked conservatory is taken from the Holmesian pastiche "The Adventure of the Sealed Room," which had been plotted by Carr but written almost entirely by Adrian Conan Doyle.

Carr's British publisher, Hamish Hamilton, must have recognized the problems in this weak detective novel, but he was an old friend and he wrote to Carr that *The Hungry Goblin* was "one of your very best." "What a high standard you maintain," he said, "despite your vicissitudes."[55] Joan Kahn, Carr's American editor, was at first at a loss what to do. She thought *The Hungry Goblin* such a weak novel that she didn't want to publish it.[56] Once again, friendship was probably of crucial importance—and also the mundane consideration that Carr's books had good sales—and *The Hungry Goblin* was published in June 1972 in the United States and in August in Great Britain. Reviews were not good, the main exception being the *Sunday Times* of London, whose reviewer, Carr's friend Edmund Crispin, said that it "is by far the best of Mr. Carr's recent books," but that comment may indicate more what he thought of the New Orleans novels than of *The Hungry Goblin*.[57] Sales were disappointing; the American edition of *The Hungry Goblin* was one of the few Carr books to be remaindered at a bargain price, and it has never been reprinted.

Carr could still write colorful prose in his short nonfiction pieces. His reviews rolled out on a steady schedule, and he also planned a series of short articles on seventeenth- and eighteenth-century crooks and rogues. He told Frederic Dannay that the articles would cover "pirates, murderers, housebreakers, roaring girls, and other wearers of the motley."[58] Carr's health, however, did not allow him to complete the series, and only the first installment (on highwaymen) was published in *Ellery Queen's Mystery Magazine* in March and April 1973. The article is so full of life that it is difficult to believe that it was written by a man emerging from an exhausting illness.

By early 1973, Carr was pretending, at least publicly, that his treatment for lung cancer did not indicate that he had been seriously ill. "Though I did have a bout of illness," he wrote to his cousin Nick Carr, "it wasn't a heart attack or (I am happy to add) anything of a serious nature." Although in the same letter he described himself as "semi-retired from my own writing career,"[59] he was already making plans for his next novel. In January 1973 he began work on a book called *Pirate's Way*, to be set in modern South Carolina, its amateur sleuth to be an English high court jurist "patterned after a barrister I used to know."[60]

Carr had only just started *Pirate's Way* when at the beginning of February 1973 he faced another health problem. "Part of this month," he wrote on February 21, "I have spent flat on my back. Not skating, not skiing, not in any way imitating old Sir Henry Merrivale, but in my own study working on a new novel, I fell and broke my left hip." He spent some time in the Greenville hospital, where the nurses treated him as a celebrity. Edna Seaman, who visited him there, was so impressed with the attention that John received that she thought, wrongly, that Clarice must have hired special nurses. Carr refused to be laid up for a lengthy time in a plaster cast, so his doctors inserted a steel rod into the broken hip. Soon he was hobbling about on a steel walker, and by the end of February he was again typing his reviews. Although the hip mended almost completely, his leg remained stiff and sometimes his balance was impaired, and Clarice remembers that he had become a semi-invalid. In April, however, he was ready to tackle *Pirate's Way*.[61]

In spite of all his determination, Carr could not write the book. Although he began a few chapters, nothing publishable was coming. But he refused to give up. "I have no intention of sinking into silence," he said in June 1974; "there are still a few more stories to spout before I finally shut up." And a year later: "I still have story plots; yes, and the skill to write them."[62] But he simply was unable to write anything longer than book reviews. In April 1974, he decided that he would find it easier to write a historical novel, and he put *Pirate's Way* aside in favor of an 1890s mystery with Arthur Conan Doyle himself being the amateur sleuth.[63] But again he couldn't manage the book, and in November he was back to *Pirate's Way*.

At the same time, Carr broached another idea to his agents—one that he had been considering at least since 1967. The best summary of the project is in a letter he wrote to David Higham in November 1974:

> Sooner or later there is another sort of chronicle I must write. Having been Honorary Secretary of the London Detection Club, as well as

President of the Mystery Writers of America in New York, I have been
acquainted with every first-class blood-and-thunder author on both
sides of the Atlantic, some of whom became close friends. The projected book will say very little about your obedient servant—I can't
flatter myself anyone would be interested—but will go on at length
about everybody else. I think I can do this, lightly yet sympatheti-
cally, without offending any writer still alive, and without embarrassing friends or relatives if the writer happens to be dead. It might be
called *Culprit Confesses*, with some sub-title not yet determined.

Higham responded enthusiastically, and so did Joan Kahn representing
Harper & Row. Carr contacted several old friends to ask for their reminiscences. But this project, like the others, was stillborn. "I seem to have
come to a halt," he admitted sadly a short while later.[64]

By September 1975, Carr had rationalized his continuing lack of productivity. It wasn't, he told Higham, "merely inertia"; it was the Internal
Revenue Service. (In fact, it was the Social Security Administration, but
the point was the same.) For every two dollars he earned over $2,520, his
Social Security benefits would decrease by one dollar. This he called a determination "to fleece taxpayers in every possible way short of actual
swindling." When he became seventy-two, however, he would collect full
benefits no matter how much he earned. In short, Carr said that he would
not publish any more books until he was seventy-two, "always provided I
live that long."[65]

Since the age of around fourteen, writing had been John Dickson
Carr's identity and his refuge; he could escape from a world he did not
like by creating another and better one in his novels and short stories.
Without this to fall back upon, he became frustrated and, in his letters, occasionally testy. Perhaps what bothered him most was that The Detection
Club's oath, whose requirement of fair play he quoted over and over in
his reviews, had been changed. For more than ten years, the club had
been admitting as members those whose main work had been in the area
of thrillers or espionage rather than detection, and around 1975 the oath
itself was revised to recognize writers of other than fair-play detection.
The detective-story writer Anthony Lejeune sent Carr an outline of the
new oath, and Carr was distressed. "Old rules are recalled," he complained in September 1975, "so that they may be the more conveniently
ignored. It's not merely my preference for old practices; I am uncomfortable when the brethren jeer at their own work."[66] It was such things as

fair play that Carr had made an anchor for his values both as a writer and as a human being, and to see The Detection Club deserting the principle was difficult to bear. Several times he told his correspondents that he was "fed up." His life had reached what he began to call "a summing up," and he felt old: "Next Sunday," he wrote in November 1975, "I celebrate—or, rather refrain from celebrating—my sixty-ninth birthday."[67]

Since late in 1974, Carr had had a recurrence of an old ailment, stiffness and pain in the back. He flew back to Mamaroneck to take treatment from Dr. Barrett, and for a few months he seemed to be on the mend.[68] During the late winter and early spring of 1975, however, the pain came back and he and Clarice flew north every month where, for a week each time, Barrett gave him injections of calcium. The residual effects of the broken hip and the back problems meant that Carr could not get along by himself, and each time he came to Mamaroneck he needed a wheelchair. By February 1976, he had become so weak that Clarice took him to the Greenville hospital for a series of tests. He was there for two or three days before the physicians told Clarice that there was nothing they could do for him. The cancer had reappeared, spread to the bones, and metastasized to affect other parts of his body. Even though the doctors spoke about the wonders of radiation treatments, they told Clarice that John's condition was almost certainly terminal and that she should make arrangements for a nursing home to care for her husband. In the latter part of February, John Dickson Carr moved to the Oakmont Nursing Home.[69]

Clarice told her daughters that their father had cancer, but although John was aware of what he faced, he continued to insist that he had only a back problem. For someone who objected to regimentation, it was galling to have to follow the schedule and rules of a nursing home. Then, it seemed that a miracle had occurred. Carr felt better; he was able to get out of bed; and though he was still weak it seemed that his cancer had gone into remission. He announced that it was a free country, and he was going to leave Oakmont. He asked his lawyers to fill out the necessary papers.

As crisis seemed to follow crisis, Clarice spent all afternoon and evening of March 9 or 10 at the nursing home trying to persuade her husband to stay there, and about one o'clock the next morning she herself felt sick. Having suffered a major heart attack, she was rushed to a hospital. Bonnie had remarried and had moved to New Zealand with her husband, James Cron, but Mary and Julia came down to Greenville. On her father's desk, Julia found the first three or four pages of a novel set on the islands off the Carolina coast. The pages had no title, but they must have represented another attempt to write *Pirate's Way*. The fragment has disappeared. Meanwhile, Carr absolutely insisted on leaving the nursing home. The doctor assured Julia that her father was too weak to go anywhere, but if willpower could make it happen, John was bound and determined to do it. He got someone to help him to a cab, and he was back at the Jones Avenue house by the first week in April. Clarice was in the hospital for three weeks and Julia, fearing that her mother did not have the strength to handle an invalid, insisted that she return with her to Mamaroneck. Mary remained to look after her father for a while, then, after hiring a young woman to come in and watch over him, brought Clarice to Mamaroneck.

Back in his study, John Dickson Carr caught up on some of his correspondence and his responsibilities as a reviewer for *Ellery Queen's Mystery Magazine*. He had missed two issues, but in April he was able to produce copy for the August 1976 issue. "Your mentor, now fully recovered from a long and tedious illness," he wrote, "once more mounts the familiar rostrum to preach."[70] Clarice was able to come back to Greenville early in June, and managed to provide the care her husband needed. When I suggested to her that it must have been a difficult time for her, she replied, "There was this strange—I can't tell you what it is—'love' is a stupid word. We were very much at one with each other, and, no, it wasn't hard at all." But physicially the situation was becoming worse. A small woman herself, Clarice found it difficult to turn John in bed and to support him while he tried to walk. Early in July, he was still hopeful after what he called "more than six months of exhausting illness." On July 22, however, he spent all day at the doctor's, and it became clear that the cancer was advancing again and that he should return to a nursing home. He had just completed his final review column, and like many of the others that had preceded it, it praised books that "never once cheat with the clues."[71]

Edna Seaman was a friend of Mrs. Carol McCarthy, who owned and managed Resthaven Geriatric Center, a nursing home well known for its care of terminally ill patients. The word had gotten around that John Dickson Carr was not easy to handle, but Mrs. McCarthy admired his books and she was willing to admit him. He had a private room at Resthaven, looking out over the trees—though Mrs. McCarthy recalls that he was not the sort of man particularly interested in scenery. He wanted to read books and watch television—especially baseball. Clarice came in every day to read to him, or just to talk while she worked on needlepoint. Despite his physical weakness, he remained mentally sharp. He talked with Mrs. McCarthy about his mother—whom he still disliked ten years after her death—his education, his experiences during World War II, and writing. His daughters and grandchildren came down to visit, and on November 30, 1976, Carol McCarthy honored his seventieth birthday with a cake and oyster stew. Clarice, Edna Seaman, and one of the Carrs' granddaughters, Michelle McNiven, were there. He was touched: "I haven't had a birthday party since I was a little boy," he said—not mentioning that he hadn't often wanted to have one.

John still did not admit that he was dying. When he received a letter from Nick Carr in December, he told Clarice to tell his cousin that he would write as soon as he was strong enough.[72] Early in 1977 it seemed on several occasions that he was near death, but he rallied. On February 27, Clarice spent all day at Resthaven and helped settle John for the night. Carol McCarthy sent Clarice home to get some rest, promising to sit with John until morning. But the end came quickly. "John," said Mrs. McCarthy, "is there anything at all that I can get for you?" "No," he answered, "everything is going to be all right." Five minutes later, he was dead.

At such times, the mind focuses on little things. Clarice returned to Resthaven, and when she saw John's body, she noticed how pale he looked, but that his hair was still the light-brown color that it had been when they were married forty-five years earlier.

Chapter 20

L'ENVOI

The funeral for John Dickson Carr was held at two o'clock on the afternoon of Wednesday, March 2, 1977, at the graveside. The day was bright and chilly. Clarice Carr had purchased two lots at Springwood Cemetery in downtown Greenville, next to the library where her husband had done much of the research for his last books. At the family's request, only a few people were present. Clarice, Mary, and Julia were there, and Julia's husband, Richard McNiven. Carol McCarthy's husband came, and so did Edna Seaman and Norvin Duncan from the local television station. The service was conducted by an Episcopal clergyman. Clarice chose a simple aboveground tomb, with CARR on the center, and on the left John's name, places and dates of birth and death, and the words "Requiescat in Pace." On the right is Clarice's name and place of birth.

The obituaries recognized that one of the great writers of detective fiction had gone. The Associated Press sent the announcement throughout the world. The BBC broadcast the news of the death of the man whose radio plays had terrified so many of its listeners. The *Uniontown Evening Standard* used three columns of its front page to eulogize Carr as one of its most important natives. *The New York Times* in its headline called him "A Master of the Mystery Novel," and the *Times* of London, in an obituary that was published anonymously but written by Anthony Lejeune, said that he

> was one of the most technically ingenious of all modern detective story writers. . . . His mind and conversation burned with fantastic ideas and sinister devices and great roaring heroes of romance. Life perhaps never quite measured up to his expectations. His books showed, in the terms of a modern fairy tale, what he wanted to be.

Edmund Crispin summarized Carr's contributions in these words: "For subtlety, ingenuity and atmosphere he was one of the three or four best detective-story writers, since Poe, that the English language has known."[1]

John Dickson Carr's legacy was his books; through them he gave, and continues to give, matchless pleasure both to puzzle fanciers and to those who agree with him that the world would be better if it reflected the standards of romance. For those of us who, like Carr, think that the ultimate mystery is whether the world is ordered and rational or chaotic, his detective stories have a power that transcends the genre.

When John Dickson Carr was asked whether he would change any part of his life, he answered, "Oh, I've been a damned fool sometimes, you know, but otherwise no."[2] The world has plenty of damned fools—all of us can claim that title—but it had only one John Dickson Carr.

Appendix 1

JOHN D. CARR III
ON REALISTIC WRITERS
IN 1922

[The following article was written by John Dickson Carr when he was fifteen years old and published in his column "As We See It," *Union-town Daily News Standard*, May 4, 1922. Unfortunately, the only known copy has damage toward the bottom of the page resulting in the loss of a few words.]

As we have had precious [sic, for "previous"] occasion to remark, we have no use for the so-called "realistic" novels which rob life of all that is beautiful and show it in distorted sordidness. The author seems to delight in thinking of disagreeable things. He is continually telling one that happiness, like Solanio's reason, is as a grain of wheat hid in a bushel of chaff; one may search all day ere he find it, and when he does find it, it is not worth the search. It does not take an author but a pessimist to write such books; surely they demand no creativeness or writers' art, when their characters are but poor, weak attempts at what might be, and when they contain not the slightest shred of plot.

Why must an author see the world through smoked glasses to be called a realist? Why is the market flooded with stuff such as *Main Street, Potterism,* and *The Beautiful and the Damned*? And prodigious wonder, why do these books rank as best-sellers?

It is child's play to write a "startling" book. Even the struggling dime-novelist, who is sweating blood to get its effusions between paper covers, is capable of writing something that because of its bad taste would find a wide sale. Were he to write a book describing the struggles of the heroine, a talented washwoman, and the hero, a respectable bootlegger, to break with society, giving a sensational account of the fight when Lord Hokum came home drunk and crowned Lady

Hokum with the umbrella stand, and, in a final blaze of glory, telling how society split into two factions over the divorce and the hero and the heroine thus wormed their way into the Four Hundred then he could retire and live happily ever after on the [words missing]. By its very senselessness; its lack of writers' art disguised behind the mask of "genius respects no rules"; and the fact that there is a certain class of the reading public which revels in such fiction, the book would create a furore in literary circles.

Because it is impossible for them to write anything better the "realists" stick to "realism." If there were more such clean, wholesome, cheerful authors as A. S. M. Hutchinson and Floyd Dell, and less fiction of this and the *Sheik* type, then the reading public would recognize how inferior is the "realistic" fol-de-rol.

It is our firm belief that it takes more writers' art to get out a really good detective story than a truckload of Fitzgerald's books. In writing the problem story the characters do not matter; the author's chief aim is to amuse. If he can create a new and ingenious plot, create a tense undercurrent of suspense that carries the reader along in spite of himself, and then produce a climax [words missing] breathless while he naively explains away all the seemingly unsolvable puzzles that have added zest to the story—then has he written a good mystery novel. Easy? It looks easy as one who has just finished a clever plot story. Misled by the fluent style of the author, he says: "Why, there would be nothing hard about writing one of those. Just get a good—" and so on.

But in reality writing a story with all these requirements is the most difficult task in the world. Slicing and amplifying; putting here and there a casual remark that, unknown to the reader, is the keynote of the plot; increasing the suspense bit by bit until the reader is being hurried along at a terrific speed; and in one astounding flash revealing the whole truth—easy? Hardly.

So it is our contention that any imitation author can write a realistic story; but it takes a true master—one who knows his reader—to write a problem novel.

Appendix 2

DOROTHY L. SAYERS'S REVIEWS OF CARR'S BOOKS

[One of the most important influences on John Dickson Carr's career was Dorothy L. Sayers's reviews of his books in the *Sunday Times*. All of Sayers's reviews of mystery fiction should be collected in one volume, but in lieu of that, I am grateful to her estate for permission to print extracts about Carr's books.]

REVIEW OF *THE MAD HATTER MYSTERY* (September 24, 1933)
"Is Mr. Carr Edgar Wallace's successor?"* inquires Mr. Carr's publisher, wistfully. The answer is "Don't ask silly questions." From the very first paragraph of *The Mad Hatter Mystery* it is abundantly clear that Mr. Carr has nothing in common with Edgar Wallace:—

> It began, like most of Dr. Fell's adventures, in a bar. It dealt with the reason why a man was found dead on the steps of Traitors' Gate at the Tower of London, and with the odd headgear of this man in the golf suit. That was the worst part of it. The whole case threatened to become a nightmare of hats.

If that is like anybody, it is like Mr. G. K. Chesterton. And in the portrait of Dr. Fell himself one may perhaps, without being too personal, trace a certain Chestertonian exuberance of outline:

*Edgar Wallace, one of the most popular thriller writers of all time, had died in 1932.

All the old genial days, all the beer-drinking and fiery moods and table-pounding conversations, beamed back at Rampole in the person of Dr. Fell. . . . There was the doctor, bigger and stouter than ever. He wheezed. His red face shone, and his small black eyes twinkled over eyeglasses on a broad black ribbon. There was a grin under his bandit's moustache, and chuckling upheavals animated his several chins. On his head was the inevitable shovel-hat; his paunch projected from a voluminous black cloak. Filling the stairs in grandeur, he leaned upon an ash-cane with one hand and flourished an umbrella with the other. It was like meeting Father Christmas or Old King Cole.

Chestertonian also are the touches of extravagance in character and plot, and the sensitiveness to symbolism, to historical association, to the shapes and colours of material things, to the crazy terror of the incongruous. Mr. Carr can lead us away from the small, artificial, brightly-lit stage of the ordinary detective plot into the menace of outer darkness. He can create atmosphere with an adjective, and make a picture from a wet iron railing, a dusty table, a gas-lamp blurred by the fog. He can alarm with an illusion or delight with a rollicking absurdity. He can invent a passage from a lost work of Edgar Allan Poe which sounds like the real thing. In short he can write—not merely in the negative sense of observing the rules of syntax, but in the sense that every sentence gives a thrill of positive pleasure. This is the most attractive mystery I have read for a long time.

REVIEW OF *THE EIGHT OF SWORDS* (March 25, 1934)
I feel that neither Mr. Punshon* nor Mr. Carr has written quite up to his usual form. . . .

"The Eight of Swords" suffers from a kind of general looseness and unevenness. There are moments of good detection, moments of brilliant character-drawing, and moments of horror and of the queer suggestiveness in which Mr. Carr excels, but there are too many moments of what I can best call, in the wireless sense of the word, "fading."

We start off with the Bishop sliding exuberantly down the banisters, but the episcopal glory grows dim in the sequel, and the tone of this noble opening is not consistently maintained. Nor does Dr. Gideon Fell ever get quite enough scope for his endearing eccentricities. The curious Mummerzet spoken by the local policeman reminds us that the author is not an Englishman, and, while it is probably no worse than English attempts at rendering American dialect, it helps to make the story stagey and unreal.

The book needs pulling together. It shines, but only by intermittent flashes, and it is by the light of those flashes that it must be read.

REVIEW OF *THE BOWSTRING MURDERS* (August 19, 1934)
"The Bowstring Murders" take place, if anywhere, in the Castle of Otranto. There is a mad old baron in a weird old castle, where corpses appear mysteriously in a great old hall filled with suits of armour, and apparitions of armed knights haunt the staircase.

*The review also discusses E. R. Punshon's *Death Among the Sun Bathers*.

The plot is of the "hermetically sealed chamber" type, and the mysteries all have a plain, physical explanation, but the style is rather Adelphi, and some of the details are not convincing. I have my doubts about the ballistics, and I *know* that a vambrace is not a kind of armour-plated skirt, but a defense for the forearm *(avant-bras)*. But there are ingenious touches here and there, and, with better handling, this might have made a good tale of the near-thriller type.

REVIEW OF *THE BLIND BARBER* (November 11, 1934)
I laughed uproariously over "The Blind Barber." But I admit that I am one of the simple-minded people who become weak and ill over the antics of Nervo and Knox, and have to be led away suffering from convulsions. Perhaps it was unrefined of me to be amused when the dignified and choleric skipper of the Queen Victoria was laid out by an impulsive but mistaken young investigator armed with a whisky bottle, and subsequently half-smothered in his own cabin by the uncontrollable blast of the Mermaid Automatic Bug-Powder Gun. But even those who only joke "wi' deeficulty" must spare a chuckle for Captain Valvick, who tells such delightful and irrelevant stories in so persuasive a Dutch [sic] accent, and for the other preposterous passengers who roam and wrestle and tumble (not always, alas! with strict sobriety) about the decks of that outraged and respectable liner. Never can a nasty, bluggy murder have been detected to an accompaniment of so much hilarious horseplay. Yet, in all the confusion, the clues are not neglected. Sixteen of them, all magnificently Chestertonian and incomprehensible, are listed by Dr. Gideon Fell. He, of course, is the god in the Carr who makes majestic descent upon the final hurly-burly to unravel the tangle; *dignus,* I am delighted to say, *vindice nodus.*

The story has all its author's usual happy touch of the grotesque, with less of the horrible and more of the farcical about it, and all his usual merits of style, and if anybody doesn't like it, I pities 'em.

REVIEW OF *THE PLAGUE COURT MURDERS* (March 17, 1935)
"Plague Court"—the words are horrid in themselves and suggestive of horrors to come. . . .

Mr. Carter Dickson belongs to the school of mystery-writers who want to make your flesh creep. . . .

"The Plague Court Murders" seems to me to show a very great advance upon Mr. Dickson's previous book, "The Bowstring Murders." It is less jerky and confused; he has got his style under better control. The tale is about a circle of people who have come under the influence of a gentleman who deals in the psychic; and the atmosphere of grotesque horror surrounding this person's murder in a "hermetically sealed chamber" is really well done.

It is the kind of thing to which you must willingly abandon yourself if you are to enjoy it; but if you like being deliciously frightened into fits you can, to quote a tailor's advertisement which once delighted me, "have a fit here." Like all "sealed chamber" mysteries, this one has a solution that takes a good deal of swallowing and demands a long-winded explanation at the end; that is the drawback to all plots of this type, except, perhaps, the famous "Mystere de la Chambre Jaune."*

*Gaston Leroux's *The Mystery of the Yellow Room.*

Mr. Dickson's burly and eccentric Sir Henry Merrivale exudes personality and—positively!—an original charm, and that is no small feat in a world where eccentric detectives are as common as blackbeetles. Also, Mr. Dickson can write; he tends to the violently picturesque, and nine times out of ten he brings it off. Incidentally (while we are fighting about syntax) he has staggered me by producing a perfectly correct gerund: "Something about the servants' hearing things in the house." Burn me! (as Sir Henry Merrivale would say) but I would forgive him more sins than one for that blessed apostrophe!

REVIEW OF *DEATH-WATCH* (March 31, 1955)

In almost ludicrous contrast to Mr. Kennedy* comes Mr. John Dickson Carr, with a new adventure of Dr. Gideon Fell. Mr. Carr has the knack of surrounding his plot and characters with a perpetual aura of excitement. Everything about them is fantastic; his people are all a little larger than human; they thrill with a kind of spiritual violence, even when they perform the most ordinary actions. His story may be too complicated, too improbable; his crimes may be performed by means and motives too far-fetched for belief; but he has the art of the genuine *frisson*. He deals with the thing that is not quite reasonable, with the thing "on the wrong side of the door," and his love of these things is so infectious that, before your judgment has time to assert itself, he has "coost the glamour over ye." I do not believe in the man who was stabbed, by so strange a contrivance, amid a household of people so unbalanced, and for so insane a motive; but between the dark and the light I am ready to listen to the voice of the enchanter and to the sinister ticking of the "Death-Watch."

Mr. Carr is an American with a passion (as it seems to me) for England, and especially for the older and more secretive parts of London. (His English diction and atmosphere are very good; only occasionally does a phrase—"rooming-house," "the defence rests"—trip him up.)

REVIEW OF *THE WHITE PRIORY MURDERS* (July 28, 1935)

Of this weeks' trio of writers, I place Mr. Dickson first, because he has succeeded in keeping the equilibrium between his plot and his writing. "The White Priory Murders" is built up on the fine old theme of the lonely corpse surrounded by an area of snow, virgin except for the tracks of the person who discovers the body. We all know that (excluding suicide and the universally despised secret passage) this problem admits of only three legitimate solutions: the time was wrong, the place was wrong, or the corpse was wrong. Mr. Dickson has handled this classical material very capably, using scrupulous fairness in deduction and concealing the identity of his criminal with considerable cunning. His group of characters contains a number of oddities, but the oddities are both interesting and believable; and he uses his skill in suggesting queerness, both of psychology and atmosphere, for the legitimate double purpose of distracting attention from the material clues and preparing our minds to accept his solution. Our fat and eccentric friend, Sir Henry Merrivale, comes in to do the final detection; but his is not the only sympathetic portrait in a collection of careful character-sketches.

*The review also discusses Milward Kennedy's *Poison in the Parish*.

REVIEW OF *THE LIFE OF SIR ARTHUR CONAN DOYLE* (February 6, 1949)
[Most of Sayers's review talks about Doyle, but it concludes with these remarks about Carr's book.]

Mr. John Dickson Carr has made a good use of the abundant material—much of it hitherto inedited—which the Doyle family have placed at his disposal. His biography is admirably complete, and clearly and well arranged. It suffers somewhat from a determined brightness of style, reminiscent of a radio feature-programme, whereby every episode is remorselessly dramatised, every chapter begins with a tableau and a flash-back, and rhetorical questions abound. But we may bear with these surface defects for the sake of the accuracy, sympathy and balanced judgment with which he has handled his subject.

Appendix 3

A THIRD SOLUTION TO
THE BURNING COURT?

If you haven't read *The Burning Court,* you should ignore this appendix. Those who have read the book will recall that Carr so carefully creates the supernatural atmosphere and has such a stunning impossible situation one can only regard him as having finally broken from his pattern of finding a rational explanation for the eerie events. Here witchcraft appears all too real, with Ted Stevens's wife, Marie, the head of a group of nondead who poison their victims. Then Gaudan Cross turns up and provides detailed and persuasive explanations of the mysteries. The guilty person, he says, is Myra Corbett, a nurse who had attended the victim, Miles Despard. As Cross finished giving his evidence, however, he dies from poison himself, obviously administered by Corbett. This was a shocking conclusion, for rarely had authors killed their detectives at the denouement, but at least the reader could return to his or her tidy world. The supernatural had again been shown to be an illusion.

But *The Burning Court* is not over. It has an epilogue giving a second explanation to the mystery: We enter Marie Stevens's mind and discover that she is a witch after all. She has murdered Miles Despard through supernatural means and stolen his body so that he would join the nondead. She muses that "it was clever of [Gaudan Cross] to pluck a physical explanation, a thing of sizes and dimensions and stone walls, out of all those things which had no explanation I was prepared to give them." But Cross had wanted her to come back to him as his lover, so she had to murder him as well. "He will return to flesh and bone presently, but I have the better of him now." Meanwhile, she plans also to make her husband one of the nondead: "He will be one of us presently, if I can transform him without pain. Or too much pain." In other words, she intends to poison Ted, but with a less painful poison than the arsenic she had used on Miles Despard. She then hears her husband return home, and "her face became the face of a pretty wife."

My brother, David L. Greene, has suggested that there is a third possible conclusion to *The Burning Court*—that Marie Stevens's musings in the epilogue show not that she is a witch but that she is mad. She may have thought herself a witch, but there is no strong evidence to prove that she was one, and some indirect evidence to the contrary. *The Burning Court* takes place in 1929, and the epilogue indicates that she plans to "transform" (i.e., kill) her husband soon. What then are we to make of the statement at the beginning of the book, "Stevens himself now admits that it is a relief to state facts, to deal with matters that can be tabulated or arranged"? In other words, Stevens was still alive in 1937, when the book was published. Even had he been poisoned and then come back as a member of the witch cult, what relief could he get by tabulating facts? If, on the other hand, he had not been poisoned, perhaps Marie was not a witch after all.

My consideration of the problems that David Greene raised about *The Burning Court* had reached the above stage when I reread *Panic in Box C*, published in 1966. In a passing reference, we discover that Ted Stevens has still not succumbed to poison: "[Phillip Knox] had lunch with Edward Stevens of Herald & Sons." *Panic in Box C* takes place during the first four months of 1965, some thirty-six years after *The Burning Court*. Has Marie Stevens merely been biding her time for all these years? Or were her thoughts at the end of *The Burning Court* the result of derangement? The true solution to *The Burning Court* may be that Myra Corbett did murder Miles Despard, exactly as Gaudan Cross said, that Cross wanted to seduce Marie but for a more human and less witchly reason, that Marie murdered him to escape his unwelcome attentions and then went mad to the extent that she believed that she was a witch.

A final note: I think Carr would be vastly amused by this attempt to undermine the epilogue of *The Burning Court*, and he wouldn't believe a word of it.

Appendix 4

JOHN DICKSON CARR—SPY?

Several recent publications have stated that John Dickson Carr was a British espionage agent during World War II, working under Maxwell Knight, known as "M." It has been alleged that, using the name "John Dickson," he infiltrated the British Communist party for MI5. The story apparently first appeared in print in Nigel West's *MI5: British Security Operations 1902–1945* (1981): "Another MI5 author who was to draw on his own experiences was John Dickson Carr, the American-born thriller writer, who served with [Sir Vernon] Kell before joining the BBC as a playwright in 1942." (Kell was director-general of MI5 until 1940.) Details were added in Anthony Masters's *The Man Who Was M, the Life of Maxwell Knight* (1984). Based on information from Olga Gray, who infiltrated the Communist party, Masters wrote: "She also met the thriller writer John Dickson Carr, another C[ommunist] Party worker, who, unbeknown to Olga, was also an MI5 agent, presumably directed by Knight."[1] Joan Miller, who was Knight's secretary during the war, mentions Carr in her memoirs, *One Girl's War, Personal Exploits in MI5's Most Secret Station* (1986):

> There is no doubt that the "M" figure of the James Bond novels owes a great deal to Maxwell Knight. . . . His closest associates at the time were Philip Brocklehurst, a delightful man who was known as Brock; the famous detective novelist John Dickson Carr (known as John Dickson in the office). . . . These four—Bill Younger, Guy Poston, Brock and John Dickson—shared an office and ran agents under M's direction.[2]

Ray Bearse and Anthony Read in *Conspirator* (1991) include Carr as one of "several agents working under cover against the communists." The story reached general mystery fans when Patricia Craig mentioned Carr's supposed MI5 connection in *The Oxford Book of English Detective Stories* (1990).

In spite of this accumulation of evidence and assertions, it is unlikely that Carr worked for British intelligence. For one thing, Carr's wife, Clarice, has no knowledge of it, pointing out that it would have been foolish for the government to give someone whose heavy drinking was so well known an assignment that would entail knowing important secrets. (On the other hand, as we now know from the Kim Philby and Guy Burgess scandal, an addiction to alcohol did not prevent some people from service with MI5.) Tony Medawar, who has done much valuable work on tracking down Carrian material, has investigated the matter. With the help of a former head of MI5 and of a British member of Parliament, Rupert Allason—who, under the pseudonym Nigel West, had set the hare running—Medawar learned that there was a World War II double agent named "Jimmy Dickson," a small-time writer with associations with the London underworld. West had confused Jimmy Dickson with Carr; once this confusion appeared in print other writers—including those who had lived through the era—continued to make the connection.

Sometime after the war, another story circulated claiming that Carr was involved with the interrogation of Rudolf Hess, the Nazi official who had parachuted into Scotland in May 1941 under the delusion that he could bring peace between Germany and Britain. The rumor of Carr's involvement probably began with the publication of J. R. Rees's *The Case of Rudolf Hess* (1948). This book, which is a study in "forensic psychology" based on the work of various doctors who had dealt with Hess during the war, does indeed acknowledge Carr's assistance. Clarice Carr, however, recalls that John knew Rees socially after the war, and that his role was limited to helping assemble the book. Although it's a good tale, and one that Carr would have liked, he had nothing to do with questioning Hess.

One small matter might be mentioned in connection with Carr-as-espionage agent. In 1938, when he applied for a renewal of his passport, the United States government placed a memorandum in his file: "A report states that John D. Carr was dismissed by the Bethlehem Steel Corporation for indiscretions and disloyalty." A handwritten note adds "apparently not same," and Carr never knew that he had been confused with an indiscreet and disloyal steelworker. His passport was renewed.

Appendix 5

THE OTHER DEAR CHARMER, A NEVER-WRITTEN CARR NOVEL

[On page 384, I alluded to the plot of a book that Carr considered but never wrote. It was replaced by *Fear Is the Same* (1956). Because this is the only unfinished Carr novel for which many details survive, I quote Carr's full description as sent to Anthony Boucher on October 8, 1954.]

Being fierily in the creative mood, I am working out the details of a novel whose theme is as follows.

The central character is a famous present-day actor: someone, for instance, like Laurence Olivier. During a debate over the dearth of good plays on the stage for nearly a hundred years—between, say, the time of Sheridan and Goldsmith and the arrival of Henry Arthur Jones, Pinero, and Shaw—this actor toys with a challenge to himself. He wonders whether he could choose a play from the stuffiest height of mid-Victorianism, say 1868, and attempt to put it on as a serious production.

He is told that he couldn't get away with it unless he burlesqued it. He retorts that to burlesque it has been tried before; it is the cheapest trick which has been tried on the stage. If he does it at all, he will stick to every word from the prompt-book of the original play, including the jokes. This time they give him the horse-laugh. He replied that there is just one way in which it might be done. Pathos and comedy differ in different generations; but fear is much the same at any time. If he chose one of the old blood-and-thunder thrillers, he might just manage it.

Well! He and his wife, actor-managers of an old theatre, arrange a production which shall copy the clothes, the sets, and the music in every detail. On the first night—his entrance does not occur until the middle of the first act—something happens to him on the way between his dressing-room and the stage. He makes his entrance: to a burst of applause, yes, and on the proper set: but amid actors he has never seen before, and under the scorching heat of gas footlights.

Even his wife, who should be playing the lead, is not on the stage. She appears—or somebody like her appears—towards the end of the act; but in a small part, and does not seem to understand when with under-the-breath remarks he attempts to discover what the hell, while still playing the act through. I need scarcely tell you what has happened to him; he is in 1868, with all the troubles that would bring to make difficult his playing. Further, he remains there. He becomes involved in a murder, whose mystery he must solve to save his own neck. He is between two women, one his wife and one his leading-lady in the play, who has died before he was born. That is why the tentative title should be *The Other Dear Charmer* or perhaps *Fear Is the Same*.

CHECKLIST OF THE
WORKS OF
JOHN DICKSON CARR

This checklist is a revised and enlarged version of "A Bibliography of the Works of John Dickson Carr," which was published in the first British and American editions of *The Door to Doom and Other Detections* (1980). Many people contributed the new information that appears here, but I should specifically thank Tony Medawar, whose researches at the BBC, the British Library, and other archives have resulted in many important discoveries, especially the location of the typescripts of Carr's stage plays and of the radio program *Cabin B-13*; Collin Southern and Robert Adey, both of whom checked many of the periodical appearances of Carr's novels in British sources; James E. Keirans, who added information on paperback editions; Chivers Press for information on their Carr publications; John Cooper, who checked the list for errors and caught several of them; and S. T. Joshi, whose bibliography published in his *John Dickson Carr, a Critical Study* (Bowling Green State University Press, 1990) should be consulted to identify many reprints of Carr's works by various publishers as well as translations of his books into many languages.

The checklist is divided into the following sections:

1. Books
    A. Published Under the Name John Dickson Carr
    B. Published Under the Pseudonym Carr Dickson
    C. Published Under the Pseudonym Carter Dickson
    D. Published Under the Pseudonym Roger Fairbairn
    E. Omnibus Editions
    F. Book Edited by John Dickson Carr
2. Short Stories, Poems, and Early Nonfiction
    A. High School and Preparatory School Publications
    B. College Publications
    C. Later Short Fiction
3. Articles and Reviews

4. Introductions to Books
5. Radio Scripts
6. Stage Plays
7. Adaptations of Carr's Works by Other Writers
8. Parodies and Pastiches (and Similar) of Carr's Works

1. BOOKS

The material following the title of each book includes first American publisher, first British publisher (British publisher is given first if that edition is dated at least a year before the American), first American paperback, first British paperback, first edition(s) in English in other countries, and any succeeding editions with noteworthy features. In several instances, Carr's novels were published in British magazines shortly before or about the same time as book publication. Although this information is still incomplete, I include it whenever possible.

A. PUBLISHED UNDER THE NAME JOHN DICKSON CARR

It Walks By Night. New York: Harper & Brothers, 1930; London: Harper & Brothers (British branch), 1930; first U.S. paperback, Pocket Books 101, 1941; first British paperback, Penguin 124, 1938.

    The first Henri Bencolin novel, narrated by Jeff Marle. This is a revised and expanded version of "Grand Guignol," *The Haverfordian*, March, April 1929.

The Lost Gallows. New York: Harper & Brothers, 1931: London: Hamish Hamilton, 1931; first U.S. paperback, Pocket Books 436, 1947. (There have been no British paperback editions.)

    The second Henri Bencolin novel, narrated by Jeff Marle.

Castle Skull. New York: Harper & Brothers, 1931; London: Tom Stacey, 1973, or Severn House, 1976;* first U.S. paperback, Pocket Books 448, 1947. (There have been no British paperback editions.)

    The third Henri Bencolin novel, narrated by Jeff Marle.

The Corpse in the Waxworks. New York: Harper & Brothers, 1932; London: Hamish Hamilton, 1932, as *The Waxworks Murder;* first U.S. paperback, Avon 33, 1943; first British paperback, Penguin 158, 1938.

    The fourth Henri Bencolin novel, narrated by Jeff Marle.

Poison in Jest. New York: Harper & Brothers, 1932; London: Hamish Hamilton, 1932; first U.S. paperback, abridged, Thriller Novel Classic 23, 1944; first U.S. paperback, unabridged, Popular Library 349, 1951; first British paperback, Penguin 250, 1940.

    The only novel featuring Patrick Rossiter, narrated by Jeff Marle. Henri Bencolin is mentioned in passing.

Hag's Nook. New York: Harper & Brothers, 1933; London: Hamish Hamilton, 1933; first U.S. paperback, Penguin (U.S. branch) 532, 1943; first British paperback, Penguin 256, 1940. A paperback edition with an introduction by Anthony Boucher was published in 1963 by Collier Books (New York). A paperback edition with an introduction by Douglas G. Greene was published in 1985 by International Polygonics (New York).

    The first Dr. Gideon Fell novel.

The Mad Hatter Mystery. New York: Harper & Brothers, 1933; London: Hamish Hamilton,

---

*The British edition was announced by Tom Stacey Publishers in 1973 and copies were printed and bound, but that firm went bankrupt before the book was officially published. Nonetheless, without proper authorization a few copies reached the market in 1974. In 1976, Severn House purchased the remaining stock and replaced the Stacey title page with a cancel giving the new publisher's name. The spine, however, retains the Stacey imprint.

1933; first U.S. paperback, Popular Library 61, 1945; first British paperback, Penguin 610, 1947.

> The second Dr. Gideon Fell novel.

The Eight of Swords. New York: Harper & Brothers, 1934; London: Hamish Hamilton, 1934; first U.S. paperback, abridged, Detective Novel Classic 32, 1944; first U.S. paperback unabridged, Berkley G-48, 1957; first British paperback, Pan G487, 1961; first Continental edition in English, Scherz Phoenix paperback 120 (Berne, Switzerland), ca. 1947–48.

> The third Dr. Gideon Fell novel.

The Blind Barber. New York: Harper & Brothers, 1934; London: Hamish Hamilton, 1934; first U.S. paperback, Penguin 528 (U.S. branch), 1943; first British paperback, Penguin 875, 1952. A paperback edition with an introduction by Anthony Boucher was published in 1962 by Collier Books (New York). A 1984 Collier reprint of this edition gives the cover title as *The Case of the Blind Barber.*

> The fourth Dr. Gideon Fell novel.

Death-Watch. New York: Harper & Brothers, 1935; London: Hamish Hamilton, 1935; first U.S. paperback, abridged, Bestseller 78, 1946; first U.S. paperback, unabridged, Dell 564, 1952; first British paperback, Penguin 914, 1953.

> The fifth Dr. Gideon Fell novel. Henri Bencolin is mentioned in passing. British editions contain a brief prefatory note not included in the American editions.

The Three Coffins. New York: Harper & Brothers, 1935; London: Hamish Hamilton, 1935, as *The Hollow Man;* first U.S. paperback, abridged, Bestseller 47, 1944; first U.S. paperback, unabridged, Popular Library 174, 1949; first British paperback, Penguin 862, 1951. A hardback edition with an introduction by Joan Kahn was published in 1979 by Gregg Press (Boston).

> The sixth Dr. Gideon Fell novel.

The Arabian Nights Murder. New York: Harper & Brothers, 1936; London: Hamish Hamilton, 1936; first U.S. paperback, Hillman Detective 1, 1944. (There have been no British paperback editions.)

> The seventh Dr. Gideon Fell novel.

The Murder of Sir Edmund Godfrey. New York: Harper & Brothers, 1936; London: Hamish Hamilton, 1936; first U.S. paperback, Dolphin C-369, 1962. (There have been no British paperback editions.) An edition with a foreword and an afterword by Douglas G. Greene was published both as a hardback and as a paperback in 1989 by International Polygonics (New York).

> An unsolved murder of 1678 investigated as a detective novel.

The Burning Court. New York: Harper & Brothers, 1937; London: Hamish Hamilton, 1937; first U.S. paperback, Popular Library 28, 1944; first British paperback, Guild 444, 1952.

> Nonseries novel of detection and witchcraft.

The Four False Weapons. New York: Harper & Brothers, 1937; London: Hamish Hamilton, 1938; first U.S. paperback, abridged, Detective Novel Classic 40, 1945; first U.S. paperback, unabridged, Popular Library 282, 1950; first British paperback, Pan G453, 1961. Serialized in the British magazine *Woman's Journal,* December 1937–April 1938.

> The fifth Henri Bencolin novel. Jeff Marle is mentioned in passing.

To Wake the Dead. London: Hamish Hamilton, 1937; New York: Harper & Brothers, 1938; first U.S. paperback, Popular Library 10, 1943; first British paperback, Pan 64, 1948; first Continental edition in English, Tauchnitz paperback 5340 (Leipzig, Germany), 1938.

> The eighth Dr. Gideon Fell novel.

The Crooked Hinge. New York: Harper & Brothers, 1938; London: Hamish Hamilton, 1938; first U.S. paperback, Popular Library 19, 1943; first British paperback, Pan GP80, 1957. Serialized in the British magazine *The Passing Show,* October 29, 1938–January 14, 1939. A hardback edition with an introduction and notes by Robert E. Briney was published in 1976 by University Extension, University of California at San Diego (Publishers, Inc.).

The ninth Dr. Gideon Fell novel.

The Problem of the Green Capsule. New York: Harper & Brothers, 1939; London: Hamish Hamilton, 1939, as *The Black Spectacles;* first U.S. paperback, Bantam 101, 1947; first British paperback, Pan 21, 1947. Serialized as *Mystery in Limelight* in the British magazine *Woman's Journal,* May–July 1939.

The tenth Dr. Gideon Fell novel.

The Problem of the Wire Cage. New York: Harper & Brothers, 1939; London: Hamish Hamilton, 1940; first U.S. paperback, Bantam 304, 1948; first British paperback, Pan 97, 1949. Serialized as *The Cage* in the British magazine *Modern Woman* November 1939–March 1940.

The eleventh Dr. Gideon Fell novel.

The Man Who Could Not Shudder. New York: Harper & Brothers, 1940; London: Hamish Hamilton, 1940; first U.S. paperback, Bantam 365, 1949. (There have been no British paperback editions.)

The twelfth Dr. Gideon Fell novel.

The Case of the Constant Suicides. New York: Harper & Brothers, 1941; London: Hamish Hamilton, 1941; first U.S. paperback, Dell 91, 1945; first British paperback, Penguin 947, 1953; first Continental edition in English, Scherz Phoenix paperback 92 (Berne, Switzerland), 1947.

The thirteenth Dr. Gideon Fell novel.

Death Turns the Tables. New York: Harper & Brothers, 1941; London: Hamish Hamilton, 1942, as *The Seat of the Scornful;* first U.S. paperback, Pocket Books 350, 1946 (printed, December 1945); first British paperback, Pan G309, 1960; first Continental edition in English, Scherz Phoenix paperback 6 (Berne, Switzerland), 1943, using the British title.

The fourteenth Dr. Gideon Fell novel.

The Emperor's Snuff-Box. New York: Harper & Brothers, 1942; London: Hamish Hamilton, 1943; first U.S. paperback, Pocket Books 372, 1946; first British paperback, Penguin 949, 1953; first Australian edition, Jaboor (Melbourne), 1944; first Continental edition in English, Scherz Phoenix paperback 24 (Berne, Switzerland), 1946. Serialized in the British magazine *Woman's Journal,* February–May 1943.

Nonseries detective novel featuring Dr. Dermot Kinross.

Till Death Do Us Part. New York: Harper & Brothers, 1944; London: Hamish Hamilton, 1944; first U.S. paperback, Bantam 793, 1950; first British paperback, Penguin 950, 1953; first Continental edition in English, Scherz Phoenix paperback 45 (Berne, Switzerland), 1946; first Indian edition in English, Thacker, ca. 1946.

The fifteenth Dr. Gideon Fell novel.

He Who Whispers. New York: Harper & Brothers, 1946; London: Hamish Hamilton, 1946; first U.S. paperback, Bantam 896, 1951; first British paperback, Penguin 948, 1953; first Continental edition in English, Scherz Phoenix paperback 102 (Berne, Switzerland), 1947.

The sixteenth Dr. Gideon Fell novel.

The Sleeping Sphinx. New York: Harper & Brothers, 1947; London: Hamish Hamilton, 1947; first U.S. paperback (noncommercial), Editions for the Armed Services 1280, 1947; first U.S. paperback (commercial), Bantam 996, 1952; first British paperback, Pan G595, 1962. Serialized in the British magazine *Woman's Own,* May 30–July 18, 1947.

The seventeenth Dr. Gideon Fell novel.

Dr. Fell, Detective, and Other Stories. New York: The American Mercury, Lawrence E. Spivak, Publisher (Mercury Mystery paperback 110), 1947. (There have been no British editions.)

A collection (edited by Ellery Queen) containing the following short stories and radio plays: "The Proverbial Murder" (Dr. Fell), "The Locked Room" (Dr. Fell),

"The Wrong Problem" (Dr. Fell), "The Hangman Won't Wait" (Dr. Fell radio play), "A Guest in the House" (Dr. Fell), "The Devil in the Summer-House" (radio play), "Will You Walk into My Parlor?" (radio play), and "Strictly Diplomatic." All of the contents of this book appear in later John Dickson Carr books. ("Will You Walk into My Parlor?" is printed in its revised British version, "Vampire Tower," in a later Carr book.)

The Life of Sir Arthur Conan Doyle. New York: Harper & Brothers, 1949; London: John Murray, 1949; first U.S. paperback, Dolphin C-117, ca. 1960; first British paperback, Pan GP20, 1953.

Biography of the creator of Sherlock Holmes.

Below Suspicion. New York: Harper & Brothers, 1949; London: Hamish Hamilton, 1950; first U.S. paperback, Bantam 1119, 1953; first British paperback, Penguin 1164, 1956.

The eighteenth Dr. Gideon Fell novel, also featuring barrister Patrick Butler.

The Bride of Newgate. New York: Harper & Brothers, 1950; London: Hamish Hamilton, 1950; first U.S. paperback, as portion of anthology, *Avon Giant Mystery Reader,* Avon G1004, 1951; first separately published U.S. paperback, Avon 476, 1952; first British paperback, Corgi G194, 1956. A hardback edition with an introduction by Peter Chambers was published in 1991 by Chivers Press (Bath). Serialized in the British magazine *Woman's Journal,* June–September 1950.

Historical detective novel, taking place in England in 1815.

The Devil in Velvet. New York: Harper & Brothers, 1951; London: Hamish Hamilton, 1951; first U.S. paperback, Bantam A1009, 1952; first British paperback, Penguin 1242, 1957.

Historical detective novel, taking place in England in 1675.

The 9 Wrong Answers. New York: Harper & Brothers, 1952; London: Hamish Hamilton, 1952; first U.S. paperback (abridged), Bantam 1325, 1955; first British paperback (abridged), Corgi 1325, 1956.*

Nonseries detective novel featuring Bill Dawson.

The Third Bullet and Other Stories. New York: Harper & Brothers, 1954; London: Hamish Hamilton, 1954; first U.S. paperback, Bantam 1447, 1956. (There have been no British paperback editions.)

A collection containing an abridged version of the title novella, which had appeared, unabridged, as a separately published paperback in 1937 under the Carter Dickson pseudonym, and the following short stories: "The Clue of the Red Wig," "The House in Goblin Wood" (Sir Henry Merrivale), "The Wrong Problem" (Dr. Fell), "The Proverbial Murder" (Dr. Fell), "The Locked Room" (Dr. Fell), and "The Gentleman from Paris." Three of these stories had previously been collected in *Dr. Fell, Detective, and Other Stories* (1947).

The Exploits of Sherlock Holmes (with Adrian Conan Doyle). New York: Random House, 1954; London: John Murray, 1954; first U.S. paperback, Ace D-181, 1956 (with front cover title, *The New Exploits of Sherlock Holmes*). In 1963, John Murray reprinted the final six stories (which were written by Doyle alone) in a paperback volume retaining the title *The Exploits of Sherlock Holmes.* In 1964, Murray reprinted the first six stories (by Carr and Doyle) in a paperback entitled *More Exploits of Sherlock Holmes.* The first complete British paperback was published by Sphere, 1978.

Twelve pastiches of Sherlock Holmes. The following stories were written by Carr and Adrian Conan Doyle: "The Adventure of the Seven Clocks," "The Adventure of the Gold Hunter," "The Adventure of the Wax Gamblers," "The Adventure of the Highgate Miracle," "The Adventure of the Black Baronet," and "The Adventure of the Sealed Room." The remaining six stories were written by Doyle alone.

Captain Cut-Throat. New York: Harper & Brothers, 1955; London: Hamish Hamilton, 1955;

*All paperbacks of *The 9 Wrong Answers* are abridged, although some do not admit the fact.

first U.S. paperback, Bantam A1472, 1956; first British paperback, Penguin 1488, 1960; serialized as *Black Sabre* in the British magazine *Argosy*, May–August 1955.

Historical detective novel, taking place in France in 1805.

Patrick Butler for the Defence. New York: Harper & Brothers, 1956; London: Hamish Hamilton, 1956; first U.S. paperback, Bantam 1682, 1957 (with a slight change in spelling of the title, *Patrick Butler for the Defense*); first British paperback, Penguin 1391, 1959.

Nonseries detective novel featuring Patrick Butler, the barrister in *Below Suspicion* (1949). Dr. Gideon Fell is mentioned in passing.

Fire, Burn! New York: Harper & Brothers, 1957; London: Hamish Hamilton, 1957; first U.S. paperback, Bantam A1847, 1959; first British paperback, Penguin 1622, 1961.

Historical detective novel, taking place in England in 1829; the first of the three volumes about the London police.

The Dead Man's Knock. New York: Harper & Brothers, 1958; London: Hamish Hamilton, 1958; first U.S. paperback, Bantam A2108, 1960; first British paperback, Penguin 1564, 1961.

The nineteenth Dr. Gideon Fell novel.

Scandal at High Chimneys. New York: Harper & Brothers, 1959; London: Hamish Hamilton, 1959; first U.S. paperback, Bantam A2155, 1960; first British paperback, Pan G537, 1962.

Historical detective novel, taking place in England in 1865; the second of three volumes about the London police.

In Spite of Thunder. New York: Harper & Brothers, 1960; London: Hamish Hamilton, 1960; first U.S. paperback, Bantam A2267, 1961; first British paperback, Penguin C2386, 1966.

The Witch of the Low-Tide. New York: Harper & Brothers, 1961; London: Hamish Hamilton, 1961; first U.S. paperback, Bantam J2559, 1963; first English paperback, Penguin C2132, 1964.

Historical detective novel, taking place in England in 1907; the third of three volumes about the London police. The British edition concludes with "Notes for the Curious," lacking in the U.S. edition.

The Demoniacs. New York and Evanston: Harper & Row, 1962; London: Hamish Hamilton, 1962; first U.S. paperback, Bantam F2767, 1964; first British paperback, Penguin C2220, 1965.

Historical detective novel, taking place in England in 1757; though never publicized as such, this book was clearly meant as a precursor to the series about the London police.

The Grandest Game in the World. [New York: Davis Publications, 1963.] (There have been no British editions in this form.)

A portion of an essay on detective fiction written about 1946 as the introduction to a never-published anthology. With a newly written postscript, it was printed in *Ellery Queen's Mystery Magazine*, March 1963, and this twenty-two-page pamphlet, limited to three hundred copies, was probably published simultaneously. The complete essay was not published until it was included in the paperback edition of *The Door to Doom* (1991).

The Men Who Explained Miracles. New York and Evanston: Harper & Row, 1963; London: Hamish Hamilton, 1964; first U.S. paperback, Pyramid R1083, 1964; first British paperback, Penguin C2513, 1966.

A collection containing the following stories: "William Wilson's Racket" (Colonel March), "The Empty Flat" (Colonel March), "The Incautious Burglar" (Dr. Fell), "Invisible Hands" (Dr. Fell), "Strictly Diplomatic," "The Black Cabinet," and "All in a Maze" (Sir Henry Merrivale). "Strictly Diplomatic" and "The Incautious Burglar" (under the title "A Guest in the House") were previously collected in *Dr. Fell, Detective, and Other Stories* (1947).

Most Secret. New York and Evanston: Harper & Row, 1964; London: Hamish Hamilton, 1964;

first U.S. paperback, Berkley S1709, 1969. (There have been no British paperback editions.)

Historical novel, taking place in England in 1670. This is a revised version of *Devil Kinsmere* (1934), which was published under the pseudonym Roger Fairbairn.

The House at Satan's Elbow. New York: Harper & Row, 1965; London: Hamish Hamilton, 1965; first U.S. paperback, Signet P3102, 1967; first British paperback, Pan, 1969.

The twenty-first Dr. Gideon Fell novel.

Panic in Box C. New York: Harper & Row, 1966; London: Hamish Hamilton, 1966; first U.S. paperback, Berkley X1587, 1968; first British paperback, Pan, 1970.

The twenty-second Dr. Gideon Fell novel.

Dark of the Moon. New York and Evanston: Harper & Row, 1967; London: Hamish Hamilton, 1968; first U.S. paperback, Berkley S1656, 1969; first British paperback, Corgi, 1970.

The twenty-third Dr. Gideon Fell novel.

Papa Là-Bas. New York and Evanston: Harper & Row, 1968; London: Hamish Hamilton, 1969; first U.S. paperback, Carroll & Graf, 1989. (There have been no British paperback editions.)

Historical detective novel, taking place in New Orleans in 1858.

The Ghosts' High Noon. New York and Evanston: Harper & Row, 1969; London: Hamish Hamilton, 1970; first U.S. paperback, Carroll & Graf, 1990. (There have been no British paperback editions.)

Historical detective novel, taking place in New Orleans in 1912.

Deadly Hall. New York and Evanston: Harper & Row, 1971; London: Hamish Hamilton, 1971; first U.S. paperback. Carroll & Graf, 1989. (There have been no British paperback editions.)

Historical detective novel, taking place in New Orleans in 1927. (Although the events begin only four days before the events of Carr's first novel, *It Walks By Night*, more than forty years have passed, and therefore *Deadly Hall* should be considered a historical novel.)

The Hungry Goblin. New York and Evanston: Harper & Row, 1972; London: Hamish Hamilton, 1972. (There have been no paperback editions.)

Historical detective novel, taking place in England in 1869.

The Door to Doom and Other Detections. New York: Harper & Row, 1980; London: Hamish Hamilton, 1981; first U.S. paperback, International Polygonics, 1991. (There have been no British paperback editions.)

A collection (edited by Douglas G. Greene) containing the following material: "'As Drink the Dead . . . ,'" "The Shadow of the Goat" (Bencolin), "The Fourth Suspect" (Bencolin), "The Ends of Justice" (Bencolin), "The Murder in Number Four" (Bencolin), "Cabin B-13" (radio play), "The Hangman Won't Wait" (Dr. Fell radio play), "The Phantom Archer" (radio play), "The Bride Vanishes" (radio play), "Will You Make a Bet with Death?" (radio play), "The Devil in the Summer-House" (radio play), "The Man Who Was Dead," "The Door to Doom," "Terror's Dark Tower," "The Adventure of the Conk-Singleton Papers" (Sherlockian playlet), "The Adventure of the Paradol Chamber" (Sherlockian playlet), "Stand and Deliver!" (essay), and "The Grandest Game in the World" (portion of an essay). Two of the radio plays were previously collected in *Dr. Fell, Detective, and Other Stories* (1947). The paperback edition of *The Door to Doom* differs from earlier printings in that it contains the first publication of the complete essay "The Grandest Game in the World."

The Dead Sleep Lightly. Garden City: Published for the Crime Club by Doubleday & Co., 1983. (There have been no British editions and no paperback editions.)

A collection (edited by Douglas G. Greene) containing nine radio scripts: "The Black Minute" (Dr. Fell), "The Devil's Saint," "The Dragon in the Pool," "The Dead Sleep Lightly" (Dr. Fell), "Death Has Four Faces," "Vampire Tower," "The Devil's Manuscript," "White Tiger Passage," and "The Villa of the Damned." A different version of

"Vampire Tower" was previously collected in *Dr. Fell, Detective, and Other Stories* (1947) as "Will You Walk into My Parlor?" The dust jacket of *The Dead Sleep Lightly* adds a subtitle: *And Other Mysteries from Radio's Golden Age.*

Crime on the Coast and No Flowers by Request. London: Victor Gollancz, 1984; New York: Berkley paperback, 1987. (There have been no British paperback editions.)

Two round-robin novellas by various mystery writers. Carr wrote the two opening chapters of the first story.

Fell and Foul Play. New York: International Polygonics, 1991. (There have been no British and no paperback editions.)

A collection (edited by Douglas G. Greene) containing the following: from *The Department of Queer Complaints* (1940), "The Other Hangman" and "Persons or Things Unknown"; from *The Third Bullet and Other Stories* (1954), "The Wrong Problem" (Dr. Fell), "The Proverbial Murder" (Dr. Fell), and "The Gentleman from Paris"; from *The Men Who Explained Miracles* (1963), "The Incautious Burglar" (Dr. Fell), "Invisible Hands" (Dr. Fell), and "The Black Cabinet"; from *The Dead Sleep Lightly* (1983), "The Black Minute" (Dr. Fell radio play) and "The Dead Sleep Lightly" (Dr. Fell radio play). The book also includes the full 1937 version of "The Third Bullet" and the following previously uncollected material: "Who Killed Matthew Corbin?" (three-part Dr. Fell radio play), "The Devil in the Summer-House" (Dr. Fell radio play differing from previously published version, which does not have Dr. Fell), and "The Dim Queen."

Merrivale, March and Murder. New York: International Polygonics, 1991. (There have been no British editions and no paperback editions.)

A collection (edited by Douglas G. Greene) containing the following: from *The Department of Queer Complaints* (1940), "The New Invisible Man" (Colonel March), "The Crime in Nobody's Room" (Colonel March), "Error at Daybreak" (Colonel March), "Hot Money" (Colonel March), "Death in the Dressing-Room" (Colonel March), "The Silver Curtain" (Colonel March), "The Footprint in the Sky" (Colonel March), "Blind Man's Hood," and "New Murders for Old"; from *The Third Bullet and Other Stories* (1954), "The House in Goblin Wood" (Sir Henry Merrivale) and "The Clue of the Red Wig"; from *The Men Who Explained Miracles* (1963), "All in a Maze" (Sir Henry Merrivale), "The Empty Flat" (Colonel March), "William Wilson's Racket" (Colonel March), and "Strictly Diplomatic." The book also contains the following previously uncollected material: "The Diamond Pentacle," "Lair of the Devil-Fish" (radio play), and "Scotland Yard's Christmas."

Speak of the Devil. Norfolk, Virginia: Crippen & Landru, Publishers, 1994.

The first publication of Carr's eight-part radio script, broadcast on the BBC in 1941. Introduction by Tony Medawar.

B. PUBLISHED UNDER THE PSEUDONYM CARR DICKSON

The Bowstring Murders. New York: William Morrow, 1933; London: William Heinemann, 1934, as by Carter Dickson; first U.S. paperback, Pocket Books 46, 1940, as by Carter Dickson; first British paperback, Guild S89, 1944, as by Carter Dickson. The original pseudonym, Carr Dickson, was restored on the 1989 Zebra paperback edition.

Nonseries detective novel featuring John Gaunt; also featuring Dr. Michael Tairlaine. Carr had originally proposed that this book be published under the pseudonym Christopher Street, but Morrow chose Carr Dickson. Carr objected, and a compromise was reached that reprints and future titles by John Dickson Carr published by Morrow would be credited to Carter Dickson.

C. PUBLISHED UNDER THE PSEUDONYM CARTER DICKSON

The Plague Court Murders. New York: William Morrow, 1934; London: William Heinemann, 1935; first U.S. paperback, Avon 7, 1941; first British paperback, Penguin 820, 1951. A paperback edition with an introduction by Douglas G. Greene was published in 1990 by International Polygonics.

The first Sir Henry Merrivale novel. The statement given in some sources that the book is subtitled "A Chief-Inspector Masters Mystery" is misleading. No such subtitle appears in the first U.S. or British editions, but it was added on a corner of the front cover of the Avon paperback, though less as a subtitle than as a description (albeit erroneous) of the contents.

The White Priory Murders. New York: William Morrow, 1934; London: William Heinemann, 1935; first U.S. paperback, Pocket Books 156, 1942; first British paperback, Penguin 811, 1951.

The second Sir Henry Merrivale novel.

The Red Widow Murders. New York: William Morrow, 1935; London: William Heinemann, 1935; first U.S. paperback, Pocket Books 86, 1940; first British paperback, Penguin 815, 1951.

The third Sir Henry Merrivale novel; also featuring Dr. Michael Tairlaine. John Gaunt, the detective in *The Bowstring Murders,* is mentioned in passing.

The Unicorn Murders. New York: William Morrow, 1935; London: William Heinemann, 1936; first U.S. paperback, Dell 16, 1943. (There have been no British paperback editions.)

The fourth Sir Henry Merrivale novel.

The Punch and Judy Murders. New York: William Morrow, 1937 (printed December 1936); London: William Heinemann, 1936, as *The Magic-Lantern Murders;* first U.S. paperback, Pocket Books 219, 1943. (There have been no British paperback editions.)

The fifth Sir Henry Merrivale novel.

The Peacock Feather Murders. New York: William Morrow, 1937, as *The Ten Teacups;* first U.S. paperback, Pocket Books 180, 1942; first British paperback, Penguin 817, 1951; first Continental edition in English, Tauchnitz paperback 5334 (Leipzig, Germany), 1938. Serialized as *Ten Teacups* in the British magazine *The Passing Show,* November 27, 1937–January 29, 1938.

The sixth Sir Henry Merrivale novel.

The Third Bullet. London: Hodder & Stoughton, 1937.

A separately published paperback novella in the series "New-at-Ninepence." Its first American publication was an abridgment in *Ellery Queen's Mystery Magazine,* January 1948, and it is this version that appeared in all subsequent reprints, including *The Third Bullet and Other Stories* (1954), until the full text was restored in *Fell and Foul Play* (1991). The novella features a nonseries detective, Colonel Marquis, whom Carr described as "probably a mental forerunner of Colonel March."

The Judas Window. New York: William Morrow, 1938 (printed December 1937); London: William Heinemann, 1938; first U.S. paperback, Pocket Books 231, 1943; first British paperback, Penguin 819, 1951. The book was also published as *The Crossbow Murder,* Berkley paperback F870, 1964. A paperback edition (using the original title) with an introduction by Douglas G. Greene was published in 1987 by International Polygonics (New York).

The seventh Sir Henry Merrivale novel. The British and American editions have many textual differences, mostly minor, but the name of one major character is different.

Death in Five Boxes. New York: William Morrow, 1938; London: William Heinemann, 1938; first U.S. paperback, abridged, Bestseller 45, 1943; first U.S. paperback unabridged, Dell 108, 1946; first British paperback, Guild 112, 1941. Serialized as *The Man With Five Secrets* in the British magazine *Home Journal,* August 2–September 17, 1938.

The eighth Sir Henry Merrivale novel.

Fatal Descent (with John Rhode). New York: Dodd, Mead, 1939; London: William Heinemann, 1939, as *Drop to His Death;* first U.S. paperback, Popular Library 87, 1947. (There have been no British paperback editions.)

Nonseries detective novel featuring Dr. Horatio Glass and Inspector Hornbeam.

The Reader Is Warned. New York: William Morrow, 1939; London: William Heinemann, 1939; first U.S. paperback, Pocket Books 303, 1945; first British paperback, Penguin 812, 1951.

> The ninth Sir Henry Merrivale novel.

And So to Murder. New York: William Morrow, 1940; London: William Heinemann, 1941; first U.S. paperback, Dell 175, 1947; first British paperback, Penguin 814, 1951. A cloth edition with an introduction by John Kennedy Melling was published in 1987 by Chivers Press (Bath). Serialized as *Two Angry People* in the British magazine *Woman's Journal,* June–September 1940.

> The tenth Sir Henry Merrivale novel.

Nine—and Death Makes Ten. New York: William Morrow, 1940; London: William Heinemann, 1940, as *Murder in the Submarine Zone;* first U.S. paperback, Pocket Books 335, 1945; first British paperback, World W840, 1959, as *Murder in the Atlantic.* A cloth edition (using the U.S. title) with an introduction by John Kennedy Melling was published in 1991 by Chivers Press (Bath).

> The eleventh Sir Henry Merrivale novel.

The Department of Queer Complaints. New York: William Morrow, 1940; London: William Heinemann, 1940; first U.S. paperback (omitting one of the non–Colonel March stories), Bestseller 34, 1942; first U.S. paperback (noncommercial, but with all the stories), Editions for the Armed Services 1069, 1946; first British paperback, Pan X208, 1963. Omitting all four of the non–Colonel March stories, the book was also published as *Scotland Yard: The Department of Queer Complaints,* Dell 65, 1944. A hardback edition of the complete book with an introduction by Richard Levinson and William Link was published in 1981 by Gregg Press (Boston).

> A collection containing the following short stories: "The New Invisible Man" (Colonel March), "The Footprint in the Sky" (Colonel March), "The Crime in Nobody's Room" (Colonel March), "Hot Money" (Colonel March), "Death in the Dressing-Room" (Colonel March), "The Silver Curtain" (Colonel March), "Error at Daybreak" (Colonel March), "The Other Hangman," "New Murders for Old," "Persons or Things Unknown," and "Blind Man's Hood."

Seeing Is Believing. New York: William Morrow, 1941; London: William Heinemann, 1942; first U.S. paperback, Pocket Books 386, 1946; first British paperback, World M854, 1959, as *Cross of Murder.* Serialized as *Invitation to a Mystery* in the British magazine *Woman's Journal,* May–August 1941.

> The twelfth Sir Henry Merrivale novel.

The Gilded Man. New York: William Morrow, 1942; London: William Heinemann, 1942; first U.S. paperback, Pocket Books 478, 1947, as *Death and the Gilded Man;* first British paperback, Pan 168, 1951.

> The thirteenth Sir Henry Merrivale novel.

She Died a Lady. New York: William Morrow, 1943 (printed December 1942); London: William Heinemann, 1943; first U.S. paperback, Pocket Books 507, 1948; first British paperback, Penguin 816, 1951; first Continental edition in English, Zephyr paperback 223 (Stockholm, Sweden), 1948.

> The fourteenth Sir Henry Merrivale novel.

He Wouldn't Kill Patience. New York: Hampton Publishing distributed by William Morrow, 1944; London: William Heinemann, 1944; first U.S. paperback, Dell 370, 1950; first British paperback, Penguin 818, 1951. Serialized as *Magicians Dine Out* in the British magazine *Woman's Journal,* December 1943–February 1944.

> The fifteenth Sir Henry Merrivale novel.

The Curse of the Bronze Lamp. New York: William Morrow, 1945; London: William Heinemann, 1946, as *Lord of the Sorcerers;* first U.S. paperback (noncommercial), Editions for the Armed Services 991, 1946; first U.S. paperback (commercial), Pocket Books 568, 1949; first British paperback, Pan 390, 1956, uses the U.S. title.

> The sixteenth Sir Henry Merrivale novel.

My Late Wives. New York: William Morrow, 1946; London: William Heinemann, 1947; first
U.S. paperback (noncommercial), Editions for the Armed Services 1246, 1947; first U.S.
paperback (commercial), Pocket Books 633, 1949; first British paperback, Pan 263,
1953; first Continental edition in English, Scherz Phoenix paperback 120 (Berne,
Switzerland), ca. 1947–1948. Serialized in abridged form as *Case of the Vanishing Brides*
in the British magazine *Woman's Journal*, April–June 1947.
The seventeenth Sir Henry Merrivale novel.

The Skeleton in the Clock. New York: William Morrow, 1948; London: William Heinemann,
1949; first U.S. paperback, Dell 481, 1951; first British paperback, Pan G162, 1958.
The eighteenth Sir Henry Merrivale novel.

A Graveyard to Let. New York: William Morrow, 1949; London: William Heinemann, 1950;
first U.S. paperback, Dell 543, 1951; first British paperback, Pan 337, 1955.
The nineteenth Sir Henry Merrivale novel.

Night at the Mocking Widow. New York: William Morrow, 1950; London: William Heinemann,
1951; first U.S. paperback, Dell 650, 1953; first British paperback, Pan G279, 1959.
The twentieth Sir Henry Merrivale novel.

Behind the Crimson Blind. New York: William Morrow, 1952; London: William Heinemann,
1952; first U.S. paperback, Dell 690, 1953; first British paperback, Pan G340, 1960. A
cloth edition with an introduction by John Kennedy Melling was published in 1990 by
Chivers Press (Bath). Serialized in abridged form in the British magazine *Argosy*, January–April 1952.
The twenty-first Sir Henry Merrivale novel.

The Cavalier's Cup. New York: William Morrow, 1953; London: William Heinemann, 1954;
first U.S. paperback, Zebra, 1987; first British paperback, Pan G412, 1960.
The twenty-second Sir Henry Merrivale novel.

Fear Is the Same. New York: William Morrow, 1956; London: William Heinemann, 1956; first
U.S. paperback, Bantam A2000, 1959; first British paperback, World HN 847, 1959.
Historical detective novel, taking place in England in 1795.

D. Published Under the Pseudonym Roger Fairbairn

Devil Kinsmere. New York: Harper & Brothers, "1934";* London: Hamish Hamilton, 1934.
(There have been no paperback editions.)
Historical novel, taking place in England in 1670. Carr later rewrote the novel
and published it under his own name as *Most Secret* (1964).

E. Omnibus Editions

Note that each omnibus edition was published only by the publisher named and that there
have been no paperback editions.

A John Dickson Carr Trio. New York: Harper & Brothers, 1957.
Contains *The Three Coffins* (1935), *The Crooked Hinge* (1938), and *The Case of the
Constant Suicides* (1941).

Three Detective Novels. New York: Harper & Brothers, 1959.
Contains *The Arabian Nights Murder* (1936), *The Burning Court* (1937), and *The
Problem of the Wire Cage* (1939).

A Dr. Fell Omnibus. London: Hamish Hamilton, 1959.
Contains *The Mad Hatter Mystery* (1933), *Death-Watch* (1935), *The Black Spectacles*
(1939), and *The Seat of the Scornful* (1941).

The John Dickson Carr Treasury. Garden City: Nelson Doubleday, n.d. [1987].
Contains *The Three Coffins* (1935) and *The Burning Court* (1936). Published for
the Doubleday Mystery Guild book club.

*The American edition was actually published in February 1935.

Four Complete Dr. Fell Mysteries. New York: Avenel Books, 1988.
>Contains *The Blind Barber* (1934), *To Wake the Dead* (1937), *The Crooked Hinge* (1938), and *The Case of the Constant Suicides* (1941).

F. Book Edited by John Dickson Carr

Arthur Conan Doyle. *Great Stories.* New York: London House and Maxwell, 1959; London: John Murray, 1959. (There have been no paperback editions.)

2. SHORT STORIES, POEMS, AND EARLY NONFICTION

In the bibliography in the first edition of *The Door to Doom,* I included not only Carr's short works but also all known reprints of them. Since that time, his short stories have appeared in so many anthologies and magazines that the list would be almost endless. This list now includes only first publications in the United States and Britain as well as alternate titles, but it no longer attempts completeness on later reprints.

A. High School and Preparatory School Publications

"The Ruby of Rameses." *The* (Uniontown High School) *Maroon and White,* Thanksgiving Edition, 1921.
>Detective story.
"The House of Terror." *The Maroon and White,* Midwinter Edition, 1922.
>Mystery story.
"The Will-o'-the-Wisp." *The Maroon and White,* Easter Edition, 1922.
>Fantasy and historical romance.
"High School News." *Uniontown Daily News Standard,* February 18, 25; March 11, 25; April 22, 1922.
>Short notes on classmates' doings, especially in the Edison Science Club.
"As We See It." *Uniontown Daily News Standard,* February 22, 23, 27; March 2, 3, 6, 7, 8, 9, 10, 11, 14, 15, 16, 17, 20, 22, 23, 24, 27, 28, 29, 30, 31; April 3, 4, 5, 6, 7, 10, 11, 12, 18, 20, 21, 26, 28, 29; May 1, 4, 5, 8, 11, 16, 17, 20, 25, 26, 31; June 8, 20, 24, 26; July 3, 17, 18, 24; August 7, 10, 18; September 16, 1922.
>Column covering various matters.
"The Marked Bullet." *The Hill Record,* March, April 1923.
>Detective story.
"The Kindling Spark." *The Hill Record,* June 1923.
>Contemporary story.
"Valley Forge, 1777." *The Hill Record,* June 1923; reprinted in *A Book of Hill School Verse,* Frederick W. Graves, ed., 1927.
>Poem.
"Ashes of Clues." *The Hill Record,* October 1923.
>Detective story.
"The Blindfold Quest." *The Hill Record,* November, December 1923, January 1924.
>Ruritanian adventure and mystery.
"Christmas Spirit." *The Hill Record,* December 1923.
>Essay.
"The Riddle of the Laughing Lord." *The Hill Record,* February 1924.
>Supernatural mystery story.
"E'en Though It Be a Cross." *The Hill Record,* April 1924.
>Mystery story.
"The Voice and the Harp." *The Hill Record,* April 1924; reprinted in *A Book of Hill School Verse,* 1927.
>Poem.

"The Cloak of D'Artagnan." *The Hill Record,* June 1924.
>
> Humorous story.

"Richard to the Crusaders Before Jerusalem." *The Hill Record,* June 1924;' reprinted in *A Book of Hill School Verse,* 1927.
>
> Poem.

"Election Night." *The Hill Record,* June 1924; reprinted in *A Book of Hill School Verse,* 1927.
>
> Poem.

"Leader." *The Hill Record,* October 15, 1924.
>
> Humorous essay.

"Candlelight: A Ghost Story of Christmas." *The Hill Record,* December 15, 1924.
>
> Supernatural story.

"The Brotherhood of Shadows." *The Hill Record,* December 15, 1924.
>
> Essay.

"The God of the Gloves." *The Hill Record,* January 22, 1925.
>
> Boxing story.

"The Land of Lost Causes." *The Hill Record,* March 5, 1925.
>
> Essay.

"The Harp of Tairlaine." *The Hill Record,* April 1925.
>
> Historical romance.

"The Gordon Djinn." *The Hill Record,* June 1925.
>
> Supernatural story.

"Helmsmen of Atlantis." *The Hill Record,* June 1925; reprinted in *A Book of Hill School Verse,* 1927.
>
> Poem.

"Hunting Song." *A Book of Hill School Verse,* 1927.
>
> Poem.

"Poets' Isle." *A Book of Hill School Verse,* 1927.
>
> Poem.

"The Passing of the Leader." *A Book of Hill School Verse,* 1927.
>
> Poem.

Snooze. This was an annual humor magazine at The Hill School. Carr was a member of its board and wrote anonymous pieces for at least one issue. A copy is known to survive but it is unavailable for examination.

B. COLLEGE PUBLICATIONS

An asterisk in front of one of the following college writings indicates an uncertain, but probable, attribution to John Dickson Carr.

"'As Drink the Dead . . .'" [published anonymously, but the initials J.D.C. are included as one of the contributors to the issue] (collected in *The Door to Doom,* 1980). *The Haverfordian,* March 1926.
>
> Mystery and historical romance.

"The Red Heels." *The Haverfordian,* April 1926.
>
> Historical romance.

"The Dim Queen" (collected in *Fell and Foul Play,* 1991). *The Haverfordian,* May 1926.
>
> Historical romance.

"The Blue Garden." *The Haverfordian,* November 1926.
>
> Historical romance.

"The Song of the Sword" [published under the name of friend and former student Frederic Prokosch]. *The Haverfordian,* November 1926.
>
> Poem.

"The Shadow of the Goat" [published anonymously] (collected in *The Door to Doom*, 1980). *The Haverfordian*, November, December 1926.
>Henri Bencolin detective story.

"The Old Romance." *The Haverfordian*, December 1926.
>Poem.

"Song of the Jolly Roger" [published under the pseudonym E.S.D.]. *The Haverfordian*, December 1926.
>Poem.

"The Devil-Gun" [published under the pseudonym Caliban]. *The Haverfordian*, December 1926.
>Supernatural mystery story.

*"That Ye Be Not Judged" [published under the name of fellow student Ira B. Rutherford]. *The Haverfordian*, December 1926.
>Historical romance.

"The Fourth Suspect" [published as "by the author of The Shadow of the Goat"] (collected in *The Door to Doom*, 1980). *The Haverfordian*, January 1927.
>Henri Bencolin detective story.

"When We Rode Down to London" [published under the pseudonym Richard Westcott]. *The Haverfordian*, January 1927.
>Poem.

"The Haunting of Tarnboys" [published under the name of fellow student Francis Jameson]. *The Haverfordian*, January 1927.
>Supernatural story.

"The Last Lullaby" [published under the initials J.D.C.]. *The Haverfordian*. February 1927.
>Poem.

"Song of the Legionary" [published anonymously]. *The Haverfordian*, February 1927.
>Poem.

"Aeroplanes' Song" [published under the pseudonym M.R.P.]. *The Haverfordian*, February 1927.
>Poem.

*"Pygmalion" [published under the pseudonym C. G. Baker]. *The Haverfordian*, February 1927.
>Contemporary story.

"The New Canterbury Tales." *The Haverfordian*, March 1927.
>Seven short stories and a framing story supposedly by eight writers whose initials are given at the beginning. Two of these sets of initials, however, are of pseudonyms (E.H. and C.G.B.), and according to Frederic Prokosch, who contributed to "The New Canterbury Tales," Carr's hand is obvious in most of the stories. The framing story is about Bencolin and other characters from early Carr stories, and it contains some detection. Two of the other stories, "The Legend of the Cane in the Dark" and "The Legend of the Softest Lips," are early versions of the main elements of later Carr stories.

"The God of the Gloves" [published under the name of fellow student George P. Rogers]. *The Haverfordian*, April 1927; reprinted from *The Hill Record*, January 22, 1925.
>Boxing story.

"The Inn of the Seven Swords." *The Haverfordian*, April 1927; reprinted with slight changes from *The Hill Record*, April 1925, where it had been entitled "The Harp of Tairlaine."
>Historical romance.

"Hunting Song" [published under the pseudonym M.R.P.]. *The Haverfordian*, April 1927; reprinted with slight changes from *A Book of Hill School Verse*, 1927. (Note that *The Haverfordian* version may have been printed before *The Hill School Verse* version, but the latter was clearly written first.)
>Poem.

"The Ends of Justice" [published anonymously] (collected in *The Door to Doom*, 1980). *The Haverfordian*, May 1927.

>Henri Bencolin detective story.

"The Deficiency Expert." *The Haverfordian*, May 1927.

>Humorous story.

*"Song of the Toy Shops" [published under the pseudonym Eric Hirth]. *The Haverfordian*, May 1927.

>Poem.

"The Dark Banner" [published under Carr's name but written by Frederic Prokosch and John Rodell]. *The Haverfordian*, January 1928.

>Historical romance.

"The Murder in Number Four" (collected in *The Door to Doom*, 1980). *The Haverfordian*, June 1928.

>Henri Bencolin detective story.

"Grand Guignol" [published anonymously]. *The Haverfordian*, March, April 1929.

>Henri Bencolin detective novella, an early version of Carr's first book, *It Walks By Night*.

C. Later Short Fiction

"The Man Who Was Dead" (collected in *The Door to Doom*, 1980). First published in *Dime Mystery*, May 1935.

>Supernatural mystery story; a rewritten version of "The Adventure of the Cane in the Dark," a part of "The New Canterbury Tales," *The Haverfordian*, March 1927.

"The Door to Doom" (collected in *The Door to Doom*, 1980). First published in *Horror Stories*, June 1935.

>Supernatural mystery story.

"Terror's Dark Tower" (collected in *The Door to Doom*, 1980). First published in *Detective Tales*, October 1935.

>Detective story.

"The Other Hangman" (collected in *The Department of Queer Complaints*, 1940, and in *Fell and Foul Play*, 1991). First published in *A Century of Detective Stories*, introduction by G. K. Chesterton (London: Hutchinson, 1935).

>Historical mystery story.

"The Wrong Problem" (collected in *Dr. Fell, Detective*, 1947, in *The Third Bullet and Other Stories*, 1954, and in *Fell and Foul Play*, 1991). First published in *The* (London) *Evening Standard*, August 14, 1936; first published in the United States with very slight changes in *Ellery Queen's Mystery Magazine*, July 1942. For the reprint of the story in *Four-and-Twenty Bloodhounds*, Anthony Boucher, ed. (New York: Simon and Schuster, 1950), Carr provided a sketch of Dr. Fell's life in the form of a "Detective's Who's Who." All printings of this story except the first use the text from *Ellery Queen's Mystery Magazine*.

>Dr. Gideon Fell detective story.

"Blind Man's Hood" (collected in *The Department of Queer Complaints*, 1940, and in *Merrivale, March and Murder*, 1991). First published in *The Sketch*, Christmas Number, 1937.

>Supernatural mystery story. Alternate title: "To Wake the Dead."

"The New Invisible Man" (collected in *The Department of Queer Complaints*, 1940, and in *Merrivale, March and Murder*, 1991). First published in *The Strand Magazine*, April 1938.

>Colonel March detective story. Alternate titles: "The Invisible Murderer" and "The Man Who Saw the Invisible."

"The Crime in Nobody's Room" (collected in *The Department of Queer Complaints,* 1940, and in *Merrivale, March and Murder,* 1991). First published in *The Strand Magazine,* June 1938. Colonel March detective story.

"Error at Daybreak" (collected in *The Department of Queer Complaints,* 1940, and in *Merrivale, March and Murder,* 1991). First published in *The Strand Magazine,* July 1938. Colonel March detective story. Alternate title: "The Lion's Paw."

"Persons or Things Unknown" (collected in *The Department of Queer Complaints,* 1940, and in *Fell and Foul Play,* 1991). First published in *The Sketch,* Christmas Number, 1938. Historical detective story.

"The Hiding Place" (collected as "Hot Money" in *The Department of Queer Complaints,* 1940, and in *Merrivale, March and Murder,* 1991). First published in *The Strand Magazine,* February 1939. Colonel March detective story. Alternate titles: "A Case for Colonel March" and "Right Before Your Eyes."

"Death in the Dressing-Room" (collected in *The Department of Queer Complaints,* 1940, and in *Merrivale, March and Murder,* 1991). First published in *The Strand Magazine,* March 1939. Colonel March detective story.

"Harem-Scarem." First published in *The* (London) *Daily Mail,* March 24, 1939. Adventure story; a rewritten version of "The Legend of the Softest Lips," a part of "The New Canterbury Tales," *The Haverfordian,* March 1927.

"The Empty Flat" (collected in *The Men Who Explained Miracles,* 1963, and in *Merrivale, March and Murder,* 1991). First published in *The Strand Magazine,* May 1939; first published in the United States in *Ellery Queen's Mystery Magazine,* May 1945. Colonel March detective story.

"The Silver Curtain" (collected in *The Department of Queer Complaints,* 1940, and in *Merrivale, March and Murder,* 1991). First published in *The Strand Magazine,* August 1939. Colonel March detective story.

"The Diamond Pentacle" (collected in *Merrivale, March and Murder,* 1991). First published in *The* (London) *Times Weekly Edition,* November 15, 1939. Detective story.

"Strictly Diplomatic" (collected in *Dr. Fell, Detective,* 1947, in *The Men Who Explained Miracles,* 1963, and in *Merrivale, March and Murder,* 1991). First published in *The Strand Magazine,* December 1939; first published in the United States in *Ellery Queen's Mystery Magazine,* January 1946. Secret service story combined with detection.

"New Murders for Old" (collected in *The Department of Queer Complaints,* 1940, and in *Merrivale, March and Murder,* 1991). First published in *The Illustrated London News,* Christmas Number, 1939. Supernatural mystery story, a rewritten version of "The Adventure of the Cane in the Dark," *The Haverfordian,* March 1927, and "The Man Who Was Dead," *Dime Mystery,* May 1935. Alternate title: "The One Real Horror."

"The Proverbial Murder" (collected in *Dr. Fell, Detective,* 1947, in *The Third Bullet and Other Stories,* 1954, and in *Fell and Foul Play,* 1991). First publication unknown, but probably 1939–40; first published in the United States in *Ellery Queen's Mystery Magazine,* July 1943. Dr. Gideon Fell detective story. Alternate title: "The Proverbial Murderer."

"Clue in the Snow" (collected as "The Footprint in the Sky" in *The Department of Queer Complaints,* 1940, and in *Merrivale, March and Murder,* 1991). First published in *The Strand Magazine,* January 1940. Colonel March detective story.

"The Locked Room" (collected in *Dr. Fell, Detective,* 1947, in *The Third Bullet and Other Stories,* 1954, and in *Fell and Foul Play,* 1991). First published in *The Strand Magazine,* July 1940; first published in the United States in *Ellery Queen's Mystery Magazine,* February 1946.

Dr. Gideon Fell detective story. Alternate title for an abridged reprint: "The Locked Door."

"A Guest in the House" (collected in *Dr. Fell, Detective,* 1947, and as "The Incautious Burglar" in *The Men Who Explained Miracles,* 1963, and in *Fell and Foul Play,* 1991). First published in *The Strand Magazine,* October 1940.

Dr. Gideon Fell detective story.

"The Clue of the Red Wig" (collected in *The Third Bullet and Other Stories,* 1954, and in *Merrivale, March and Murder,* 1991). First published in *The Strand Magazine,* December 1940; first published in the United States in *Ellery Queen's Mystery Magazine,* December 1948.

"William Wilson's Racket" (collected in *The Men Who Explained Miracles,* 1963, and in *Merrivale, March and Murder,* 1991). First published in *The Strand Magazine,* February 1941; first published in the United States in *Ellery Queen's Mystery Magazine,* November 1944.

Colonel March detective story.

"The House in Goblin Wood" (collected in *The Third Bullet and Other Stories,* 1954, and in *Merrivale, March and Murder,* 1991). First published simultaneously in *Ellery Queen's Mystery Magazine,* November 1947, and *The Strand Magazine,* November 1947.

Sir Henry Merrivale detective story.

"The Gentleman from Paris" (collected in *The Third Bullet and Other Stories,* 1954, and in *Fell and Foul Play,* 1991). First published in *Ellery Queen's Mystery Magazine,* April 1950; first published in Britain in *Majority 1931–1952* (London: Hamish Hamilton, July 1952). For the reprint of the story in *Crimes and Misfortunes,* J. Francis McComas, ed. (New York: Random House, 1970), Carr provided a brief preface.

Historical detective story.

"The Black Cabinet" (collected in *The Men Who Explained Miracles,* 1963, and in *Fell and Foul Play,* 1991). First published in *Twenty Great Tales of Murder,* Helen McCloy and Brett Halliday, eds. (New York: Random House, 1951); the first British publication was probably in the U.K. edition of this book (London: Hammond, 1952), though it may have appeared about the same time in *MacKill's Mystery Magazine,* December 1952.

Historical mystery and suspense.

"The Adventure of the Seven Clocks" (collected in *The Exploits of Sherlock Holmes,* 1954). First published in *Life,* December 24, 1952; first published in Britain in *The* (London) *Evening Standard,* January 21, 22, 23, 1954.

Sherlock Holmes pastiche by Carr and Adrian Conan Doyle.

"The Adventure of the Black Baronet" (collected in *The Exploits of Sherlock Holmes,* 1954). First published in *Collier's,* May 23, 1953; first published in Britain in *The* (London) *Evening Standard,* October 1, 2, 3, 1953.

Sherlock Holmes pastiche by Carr and Adrian Conan Doyle.

"The Adventure of the Gold Hunter" (collected in *The Exploits of Sherlock Holmes,* 1954). First published in *Collier's,* May 30, 1953; first published in Britain in *The* (London) *Evening Standard,* October 8, 9, 10, 1953.

Sherlock Holmes pastiche by Carr and Adrian Conan Doyle.

"The Adventure of the Highgate Miracle" (collected in *The Exploits of Sherlock Holmes,* 1954). First published in *Collier's,* June 6, 1953; first published in Britain in *The* (London) *Evening Standard,* October 5, 6, 7, 1953.

Sherlock Holmes pastiche by Carr and Adrian Conan Doyle.

"The Adventure of the Sealed Room" (collected in *The Exploits of Sherlock Holmes,* 1954). First published in *Collier's,* June 13, 1953; first published in Britain in *The* (London) *Evening Standard,* September 28, 29, 30, 1953.

Sherlock Holmes pastiche by Carr and Adrian Conan Doyle.

"The Adventure of the Wax Gamblers" (collected in *The Exploits of Sherlock Holmes*, 1954). First published in *Collier's*, June 20, 1953.

>Sherlock Holmes pastiche by Carr and Adrian Conan Doyle.

"Crime on the Coast." *The* (London) *News Chronicle*, August 3–17, 1954. Published in book form as *Crime on the Coast and No Flowers by Request* (London: Victor Gollancz, 1984; New York: Berkley paperback, 1987).

>Round-robin mystery novella, the first two chapters of which were written by Carr, and the other chapters by Valerie White, Laurence Meynell, Joan Fleming, Michael Cronin, and Elizabeth Ferrars.

"Ministry of Miracles" (collected as "All in a Maze" in *The Men Who Explained Miracles*, 1963, and in *Merrivale, March and Murder*, 1991). First published in *The Housewife*, January, February, March, 1956; first published in the United States in *Ellery Queen's Mystery Magazine*, March 1956, as "The Man Who Explained Miracles."

>Sir Henry Merrivale detective novelette.

"King Arthur's Chair" (collected as "Invisible Hands" in *The Men Who Explained Miracles*, 1963, and in *Fell and Foul Play*, 1991. First published in *Lilliput*, August 1957; first published in the United States with slight changes in *Ellery Queen's Mystery Magazine*, April 1958, as "Death by Invisible Hands." All printings of this story except the first use the text from *Ellery Queen's Mystery Magazine*.

>Dr. Gideon Fell detective story.

"Detective's Day Off" (collected under Carr's original title, "Scotland Yard's Christmas," in *Merrivale, March and Murder*, 1991). First published in *Weekend*, December 25/29, 1957.

>Christmas detective story.

Note that a novella, *The Third Bullet* (1937), was first published as a separate volume under the Carter Dickson pseudonym, and it is therefore included in the "Books" section of this bibliography.

3. ARTICLES AND REVIEWS

"Unsolved Mysteries of Real Life No. 5, Mystery of the 'Florodoro' Girl." *The* (London) *Star*, July 30, 1937.

>Following an unsigned article about the murder trial of Nan Patterson in 1902, Carr suggests a solution to the mystery.

"The Lure of Detective Fiction." *The* (London) *Morning Post*, August 30, 1937.

>The appeal of amateur detectives in fiction.

". . . And Things That Go Bump in the Night." *Woman's Journal*, December 1938.

>Ghosts in fact and fiction.

"It's a Dare!" *Radio Times*, September 3, 1943.

>Brief article introducing the radio series *Appointment With Fear*.

"Magicians' Progress." *Radio Times*, July 14, 1944.

>Article introducing the radio program "Magicians' Progress."

"The New Mysteries." *Clue*, May 1948.

>Reviews by various writers; Carr reviewed *The Murder of Maria Marten*.

"Hammock Companions." *The New York Times Book Review*, August 1, 1948.

>Reviews by various writers; Carr reviewed Arthur Machen's *Tales of Horror and the Supernatural*.

"When Conan Doyle was Sherlock Holmes." *Harper's*, January 1949, and *The Strand*, January 1949, as "Conan Doyle, Detective."

>A portion of Carr's biography of Sir Arthur Conan Doyle, which was published at about the same time.)

"A Mystery Addict Speaks His Mind." Published on the back panel of the dust jacket of the Mystery Guild book club edition of *Night at the Mocking Widow*, 1950.

>Brief discussion of types of mystery fiction.

"With Colt and Luger." *The New York Times Book Review,* September 24, 1950.
>Review of Raymond Chandler's *The Simple Art of Murder.*
"Did Dickens Murder Drood?" *The New York Times Book Review,* March 25, 1951.
>Review of Richard M. Baker's *The Drood Murder Case.*
"Holmes Wouldn't Recognize It." *The New York Times Magazine,* February 21, 1954.
>Early and modern Scotland Yard.
"Connoisseurs in Crime." *Woman's Journal,* March 1955.
>Brief anecdotes about Agatha Christie, Margery Allingham, and Michael Gilbert.
"Story Development." *The Mystery Writer's Handbook,* Herbert Brean, ed. New York: Harper & Brothers, 1956.
>Speech on plot development.
"Another Glass, Watson." *The Sherlock Holmes* (exhibition catalogue). London: Whitbread, 1957.
>Sherlock Holmes's drinking habits.
"The Sherlock Holmes." *House of Whitbread,* Spring 1958.
>A pub named after Sherlock Holmes.
"Let Us Have Nightmares." *Kenyon Review,* Summer 1960.
>Review of Colin Wilson's *Ritual in the Dark.*
"The Grandest Game in the World." About half of this essay was published in *Ellery Queen's Mystery Magazine,* March 1963, and (probably simultaneously) as a separate pamphlet edition; this version was collected in the first American and British editions of *The Door to Doom* (1980 and 1981). The complete essay was first published in the paperback edition of *The Door to Doom* (1991).
>Essay on detective fiction.
"Murder-Fancier Recommends." *Harper's,* July 1964, July 1965, July 1966, July 1967.
>Book review column.
"Hail, Holmes!" *The New York Times,* February 14, 1965.
>The continuing appeal of Holmes and Watson.
Untitled speech at the University of North Carolina. *The Bookmark, Friends of the University of North Carolina Library,* No. 38, September 1968.
>Discussion of detective story writers.
"Best Mysteries of the Month." *Ellery Queen's Mystery Magazine,* January 1969–April 1970; retitled "The Jury Box," May 1970–February 1971, April 1971–May 1976, August–October 1976.
>Book review column, interspersed with reminiscences and anecdotes.
"Stand and Deliver!" *Ellery Queen's Mystery Magazine,* March, April, 1973; collected in *The Door to Doom,* 1980.
>Seventeenth- and eighteenth-century highwaymen.
"Sound Lad." *New Statesman,* April 6, 1973.
>Review of Kingsley Amis's *The Riverside Villa Murders.*
"John Dickson Carr's Solution to *The Mystery of Edwin Drood.*" *The Armchair Detective,* n.d. (October 1981).
>A letter from Carr to Lillian de la Torre, written in 1949, suggesting a solution to Charles Dickens's unfinished mystery.

4. INTRODUCTIONS TO BOOKS

Torquemada [pseudonym of E. Powys Mathers]. *112 Best Crossword Puzzles.* London: Pushkin Press, 1942.
Arthur Conan Doyle. *The Lost World and The Poison Belt.* London: Eyre & Spottiswoode, 1950.
Arthur Conan Doyle. *The Valley of Fear.* New York: Bantam, 1950.
Mystery Writers of America. *Maiden Murders.* New York: Harper & Brothers, 1952.

Arthur Conan Doyle. *The Complete Sherlock Holmes.* Garden City: Doubleday, 1953.
　　Carr's introduction appears only in the limited edition.
John Williams. *Suddenly at the Priory.* London: Heinemann, 1957.
Arthur Conan Doyle. *The Poison Belt.* New York: Macmillan, 1964.
Arthur Conan Doyle. *The Maracot Deep.* New York: W. W. Norton, 1968.

5. RADIO SCRIPTS

"Who Killed Matthew Corbin?, A Detective Problem." BBC, 3 episodes, December 27, 1939;
　　January 7, January 14, 1940. The script was printed in *Fell and Foul Play,* 1991.
　　　　Dr. Fell.
"The Black Minute." BBC, February 13, 1940; October 18, 1941. The script was printed in
　　Ellery Queen's Mystery Magazine, May 1983, in *The Dead Sleep Lightly,* 1983, and in *Fell
　　and Foul Play,* 1991.
　　　　Dr. Fell.
"The Devil in the Summer-House." BBC, October 15, 1940; *(Mystery Playhouse)* July 21, 1947.
　　(Dr. Fell.) Carr shortened the script from an hour to thirty minutes and omitted Dr.
　　Fell for U.S. broadcast. CBS *(Suspense),* November 3, 1942. The British script was
　　printed in *Fell and Foul Play,* 1991; the U.S. script was printed in *Ellery Queen's Mystery
　　Magazine,* September 1946, *Dr. Fell, Detective,* 1947, and *The Door to Doom,* 1980.
"Speak of the Devil." BBC, 8 episodes, February 10, 17, 24, March 3, 10, 17, 24, 31, 1941. The
　　entire script was published as a separate book by Crippen & Landru, 1994.
"Never Tell Parents the Truth." BBC, July 6, 1941; November 22, 1943.
"Lord of the Witch Doctors." BBC, September 13, 1941; CBS *(Suspense),* October 27, 1942.
　　　　For the BBC version, Carr used the nom-de-air Robert Southwell.
"Black Market." BBC, October 7, 1941.
　　　　Propaganda script by Carr and Robert Westerby.
"Four Smart Girls." BBC, November 12, 1941. Carr reworked the script, and it was broadcast
　　as "Civilians' War No. 41, Women on the Guns/Gun-Site Girl." BBC, February 27, 1942.
　　　　Propaganda script.
"Britain Shall Not Burn, a Play for the Times." BBC, December 12, 1941.
　　　　Propaganda script.
"The Man in the Iron Mask, A Historical Detective-Story." BBC, January 5, 1942.
"Europe in Chains No. 14, They Strike at Night." BBC, January 6, 1942.
　　　　Propaganda script.
"Starvation in Greece." BBC, February 6, 1942.
　　　　Propaganda script.
"You're Not Behind the Plow." BBC, February 15, 1942.
　　　　Propaganda script.
"Black Market." BBC, March 6, 1942.
　　　　Propaganda script, but not related to earlier BBC script, also called "Black Mar-
　　ket."
"Europe in Chains No. 9, Denmark Occupied." BBC, March 16, 1942.
　　　　Propaganda script. I have found no evidence why No. 9 was broadcast after
　　No. 14.
"Escape to Freedom No. 1, The Adventure of the Three French Students." BBC, March 21, 1942.
　　　　Propaganda script.
"Inspector Silence Takes the Underground." BBC, March 25, 1942.
"Escape to Freedom No. 4, Men of Sparta." BBC, April 11, 1942.
　　　　Propaganda script.
"Escape to Freedom No. 7, Fifth Time Lucky." BBC, May 2, 1942.
　　　　Propaganda script.

"Black Gallery No. 4: Heinrich Himmler." BBC, June 4, 1942.
> Propaganda script.

"Will You Make a Bet with Death?" CBS *(Suspense)*, November 10, 1942; BBC *(Appointment With Fear)*, October 14, 1943; October 16, 1945. The script was printed in *Ellery Queen's Mystery Magazine*, April 1954, and in *The Door to Doom*, 1980.

"Menace in Wax." CBS *(Suspense)*, November 17, 1942; BBC *(Appointment With Fear)*, November 18, 1943. The script was printed in *Espionage* magazine, October 1985.

"The Body Snatchers." CBS *(Suspense)*, November 24, 1942; BBC *(Appointment With Fear)*, September 30, 1943.

"The Bride Vanishes." CBS *(Suspense)*, December 1, 1942; BBC *(Appointment With Fear)*, as "Into Thin Air," September 21, 1943; September 11, 1945; CBS *(Cabin B-13)*, December 12, 1948. The script was printed in *Ellery Queen's Mystery Magazine*, September 1950, and in *The Door to Doom*, 1980.

"Till Death Do Us Part." CBS *(Suspense)*, December 15, 1942; BBC *(Appointment With Fear)*, as "The Man Who Died Twice," November 11, 1943; September 25, 1945; CBS *(Cabin B-13)*, December 19, 1948.

"Nothing Up My Sleeve." CBS *(Suspense)*, January 5, 1943. (Based on Carr's story "The Hiding Place.")

"The Pit and the Pendulum." CBS *(Suspense)*, January 12, 1943; BBC *(Appointment With Fear)*, September 18, 1943; May 4, 1944; CBS *(Suspense)*, November 28, 1947; November 10, 1957; June 7, 1959.
> Based on the Edgar Allan Poe story.

"The Devil's Saint." CBS *(Suspense)*, January 19, 1943; BBC *(Appointment With Fear)*, October 21, 1943; CBS *(Cabin B-13)*, as "The Sleep of Death," December 26, 1948. The script was printed in *The Dead Sleep Lightly*, 1983.

"The Hangman Won't Wait." CBS *(Suspense)*, February 9, 1943; BBC *(Appointment With Fear)*, as "The Clock Strikes Eight," May 18, 1944; October 2, 1945. The script was printed in *Ellery Queen's Mystery Magazine*, September 1944, *Alfred Hitchcock's Fireside Book of Suspense*, 1947, *Dr. Fell, Detective*, 1947, *Alfred Hitchcock's Stories Not for the Nervous*, 1965, and *The Door to Doom*, 1980.
> Dr. Fell.

"Will You Walk into My Parlor?" CBS *(Suspense)*, February 23, 1943; BBC *(Appointment With Fear)*, a revised version called "Vampire Tower," May 11, 1944. The U.S. script was printed in *Ellery Queen's Mystery Magazine*, September 1945, and in *Dr. Fell, Detective*, 1947. The British script was printed in *The Dead Sleep Lightly*, 1983.

"The Phantom Archer." CBS *(Suspense)*, March 9, 1943; BBC *(Appointment With Fear)*, November 4, 1943. The script was printed in *Ellery Queen's Mystery Magazine*, June 1948, and in *The Door to Doom*, 1980.

"Cabin B-13." CBS *(Suspense)*, March 16, 1943; November 9, 1943; BBC *(Appointment With Fear)*, September 11, 1943; October 9, 1945; December 24, 1952. The script was printed in *Ellery Queen's Mystery Magazine*, May 1944, *20th Century Detective Stories*, Ellery Queen, ed., 1948; *Suspense*, Spring 1951, as "Honeymoon Terror" (using what appears to have been a later script), and in *The Door to Doom*, 1980.

"The Customers Like Murder." CBS *(Suspense)*, March 23, 1943; BBC *(Appointment With Fear)*, October 7, 1943. The script was printed in *Ellery Queen's Mystery Magazine*, April 1952.

"The Dead Sleep Lightly." CBS *(Suspense)*, March 30, 1943; the BBC version, August 28, 1943, was longer and it features Dr. Fell. (Note that the surviving BBC script is for the Overseas Service in 1943; Carr wrote it in 1941, and it is possible that the play was broadcast that year on the Home Service; in any case it was written before the U.S. version.) The British version of the script was printed in *The Dead Sleep Lightly*, 1983, and in *Fell and Foul Play*, 1991.

"Fire Burn and Cauldron Bubble." CBS *(Suspense)*, April 6, 1943: BBC *(Appointment With Fear)*, October 28, 1943; September 18, 1945.

"The Moment of Darkness." CBS *(Suspense)*, April 20, 1943.

"Death Flies Blind." CBS *(Suspense)*, May 4, 1943; BBC *(Appointment With Fear)*, April 20, 1944.

"Mr. Markham, Antique Dealer." CBS *(Suspense)*, May 11, 1943; BBC *(Appointment With Fear)*, as "The Speaking Clock," April 13, 1944; CBS *(Suspense)*, as "The Dealings of Mr. Markham," June 29, 1945, and November 2, 1958. The script was printed in *Rogues' Gallery*, Ellery Queen, ed., 1948.

"Five Canaries in the Room." CBS *(Suspense)*, June 8, 1943; BBC *(Appointment With Fear)*, as "The Case of the Five Canaries," November 13, 1945.

Based on Carr's story "The Crime in Nobody's Room."

"The Man Without a Body." CBS *(Suspense)*, June 22, 1943.

"The French Fight On." BBC, July 14, 1943.

Propaganda script by Carr and Robert Barr.

"A Corner in Crime No. 3, The Riddle of the Cabin Cruiser." BBC *(Here's Wishing You Well Again)*, November 18, 1943.

"A Corner in Crime No. 5, The Riddle of the Poisoned Cocktail." BBC *(Here's Wishing You Well Again)*, December 16, 1943.

"Vex Not His Ghost." BBC *(Appointment With Fear)*, January 6, 1944; November 30, 1944.

"The Tell-Tale Heart." BBC *(Appointment With Fear)*, January 13, 1944.

Based on the Edgar Allan Poe story.

"The Room of the Suicides." BBC *(Appointment With Fear)*, January 20, 1944; CBS *(Cabin B-13)*, a heavily revised version called "The Dead Man's Knock." November 28, 1948.

"The Sire de Malatroit's Door." BBC *(Appointment With Fear)*, January 27, 1944.

Based on the Robert Louis Stevenson story.

"The Dragon in the Pool." BBC *(Appointment With Fear)*, February 3, 1944. The script was printed in *The Dead Sleep Lightly*, 1983.

"The Man Who Was Afraid of Dentists." BBC *(Appointment With Fear)*, February 10, 1944.

"The Silent Battle No. 1: They Saw Him Die." BBC, February 16, 1944.

Propaganda script.

"The Silent Battle No. 2: The Midnight Edition." BBC, February 23, 1944.

Propaganda script.

"The Silent Battle No. 3: Death Whistles a Tune." BBC, March 1, 1944.

Propaganda script.

"The Silent Battle No. 4: Army of Shadows." BBC, March 8, 1944.

Propaganda script.

"The Silent Battle No. 5: The Blood Is Our Repayment." BBC, March 15, 1944.

Propaganda script.

"The Silent Battle No. 6: Secret Radio." BBC, March 22, 1944.

Propaganda script.

"A Watcher by the Dead." BBC *(Appointment With Fear)*, April 27, 1944.

Based on the Ambrose Bierce story.

"New Judgment: John Dickson Carr on Edgar Allan Poe." BBC, May 22, 1944.

"Magicians' Progress." BBC, July 21, 1944.

"The Scandalous Affair of the Queen's Necklace." BBC, August 25, 1944.

"I Never Suspected." BBC *(Appointment With Fear)*, October 5, 1944.

"The Devil's Manuscript." BBC *(Appointment With Fear)*, October 12, 1944. The script was printed in *The Dead Sleep Lightly*, 1983.

Based on the Ambrose Bierce story "The Suitable Surroundings."

"Death Has Four Faces." BBC *(Appointment With Fear)*, October 19, 1944. The script was printed in *The Dead Sleep Lightly*, 1983.

Based on Carr's story "The Silver Curtain."

"The Purple Wig." BBC *(Appointment With Fear)*, October 26, 1944.
> Based on the G. K. Chesterton story.

"He Who Whispers." BBC *(Appointment With Fear)*, November 2, 1944.

"The Curse of the Bronze Lamp." BBC *(Appointment With Fear)*, originally scheduled for November 9, 1944, but preempted by a speech by Winston Churchill; it was broadcast December 7, 1944; CBS *(Cabin B-13)*, November 14, 1948.

"The Great Cipher." BBC *(Appointment With Fear)*, November 16, 1944.
> Based on the Melville Davisson Post story.

"The Gong Cried Murder." BBC *(Appointment With Fear)*, December 14, 1944; CBS *(Cabin B-13)*, a heavily revised version called "The Footprint in the Sky," September 7, 1948.
> Based on Carr's story "Clue in the Snow."

"Lair of the Devil-Fish." BBC *(Appointment With Fear)*, December 21, 1944; CBS *(Cabin B-13)*, November 21, 1948. The script was printed in *Merrivale, March and Murder*, 1991.

"The Oath of Rolling Thunder." BBC *(Appointment With Fear)*, December 28, 1944.

"The Adventure of the Speckled Band." BBC, May 17, 1945; December 27, 1948; September 25, 1956. The script was printed in *The Baker Street Journal*, June 1982.
> Based on the Arthur Conan Doyle story.

"Corner in Crime No. 9: The Bravo Mystery." BBC, October 18, 1945.

"He Wasn't Superstitious." BBC *(Appointment With Fear)*, originally scheduled for October 23, 1945, but preempted by Churchill and Montgomery, and broadcast on October 30, 1945.
> Based on Ambrose Bierce's "The Man and the Snake."

"The Man With Two Heads." BBC *(Appointment With Fear)*, November 6, 1945; CBS *(Cabin B-13)*, December 5, 1948.
> Based on Carr's stories "The Adventure of the Cane in the Dark," "The Man Who Was Dead," and "New Murders for Old."

"A Razor in Fleet Street." CBS *(Cabin B-13)*, July 5, 1948. A revised version of the script, called "an entertainment in four tableaux," was published in *The London Mystery Magazine*, February/March 1952. This revised version, but with the original title, "A Razor in Fleet Street," was reprinted in *The Art of the Impossible* (U.S. title, *Murder: Impossible*), Jack Adrian and Robert Adey, eds., 1990.

"The Man Who Couldn't Be Photographed." CBS *(Cabin B-13)*, July 12, 1948; October 31, 1948; BBC *(Appointment With Fear)*, July 26, 1955; August 12, 1957.

"Death Has Four Faces." CBS *(Cabin B-13)*, July 19, 1948.
> Not related to earlier BBC script with the same name.

"The Blindfolded Knife-Thrower." CBS *(Cabin B-13)*, July 26, 1948.

"No Useless Coffin." CBS *(Cabin B-13)*, August 2, 1948.
> Based on Carr's story "The House in Goblin Wood."

"The Nine Black Reasons." CBS *(Cabin B-13)*, August 9, 1948.

"The Count of Monte Carlo." CBS *(Cabin B-13)*, August 16, 1948.

"Below Suspicion." CBS *(Cabin B-13)*, August 23, 1948.

"The Power of Darkness." CBS *(Cabin B-13)*, August 31, 1948; BBC *(Appointment With Fear)*, as "The Villa of the Damned," August 30, 1955; September 9, 1957. Printed in *The Dead Sleep Lightly*, 1983.

"The Man with the Iron Chest." CBS *(Cabin B-13)*, September 14, 1948.

"The Street of Seven Daggers." CBS *(Cabin B-13)*, October 3, 1948.

"The Dancer from Stamboul." CBS *(Cabin B-13)*, October 10, 1948; January 2, 1949.

"Death in the Desert." CBS *(Cabin B-13)*, October 17, 1948.

"The Island of Coffins." CBS *(Cabin B-13)*, October 24, 1948.

"A Most Respectable Murder." CBS *(Cabin B-13)*, November 7, 1948.

"The Dead Man's Knock." BBC *(Appointment With Fear)*, August 9, 1955; August 26, 1957.
> Not related to earlier CBS *(Cabin B-13)* script with the same name, which was, in fact, a revised version of the BBC "The Room of the Suicides."

"White Tiger Passage." BBC *(Appointment With Fear)*, August 2, 1955; August 19, 1957. Printed in *The Dead Sleep Lightly*, 1983.

"The Sleuth of Seven Dials." BBC *(Appointment With Fear)*, August 16, 1955; September 2, 1957.

"Till the Great Armadas Come." BBC *(Appointment With Fear)* August 20, 1955; September 16, 1957.

John Dickson Carr often appeared on British radio to introduce shows, to be interviewed, and to participate in panel discussions. With Val Gielgud and others, he appeared on *BBC Close Up No. 19*, "How a Radio Play Is Produced," September 29, 1943. He was a guest on a quiz called "Puzzle It Out" on *Here's Wishing You Well Again*, May 31, 1945. He edited and was a contestant on *Detective Quiz: Corner in Crime*, numbers 1, 2, and 3, August 2, August 30, and September 27, 1945. On September 18, 1945, he was a guest on *The Michael Howard Show*, and on July 11, 1946, he was a guest expert on *Call Yourself a Detective*, a series written by Ernest Dudley in which solutions were proposed to whodunit sketches. He was interviewed on *Radio Newsreel*, July 12, 1947, about the discovery of a supposed Conan Doyle story. He and Christianna Brand discussed the topic of mystery writing for the North American Service of the BBC, March 31, 1955. On the BBC show *Connoisseurs of Crime*, Carr introduced a fictional case, "The Mystery of the Yellow Room" (November 29, 1957), and a real-life one, "Who Killed Charles Bravo?" (December 5, 1957). He was a guest on *These Foolish Things*, a nostalgia show, on July 11, 1958. He narrated "The Good Giant" about Sir Arthur Conan Doyle on the BBC's Scottish Home Service, May 20, 1959. In the United States, he was host of Mutual's *Murder by Experts*, beginning June 18, 1949.

6. STAGE PLAYS

Arms and the God, by Carr and Sheldon Dick. Produced at the Dell Theatre, The Hill School, Pottstown, Pennsylvania, 1924 or 1925.

The Stewed Prince of Haverburg, a satire on *The Student Prince*, performed by the freshman class at Haverford College, Haverford, Pennsylvania, Fall 1926.

Inspector Silence Takes the Air, by Carr and Val Gielgud; opened on April 20, 1942, at the Pier Pavilion, Llandudno.

Thirteen to the Gallows, or Out of Town Tonight, by Carr and Val Gielgud; opened on April 17, 1944, at the Royal Theatre, Leicester.

Intruding Shadow. Toured under the general title *Appointment With Fear*, along with the play listed below and a farce called *Prize Onions*, which was not by Carr. Opened on April 2, 1945, at the Palace Theatre, Westcliff.

She Slept Lightly. Toured with *Intruding Shadow*, listed above.

"The Adventure of the Conk-Singleton Papers." A playlet parodying Sherlock Holmes, performed at the Mystery Writers of America annual meeting, April 1948. The script was printed in *The Unicorn Mystery Book Club News*, vol. 1, no. 9 (undated, 1949), as by Dr. John H. Watson; it was reprinted with very slight changes under Carr's name in *Ellery Queen's Mystery Magazine*, October 1968, and in *The Door to Doom*, 1980.

"The Adventure of the Paradol Chamber." A playlet parodying Sherlock Holmes, performed at the Mystery Writers of America annual meeting, April 1949, and at The Detection Club, October 12, 1955. The script was printed in *The Unicorn Mystery Book Club News*, vol. 2, no. 3 (undated, 1949), under Carr's name; it was reprinted with very slight changes in *Ellery Queen's Mystery Magazine*, February 1950, *Ellery Queen's Annual*, 1965, *The Baker Street Journal*, September 1965, *Ellery Queen's Minimysteries*, 1969, and *The Door to Doom*, 1980.

7. ADAPTATIONS OF CARR'S WORKS BY OTHER WRITERS

Several of John Dickson Carr's novels and short stories have been adapted by other scriptwriters for radio broadcast. The following are known.

"The Burning Court." Adapted by Harold Medford from the Carr novel. CBS *(Suspense)*, June 17, 1942; rebroadcast June 14, 1945.
"Death in the Dressing Room." Adapted from the Carter Dickson short story. Mutual *(Murder Clinic)*, September 29, 1942.
"The Locked Room." Adapted from the Carr short story. CBS *(Suspense)*, January 27, 1944.
"You Have Been Warned." Adapted by Julian McLaren-Ross from the Carter Dickson novel *The Reader Is Warned*. BBC, 6 parts, February 19, 26, March 5, 12, 19, 26, 1958.
"Fire, Burn!" Adapted by John Keir Cross from the Carr novel. BBC, July 5, 1958.
"The Hollow Man." Adapted by John Keir Cross from the Carr novel. BBC, January 10, 1959.
"He Wouldn't Kill Patience." Adapted by John Keir Cross from the Carter Dickson novel. BBC, April 4, 1959.
"Blind Man's Hood." Adapted by Michael and Mollie Hardwick from the Carter Dickson short story. BBC, April 18, 1963.

The following adaptations of Carr novels and stories have appeared on television.

"The Devil in Velvet." Adapted by Sumner Locke-Elliott from the Carr novel. CBS *(Westinghouse Studio One)*, January 7, 1952.
"The Adventure of the Black Baronet." Adapted by Michael Dyne from the short story by Carr and Adrian Conan Doyle. CBS *(Suspense)*, May 26, 1953.
Colonel March of Scotland Yard. Twenty-six half-hour episodes based on the Carter Dickson book *The Department of Queer Complaints*. Fountain Films, Middlesex, England, 1953. Distributed by Official Films to U.S. television beginning in 1954.
"The Seat of the Scornful." Adapted by Ted Allan from the Carr novel. BBC, April 15, 1956.
"Cabin B-13." Adapted from the Carr radio play. CBS *(Climax)*, June 26, 1958.
"The Burning Court." Adapted by Kelley Roos from the Carr novel. NBC *(Dow Great Mysteries)*, April 24, 1960.
"The Gentleman from Paris." Adapted by Troy Kennedy Martin and Michael Imison from the Carr short story. BBC *(Storyboard)*, July 28, 1961.
"The Judas Window." Adapted by Dick Sharples from the Carter Dickson novel. BBC *(Detective)*, April 23, 1964.
"The Man Who Couldn't Be Photographed." BBC *(Plunder)*, May 12, 1966.
　　　　The series, described as "a weekly raid on the archives of BBC television," included an excerpt from the Carr radio play.
"And So to Murder." Adapted by Paul Wheeler from the Carter Dickson novel. BBC *(Detective)*, October 26, 1969.
"Les Yeux en Bandoulière." Adapted by Daniel Depland from the Carr novel *The Problem of the Green Capsule*. FR3, France *(Le Masque)*, 1988.

Between September 28 and November 16, 1960, ITV England broadcast a serial version of Charles Dickens's unfinished novel, *The Mystery of Edwin Drood*. The script by John Keir Cross was based on a solution to the novel propounded by John Dickson Carr, and Carr was given credit in the series.

The following movies have been based on Carr's stories:
Appointment With Fear. A film made up of three short subjects: "The Clock Strikes Eight," "The Gong Cried Murder," and "The House in Rue Rapp," all based on Carr radio scripts (the third on "Death Has Four Faces," the radio version of the short story "The Silver

Curtain"). British Foundation, 1946. Screenplay by Roy Clark. Directed by Ronald Haines. With Valentine Dyall.

The Man in Black. A film based on the radio series *Appointment With Fear,* but the story is not taken from any of Carr's scripts. Hammer Films, 1950. Screenplay by John Giling and Francis Searle. Directed by Francis Searle. With Valentine Dyall.

The Man with a Cloak. Based on Carr's short story "The Gentleman from Paris." MGM, 1951. Screenplay by Frank Fenton. Directed by Fletcher Markle. With Joseph Cotten, Leslie Caron, Barbara Stanwyck, and Jim Backus.

Colonel March Investigates. This film combines three of the episodes that would appear on *Colonel March of Scotland Yard:* "Hot Money," "Death in the Dressing Room," and "The New Invisible Man." Criterion Films, 1952. Screenplay by Leo Davis. Directed by Cyril Enfield. With Boris Karloff, Ewan Roberts, and Sheila Burrell.

Dangerous Crossing. Based on Carr's radio play "Cabin B-13." Twentieth Century-Fox, 1953. Screenplay by Leo Townsend. Directed by Joseph M. Newman. With Jeanne Craine and Michael Rennie.

That Woman Opposite. Based on Carr's novel *The Emperor's Snuff-Box.* Monarch Films, 1957. Released in the United States as *City After Midnight.* RKO, 1959. Screenplay by Compton Bennett. Directed by Compton Bennett. With Phyllis Kirk, Dan O'Herlihy, Petula Clark, and Wilfred Hyde-Whyte.

La Chambre Ardente. Based on Carr's novel *The Burning Court.* UFA-Comacico (France), 1961. Released in the United States as *The Burning Court.* Translux, 1963. Screenplay by Julien Duvivier and Charles Spaak. Directed by Julian Duvivier. With Jean-Claude Brialy, Nadja Tiller, and Perrette Pradier.

Treacherous Crossing. Based on Carr's radio play "Cabin B-13." O.T.M.L. Productions in association with Wiltshire Coast Productions. A "World Premier Movie," first broadcast on the USA cable television network, April 8, 1992. Screenplay by Elisa Bell. Directed by Tony Warmby. With Lindsay Wagner, Angie Dickinson, and Jeffrey de Munn.

8. PARODIES AND PASTICHES (AND SIMILAR) OF CARR'S WORKS

Alex Atkinson. "Chapter the Last, Merriman Explains." *Punch,* August 15, 1951. Reprinted in *The Art of the Impossible* (U.S. title *Murder: Impossible*), Jack Adrian and Robert Adey, eds., 1990.

    A parody of golden-age crime fiction, especially Carr and Sir Henry Merrivale.

E. G. Ashton. "International Investigators, Inc." *Ellery Queen's Mystery Magazine,* February 1952.

    Dr. Gideon Fell is one of the members of International Investigators, Inc.

W. Heidenfeld. "The Unpleasantness at the Stooges Club." *Ellery Queen's Mystery Magazine,* February 1953.

    Dr. Fell and Sir Henry Merrivale attend the First International Congress of Fictional Sleuths, while the stooges of great detectives investigate a locked-room murder.

R. G. S. Price. "'Tec's Twilight." *Ellery Queen's Mystery Magazine,* September 1953 (story copyright, 1951).

    Dr. Fell is one of many sleuths mentioned in this short-short.

Arthur Porges. "Her Last Bow." *Ellery Queen's Mystery Magazine,* February 1957. Reprinted as "An Adventure of Stately Homes" in Arthur Porges's *Three Porges Parodies and a Pastiche,* 1988.

    A double-barreled parody of Sherlock Holmes and Sir Henry Merrivale.

Morton Wolson. "The Glass Room." *Ellery Queen's Mystery Magazine,* September 1957.

    A brief parody of an H.M. case is given within a larger story.

John F. Suter. "The Unlocked Room." *Ellery Queen's Mystery Magazine,* July 1960.

    The impossible murder of Jon Dickens Carbon is solved by Colonel Goliath Perrivale.

Arthur Porges. "Another Adventure of Stately Homes." *The Saint Mystery Magazine*, September 1964. Reprinted in Arthur Porges's *Three Porges Parodies and a Pastiche*, 1988.

> A parody of Holmes and H.M.

William Brittain. "The Man Who Read John Dickson Carr." *Ellery Queen's Mystery Magazine*, December 1965.

> A story about how reading Carr creates a locked room.

Priscilla Dalton (pseudonym of Michael Avallone). *The Silent, Silken Shadows*. New York: Paperback Library, 1965.

> A gothic romance with Henrietta Merrivale as a main character.

Handon C. Jorricks (pseudonym of Norma Schier). "Hocus-Pocus at the Drumis-Tree." *Ellery Queen's Mystery Magazine*, April 1966. Reprinted in Norma Schier's *The Anagram Detectives*, 1979.

> An anagrammatic pastiche of a Sir Henry Merrivale case.

Anthony Shaffer. *Sleuth*. Produced in London, February 12, 1970, and in New York, November 12, 1970; script printed London: Boyars, 1970, and as part of *Best Mystery and Suspense Plays of the Modern Theatre*, Stanley Richards, ed., New York: Dodd, Mead, 1971.

> The play begins with quotations from a mystery solved by St. John Lord Merridew, based on one of the rejected solutions to *The Problem of the Wire Cage*.

Jon L. Breen. "The House of the Shrill Whispers." *Ellery Queen's Mystery Magazine*, August 1972. Reprinted in Jon L. Breen's *Hair of the Sleuthhound*, 1982.

> A parody of Carr's stories, featuring Sir Gideon Merrimac.

Elaine Budd. "The Second Scandal." *Skullduggery*, April 1980.

> A story about the Gideon Fell Society, based on the genuine Carr Society.

Bill Pronzini. "The Problem of the Black Road." *Collecting Paperbacks?* n.d. [1981].

> An article describing the discovery of *The Problem of the Black Road* by Carr under the pseudonym of Philip Jacoby. The book featured "a wild adventure set in Scotland and involving an insane midget, a one-eyed fat man, a mysterious goatlike figure, two grisly murders, and the fantastic disappearance of an entire circus troupe (including two elephants) from a 'black road.'" Only a few fans realized that the article was an imaginative hoax.*

Carr appears briefly as a character in two mysteries set in part at Mystery Writers of America meetings: Robert Arthur, "The 51st Sealed Room, or the MWA Murder," *Ellery Queen's Mystery Magazine*, October 1951; and Brett Halliday, *She Woke to Darkness*, New York: Torquil, 1954.

---

*With Pronzini's permission, Edward D. Hoch used part of the "Black Road" plot in "The Bad Samaritan," *Alfred Hitchcock's Mystery Magazine*, December 9, 1981. In homage to Carr, the detective who solves the disappearance of the circus in Hoch's story is G. K. Chesterton, the model for Dr. Fell.

Notes

John Dickson Carr's letters are preserved in several archives: Contracts and correspondence with Harper and Brothers and with Hamish Hamilton Ltd. are in the possession of those companies; radio scripts and BBC letters (to Val Gielgud, John Cheatle, Moray McLaren, and others) and memoranda are in the BBC archives; correspondence with his British agents, Pearn, Pollinger & Higham (and their successors, David Higham Associates), from 1951 through 1965 is at the Harry Ransom Humanities Research Center, the University of Texas at Austin, and later material is in the files of David Higham Associates; correspondence with his American agents, Rene de Chochor and James Oliver Brown, is in the James Brown Associates Records, Rare Book and Manuscript Library, Columbia University; letters to and from Anthony Boucher are in the William A. P. White Papers, Lilly Library, Indiana University; letters to and from Frederic Dannay are at the Harry Ransom Humanities Research Center, University of Texas at Austin; letters to Dorothy L. Sayers are at the Marion E. Wade Center, Wheaton College; and letters to Clayton Rawson are owned by Rawson's family. Locations of this material will be given in the following notes only in instances where there might be some uncertainty. Other letters cited in the notes are in the possession of their recipients unless stated otherwise.

Personal communications to me are identified as either letter (L) or interview (I) with the dates.

Carr's books have appeared in so many different printings with different paginations that citing quotations by page number would not be helpful. I have therefore followed S. T. Joshi's lead in giving chapter (or other division) rather than page number. (When the location of a quotation is obvious from the context, I do not give a separate citation.)

I use some short forms in the notes: DNS = *Uniontown Daily News Standard*; EQMM = *Ellery Queen's Mystery Magazine*; Joshi = S. T. Joshi, *John Dickson Carr, a Critical Study* (Bowling Green, Ohio: Bowling Green State University Popular Press, 1990); Taylor = Robert Lewis Taylor, "Two Authors in an Attic," *The New Yorker*, 2 parts, September 8 and 15, 1951; JDC = John Dickson Carr.

PREFACE

1. *The Murder of Sir Edmund Godfrey*, Preface.
2. *Hag's Nook*, Chapter 1.
3. Clarice Carr (I), September 8, 1988.
4. *The Bowstring Murders*, Chapter 1.
5. Back dust jacket panel of the first United States edition of *The Three Coffins*, courtesy William Dunn.
6. Clarice Carr (I), September 8, 1988.
7. Clarice Carr (I), January 15, 1990.
8. EQMM, June 1975, p. 110.
9. Introduction to A. Conan Doyle, *The Lost World and The Poison Belt* (London: Eyre & Spottiswoode, 1950), p. v.
10. *The Life of Sir Arthur Conan Doyle*, Introduction.
11. *The Eight of Swords*, Chapter 1.
12. *The Crooked Hinge*, Chapter 20.

1. UNIONTOWN

1. *Poison in Jest*, Chapter 1.
2. Edward Dumbauld (L), October 4, 1988; Mrs. Mary Rosboro Carroll (I), August 25, 1988; and Mrs. Winifred Woodfill (I), August 25, 1988.
3. John W. Jordan and James Hadden, *Genealogical and Personal History of Fayette and Greene Counties, Pennsylvania*, I (New York: Lewis Publishing Co., 1912), p. 55.
4. Edward Dumbauld, "Recollections of John Dickson Carr," typescript dated August 15, 1988; JDC's autobiographical notes, ca. July 1954 (Higham files, University of Texas at Austin).
5. Inscription in a copy of the first United States edition of *The Lost Gallows*, courtesy Wooda (Nick) Carr.
6. *Poison in Jest*, Chapters 1, 4.
7. Julia McNiven (I), September 5, 1989.
8. Edward Dumbauld, "Recollections of John Dickson Carr."
9. Mary White Hubbard to Edward Dumbauld, September 28, 1988; Anna B. Jones (L), August 26, 1988.
10. DNS, November 6, 1912; *New York Times*, November 6, 1912.
11. DNS, October 25, 1914.
12. Howard Haycraft, *Murder for Pleasure* (New York: D. Appleton-Century, 1941), pp. 199–200, clearly based on publicity material prepared by JDC for Harper & Bros. A shorter version appears on the back dust jacket panel of the first United States edition of *The Three Coffins*.
13. *The Ghosts' High Noon*, Chapter 2, and "Notes for the Curious"; Julia McNiven (I), September 5, 1989.
14. DNS, November 4, 1914; *New York Times*, November 4, 1914.
15. Jordan and Hadden, *Genealogical and Personal History*, p. 56.
16. JDC to Nelson Bond, March 8, 1968 (in the possession of Rosalie Abrahams); Edward Dumbauld (L), August 15, 1988; Anna B. Jones (L), August 26, 1988, and (I) August 30, 1988; Julia McNiven (I), October 20, 1988.
17. Clarice Carr (I), May 1, 1990; JDC to Dorothy L. Sayers, March 16, 1937.
18. "As We See It," DNS, March 17, 1922.
19. "As We See It," DNS, September 16, 1922.
20. *The Cavalier's Cup*, Chapters 5, 9, 13.
21. Anna B. Jones (L), August 26, 1988.
22. Philip Carr (I), August 10, 1988.
23. Julia McNiven (I), October 20, 1988.
24. Carol McCarthy (I), February 27, 1990.

25. Application for admission to The Hill School, August 8, 1922 (Hill School files).
26. "As We See It," DNS, June 20, 1922; see also DNS, July 25, 1922.
27. *The Ghosts' High Noon,* Part 4, and "Notes for the Curious."
28. "As We See It," DNS, June 8 and 24, 1922.
29. Mary Rosboro Carroll (I), August 25, 1988; John Messmore, Sr. (I), November 3, 1988.
30. Mary Rosboro Carroll (I), August 25, 1988; Anna B. Jones (I), August 30, 1988.
31. "As We See It," DNS, April 4, 1922, May 5, 1922. "The Grandest Game in the World," *The Door to Doom,* p. 317.
32. "As We See It," DNS, March 15, 1922; April 4, 1922.
33. Winifred Woodfill (I), August 25, 1988; Edward Dumbauld, "Recollections of John Dickson Carr."
34. Winifred Woodfill (I), August 25, 1988.
35. Edward Dumbauld, "Recollections of John Dickson Carr."
36. *Dark of the Moon,* Chapter 5.
37. "Election Night," *A Book of Hill School Verse, 1920–1926,* Frederick W. Graves, ed. (New York: Macmillan, 1927), pp. 126–27.
38. JDC's autobiographical notes, ca. July 1954 (Higham files).
39. The legend about JDC's grandfather owning the newspaper appears in JDC's autobiographical notes, ca. July 1954, and a version of it is printed in Taylor, Part 1, along with an imaginative version of the Ignatz claims and the statement that John was writing for the paper at the age of eleven. These stories are repeated in Joshi, p. 1. JDC denied the story about writing at the age of eleven in a letter to Otto Penzler, September 14, 1973.
40. "As We See It," DNS, March 14, 1922.
41. "As We See It," DNS, April 10, 1922.
42. "As We See It," DNS, March 8, 1922.
43. "As We See It," DNS, April 12, 1922; May 16, 17, 25, and 26, 1922.
44. Dust jacket of *The Three Coffins.*
45. Frank Joslyn Baum and Russell P. MacFall, *To Please a Child, a Biography of L. Frank Baum* (Chicago: Reilly & Lee, 1961), pp. 123–24; Julia McNiven (I), October 20, 1988.
46. *It Walks By Night,* Chapter 5.
47. "As We See It," DNS, April 28 and 29, 1922.
48. Anna B. Jones (L), August 26, 1988; "As We See It," DNS, March 23, 1922; April 4, 1922; JDC to Nelson Bond, March 8, 1967.
49. JDC to Nelson Bond, March 8, 1968.
50. JDC to Eleanor Sullivan, July 7, 1976.
51. "As We See It," DNS, April 4, 1922.
52. *It Walks By NIght,* Chapter 12.
53. JDC to Nelson Bond, March 3, 1968.
54. Ibid.
55. EQMM, May 1970, p. 95; EQMM, September 1972, p. 106.
56. *The Three Coffins,* Chapter 17; EQMM, November 1972, p. 84.
57. EQMM, July 1948, p. 35.
58. "As We See It," DNS, June 26, 1922.
59. *The Plague Court Murders,* Chapters 8, 13; *The Mad Hatter Mystery,* Chapter 9; Larry L. French, "The Baker Street-Carrian Connection: The Influence of Sherlock Holmes on John Dickson Carr," *The Baker Street Journal,* March 1979, pp. 6–10.
60. Untitled speech at the University of North Carolina, *The Bookmark,* September 1968, p. 15; JDC to "Alan," August 7, 1967 (in the possession of Benjamin F. Fisher IV); JDC to Nelson Bond, June 4, 1969 (in the possession of Rosalie Abrahams).
61. Douglas G. Greene, "A Mastery of Miracles: G. K. Chesterton and John Dickson Carr," *The Chesterton Review,* August 1984, pp. 307–15.
62. JDC to Nelson Bond, June 4, 1969.
63. "As We See It," DNS, August 8, 1922.

64. "As We See It," DNS, March 23, 1922; May 4, 1922. See also Appendix 1.
65. "As We See It," DNS July 7, 1922.
66. "As We See It," DNS, March 23, 1922; April 29, 1922.
67. *Dark of the Moon*, Chapter 2.
68. *The Haverfordian*, March 1927, pp. 271–73.
69. Edward Dumbauld, "Recollections of John Dickson Carr."
70. "As We See It," DNS, August 7, 1922.

2. THE HILL AND HAVERFORD

1. J. H. Alleman to the headmaster, Hill School, August 7, 1922 (Hill School files); DNS, August 21, 1922; September 18, 1922; Herbert S. MacDonald (L), October 4, 1988.
2. *Poison in Jest*, Chapter 1.
3. Carol McCarthy (I), February 27, 1990.
4. Paul Chancellor, *The History of the Hill School, 1851–1976* (Pottstown: The Hill School, 1976), pp. 24, 108, and plates 18 and 19.
5. Records from The Hill School sent to John Carr Duff, January 1929 (copies in Hill School files); JDC's autobiographical notes, ca. July 1954 (Higham files).
6. "Leader," *The Hill Record*, October 15, 1924.
7. William B. Willcox (L), June 21, 1981; January 11, 1982.
8. Julia McNiven (I), September 5, 1989; Alan Wykes (interview with Tony Medawar), July 1989; Clarice Carr (I), November 20, 1989.
9. Julia McNiven (I), September 5, 1989; JDC to Francis Wilford-Smith, November 12, 1967.
10. *Death-Watch*, Chapter 1; Daniel P. Mannix, "Commentary," *The Baum Bugle*, Spring 1987, pp. 15–16.
11. Herbert S. MacDonald (I), October 10, 1988; *The Dial*, Hill School yearbook, 1925, p. 54; *The* [Hill School] *News*, April 23, 1925.
12. "Leader," *The Hill Record*, October 15, 1924.
13. William B. Willcox (L), June 21, 1981; January 11, 1982.
14. Chancellor, *The History of the Hill School*, pp. 46–55.
15. Dust jacket of *The Three Coffins*.
16. Wooda N. Carr to Boyd Edwards, headmaster, The Hill School, September 19, 1925; Hill School records sent to John Carr Duff, February 8, 1929 (Hill School files).
17. Wooda N. Carr to Boyd Edwards, September 19, 1925; Clarice Carr (I), November 20, 1989; Bonita Cron (L), March 18, 1992. Harvard has checked its official records and its student directory, and "unfortunately neither source indicated that John D. Carr III attended Harvard University for any amount of time." Rebecca J. Bates, curatorial assistant, Harvard University Archives (L), October 31, 1990.
18. Frederic Prokosch, *Voices, A Memoir* (New York: Farrar, Straus, and Giroux, 1983), p. 14.
19. Frederic Prokosch (L), June 18, 1988; July 12, 1988; March 2, 1989; *Voices*, pp. 16–17.
20. Joe MacNamee (I), June 15, 1989; Herbert Ensworth (I), June 29, 1989; Bea McDade (I), January 24, 1989; March 11, 1989; Samuel Cook (I), July 6, 1989.
21. Bea McDade (I), January 24, 1989; March 11, 1989.
22. James Partington, Jr. (L), June 5, 1989; (I) June 15, 1989.
23. Bea McDade (I), January 24, 1989; March 11, 1989; Taylor, Part 1; *The Eight of Swords*, Chapter 14.
24. Joshi, pp. 9, 76.
25. "'As Drink the Dead . . . ,'" *The Door to Doom*; "The Dim Queen," *Fell and Foul Play*.
26. Haverford *Alumni News*, undated clipping (1949).
27. Frederic Prokosch (L), March 2, 1989; Frederic Prokosch to John Rodell, May 15, 1989.
28. Frederic Prokosch (L), March 2, 1989.
29. Francis C. Jameson (L), July 12, 1989.
30. *The Record*, 1929, p. 115.
31. Ibid.

32. "The Deficiency Éxpert," *The Haverfordian,* May 1927, p. 355.
33. "The Murder in Number Four," *The Door to Doom.*
34. "The Fourth Suspect," *The Door to Doom.*
35. Frederic Prokosch (L), July 12, 1988.
36. At my request, Professor Robert Greenfield, who is writing a book about Prokosch, examined "The New Canterbury Tales," and he agrees that Prokosch wrote two of the legends—"The Legend of the Neckband of Carnellians" and "The Legend of the Hand of Ippolita."
37. Joshi, p. 85.
38. Samuel Cook (I), July 6, 1989; Walter Sondheim, Jr. (I), June 29, 1989.
39. Dr. Herbert Ensworth (I), June 29, 1989.
40. Joe MacNamee (L), June 6, 1989; (I), June 15, 1989; Carr's grades are from a photostat of Carr's record supplied by Haverford College.
41. James Partington, Jr. (L), June 5, 1989; (I) June 29, 1989; Dr. Herbert Ensworth (I), June 29, 1989.

3. Paris, Columbia Heights—and the Satanic Bencolin

1. Kenneth Allsop, "The Man Who Enjoys Slapstick with His Corpses," *The Daily Mail,* August 2, 1961; JDC's autobiographical notes, ca. July 1954.
2. James Partington, Jr. (L), June 5, 1989; (I) June 15, 1989.
3. JDC to Richard Clark, July 8, 1967.
4. Photograph in possession of James Partington, Jr.
5. DNS, February 4, 1928.
6. Publicity material in Penguin Books editions of Carr's novels.
7. Taylor, Part 1; Haycraft, *Murder for Pleasure,* p. 200; Haverford Alumni News, undated clipping (1949).
8. DNS, February 4, 1928.
9. "Grand Guignol," *The Haverfordian,* April 1929, p. 260.
10. *It Walks By Night,* Chapter 8.
11. Alsop, *The Daily Mail,* August 2, 1961; Taylor, Part 1.
12. DNS, March 29, 1928.
13. *The Haverfordian,* March 1928, pp. 263–64; John S. Rodell (L), June 12, 1989; (I) June 19, 1989; (L) June 28, 1989.
14. Nicolas Barker, *The Butterfly Books* (London: Bertram Rota, 1987), p. 54. On Prokosch, also see his memoir, *Voices,* and Radcliffe Squire, *Frederic Prokosch* (New York: Twayne, 1964), and Robert Greenfield's forthcoming critical study.
15. JDC to Anthony Boucher, March 14, 1942.
16. Joshi, p. 134.
17. John Carr Duff to The Hill School, January 18, 1929; Hill School to Duff, February 8, 1929 (Hill School files).
18. Walter J. (Buzz) Storey (I), August 10, 1988; Clarice Carr (I), March 22, 1990; JDC to Otto Penzler, September 14, 1973.
19. Taylor, Part 1; Edward Delafield (I), July 6, 1988.
20. The contract is in the files of Harpers-Collins.
21. This copy is in the possession of the Uniontown Public Library.
22. JDC to Christopher Morley, dated "Friday" (University of Texas at Austin).
23. *It Walks By Night,* Chapter 5.
24. Ibid., Chapter 7.
25. Ibid., Chapter 2, 8.
26. Ibid., Chapter 11.
27. Ibid., Chapter 13.
28. Ibid.
29. Ibid., Chapter 4.

30. Ibid., Chapter 1.

31. Ibid., Chapter 4.

32. Edward Delafield (I), August 9, 1988.

33. *It Walks By NIght,* Chapter 8.

34. *Spectator,* April 5, 1930; *New York Times,* February 23, 1930; *Saturday Review of Literature,* April 5, 1930; *Evening Standard,* March 27, 1930, reprinted in *Arnold Bennett: The Evening Standard Years,* Andrew Mylett, ed. (London: Chatto & Windus, 1974).

35. Edward Delafield (I), July 6, 1988; April 20, 1989; John Murray Reynolds (I), August 21, 1988; Clarice Carr (I), November 20, 1989. Ray Stanich (L), January 16, 1990, has sent me a description of the current neighborhood.

36. JDC to Wooda (Nick) Carr, June 23, 1974.

37. Edward Delafield (L), February 13, 1982; John Murray Reynolds (L), April 23, 1982; (I) August 21, 1988.

38. JDC to Otto Penzler, September 14, 1973.

39. Taylor, Part 1; Joshi, p. 2.

40. JDC to Passport Office, January 6, 1933 (Passport Office files); John Murray Reynolds (I), November 21, 1991.

41. Taylor, Part 1; confirmed by Edward Delafield (L), February 13, 1982.

42. Edward Delafield (L), undated, late 1981; John Murray Reynolds (I), August 21, 1988.

43. Edward Delafield (I), August 9, 1988.

44. Taylor, Part 1; Edward Delafield (I), April 20, 1989.

45. John Murray Reynolds (L), April 23, 1982; (I) November 20, 1989; Edward Delafield (I), August 9, 1988.

46. John Murray Reynolds (I), November 20, 1989.

47. John Murray Reynolds (L), April 23, 1982. Other stories are from Taylor, Part 1, confirmed and corrected by Edward Delafield (L), February 13, 1982.

48. The date is in JDC's passport application (Passport Office files). Harper's (Bissel) to JDC, May 16, 1930; Hamish Hamilton to JDC, February 23, 1937; November 26, 1952.

49. O'Neil Kennedy, *Bachelor Abroad* (Uniontown: The News Publishing Company, 1930), pp. 26, 49–50; Carr to Bissel, undated (May or early June 1930). I am grateful to Roland Lacourbe for information on the Hotel La Bourdonnais.

50. Kennedy, *Bachelor Abroad,* p. 16.

51. Ibid., pp. 17, 51.

52. Ibid., pp. 27–28, 30–33, 43.

53. Ibid., pp. 57–58, 66–70.

54. Ibid., pp. 70–71, 81; Clarice Carr (I), September 8, 1988.

55. Kennedy, *Bachelor Abroad,* pp. 61–67. My copy of Ruland's *Legends of the Rhine* is signed by its owner "S. S. Kaiser Wilhelm on the Rhine July 8, 1926."

56. Kennedy, *Bachelor Abroad,* pp. 79–80; *The Corpse in the Waxworks,* Chapter 2.

57. Kennedy, *Bachelor Abroad,* pp. 8, 81.

58. Clarice Carr (I), September 8, 1988; (I) March 22, 1990; (I) October 22, 1990; John Murray Reynolds (I), August 21, 1988.

59. Lillian de la Torre (L), July 1, 1988; John Murray Reynolds (I), August 21, 1988.

60. Clarice Carr (I), March 22, 1990; Julia McNiven (I), September 8, 1988.

61. Clarice Carr (I), September 8, 1988; March 22, 1990; October 22, 1990.

62. Bissel of Harpers to JDC, May 16, 1930; JDC to Bissel, undated, probably May or early June 1930; Carr to Hamish Hamilton, April 1, 1935; JDC to Clayton Rawson, undated, 1939. It is just possible that the phrase "Miss Death" refers to a gallows, and therefore that this was a working title for *The Lost Gallows.* It seems more likely, however, that Carr's references to having torn up large portions of his second book and having been unable to sell an American novel refer to *Miss Death.*

63. Taylor, Part 1; Edward Delafield (L), February 13, 1982. The first contract signed under this new arrangement, dated July 7, 1931, lacks the final pages giving the royalty guaran-

tees. The next contract, September 6, 1934, specifies the one-hundred-dollar-a-month figure.

64. John Murray Reynolds (L), April 23, 1982.
65. Julia McNiven (I), September 8, 1988.
66. *The Lost Gallows,* Chapter 1.
67. *Castle Skull,* Chapter 2.
68. *The Lost Gallows,* Chapter 2.
69. *The Corpse in the Waxworks,* Chapter 1.
70. *The Lost Gallows,* Chapters 6, 16.
71. Ibid., Chapter 5.
72. *The Corpse in the Waxworks,* Chapter 5.
73. *The Lost Gallows,* Chapter 3.
74. Joshi, p. 14.
75. *The Lost Gallows,* Chapter 18.
76. Ibid., Chapters 5, 14.
77. LeRoy Panek, *Watteau's Shepherds, The Detective Novel in Britain, 1914–1940* (Bowling Green, Ohio: Bowling Green State University Popular Press, 1979), p. 146.
78. *The Corpse in the Waxworks,* Chapter 11.
79. JDC to Hamish Hamilton, November 6, 1935.
80. Anna B. Jones (L), August 26, 1988.
81. JDC to Hamish Hamilton, April 1, 1935.
82. *Poison in Jest,* Chapter 11.
83. Ibid., Chapter 12.
84. Both Joshi, pp. 52–54, and Panek, pp. 149–50, have good discussions of Rossiter.
85. *Poison in Jest,* Chapter 18.
86. John Murray Reynolds (L), April 23, 1982; (I) August 21, 1988; (I) October 10, 1988; Julia McNiven (I), September 8, 1988; Clarice Carr (I), November 2, 1988; November 20, 1989.
87. *Hag's Nook,* Chapter 16.
88. Edward Dumbauld, "Recollections of John Dickson Carr"; Julia McNiven (I), September 8, 1988; Clarice Carr (I), March 22, 1990; November 12, 1990.
89. Julia McNiven (I), September 5, 1989.
90. Edward Dumbauld, "Recollections of John Dickson Carr"; Bissell to JDC, November 16, 1932; Bissel to JDC, January 4, "1932" (recte 1933); Edward Delafield (I), July 6, 1988. The Nicholas Wood name in taken from Chris Steinbrunner and Otto Penzler, eds., *Encyclopedia of Mystery and Detection* (New York: McGraw-Hill, 1976), p. 63, which is based on material sent by Carr to Penzler. The Street name is in JDC to Hamish Hamilton, November 12, 1935.
91. Clarice Carr (I), November 29, 1988; November 12, 1990.

4. INTERLUDE—JOHN DICKSON CARR AND DETECTIVE FICTION

1. Most histories of detective fiction are either much too general or have a debatable theme—by which I mean that they're wrong. The following, however, can be recommended: Howard Haycraft, *Murder for Pleasure* (1941), Julian Symons, *Mortal Consequences* (1972; 2d edition, as *Bloody Murder,* 1975), and LeRoy Panek, *An Introduction to the Detective Story* (1987).
2. Richard D. Altick, *Victorian Studies in Scarlet* (New York: W. W. Norton, 1970), p. 10.
3. "The Lure of Detective Fiction," London *Morning Post,* August 30, 1937.
4. Ronald Knox, Introduction to *The Best Detective Stories of the Year 1928,* Ronald Knox and H. Harrington, eds. (New York: Horace Liberight, 1929).
5. Van Dine's rules are quoted from material published in his *The Winter Murder Case* (New York: Charles Scribner's, 1939).
6. There has been much debate about the date of the founding of The Detection Club. Carr always thought it was 1932, based on the date of their bylaws. But John Rhode, in the in-

troduction to a club anthology, *Detection Medley* (1939), says that it grew out of dinners held by Anthony Berkeley in 1928; a letter from The Detection Club was printed in the *Sunday Times* in 1930; and their round-robin novel, *The Floating Admiral,* was published in 1931. The problem has been solved by a collection of early Detection Club material described in Ferret Fantasy catalogue Q91, December 1990, p. 26. Among the documents are a letter from Berkeley to G. K. Chesterton, December 27, 1929, proposing such a club, and a list of "members to date" dated January 4, 1930. Clearly it began at the very end of 1929 or in the first days of 1930.

7. "The Grandest Game in the World," *The Door to Doom,* p. 316.
8. "The Lure of Detective Fiction," *Morning Post,* August 30, 1937.
9. "The Grandest Game in the World," *The Door to Doom,* pp. 308–12.
10. Harold Q. Masur (L), October 5, 1988.
11. "Writing the Mystery Story, First New York Craft Session" (Mystery Writers of America papers, Mugar Memorial Library, Boston University).
12. *The Three Coffins,* Chapter 17.
13. "Murder Fancier Recommends," *Harper's Magazine,* July 1965, p. 105.
14. JDC to Frederic Dannay, October 20, 1941.
15. "The Grandest Game in the World," *The Door to Doom,* p. 321.
16. JDC to Frederic Dannay, May 26, 1946.
17. "With Colt and Luger," *New York Times,* September 24, 1950; Raymond Chandler, *Selected Letters* (London: Jonathan Cape, 1981), p. 238.
18. JDC to Frederic Dannay, September 17, 1946.
19. "A Mystery Addict Speaks His Mind," on the dust jackets of book-club editions of *Behind the Crimson Blind, Night at the Mocking Widow,* and probably other books.
20. Basil Hogarth, *Writing Thrillers for Profit* (London: A. & C. Black, 1936), p. 88.
21. Helen R. Tiffany, "Pacifying the Public with Mysteries," *Publishers Weekly,* August 24, 1935, p. 498.

5. ENGLAND AND THE COMING OF SIR HENRY MERRIVALE

1. Unless otherwise stated, details about the Carrs' life in London and Bristol are from Clarice Carr (I), September 28, 1981; November 29, 1988; April 20, 1989; January 15, 1990; February 4, 1991.
2. Roy Cleaves (I), September 8, 1990.
3. *The Mad Hatter Mystery,* Chapter 3.
4. Leonard Huckman (interview with James E. Keirans), March 16, 1989; Clarice Carr (I), April 20, 1989.
5. Hogarth, *Writing Thrillers,* p. 88.
6. JDC to Francis Wilford-Smith, July 17, 1969.
7. "Magicians' Progress," *Radio Times,* July 14, 1940.
8. References to dummies are in the JDC-Hamilton correspondence, March 17 and 19, October 1, 1936; April 13, 1938; May 9, 1939. The cutting of the text of *The Murder of Sir Edmund Godfrey* is in JDC to Hamish Hamilton, May 31, June 9, 1936.
9. Chapter 17 of both *The Three Coffins* (U.S.) and *The Hollow Man* (U.K.).
10. Roy Cleaves (I), September 8, 1990.
11. Wycliffe A. Hill, *The Plot Genie, General Formula* (Hollywood: Gagnon Company; 5th ed., 1935).
12. JDC mentioned that he based the situation in *The White Priory Murders* on a puzzle book in an inscription of Frederic Dannay's copy of the book, now in the library of the University of Texas at Austin. Though not mentioned by JDC, *The Baffle Book* seems to have been the source.
13. Clarice Carr (I), March 5, 1987; July 6, 1988; February 4, 1991; July 23, 1991; Lillian de la Torre (L), July 1, 1988.
14. Clarice Carr (I), November 29, 1988; May, 1990; Hamish Hamilton to JDC, July 24, 1935.

15. JDC to Hamish Hamilton, September 9, 1936; October 22, 1937; Clarice Carr (I), May, 1990; April 9, 1981.
16. *The Bowstring Murders,* Chapter 12.
17. Ibid., Chapters 5, 8, 17.
18. Ibid., Chapters 17, 18.
19. Ibid., Chapter 4.
20. Ibid., Chapter 12.
21. *Sunday Times,* August 19, 1934.
22. JDC to Hamish Hamilton, November 12, 1935.
23. In going through the remains of her father's library, Julia McNiven found a copy of this book; (I) February 12, 1992. I am grateful to Tony Medawar for the reference to Sir Henry Marquis.
24. JDC to Francis Wilford-Smith, July 17, 1969.
25. *The Plague Court Murders,* Chapter 13.
26. Ibid., Chapter 16.
27. *The Red Widow Murders,* Chapters 15, 17, 20.
28. JDC to Hamish Hamilton, November 12, 1935.
29. *The Plague Court Murders,* Chapter 3.
30. *The Unicorn Murders,* Chapter 4.
31. G. H. Webster, "An Analytical Chart of the Stories of John Dickson Carr" (typescript, 1990). I am indebted to Mr. Webster for permission to use this valuable critical tool.
32. *The Red Widow Murders,* Chapter 1.
33. These quotations are from the opening chapters of *The Bowstring Murders, The Plague Court Murders,* and *The White Priory Murders.*
34. *The Unicorn Murders,* Chapter 18.
35. Ibid., Chapter 2.
36. Contracts, September 1934 and July 1935 (Hamilton files).
37. JDC to Hamish Hamilton, November 11, 1935; Hamilton to JDC, November 11, 1935.
38. JDC to Hamish Hamilton, November 12, 1935.
39. JDC to Hamish Hamilton, July 10, 1936; contract with William Morrow, May 19, 1936 (Ann Watkins papers, Columbia University).
40. Hamish Hamilton to JDC, July 9, 1936; JDC to Hamilton, July 10, 1936; Hamilton to JDC, July 13, 1936; JDC to Hamilton, July 17, 1936.

6. FELL CRIMES AND MORE MERRIVALE MURDERS

1. *Death-Watch,* Chapter 12.
2. Anthony Boucher (ed.), *Four-&-Twenty Bloodhounds* (New York: Simon & Schuster, 1950), p. 55. Carr contributed a "Detective's Who's Who" to this anthology giving Dr. Fell's publications.
3. *Hag's Nook,* Chapter 9.
4. Ibid., Chapter 15.
5. *The Mad Hatter Mystery,* Chapter 10.
6. Ibid., Chapter 1.
7. Taylor, Part 2.
8. "Mystery Out of the Ordinary," *Sunday Times,* September 24, 1933.
9. Taylor, Part 2.
10. *The Eight of Swords,* Chapter 4.
11. Ibid., Chapter 3.
12. Ibid., Chapter 9.
13. Ibid., Chapters 13, 18.
14. *The Blind Barber,* Chapters 1, 2.
15. JDC to Hamish Hamilton, January 2, 1935; Hamilton to JDC, January 3, 1935; Eugene Saxton to JDC, March 20, 1935 (all in Hamilton files).

16. *The Three Coffins,* Chapter 17.
17. *Death-Watch,* Chapters 8, 20.
18. Ibid., Chapter 22.
19. "Restrained and Fantastic," *Sunday Times,* March 31, 1935.
20. JDC to Hamish Hamilton, April 1, 1935.
21. *Death-Watch,* Chapter 22.
22. JDC to Hamish Hamilton, January 2, 1935; February 12, 1935.
23. JDC to Hamish Hamilton, March 10, 1935; Hamilton to JDC, July 24 and 30, August 20, 1935.
24. *The Plague Court Murders,* Chapter 6; *The Crooked Hinge,* Chapter 2.
25. *The Three Coffins,* Chapter 17.
26. Ibid., Chapter 3.
27. Joshi, pp. 32–33.
28. Edward D. Hoch, ed., *All But Impossible! An Anthology of Locked Room and Impossible Crime Stories* (New Haven: Ticknor & Fields, 1981), pp. ix–xi. Four additional Carr novels appeared in the top fifteen: *The Crooked Hinge, The Judas Window, The Peacock Feather Murders,* and *He Wouldn't Kill Patience.*
29. JDC to Hamish Hamilton, October 2, 1935.
30. Hamish Hamilton Ltd. to Jacqueline Korn of David Higham Ltd., December 22, 1966; Anthony Lejeune (L), August 31, 1991.
31. *The Arabian Nights Murder,* Chapters 6, 10.
32. Ibid., Chapter 1.
33. *The Punch and Judy Murders,* Chapter 1.
34. JDC to Douglas G. Greene, December 13, 1967.
35. *The Ten Teacups,* Chapter 1.
36. *The Judas Window,* Chapters 3, 18.
37. *Death in Five Boxes,* Chapter 6.
38. Haycraft, *Murder for Pleasure,* p. 201.
39. Dust jacket of first British edition, *The Magic Lantern Murders,* courtesy Robert C. S. Adey.
40. *The Punch and Judy Murders,* Chapter 6.
41. *The Peacock Feather Murders,* Chapters 2, 7, 13.
42. G. K. Chesterton, *The Club of Queer Trades* (London: Darwin Finlayson, 1960), p. 9; originally published in 1905.
43. E. F. Bleiler, "Some Thoughts on Peacock Feet," *The Mystery Fancier,* May/June 1982, pp. 13, 14–21.
44. Joshi, p. 46; Robert Adey, *Locked Room Murders and Other Impossible Crimes* (Minneapolis: Crossover; 2d ed., 1991), p. 313.
45. *The Judas Window,* Chapter 4.
46. Clarice Carr (I), March 5, 1987.
47. Christianna Brand (L), May 29, 1981.
48. Bleiler, "Some Thoughts on Peacock Feet," p. 14.
49. Joshi, p. 47.
50. *The Reader Is Warned,* Part 4, Chapter 20.

7. WITCHCRAFT

1. *The Crooked Hinge,* Chapter 17.
2. Ibid.
3. JDC to Francis Wilford-Smith, June 4, 1969.
4. Hamish Hamilton to JDC, July 24, 1935.
5. Hamish Hamilton to JDC, November 2, 1935.
6. JDC to Hamish Hamilton, November 6, 1935.
7. JDC to Hamish Hamilton, March 19, 1936; Hamilton to JDC, March 20, 1936.
8. JDC to Hamish Hamilton, March 24, 1936.

9. JDC to Hamish Hamilton, October 5 and 28, 1936.
10. *The Burning Court,* Chapter 7.
11. Ibid., Chapters 1, 3.
12. Ibid., Chapter 7.
13. Ibid., Epilogue.
14. Anthony Boucher to JDC, January 15, 1939; JDC to Boucher, February 7, 1939; Boucher to JDC, April 4, 1940; JDC to Boucher, April 23, 1940; JDC to Francis Wilford-Smith, June 4, 1969.
15. JDC to Hamish Hamilton, April 1, 1937.
16. *The Four False Weapons,* Chapters 5, 6, 8, 10.
17. Ibid., Chapter 1.
18. J. King of Hamilton Ltd. to JDC, June 17, 1937; JDC to King, July 3, 1937; JDC to Hamish Hamilton, July 27, 1937; September 28, 1937; Hamilton to JDC, October 5, 1937; December 14, 1937; Higham sales books, as transcribed by Tony Medawar.
19. JDC to Hamish Hamilton, undated (March 24, 1938); Hamilton to JDC, March 25, 1938; *The Crooked Hinge,* Chapter 16.
20. James Kingman, "John Dickson Carr and the Aura of Genius," *The Armchair Detective,* Spring 1981, pp. 166–67.
21. JDC to John McAleer, January 19, 1974; Robert Bruce Montgomery, "Edmund Crispin," *The Armchair Detective,* Spring 1979, pp. 183–85.
22. Hamish Hamilton to JDC, November 22, 1938; JDC to Hamilton, December 8, 1938. The letters are so vague, however, that they might be read to indicate that Carr came up with a list of titles—Harpers picked one, Hamilton another.
23. *The Problem of the Green Capsule,* Chapters 1, 4.
24. Ibid., Chapters 13, 15.
25. *The Problem of the Wire Cage,* Chapters 1, 3.
26. Ibid., Chapter 14.
27. Anthony Boucher to JDC, April 4, 1940; JDC to Boucher, April 23, 1940.

8. THE LURE OF HISTORY, THE DETECTION CLUB, AND A COLLABORATION

1. *The Murder of Sir Edmund Godfrey,* Preface.
2. Ibid.
3. *Devil Kinsmere,* L'Envoi.
4. *Deadly Hall,* Chapter 1.
5. *Sunday Times,* November 6, 1938.
6. JDC to Hamish Hamilton, July 31, 1936.
7. *The Murder of Sir Edmund Godfrey,* Preface and Interlude.
8. *Devil Kinsmere,* Chapter 1.
9. *The Murder of Sir Edmund Godfrey,* Preface.
10. JDC to Douglas G. Greene, February 6, 1971.
11. Hamish Hamilton to JDC, April 3, 1935; Eugene Saxton of Harpers to JDC, March 20, 1935 (Hamilton files).
12. *Devil Kinsmere,* Editor's Note.
13. Ibid., Chapters 11, 17.
14. JDC to Hamish Hamilton, January 2 and 8, 1935.
15. JDC to Hamish Hamilton, April 1, 1935; Hamilton to JDC, April 3, 1935.
16. Roy Cleaves (I), September 8, 1990; Clarice Carr (I), February 4, 1991.
17. JDC to Hamish Hamilton, January 2, 1935; Hamilton to JDC, January 3, 1935.
18. Contract in Hamilton files; JDC to Hamish Hamilton, November 12, 1935.
19. Clarice Carr (I), August 10, 1988.
20. JDC to Hamish Hamilton, July 17, 1935; August 15, 1935; December 18, 1935.
21. JDC to Hamish Hamilton, March 19, 1936; May 4, 1936; Hamilton to JDC, May 27, 1936; JDC to Hamilton, May 31, 1936; June 9, 1936.

22. JDC to Hamish Hamilton, May 31, 1936; June 9, 1936.
23. Jacques Barzun and Wendell Hertig Taylor, *A Catalogue of Crime* (New York: Harper & Row, 1971), p. 633.
24. *The Murder of Sir Edmund Godfrey,* Preface.
25. Thomas de Quincey, *Miscellaneous Essays* (Boston: Ticknor, Reed and Fields, 1851), p. 16.
26. *The Murder of Sir Edmund Godfrey,* Chapter 4.
27. JDC to Hamish Hamilton, July 31, 1936; Hamilton to Cass Canfield of Harpers, August 5, 1936 (Harpers files); *Publishers' Weekly,* June 13, 1936, p. 2334.
28. Canfield to Hamish Hamilton, February 18, 1937 (Harpers files).
29. Ibid.; Hamish Hamilton to JDC, October 5, 1937; January 4, 1938; contract in Hamilton files.
30. Lillian de la Torre (L), July 1, 1988. At this time, however, Carr had only one daughter in college.
31. Untitled speech, *Bookmark,* September 1968, p. 16; Hamish Hamilton to JDC, February 21, 1936; JDC to Janet Hitchman, April 2, 1974 (Mugar Library, Boston University).
32. EQMM, September 1970, p. 98.
33. Gladys Mitchell (L), June 23, 1981.
34. Clarice Carr (I), June 8, 1989.
35. JDC to Janet Hitchman, April 2, 1974; JDC to Francis Wilford-Smith, November 12, 1967.
36. JDC to Allen J. Hubin, January 8, 1969.
37. EQMM, July 1972, p. 87; JDC to Allen J. Hubin, printed in *The Armchair Detective,* July 1979, pp. 279–80.
38. Introduction to *The Floating Admiral* (Boston: Gregg Press, 1979), pp. xi—xii.
39. JDC to Allen J. Hubin, *The Armchair Detective,* July 1969, pp. 279–80.
40. EQMM, December 1970, p. 101.
41. EQMM, September 1970, p. 98.
42. EQMM, August 1970, p. 65.
43. EQMM, May 1970, p. 95.
44. JDC to Hamish Hamilton, November 12, 1935; *A Century of Detective Stories* (London: Hutchinson, 1935), p. [387].
45. JDC to Allen J. Hubin, November 28, 1968.
46. JDC to Dorothy L. Sayers, September 15, 1937 (Marion E. Wade Collection at Wheaton College Library).
47. JDC to Frederic Dannay, October 20, 1941 (University of Texas at Austin).
48. JDC to Hamish Hamilton, March 5, 1936.
49. JDC to Sayers, December 23, 1936.
50. Gladys Mitchell (L), June 23, 1981; JDC to Dorothy L. Sayers, September 15, 1938; JDC to Val Gielgud, May 2, 1939 (BBC archives); EQMM, October 1970, pp. 75–76.
51. EQMM, November 1970, pp. 126–27.
52. EQMM, February 1971, pp. 99–100.
53. "Corner in Crime No. 9: The Bravo Mystery," October 18, 1945, p. 25 (BBC archives); Introduction to John Williams, *Suddenly at the Priory* (London: Heinemann, 1957), pp. ix–xi.
54. "Let Us Have Nightmares," *The Kenyon Review,* 1960, pp. 509–14.
55. Bonita Cron (I), February 4, 1991; Clarice Carr (I), February 4, 1991.
56. Ibid.; JDC to Dorothy L. Sayers, February 28, 1937; March 16, 1937.
57. "Unsolved Mysteries of Real Life, No. 5, Mystery of the 'Florodora' Girl," *The Star,* July 30, 1937.
58. *Seeing Is Believing,* Chapter 20.
59. JDC to Dorothy L. Sayers, undated (late 1937/early 1938).
60. JDC to Hamish Hamilton, November 22, 1937; Clarice Carr (I), February 4, 1991; April 8, 1991. My thanks to Dr. James E. Keirans, who took photographs of 90 Eton Rise in 1985.
61. "Connoisseurs in Crime," *Woman's Journal,* March 1955; Clarice Carr (I), January 15, 1990; JDC to Francis Wilford-Smith, November 12, 1967.

62. Barry Mann (secretary of the Savage Club) to Tony Medawar, March 4, 1989; Clarice Carr (I), February 4, 1991. On club life and the Savage in particular, see two entertaining books: Charles Graves, *Leather Armchairs, The Book of London Clubs* (New York: Coward, McCann, 1963) and Anthony Lejeune, *The Gentlemen's Clubs of London* (No place: Dorset, 1984).
63. The United States contract is in my possession; the British contract is in Higham files.
64. Clarice Carr (I), January 29, 1981; Janaury 25, 1989.
65. *Fatal Descent*, Chapter 1.
66. Ibid., Chapter 5.
67. Ibid., Chapters 1, 2, 8; John Dickson Carr, "Powys Mathers—An Impression," in Torquemada, *112 Best Crossword Puzzles* (London: Pushkin, 1942), p. 30.
68. *Fatal Descent*, Chapter 19.
69. *Los Angeles Times*, January 15, 1939; Anthony Boucher to JDC, January 15, 1939; JDC to Boucher, February 7, 1939.

9. MINIATURE MURDERS

1. For information in this genre, see Robert Kenneth Jones, *The Shudder Pulps* (West Linn, Oregon: Fax Collectors Editions, 1975).
2. In a conversation with Reynolds, November 11, 1991, he recalled that he was writing for Popular Publications at this time, but he did not remember introducing Carr to an editor there. Nonetheless, Reynolds thinks it logical that he would have done so.
3. Ryerson Johnson (L), July 19, 1989.
4. JDC to Rick Sneary, August 12, 1970.
5. Harry Steeger (I), April 5, 1989; see also Jones, *The Shudder Pulps*, p. 116.
6. "The Man Who Was Dead," *The Door to Doom*, pp. 223, 236.
7. "The Door to Doom," *The Door to Doom*, p. 232.
8. JDC to Frederic Dannay, December 16, 1946.
9. JDC to Hamish Hamilton, March 27, 1935; April 1, 1937, referring to a project proposed "a few years ago."
10. Harry Steeger (I), June 8, 1989; (L) August 28, 1989; *Publishers' Weekly*, December 8, 1934; February 2, 1935; April 6, 1935; August 19, 1935; August 17, 1935; September 21, 1935; December 7, 1935.
11. Contract, September 6, 1934 (Hamilton files).
12. Hamish Hamilton to JDC, June 20, 1935; July 2, 1935; JDC to Hamilton, July 17, 1935.
13. "Terror's Dark Tower," *The Door to Doom*, pp. 258–59.
14. JDC to Hamish Hamilton, March 10, 1935; Anthony Boucher to JDC, January 9, 1941; Joshi, p. 78.
15. "The Wrong Problem," *The Third Bullet and Other Stories;* quoted from the Harper edition, pp. 135, 137, 149.
16. JDC to Francis Wilford-Smith, June 4, 1969.
17. JDC to Francis Wilford-Smith, July 16, 1969; Anthony Lejeune (L), August 31, 1991.
18. ". . And Things That Go Bump in the Night," *Woman's Journal*, December 1938.
19. Carr gives the spelling both as "Buff" and, incorrectly, as "Bluff" in the magazine printing of the story. In the book version *(The Department of Queer Complaints)* the wrong spelling is used throughout.
20. JDC to Frederic Dannay, December 16, 1946.
21. Richard Dalby and Rosemary Pardoe, eds., *Ghost and Scholars, Ghost Stories in the Tradition of M. R. James* (London: Crucible, 1987).
22. *The Third Bullet;* quoted from the 1937 edition, pp. 34–35.
23. JDC to Frederic Dannay, October 21, 1946; Joshi, p. 55; Barzun and Taylor, *A Catalogue of Crime*, p. 471.
24. EQMM, January 1948, pp. 4–5.
25. JDC to Frederic Dannay, September 17, 1946.

26. *The Department of Queer Complaints;* quoted from the first British and American editions, pp. 2, 59, 139; JDC to Allen J. Hubin, November 28, 1968.
27. G. K. Chesterton, *The Innocence of Father Brown* (New York: John Lane, 1911), p. 156; "William Wilson's Racket," *The Men Who Explained Miracles;* quoted from the Harper edition, p. 9; "The Footprint in the Sky," *The Department of Queer Complaints,* p. 38.
28. *The Department of Queer Complaints,* p. 112.
29. JDC to John Cheatle of the BBC, December 17, 1940.
30. JDC to Frederic Dannay, October 20, 1941; December 16, 1946.
31. Lady Wykeham (L), July 20, 1989.
32. Contract in the possession of Priestley's agents, Peters, Fraser, & Dunlop.
33. Clarice Carr (I), January 25, 1989.
34. JDC to Clayton Rawson, undated (middle of 1939).
35. *New York Times,* June 16, 1939.
36. Higham sales books; transcribed by Tony Medawar.
37. JDC to Clayton Rawson, undated.
38. Clarice Carr (I), September 8, 1988; December 4, 1989; May 1990; February 4, 1991; Julia McNiven (I), September 8, 1988; clipping of photos in DNS, sent to me by Wooda N. (Nick) Carr.
39. Clarice Carr (I), May 1990; John Murray Reynolds (I), July 6, 1988; JDC to Dorothy L. Sayers, September 25, 1939; JDC to Moray McLaren of the BBC, September 25, 1939; JDC to Clayton Rawson, February 28, 1941; DNS, August 31, 1939.
40. "The Proverbial Murder," *The Third Bullet and Other Stories;* quoted from the Harper edition, pp. 168–69.
41. *The Reader Is Warned,* Chapter 20.
42. Van Gielgud, *Years in the Mirror* (London: The Bodley Head, 1965), p. 106. Gielgud's diary entry seems to be confused. It is dated October 4, 1940, and part of the entry clearly refers to that year. On the other hand it says that Carr has just returned to England, which would make the year 1939, not 1940. Perhaps Gielgud wrote up notes for two years as a single entry.

10. WAR AND THE SOUND OF MYSTERY

1. JDC to Frederic Dannay, July 28, 1944.
2. John Murray Reynolds (L), April 23, 1982.
3. JDC to Frederic Dannay, July 28, 1944.
4. "It's a Dare!" *Radio Times,* September 3, 1943.
5. Ernest Dudley (L), July 10, 1991.
6. JDC to Val Gielgud, May 2, 1939.
7. Moray McLaren to Val Gielgud, May 3, 1939; Gielgud to JDC, May 3, 1939; memoranda from M. T. Candler, May 22, 1939; June 2, 1939.
8. "Who Killed Matthew Corbin?," *Fell and Foul Play,* pp. 23–24.
9. JDC to John Cheatle, December 29, 1939; Cheatle to JDC, January 4, 1940.
10. JDC to Moray McLaren, September 25, 1939; JDC to John Cheatle, December 29, 1939.
11. JDC to Val Gielgud, February 9, 1940.
12. "The Black Minute," *Fell and Foul Play,* p. 101.
13. Tony Medawar, "Serendip's Detections: 2, Mr. Nigel Strangeways and the Detection Club," *CADS: Crime and Detective Stories* 9 (July 1988), pp. 22–25.
14. Memorandum from M. T. Candler, September 3, 1940; memorandum from John Cheatle, September 5, 1940.
15. Memorandum from Candler, August 23, 1940.
16. "Speak of the Devil," Episode 1, p. 1. (All quotations from unpublished BBC plays are from scripts in the BBC archives.)
17. Ibid., Episode 4, p. 8.
18. JDC to Val Gielgud, undated (February 1941).

19. JDC to Clayton Rawson, February 28, 1941.

20. Rosemary Cooper of Pearn, Pollinger & Higham to Val Gielgud, February 12, 1941; BBC to Cooper, February 14, 1941.

21. "The Dead Sleep Lightly," *Fell and Foul Play*, p. 168.

22. Joshi, p. 120.

23. Tony Medawar, "Serendip's Detections III, The Pursuit of Silence," *CADS: Crime and Detective Stories* 10 (January 1989), pp. 3–7.

24. Memoranda from Stephen Potter, September 24 and 29, 1941; Potter to Robert Westerby, September 20, 1941.

25. "Black Market" (1941 version), p. 27.

26. Taylor, Part 2.

27. "Starvation in Greece," pp. 23–24.

28. "Black Gallery No. 4: Heinrich Himmler," pp. 6, 8, 10.

29. "Denmark Occupied," pp. 3, 6, 8, 9.

30. "They Strike at Night," p. 11.

31. JDC to Richard Clark, February 16, 1968.

32. JDC to Clayton Rawson, February 28, 1941; JDC to Anthony Boucher, March 1, 1941; JDC to Frederic Dannay, October 20, 1941. Clarice Carr (I), April 8, 1991, confirms that he was confident about the outcome of the war in private as well.

33. Julia McNiven (I), September 8, 1988; Clarice Carr (I), May 1990.

34. Clarice Carr (I), May 1990.

35. JDC to Anthony Boucher, March 1, 1941; Nancy Pearn to Gielgud, September 23, 1940; Gielgud to JDC, September 27, 1940; JDC to Dannay, October 20, 1941; Clarice Carr (I), April 8, 1991; Taylor, Part 2.

36. Taylor, Part 2; J. King of Pearn, Pollinger & Higham to JDC, November 1 and 29, 1940; JDC to Clayton Rawson, February 28, 1941.

37. Nancy Pearn to Val Gielgud, December 3, 1940; JDC to Clayton Rawson, February 28, 1941; JDC to Anthony Boucher, March 1, 1941; JDC to Harper & Bros., quoted in Haycraft, *Murder for Pleasure*, p. 204; Clarice Carr (I), June 8, 1989.

38. Nancy Pearn to Val Gielgud, December 3, 1941; JDC to Anthony Boucher, March 14, 1942; Clarice Carr (I), June 8, 1989; March 22, 1990; Julia McNiven (I), February 27, 1989.

39. JDC to Clayton Rawson, February 28, 1941; JDC to Anthony Boucher, March 1, 1941; JDC to Val Gielgud, January 1, 1941, and two undated letters from February to early March, 1941.

40. JDC to Val Gielgud, undated (about March 18, 1941).

41. JDC to John Cheatle, undated (early January 1942); JDC to Anthony Boucher, March 14, 1942.

42. For example, in a short story, "The Locked Room," published in July 1940.

43. BBC memorandum, February 5, 1942.

44. Clarice Carr (I), June 8, 1989; May 1990; April 8, 1991; Julia McNiven (I), April 10, 1991.

45. JDC to Frederic Dannay, October 20, 1941.

46. Francis M. Nevins, Jr., and Ray Stanich, *The Sound of Detection: Ellery Queen's Adventures on Radio* (Madison, Indiana: Brownstone Books, 1983).

47. CBS press release, November 2, 1942 (*Washington Post* archives, courtesy Christopher Lee Phillips).

48. Transcribed from audiotape of "Menace in Wax."

49. Julia McNiven (I), April 10, 1991.

50. Francis M. Nevins, Jr., "The Sound of Suspense, John Dickson Carr as a Radio Writer," *The Armchair Detective*, October 1978, pp. 335–38.

51. Tony Medawar and James E. Keirans, "Suspense on the High Seas," *The Armchair Detective*, Fall 1991, p. 433.

52. "The Devil's Saint," *The Dead Sleep Lightly*, p. 41.

53. "Will You Walk Into My Parlor?" *Dr. Fell, Detective, and Other Stories*, p. 95.

54. Val Gielgud to JDC, February 25, 1952.
55. Quoted from BBC script under the title "The Man Who Died Twice," pp. 3, 4, 13, 17.
56. *Seeing Is Believing*, Chapter 16.
57. Clarice Carr (I), January 25, 1989; November 20, 1989; January 15, 1990; Julia McNiven (I), February 27, 1989; April 8, 1991.
58. Alfred Goodman Gilman, Louis S. Goodman, and Alfred Gilman, eds. *The Pharmacological Basis of Therapeutics* (6th ed.), pp. 339; 361–63. I am grateful to Dr. Susan Mandell for information on chloral hydrate.
59. Julia McNiven (I), February 27, 1989; Clarice Carr (I), March 26, 1990; May 1990.
60. JDC to Wooda N. Carr II, "Labor Day," 1975; Clarice Carr (I), November 20, 1989; April 26, 1990.

11. WAR AND THE PUZZLE TALE

1. Joshi's bibliography includes an admittedly incomplete list of translations, pp. 147–64.
2. Joshi, pp. 92–95.
3. "It's a Dare!" *Radio Times*, September 3, 1943.
4. JDC to Clayton Rawson, February 28, 1941.
5. *The Case of the Constant Suicides*, Chapter 15.
6. *Death Turns the Tables*, Chapter 20.
7. "The Grandest Game in the World," *The Door to Doom*, p. 324.
8. *The Three Coffins*, Chapter 1.
9. *Seeing Is Believing*, Chapters 1, 20.
10. Anthony Boucher to JDC, January 31, 1942; JDC to Boucher, March 14, 1942.
11. *Nine—and Death Makes Ten*, Chapter 3.
12. Clarice Carr (I), April 20, 1989; Lady Wykeham (L), July 20, 1989.
13. Eugene Saxton of Harpers to JDC, March 12, 1940 (Higham files); Saxton to Margot Watson of Ann Watkins, Inc., March 12, 1940 (Harpers files).
14. JDC to Richard Clark, July 8, 1967.
15. *The Case of the Constant Suicides*, Chapter 9.
16. JDC to Howe of Hamish Hamilton, January 17, 1941.
17. *The Seat of the Scornful*, Chapter 8; see also Chapter 10.
18. Ibid., Chapter 4.
19. J. King of Hamish Hamilton to JDC, April 8, 1941; June 1, 1941.
20. Geoff Webster's unpublished "An Analytical Chart of the Stories of John Dickson Carr" first pointed out that *The Emperor's Snuff-Box* "might have been a Colonel March story with added 'psychology.'"
21. *The Emperor's Snuff-Box*, Chapter 2.
22. Ibid., Chapter 1.
23. JDC to Anthony Boucher, March 14, 1942.
24. Ann Watkins's summary of accounts for *The Emperor's Snuff-Box*, December 31, 1944 (Columbia University); J. King to JDC, January 13, 1945; J. King to JDC, May 3, 1946.
25. Higham sales books.
26. *Seeing Is Believing*, Chapter 10.
27. *She Died a Lady*, Chapter 1.
28. Ibid., Chapter 17.
29. Ibid., Chapters 3, 4.
30. Ibid., Chapters 5, 7.

12. DRAMA—STAGE, RADIO, AND LIFE

1. "Second Thoughts [to The Grandest Game in the World]—after 17 Years," *The Door to Doom*, p. 325.
2. JDC to Frederic Dannay, July 28, 1944.
3. Clarice Carr (I), January 15, 1990.

4. Christianna Brand (L), May 29, 1981.
5. "The Count of Monte Carlo," radio script for the series *Cabin B-13* (Library of Congress, CBS Box 134).
6. *Captain Cut-Throat*, Chapter 4; *In Spite of Thunder*, Chapter 18.
7. Ernest Dudley (I), September 22, 1990.
8. John Murray Reynolds (I), July 6, 1988.
9. Clipping sent to me by Judge Edward Dumbauld, summarizing a news story from Uniontown of May 8, 1944; Clarice Carr (I), January 15, 1990.
10. Clarice Carr (I), November 20, 1989; JDC to Frederic Dannay, May 24, 1944.
11. JDC to Frederic Dannay, July 28, 1944.
12. Joshi, pp. 17, 47, 56, 71.
13. JDC to Francis Wilford-Smith, September 10, 1967.
14. *The Haverfordian*, March 1927, pp. 227, 271.
15. *The Lost Gallows*, Chapter 12.
16. *The Bowstring Murders*, Chapter 15.
17. *The Eight of Swords*, Chapters 8, 14.
18. *The Unicorn Murders*, Chapters 1, 16.
19. *The Mad Hatter Mystery*, Chapter 13.
20. Ibid., Chapter 10.
21. *Till Death Do Us Part*, Chapter 1.
22. JDC to Jan Broberg, February 2, 1963.
23. *Till Death Do Us Part*, Chapters 10, 12, 17.
24. Information from Dr. James E. Keirans's valuable but still unpublished chronology of the Dr. Fell stories.
25. *Till Death Do Us Part*, Chapter 1.
26. Cass Canfield to JDC, September 25, 1944 (Higham files); Ann Watkins Company's summary of accounts, December 31, 1944 (Columbia University).
27. Higham files, transcribed by Tony Medawar; Anthony Boucher to JDC, September 4, 1948 ("whatever became of the novel of BBC which Harper's once announced for publication").
28. *He Wouldn't Kill Patience*, Chapter 2.
29. Ellery Queen, *In the Queen's Parlor* (New York: Biblo & Tannen, 1969), pp. 30–31; JDC to Clayton Rawson, February 28, 1941.
30. *He Wouldn't Kill Patience*, Epilogue.
31. JDC to Frederic Dannay, August 27, 1943.
32. Ibid.; Val Gielgud, *Years of the Locust* (London: Nicholson & Watson, 1945), p. 180.
33. Ernest Dudley (I), September 22, 1990.
34. JDC to Frederic Dannay, August 27, 1943.
35. Gielgud, *Years of the Locust*, p. 180; Gale Pedrick, ed., *Radio and Television Jubilee Issue Annual*, p. 99; BBC memorandum, November 24, 1943.
36. The playlets are in the BBC's Play Library. See also Howard Agg of the BBC to JDC, November 9, 1943.
37. Memorandum from B. E. Nicholls, December 3, 1943.
38. "The Man with Two Hands," pp. 7, 9. (All the following scripts are in the BBC's Play Library.)
39. "The Sire de Malatroit's Door," pp. 1, 12.
40. "The Oath of Rolling Thunder," p. 4.
41. "The Dragon in the Pool," *The Dead Sleep Lightly*, p. 55.
42. "He Who Whispers," p. 7.
43. "The Curse of the Bronze Lamp," pp. 4, 14, 16.
44. "Vex Not His Ghost," pp. 4, 9.
45. Swedish newspaper interviews summarized and translated by Johan Wopenka (L), October 11, 1990. I am most grateful to Mr. Wopenka.

46. *The Third Bullet;* quoted from the 1937 edition, p. 126.
47. "New Judgment: John Dickson Carr on Edgar Allan Poe," p. 20.
48. JDC to Frederic Dannay, July 28, 1944; "The Scandalous Affair of the Queen's Necklace," pp. 2, 7.
49. For details about this radio play, see Douglas G. Greene, "Adolph Hitler and John Dickson Carr's Least-Known Locked Room," *The Armchair Detective,* undated (1981).
50. Kay Hutchings (Librarian of the Garrick Club) to Tony Medawar, July 4, 1989, August 9, 1989; JDC to Hamish Hamilton, June 1, 1944; JDC to Pearn, Pollinger & Higham, March 13, 1951; David Higham to JDC, March 15, 1951; Graves, *Leather Armchairs,* pp. 52–55; Lejeune, *The Gentlemen's Clubs of London,* pp. 121–27.
51. Val Gielgud to Carr, January 9, 1942.
52. JDC to Anthony Boucher, March 14, 1942; *Radio Times,* April 3 and 24, 1942; Tony Medawar, "Serendip's Detections III, The Pursuit of Silence," *CADS: Crime and Detective Stories* 10, January 1989, pp. 3–7.
53. *Inspector Silence Takes the Air,* Act II, p. 20; Act III, p. 4.
54. *The Stage,* April 30, 1942.
55. Ibid., April 20, 1944; September 20, 1945; JDC to Gielgud, undated (July 1942); Medawar, "Serendip's Detections III."
56. *The Stage,* April 20, 1944.
57. *Thirteen to the Gallows,* Act II, p. 6.
58. *The Stage,* April 12, 1945; Medawar, "Serendip's Detections III."
59. *Intruding Shadow,* pp. 33–34.
60. Medawar, "Serendip's Detections III," p. 7.
61. Ibid. June Whitfield, who played the mysterious young woman in the play, wrote briefly of her memories to Tony Medawar, June 24, 1988, and sent an undated review of *Appointment With Fear* and programs from Palace Theatre, Westcliff (April 2, 1945), and the Arts Theatre of Cambridge (April 9, 1945).
62. Val Gielgud to JDC, August 29, 1946; JDC to Gielgud, undated (September 1946).
63. M.V. Ltd. to JDC, October 14, 1955 (Higham files); James Oliver Brown to JDC, November 28, 1955.
64. JDC to Frederic Dannay, "VE-Day, 1945."

13. THE POSTWAR WORLD AND THE LIFE OF DOYLE

1. Joan Kahn, Introduction to *The Three Coffins* (Boston: Gregg Press, 1979), p. vi.
2. JDC to Department of State, November 7, 1945; G. Grant McKenzie of British embassy to Department of State, December 4, 1945 (Passport Office files).
3. "Speaking of Crime," EQMM, April 1946, p. 47.
4. "Having Impossible Time," EQMM, September, 1946, p. 60.
5. Clarice Carr (I), March 26, 1990; Edward Delafield (L), undated (1981); (I), August 9, 1988; G. Grant McKenzie to Department of State, December 4, 1945; Nancy Pearn to Ann Watkins Company, January 6, 1946.
6. JDC to Frederic Dannay, undated (about January 1946); June 16, 1946; September 17, 1946.
7. JDC to Frederic Dannay, September 17, 1946; EQMM, November 1947, pp. 20–22.
8. "The House in Goblin Wood," *The Third Bullet and Other Stories,* pp. 116–17.
9. *Till Death Do Us Part,* Chapters 8, 16.
10. "A Mystery Addict Speaks His Mind," from the jackets of Mystery Guild books.
11. The problem was pointed out to me by Edward D. Hoch, who in turn heard about it from Joseph Commings.
12. EQMM, November 1947, p. 4.
13. JDC to Frederic Dannay, June 16, 1946; August 26, 1946; Ellery Queen, Introduction to *Dr. Fell, Detective, and Other Stories* (New York: The American Mercury, Lawrence E. Spivak, 1947), p. 7.

14. JDC to Frederic Dannay, "V-E Day, 1945"; EQMM, April 1946, p. 47.

15. Brand's memories are given in two accounts: undated letter to Larry L. French; undated (May 29, 1981) letter to DGG.

16. JDC to Frederic Dannay, October 21, 1946; Christianna Brand, Introduction to *The Floating Admiral* (Boston: Gregg Press, 1979), pp. ix–x; Brand (L), May 29, 1981.

17. Geoffrey Bush (L), February 17, 1989; March 11, 1989; Clarice Carr (I), February 23, 1989; Geoffrey Bush, *An Unsentimental Education*, pp. 20–21, reference courtesy of David Whittle, who is writing a biography of Crispin.

18. Crispin to Larry L. French, March 24, 1978; printed in his fanzine, *Culprit Confesses* 25 (1978).

19. Julia McNiven, "With Christmas 1945, Came the Gift of Literature," *Farmington* (Connecticut) *Valley Herald*, November 26, 1986.

20. JDC to Frederic Dannay, October 21, 1946; December 2, 1946; Clarice Carr (I), April 20, 1989; July 23, 1991; Adrian Doyle to Denis Doyle, November 19, 1946. I am indebted to Richard Lancelyn Green for transcriptions of the Adrian Conan Doyle letters in his collection.

21. Clarice Carr (I), April 20, 1989; July 23, 1991; JDC to Frederic Dannay, October 21, 1946; September 22, 1947; December 16, 1946; JDC to Lawrence G. Blochman, December 28 [1951] (in my possession).

22. JDC to Val Gielgud, September 15, 1949.

23. JDC to Frederic Dannay, May 26, 1946; August 26, 1946.

24. On Adrian Conan Doyle, see Jon L. Lellenberg, *Nova Fifty-Seven Minor* (Bloomington, Indiana: Gaslight, 1990); also Clarice Carr (I), January 25, 1989.

25. Howard Lachtman, "The Ideal Storybook Hero," *The Quest for Sir Arthur Conan Doyle, Thirteen Biographers in Search of a Life*, Jon L. Lellenberg, ed. (Carbondale: Southern Illinois University Prsss, 1987), pp. 111–24; Michael Harrison (L), May 3, 1989; September 27, 1989; Larry L. French, ed. *Notes for the Curious, a John Dickson Carr Memorial Journal* (Carrian Press, 1979), pp. 17–18.

26. JDC to "Mr. Keddie," September 7, 1945 (in my possession).

27. JDC to Frederic Dannay, July 28, 1944; Taylor, Part 2.

28. Adrian Doyle to Denis Doyle, May 14, 1945; April 20, 1946; December 7, 1946.

29. Adrian Doyle to Denis Doyle, December 5 and 10, 1946; January 24, 1947; April 17, 1947.

30. Clarice Carr (I), July 23, 1991.

31. *The Life of Sir Arthur Conan Doyle*, Foreword; JDC to Frederic Dannay, June 12, 1947.

32. *Times Literary Supplement*, July 5, 1947; JDC to Frederic Dannay, June 12, 1947; August 6, 1947; "Sherlock Back in 1947 Bank Safe Mystery," *Daily Mail*, July 12, 1947; Adrian Doyle to Denis Doyle, April 27, 1947; November 9, 1948.

33. Harpers contract (both Harpers and Higham files); Murray contract (Higham files); Adrian Doyle to Denis Doyle, April 17, 1947; JDC to Frederic Dannay, June 18, 1947; August 6, 1947.

34. John Murray contract; Harpers contract; Adrian Doyle to JDC, June 8, 1948 (Harpers files); Adrian Doyle to Winston Churchill, February 4, 1991 (carbon in the Richard Lancelyn Green collection).

35. Adrian Doyle to JDC, June 8, 1948; *The Life of Sir Arthur Conan Doyle*, Murray first edition, p. 15; Harpers first edition, p. 4.

36. Adrian Doyle to Denis Doyle, April 22, 1947; November 9, 1948; JDC to John Grey Murray, February 27, 1948; "A Line O' Type of Two," *Chicago Tribune*, September 9, 1948; "The Editor's Gas-Lamp," *The Baker Street Journal*, January 1949, p. 3. I am grateful to Peter Blau for photocopies of articles and reviews in his collection.

37. *The Life of Sir Athur Conan Doyle*, Foreword.

38. Ibid., Chapter 3.

39. Howard Lachtman, "The Ideal Storybook Hero."

40. *The Life of Sir Arthur Conan Doyle*, Chapter 5.

41. Ibid., Chapters 1, 2, 5, 7, 8.
42. Lachtman, pp. 113–14, 124.
43. *The Life of Sir Arthur Conan Doyle,* Chapters 1, 13.
44. Ibid., Chapter 15.
45. *Chicago Tribune,* September 9, 1948.
46. *The Life of Sir Arthur Conan Doyle,* Chapters 15, 21.
47. Lachtman, p. 111.
48. Dame Jean Conan Doyle, Foreword to Lellenberg, ed., *The Quest for Sir Arthur Conan Doyle,* p. xiii.
49. Charles Renshaw, Jr., "There Was a Dr. Watson," *The American Weekly,* March 20, 1949, p. 4.
50. JDC to Adrian Doyle, May 4, 1949 (John Murray Ltd. files).
51. "First Time for Everything," undated clipping, perhaps from *New York Herald Tribune,* ca. early January 1949; courtesy of Peter E. Blau; JDC to Adrian Doyle, May 4, 1949.
52. *The Baker Street Journal,* January 1949, pp. 3–4.
53. *San Francisco Chronicle,* January 30, 1949; *New York Herald Tribune Weekly Book Review,* February 6, 1949; *St. Louis Globe-Democrat,* March 6, 1949; *Sunday Times,* February 6, 1949; *Providence Journal,* February 9, 1949; *The New Republic,* February 14, 1949.
54. Adrian Doyle to Denis Doyle, June 10, 1949.
55. JDC to editor of *New English Review,* May 4, 1949 (carbon in John Murray Ltd. files).
56. *Daily Telegraph,* February 4, 1949; Adrian Doyle to John Grey Murray, February 18, 1949, enclosing Adrian Doyle to Harold Nicolson, undated (John Murray files).
57. Information from Peter E. Blau, based on *New York Times,* March 13 through April 17, 1949; JDC to Adrian Doyle, May 5, 1949; JDC to Val Gielgud, September 15, 1949; "Writers Award 'Edgars,'" *New York Times,* April 21, 1950.

14. MAMARONECK

1. JDC to Frederic Dannay, September 22, 1947; JDC to Val Gielgud, September 15, 1949.
2. Clarice Carr (I), July 23, 1991; August 2, 1991; Julia McNiven (I), September 5, 1989; JDC to Val Gielgud, September 15, 1949; Taylor, Part 1; photograph of house by Dr. James E. Keirans.
3. JDC to Val Gielgud, September 15, 1949.
4. *A Graveyard to Let,* Chapters 3, 8, 9.
5. Julia McNiven (I), February 27, 1989.
6. *A Graveyard to Let,* Chapters 4, 5.
7. Catherine Rawson (L), March 13, 1989; (I), May 9, 1989.
8. Hugh Rawson (I), January 24, 1989.
9. Ibid.; Catherine Rawson (I), May 9, 1989; Hugh Rawson, Introduction to *Death from a Top Hat* (New York: International Polygonics, 1986).
10. Lillian de la Torre (L), July 1, 1988.
11. Dorothy Salisbury Davis (L), October 31, 1988; Lillian de la Torre (L), November 17, 1988.
12. Minutes of Board of Directors, April 7, 1948 (MWA papers, Mugar Memorial Library, Boston University); "Mystery Writers Elect/John Dickson Carr Made Head of Country's Thrill Authors," *New York Times,* February 8, 1949; Harold Q. Masur (L), October 5, 1988; July 3, 1989.
13. Edward D. Hoch (L), May 23, 1979.
14. The playlet was printed in *The Unicorn Mystery Book Club News,* undated [1949], photocopy kindly supplied by Edward D. Hoch; Catherine Rawson (I), May 9, 1989; Harold Q. Masur (L), July 3, 1989.
15. *The Adventure of the Paradol Chamber,* in *The Door to Doom,* p. 282.
16. JDC to Val Gielgud, September 15, 1949; "Death Has Four Faces." (All *Cabin B-13* plays from Library of Congress, CBS, Box 134.) I am grateful to Ray Stanich for copies of press releases about *Cabin B-13.*
17. "A Razor in Fleet Street."

18. Steinbrunner and Penzler, *Encyclopedia of Mystery and Detection*, p. 64.
19. Ellery Queen, *Queen's Quorum* (New York: Biblo & Tannen, 1951), p. 22. According to Queen, Shaw's story was written in 1879 but never published. It was mentioned in *John O'London's Weekly*, November 16, 1945, so it is possible that Carr learned of the gimmick from that source, though Gross seems more likely.
20. "The Man Who Couldn't Be Photographed," BBC version of play, p. 6.
21. JDC to Val Gielgud, September 15, 1949.
22. CBS press releases, November 14, 11, and 17, 1948, December 12 and 26, 1948.
23. JDC to Val Gielgud, September 15, 1949.
24. Memorandum from N. G. Luker, July 6, 1949 (BBC archives); Val Gielgud to JDC, August 3, 1949; September 20, 1949; Nancy Pearn to Gielgud, October 4, 1949; Jean LeRoy of Pearn, Pollinger & Higham to Gielgud, October 5, 1949; memoranda from Martyn C. Webster, October 19 and 24, 1949; Webster to Nancy Pearn, October 26, 1949.
25. JDC to Adrian Doyle, May 4, 1949; Julia McNiven (I), February 27, 1989.
26. JDC to Frederic Dannay, June 16, 1946.
27. JDC to Frederic Dannay, August 26, 1946.
28. JDC to Frederic Dannay, December 2, 1946.
29. Hamish Hamilton to JDC, December 2, 1946; JDC to Hamilton, n.d. (December 5, 1946).
30. *He Who Whispers*, Chapter 1; *My Late Wives*, Chapter 6; *The Sleeping Sphinx*, Chapter 17; *The Skeleton in the Clock*, Chapter 1; *Below Suspicion*, Chapters 10, 13, 18.
31. *He Who Whispers*, Chapter 13.
32. Ibid., Chapter 18.
33. Ibid., Chapter 20.
34. *The Sleeping Sphinx*, Chapter 1.
35. Ibid., Chapter 4.
36. *A Catalogue of Crime*, p. 108.
37. *Below Suspicion*, Chapters 2, 4.
38. Ibid., Chapter 19; "The Grandest Game in the World," *The Door to Doom*, pp. 323–24.
39. Julia McNiven (I), September 23, 1991.
40. *Below Suspicion*, Chapter 3.
41. JDC to Frederic Dannay, August 26, 1946.
42. JDC to Francis Wilford-Smith, July 19, 1967; September 10, 1967.
43. JDC to Frederic Dannay, "V-E Day, 1945"; September 17, 1946.
44. J. J. H. Gaute and Robin Odell, *The New Murderer's Who's Who* (New York: International Polygonics, 1989), pp. 186–88.
45. *The Skeleton in the Clock*, Chapter 2.
46. Ibid., Chapter 1.
47. *Night at the Mocking Widow*, Chapters 12, 13.
48. "The Grandest Game in the World," full version in the revised edition of *The Door to Doom* (New York: International Polygonics, 1991), pp. [341–42].
49. *Night at the Mocking Widow*, Chapter 21.
50. Quoted in Haycraft, *Murder for Pleasure*, p. 200.

15. RESTORATION RAKES, REGENCY BUCKS, AND SHERLOCKIAN EXPLOITS

1. JDC to Jan Broberg, February 2, 1963.
2. *The Devil in Velvet*, Chapter 1.
3. JDC to James O. Brown, April 22, 1955.
4. *The Devil in Velvet*, Chapter 1.
5. *The Bride of Newgate*, Chapters 1, 4, 8; *The Devil in Velvet*, Chapter 2.
6. Tony Medawar and James E. Keirans, "Suspense on the High Seas," *The Armchair Detective*, Fall 1991, pp. 427, 437.
7. *The Bride of Newgate*, Chapter 1.
8. EQMM, September 1949, pp. 26–27; reprinted in Ellery Queen, *In the Queen's Parlor* (New

York: Biblo & Tannen, 1969), pp. 27–28; Edward D. Hoch (L), December 7, 1981. Hoch himself solved the vanishing furniture problem in "The Theft of the White Queen's Menu," EQMM, March 1983.

9. JDC to Anthony Boucher, October 30, 1962; JDC to John Curran, August 8, 1975.

10. *The Bride of Newgate*, Chapters 12, 16.

11. Ibid., Chapters 21, 23.

12. This fact was pointed out to me by Gary G. Brockman.

13. A note in Higham files, June 15, 1951, says that "Clarice sold a short story film—'The Gentleman from Paris' for $5000." Clarice herself believes that the amount was $10,000; Clarice Carr (I), September 23, 1991.

14. Richard McNiven (I), August 30, 1988; Clarice Carr (I), January 25, 1989; JDC to Val Gielgud, undated (late December 1954–early January 1955).

15. Adrian Conan Doyle, *Heaven Has Claws* (New York: Random House, 1953), pp. 3–14.

16. *Behind the Crimson Blind*, Chapter 3.

17. Ibid., Chapters 7, 18.

18. Clarice Carr (I), December 4, 1989.

19. Julia McNiven (I), January 11, 1990; Clarice Carr (I), September 23, 1991.

20. *The Devil in Velvet*, Chapter 18.

21. Ibid., Chapter 2.

22. I am grateful to John W. Campanella for informing me of the existence of this program.

23. Clarice Carr (I), September 23, 1991.

24. JDC to David Higham, cable, March 13, 1951.

25. Richard McNiven (I), August 30, 1988; September 5, 1989.

26. *The 9 Wrong Answers*, Chapter 9.

27. JDC to Lawrence Blochman, December 28 [1951] (in my possession).

28. Val Gielgud to David Higham, July 13, 1951 (BBC archives); BBC memoranda, September 18 and 24, 1951.

29. JDC to Blochman, December 28 [1951]; Mary Howes (I), January 8, 1990; Clarice Carr (I), September 23, 1991. The treatment of animals is also mentioned in Adrian Conan Doyle, *Heaven Has Claws*, p. 11.

30. David Higham to Helen Strauss, December 20, 1951; Jean LeRoy of Pearn, Pollinger & Higham to Val Gielgud, January 1, "1951" [recte, 1952]; JDC to Gielgud, no date [about February 1952]; Clarice Carr (I), September 23, 1991.

31. Val Gielgud to C. Lefeaux, April 30, 1952.

32. Herbert Brean, "How Holmes Was Reborn," *Life* magazine, December 24, 1952, pp. 62–64.

33. Adrian Doyle to Denis Doyle, July 25, 1952; November 9 and 10, 1952; March 13, 1953; Denis Doyle to Adrian Doyle, December 16, 1952 (Richard Lancelyn Green collection).

34. Vincent Starrett, "Books Alive," *Chicago Sunday Tribune*, September 7, 1952; "New Sherlock Holmes Tales Are Written," *San Francisco Chronicle*, August 24, 1952; David Dempsey, "In and Out of Books," *New York Times Book Review*, September 14, 1952; *The Third Degree*, September 1952 (references courtesy of Peter E. Blau); David Higham to JDC, August 20, 1952; Rene de Chochor to Pearn, Pollinger & Higham, August 21, 1952; Higham to Chochor, August 27, 1952; Higham to JDC, August 27, 1952; JDC to Higham, no date [October 5, 1952]; Higham to JDC, October 10, 1952; Higham to Chochor, October 10, 1952; Chochor to Higham, October 15, 1952; Higham to Chochor, October 17, 1952; Higham to JDC, October 17, 1952; Chochor to JDC, October 23, 1952; JDC to Higham, November 5, 1952; Higham to JDC, November 11, 1952.

35. Clarice Carr to Laurence Pollinger, no date [early September 1952]; Val Gielgud, memorandum, August 14, 1952; JDC to David Higham, no date [October 5, 1952].

36. Contract, September 22, 1947 (Hamilton files); David Higham to JDC, June 12, 1951; JDC to Higham, November 20, 1952; Cass Canfield to JDC, December 30, 1952.

37. Hamish Hamilton to JDC, November 18, 1952; JDC to Hamish Hamilton, November 20, 1952.

38. JDC to David Higham, November 20, 1952; Higham to JDC, November 25, 1952; Hamish Hamilton to JDC, November 26, 1952; December 11, 1952; Cass Canfield to JDC, December 30, 1952.

39. JDC to David Higham [October 5, 1952]; Adrian Doyle to Denis Doyle, October 23, 1952; October 30, 1952; JDC to Higham, November 5, 1952; Adrian Doyle to Denis Doyle, January 2, 1953.

40. BBC memorandum from C. LeFeaux, August 12, 1952; Val Gielgud to Jean LeRoy of Pearn, Pollinger & Higham, December 2, 1952; LeRoy to Gielgud, December 9, 1952; Clarice Carr (I), January 25, 1989; September 23, 1991; Adrian Doyle to Denis Doyle, March 13, 1953.

41. Camille Benoist to Denis Doyle, October 6, 1953; Adrian Doyle to Dennis Doyle, October 13, 1953; memorandum from Gielgud, October 14, 1953.

42. Rene de Chochor to JDC, April 8, 1954; June 4, 1954.

43. "Dottle from Baker Street," *Time*, April 5, 1954; Vincent Starrett, "Sherlock Is Back—or Is He?" *Chicago Tribune*, April 4, 1954; Anthony Boucher, "Criminals at Large," *New York Times Book Review*, April 11, 1954; "From the Editor's Commonplace Book," *The Baker Street Journal*, April 1955 (references courtesy *Chicago Tribune* and Peter Blau).

44. "The Adventure of the Wax Gamblers," *The Exploits of Sherlock Holmes*.

45. Clarice Carr (I), January 25, 1989; September 23, 1991; Julia McNiven (I), September 23, 1991.

46. JDC to Anthony Boucher, October 8, 1954; JDC to Rene de Chochor, June 1, 1954.

47. JDC to Rene de Chochor, February 9, 1954; JDC to David Higham, March 6, 1954; JDC to Chochor, March 6, 1954; June 6, 1954.

48. JDC to Anthony Boucher, October 8, 1954.

49. Boucher is quoted in EQMM, April 1953, p. 60.

50. Rene de Chochor to JDC, February 4, 1954; JDC to Chochor, February 9, 1954.

51. Clarice Carr (I), September 28, 1981; Julia McNiven (I), February 27, 1989; memorandum in Pearn, Pollinger & Higham files, May 17, 1951; Clarice Carr to David Higham, September 5, 1952; JDC to Higham, November 5, 1952; *The Cavalier's Cup*, Chapter 18.

52. *Behind the Crimson Blind*, Chapter 2.

53. Ibid., Chapters 15, 18.

54. Ibid., Chapters 18, 19.

55. *The Cavalier's Cup*, Chapter 15.

56. *Behind the Crimson Blind*, Chapters 2, 7, 18.

57. *The Cavalier's Cup*, Chapters 6, 9.

58. *Behind the Crimson Blind*, Chapter 15.

59. Ibid., Chapter 9.

60. Ibid., Chapters 10, 11, 16, 17, 19.

61. Julia McNiven (I), February 27, 1989.

62. *The White Priory Murders*, Chapter 12.

63. *The Cavalier's Cup*, Chapter 18.

16. RETURN TO LONDON

1. JDC to Rene de Chochur, January 12, 1954.

2. Autobiographical notes, ca. July 1954 (Higham files).

3. JDC to David Higham, March 6, 1954; photograph by Dr. James E. Keirans, 1988.

4. Christianna Brand (L), May 29, 1981.

5. JDC to Janet Hitchman, April 2, 1974 (Muger Memorial Library, Boston University); Michael Gilbert (L), September 1, 1988.

6. Brand, Introduction to *The Floating Admiral*, p. xii; Alan Wykes, interview with Tony Medawar, July 1989; Sir Kingsley Amis (L), July 5, 1988.

7. *Daily Mail*, August 17 and 1955; *The Washington Post*, August 18, 1955; Christianna Brand

to Larry L. French, no date [ca. 1979]; Brand (L), May 29, 1981; Brand to Mauro Boncam-
pagni, no date [1984], Brand, introduction to *The Floating Admiral*, pp. xii–xiii; Michael
Avallone (L), February 9, 1991.

8. Rene de Chochor to JDC, February 10, 1954; October 25, 1954.

9. Memoranda from Val Gielgud, October 26, 1954; November 4, 1954; Gielgud to JDC, No-
vember 1 and 4, 1954; January 5, 1955; JDC to Gielgud, no date [late December 1954–early
January 1955]; Gielgud to JDC, January 5, 1955; Eric Evens, assistant script editor, to JDC,
March 17, 1955; David H. Godfrey to JDC, July 14, 1955; *The 9 Wrong Answers*, Chapter 16.

10. Jean LeRoy to Martin Esslin, BBC, December 12, 1963; Richard Imison to LeRoy, January
30, 1964; LeRoy to Imison, January 31, 1963 (BBC archives); LeRoy to JDC, July 17, 1964
(Higham files); JDC to LeRoy, July 27, 1964; LeRoy to Imison, August 4, 1964; memorandum, Higham files, August 12, 1964; LeRoy to JDC, September 9, 1964; LeRoy memorandum, to JDC, November 4, 1964; JDC to LeRoy, November 9, 1964; LeRoy to JDC, November 12, 1964; JDC to LeRoy, November 25, 1964; LeRoy to Imison, November 27,
1964; Imison to Hilton Ambler of Higham, November 30, 1964 (BBC archives); Imison to
Ambler, December 15, 1964 (BBC archives). Carr's outline of the series is undated, but enclosed with his letter of November 25, 1964.

11. Medawar and Keirans, "Suspense on the High Seas," *The Armchair Detective*, Fall 1991, p.
437.

12. Higham memorandum, March 1954; Dr. Mohr to Pearn, Pollinger & Higham, January 3,
1956; Higham memoranda, January 17, 1956; February 6, 1956; Higham to JDC, March
16, 1956; Higham notes, May 16 and 17, 1956; Higham memorandum, May 18, 1956; JDC
to Lillian de la Torre, February 13, 1949, printed in *The Armchair Detective*, no month, 1981,
pp. 291–94.

13. JDC to de Rene Chochor, June 1, 1954; Chochor to JDC, June 4, 1954; JDC to Jean LeRoy,
undated (about June 13, 1954).

14. JDC to Rene de Chochor, March 6, 1954; Chochor to JDC, July 26, 1954; JDC to Chocor,
February 9, 1954; June 28, 1954.

15. *TV Guide*, undated clipping (1954); Richard Meyers, *TV Detectives* (San Diego: A. S.
Barnes, 1981), pp. 31–32. I am grateful to Francis M. Nevins, Jr., for a log of the episodes.

16. JDC to Rene de Chochor, June 28, 1954; Chochor to JDC, July 1, 1954; August 31, 1954;
September 23, 1954; October 7, 1954.

17. *Crime on the Coast & No Flowers By Request* (London: Victor Gollancz, 1984), pp. 3, 6; Jean
LeRoy to JDC, July 5, 1954; Elizabeth Ferrars (L), August 13, 1981.

18. JDC to Anthony Boucher, October 8, 1954.

19. Clarice Carr to Laurence Polinger, no date (early September 1952); Hamish Hamilton to
JDC, November 18, 1952; JDC to Hamilton, November 20, 1952; JDC to Rene de Chochor,
September 5, 1954.

20. JDC to Anthony Boucher, October 8, 1954; JDC to Rene de Chochor, October 7, 1954.

21. Cass Canfield to JDC, December 1, 1954 (Columbia University); Rene de Chochor to JDC,
December 17, 1954; JDC to Chochor, December 29, 1954; Chochor to JDC, January 27,
1955; James O. Brown to JDC, March 24, 1955; JDC to Brown, April 3 and 22, 1955; Brown
to JDC, May 6, 1955.

22. JDC to Rene de Chochor, October 7, 1954.

23. JDC to Chochor, November 1, 1954; Jean LeRoy to JDC, January 27, 1956; JDC to James O.
Brown, April 3, 1955; Alan Wykes to JDC, April 28, 1956 (Higham files).

24. Naome Walsh of *Collier's* magazine to Brown, July 1, 1955; Brown to JDC, August 2, 1955;
Carr to Brown, August 7, 1955; JDC to Francis Wilford-Smith, September 10, 1967.

25. "All in a Maze," *Merrivale, March and Murder*, pp. 51–52.

26. Ibid., pp. 35–36, 41, 54.

27. Higham memorandum, May 16, 1956; JDC to James O. Brown, November 1, 1956; JDC to
Brown, December 9, 1956; Higham memoranda, June 1957, March 26, 1958; David

Higham to JDC, January 19, 1959; JDC to Higham, January 27, 1959; December 28, 1959; February 6, 1960; December 20, 1960; JDC to Brown, January 25, 1961; "Washington's Brithday," 1961.

28. JDC to James O. Brown, January 25, 1961; Higham memorandum, September 15, 1961.
29. JDC to David Higham, February 22, 1962.
30. David Higham to JDC, May 4, 1962; JDC to Higham, May 18, 1962; Higham memorandum, August 13, 1963.
31. Higham memorandum, December 7, 1954; David Higham to JDC, December 16, 1954; JDC to James O. Brown, April 3, 1955; Brown to JDC, April 14 and 16, 1955; JDC to Brown, April 22, 1955.
32. JDC to Rene de Chochor, postcard from Copenhagen, October 31, 1954; JDC to Chochor, November 1, 1954.
33. *Fear Is the Same*, Chapters 1, 3, 11, 15, 16.
34. JDC to Anthony Boucher, October 8, 1954; Boucher to JDC, April 28, 1955; *Fear Is the Same*, Chapter 3.
35. *Fear Is the Same*, Chapters 7, 15.
36. Ibid., Chapter 18; Joshi, pp. 69–70.
37. *Fear Is the Same*, Chapter 18.
38. Ibid.
39. Ibid., Epilogue.
40. JDC to James O. Brown, "Washington's Birthday," 1961.
41. I purchased my copy at that time from the publisher.
42. JDC to James O. Brown, April 22, 1955.
43. JDC to Jan Broberg, February 2, 1963; "John Dickson Carr: 'Dodsstraffet avyskyvart det far mig att ma illa,'" *Expressen*, July 15, 1955; "Varldsberomd deckare skriver," *Expressen*, July 17, 1955. I am grateful to Johan Wopenka, who supplied not only photocopies of the articles but also translations of the key sections.
44. Ake Runnquist (L), October 30, 1990.
45. Cass Canfield to JDC, August 26, 1955 (Columbia University); David Higham to JDC, September 20, 1955; Hamish Hamilton to JDC, October 28, 1955.
46. *Patrick Butler for the Defence*, Chapter 1.
47. Ibid., Chapters 10, 12, 19.
48. Memorandum from Hamish Hamilton, June 11, 1956.
49. Higham memorandum, undated (about January 20, 1956); David Higham to JDC, January 20, 1956; Higham notes, May 16, 1956; Higham memorandum, May 17, 1956; Higham to JDC, May 29, 1956; contract, July 24, 1956 (Hamilton files).
50. JDC's passport gives the dates (courtesy Clarice Carr); James O. Brown to JDC, July 12, 1956.
51. Memorandum from Hamilton, June 11, 1956 (Higham files); JDC to James O. Brown, November 1, 1956; Hamilton to JDC, November 5, 1956; Brown to JDC, December 14, 1956.
52. JDC to James O. Brown, November 1, 1956; Brown to JDC, November 19 and 27, 1956; December 14 and 20, 1956.
53. JDC to Jan Broberg, February 2, 1963; JDC to Douglas G. Greene, December 13, 1967; Higham memorandum, May 29, 1957.
54. *Fire, Burn!* Chapters 1, 8.
55. Ibid., Chapters 13, 18.
56. Ibid., Chapter 6.
57. Ibid., Chapters 13, 18.
58. JDC to James O. Brown, December 9 (1956).
59. JDC to David Higham, January 27, 1959.
60. JDC to Douglas G. Greene, December 13, 1967.
61. *The Dead Man's Knock*, Chapters 3, 17.
62. JDC to Jan Broberg, February 2, 1963.

17. RETURN TO MAMARONECK—AND ELSEWHERE

1. *The Daily Mail,* July 27, 1956; *The Washington Post,* July 28, 1956.
2. Julia McNiven (I), September 5, 1989; Clarice Carr (I), November 20, 1989; *The Evening Standard,* June 24, 1958.
3. JDC to James O. Brown, December 9, 1956.
4. Mary Howes (I), December 6, 1989; November 26, 1991; Julia McNiven (I), November 19, 1991; JDC to Bruce Montgomery, undated (spring 1958) (uncatalogued Montgomery papers, Bodleian Library; transcription, courtesy of David Whittle).
5. *The Evening Standard,* June 24, 1958; *The Daily Telegraph,* July 2, 1958.
6. Julia McNiven (I), September 5, 1989; November 19, 1991; photograph, 1990, by Dr. James E. Keirans.
7. Mary Howes (I), December 6, 1989; November 26, 1991.
8. Mary Cantwell, "Close to Home," *The New York Times,* April 27, 1989; Cantwell (L), May 12, 1989.
9. Julia McNiven (L), January 11, 1990; December 13, 1991.
10. JDC to David Higham, January 27, 1959.
11. Ibid.; David Higham to JDC, February 3, 1959; Introduction to Arthur Conan Doyle, *Great Stories* (London: John Murray, 1959), p. 8.
12. *Scandal at High Chimneys,* Chapter 11.
13. Ibid. (in this case, I shall also give page numbers to the Harpers edition), Chapters 4 (pp. 29, 37, 38), 5 (pp. 43, 48–49), 6 (p. 66), 8 (p. 77), 9 (p. 90), 11 (p. 115), 12 (p. 118), 13 (p. 138), 14 (p. 144), 16 (p. 175).
14. Ibid., Chapter 13.
15. Ibid., Chapter 1.
16. JDC to David Higham, January 27, 1959; December 28, 1959.
17. *In Spite of Thunder,* Chapters 3, 4, 6.
18. Ibid., Chapter 1.
19. Ibid.
20. Ibid., Chapter 6.
21. JDC to David Higham, July 13, 1959; December 28, 1959; February 6, 1960; Introduction to Doyle, *Great Stories,* p. 9.
22. JDC to Bonita Carr, May 18, 1960; June 1, 1960.
23. JDC to the *Kenyon Review,* May 3, 1960 (in my possession); JDC to Wooda N. Carr, May 31, 1960; Julia McNiven (I), January 11, 1990; November 19, 1991; Mary Howes (I), December 6, 1989; November 26, 1991.
24. JDC's passport (courtesy Clarice Carr); JDC to David Higham, December 20, 1960; JDC to James O. Brown, January 25, 1961.
25. JDC's passport; JDC to David Higham, November 6, 1960; JDC to James O. Brown, undated (November 1960).
26. JDC to James O. Brown, October 17, 1960.
27. Therese Morrisroe of NBC to JDC, August 17, 1960 (Brown Associates Records at Columbia University); James O. Brown to JDC, October 7, 1960; JDC to Brown, October 17, 1960.
28. Roland Lacourbe (L), December 12, 1991; Maurice Renault of Club du Livre Policier to Sheila Watson of Higham Associates, November 29, 1960; David Higham to JDC, December 5, 1960.
29. JDC to David Higham, November 6, 1960; December 20, 1960.
30. JDC's passport; JDC to David Higham, April 21, 1961; postcard, undated (end of April 1961); June 12, 1961; September 7, 1961; *The Daily Mail,* August 2, 1961.
31. Julia McNiven (I), February 27, 1989; December 13, 1991; Clarice Carr (I), April 20, 1989; March 26, 1990; photograph, 1990, by Dr. James E. Keirans.
32. JDC to David Higham, February 22, 1962.
33. Katherine Rawson (L), March 13, 1989. Hugh Rawson has kindly summarized his father's notes on this project (L), February 3, 1990.

34. *The Witch of the Low-Tide,* Chapter 15.
35. David Higham to JDC, July 27, 1961.
36. *The Witch of the Low-Tide,* Chapter 1. Joshi, p. 72, says of this book that "there are so few references to any social or political events of the Edwardian age that this work hardly deserves to be called an historical novel at all." References to "events" strikes me as too narrow a way to define historical novels. *The Witch of the Low-Tide* is filled with references to things one might hear or see or smell in 1907.
37. *The Witch of the Low-Tide,* Chapter 11.
38. Ibid., Chapter 12.
39. Ibid., Chapter 10.
40. JDC to David Higham, May 18, 1962.
41. *The Demoniacs,* Chapter 14.
42. Anthony Boucher to JDC, October 7, 1962; JDC to Boucher, October 30, 1962.

18. THE LAST WANDERINGS

1. Clarice Carr (I), March 26, 1990. I have been unable to discover the exact date of the stroke.
2. JDC to David Higham, May 18, 1962; Phillip Carr (I), August 10, 1988; Edward Dumbauld, "Recollections of John Dickson Carr," August 15, 1988; Clarice Carr (I), February 23, 1989.
3. David Higham to JDC, May 4, 1962; JDC to Higham, May 18, 1962; January 15, 1962; February 10, 1963; Higham memoranda, December 13, 1962; February 10, 1963; JDC to Jan Broberg, February 2, 1963.
4. JDC to David Higham, February 10, 1963.
5. Clarice Carr (I), March 26, 1990; Julia McNiven (I), August 4, 1988; February 27, 1989; Richard McNiven (I)), August 30, 1988; September 5, 1989; JDC to Lee Wright, March 18, 1966 (Columbia University).
6. Julia McNiven (I), February 27, 1989; Holly Magill (I), November 20, 1989.
7. Clarice Carr (I), March 26, 1990; JDC to David Higham, August 30, 1963.
8. JDC's passport; JDC to Bonita Carr, June 30, 1963; JDC to David Higham, August 30, 1963; Clarice Carr (I), March 26, 1990; Mary Howes (I), December 6, 1989; November 26, 1991.
9. *The House at Satan's Elbow,* Chapter 5.
10. Clarice Carr (I), March 26, 1990; November 19, 1991; JDC to David Higham, October 23, 1963; May 31, 1964.
11. David Higham to JDC, October 21, 1963; JDC to Higham, October 23, 1963; November 13, 1963; Alan Wykes, interview with Tony Medawar, July 1989; programs from Writers' Summer School, August 1956 and August 1957, courtesy of Philippa Boland.
12. David Higham to JDC, October 25, November 11 and 22, 1963; Higham to Colston Leigh, telegram, November 26, 1963; Higham to JDC, November 26 and 29, 1963; JDC to Jean LeRoy, November 9, 1964.
13. JDC to Bonita Carr, November 18, 1962.
14. JDC to David Higham, October 23, 1963; JDC to Jacqueline Korn of Higham Associates, February 29, 1964; Julia McNiven (I), August 4, 1988; February 27, 1989; September 5, 1989.
15. Higham memorandum, May 14, 1964.
16. Inscription on copy (Item 87) in Pepper & Stern Catalogue O, 1986; JDC to Douglas G. Greene, February 6, 1971.
17. Joshi, pp. 67–68.
18. *Devil Kinsmere,* Editor's Note; *Most Secret,* Editor's Note.
19. *Devil Kinsmere,* Chapter 2; *Most Secret,* Chapter 2.
20. JDC to David Higham, May 21, 1964.

21. JDC to Jean LeRoy, November 9, 1964; David Higham to JDC, July 27, 1965; JDC to Higham, August 8, 1965.
22. *Dark of the Moon,* Chapter 4.
23. *The House at Satan's Elbow,* Chapter 4.
24. *Deadly Hall,* Chapter 16.
25. *Panic in Box C,* Chapters 9, 13, 14.
26. *Dark of the Moon,* Chapters 1, 3.
27. *The House at Satan's Elbow,* Chapter 3.
28. *Dark of the Moon,* Chapter 12; *Deadly Hall,* Chapter 1.
29. *The House at Satan's Elbow,* Chapters 1, 2.
30. Clarice Carr (I), January 15, 1990.
31. JDC to Francis Wilford-Smith, July 19, 1967; JDC to DGG, December 13, 1967; JDC to "Monica" of Higham Associates, "Whit Sunday, 1965."
32. Holly Magill (I), Arthur Magill (I), November 20, 1989.
33. *Panic in Box C,* Chapter 1.
34. *Greenville Piedmont,* March 24, 1965; Penny Forrester, Greenville Public Library (I), November 30, 1989.
35. Holly Magill (I), Arthur Magill (I), November 20, 1989; Edna Seaman, November 29, 1989.
36. JDC's passport; Clarice Carr (I), January 15, 1991; Harriet Doar, "John Dickson Carr," *Charlotte Observer,* October 1, 1967; photograph of Knoxbury Terrace house, 1987, by Dr. James E. Keirans.
37. JDC to David Higham, May 15, 1965; August 9, 1965. The date of JDC's leaving England is uncertain. He wrote a letter from Lymington on Whitsunday, 1965, which fell on June 13 that year, saying that he was leaving on the coming Wednesday. His passport, however, which is certainly accurate, indicates that he left on June 5. Perhaps as a non-church-goer, he miscalculated the date of Whitsunday.

19. GREENVILLE INDIAN SUMMER

1. JDC to David Higham, September 27, 1965; JDC to Richard Clark, July 8, 1967; JDC to Francis Wilford-Smith, July 19, 1967; JDC to "Allan," August 7, 1967 (in the possession of Benjamin F. Fisher); JDC to Douglas G. Greene, December 13, 1967; JDC to Robert L. Fish, January 6, 1968 (Mugar Memorial Library, Boston University); JDC to Wooda N. Carr, January 23, 1973.
2. Fred Van Deventer, "'Y'all Come,' Says Local British Author," *Greenville News,* March 31, 1968.
3. JDC to David Higham, September 27, 1965; Van Deventer, "'Y'all Come,'" *Greenville News,* March 31, 1968; JDC to Nelson Bond, December 7, 1966 (in the possession of Rosalie Abrahams).
4. JDC to Francis Wilford-Smith, July 19, 1967; JDC to Roger Machell of Hamish Hamilton Ltd., September 2, 1969.
5. JDC to David Higham, August 8, 1965.
6. Edna Seaman (I), November 20, 1989.
7. "Second Thoughts [to The Grandest Game in the World]—after 17 Years," *The Door to Doom,* Harpers and Hamilton editions, p. 325; International Polygonics edition, p. [345].
8. Holly Magill (I), November 20, 1989.
9. Julia McNiven (I), February 12, 1992; Doar, "John Dickson Carr," *Charlotte Observer,* October 1, 1967; Van Deventer, "'Y'all Come,'" *Greenville News,* March 31, 1968.
10. JDC to David Higham, September 27, 1965; Julia McNiven (I), February 10, 1992.
11. Doar, "John Dickson Carr," *Charlotte Observer,* October 1, 1967; Clarice Carr (I), November 20, 1989; January 15, 1990; JDC to Francis Wilford-Smith, March 3, 1968.
12. JDC to Francis Wilford-Smith, July 17, 1969.

13. JDC to Robert Bloch of the Mystery Writers of America, May 1, 1970 (in possession of Hugh Rawson).
14. *Punch,* August 15, 1951, pp. 172–73. The story is most readily available in *The Art of the Impossible,* Jack Adrian and Robert Adey, eds. (London: Xanadu, 1990), pp. 300–302 (U.S. edition, *Murder: Impossible;* New York: Carroll & Graf, 1990).
15. Norma Schier's inscription in my copy of her *The Anagram Detectives* (New York: Mysterious Press, 1979); Schier (I), January 15, 1990.
16. Jon L. Breen, *Hair of the Sleuthhound* (Metuchen, N.J.: Scarecrow, 1982), pp. 60–69.
17. JDC to Douglas G. Greene, December 13, 1967.
18. Bonita Cron (L), January 6, 1991.
19. JDC to Francis Wilford-Smith, September 10, 1967.
20. JDC to Francis Wilford-Smith, July 19, 1967; November 12, 1967; JDC to Douglas G. Greene, December 13, 1967; JDC to Richard Clark, December 13, 1967; February 16, 1968.
21. JDC to Lee Wright, March 18, 1966 (Columbia University); JDC to Douglas G. Greene, December 13, 1967; JDC to Rick Sneary, May 8, 1970; JDC to Douglas G. Greene, February 6, 1971.
22. JDC to Richard Clark, July 8, 1967; Doar, "John Dickson Carr," *The Charlotte Observer,* October 1, 1967.
23. *Panic in Box C,* Chapters 2, 7, 8, 13.
24. Ibid., Chapter 13.
25. JDC to Francis Wilford-Smith, March 3, 1968.
26. JDC to Norma Schier, "Day Before Hallowe'en, 1966."
27. *Dark of the Moon,* Chapters 2, 18, 20.
28. JDC to Douglas G. Greene, December 13, 1967.
29. JDC to Francis Wilford-Smith, March 3, 1968.
30. *New York Times,* November 10, 1968; *Book World,* December 29, 1968.
31. *Papa Là-Bas,* Chapter 2.
32. *Dark of the Moon,* Chapter 9; JDC to Francis Wilford-Smith, March 3, 1968.
33. Joshi, pp. 66–67.
34. *Papa Là-Bas,* Chapters 11, 14, 17.
35. JDC to Cass Canfield of Harper & Row, September 9, 1968.
36. *The Ghosts' High Noon,* Chapters 1, 11; *Deadly Hall,* Chapter 15.
37. *Deadly Hall,* Chapter 1.
38. Ibid., Chapters 1, 5, 7.
39. *Saturday Review,* March 27, 1971.
40. *National Review,* October 8, 1971.
41. JDC to Lee Wright, September 9, 1968 (Columbia University).
42. EQMM, January 1966, p. 151.
43. James E. Keirans, "The Jury Box," *The Armchair Detective,* Summer 1991, pp. 368–73.
44. EQMM, August 1969, p. 53, and February 1970, p. 130.
45. EQMM, October 1970, p. 76.
46. EQMM, February 1972, p. 107.
47. EQMM, October 1976, p. 124.
48. EQMM, November 1971, p. 94.
49. EQMM, October 1969, p. 104; Doar, "John Dickson Carr," *Charlotte Observer,* October 1, 1967; cf. *Deadly Hall,* Chapter 12.
50. Julia McNiven (I), February 27, 1989; Clarice Carr (I), February 23, 1989.
51. JDC to Roger Machell of Hamish Hamilton Ltd, September 20, 1970.
52. David Higham to JDC, July 5, 1971; September 13, 1971; JDC to Higham, September 20, 1971; Bonita Cron (I), February 4, 1991; Julia McNiven (I), August 4, 1988; April 10, 1991; Clarice Carr (I), February 23, 1989; March 26, 1990.
53. JDC to Eleanor Sullivan of EQMM, November 23, 1970.
54. JDC to Hamish Hamilton, January 7, 1973.

55. Hamish Hamilton to JDC, January 2, 1973.
56. Francis M. Nevins, Jr., to Joan Kahn, March 9, 1972 (carbon in the possession of Francis Nevins).
57. *Sunday Times,* November 12, 1972.
58. EQMM, March 1973, p. 54.
59. JDC to Wooda N. Carr, January 23, 1973.
60. JDC to David Higham, January 7, 1973.
61. Edna Seaman (I), November 20, 1989; Clarice Carr (I), March 26, 1990; JDC to Eleanor Sullivan, February 21, 1973; JDC to David Higham, appended to Higham's letter of February 20, 1973; JDC to Higham, April 7, 1973; November 20, 1974.
62. JDC to Wooda N. Carr, June 23, 1974; JDC to David Higham, September 8, 1975.
63. JDC to Otto Penzler, April 23, 1974.
64. JDC to Francis Wilford-Smith, November 12, 1967; JDC to David Higham, November 20, 1974; Higham to JDC, November 27, 1974; April 3, 1975; JDC to Otto Penzler, June 12, 1975.
65. JDC to David Higham, September 8, 1975. I am very grateful to my brother, Paul E. Greene, a Social Security agent, for explaining this situation. Paul points out that Carr's accountant could have shown him all sorts of ways around the provision, including making the assertion that he worked only a month or two each year, and collecting Social Security benefits for the remaining ten or eleven months.
66. JDC to Anthony Lejeune, September 2, 1975. The honorary president of The Detection Club, H. R. F. Keating, has kindly sent me a copy of the revised ritual.
67. JDC to John Curran, August 8, 1975; JDC to Eleanor Sullivan, November 18, 1975; JDC to Otto Penzler, December 4, 1975.
68. JDC to David Higham, November 20, 1974.
69. Details on the following pages about John Dickson Carr's final illness are from Carol McCarthy (I), February 27, 1990; Clarice Carr (I), December 4, 1989; March 26, 1990; Julia McNiven (I), September 5, 1989; February 10 and 12, 1992.
70. EQMM, August 1976, p. 131.
71. JDC to Eleanor Sullivan, July 7, 1976; JDC to Eleanor Sullivan, telegram, July 21, 1976; EQMM, October 1976, p. 125.
72. Clarice Carr to Wooda Nicholas Carr, Christmas card, mailed December 11, 1976.

21. L'Envoi

1. *Uniontown Evening Standard,* March 1, 1977; *New York Times,* March 2, 1977; *Times,* March 2, 1977; *Times,* March 12, 1977. I am grateful to Edna Seaman for a photograph of the tomb.
2. Van Deventer, "'Y' all Come,'" *Greenville News,* March 31, 1968.

Appendix 4

1. Anthony Masters, *The Man Who Was M, the Life of Maxwell Knight.* (Oxford: Basil Blackwell, 1984), p. 35.
2. Joan Miller, *One Girl's War, Personal Exploits in MI5's Most Secret Mission* (London: Brandon, 1986), pp. 17–18.

Index

The following abbreviations are used in reference to Carr's writings: nov=novel; ss=short story; rp=radio play; po=poem; e=essay or newspaper column; pt=proposed title. Only the most important of Carr's fictional characters are indexed, and for Bencolin, Fell, and Merrivale, the references are limited to significant discussions. In addition, only a few major references to Clarice Carr are noted, because, from the time of her marriage to John Dickson Carr, she appears throughout the biography.